Wolfram Baur, Sylvia Kalina,
Felix Mayer, Jutta Witzel (Hrsg.)

Übersetzen in die Zukunft

*Herausforderungen der Globalisierung
für Dolmetscher und Übersetzer*

*Tagungsband der Internationalen
Fachkonferenz des Bundesverbandes der
Dolmetscher und Übersetzer e.V. (BDÜ)*

Berlin, 11.–13. September 2009

Verlegt vom
Bundesverband der Dolmetscher
und Übersetzer e.V. (BDÜ)

Wolfram Baur, Sylvia Kalina,
Felix Mayer, Jutta Witzel (Hrsg.)

Übersetzen in die Zukunft

*Herausforderungen der Globalisierung
für Dolmetscher und Übersetzer*

*Tagungsband der Internationalen
Fachkonferenz des Bundesverbandes der
Dolmetscher und Übersetzer e.V. (BDÜ)*

Berlin, 11.-13. September 2009

Die Deutsche Bibliothek – CIP-Einheitsaufnahme

**Übersetzen in die Zukunft – Herausforderungen der
Globalisierung für Dolmetscher und Übersetzer**
Tagungsband der Internationalen Fachkonferenz des
Bundesverbandes der Dolmetscher und Übersetzer e.V. (BDÜ),
Berlin, 11.–13. September 2009

Verlegt vom Bundesverband der Dolmetscher und Übersetzer e.V. (BDÜ).
ISBN 978-3-938430-24-8

© 2009 Bundesverband der Dolmetscher und Übersetzer e.V. (BDÜ), Berlin
Lektorat: Karl-Heinz Trojanus, Saarbrücken • Satz: Thorsten Weddig, Essen
Druck: Schaltungsdienst Lange oHG, Berlin

Inhalt

Geleitwort des BDÜ-Präsidenten

Fünfzehn Jahre sind vergangen, seitdem die Teilnehmer der letzten großen Konferenz des Bundesverbandes der Dolmetscher und Übersetzer (BDÜ) im Jahr 1994 in der Stadthalle zu Bonn-Bad Godesberg in Vorträgen und Diskussionen „Das berufliche Umfeld des Dolmetschers und Übersetzers" analysierten.

In diesen 15 Jahren haben sich das Berufsbild wie auch das Umfeld unseres Berufsstandes infolge der fortschreitenden Globalisierung rasant gewandelt, und dieser Wandel hält weiter an: Immer kürzere Termine zur Übersetzung mehrsprachiger Dokumentationen, zunehmender Kostendruck, Zusammenarbeit in virtuellen Teams, Beherrschung einer Vielzahl technischer Werkzeuge, Dolmetschen bei Videokonferenzen – all dies sind nur einige der neuen Anforderungen an den Berufsstand.

Wie groß der Diskussionsbedarf in unserer Branche ist, zeigt sich an der überwältigenden nationalen und internationalen Resonanz auf den vom BDÜ herausgegebenen „Call for Papers" und auf die Ankündigung der internationalen Fachkonferenz **„Übersetzen in die Zukunft – Herausforderungen der Globalisierung für Dolmetscher und Übersetzer"**, die der BDÜ nun vom 11.–13. September 2009 im Henry-Ford-Bau der Freien Universität Berlin ausrichtet. Bis zum Jahresende 2008 hatten Referenten aus der ganzen Welt über 150 Vorschläge für Vorträge und Workshops eingereicht, sieben Wochen vor der Konferenz lagen bereits über 1.450 Anmeldungen aus fast 40 Ländern rund um den Globus vor. Neben vielen freiberuflich tätigen Kolleginnen und Kollegen verzeichnet die Liste der Teilnehmer und Referenten zahlreiche Vertreter von Übersetzungsunternehmen, Sprachendiensten großer Unternehmen, von institutionellen Sprachendiensten, Auftraggebern von Übersetzungs- und Dolmetschleistungen, Schwesterverbänden aus der Fédération Internationale des Traducteurs (FIT) sowie von Ausbildungsinstituten für Dolmetscher und Übersetzer.

Die im vorliegenden Tagungsband zusammengefassten Vorträge und kurz beschriebenen Workshops und Podiumsdiskussionen spiegeln das breite Spektrum der neuen Herausforderungen an unseren Berufsstand und an jeden einzelnen von uns wider, analysieren sie aus verschiedenen Blickwinkeln und versuchen, Antworten und Hinweise zu geben, wie diese Herausforderungen erfolgreich gemeistert werden können.

Mit dieser internationalen Fachkonferenz will der BDÜ einen Beitrag dazu leisten, dass unser Berufsstand auch „in die Zukunft übersetzt". Der Dank dafür, dass dies gelingen kann, gebührt vor allem Ihnen, den Referenten und Teilnehmern dieser Konferenz – denn Sie sind es, die mit Ihrem Engagement für unseren Beruf, Ihrem Wissen, Ihrem Erfahrungsschatz und Ihrer Bereitschaft, all dies in Vorträgen, Diskussionen und Gesprächen bei der Konferenz mit Kollegen zu teilen, diese Konferenz mit Leben erfüllen, ja sie überhaupt erst möglich machen!

Dank gebührt ferner den zahlreichen Kolleginnen und Kollegen aus dem BDÜ, die nicht nur die Konferenz selbst, sondern auch die Fachmesse und Stellenbörse sowie die breitgefächerte Öffentlichkeitsarbeit zu dieser Konferenz unter der Gesamtleitung von Wolfram Baur – BDÜ-Vizepräsident und Initiator dieses Großprojekts – konzipiert, vorbereitet und in die Tat umgesetzt haben, den rund vierzig Kolleginnen und Kollegen aus dem Verband der Konferenzdolmetscher im BDÜ (VKD-BDÜ) e.V., die durch ihren ehrenamtlichen Dolmetscheinsatz bei der Konferenz für eine reibungslose Verständigung unter den internationalen Teilnehmern sorgen, den Mitarbeiterinnen der BDÜ Service GmbH, in deren Händen die organisatorische Vorbereitung und Durchführung der Konferenz liegt, und nicht zuletzt den Herausgebern dieses Tagungsbandes, die durch die sorgfältige Auswahl und Zusammenstellung der Vorträge, Workshops und Podiumsdiskussionen das Programm der Konferenz maßgeblich mitgestaltet und in Form des vorliegenden Tagungsbands dokumentiert haben.

Johann J. Amkreutz
Präsident des Bundesverbandes der
Dolmetscher und Übersetzer e.V. (BDÜ)
im Juli 2009

Vorwort der Herausgeber

„Übersetzen in die Zukunft" – das Thema der internationalen Fachkonferenz, die der Bundesverband der Dolmetscher und Übersetzer e.V. (BDÜ) vom 11.–13.9.2009 in Berlin ausrichtet, ist vielversprechend. Manche mögen sagen vollmundig. Kann der BDÜ dieses Versprechen einlösen?

Wir meinen: ja. Die Beiträge in diesem Tagungsband beweisen es. Freiberufliche Übersetzer und Dolmetscher, Vertreter von Übersetzungsunternehmen, von nationalen und internationalen Institutionen und Sprachendiensten, Berater, Betriebswirtschaftler, Juristen und Wissenschaftler analysieren veränderte Arbeitsbedingungen, Berufsprofile und Perspektiven der Branche aus ihrer jeweiligen Sicht. Hierbei spielen insbesondere die Globalisierung, die technologischen Entwicklungen und neue berufliche Anforderungen eine Rolle. Die Autoren vermitteln ihr Bild der zukünftigen Übersetzungs- oder Dolmetschprozesse, der Teamarbeit, des beruflichen Selbstverständnisses, der Qualitätskontrolle und -sicherung usw. Dabei entsteht die Vision von teamfähigen Experten für transkulturelle Kommunikation und bestimmte Fachgebiete, die Vision von belastbaren, gewissenhaften und kenntnisreichen Dolmetschern. Beide beherrschen die technologischen Mittel und Methoden virtuos und betreiben Informations- und Wissensmanagement.

Der Tagungsband spiegelt die sieben Themenschwerpunkte der Konferenz wider. Die Vorträge, Workshops und Podiumsdiskussionen wurden einem dieser Schwerpunkte zugeordnet, wobei manche Themen inhaltlich unter mehrere Schwerpunkte fallen. Er umfasst Manuskripte und Zusammenfassungen der Vorträge und Hauptreden, die Grußworte sowie Einführungen in die Themen der Workshops und Podiumsdiskussionen. Da die Vortragenden aus Deutschland und der ganzen Welt kommen, liegen die Beiträge auf Deutsch, Englisch oder Französisch vor. Naturgemäß stellt der Tagungsband eine Momentaufnahme vor der Konferenz dar und enthält daher Langfassungen, Manuskripte sowie kürzere Beiträge oder auch Abstracts. Die Podiumsdiskussionen und Workshops können in diesem Tagungsband nur kurz vorgestellt werden – von ihren Erkenntnissen profitieren zunächst nur die aktiven Teilnehmer der Konferenz.

Die Herausgeber des Tagungsbands repräsentieren die Auswahlkommission für die Beiträge der Konferenz. Aus mehr als 150 Vorschlägen, die auf den Call for Papers des BDÜ hin eingingen, wurden 76 Abstracts, elf Workshops und drei Podiumsdiskussionen ausgewählt. Hauptkriterien bei den Entscheidungen waren die aktuelle und künftige Relevanz für den Berufsstand und die Neuheit des behandelten Themas. Einige Vortragsvorschläge wurden im Rahmen der Podiumsdiskussionen berücksichtigt, denn zentrale und strittige Fragen lassen sich so besser diskutieren. Wichtige Anhaltspunkte für die Aktualität und Bedeutung eines Themas sowie das Interesse der potenziellen Teilnehmer der Konferenz lieferte die „Favoritenwahl" auf der Konferenz-Website www.uebersetzen-in-die-zukunft.de. Bis Mitte Januar 2009 hatten mehr als 700 Interessenten auf der Konferenzseite im Internet in anonymisierter Form die Vorträge markiert, die sie besonders interessierten.

Wir freuen uns, dass bei der internationalen Konferenz des BDÜ und damit auch in diesem Tagungsband so viele unterschiedliche Akteure den Beruf und die Zukunft der Übersetzer und Dolmetscher aus unterschiedlichen Blickwinkeln beleuchten. Insbesondere die Grußworte und Hauptreden zeugen von hohem Respekt vor Übersetzern und Dolmetschern und von der großen ideellen und wirtschaftlichen Bedeutung ihrer Arbeit: Ein Beitrag bezeichnet sie als „Hidden Champions".

Lassen Sie sich von diesem Tagungsband inspirieren und motivieren – vor, während und nach der Konferenz.

Die Herausgeber

Essen, Köln, München, Nürtingen, im Juli 2009

Grußworte

Grußwort von Hartmut Schauerte

*Mitglied des Deutschen Bundestages, Parlamentarischer Staatssekretär
beim Bundesminister für Wirtschaft und Technologie und Beauftragter
der Bundesregierung für den Mittelstand*

**Grußwort aus Anlass der 1. Internationalen Fachkonferenz des Bundesverbandes der Dolmetscher und Übersetzer e.V. (BDÜ) „Übersetzen in die Zukunft –
Herausforderungen der Globalisierung für Dolmetscher und Übersetzer!"
vom 11.–13. September 2009 an der Freien Universität Berlin**

Dolmetschen und Übersetzen sind uralte Kulturtechniken: sie dienen nicht nur der Wirtschaft, sondern auch der Technik, dem Film, der Literatur, der Justiz und natürlich nicht zuletzt der Diplomatie und der Politik. Übersetzer und Dolmetscher sind die unentbehrlichen Mittler zwischen den Völkern im globalen Dorf, wobei Sie sich auch den Herausforderungen der Globalisierung zu stellen haben. Daher lautet das Motto Ihrer Veranstaltung zu Recht: „Übersetzen – in die Zukunft".

Der BDÜ ist mit über 5.500 Mitgliedern der größte Berufsverband Ihrer Branche in Europa. Der deutsche Übersetzungs- und Dolmetschmarkt, im Herzen der europäischen Sprachenvielfalt gelegen, ist einer der weltweit interessantesten Translationsmärkte. Über 90% der Mitglieder des BDÜ sind freiberuflich tätig. Als Mittelstandsbeauftragter der Bundesregierung unterstütze ich Ihre Interessen mit Nachdruck und habe daher gerne die Schirmherrschaft für diese erste internationale Konferenz Ihres Verbandes übernommen. Sie leisten als Freiberufler und Mittelständler in Deutschland einen ganz wesentlichen Beitrag für Wirtschaft und Gesellschaft. Sie tragen in besonderem Maße Verantwortung, wenn Sie Ihre sprachmittlerischen Dienstleistungen vom Standort Deutschland weltweit anbieten.

Der BDÜ unterstützt die Professionalisierung des Berufsstandes. Er schafft für seine Mitglieder verbindliche Standards, berät den Berufsnachwuchs, bildet fort und begleitet seine Mitglieder bei Veränderungsprozessen und neuen Herausforderungen wie z.B. fortschreitende Technisierung und zunehmender internationaler Wettbewerb der Anbieter, globaler Einkauf von Übersetzungsleistungen, immer kürzere Lieferfristen, Englisch als Lingua franca, rechnergestütztes Übersetzen, neue Konferenz- und Dolmetschmodalitäten und Arbeiten in virtuellen Teams.

Das klassische Berufsbild des Dolmetschers und Übersetzers wird neu ausgerichtet. Der Berufsanfänger kann nicht mehr mit einer sicheren Festanstellung in Großunternehmen oder Behörden rechnen. Deutsche Unternehmen decken ihren Bedarf an Übersetzungen und Verdolmetschungen überwiegend durch Beauftragung externer Experten ab. Als etablierte mittelständische Dienstleister oder Existenzgründer zeigen Sie Mut und Ortsunabhängigkeit. Sie positionieren sich neu, setzen auf innovative Translationstechnologien und Qualitätssicherung, um auf hohem Niveau korrekt, stilsicher, zielgruppengerecht und wettbewerbsorientiert zu arbeiten.

Die erste internationale Fachkonferenz des BDÜ bietet ein Forum, auf dem Sie sich als Sprachmittler, Kommunikationsprofis und freiberuflich tätige Unternehmer präsentieren und im unmittelbaren Kontakt mit Wettbewerbern und Kunden für die künftigen Herausforderungen fit machen können.

Ich wünsche allen Konferenzteilnehmern eine gute Veranstaltung mit anregenden Gesprächen und Diskussionen, neuen Geschäftskontakten und dem BDÜ sowie Ihrer gesamten Branche für die Zukunft viel Erfolg.

Ihr
Hartmut Schauerte

Mitglied des Deutschen Bundestages,
Parlamentarischer Staatssekretär beim Bundesminister
für Wirtschaft und Technologie und Beauftragter der
Bundesregierung für den Mittelstand

Welcoming Statement of Hartmut Schauerte

Member of the German Parliament, Parliamentary State Secretary to the Minister of Economics and Technology, and Government Commissioner for Small and Medium-sized Enterprises

Welcoming Statement to the 1st International Conference of the Federal Association of Interpreters and Translators (BDÜ) "Interpreting the Future – Challenges for Interpreters and Translators Arising from Globalisation", September 11 to 13, 2009, Freie Universität Berlin

Interpreting and translating are ancient crafts practised not only for the benefit of business, but also in engineering, the film industry, literature, justice and, of course, the worlds of diplomacy and politics. Translators and interpreters are essential mediators between the communities that populate the global village. Like others, they also have to address the challenges of globalisation within their profession. Against this background, "Interpreting the Future" is an apposite title for their conference.

With more than 5,500 members, the BDÜ is the industry's largest professional association in Europe. Occupying a place at the heart of Europe's multilingual culture, the German translation and interpreting market ranks among the most fascinating in the world. More than 90% of BDÜ members are freelances. As the government commissioner for small and medium-sized enterprises, I am committed to supporting their interests and was therefore delighted to accept the invitation to serve as a patron of their association's inaugural international conference. Translators and interpreters working as freelances and entrepreneurs make a significant contribution to the German economy and society. They accept a special responsibility by offering their language services from Germany to a global audience.

The BDÜ is fostering the development of professionalism within the industry. It creates binding standards for its members, advises the upcoming generation of practitioners, offers continuing development programmes, and provides guidance on change processes and new challenges. Topical issues include the irresistible rise of technology, growing international competition among providers, the global procurement of translation services, shortening deadlines, the role of English as a lingua franca, computer-aided translation, new conference and interpreting arrangements, and working in virtual teams.

The translating and interpreting professions are being redefined. Those seeking to enter the profession can no longer expect to find a permanent position with a large company or public authority. German enterprises satisfy their demand for translation and interpreting largely by engaging outside specialists. Established small and medium-sized service providers and new entrants alike are willing to take risks and work wherever required. They are flexible and embrace innovative translation technologies and quality assurance in order to maintain high standards, pursue stylistic excellence, address target groups appropriately and remain competitive.

The BDÜ's first international conference is a place where linguists, communication professionals and freelances can present their services and, in the company of their competitors and customers, prepare for the challenges that lie ahead.

I hope that all those attending this conference will enjoy the proceedings, engage in stimulating conversation and discussion, and establish new business contacts. I wish the BDÜ and the whole of your industry every success in the future.

Yours sincerely,
Hartmut Schauerte

Member of the German Parliament,
Parliamentary State Secretary to the Minister of Economics
and Technology, and Government Commissioner for Small
and Medium-sized Enterprises

Grußwort von Wolfgang Steimels

Präsident des Bundessprachenamtes

Grußwort aus Anlass der Internationalen Fachkonferenz des Bundesverbandes der Dolmetscher und Übersetzer e. V. (BDÜ) „Übersetzen in die Zukunft – Herausforderungen der Globalisierung für Dolmetscher und Übersetzer" vom 11.–13. September 2009 an der Freien Universität Berlin

Seit vielen Jahren ist das Bundessprachenamt dem Bundesverband der Dolmetscher und Übersetzer als außerordentliches Mitglied eng verbunden. Hinter diesem außerordentlichen Mitglied steht eine Bundesoberbehörde mit rund 1.000 Mitarbeiterinnen und Mitarbeitern, die im Übersetzerbereich mehr als 25 Sprachen abdecken und im Lehrbetrieb fast 50 Sprachen unterrichten. Hinzu kommen Dolmetschleistungen von rund 33.000 Stunden pro Jahr. Vor diesem Hintergrund habe ich mich als Präsident des Bundessprachenamtes besonders gefreut, als mir eine Schirmherrschaft über die Konferenz zum Thema „Übersetzen in die Zukunft – Herausforderungen der Globalisierung für Dolmetscher und Übersetzer" angetragen wurde. Ich sehe diese Schirmherrschaft als eine Bekräftigung der guten Beziehungen zwischen dem BDÜ und meinem Amt, die traditionell in einem regen Gedankenaustausch deutlich werden.

Die überwältigende Resonanz, die diese BDÜ-Konferenz im In- und Ausland findet, zeigt, wie aktuell die Themen, die hier von einem Fachpublikum diskutiert werden, für den Berufsstand sind. Aber nicht nur die Profis sind angesprochen. Vielmehr bietet diese internationale Fachkonferenz über die Medienpräsenz auch ein Forum, um die anspruchsvollen und vielfältigen Tätigkeiten des Dolmetschens und Übersetzens einer interessierten Öffentlichkeit näherzubringen.

Angesichts einer zunehmend globalisierten Welt offenbart der Blick in die Zukunft vielfältige Herausforderungen, denen sich auch alle Übersetzerinnen und Übersetzer sowie Dolmetscherinnen und Dolmetscher stellen müssen – ganz gleich, ob sie freiberuflich arbeiten oder nicht. Für die im Bundessprachenamt tätigen Mitarbeiterinnen und Mitarbeiter bedeutet Globalisierung vor allem, dass sich unsere Auftraggeber – allen voran die Bundeswehr – neuen Aufgaben in vielen Teilen der Welt stellen, was eine fortlaufende Anpassung unserer sprachmittlerischen Dienstleistungen zur Folge hat. So sind beispielsweise bei allen Auslandseinsätzen der Bundeswehr auch Sprachmittler des Bundessprachenamtes vor Ort im Einsatz.

Es sind aber nicht nur geänderte politische Parameter, auf die wir mit der Ausrichtung unserer Serviceleistungen reagieren. Vielmehr zeigen sich die Auswirkungen der Globalisierung auch im Bereich technischer Übersetzungen wie beispielsweise der Interaktiven Elektronischen Technischen Dokumentation. Hier gilt es, stets mit den Neuerungen Schritt zu halten, um so unserem Anspruch, leistungsfähiger und unverzichtbarer Dienstleister für unsere Auftraggeber zu sein, gerecht zu werden.

Ich bin zuversichtlich, dass die Fülle der Fachbeiträge dieser Konferenz uns helfen wird, die Erfordernisse der Zukunft zu erkennen. Daher beglückwünsche ich den

BDÜ zu dieser Veranstaltung und wünsche den Konferenzteilnehmerinnen und Konferenzteilnehmern interessante Vorträge und Diskussionen, damit wir alle die Herausforderungen der Globalisierung annehmen und den richtigen Weg in die Zukunft einschlagen können.

Wolfgang Steimels
Präsident des Bundessprachenamtes

Welcoming Statement of Wolfgang Steimels

Director of the Federal Office of Languages (Bundessprachenamt)

Welcoming Statement to the international conference of the Federal Association of Interpreters and Translators *Interpreting the Future – Challenges for Interpreters and Translators Arising from Globalisation* **from 11 to 13 September 2009, Freie Universität Berlin**

The Federal Office of Languages has been an associate member of the Federal Association of Translators and Interpreters for many years. Excellent ties exist between the two institutions. Behind this "associate member" is a higher federal authority with around 1,000 employees, translating in more than 25 languages and teaching almost 50 languages. Furthermore, our Office clocks up around 33,000 hours of interpreting each year. As Director of the Federal Office of Languages I was delighted to be invited to become a patron of this conference, *Interpreting the Future – Challenges for Interpreters and Translators Arising from Globalisation*. I see this patronage as confirming the good relations between the Federal Association and my Office that have traditionally been articulated in a lively exchange of ideas.

The overwhelmingly positive response to this conference both at home and abroad demonstrates just how crucial the issues discussed here by the experts are for the profession at present. However, this international conference is not just for the "pros". With its media presence, it also provides a forum for an inquisitive public to discover more about the demanding and multifaceted work of interpreters and translators.

Interpreting the Future reveals the multiplicity of challenges that both translators and interpreters face in a world of increasing globalisation – whether working freelance or in-house. For the staff of the Federal Office of Languages, globalisation means primarily that our customers – first and foremost the German Armed Forces – are facing new tasks in many parts of the world. This requires constant adaptation of the translation and interpreting services we provide. As one example, linguists from the Federal Office of Languages are now deployed on all German Armed Forces operations abroad.

However, it is not just the changed political landscape that we must respond to when realigning our services. The impact of globalisation can also be seen in technical translation, for example, with Interactive Electronic Technical Documentation. In this sense it is vital that we keep up with the latest developments and thus do justice to our claim: to be an efficient and indispensable service provider to our customers.

I am confident that the wealth of expert contributions at this conference will help us to recognise the demands of the future. In this vein I would like to congratulate the Federal Association of Interpreters and Translators on the event. I hope that everybody attending the conference will enjoy some interesting presentations and discussions, so that we are all able to meet the challenges of globalisation and steer the right course to the future.

Wolfgang Steimels

Director of the Federal Office of Languages (Bundessprachenamt)

Grußwort von Klaus Wowereit

Regierender Bürgermeister von Berlin

Grußwort des Regierenden Bürgermeisters von Berlin, Klaus Wowereit, an die Teilnehmer der Internationalen Fachkonferenz „Übersetzen in die Zukunft", Berlin 11.–13. September 2009

Die Welt rückt im Zeitalter der Globalisierung zusammen. Immer mehr Menschen unterschiedlicher Sprache und Kultur begegnen sich. Der Austausch in Politik, Wirtschaft und Wissenschaft nimmt zu, gleichzeitig aber auch die Schwierigkeit der Kommunikation über sprachliche und kulturelle Barrieren hinweg. Allein die Europäische Union besteht aus 27 Mitgliedsstaaten mit 23 offiziellen Amtssprachen. Da werden professionelle Brückenbauer gebraucht, also Dolmetscher und Übersetzer, die den Zugang zu einer anderen Welt eröffnen und so dazu beitragen, dass Begegnung auch mit gegenseitigem Verstehen einhergeht.

Ich freue mich, dass die Konferenz „Übersetzen in die Zukunft – Herausforderungen der Globalisierung für Dolmetscher und Übersetzer" in Berlin stattfindet. Wir blicken in diesem Jahr auf 20 Jahre Fall der Mauer zurück. Seit diesem epochalen Ereignis hat sich Berlin zu einer weltoffenen und von kultureller Vielfalt geprägten Hauptstadt in der Mitte Europas entwickelt, die auf viele Kreative und Talente aus aller Welt eine große Anziehungskraft ausübt. Schon bei einem Schritt auf die Straße ist man enormer sprachlicher Vielfalt ausgesetzt. In welcher Sprache auch immer die Teilnehmerinnen und Teilnehmer der Dolmetscher- und Übersetzertagung arbeiten, in Berlin werden sie Menschen finden, die in ihr als Muttersprache zuhause sind.

Berlin bietet ideale Bedingungen für eine erfolgreiche Tagung und zählt zu den beliebtesten Tagungsorten weltweit. Weil sich Berlin als Hauptstadt, Messeplatz und Sitz zahlreicher Botschaften und internationaler Firmenrepräsentanzen zunehmend zu einem Ort der internationalen Begegnung in Politik, Kultur und Wissenschaft entwickelt, wächst auch die Nachfrage nach Sprachdienstleistungen. Die Folge ist, dass hier immer mehr Übersetzer und Dolmetscher eine feste oder freie Beschäftigung finden.

Im Namen des Senats von Berlin heiße ich Sie also sehr herzlich willkommen zu dieser Konferenz in der deutschen Hauptstadt. Ich wünsche Ihnen eine fachlich ergiebige Tagung und anregende Begegnungen sowie einen angenehmen Aufenthalt in Berlin, an den Sie sich stets gerne erinnern werden.

Klaus Wowereit
Regierender Bürgermeister von Berlin

Welcoming Statement of Klaus Wowereit

Governing Mayor of Berlin

Welcoming Statement of the Governing Mayor of Berlin, Klaus Wowereit, to the participants of the international conference "Interpreting the Future – Challenges for Interpreters and Translators Arising from Globalisation", September 11 to 13, 2009, Freie Universität Berlin

Globalisation is a process that is bringing the world closer together. More and more people are engaging with each other across language and cultural boundaries. While political, business and academic exchanges intensify, the difficulties of communicating in different languages and against diverse cultural backgrounds become more apparent. The European Union alone consists of 27 member states and recognises 23 official languages. These circumstances call for professional bridge-builders, for interpreters and translators, capable of giving access to other worlds and facilitating mutual understanding among peoples.

I am delighted that the conference "Interpreting the Future – Challenges for Interpreters and Translators Arising from Globalisation" is taking place in Berlin. This year is the 20th anniversary of the fall of the Berlin Wall. Since this epoch-making event, Berlin has emerged as a cosmopolitan capital city at the heart of Europe, a melting pot of cultural diversity and a home to countless creative and talented people from all over the globe. Even as you walk down the street, you are exposed to an enormous variety of languages. Irrespective of the working languages of the translators and interpreters attending the conference, participants will have every opportunity to meet native speakers of those languages in Berlin.

Berlin is an ideal venue for a successful conference and ranks among the most popular congress cities worldwide. As the capital develops as a trade convention centre, the seat of numerous embassies and international corporations' offices, and a meeting place for the world's politicians, businesspeople and academics, the demand for language services is growing as well. As a consequence, more and more translators and interpreters are employed or work as freelances in the city.

On behalf of the Berlin Senate, it therefore gives me great pleasure to welcome you to this conference in the German capital. I am sure that you can look forward to a stimulating programme, inspiring meetings and a very pleasant and memorable stay in Berlin.

Klaus Wowereit
Governing Mayor of Berlin

Grußwort von Dr. Ulrich Oesingmann

Präsident des Bundesverbandes der Freien Berufe (BFB)

BFB-Präsident Dr. Ulrich Oesingmann anlässlich der BDÜ-Fachkonferenz „Übersetzen in die Zukunft – Herausforderungen der Globalisierung für Dolmetscher und Übersetzer"

Sehr geehrte Damen und Herren,

sicherlich könnte man mit viel bösem Willen die nachfolgenden Zeilen auch Sprachakrobat Ernst Jandl, übrigens ebenfalls Übersetzer, zuschreiben. Doch das, was nun folgt, ist, wie Sie alle wissen, keine Kunst, sondern grober Unfug. In Anlehnung etwa an wunderliche „laufmaschinenfreie Strumpfhosen" fanden wir nachfolgenden Übersetzungsfehler doch zumindest von den Begriffen her passend für Ihre internationale Fachkonferenz:

Viele sprache statatur ist benutzbar: Englisch, Deutshc, Franzozisch, Spanisch, Italische, und Swedisch.

Hier mag sich der Verbraucher mit ein wenig Verstand die mehrsprachige PC-Tastatur noch selbst erschließen. Doch wenn wichtige Texte von Unqualifizierten übersetzt oder gar nur noch durch einen Übersetzungscomputer gejagt werden, könnte dies weitreichende Folgen haben und könnten Bedienungsfehler von Maschinen etwa auch Menschenleben gefährden. Kaum auszudenken, wenn Medikamente derart stümperhafte Beipackzettel hätten. Aber mit Ihrer Leistung bürgen Sie als Übersetzer für eine Qualität, gemeinsam mit Freiberuflern wie dem verschreibenden Arzt und dem aushändigenden Apotheker.

Nicht nur das geschriebene Wort, auch das gesprochene Wort ist Ihr Metier. Von Afrikaans bis Weißrussisch machen Sie uns die Welt verständlicher. Hier ist Ihr Stellenwert außergewöhnlich. Ein falscher Begriff, eine verzerrte Tonlage, bei internationalen Krisengesprächen könnte dies zu riskanten Verwicklungen führen.

Wer erinnert sich nicht an die berühmten Worte von John F. Kennedy: „ICH BIN EIN BERLINER." Kaum auszudenken, hätte man dies als „Ich möchte gerne einen Berliner" übersetzt. Kennedy muss bereits gewusst haben, wie anspruchsvoll der Dolmetscher in puncto Aufnahmefähigkeit und Reaktionstempo arbeitet. Denn Kennedy sagte damals nicht nur den legendären Satz, sondern auch „Ich bin dem Dolmetscher dankbar, dass er mein Deutsch noch besser übersetzt hat". Mit Ihrem Sprachgefühl unterstützen Sie also nicht nur die Wirtschaft und Verwaltung, sondern auch Organisationen und Politik und dabei, das darf ich erahnen, ist diplomatisches Geschick gefordert.

Sie könnten Ihre Leistungen nicht erbringen, würden Sie die beherrschten Sprachen nicht auch leben und denken. Dazu können wir nur sagen, Hochachtung! Auch mit Blick auf unsere Volkswirtschaft sind Sie zweifelsfrei so etwas wie die viel zitierten „Hidden Champions"! Denn gerade Ihre Arbeit unterstützt den Exportweltmeister

Deutschland. Die Ausfuhr hochwertiger Güter und qualifizierter Dienstleistungen kann nur gelingen, wenn die Kommunikation und Information ebenso anspruchsvoll ist. Und Garanten unseres Rechtsstaates etwa sind zudem die Gerichtsdolmetscher unter Ihnen, ermöglichen Sie sprachunkundigen Ausländern doch rechtliches Gehör.

Freiberuflichkeit und der Berufsstand des Übersetzers sowie Dolmetschers sind unverrückbar miteinander verknüpft. Erbringen Sie doch aufgrund Ihrer besonderen beruflichen Qualifikation Ihre geistig-ideellen Leistungen tagtäglich persönlich, eigenverantwortlich und fachlich unabhängig – und zwar nicht nur im Interesse Ihrer direkten Auftraggeber, sondern insbesondere im Interesse der Allgemeinheit.

Sie sind unsere Lotsen in einer globalisierten Welt und bei allen Smileys und Sonderzeichen, auf die man sich global-lingual einigt, ist es Ihre Sprachkompetenz, die umfassendes Verstehen ermöglicht und damit Verständnis schafft. Ohne Sie gäbe es etwa die Europäische Union gar nicht, weil Sprachbarrieren blieben und sie keine Eigenständigkeit entwickeln könnte. Ich bin stolz, Sie in den Reihen des BFB zu wissen. Ich wünsche Ihnen gutes Gelingen für Ihre Fachtagung und einen ergiebigen Austausch mit dem Ziel der weiteren Professionalisierung und Weiterentwicklung Ihres Berufsstandes!

Mit herzlichen Grüßen
Dr. Ulrich Oesingmann

Präsident des Bundesverbandes
der Freien Berufe (BFB)

Welcoming Statement of Dr. Ulrich Oesingmann

President of the Bundesverband der Freien Berufe (BFB)

**Welcoming Statement of BFB President Dr. Ulrich Oesingmann
to the BDÜ conference Interpreting the Future – Challenges for
Interpreters and Translators Arising from Globalisation**

Ladies and gentlemen,

Although it would be unkind, the following lines could be ascribed to the linguistic experimentalist and translator Ernst Jandl. As you will appreciate, they have nothing in common with art, but constitute pure nonsense. Calling to mind magnificent mistranslations, such as "Our wines leave you nothing to hope for", we came across this passage, which seeks at least to use words fit for this conference.

> *Viele sprache statatur ist benutzbar: Englisch, Deutshc, Franzozisch, Spanisch, Italische, und Swedisch*

The user of these operating instructions for a computer keyboard will probably work things out for himself, but the practice of having important texts translated by non-professionals or even simple software can have severe repercussions. Machine operating errors can endanger human life. The consequences of a similarly bungled patient information leaflet do not bear thinking about. As translators, you are guarantors of quality alongside other self-employed professionals in the value chain, including the prescribing physician and the dispensing pharmacist.

Your field is not only the written, but also the spoken word. From Afrikaans to Yiddish, you enable us to make better sense of the world. You occupy an exceptional position – an inappropriate word or tone of voice can give rise to serious complications in international crisis talks.

Who can forget the famous words of John F. Kennedy, "ICH BIN EIN BERLINER"? It's just as well he wasn't advised to use the words, "Ich möchte gerne einen Berliner" or "I WOULD LIKE A DOUGHNUT". Kennedy must already have understood his interpreter's ability to absorb information and respond quickly. Not only did Kennedy utter those memorable words, but he also thanked his interpreter in public by saying, "I appreciate my interpreter translating my German." Your feeling for language assists not only business and public authorities, but also a variety of organisations, including in politics, where, I suspect, a good deal of diplomacy is required.

You would not be able to perform your services if you did not also live and breathe your chosen languages. I am full of admiration for what you do. In view of how you support our national economy as well, you can certainly be described as hidden champions. Your work shores up the world-beating export record of the German economy. We can succeed in exporting first-rate goods and services only if communication takes place and information is exchanged according to similarly high quality standards. Court interpreters, moreover, champion the rule of law by enabling those who do not speak German to be heard in court.

Self-employment goes hand in hand with the occupations of translator and interpreter. Every day, you use your professional and intellectual skills in person, on your own responsibility and without bias, not only on behalf of your customers, but also in the interests of the public at large.

You serve as pilots in an age of globalisation and, notwithstanding the universality of emoticons and other symbols, it is your linguistic proficiency that facilitates comprehensive understanding and, therefore, mutual sympathy. The European Union could not exist without you because language barriers would impede its autonomy. I am proud that you are part of the community of self-employed professionals that I represent. Enjoy the rewards of your conference and engage in a stimulating exchange of opinions with your colleagues, while fostering further professionalism and the development of your industry.

Yours sincerely,
Dr. Ulrich Oesingmann

President of the Bundesverband
der Freien Berufe (BFB)

Vorträge der Hauptredner

Prof. Dr. Dr. hc. mult. Jutta Limbach

1994–2002: Präsidentin des Bundesverfassungsgericht;
bis 2007: Vorsitzende des Deutschen Sprachrats;
2002–2008: Präsidentin des Goethe-Instituts

Mario Ohoven

Präsident des Bundesverbandes mittelständische Wirtschaft (BVMW)

Karl-Johan Lönnroth

Generaldirektor der Generaldirektion Übersetzung (DGT)
der Europäischen Kommission

Donald A. DePalma

Leiter des Forschungsbereichs des Beratungs- und Forschungsunternehmens
Common Sense Ad-vi-sory Inc. (CSA)

Marion Boers

Präsidentin der Fédération Internationale des Traducteurs (FIT)

Hat Deutsch eine Zukunft? – Unsere Sprache in der globalisierten Welt

Prof. Dr. Dr. hc. mult. Jutta Limbach

In ihrem Vortrag zur Eröffnung der Konferenz stellt die ehemalige Präsidentin des Bundesverfassungsgerichts, Vorsitzende des deutschen Sprachrats und Präsidentin des Goethe-Instituts Kernaussagen ihres 2008 erschienenen Buchs *„Hat Deutsch eine Zukunft? – Unsere Sprache in der globalisierten Welt"* vor.

Das Redemanuskript lag zum Zeitpunkt der Drucklegung noch nicht vor. Sie können es jedoch – vorbehaltlich der Zustimmung der Rednerin – voraussichtlich ab November 2009 auf der Konferenz-Website unter *www.vortraege.uebersetzen-in-die-zukunft.de* als PDF-Datei abrufen.

Bitte geben Sie dafür folgenden Zugangscode ein: *X2JK2009*.

Verständigung in einer globalisierten Welt

Mario Ohoven

Präsident des Bundesverbandes der Mittelständischen Wirtschaft (BVMW)

In seinem Vortrag kommentiert Mario Ohoven die Rolle von Sprachmittlerleistungen für die Wirtschaft und insbesondere die Anforderungen des Mittelstands.

Das Redemanuskript lag zum Zeitpunkt der Drucklegung noch nicht vor. Sie können es jedoch – vorbehaltlich der Zustimmung des Redners – voraussichtlich ab November 2009 auf der Konferenz-Website unter *www.vortraege.uebersetzen-in-die-zukunft.de* als PDF-Datei abrufen.

Bitte geben Sie dafür folgenden Zugangscode ein: *X2JK2009*.

The challenges facing international organisations' language services

Karl-Johan Lönnroth

Directorate-General for Translation of the European Commission

1 Introduction

Language services play a vital, but not always visible or recognised, role in international decision-making processes; decisions taken by the United Nations, the European Union, the International Monetary Fund or the World Bank affect citizens around the world. And in today's globalised world, information about those decisions and their impact reaches the man-in-the-street almost instantly. By providing multilingual information to the citizens and all other interested parties, language services play their part in boosting transparency, democracy and legitimacy.

In a changing world, international organisations have likewise had to change, and the same goes for those organisations' language services.

Some might see these challenges as threats. Another way of looking at them, though, is as opportunities – a chance to enhance an organisation's performance.

This paper gives a brief historical overview of multilingualism in Europe, taking into account the major technological and linguistic developments which are inevitably linked in a globalised world, before discussing the challenges faced by international organisations' language services and the responses the European Commission's Directorate-General for Translation (DGT) has come up with.

Striving for legitimacy, openness and citizen-oriented service in the EU, DGT provides the European Commission with high-quality language-related services for its written communication, operating with 23 official languages, i.e. 506 language pairs.

DGT's own experience, problems and solutions might well prompt other organisations to use them and adapt them to their work environment.

The European Union is built on the concept of multilingualism. It is one of the EU's key features, embodied in the treaties and in the very first regulation of 1958. Indeed, multilingualism is an essential part of the EU's values of equality between languages, cultures and nations.

But it was not always like this in Europe: the 17th, 18th and 19th centuries were characterised by the rise of nation-states (where the idea of 'one country, one people, one language' prevailed), by the access of broader sections of the population to education, and by the growth of public communication. These combined factors led to a situation where language boundaries came to coincide more or less with political borders. Mercantilism and colonialism strengthened this trend. The explorers, conquerors, missionaries and merchants all brought with them their own language, to facilitate trade, administration and the import of the culture of their country of origin – thereby underpinning political domination. Political hegemony was thus accompanied by language hegemony. But today, the 19th and 20th century vision of the nation-state is giving way to a more dynamic and fluid reality.

In major cities in Europe and across the globe we can see street signs, administrative notices and advertisements written in a multitude of languages which are not the official language of the country. The eye, nose and ear catch the sounds and fragrance of vibrant ethnic communities, with their cooking, their habits, their tongue and their religion. Local authorities realised long ago that multilingual communication is a prerequisite for social cohesion – the very survival of their community. The growing mix of languages, religions, racial and cultural backgrounds affects the European Union as a whole, as well as each of its constituent parts.

Monolingual classes in schools are becoming a rarity, with almost 10% of pupils speaking different languages at home and at school, while mixed-language families are becoming more and more common. Television, radio and the Internet, low-cost flights and exchange programmes expose Europeans more and more to other languages, mindsets and traditions. Ethnic radio stations proliferate. One example is the 'Funkhaus Europa' which, I understand, broadcasts in 15 languages.

2 Technological changes, globalisation and the language industry

As early as 1939, the world saw the beginning of a technological revolution as the first prototypes of modern computers were built by the English mathematician Alan Turing. Since, the information society has made enormous strides, but computer science and the language industry have never lost sight of one another.

Nowadays, the global economy plays a growing role in determining the development of both the language industry and technological change. With more and more countries enjoying free trade, the creation of GATT and, more recently, of the World Trade Organisation, and the subsequent signature of a host of multilateral agreements, the economic landscape has undergone a dramatic change. In this new context, businesses and customers use delocalised services in many industries. If you book a flight by telephone, for instance, you may be dealing with an airline representative who is thousands of miles away.

This marked reshaping of the economic scene has had significant consequences for all concerned. From the linguistic point of view, the most obvious one is the need for people to be able to interact with each another.

It has been shown that a lack of language skills can seriously hinder the international ambitions of smaller and larger companies.

However, the ability to negotiate a deal by speaking another language is just one part of the challenge. If customers are to be reached wherever they are, products and services must be localised. And it is at this point that the professionals must come in – to ensure that not only the language, but also cultural differences, traditions and sensitivities are taken properly into account.

3   International organisations' language services

The golden age of international organisations was between 1945 and the 1970s. After World War Two, there was agreement that international cooperation was an important instrument for preventing or at least containing conflicts. Funding for those organisations was largely available. Since then, a succession of crises has changed this: international organisations are increasingly affected by public deficits and indebtedness, leading to calls for more accountability, efficiency and transparency. International organisations are now under greater scrutiny by budgetary authorities and the public than they were fifty years ago.

Translation services face the same challenges, but they have an additional 'handicap' since their role is not always clear or recognised within international organisations. Translation is often considered to be merely a 'support service' and a necessary evil, rather than an integral part of the business and policy processes, and is therefore often little more than an afterthought. The upshot of this may be that decisions taken at a higher management or political level do not take sufficiently account of the specificities of translation. In translation services, for example, the internal redeployment of people to meet shifting needs is more complex than elsewhere, since it is not normally possible to move, say, a French translator to the English translation department and maintain the same level of quality and productivity.

The main challenges faced by international organisations' translation services all over the world include a higher demand for translation, and pressure to reduce costs and work more efficiently, i.e. do more with fewer staff, to tighter deadlines, and without due consideration of the way the translation profession works.

Indeed, the temptation is often to judge translation services by the volume of their output, i.e. the number of pages produced. Other services are less likely to be judged on that criterion: it would be hard to imagine a policy department being judged by the volume of its proposals or reports.

Other temptations arise from underestimating the intellectual dimension of the translation profession, and pipedreams that technological miracles such as machine translation and organisational quick fixes, e.g. offshoring, will solve the broader challenges of international organisations.

The real challenge is to redirect the debate towards real and effective productivity and organisational improvements and to be clear about what can be expected from IT support or from external translation providers.

While translation is to a certain extent an activity which needs no further justification, translation services in international organisations will have to learn an additional language: that of the auditors and budgetary authorities. Only by providing hard facts about their added value, as other services do, will translation services have any chance of earning the recognition they deserve and muster the support they need to defend their interests. For some, this will require a change in mentality; others have already gone some distance down this road.

4   DGT's responses to the challenges

Multilingualism is one of the basic principles and key features of the European Union, guaranteeing cultural and linguistic diversity, equal treatment between peoples and individuals in Europe, and the right of citizens and entities to interact with European Union institutions in any of the official languages.

Translation is not a single, homogeneous product: it takes various forms, depending on the customer's needs. Language-related services include, over and above mainstream translation, Web translation and Web editing, the editing of original texts, terminology, summaries (oral and written), localisation, and the provision of all manner of linguistic advice.

With about 2500 staff, DGT is the largest public translation service in the world. It translates into the 23 official EU languages, producing something like 1.8 million pages a year.

DGT's size brings both advantages and disadvantages. On the one hand it gives us some leeway to allocate resources to translation support activities, like editing, Web translation, terminology, and the European Master's in Translation university programme.

On the other, being the largest service in the European Commission means that it is exposed to particular scrutiny over its efficiency and productivity.

The European Commission and its departments are DGT's immediate clients. But the EU legislators – the European Parliament and the Council of the European Union – are direct addressees, and the citizens are the ultimate beneficiaries. The Commission and its translation service are not an end in themselves but a key enabler. By giving citizens and representative entities access to the information they need to make an informed judgment on the European Union's policies, DGT plays a part – and helps the rest of the Commission to play its part – in making the EU open to the world. In turn, openness and transparency are a prerequisite if people are to enjoy their rights and if the democratic process is to work satisfactorily in the European Union.

DGT's challenges can be summarised as follows:

1. The need to meet the Commission's legal obligations as regards translation in an enlarged Union, where the number of official EU languages has more than doubled since 2004.

2. The determination to provide the highest quality, particularly in legislative texts, but also in texts destined for the general public.

3. The need to communicate and 'market' its services and to provide clear information on DGT's performance and added value.

4.1 The Commission's legal obligations – not lost in translation

Linguistic diversity is a value in itself, and its preservation a sign of respect for the cultural identities of the EU's citizens. It is also a democratic right. Accordingly, the language services in the EU, including DGT, work under an official, legal language regime which is enshrined in the EC Treaty and in the first Regulation adopted by the European Community (Regulation No 1 of 1958).

This means that there are legal obligations as regards translation, which poses a formidable challenge, as publication and entry into force of EU laws depends on those texts being available in all official EU languages. There have been cases where EU acts have been challenged before the European Court of Justice for breach of the principle of equal treatment of official languages.

On the other hand, this language regime provides a strong and objective justification for the EU's translation services. There will always be a need for a critical mass of in-house translators who are familiar with EU policies, legislation and terminology, to deal with the Institutions' legal obligations as regards translation. All the more so since legal acts and documents which define the rights and obligations of citizens and other interested parties must be available in all official languages and these language versions must be of the highest quality to ensure legal certainty and a satisfactory level of implementation.

Language services of other international organisations which do not enjoy this sound justification have in some cases been hit harder than non-linguistic services in recent downsizing operations.

DGT's work is highly dependent on the Commission's changing political agenda and on developments in the Commission's policies. This means that translation demand in the long term is highly unpredictable, and that in the short term there are peaks and troughs at certain times of the year.

Moving from 11 official languages in 2003 to 20 in 2004 and 23 in 2007 was a massive challenge, which the Commission has overcome with the instrumental contribution of DGT.

Given the magnitude of the challenge, DGT had to tackle it on many fronts: managing the demand for translation was seen as a strategic need to preserve the balance between the legal obligations to translate and the available capacity. It meant curbing unnecessary requests, and hence conducting a complete overhaul of what we meant by priority documents, tailoring the language target to legal and political needs, establishing volume ceilings for each type of document, and getting involved in the policy-cycle of the Commission to ensure better planning. Obviously, this strategic approach had to be carried out in partnership between DGT and its requesters, the Commission's various departments.

DGT also took a critical look at the way it worked, and brought in strong measures to use additional resources effectively, such as freelance translation, with a view to boosting its productivity. The combination of external and internal action is designed to ensure the sustainability of the language regime in the European Union.

Now, five years after the introduction of the Commission's revamped translation strategy, the conclusion is that it has worked: demand for translation is manageable. DGT has established itself as the Commission's hub for translation and is involved at an earlier stage in the planning of the Commission's Work Programme, so as to ensure that translation is taken into account in the Commission's overall planning.

By showing it could cope with this doubling of the number of official EU languages, DGT turned a potential threat into an opportunity: it did not just try to go on as before (before the 2004 enlargement, that is); nor did it ignore the challenge that enlargement had engendered. Instead, it went for a radical change. And the upshot of that is that translation is now better integrated into the planning and the work of the Commission and other institutions.

4.2 Ensuring and enhancing quality

Because translation is so supremely important in terms of legal certainty, accuracy for financial operations, equal treatment of citizens before the law and the need for people to enjoy their rights and meet their obligations in the European Union, translated documents must be of the very highest quality.

It follows that DGT must provide high-quality translations; its reputation depends on the quality of its services. Not content with this, DGT has launched a Total Quality Management exercise, which is based on the pursuit of excellence and which covers all aspects of DGT, from recruitment and training to translation and revision. A key dimension of this exercise is the 'Quality in Translation-Programme', which is running in parallel and which focuses on the translation process itself. This has resulted in a broadly conceived quality reform programme, covering 22 areas of action in all.

Good quality starts with good people. This is why DGT, along with the rest of the European Commission, has a formal recruitment procedure for its in-house staff which is both transparent and demanding. It takes the form of open competitions, organised by the European Communities Personnel Selection Office (EPSO). Announcements are published in the Official Journal of the European Union and on the EPSO Website.

Once recruited, translators need to be given careful training if they are to achieve top quality. DGT has a higher number of training days per person than the Commission average.

High quality also means timely delivery of translations. DGT has a deadline compliance rate of more than 93 %.

A recent customer satisfaction survey has shown that a large majority (more than 80 %) of respondents rate the service provided by DGT as good or very good, and more than half factor in enough time for translation before a particular dossier enters the decision-making procedure. Editing of originals, Web translation and written summaries are particularly popular services.

The survey also showed that respondents are keen on stronger communication between document authors and translators. DGT has taken good note of this issue, and will make every endeavour to tackle it. In fact, it has been pushing for a long time for greater awareness among requesting services of the need for translators to be more closely involved in the process of document creation. Now, the requesting services themselves are voicing this need.

DGT has a robust and reliable IT environment and technical support network, these being indispensable if we are to maximise quality and productivity. DGT provides and maintains a number of high-end computer aid tools including terminology bases, translation memories, librarian tools, documents workflow systems, and so on.

In his presentation, pointedly entitled 'Translation services taken to the extreme', my colleague Josep Bonet will tell you in detail about DGT's complex workflow system and the wide array of tools available. Other important issues he will be touching on include the mechanisms we have for vetting and guaranteeing data quality and the importance of training.

One of the consequences of globalisation and of the increasing range of languages spoken by staff is that as English increasingly becomes the lingua franca, the quality of original texts is tending to decline. By creating an editing service, DGT has adopted a proactive approach to the problem of substandard originals; as well as editing on request, it identifies important, priority documents that would benefit from editing and offers its services where appropriate. DGT's Editing Service is thus acquiring a reputation across the Commission. Priority is given to legislative texts and major policy documents, and the number of editing requests has been growing steadily since the service was put in place.

DGT has also helped set up a Task Force composed of representatives from key Commission services, which aims to promote clear writing in the Commission, the idea being that if the originals are clear, they are easier to translate and clearer for the EU citizen. This project links in with the overall Commission's Better Regulation initiative and its Action Plan on Communicating Europe, the 'Plan D for Democracy, Dialogue and Debate'.

DGT is establishing networks with translation and language services in the Member States (e.g. Italy, Slovakia, Romania) in order to develop terminology exchanges, monitor the way languages are changing and strengthen the links with national partners, which may be authoritative entities in terms of setting language standards.

4.3 DGT's services and added value – Communication and 'marketing'

It is not enough to deliver quality and efficiency; it also has to be registered and recognised by clients, other interested parties and budget authorities. To be a force to be reckoned with, and to attain a high profile, we have to speak the 'language' of managers and auditors. DGT has introduced a scoreboard system and performance indicators and has developed advanced tools for measuring the service's production. For example, we have made significant progress in terms of work rate, boosting average productivity from 5.7 pages to 6.25 pages per translator per day. The main beneficiary of this approach, however, is the service itself, being able to focus on the essential, allocate resources to priority tasks and improve its own quality.

DGT attaches great importance to communicating its services to its clients and to the decision-makers. One real success story has been the introduction of a specialised unit for Web translations, which has received enthusiastic reactions from its clients. Here, DGT's activity is directly linked with one of the Commission's top priorities: improving the way it communicates with the EU citizens.

In addition, DGT has organised information sessions for the other Directorates-General on the European Commission's language regime and the practical implications, and has gone out and advertised its newly established Editing Service. DGT also organises Commission-wide workshops on clear writing, training sessions on how to write for the Web and joint initiatives to improve the quality and workflow of the Commission's press releases and citizens' summaries of EU legislation.[1]

For documents falling outside the scope of the translation strategy, DGT has concluded Service Level Agreements (SLAs), which have raised awareness of the Commission's multilingual environment and of the need to factor it into partner departments' work. At the same time, it has boosted DGT's image as a customer-friendly service provider delivering services beyond its legal obligations.

DGT's communication and 'marketing' are not limited to activities within the Commission; the external component is equally important.

Every year, DGT uses the European Day of Languages (26 September) to promote the translation profession, and takes an active part in the Open Day organised annually by the European Commission on 9 May, Europe Day. By building networks with universities, DGT is helping to develop the translation profession and the labour market. For example, DGT is also promoting the European Master's in Translation, to build up the labour market for translators, the harmonisation and honing of translators' skills, including the ability to use IT tools, and working towards the professionalisation of the translation industry and a smooth transition from studenthood to working life.

DGT regularly sends experienced translators to universities in and outside the EU to give lectures on translation in the EU institutions, in exchange for the opportunity to follow classes at those universities.

In a further initiative to raise the profile and attractiveness of the translation profession, to draw attention to language learning in schools and to have a long-term impact on the labour market for linguists, DGT decided in 2007 to organise a regular translation contest for secondary schools called *Juvenes Translatores*. Following the success of the first project, that spawned a second and a third edition, secondary schools in some Member States indeed decided to enhance the teaching of foreign languages.

Another way in which DGT contributes to the Commission's communication policy is by assigning translators to the EC's Representations in the Member States. Their main tasks consist of translating and localising press releases and memos, reaching out to the public. They also establish and develop contacts with the national and local authorities, education institutions, the media and civil society.

At the international level DGT is helping to build up the language services of the African Union and has received requests for cooperation on translation and terminology from the Arab League, South Africa, China, Russia, Canada and the **Caribbean** Regional Information and **Translation** Institute (CRITI). The DGT also plays a part in the exchange of best practices in international *fora* of language services, with a

---

[1] Citizens' summaries explain Commission proposals to the general public. They are drafted specifically for publication on Europa, the European Commission's portal. The Web unit of DGT edits them, and the language used should be simple and concise. They can also be adapted for print publication (e.g. factsheets, leaflets). They should not exceed 2600 characters.

view to enhancing the visibility of the profession, strengthening the role and influence of these services, and improving the quality of the translation process.

These initiatives have raised DGT's profile and people's awareness of the translation process and its constraints. At the same time, they have succeeded in correcting some misconceptions about translation among requesters and all manner of interested parties inside and outside the Commission.

Conclusions

Over the last five years, DGT has consistently sought to look beyond its core business and has become more involved in the Commission's political process, by providing input for draft proposals discussed among the Commission's services and by becoming more active internationally.

The result is that DGT is now recognised as a serious discussion partner in the Commission's decision-making process, and both globally and internally as a centre of excellence on translation and language matters.

DGT's core business is – and must remain – translation, at the service of the other departments of the European Commission and the European citizens, but by broadening its horizons internationally and involving itself more in the Commission's work it has managed to demonstrate its added value, and has achieved better recognition of the translation profession.

The role of language and translation services in a global economy

Donald A. DePalma

President, Common Sense Advisory, Inc.

Abstract

In this presentation, Dr. DePalma will outline the importance of translation and localization for businesses operating beyond their borders. He will discuss Common Sense Advisory's research on the language services industry, participants in its multi-tier structure, and the major trends driving language service providers and translators.

Introduction

The business of providing language services like translation and localization is critical to global commerce, branding, and other communication. Globalization has made interpretation, dubbing for TV and film, and translation of documents, software, product information, and websites commonplace items on any knowledge worker's task list. But as a US$14 billion industry, it remains highly fragmented, a bit obscure, and even difficult for some companies to justify in a down economy.

Before I begin, I would like to point out an interesting phenomenon that results from these market characteristics. Many translators and localization project managers tend to think of themselves as simply renderers of words or traffic police for language projects. I have long contended that this characterization misses the bigger picture. These people should think of themselves as "global communicators" who are responsible for making a product usable or explaining a company's value proposition.

Therefore, in today's keynote, I will talk about the strategic need for language services in any company selling to biz buyers or consumers, outline the structure of the industry that meets this need, and outline the key trends driving the practice.

1 Language matters for business buyers and consumers

I have the luxury here of speaking to an audience that understands the importance of communicating in other languages, but I'm not sure that everyone truly comprehends the value of speaking to people in their right language across a full product buying cycle. I happen to have data that demonstrates this value.

The data that I will present in the next few minutes is from a large-scale survey that we conducted in English, but we should consider that English is a proxy for any language. We contend that we would see the same, if not greater, levels of concern and higher costs for goods delivered in languages that are not as widely spoken as English. For example, Western Europeans and Asians regularly target U.S. audiences, most of them doing so in English. We believe that the findings represent best practices for doing business in any language in any foreign market – for example, Japanese selling to Germans and Czechs selling to Thais.

One of the most common refrains that we hear from software vendors and from too many enterprise planners in non-Anglophone countries is that "their buyers and developers can handle English." They tell us that as long as the products can ingest, manage, and publish information in other languages, that's fine. However, "our content management (or database or ERP) administrators and application developers can get along just fine with English, thank you." How valid is this point of view?

Unlocalized products cost more to buy, maintain, and enhance

At Common Sense Advisory, we have long held this position to be suspect. We talk a lot with companies around the world and find that many do employ lots of Anglophone staff in their IT departments and that English might be the "official" corporate language. However, when we probe deeper, we hear about the increased expense of running English-only products. They tend to pay more for bilingual developers and to provide support and training for English-language products. Furthermore, the availability of fully trained, competent developers for your favorite CMS might be lower in a given country, thus raising the total cost of ownership for that product. We find that this "English-only tax" rises as you go further south or east in Europe, or head off to Asia. Obviously, a German-only product would not do very well outside the German-speaking zone.

What's the solution? We always argue for buying localized software; that is, products whose interfaces and documentation have been translated, and whose features have been adapted to the business, cultural, or logistical needs of its target markets. In an ideal world, you'll find that the supplier for your U.S. headquarters' CMS also supports French, German, Japanese, and Russian variants, with the administrative interfaces and developer tools adapted for use in those markets.

This capability lowers the cost of developing, deploying, and managing applications in your IT centers around the world. If all variants share the same data model and underlying technology, then this internationalized stack will let you deploy the right tools to the right people in the right countries. Sound familiar? That's the goal of other corporate initiatives like customer relationship management, personalization, and website globalization. Why shouldn't administrators and developers benefit, too, from the same intention to provide tailored information and interfaces?

Testing the hypothesis that localization matters

We decided to test our hypothesis more systematically, so we polled 351 business-people in eight non-Anglophone countries about the software they buy for their firms.

One of our goals in undertaking this research was to see whether software vendors could increase their sales by localizing their products and websites.

We selected a cross-section of countries around the world, aiming for a representative mix of markets for which companies frequently localize their products (France, Germany, Japan, and Spain), attractive developing markets (China and Russia), and locales for which English is often thought to be sufficient for most offerings (Sweden).

The need for localization spans the entire buying cycle

We asked our respondents about eight factors in the buying cycle where localization plays a role. The initial decision to purchase a given product over another begins with marketing literature and technical specifications. Usability enters the equation, with both user interface and product documentation. Technical support rounds out the buying cycle for when things don't quite work the way that the manual says they should.

First, let's look at marketing materials. Items such as printed brochures, website descriptions, Flash animations, and testimonials grab the interest of potential buyers. Then they move the prospects from consideration to purchase, helping them understand a product's value proposition.

We asked our survey respondents to agree or disagree with the statement, "Having printed marketing and other collateral material in my language makes my organization more likely to purchase a software product." Across our entire sample, more than 80 percent told us they agree with that statement. As we expected, the outlier here was Sweden, with just 60 percent of respondents preferring marketing materials in their own language. If marketers accept the conventional wisdom that English is enough for Sweden, they still leave three out of five buyers on the outside looking in. That's not good for long-term sales. The other seven countries all came in at 80 percent or higher.

We also asked about the desirability of adapting the product interfaces to the linguistic, business, logistical, and cultural nuances of the country in which it is sold. This process involves a range of system components:

- **End-user interface.** About 85 percent of buyers see the value of having a localized user interface. Without access to all the capabilities of a product, they might use fewer options, rely more on defaults, and experiment less with product features. Respondents from Brazil, China, and Japan led the charge for localized interfaces.

- **Server and web-hosted software.** As companies expand eastward and southward into Europe and Asia, more than 80 percent of our respondents think that both sides of the network connection should speak the local language. Respondents from China and Brazil are more likely to buy client/server or web-hosted software when it has been localized to national practices. Russians and Swedes were less committed to localized goods, but the majority in both countries preferred localized server products.

- **Application development.** Nearly 80 percent of our respondents prefer to buy programming tools that have been adapted to local practices. Localized software allows a wider range of developers – including those not conversant in foreign languages – to create value-added applications for their companies. This capability is especially important for an enterprise product meant to be integrated with other applications such as database, content management, and enterprise resource planning. Buyers from China prefer localized tools the most, while Swedes are the most English-tolerant.

Proficiency influences purchase decisions

Our respondents told us that having information in their languages, from first contact to post-sales support, made them more likely to purchase a product. As a final test for localization preferences, we aggregated the proficiency data for end users, administrators, and developers into a single number. Then we analyzed the buyer responses to the questions of whether these various constituencies could handle English-language products, yielding the percentage for that cohort in **Table 1**. Depending on the country, our respondents feel that 33 to 69 percent of this user cohort lack the language skills required to use English-language software.

Then we combined the various components that make up a product offering – translated information, localized software, and in-language technical support – to create an index of purchasing "desirability" from a localization perspective. The third column of **Table 1** lists the percentage of buyers who, when considering all the descriptive, functional, and supporting elements of a complex product like software, told us they would be more likely to buy that product if localized. The numbers range from four out of five in Sweden to nearly everyone in Germany, Russia, and Spain to all buyers in Brazil, China, France, and Japan.

	Percent of end users, administrators, and engineers with inadequate English-language skills	Percent of buyers who prefer to purchase products with the full assemblage of components translated and localized
Brazil	56%	100.0%
China	41%	100.0%
France	33%	100.0%
Germany	36%	98.2%
Japan	69%	100.0%
Russia	53%	97.8%
Spain	53%	96.7%
Sweden	50%	80.0%

Table 1: Summary of Buying Preferences, by Country
Source: Common Sense Advisory, Inc.

Does localization matter?

Once we did the math across our eight countries, user groups, and components, we had no doubt that localization does matter. Without adapting products to local needs, manufacturers leave anywhere from a third to two-thirds of their audience not able to take full advantage of the software they're using and causing additional support burdens to their companies, thus increasing the total cost of ownership.

What did our survey tell us? Most business buyers will not give full consideration to a product unless it has been localized from top to bottom. That means that products without translated materials stand just a one-in-five chance of making it to the short list. The big question for any corporation is whether it can afford to ignore 80 percent of its potential market?

2   The language services industry satisfies much of the demand

The result is that a company doing business in any of the planet's nearly 200 countries needs to produce marketing material, product information, and websites in 8,000-plus spoken languages. Most will restrict themselves to the 17 languages of the world's 25 biggest economies, but even that less ambitious task requires large numbers of translators – or much more productive ones. The upside of selling internationally is enormous. However, monetizing those global opportunities requires a lot of translation across those eight axes of the sales cycle.

The required translation, localization, and interpretation activities happen in a variety of ways. Some companies and government agencies have in-house departments that do the work. Others rely on individual contractors who are hired singly or in bulk to do the job, as required. And still others contract with language service providers (LSPs) to do the work.

All told, our research has found that roughly 90 percent of companies or government agencies outsource some or all of their translation. The reasons for vending out translation and localization mostly come down to one fundamental issue – fixed costs. It's very expensive to keep people on your payroll, so many organizations prefer to transfer these fixed labor costs to service providers. Thus, translation becomes a variable cost that is incurred only when some project is undertaken, not as an everyday payment to full-time translators on the weekly payroll.

What they do and how they do depends on the needs of the buyer. And how the market for such service operates is interesting. It is like many other professional services such as accounting or legal in that they are delivered by humans, typically aided by a variety of technologies. In the case of language services, those tools range from common desktop productivity software such as Word and Excel to specialized computer-aided translation tools on the desktop or on a server.

The fragmented market for language services

I would characterize the market for translation, localization, and interpreting services itself as Balkanized or fragmented. The industry provides a wide range of language services, with the individual firms focusing variously on translation, localization, interpretation, or all three segments.

The language services market can be thought of as consisting of at least four tiers: 1) The six highest-ranked companies on the list report annual revenue in excess of US$200 million; 2) the second tier includes seven companies in the US$106-166 million range; 3) the third tier reports revenues from US$20 million to 60 million in revenue; and 4) the fourth tier represents thousands of smaller companies and hundreds of thousands of individual translators or freelancers who contract to do much of the work for those larger firms.

Where are these companies located? Twenty or even ten years ago, there was a close correlation between geographic location of buyer and seller. The Internet has removed that obstacle, such that language services is now a global business. Our list for 2008 includes suppliers from 15 countries across the globe: the U.S. (9), U.K. (4), Belgium (2), Japan (2), Sweden (2), Switzerland (2) and China, Czech Republic, Finland, France, Ireland, Italy, Luxembourg, Netherlands, and Spain (one each). While American and British companies still dominate the rankings, Asia continues to expand its share of dominant players with a total of three LSPs from China and Japan.

The evolving market for language services

The market is constantly evolving, and there are a few facts that ensure that it will continue to make it interesting to observe, whether you are a buyer, linguist, or economist:

- **The top suppliers account for too little revenue.** Mature markets typically consist of a few large players and many smaller ones. By this metric, the language services market is not that mature despite being around for decades. The 30 largest language service providers (LSPs) booked just 26.6 percent of the US$14.25 billion revenue earned by the industry in 2008. That means thousands of smaller firms brought in the balance of that nearly 10 billion dollars in annual turnover. That fragmentation of revenue ensures continued fluctuation in company size and composition.

- **Acquisitions generate new suppliers.** With each purchase of an LSP, staff from the acquired firm tends to get squeezed out or find their roles diminished to the point of meaninglessness – so executives and operational managers start their own agency because it's sometimes easier than finding a job with another company. Barriers to entry are low, although ongoing operations prove more difficult to manage. Their desire to keep running the show perpetuates the cycle of Balkanization. Meanwhile, every translator on the planet dreams of hanging out his own shingle to yield more than the share of translation fees that a freelancer receives.

- **The diverse needs of clients perpetuate the fragmentation.** Every buyer needs something different. Some are public agencies, most are commercial operations; some jobs are big, many are small; some firms are satisfied with just Asian tongues, others demand 36 languages from around the world; some need very specialized work, others rely on generalists. This is why the market is so Balkanized. It's not just about market efficiency, but also about the various needs being filled – from provisioning service departments to enabling global brand management to powering customer experiences across the planet.

Outlook for the language services market

Last year, acquisitions continued to fuel the growth of some companies in the sector, although most LSPs in our top three tiers of ranking reported significant organic growth from the increased demand for their language services.

Across the market we see demand growing at more than 10 percent per year, driven by national regulations, website and product localization, and consumer need for more information in their own language. But at the same time, we see industry growth holding steady at below 10 percent. Why this discrepancy? In this highly competitive market, most productivity gains benefit the customer, not the LSP. We do not find price erosion in core metrics like price per new word, but we do see the impact of translation automation and reduced publishing costs from XML conversion. LSPs are literally doing more for less but for less effort.

Participants in the language services ecosystem

Do you remember the transfer of fixed labor costs from the buyer to the supplier? The LSP does the same thing, employing most of its translators as contractors. Therefore, they mitigate their cost of labor by transferring the risk to the freelancer community. It's in the best interests of the freelancers to be very active in their search for contracts among the LSPs. We find that most freelancers will have relationships with 10 or 15 agencies, although most will work for just three or four. The ecosystem that has evolved around the delivery of language services has a certain efficiency, but not necessarily a fairness in the distribution of risk and reward.

3 Major trends driving service providers and translators

As companies strive to grow in new markets around the world, they need to transform and deliver the content. That means not only translating but also adapting information to its most usable form. Looking out over the next few years, translators and the companies they work for will face new challenges and opportunities in making sure that they communicate value to global audiences. That mandate will include new tasks that will make tomorrow's translator a more strategic component of a company's international business strategy. It means that they'll be dealing with things such as:

- **Translation for new devices.** Each content receiver – paper, web, mobile phone, car navigation screen, or heretofore unthought-of-technology – complicates the information architecture with specific formatting, content, literacy, dialectal, and device requirements. Each additional language or national regulation squares the complexity of making sure that unified corporate messages are sent and received in the intended form.

- **New information management strategies.** Companies in the high-tech and advanced manufacturing sectors are deconstructing documents into thousands of small XML- or DITA-based units that might show up in any of their distribution formats – paper, web, mobile phones, navigation systems, game stations, or wherever there's a network connection. This new architecture results in almost limitless streams of translation units, each needing to be tagged, rendered, and otherwise processed.

- **Machine translation.** Like it or not, software-driven machine translation is a tool to be used by translators to improve their productivity. We figure that 99.44 percent of information in most firms, governments, and other organizations will never be translated. That zero translation (ZT) means that most firms do little more than translate their "About Us" page or whatever content national regulations require. Companies tell us that in an ideal world they would translate everything, so an increasing number will experiment with automated translation to bridge the gap. There will never be enough translators or Euros to translate everything that should be translated, so more technology will be one of the solutions.

Bibliography

of referenced Common Sense Advisory research:

"The state of freelance translation," June 2009

"Localization matters: Why adapting products and websites to local market needs means good business," November 2008

"Evolution and revolution in translation management," May 2008

"On the web, some countries matter more than others," September 2007

"Consolidation in the language services market," July 2007

"Can't read, won't buy: Why language matters on global websites," September 2006

"Language services: Supply-side outlook," January 2006

"Beggars at the globalization banquet," November 2002

Donald A. DePalma is the founder and chief research officer of the research and consulting firm Common Sense Advisory, and author of the premier book on business globalization "Business without borders: A strategic guide to global marketing."

The world in translation

Marion Boers

President of the International Federation of Translators

Introduction

Translation is as old as humanity itself. Is it not then surprising that we are still struggling to gain the recognition that we deserve as the guardians of cultural diversity and mediation? Translators and interpreters have been used throughout history to further the aims of various sectors – trade, religion, politics, etc. – and yet the translator was generally viewed simply as a minion in this process, although we all know how vital their role in fact is.

Technological advances and globalisation have seen the world change tremendously over the past decades. This has had both positive and negative spin-offs for our profession, and although our core activity may not have changed much there have been tremendous changes in the way we carry out that activity and the expectations on the part of both the professionals and their clients.

Status and recognition of the profession worldwide

So where do professional translators and interpreters fit into this globalised world of ours? Are they given any more recognition than they were in early times?

I think they are – but we are still a long way from the proper recognition due to our profession. There are a few countries in the world – Canada, Argentina and Denmark among them – where legal status has been awarded to the profession of translator, generally the result of years of lobbying by the leading members of the profession. This means that in those countries no one may practise as a translator (I use the term in its wider sense to include written and oral translation) without having met certain requirements, and in return they are accorded the professional respect that reflects the path that had to be followed to reach this level of expertise.

In most countries, though, anyone who has mastered two languages can tout themselves as a translator. Here it is up to the practitioners themselves to create conditions under which they are shown respect and acknowledged as experts. Unfortunately, this is easier said than done. One way to help achieve this goal is through the establishment of translators associations, which are then able to undertake promotional work, helping to raise awareness of the profession and the expertise required by practitioners. Very often, one of the vehicles used by such associations will be some system of accreditation. This may not have official status, but it does say to the world out there: "The work we do is important and we want to make sure the people who do that work are competent." This surely sends a message to clients that they should use an accredited or certified translator, or accept the consequences.

Many of FIT's member associations have put systems of accreditation into place. Current FIT vice-president Jiri Stejskal, when he headed FIT's Committee for Information on the Status of the Translation & Interpretation Profession, undertook a survey among FIT member associations on which of them offered accreditation and what this comprised. Roughly half of the associations that participated in the survey offer some form of accreditation or certification. The study revealed that the procedures employed in different countries vary widely, but there are certain common patterns, especially as regards the reason for introducing these systems. One of the four main purposes of certification is to elevate the status of the profession. (The other three are to establish standards of professional practice; to satisfy public demand for standards; and to extend the 'shelf life' of academic degrees through continuous professional development.)

It is an unfortunate fact of life that in most parts of the world the job of raising the status and recognition of the profession is left to translators themselves. In February this year I was privileged to attend a Salzburg Global Seminar on literary translation and what can be done to promote it. It was an eye-opening experience for me and certainly there it was clear that translators and translation are not held in particularly high regard. One of the speakers discussed the results of a recent survey of levels of payment of literary translators undertaken by the European Council of Literary Translators' Associations (CEATL), which revealed shocking figures of how poorly literary translators are remunerated in comparison with other occupations. Of course we can equate this poor pay with low status. Clients in the business world may be more willing to pay a living wage, but time and again we come across the phenomenon of the job going to the lowest bidder rather than the most competent one.

One of the very positive outcomes of the Salzburg Seminar was a series of recommendations and ideas aimed at promoting literary translations. Many of these could be extended to translation in general and if associations and individuals work at implementing them there could definitely be a spin-off in improved status for translators across the world.

I believe that globalisation has and will have a positive effect on the status of translation in the world, although it will not resolve the problems related to it or make it go away. However, the fact that the world has become so much smaller and the need to be able to communicate across borders and languages has increased brings with it a realisation of the need to have competent linguists to put your message across, to help seal the deal, to grow your business.

We also see an increased awareness of translation – and the need for good translation and competent translators – through the work of international and regional bodies around the world. Here in Europe everyone is aware of the work of the European Community, and the expense of the translation that is such a necessary part of the EC's work regularly comes under the spotlight. Though required in its constitution, the matter still makes waves every time a new country joins the EC and the pool of languages that has to be accommodated increases. Much the same applies to the work of the UN, though the number of languages is more limited there. However, the question is beginning to have relevance in other parts of the world too, where it has not traditionally been considered. The African Union is increasing its range of work and so is requiring more and more to be done in the language field. A Pan-African

Parliament was instituted a few years ago and suddenly decisions had to be made about interpreting and the provision of documentation in the different languages used. In Asia, the Association of South-East Asian Nations (ASEAN) has adopted English as its working language, but there is beginning to be a feeling that perhaps this is not the right course to follow. At a recent FIT EC meeting, we were addressed by a professor involved in translation in Thailand and there are moves there to develop Thailand as a language hub for Asia. We are all inclined to view developments within our own restricted sphere, and it is interesting to see that similar developments take place around the world – possibly at different rates and at different times, but often involving the same steps.

Challenges

What are the challenges for translators that result from globalisation?

As I have already mentioned, globalisation means the world has become more aware of translation and the need for good translation. This should translate into an increased amount of work becoming available. However, it also brings a number of challenges.

A major challenge facing translators, especially in developed countries, is that of pricing. A global market means having to compete across the world, not only within your own region. We have already mentioned that translation is not a particularly lucrative occupation at the best of times. Now a client is able to source a translator in India or in Ecuador to undertake their work. Costs of living in these areas are far lower than in Europe or America and there are different expectations as to what one should be earning. The work ethic is also different. So the client outsources his translation to the East, where he benefits from lower labour costs, from the difference in time zones, which means his translation is produced overnight and he loses no time, and from the willingness to work overtime without much extra compensation in order to secure the job. Whether this is 'right' or 'fair' or 'acceptable' I cannot say, but it is a fact of life that comes in the wake of globalisation and so we have to find a strategy for dealing with it. From the perspective of the translators in the less developed parts of the world, it brings wonderful opportunities, especially for those working in world languages. They are able to work at better rates than they may be able to locally and hopefully this situation goes hand in hand with an improvement in skills and status.

Our modern lifestyle – with everything available on demand – results in expectations of 'on-demand' translation too. Clients do not understand what goes into producing a translation and expect it to happen at the push of a button. So we face the challenge of 'better-educated' clients, who are becoming aware of things like machine translation and computer-assisted translation and assume that this means the translator is able to produce the goods in half the time they would have a few years ago. How are translators going to deal with this – work longer and longer hours in order to keep their clients happy or lose out to translators in different time zones who can deliver the goods?

With this emphasis on speed and competitive pricing, what happens to quality? For a start, we all know as professional translators that time and price pressures result in a sacrificing of quality. If you are being pushed to deliver within unrealistic time frames, the final check or proofreading goes by the board. If you are not being paid the equivalent of a professional wage, it is likely that you will not put as much effort into the final product as you would if you were being properly remunerated. This is not always the case, as in my experience language practitioners are perfectionists and often go the extra mile whether it is called for or not, but if you are juggling time and money constraints quality will definitely suffer.

A related aspect is qualifications and the standards applied in this regard. In an unregulated environment, every country, every region, virtually every university will develop their own qualifications and standards. How do we ensure that these correspond with one another, so that at the end of the day clients receive a quality product, wherever they have sourced their work? How do we know whether translators in all parts of the world even have formal training – is this in fact even necessary? Globalisation means that we are looking at things like this and it also means that teachers of translation have easier access to one another's programmes and know what is being done in other parts of the world. One hopes that this means in time a generally accepted standard of qualification will develop across the world, but such things take time. At present there is work in Europe on a European Masters in Translation and in Interpreting, and those involved will undoubtedly tell us a lot of work goes into reaching agreement on the different elements, even within a single region that has been cooperating for many years. How much more difficult will it be to reach consensus on levels of training or production in areas where the translation profession is still relatively young on a global scale – such as India, Thailand, Nigeria, Guatemala – and then to bring these into line with accepted standards elsewhere.

There are other aspects of quality and qualifications that come into play when we look at things at a global level. The developed world considers translation from the perspective of an ordered society, with established languages and plenty of resources like dictionaries – and expects the rest of the world to meet those standards. But other areas of the world do not necessarily have the luxury of such a settled background. Take my own country as an example. South Africa is regarded as a First World country, even though we are still in developing mode in many respects. We have an extremely liberal constitution that grants official status to 11 languages. Only one of those – English – is a world language. A second – Afrikaans – is at an advanced level of development. The other nine are indigenous African languages at varying stages of development, but even the best developed of them have a long way to go. Don't make the mistake of thinking that these are unsophisticated languages and wonder why there should be a fuss at all. They are in fact languages with very complicated structures and are a challenge for a non-native to learn. However, they are not fully standardised, which means there can be vehement disagreement between translators on what is correct or acceptable and what not. Then there is the problem of a lack of terminology for a wide range of fields that have not been traditional in African culture. So the African translator in South Africa faces a far more challenging work environment than someone working in languages like French, German and English. Add to this the wide range of basic needs in South Africa – education and health facilities, housing, employment opportunities – and it is no surprise to find that there is very little money to spend on making sure that the necessary development work is being done for these languages so that they can play the role they have been allocated through their status as official languages. No one polices the implementation of the language frameworks, and it is left to the individual translators to solve problems of terminology and form – messages need to go to the people and so a solution has to be found. I am sure there are many other parts of the world that face similar obstacles; I use this as an illustration because it is one I am familiar with.

Another example of the challenges arising from globalisation that one may not think of is the balancing of culture and traditions across the world. Of course this has always been an essential element of translation and is why we are known as cultural mediators. But again, cultural mediation is not too complicated when cultures and languages from a fairly homogenous region are concerned. Globalisation, however, means exposing some societies to very foreign concepts. The HIV/AIDS pandemic, for example, has required some very straight talking in efforts to curb the spread of this disease. For a Westerner, there is no problem listening to a talk or reading an information brochure that names the intimate body parts and functions. In African society this is taboo – it is simply not done, particularly in mixed society. So what does a translator do when requested to translate seemingly innocuous health pamphlets dealing with these matters? A non-local client will have no idea of the stress they will be causing to the translator – and this in an apparently developed country with international values and procedures!

A further challenge accompanying the flattening of the world through globalisation is an expectation that service providers will have the latest technology at their disposal. This again highlights discrepancies and inequalities in different parts of the world. Europeans and Americans assume that the majority of translators today work with CAT tools. It makes sense – they enable translators to remain competitive by increasing their output, while at the same time increasing consistency in the translations. I am constantly surprised at the number of unsolicited approaches I receive from overseas translation services looking for translators to add to their books, and very often stipulating that such persons must use a CAT tool, SDL Trados being the most common one. Now for a South African Trados is outrageously expensive. Add to that the fact that few South African translators are able to specialise and work largely in one narrow field, and this puts Trados out of the reach of many. I can imagine that similar situations prevail in other less developed countries as well, raising the question of how one can marry the price of this undoubtedly useful technology with local price levels in different countries. One cannot argue that the tools are not useful, and with global organisations requiring multilingual versions of documentation around the world it makes sense to use these programs, but the producers perhaps need to make some adjustments, depending on their markets. In South Africa, for example, we find that translators are beginning to use CAT tools, but that WordFast is more popular, because it is more affordable.

Globalisation and technological advances have also had some rather negative effects in our profession. We have seen a sharp rise in the problems faced by translators and interpreters in conflict and post-conflict areas. I am sure everyone is aware of the dangers faced by interpreters working for foreign armed forces or the media in places like Iraq. These regularly make the news and as far back as the time of the 2005 FIT World Congress FIT issued a press release highlighting the plight of these linguists and urging the authorities involved to provide them and their families with adequate protection. One of the FIT vice-presidents at the time, Bente Christensen, was very involved through International PEN in arranging asylum for some Iraqi interpreters. The situation does not seem to have improved, though. In November last year the American Translators Association petitioned the US government to rethink a policy prohibiting interpreters in Iraq from wearing ski masks to hide their identities. This year FIT has received direct requests from translators for support in asylum applications resulting from persecution because of their professional activities, one from a country in Africa and another from the Indian subcontinent. It is indeed concerning that at a time when the world is opening up and coming closer together, translators and interpreters should be persecuted and killed because of the work they do to bridge barriers between peoples and nations. I certainly take my hat off to those who face these dangers.

Looking forward

Where does the International Federation of Translators (FIT) fit into this globalised world? What is its role in relation to the profession?

As an international organisation, FIT operates at a global level and translators and interpreters should not expect to gain direct, tangible benefits from their own associations' membership of FIT. FIT's role is essentially to represent the profession at an international level and to help protect translators' interests at that level. The results of such work do trickle down and benefit the individual, but more through increased visibility and status than identifiable projects and money in their pockets.

FIT should not be duplicating or taking on the roles of national and local translators associations. So don't expect us to be organising local events or trying to improve the conditions of translators and interpreters at a local level.

FIT's strength and value lies in its international nature. It is supported by associations and individuals across the globe and as such has access to a variety of resources. I see three main areas in which FIT can serve the translation community in the coming years.

Firstly FIT can act as a clearing house for information from around the world. The FIT Secretariat receives a tremendous amount of information from organisations around the world. In addition, our own members can use their membership of FIT to promote their own activities and share experiences. We are fortunate to have on our current Council a member who has taken on the task of supervising the FIT Website and already it contains a great deal more up-to-date news and information than in the past. We hope to expand the usage of this avenue and other means of electronic communication to pass useful information on to our members, which in turn can pass it on to their members. In this way we can all share in the news from the global village. If associations pass this information on to their members, it will enable translators and interpreters around the world to be up to date with international trends and happenings – knowing what products are available, what events are taking place, what trends are emerging, what the outcomes and recommendations of conferences and other events are, and so on.

A second area in which FIT can play a valuable role – and one I would like to see strengthened over the next few years – is in making available information on best practice around the world. This could take a number of forms, but with access to expertise from all corners of the world it should be possible to collect common documents and information on best practice and distil these into international guidelines. When I attended the Salzburg Global Seminar earlier this year, I committed FIT, through its committees on literature and copyright, to help collect and make available model contracts for literary translators. The Council has also suggested that it would be useful to collect and make available the most important documents relating to best practice in the profession produced by our member associations. I know that FIT Europe has been doing a lot of work collecting information on standards and on debt-collecting around the continent – this type of information can also be made available to other members and supplemented with equivalent information from other parts of the world. Having such documentation readily available will also assist new associations when they set themselves up.

The third area where FIT can play a role is related to this. With its contacts all over the world, FIT should be able support dialogue between different parts of the globe. We can put members in contact with one another if they need assistance on specific matters. We can create discussion forums that span continents. We can interact with related international and regional organisations like those for conference interpreters (AIIC), localisation (GALA) and translation companies (EUTAC, ALC, ATC, etc.) and find common ground and areas for cooperation.

However, for FIT to achieve anything at all we need YOUR help. FIT itself has very limited resources and only a part-time secretariat. To make things happen it relies on the generosity of its members and their members: people who make themselves available to serve on the FIT Council and committees, volunteering their time and expertise to further the profession. Although the Council is the most visible organ of FIT, in fact most of the *real* work occurs in the committees. They represent the various areas of interest to members and they drive the action to meet the needs of members in those areas. So I appeal to you all to play your part in helping FIT achieve its objectives and raise the profile of translation around the world by accepting nomination to the FIT committee that best suits your interests. The term of office is only three years (though you may serve for a maximum of nine if you wish!), so it's not a life sentence, and it gives you the opportunity to make a contribution to the profession that has sustained you.

May I take this opportunity to thank all those who are currently serving within FIT and all our member associations for their continued support, and I invite you to let us know how you think FIT can serve its members better in the future.

Bibliographical details

Gouadec, Daniel (2007). *Translation as a Profession.* Amsterdam/Philadelphia: John Benjamins Publishing Company.

Stejskal, Jiri (2005). *Survey of the FIT Committee for Information on the Status of the Translation & Interpretation Profession.* USA: FIT.

Vorträge, Workshops und Podiumsdiskussionen

Themenblöcke

I. Auswirkungen der Globalisierung auf den Übersetzungs- und Dolmetschmarkt

Entwicklungen des Marktes

Was erwarten Kunden von Übersetzungsanbietern? Kundenanforderungen im Wandel

Frank Fleury

Fleury & Fleury Consultants, tekom

info@fleuryfleury.com

Warum kaufen Unternehmen Übersetzung ein?

Der Markt für Übersetzung ist bereits seit vielen Jahren im Wandel. Übersetzungsanbieter, ganz besonders Freelancer, stehen immer häufiger vor großen Schwierigkeiten, wenn es darum geht, Kunden zu gewinnen, auf Dauer zufrieden zu stellen und ihre Arbeit gewürdigt zu sehen. Auch Agenturen sehen sich einer zunehmenden internationalen Konkurrenz und hohem Preisdruck ausgesetzt. Diesen Schwierigkeiten versuchen Übersetzungsanbieter vor allem auf fachlicher Ebene durch Spezialisierung und erhöhte formale Qualifikation zu begegnen.

Diese Maßnahmen decken einen wichtigen Aspekt der professionellen Wahrnehmung des Berufs durch Kunden ab. Sie allein treffen jedoch noch nicht die Anforderungen von Unternehmen an Übersetzungsanbieter. Sie reichen darum nicht aus, eine professionellen Würdigung, wie sie Übersetzer gerne erfahren würden, zu erreichen.

Zur Veranschaulichung mag folgendes Beispiel dienen: Wer würde einen Staubsauger kaufen, nur weil jemand an der Haustür klingelt und ihm zeigt, dass er Staubsauger zu verkaufen hat? Auch Hinweise auf eine besonders schöne Düse oder auf besondere Saugkenntnisse des Vertreters helfen selten. Menschen kaufen Staubsauger gewöhnlich nicht um ihrer selbst willen.

Zwischen Unternehmen und Übersetzungsanbietern verhält es sich ähnlich: Sie kaufen Übersetzung nur selten schon deshalb ein, weil ein Übersetzungsanbieter in Erscheinung tritt und auf seine Spezialisierung und Qualifikation hinweist. Denn Unternehmen existieren nicht in einem Vakuum, von wo aus sie hin und wieder Übersetzungsaufträge an die Umgebung senden. Sie befinden sich in einem Beziehungsgeflecht im Dreieck Markt-Unternehmen-Übersetzungsanbieter, das bestimmte Anforderungen an sie stellt, die sie zu erfüllen versuchen. Sie haben zudem die Auswahl zwischen einer Vielzahl von Übersetzungsanbietern, die ebenfalls qualifiziert sind, und das weltweit.

Konkret bedeutet das, dass Unternehmen auf bestimmten Märkten tätig sind, wo sie Produkte oder Dienstleistungen verkaufen wollen, um Gewinne zu erwirtschaften. Dazu müssen sie bestimmte Voraussetzungen erfüllen, beispielsweise schlicht von ihren Kunden verstanden werden oder rechtlichen Vorgaben genügen. Übersetzung ist für Unternehmen also kein möglichst perfekt zu erfüllender Selbstzweck, sondern bedeutet die Bewältigung einer Voraussetzung, die Erfüllung einer Aufgabe. Sie ist Mittel zum Zweck. Da es in erster Linie um die Erfüllung dieses Zwecks geht, bestimmt dieser die Anforderungen an die Übersetzung und den Übersetzungsanbieter.

Was ist erfolgsrelevant für Unternehmen?

Auf ihren Märkten sehen sich Unternehmen indessen vor große Herausforderungen gestellt: Durch die allgegenwärtige Informationstechnologie wird es immer einfacher und günstiger, Informationen überall hin zu transportieren und zu verarbeiten. Technisierung und Automatisierung nehmen zu. Geschäftsprozesse und Organisationen werden laufend angepasst. Innovationsschübe folgen in immer kürzeren Zeitabständen. Diese Entwicklungen werden weiter getrieben und beschleunigen sich zusehends. Folge ist eine Zeitverknappung, die zu einer Beschleunigung der Geschäftsprozesse selbst und zu einem kürzerem Time-To-Market führt. Flankiert wird die Entwicklung durch eine fortschreitende rechtliche Regulierung, die ein Umdenken etwa in Haftungsfragen erfordert, eine Globalisierung von Märkten und Kapital sowie internationale und interkulturelle Zusammenarbeit. Dadurch ändert sich das Wettbewerbsumfeld drastisch. Praktisch jeder, der entsprechendes Kapital mobilisiert und über Know-how und Risikobereitschaft verfügt, kann heute weltweit am Wirtschaftsleben teilnehmen. Die Marktspielregeln ändern sich dadurch immer weiter, beispielsweise durch die Nutzung neuer Medien. Hinzu kommt eine allgemeine Geldverknappung unter anderem durch Preisverfall, Kriege und Wirtschaftskrisen.

Unternehmen reagieren darauf im Wesentlichen dadurch, dass sie die sich verändernden Marktspielregeln antizipieren und adaptieren, die betriebliche Leistung (Produktivität und Qualität) in allen Bereichen – auch in der Übersetzung – verbessern, ihre Lern- und Arbeitsgeschwindigkeit an die Veränderungsgeschwindigkeit anpassen und in immer kürzeren Abständen Innovationen hervorbringen.

Die betriebliche Leistung lässt sich durch eine Projekt-, Prozess- und Organisationsstruktur verbessern, die ständig an die Anforderungen angepasst und optimiert wird. Innerhalb einer solchen Struktur ist die Übersetzung Teil einer Prozesskette, mit definierten Schnittstellen zu anderen Teilen. Entsprechend wird sie als optimierbarer Prozessschritt im „magischen Dreieck" von definierten Zeit- und Qualitätszielen und Kosten sowie als Risikofaktor betrachtet.

So führt etwa eine standardisierte und nachvollziehbare Vorgehensweise zu höherer Effizienz sowie zu weniger Fehlern und Kosten. Klare Verantwortlichkeiten in der Projektdefinition minimieren redundante Tätigkeiten und zeitraubende Abstimmungen. Umfassende IT-Unterstützung ist der größte Hebel für Kostensenkungen und Voraussetzung für die Bewältigung immer weiter wachsender Datenmengen, etwa mit Hilfe von Autoren-, Terminologiemanagement- und Translation-Memory-Systemen oder Automatisierung. Ohne sie ist Übersetzung für Unternehmen darum meist kaum noch vorstellbar. Die Zusammenführung von Aufgaben aus verschiedenen Abteilungen und die effiziente Integration von externen Einheiten in den Gesamtprozess erschließen weitere Einsparpotenziale. All diese Maßnahmen zielen auf fortgesetzte internationale Konkurrenzfähigkeit unter enormem Preisdruck. Industrieunternehmen und Mittelständler haben sie entweder bereits weitgehend verinnerlicht oder setzen sie gerade um.

Auch das Outsourcing der Übersetzung an Übersetzungsanbieter dient der Verbesserung der betrieblichen Leistung: Neben der Erweiterung des Kundenkreises durch neue Sprachen und der Nutzung von nicht im Unternehmen vorhandenem Know-how spielen Erwartungen an die Verkürzung des Time-To-Market durch schnellere Auftragsabwicklung, Kostenreduzierung durch effizientere Projektabwicklung, Erhöhung der Kapazitäten, Sicherstellung von Produkt-, Prozess- und Servicequalität, Planbarkeit und Risikominimierung eine zentrale Rolle. Übersetzer und Agenturen werden entsprechend nach Kriterien wie Fachkenntnis, Erfahrung, Kapazität, Preis und IT-Unterstützung in Ranglisten eingeordnet.

Wo stehen die Übersetzer?

Dem steht jedoch zurzeit kein Berufsbild des Übersetzers gegenüber, das es erlaubt, diesen Zielen der Unternehmen auf Augenhöhe zu begegnen. Seine Ausbildung vermittelt zudem kein Selbstverständnis, das all die zusätzlichen Kenntnisse und Fertigkeiten integriert, die heute für jeden Selbständigen Voraussetzung sind, um auf einem weltweiten Markt zu bestehen.

So konzentrieren sich heute immer noch viele Übersetzer beinahe ausschließlich auf ihre translatorische Kompetenz. Sich als Teilnehmer einer Prozesskette zu sehen, fällt manchen genau so schwer, wie die sich daraus ergebenden Forderungen an Schnittstellen und Prozessmanagement zu erfüllen. Viele Übersetzer tun sich mit Technologieeinsatz, der von Unternehmen zunehmend aus betrieblicher Notwendigkeit vorausgesetzt wird, schwer. Sie kennen die Texterstellungsprozesse in Unternehmen nur bedingt und können ihren Kunden darum keine entsprechende Unterstützung geben oder kompetenter Lösungspartner sein. Service und Kommunikation, Kernprozesse beruflicher Tätigkeit, werden oft genau so vernachlässigt wie eine weitreichende Vernetzung und Kooperation untereinander.

Diese Schieflage hat weitreichende Folgen: Introvertiert, eigenbrötlerisch, technik- und innovationsfeindlich, ohne betriebswirtschaftliches Verständnis, besserwisserisch, schnell beleidigt und aggressiv, fortbildungsfeindlich, kontaktarm, unzuverlässig bei Terminen, schwierig im Umgang, wenig anpassungsfähig an existierende Prozesse – dies sind nur einige von vielen negativen Bildern, mit denen sich Übersetzer nach Aussage von Teilnehmern unserer Seminare konfrontiert sehen. Auch wenn diese Eindrücke nur durch einen Teil der Übersetzer erzeugt werden, sind sie doch so stark, dass sie das Image im Allgemeinen nachhaltig prägen und ein Bild von Professionalität, Kompetenz und hohem Nutzwert der Dienstleistung nicht entstehen lassen.

Einen entsprechend schweren Stand haben Übersetzer bei ihren Kunden, wenn es um die Anerkennung ihrer Leistung, das Verständlichmachen von Anforderungen und Schwierigkeitsgraden auf Übersetzerseite, oder das Durchsetzen von Preisen geht. Sie werden oft nicht einmal angehört oder wissen nicht, wie Sie professionell überzeugen können. Das Bild vom einsamen Übersetzer, der am Küchentisch bei einer Tasse Tee und mit der Katze auf dem Schoß „mal eben" übersetzt ist genau so verbreitet wie die Einschätzung des Übersetzens als Hobby, das man für ein Taschengeld nebenbei betreibt. Dementsprechend empfinden sich Übersetzer im Verhältnis zu Unternehmenskunden häufig als untergeordnet, nicht ernst genommen, per se unterlegen und als Spielball von Launen.

Perspektiven

Die Erkenntnis dieses misslichen Zusammenhangs ist zugleich der Schlüssel zu seiner Überwindung: Mindestens genauso wichtig wie die translatorische Kompetenz ist die Fähigkeit, die übrigen Anforderungen zu erfüllen, deren Bedeutung immer weiter wächst. Übersetzungsagenturen füllen genau dieses Vakuum aus. Sie sind im besten Falle anpassungsfähige Kommunikations- und Prozessprofis, die ihren Kunden flexible Unterstützung anbieten, einschließlich informationstechnischer Mittel bis hin zu speziellen Plattformen und einer für Kunden transparenten internen Verarbeitung der ausgetauschten Daten. Vieles davon können Freelancer aus Kapazitäts- und Kostengründen nicht leisten. Insofern bieten Agenturen auch Übersetzern, die bestimmte Anforderungen von Unternehmen nicht erfüllen können oder wollen, eine Möglichkeit, sich dennoch auf einem bestimmten Gebiet zu betätigen.

Die Erfüllung der Anforderungen setzt bei allen Übersetzungsanbietern, Agenturen wie Freelancern, neben Fachkompetenz Zuverlässigkeit, Vertrauenswürdigkeit, aber auch Flexibilität und Entwicklungsfähigkeit voraus. Sie können der Situation und den Anforderungen auf zwei Ebenen begegnen:

Marktpositionierung

Durch fachliche Spezialisierung und Finden einer Nische erhöhen sich die Chancen auf Aufträge deutlich. Haftungsrechtliche Fragen etwa erfordern zunehmend spezifische Fachkenntnisse.

Zentral ist die Frage nach dem beruflichen Selbstverständnis. Es ist essenziell, dass sich Übersetzungsanbieter über die Übersetzungstätigkeit hinaus statt als „Ausführer" verstärkt als Unternehmer in eigener Sache begreifen und sich aktiv mit den damit zusammenhängenden Fragen befassen. Dazu gehört auch, neue Entwicklungen aktiv aufzunehmen und zu integrieren, das eigene Berufsbild und Selbstverständnis ständig mit den sich verändernden Randbedingungen weiter zu entwickeln, statt sich von den Entwicklungen vor sich hertreiben zu lassen und sich darüber zu beschweren. Neue technologische Entwicklungen etwa bedeuten nicht automatisch eine Bedrohung für Übersetzer, sondern können, frühzeitig adaptiert oder sogar aktiv mit vorangetrieben, Übersetzungsanbieter dabei unterstützen, die Anforderungen der Kunden zu erfüllen und sich so am Markt zu behaupten. Durch eine Entwicklung mit den Anforderungen können sich Übersetzungsanbieter mit zusätzlichen Kenntnissen in Technologie, Prozessen und Wissensmanagement als Fachleute für den Prozessschritt Übersetzung etablieren, wie es die erfolgreicheren unter den Agenturen bereits tun. Dies bedeutet auch, strategische unternehmerische Entscheidungen in die Hand zu nehmen.

Dies setzt mehrerlei voraus: Wegen der vielzitierten „Halbwertszeit" des Wissens hat eine formale Ausbildung immer mehr einen eher initialen Wert. Um die Entwicklung vom „fertigen" Übersetzer zum lebenslang lernenden Wissensarbeiter und -manager kommt darum niemand mehr herum; Weiterbildung ist längst Erfolgsvoraussetzung. Des Weiteren werden konsequente Anforderungsermittlung, überzeugende Kundenorientierung und interdisziplinäres Mitdenken immer wichtiger, um genau die geforderten Ziele zu erreichen. Dies gilt auch im Verhältnis zwischen Freelancern und Agenturen, die ebenfalls im Wettbewerb und unter Preisdruck stehen. Darüber hinaus gewinnt Vernetzung an Bedeutung, etwa um Ausfallrisiken abzuwenden oder Aufträge zu schultern, für die nicht die fachlichen oder sprachlichen Voraussetzungen vorliegen.

Schließlich werden auch Fertigkeiten der Kommunikation, Gesprächs- und Verhandlungsführung sowie gut durchdachter Service immer unverzichtbarer. Entgegen der landläufigen Meinung sind viele Unternehmen bereit, Service, der ihnen nützt und ihnen überzeugend verkauft wird, zu honorieren. Entsprechend ist die gezielte Entwicklung sog. Soft Skills, Flexibilität und die Übernahme der Verantwortung für die Voraussetzungen der eigenen professionellen Dienstleistung entscheidend. So wird aus dem Übersetzungsanbieter ein integrierter und wertvoller Prozesspartner, ein Helfer und Mitdenker, statt bloß ausführender Kostenfaktor zu sein.

Daneben kann auch das Honorarkonzept überdacht werden: Wäre es beispielsweise sinnvoll, Wort- oder Zeilenpreise nach Fach, Qualitätsanforderung und Schwierigkeit zu differenzieren?

Auch das Dienstleistungsportfolio kann erweitert und differenziert werden. Neue Tätigkeitsfelder entstehen, wie etwa Terminologiearbeit oder Post-Editing, das durch das Vordringen der Maschinenübersetzung entstanden ist und am Markt bereits aktiv nachgefragt wird.

Interne Optimierung

Auf der anderen Seite können auch die eigenen Prozesse meist deutlich optimiert werden.

IT-Unterstützung kann dabei helfen, den Projektmanagement-Overhead zu verringern, wenn durch den Einsatz von TM-Systemen immer mehr kleinere Übersetzungsaufträge eingehen, und so den Durchsatz erhöhen.

Neue Technologien können für eigene Zwecke genutzt werden, beispielsweise preisgünstige Machine Translation Tools, die auch von kleineren Anbietern sinnvoll selbst angewendet werden können, um den Aufwand und die eigenen Kosten für bestimmte Aufträge zu senken. Eine durchdachte Standardisierung der Einzelaufgaben bringt Schnelligkeit und Sicherheit.

Diese und andere Maßnahmen zur Kostensenkung und Effizienzsteigerung können helfen, den Kostendruck, der von den Unternehmenskunden oder Agenturen an die Übersetzungsanbieter weitergereicht wird, aufzufangen und Unternehmen Partner bei der Kostensenkung zu sein, ohne die eigene Lebensgrundlage aufzugeben.

Fazit

Erfolgreiche Übersetzungsdienstleistung bedeutet heute mehr als Anbieten und kompetentes Durchführen von Übersetzung. Proaktives Anforderungsmanagement, professionelle Kommunikationstechniken und durchdachter Service sind wichtige Schlüssel, um professionell und kompetent wahrgenommen zu werden, handeln zu können und nicht überrollt zu werden. Ebenso wichtig ist die vorausschauende technologische Kundenunterstützung bis hin zur Prozessautomatisierung. Immer stärker ist der auf Augenhöhe professionell und umfassend agierende Übersetzungsunternehmer als Lösungsanbieter und Prozessbegleiter gefragt.

Im internationalen Wettbewerb erfolgreich bestehen

Andreas Schiemenz

Fundraising Factory GmbH

aschiemenz@gmx.net

Wettbewerb im globalen Umfeld

Die Welt wird immer kleiner. Die Kommunikationsinstrumente ermöglichen uns einen Austausch mit Gesprächspartnern überall auf der Welt ohne Zeitverzögerung. Durch Internet, E-Mails, Skype, Videokonferenzen und vielen anderen Kommunikationsmethoden sind fast alle Kommunikationshürden überwunden.

Auch im Informationsmanagement ist die Globalisierung der Märkte spürbar. Wir erfahren im Internet, wie sich die Hotelpreise am Central Park in New York verändern, wir können den Flug nach Neuseeland über eine britische Reiseagentur günstiger buchen und wissen natürlich auch, welche Eintrittspreise im Legoland auf uns warten.

Die Welt scheint transparenter und schneller geworden zu sein. Aber trotzdem führt die unbegrenzte Verfügbarkeit von Informationen nicht dazu, dass die Menschen besser informiert sind. Im Gegenteil, die Informationsflut führt zu einer verstärkten Unsicherheit. Zu viel an Input führt dazu, dass die zur Verfügung stehenden Informationen nicht mehr bewertet werden können. Weniger ist eben doch mehr.

Globalisierte Märkte sind Übersetzermärkte

Der weltweite und fast unbegrenzte Handel von Produkten und Dienstleistungen hat die Ländergrenzen als Marktgrenzen aufgehoben. Die Zollgrenzen sind weitestgehend abgeschafft, es wurden länderübergreifende Binnenmärkte geschaffen, und im interkontinentalen Handel wurden zahlreiche Ein- und Ausfuhrbestimmungen novelliert.

Laut der Bundesbank hat allein die Bundesrepublik Deutschland im Jahr 2008 Waren im Wert von 813,46 Mrd. € importiert und im Wert von 990,16 Mrd. € exportiert. Laut Wikipedia wurden 2007 weltweit Waren im Wert von 13.950 Mrd. US-$ exportiert.

Gewinner dieses weltweiten Austausches sind alle. Die Unternehmen, da sich die Märkte vergrößert haben, die Verbraucher, weil es einen größeren Wettbewerb gibt, und die Übersetzer, weil alle Gruppen miteinander kommunizieren müssen.

Der internationale Wettbewerb ist also die Grundlage des wirtschaftlichen Erfolgs von Übersetzern und Dolmetschern. Denn der Anteil an Auftraggebern aus der Wirtschaft ist wesentlich höher als öffentliche und private Auftraggeber zusammen.

Wettbewerbsdruck auf den Märkten

Doch mit dem wachsenden Welthandel und den grenzenlosen Kommunikationsmöglichkeiten, hat sich auch der Wettbewerb im Übersetzermarkt geändert. Zwar sind alle Dienstleister sehr dankbar, dass nun auch die Möglichkeit besteht, die Leistungen im Ausland zeitnah anzubieten. Doch die Freude über den gleichzeitig zunehmenden Wettbewerb von Kollegen aus dem Ausland ist überschaubar.

Denn trotz Globalisierung gibt es regionale, länderspezifische Unterschiede. So unterscheiden sich Kaufkraft und Einkommen selbst in den EU-Ländern erheblich – und somit der Preis für eine Übersetzung. Es gibt keine einheitlichen Ausbildungs- und Berufsausbildungsrichtlinien, keine verbindlichen Qualitätsrichtlinien. Selbst die Grundlage der Preisfindung ist nicht einheitlich, mal wird in Wörtern, mal in Zeilen oder gar im Stunden abgerechnet.

Positionierung im globalen Markt

Doch Heulen und Zähneklappern hilft hier wenig. Wer sich für den Beruf des Übersetzers entschieden hat, der muss sich naturgegeben auch dem internationalen Wettbewerb stellen. Erfreulicherweise gibt es drei Stellschrauben, mit denen ein Anbieter seinen internationalen Erfolg beeinflussen kann:

1. Die eigene Marktpositionierung
2. Die potentiellen Kunden
3. Die angebotenen Leistungen

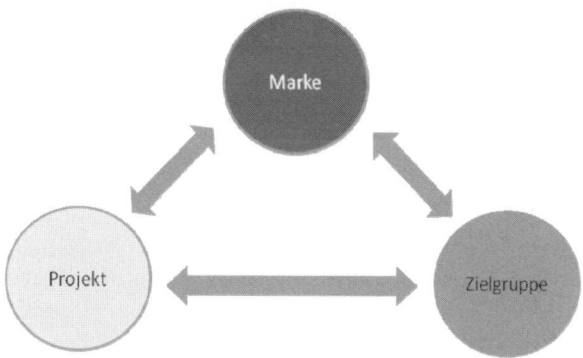

Eindeutiges Branding vereinfacht die Akquise

Im Marketing wird vom Branding gesprochen, wenn es darum geht, wie sich ein Unternehmen am Markt positioniert. Und dabei ist es vollkommen unerheblich, ob es sich um einen börsennotierten Konzern oder um einen freiberuflichen Übersetzer handelt.

Entscheidend ist, ob der Übersetzer als Anbieter am Markt überhaupt wahrgenommen wird. Der künftige Kunde muss eben wissen, dass es den Anbieter gibt. Der Aufbau einer Marke ist für einen Übersetzer genauso einfach und genauso schwer, wie für eine Automarke. Der große Vorteil für den Übersetzer liegt in seiner Spezialisierung. Er wird nicht alle Sprachkombinationen anbieten, sondern nur die, die er wirklich beherrscht. Und er wird nicht in allen Fachgebieten arbeiten, sondern da, wo er sich auskennt.

Je deutlicher das Profil, desto größer ist die Abgrenzung zum Wettbewerb. Und je klarer das Angebotsspektrum, desto klarer auch die Zielgruppen.

Wer den Kunden kennt, kennt auch dessen Präferenzen

Nicht jeder Mensch auf diesem Planet ist Kunde für einen Übersetzer. Vielmehr lassen sich die potentiellen Kunden auf Grund des Leistungsspektrums deutlich eingrenzen. Ein Übersetzer mit der Sprachkombination Deutsch – Französisch und mit dem Schwerpunkt „erneuerbare Energien" hat eine klare Vorstellung davon, in welchen Ländern (nämlich den deutsch- und französischsprachigen) welche Unternehmen anzusprechen sind.

Aus dieser banalen Erkenntnis lässt sich eine Menge ableiten. Zum einen gibt es eine gute Übersicht über die potentiellen Kunden, nämlich die Anzahl von Unternehmen aus dem Bereich der erneuerbaren Energien in den definierten Ländern. Ebenfalls lässt sich an einem solchen Zielgruppenprofil erkennen, über welche Kommunikationswege sich diese Unternehmen erreichen lassen. Das können z.B. die Branchenveranstaltungen wie Fachmessen und Symposien sein, die Internetportale oder die nationalen Fachzeitschriften.

Leistungen, wie Kunden es sich vorstellen

Übersetzung ist nicht gleich Übersetzung. Jeder Dienstleister hinterlässt seine Handschrift, jeder Auftraggeber hat seine eigenen Vorstellungen. Aber es gibt wenige Dienstleistungen auf der Welt, von denen der Auftraggeber so wenig weiß wie von der Leistung der Übersetzung.

Natürlich muss ein Auftraggeber nicht wissen, wie ein Übersetzer arbeitet, welche Anforderungen an den Berufsstand gelten. Aber es hilft doch sehr, wenn der Übersetzer seine Leistungen in einer Wertigkeit anbietet, die eine Übersetzung verdient hat. Nur so wird aus einer Übersetzung ein individuelles und nutzenbringendes Produkt.

Eingebunden im Marketingdreieck

Marketing heißt, mit den Marktakteuren im ständigen Dialog zu stehen. Die Marktakteure sind zum einen die oben skizzierten Zielgruppen, der Anbieter und der Wettbewerb. In diesem Marketingdreieck wirkt sich das Verhalten eines Akteurs immer auf die anderen beiden Akteure aus.

Entwickelt sich der Markt der Zielgruppen schlechter und die Umsätze gehen zurück, so wirkt sich das auf den Anbieter und den Wettbewerb in sinkenden Einnahmen aus. Verstärkt dann der Wettbewerb seine Kommunikation mit den Kunden im Rahmen einer Kundenbindungskampagne, so fällt es dem Anbieter schwerer, die Kunden an sich zu binden. Reagiert nun der Anbieter mit Preisdumping auf diese Situation, so muss der Wettbewerb seine eigene Preispolitik überdenken.

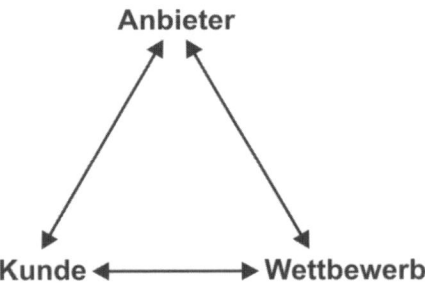

Individuelles Marketing

Damit ein Übersetzer im internationalen Wettbewerb bestehen kann, benötigt er ein individuelles Marketing. Der Dialog zwischen dem Anbieter und den Zielgruppen darf nicht standardisiert sein, sondern muss die Stärken des Anbieters deutlich in den Vordergrund stellen. Gleichzeitig bedeuten diese Stärken für die Zielgruppen Vorteile, die sich wiederum in deren Wettbewerb vorteilhaft auswirken werden.

Genauso wenig, wie sich die Inhalte des Marketings vereinheitlichen lassen, genauso wenig stehen die Marketinginstrumente fest. Natürlich gibt es Instrumente, die alle Anbieter vorhalten müssen. Dazu gehört eine aussagefähige Website und professionelle Geschäftsunterlagen wie Briefpapier und Visitenkarte. Doch diese Tools verbindet ein Erscheinungsbild und eine eindeutige Zuordenbarkeit zum Anbieter.

Aber alle anderen Marketingtools hängen von den einzelnen Übersetzern und deren Positionierungsstrategien ab. Während der Anbieter A auf Anzeigen nicht verzichten kann, um seine Bekanntheit im Markt zu steigern, akquiriert Anbieter B nur über das Telefon. Einem anderen Übersetzer liegt mehr die Kundenansprache per Brief und ein Übersetzungsbüro investiert in Onlinemarketing.

Es gibt also keinen Königsweg im internationalen Wettbewerb. Aber es gibt große Chancen, die eigenen Stärken zu nutzen und sich im Wettkampf um Kunden zu positionieren.

Current trends in the translation industry and what they mean to all of us

Oleg Rudavin

Freelancer

orudavin@gmail.com

Disclaimer: The situation as it is described below reflects the views of a freelance translator. The same trends and their consequences may be viewed and assessed differently by small/medium agency owners, MLV's or end clients.

First, a few common truths. Trivial as they are, these facts often help us better understand what is happening in our professional lives and environment.

- By definition, the translation industry cannot be self-sustaining. We don't make our own product to later sell it to translation consumers; instead, we fully depend on the activities in various sectors of the world economy and sometimes, political relations between countries. Here are a few simple examples to illustrate it. Ukraine is among those most affected by the current crisis; and the result is a noticeable decrease in the inflow of jobs into Ukrainian. Or, ambitious oilfield development projects were hastily launched last year when the price reached almost $US 150 per barrel – only to be frozen or put on low profile when it dropped to nearly $US 30.

- The most popular geometric figure to be found in the structure of the modern society and economy is a pyramid. It's actually a very stable construction, and the only drawback with it is the weight distribution: the load is highest at the bottom and almost non-existent at the top. In economic reality, we frequently see slightly misshaped pyramids withy very broad foundations (formed by actual doers) and narrowed peaks (decision-makers, business owners, top managers, CEOs) with the administrative layer(s) in between.

- For all players, one of the most important motives of our professional or business activities is of a financial nature. The difference is in the degree: while translators make their living, agencies make their own living better, and agency owners make their own living the best.

Now, introduction dealt with, let's get back to the immediate topic of the presentation.

Indeed, there is an entire spectrum of expectations among the major players in the market – from cheerful optimism to sheer pessimism. Often, it's a matter of perception; in other instances, certain trends do mean serious changes (like those in the quality of translation jobs, or a new translator's profile). Personally, as a freelancer, I see very little room for optimism in the new structure of the translation industry we'll all soon find ourselves in. The changes taking place make me sad because I love my profession and have been enjoying it immensely... until recently. These changes, they alter the very essence of the profession, and I can't say that I like the coming model.

The three things that are of major importance for the industry are: globalization, technological progress and market consolidation.

The consequences of globalization in the translation market are numerous and diverse. As a result of globalization, the demand for translation services is increasing quite rapidly. A while back, goods or services were mostly sold, consumed or used locally and occasionally exported to other linguistic locations. Today, an increasing proportion of goods and services are intended for global sales, and this global commercial suitability becomes obvious at the moment of their conception. Wiser clients take this into account and plan for translation expenses in advance. They understand the linguistic component of their products is about the only thing that makes them stand out from among similar goods or services.

A higher demand for translation services means more work for us translators. Well, at the end of the day it's indeed so; but the nature of the demand is also changing, and an increasing part of the new jobs will not be the kind of jobs to be handled by freelancers. They will be too big in size – sometimes millions of words – or the schedules are going to be too tight, and often, it's going to be translation into a dozen or more languages. It's exactly the type of jobs to be handled by large international MLV's – in other words, by translation corporations.

We didn't have any 15 or 10 years ago, did we? I doubt so: the Internet connection was slower, more expensive and not as easily accessible as now in many parts of the world. But technological progress can't be stopped, and now a translator living on the other side of the globe is just a few clicks away.

The increasing demand, global availability and affordability of Internet and market globalization were the primary reasons for the emergence of translation corporations. Yet another encouraging factor is the easiness of it. Indeed, the conditions are enviable: a large company can consist of top managers and middle-tier administrators like PM's only, with no production facilities, no machines, no insurance or social package for the actual doers scattered all over the world; and the doers are supposed to have their own production tools and software. It's like Lufthansa accepting only pilots with their own Boeings... The fact that some of the MLV's (Multi-Language Vendors) are also developers and owners of CAT tools adds to the irony of the situation. "We only accept pilots with their own aircraft – and you must buy one from us!"

According to certain estimates, the 30 largest language service companies get about 20% of the revenues generated in the translation industry, and some of them boast about an annual growth of 20% to 50%. If the trend continues, we'll soon see them in charge of a half, and a bit later – in a pessimistic scenario, in three to four years – of three quarters of the jobs, with small and medium agencies acting as subcontractors, and freelancers being virtually excluded from the process or at least separated from the end clients.

Essentially, there's nothing wrong in working for translation agencies, with the exception of their rates which are commonly not as high as those paid by direct clients. But it becomes different with translation corporations. As a translation agency moves along the road of transformation from a medium-sized into a large one and then into a corporation, a change of priorities happens.

What's the purpose that I set for myself as a freelance translator? Well, I earn my income by doing what I like doing and can do well. A small or medium translation agency is supposed to streamline the process via distribution of responsibilities across specialized resources (translators, proofreaders & editors, administration, accounting, logistics, etc) while bringing higher revenues to the owner. Unlike these, corporations are basically structures intended for making a comfortable living for their owners and/or top managers. Period.

During a discussion at a recent conference, the manager of one of the largest translation companies in Russia was cynically sincere: he said that freelance translators are tools the agencies use to make money for themselves – kind of human-mechanical revenue-generating machines. By his book, machines (=translators) that want to be busy must be cheap and reliable (the list of requirements is not complete of course). This approach is steadily gaining popularity, and translators are categorized as expenditure items which any for-profit company will always be trying to minimize.

No doubt freelancing as a business model is not very efficient and has its limitations. My turnaround would not normally exceed the standard three or four thousand words a day, nor can I handle three target languages as one bunch, and the full cycle (translation, editing/proofreading and probably occasional QA) would require third party involvement. In the same way, a smaller agency would not digest a few million words in a dozen languages within a few weeks or even months. So obviously, we can distinguish "freelance", "agency" and "MLV's jobs" – and there are plenty of them for each. Unfortunately, no agency/MLV would ever decline an offer of a "pure freelancer's" job like 4,500 words in an MS Word.doc format to be delivered in 3 days. The question is, from the end client's side, what added value would an agency offer to the end client in this case? None I'm afraid, especially if the agency is of the box-shifter type. To see how numerous they are, just google the phrase "we translate all languages" – the result may come as a surprise.

That's exactly the situation when freelance translators and agencies are competitors; and I suspect that, as a freelancer, I'm unlikely to win in the competition with agencies and big language service companies in the long run.

The nature of the demand is undergoing serious transformations, too. Many of us translate millions and millions of words that will never be read. In this artificial world of today, common sense is often replaced with excessively detailed instructions. Hence the "don't-put-your-finger-into-the-electric-socket" or "wearing your headset while scuba-diving will result in irrevocable damage of the device and make the warranty void" bits and pieces in every manual; hence the nearly illegible language of marketing materials; awkward names for innovative features and functions invented in an attempt to catch the buyers' attention; hence the software strings and acronyms which are not understood even by the authors themselves. With every year, texts I translate get worse in the meaning and in nine cases out of ten leave a bad marketing aftertaste.

Then, there's technological progress taking its toll. As a translator, I'm expected to own and be able to work with a number of software products, have basic understanding of codes, and possess a range of other skills to be eligible as a translation service provider. On top of that, the list of requirements is repeatedly followed by "give us your best rate" refrain.

The jobs are getting more complex. Translators with linguistic backgrounds find it increasingly difficult to get themselves settled in specialized areas as the areas themselves are becoming ever more sophisticated. Second education in the relevant field and on-site hands-on experience help us out, and I suggest that those contemplating translation as their future profession should consider getting a second specialized education as well or acquire specialization first while working at their language skills in parallel. As opposed to linguists, specialists will be in higher demand.

To illustrate the trend, let's have a look at a more or less typical job offer:

"XXX seeking experienced professional translators who are attorneys or have formal legal and medical training to translate agreements related to XXX. Experience in the translation of such agreements is a major plus. Five years professional translation experience minimum – ten or more ideal. Trados or compatible translation tool a must. Translators must be available to begin work immediately. Interested translators should send a detailed resume outlining translation experience, subject-area expertise, Trados rates and other supporting information."

In the former Soviet Union, it took five years to get an academic linguistic or legal education, and seven years to get training in medicine. That means that to be an ideal candidate for the job, I should have spent 17 years studying and the next 10 years gaining experience, be ready to accept reduced rates for repetitions/fuzzies and to crown it all, be unemployed to be able to start immediately. With all due respect, isn't that a bit too much?

Taking on a more serious note, specialization is the key to success right now and will be even more so in the future: expert knowledge will probably override linguistic skills.

Looming in the dark future of the translation industry is an ugly ghost of machine translation. Though it's not a red level alert yet, machine translation is getting better and presently it's used quite extensively, for example, by web-page visitors for translating page content. This factor surely has to be considered for long-term planning. MT is unlikely to replace human translation anytime soon. At the same time, properly combined with CAT tools and human involvement, machine translation can in fact be a step in the right direction, especially if it's used wisely and for the right purposes. Like, for example, translation of machine-generated texts. Why not? Those who translate manuals for household appliances might have noticed the similarity of certain parts; after all, the safety warnings, connection to power and button-pushing process are more or less the same irrespective of the actual device – be it a TV, microwave oven or lawn grass trimmer. Why not use machines to generate the content of all these user's manuals, with human post-editing?

In its core, machine translation is akin to combining harvesters in agriculture: they do the hard job of taking the wheat crop but they don't make flour or bread. In the same manner, MT might, in a few years, be used to produce "raw translations".

Lack of universally and internationally accepted standards applicable to the translation industry and products brought a lot of easy riders into translation. Luckily, there's progress in this area. At the same time, only a minor part of end clients or translation consumers really understand what translation is about and what it should be like. Many translation service buyers do not differentiate between bilingualism and professional translation ability; frequently, they believe that a newspaper article about a movie star caught driving drunk and the operation manual for a hemodialysis machine – well, away with extremism; let it be a car washer service manual – can be translated in the same manner and probably by the same bilingual person. Education the client about translation as a product and a profession, about the translation process and intent can do good to all parties.

One of our practical worries and a topic for endless (and mostly useless) discussions is what's going to happen with the translation rates. In fact, the downward pressure is really strong. First, as already mentioned, agencies are and will always be trying to cut their expenses thus increasing the margin. Many of us have received emails from our clients telling us how they tried to keep the existing rates unchanged and why they finally decided to chip off a few cents, at times accompanied with a promise of larger volumes. During the past 8 months, I agreed only once to reduce my rate with a single UK client and that had to do with the exchange rate rather than anything else. In all other cases, my answer was no, and the best (and best-paying) clients of mine didn't even touch on the issue.

Then, many language combinations feel the impact of translators coming from cheaper local markets. I guess an explanation is needed here. It's not only or exactly the cheaper living standards or worse economic situation that encourages translators from less developed countries to work for lower rates. In fact, we are operating in very different economic and taxation environments. As an illustration, under the present taxation scheme applied in Ukraine, I can earn UAH 500,000 annually (roughly € 4,000 a month) and pay a fixed monthly tax of ca. € 9 – about 0.225%. With this arithmetic, I can charge € .10 and earn more than a translator charging € .14 and paying 30% in taxes.

This pressure is mostly limited to those language pairs where we have translators working from countries belonging to very different markets – for example combinations with target languages such as Spanish or Russian. Of course a client who needs translation of the same German document into Swedish and Ukrainian might be wondering why he has to pay the Swedish translator four times the amount he pays to the Ukrainian one. But the German into Swedish translation community is not over-populated and he'll have no choice but to accept the rate. With various language pairs, the situation is not the same, but in many cases, a client can choose within a wide range of rates.

Nevertheless, we'll soon be facing a certain leveling of translation rates throughout language combinations and regions. The prevailing rate will vary from market to market, but the average price – whatever it is – will go down, especially for non-specialized areas.

Worth mentioning is another very interesting trend: the growing gap between the demand for translation services and availability of good translators capable of hand-ling them properly. It gets absurd at times: an agency wins a tender and gets a contract worth a few millions and then discovers that there are no translators capable, available or willing to do the job. In my personal experience it was even more ironic. A Mos-cow agency seduced a client I'd been working for offering them a price 2 cents lower than mine. A few days later the agency contacted me with a cooperation invitation – as you might have already guessed, at a rate about 30% of what the end client was paying me; but the irony was, they ended up paying my rate as they couldn't find another translator for the job!

This gap is a very good opportunity for the best translators. They are the ones who needn't worry about their future: the niche for high-end services is there to remain. On the other side of the coin, the agencies will inevitably use translators with substandard quality and present the product as "standard", thus contributing to the general deterio-ration of the quality in the entire industry. Which tendency wins in the long run is to be seen.

One more trend to consider is translation memory sharing. This topic was quite hot a while ago. In my view this is something which could optimize the translation process a lot for certain projects – provided the issues such as confidentiality, non-disclosure, copyright, final liability and quality are addressed.

At the end of the presentation, I will try to get my crystal ball rolling and draw a futuristic picture of what the translation market is going to be like in, say, ten or fifteen years from now – unless a new and more severe crisis brings mankind back to common sense:

Globalization has reached the most remote parts of the world, and there's at least one office representing the Big Ten – a dozen translation corporations controlling 90% of the market – in any three neighboring countries, including Africa.

Many jobs which are common today have completely disappeared: the largest brands require that their products are registered online and the right to use their products is only granted after the buyer checks two boxes: "I accept the Terms and Conditions" and "I have read and understood the user manual". Manuals are displayed on their sites in different languages. Their translation is a mixture of MT based on huge translation memories accumulated over the years, crowdsourcing and a little bit of human post-editing; consumers got used to the not-so-good quality as they usually don't read that stuff anyway.

In certain sectors – industrial, engineering, construction – machine translation almost completely replaced our human translators because human translation became prohibitively expensive for many businesses. In a few sensitive domains though, MT is not allowed at all.

In a translator's profile, specialized knowledge is more important than the linguistic background. For the most sensitive translations, working teams are created consisting of a specialist with suitable knowledge of the language and a linguist to help the former get over language problems. The problems are few though: standards imposed for written documentation require that they are written in simple easy-to-comprehend language thus eliminating misinterpretation.

Translation is a rare profession (as any other manual labor). A few remaining translators are very well paid, but their services are needed less and less from year to year…

This is where we are heading if we continue using our mental abilities exclusively to obey instructions, cherishing the in-house mindset of ours and willingly turning ourselves into money-making machines for those interested only in their own profits.

Can there still be another future for us? Let's wait and see…

Positionierung des Übersetzers am Markt

Übersetzen wird abwechslungsreicher und lukrativer

Barbara Sabel

trans-agrar

sabel@trans-agrar.com

Abstract

In Fortsetzung des Schlusswortes von Friedrich Krollmann beim BDÜ-Kongress 1994 in Bonn, in dem cr inhaltlich sagte, dass es in Zukunft weniger Wald- und Wiesen-übersetzer und stattdessen kleine, aber feine Boutiquen für Maßgeschneidertes geben werde, will dieser Vortrag vor Augen führen, mit welch einfachen Mitteln Übersetzer-Innen das immense Potenzial der Globalisierung nutzen können.

Dabei kreist der Vortrag um drei Dreh- und Angelpunkte:

Punkt eins gibt Einblicke in das sich ändernde Bewusstsein der Industrie in Bezug auf Übersetzungen sowie in subtile Problemstellungen innerhalb der Dokumentationspro-zesse mittelständischer Global Players und zeigt auf, welche Profilierungschancen hier für SprachdienstleisterInnen liegen. Dabei sollen auch Einsichten aus der eigenen Praxis in Bezug auf Praxisrelevanz der Ausbildung als Denkanstoß für die Lehre in den Raum gestellt werden.

Punkt zwei zeigt einmal mehr die Notwendigkeit des Selbstmarketings auf der Grundlage des persönlichen, fachlichen und unternehmerischen Selbstverständnisses (auch im Vergleich zu anderen Branchen) sowie vor dem Hintergrund translatorischer Ausbildung und Berufsausübung auf. Dazu wird das im Flyer „Call for Papers" aufgestellte Szenario (kürzere Termine, Kostendruck, Honorarerosion, weltweiter Einkauf von Leistungen etc.) in Frage gestellt, und es werden Perspektiven für Klein-unternehmen aufgezeigt, aus denen heraus solche Herausforderungen an Relevanz verlieren.

Punkt drei regt zur kritischen Selbstbetrachtung an und zeigt Möglichkeiten auf, wie professionelle SprachmittlerInnen sich von ihren semiprofessionellen KonkurrentIn-nen erfolgreich abgrenzen können. Außerdem werden die bestehenden Honorarkon-zepte hinterfragt und neue Ansätze und Optionen speziell für kleine, aber professionelle SprachdienstleisterInnen angedacht. Darüber hinaus wird aufgezeigt, durch welches erweiterte Engagement der Verband der Übersetzungsbranche gute Dienste erweisen könnte.

The effects of globalization on the Globalization, Internationalization, Localization and Translation Industry (GILT)

Florian Willer

Diplom-Technikübersetzer (BDÜ)

florian@linguatechnica.com

Introduction

Presentation and discussion of a worldwide survey on the effects of globalization on the GILT industry with special focus on technology solutions for „nomadic" freelancers. Globalization is one of the buzzwords of the 21st century. This widely used notion also stands for change in the way people live and work. Furthermore, this change abounds in the GILT industry. With more than 1,400 translators and roughly 100 translation and localization agencies interviewed, the presentation will examine not only the demographic characteristics of in-house and freelance translators and their satisfaction in their working environment, but also advantages agencies realize when employing freelance contractors as well as other factors. All questions have been subjected to regional nuances. Learn what freelance translators really are about. How do they feel about their working conditions? Find out the pros and cons agencies see when outsourcing. What factors are important to them when opening new branches? The processes for localization on the client side and the advantages clients realize in outsourcing localization projects will also be elaborated on in the presentation.

Part two of the presentation focuses on recent developments and technology solutions that assist freelance translators when working independent of their location. This includes communication tools, management tools and other work-related solutions.

What is globalization?

> *Globalization is an overused term than can be given a wide variety of meanings. (Soros 2002: 1)*

In this article, globalization is defined as the process of increasing worldwide networking of national markets and societies due to developments in information and communication technologies and the increasingly liberal world trade.

Historic overview

Global trade has been around for a long time, just think of ivory from Africa, silk from China, or spices from Asia that were an important status symbol in the past. However, this cannot be compared to technical developments since the end of World

War II such as the introduction of container shipping and reduced communication costs that enable today's business to be independent of time and location. Frances Cairncross refers to this development as „Death of Distance" (Huws/Jagger/Bates 2001: 1). Furthermore, the introduction of global agreements and organizations (e.g. GATT, WTO, IMF) „facilitates the international exchange of goods and services among willing partners" (Soros 2002: 15).

Internet

The Internet and communication solutions such as e-mail, FTP or telework over VPNs epitomize the recent development of globalization and break down geographic barriers. „For the first time in centuries, religious affinities are becoming more significant than national bonds" (Cunningham/Fröschl 1999: 65). But this process also leads to new problems, especially in poorer regions: „It can create new barriers such as those created by access (or lack of access) to telecommunications" (Cunningham/Fröschl 1999: 49). Broadband, for instance, is only available in about half of the world's countries if you don't count satellite access (Ermert 2004: 40). Modern Internet-based communication solutions are especially suitable for the GILT industry as all data is available in digital format and can be transferred to virtually any point in the world without delay, and contractors from around the world can work on the same project at the same time.

Telework

Historically, people did not have the freedom to choose the community in which they lived. But starting with the Industrial Revolution, people increasingly migrated to other geographic areas. In recent years, the ease of transportation has accelerated these migratory patterns. (Cunningham/Fröschl 1999: 45)

Today, global networks and electronic file transfer solutions allow an independent selection of location in various industries and lead to different forms of telework: home-based, mobile, telecenter-based and on-site. „Historically, such global access was reserved for only the very largest multinational organizations, which could afford the physical infrastructure to support such operations" (Cunningham/Fröschl 1999: 49). Almost two thirds of telework positions in Germany are held by men, and telework is not only suitable for simple jobs. More than one third are management positions, and almost two thirds of all teleworkers have a university degree (Bundesministerium für Arbeit und Sozialordnung/German Ministry for Labor and Social Affairs 2001: 10).

Telework offers various advantages for individuals such as better integration of job, family and recreation, increased creativity and performance thanks to a quiet and flexible atmosphere at home, or time savings thanks to less commuting. It also offers advantages for employers such as increased desirability for applicants, increased productivity, or cost savings thanks to reduced space and energy requirements.

Globalization, internet, and the translation and localization industry

The Internet is not only dependent on technology; it is an enabler of the application of technology to business and other uses. (Cunningham/Fröschl 1999: 87)

The development of the Internet has led to a sustainable change in the way projects are handled in the translation and localization industry over the past two decades. The GILT industry is an exception in the service industry as all data is transferred electronically and details of a project can be discussed on the phone or by e-mail. Furthermore, the daily availability of news, TV shows and movies in any language can help delay the loss of mother tongue significantly.

Until the middle of the eighties, organizations did not outsource translation and localization projects to external service providers, but had internal language and translation departments. This meant that most translators were employed by organizations in different fields, often in a very small team, and only handled jobs for their employer, mainly as hardcopies. To save costs and due to the increasing complexity and extent of translation projects, these organizations started outsourcing projects to specialized service providers. At the same time, the Internet went public (ARPANET was switched off and the first commercial operator for dial-up connections started operating in 1990).

Today, global organizations rely on multilanguage vendors (MLVs) to translate all their content such as manuals, software strings, websites, or packaging and marketing material into various languages with a single partner. These MLVs, in turn, outsource projects to local branches and translators all over the world.

Survey results

The survey was conducted between January and April 2004. A total of 1,490 questionnaires from 85 countries has been evaluated. Below is an overview of the results, detailed results including diagrams and tables can be found in „Übersetzen und Globalisierung" (ISBN 9783938430187), available in English shortly.

Translators

- Majority works freelance
- 60% are women, 40% men
- Women are younger than men
- Translators generally younger in Africa, Asia and South/Central America than in rest of world
- E-mail is primary means of communication
- 80% of freelancers never meet their employer, although 60% work for employers in their country of residence

- 97% work at home
- 93% are satisfied with their hours of work
- Over 20% not satisfied with their social security situation

Agencies

- Most agencies regularly resort to freelance contractors, even MLVs with more than 100 employees
- E-mail is primary means of communication
- Only few freelance contractors work in-house at the agency's location
- 70% say contractor's country of residence is not important, only 19% say translator must live in country of mother tongue
- Cost savings for energy, rent etc. when using freelance contractors
- Access to remote know-how is important factor
- Satisfied with quality, but communication problems due to different time zones

Clients

- Mainly use MLVs/SLVs, rarely freelance contractors
- Some complete translation/localization projects in-house (small projects or documents for internal use)
- Even large organizations that need translations into more than 30 languages sometimes resort to freelance contractors
- Location of contractor is not important
- Satisfied with quality and delivery times of freelance contractors
- Vendor selection has no influence on satisfaction regarding quality of translations, quality of service or delivery times

Solutions for nomadic freelancers

There is a large variety of tools to simplify the daily life of freelance translators such as Internet-based phone providers, phone answering services, server-based project management systems, online backup systems, mobile access devices etc. The live presentation included examples and a discussion, but this market changes rapidly, so no specific solutions are mentioned here. Please do not hesitate to contact me if you have any questions.

Bibliography

Bundesrepublik Deutschland. Ministerium für Arbeit und Sozialordnung, Ministerium für Wirtschaft und Technologie, Ministerium für Bildung und Forschung. (2001):

Telearbeit. Leitfaden für flexibles Arbeiten in der Praxis. Braunschweig: Westermann.

Cunningham, P. & Fröschl, F. (1999): *Electronic Business Revolution.* Berlin: Springer.

Ermert, M. (2004): „Scheideweg, Die Weltinformationsgesellschaft zeigt wenig Visionen und schwachen politischen Willen": *c't* [01/04]: 40–42.

Huws, U./Jagger, N./Bates, P. (2001): *Where the Butterfly Alights. The Global Location of eWork.* Brighton, UK: Institute for Employment Studies.

Soros, G. (2002): *George Soros on Globalization.* Oxford: PublicAffairs Ltd.

Willer, F. (2006): *Übersetzen und Globalisierung.* Berlin: BDÜ.

Corporate pawns or "free"-lancers? Translators and translation technology

Dr. Jost Zetzsche

International Writers' Group

jzetzsche@internationalwriters.com

Abstract

For many translators, the development of translation technology in the last 15 years or so has been largely dominated by the interests of translation buyers and medium to large language service providers. Though individual translators use translation technology, many feel powerless to shape the future of the technology that constitutes their work environment. Is this an accurate perception? If not, what can be done to change that perception? And if that feeling of powerlessness is accurate, what can be done to change the situation?

While pondering these questions, Zetzsche will discuss the role of translation professionals' self-image, open standards, and the future of translation technology. He will also present the results of a survey sponsored by the ATA and FIT on the role of technology in the lives of today's translators.

Internationale Netzwerke bilden

Interkontinentale Geschäftstätigkeit als Sprachmittler ... aus USA-Perspektive

Marita Marcano

Diplom-Übersetzerin (BDÜ, ATA)

mmarcano@mm-translations.com

1 Einleitung

Dieser Vortrag soll einen komparativen Vergleich der Situation der freiberuflichen Sprachmittler in Deutschland und den USA sowie Tipps zur länderübergreifenden Zusammenarbeit bieten und beruht auf meinen persönlichen Erfahrungen, Eindrücken und Recherchen. Nach zehnjähriger Festanstellung als Übersetzerin bei einem internationalen Telekommunikationskonzern in Deutschland habe ich den Weg der Freiberuflichkeit eingeschlagen und seitdem jeweils einige Jahre in den Niederlanden, in Deutschland und in den USA als Übersetzerin gearbeitet.

2 Wie hat sich das Ausbildungsangebot für Sprachmittler in den USA in den vergangenen Jahren entwickelt?

In Deutschland haben Hochschulstudiengänge in Übersetzen und Dolmetschen und der Beruf des Übersetzers und Dolmetschers eine lange Tradition, während diese Berufe in den USA erst eigentlich mit der Globalisierung ins Licht der Öffentlichkeit gerückt sind. In den USA sind die meisten freiberuflichen Sprachmittler Quereinsteiger und es wird immer noch argumentiert, dass es ja nur wenige Ausbildungsmöglichkeiten für Übersetzer und Dolmetscher gebe. Stimmt das noch?

Vor 25 Jahren, als ich mein Übersetzerdiplom abgelegt habe und anschließend ein Jahr als Austauschstudentin in die USA gegangen bin, gab es meines Wissens nach in den USA tatsächlich nur zwei Universitäten, die ein Übersetzerstudium anboten: das *Monterey Institute of International Studies* (www.miis.edu, 1955 gegründet*)* in Kalifornien und die *Georgetown University* in Washington, DC. Das hat sich aber in der jüngsten Vergangenheit, vor allem mit der Globalisierung, sehr verändert. Heute gibt es um die 20 Universitäten mit Studienangeboten in Übersetzen und/oder Dolmetschen, davon 10, die einen Master-Abschluss anbieten. An der *Kent State University* in Solon, Ohio, kann außerdem seit Neustem ein PhD-Abschluss erworben werden. Informationen über die Ausbildungsinstitute in den USA gibt es hier:

www.gradschools.com/Subject/Translation-and-Interpretation/379.html.
Wird das größere Ausbildungsangebot auch entsprechend wahrgenommen?

Mein persönlicher Eindruck ist, dass es unter den jüngeren freiberuflichen Übersetzern und Dolmetschern zwar jetzt mehr Personen mit einer einschlägigen Ausbildung gibt, dass aber eine solche Ausbildung von der Mehrheit der schon auf dem freien Markt etablierten Freiberufler immer noch nicht als zur Ausübung des Berufs notwendig betrachtet wird.

3 Berufsverbände – Vergleich zwischen BDÜ und ATA

3.1 ATA

Die *American Translators Association* (ATA) hat über 10.000 Mitglieder in ca. 90 Ländern.

Laut einer ATA-Umfrage vor einigen Jahren hat nur ca. ein Viertel aller Mitglieder einen übersetzungs- oder sprachenbezogenen höheren Abschluss. Die überwiegende Mehrheit sind Quereinsteiger, von denen viele zwar einen Hochschulabschluss haben, der aber nicht sprachenbezogen ist (z. B. Juristen, Mediziner, Physiker, Steuerberater etc.).

Laut den *ATA Bylaws* kann jeder Mitglied werden, der irgendein Interesse an Übersetzen und/oder Dolmetschen hat. Es gibt verschiedene Mitgliedskategorien, zum Beispiel:

Associate: Status für alle Interessierten, für den keinerlei Bedingungen erfüllt werden müssen. *Associate*-Mitglieder können aber nicht an Vorstandssitzungen teilnehmen und auch nicht wählen.

Active: Status für US-Staatsbürger oder *Legal Permanent Residents*. Für diesen Status muss man entweder die ATA-Prüfung bestehen oder ein paar Jahre berufliche Tätigkeit und/oder einen Abschluss irgendwelcher Art in Übersetzen und/oder Dolmetschen oder in Fremdsprachen nachweisen, was durch *Peer Review* (Prüfung durch Fachkollegen) überprüft wird. *Active*-Mitglieder haben volle Verbandsrechte, können an Vorstandssitzungen teilnehmen und wählen.

Corresponding: Dieser Status ist für aktive Mitglieder, die weder US-Staatsbürger noch *Legal Permanent Residents* sind. Es gelten die gleichen Rechte und Mitgliedschaftsanforderungen wie für *Active*-Mitglieder.

Außerdem können auch Agenturen Mitglied werden.

Die ATA bietet als Qualifikationsnachweis das *ATA Certification Exam* an, das aber nur von der ATA selbst anerkannt wird. Es ist nicht international anerkannt und wird bei Kündigung der Mitgliedschaft ungültig. Damit diese Prüfung gültig bleibt, müssen die Mitglieder, die die Prüfung erfolgreich abgelegt haben, jetzt jedes Jahr eine bestimmte Punktzahl für Weiterbildungsmaßnahmen bei der ATA einreichen. Tun sie das nicht, wird die Prüfung ebenfalls ungültig.

Diese Prüfung braucht man aber für eine *Active-* oder *Corresponding*-Mitgliedschaft nicht, wenn man einen Übersetzer-/Dolmetscherabschluss und/oder genügend Berufserfahrung nachweisen kann.

Alle Einzelheiten über die Mitgliedschaft können auf der ATA-Website in den *ATA Bylaws* unter *Article III Membership* nachgelesen werden.

Die ATA bietet verschiedene Divisions, die allen Mitgliedern kostenlos offenstehen, z. B. die *German Language Division* (GLD) mit 1.069 Mitgliedern.

Für weitere Informationen über die ATA möchte ich auf den Vortrag *ATA – The next 50 years* meines ATA-Kollegen und derzeitigen *ATA President-elect* Nicholas Hartmann auf dieser Konferenz verweisen.

3.2 BDÜ

Der Bundesverband der Übersetzer und Dolmetscher (BDÜ) hat über 6.000 Mitglieder.

Alle Mitglieder müssen vor Aufnahme in den Verband ihre fachliche Qualifikation nachweisen, wozu bis vor kurzem ein Hochschulabschluss in Übersetzen und/oder Dolmetschen oder ein gleichwertiger ausländischer Abschluss, eine Prüfung vor einem staatlichen Prüfungsamt oder ein IHK-Abschluss von bestimmten (nicht allen) Industrie- und Handelskammern gehörte. Neuerdings werden auch Bewerber mit einem fachfremden Hochschulabschluss, nachgewiesenen ausreichenden Sprachkenntnissen und Berufserfahrung bei Erfüllung aller Anforderungen akzeptiert, worüber durch die Bundesaufnahmekommission des Verbands entschieden wird.

Aufgrund der Aufnahmebedingungen des BDÜ haben die meisten BDÜ-Mitglieder einen übersetzungs- oder sprachenbezogenen höheren Abschluss.

4 Abrechnung von Übersetzungen in Deutschland und USA

In den USA werden Übersetzungen normalerweise nach der Anzahl der Ausgangswörter abgerechnet, es sei denn, man einigt sich auf einen Pauschalpreis oder auf einen Preis pro Zeiteinheit.

In Deutschland wird meistens nach der Anzahl der Zielzeilen abgerechnet. Software wird jedoch ebenfalls nach der Anzahl der Ausgangswörter berechnet.

Um es dem Kunden möglichst einfach zu machen, sollte man sich an die Abrechnungsweise im jeweiligen Land des Kunden anpassen.

5 Was weiß der potenzielle amerikanische Direktkunde über die Tätigkeit von Übersetzern und Dolmetschern?

Auf einen Nenner gebracht: sehr wenig. Obwohl die ATA schon viel Aufklärungsarbeit geleistet hat, kennen die wenigsten den Unterschied zwischen Übersetzern und

Dolmetschern und die meisten wissen nicht einmal, was ein *translator* denn eigentlich genau macht und wozu man diesen braucht. Jeder hat da ein bisschen eine andere Vorstellung, abhängig von seinen persönlichen Erfahrungen. In den Medien ist meist nur die Rede von *translators*, auch dann, wenn ein Dolmetscher gemeint ist. Wenn ein Dolmetscher tatsächlich als *interpreter* bezeichnet wird, dann wird aber im Anschluss garantiert dessen Tätigkeit mit *to translate* beschrieben, z. B. *They hired an interpreter to translate the conversation.*

Das bedeutet für uns, dass wir als Sprachmittler bei amerikanischen Kunden viel mehr Aufklärungsarbeit leisten müssen. Wir müssen sie viel stärker „an die Hand nehmen", als das bei den meisten deutschen Direktkunden in der Wirtschaft der Fall ist. Ein sehr nützliches Tool zur Kundenaufklärung ist die Einkaufshilfe für Übersetzungsdienstleistungen *Translation: Getting it right (Übersetzung – keine Glückssache)*, die in mehreren Sprachen (EN, FR, DE, CZ, NL, IT) von der Website des *Institute of Translation and Interpreting* (ITI) (www.iti.org.uk/ indexMain.html) oder der ATA (www.atanet.org/publications/getting_it_ right.php) heruntergeladen und im Bedarfsfall an potenzielle Auftraggeber weitergereicht werden kann.

6 Wie kann man dem Kunden auf der jeweils anderen Seite des großen Teichs entgegenkommen, damit er die geografische Entfernung gar nicht wahrnimmt?

Machen Sie dem Kunden auf der anderen Seite des großen Teichs die Zusammenarbeit mit Ihnen so leicht wie möglich und kommen Sie ihm so weit entgegen, wie es technisch und praktisch möglich und machbar ist.

6.1 Leicht erreichbar sein

6.1.1 Anpassung an unterschiedliche Zeitzonen

Zwischen Deutschland und den USA gibt es einen Zeitunterschied von mindestens 6 (Ostküste) und maximal 10 Stunden (Alaska). Wenn Sie also nicht in derselben Zeitzone wohnen wie der Kunde, können Sie dem Kunden das Gefühl vermitteln, dass Sie ihm zeitzonenmäßig entgegenkommen. Für mich in USA (Ostküste) bedeutet das, dass ich meinen Arbeitstag nicht erst um 9.00 Uhr, sondern vielleicht schon um 7.00 Uhr oder früher beginne, damit ich Anfragen aus Europa möglichst früh beantworten kann. Umgekehrt habe ich in Deutschland meinen PC bis 23.00 Uhr angelassen und nach meinem offiziellen Geschäftsschluss immer wieder in meinen E-Mail-Posteingang geschaut, um zu den Geschäftszeiten meiner US-Kunden erreichbar zu sein und schnell reagieren zu können. Dabei ist aber zu bemerken, dass die Zusammenarbeit mit Kunden an der US-Westküste wegen des großen Zeitunterschieds von Deutschland aus etwas schwieriger ist.

6.1.2 Leichte Erreichbarkeit am Arbeitsplatz

Mittlerweile ist es selbstverständlich, dass wir an unserem normalen Arbeitsplatz telefonisch und per E-Mail erreichbar und während unserer Geschäftszeiten durchgehend online sind, um immer sofort auf neue E-Mails reagieren zu können.

Sprachmittler mit Standort in den USA können auf ihrer Website außerdem den Kunden darauf aufmerksam machen, dass Telefongespräche von Deutschland in die USA über Call-by-Call-Nummern sogar billiger sind als Gespräche innerhalb Deutschlands. Führen Sie den Kunden direkt zu diesen Nummern, indem Sie auch die Links zu den entsprechenden Websites angeben, wo diese Nummern zu finden sind, zum Beispiel www.teltarif.de oder www.verivox.de.

Dementsprechend können Sprachmittler mit Standort in Deutschland Kunden in den USA den Tipp geben, dass Auslandsgespräche über Telefonkarten wesentlich billiger sind als über ihre reguläre Telefongesellschaft. Es gibt auch Telefonkartendienste übers Internet, wo man sich mit einer Kreditkarte registriert und dann – wie bei einer echten Telefonkarte – eine Einwahlnummer für diesen Service und eine eigene PIN-Nummer erhält. Das Konto kann mit Kreditkarte online immer wieder neu aufgeladen werden.

Außerdem gibt es über VoIP-Dienste wie zum Beispiel Skype die Möglichkeit zum kostenlosen Telefonieren und Abhalten von Videokonferenzen.

6.1.3 Leichte Erreichbarkeit bei Abwesenheit vom Arbeitsplatz

Im Zeichen der Globalisierung brauchen wir Sprachmittler jetzt nicht mehr immer an unserem Schreibtisch zu sitzen, sondern können überall erreichbar sein, wenn wir technisch dementsprechend ausgerüstet und organisiert sind. Mit den heutigen technischen Möglichkeiten sind Sprachmittler nicht mehr an ihren Bürostandort gebunden, sondern können bei guter Organisation auch unterwegs und länderübergreifend arbeiten.

Wenn Sie zu Ihren normalen Geschäftszeiten nicht am Arbeitsplatz erreichbar sind, sollten Sie in Ihrem eigenen Interesse dafür sorgen, dass der Kunde das entweder weiß und/oder dass er sich über ein anderes Kommunikationsmedium mit Ihnen in Verbindung setzen kann.

Sie sollten auf alle Fälle für Ihre geschäftliche E-Mail-Adresse einen Autoresponder einrichten, damit der Kunde weiß, dass Sie möglicherweise nicht sofort antworten werden.

Wenn Sie viele telefonische Kundenkontakte haben, sollten Sie Ihr Telefon auf Ihr Mobiltelefon umstellen.

Welche technischen Lösungen und Möglichkeiten gibt es, damit Ihr Kunde vielleicht nicht einmal wahrnimmt, dass Sie nicht zu Hause am PC sitzen, sondern zum Beispiel gerade in der Karibik in einer Strandbar unter Palmen einen Mojito schlürfen, während Sie seinen neuen Auftrag per E-Mail entgegennehmen?

6.1.3.1 E-Mail unterwegs empfangen und beantworten

Wenn der Kundenkontakt hauptsächlich über E-Mail stattfindet, könnten Sie sich einen Blackberry oder ein anderes Smartphone mit E-Mail-Empfang in Echtzeit (z. B. Motorola Moto Q 9c) zulegen. Damit können Sie Ihre E-Mails auch unterwegs empfangen und beantworten, auch im Ausland. Wenn Sie in den USA wohnen, brauchen Sie bei Besitz eines solchen Smartphones an manchen Tagen vielleicht nicht ganz so früh aufzustehen, denn Sie können schon vor dem Aufstehen Ihre E-Mails lesen und sich noch ein bisschen mehr Schlaf gönnen, wenn Sie keine dringende Anfrage aus Europa beantworten müssen.

Mit einem Smartphone können Sie mit einem Datenvertrag Ihre E-Mails jederzeit überall in Echtzeit automatisch empfangen und dann beantworten. Selbst angehängte Dateien können bei Installation eines entsprechenden Programms auf dem Smartphone angezeigt werden, wobei der Lesekomfort allerdings eingeschränkt ist. Es reicht jedoch aus, um einem Kunden umgehend antworten zu können, ob Sie den angebotenen Auftrag annehmen können oder nicht. So haben Sie auch im Urlaub durchgehend Zugriff auf Ihre E-Mails und können Kundenaufträge für nach dem Urlaub annehmen, ohne dass Sie ein Notebook mit sich herumschleppen oder am Urlaubsort nach einem Internetcafé suchen müssen. Über einen Daten- und Internetvertrag können Sie mit einem Smartphone auch im Internet surfen.

Bei Deutschlandreisen habe ich mein altes Triband-Handy mit einer deutschen SIM-Karte und meinen Blackberry dabei. Über mein deutsches Mobiltelefon bin ich dann für alle zum deutschen Prepaid-Tarif telefonisch erreichbar, und über den Blackberry kann ich alle meine geschäftlichen E-Mails jederzeit und überall lesen und beantworten. Um hohe Roaminggebühren zu vermeiden, schalte ich den Blackberry jedoch nur zum Lesen und Beantworten meiner E-Mails ein und anschließend sofort wieder aus, damit ich keine Telefongespräche erhalte. So fallen Auslands-Roaminggebühren nur für meinen Datenverkehr an. Diese beliefen sich bei meinem letzten dreiwöchigen Deutschlandaufenthalt auf knapp 10 Dollar. Die deutsche Telefon-SIM-Karte muss innerhalb eines Jahres neu aufgeladen werden, sonst verfällt sie.

In den USA kann man ebenfalls eine Prepaid-SIM-Karte erwerben, damit man zu Inlandstarifen immer erreichbar ist. Eine billigere Lösung sind jedoch jetzt die Einweg-Prepaid-Handys, die es überall (z. B. bei Wal-Mart oder Sam's Club) zu kaufen gibt. Diese muss man zwar innerhalb von 60 oder 90 Tagen wieder aufladen, damit sie funktionsfähig bleiben, aber auch wenn man das nicht tut, lohnt sich der Kauf. Eine SIM-Karte ohne Minuten kostet beispielsweise um die 25 Dollar. Ein Prepaid-Handy erhält man dagegen inklusive z. B. 60 Minuten schon für um die 20 Dollar.

6.1.3.2 Internetzugang und Arbeiten unterwegs und im Ausland

Wenn Sie mit dem Notebook unterwegs arbeiten möchten, benötigen Sie einen schnellen Internetzugang, wozu Ihr Notebook mit einer WLAN-Funktion, auch WiFi genannt, ausgestattet sein sollte. Bei Apple heißt diese Funktion „AirPort". Über das WLAN in Ihrem Notebook können Sie dann eine drahtlose Verbindung zum Internet herstellen, am besten über einen Hotspot oder einen Surfstick. Vergessen Sie außerdem nicht den erforderlichen Adapterstecker für das jeweilige Land, in dem Sie arbeiten möchten, damit der Notebookstecker auch in die Wandsteckdose passt.

Hotspots

Ein Hotspot ist ein Einwählpunkt zur drahtlosen Verbindung mit dem Internet.

An manchen Standorten kann man auch ohne Hotspot zu einem ungeschützten drahtlosen Netzwerk in der näheren Umgebung eine Verbindung unterschiedlicher Qualität herstellen, was zwar zum gelegentlichen Abrufen von E-Mails nützlich sein kann, aber nicht zum längeren Surfen und zu Arbeitszwecken zu empfehlen ist.

In den USA und in Deutschland gibt es zum drahtlosen Surfen im Internet kostenlose und gebührenpflichtige öffentliche Hotspots. Kostenlose Hotspots finden Sie in manchen Restaurants wie beispielsweise *Panera Bread*, auf Flughäfen und Camping-plätzen, in Hotels, Stadtbüchereien etc.

- Kostenlose Hotspots in USA: www.wififreespot.com/
- Kostenlose Hotspots weltweit: www.free-hotspot.com/
- Hotspots weltweit nach Art des Standorts: http://usatoday.jiwire.com/ hotspot-hot-spot-directory-browse-by-location.htm
- Internationales Hotspot-Verzeichnis: www.hotspot-locations.com/

Surfsticks (*wireless USB modems, speed sticks*)

Ein Surfstick ist ein UMTS-Funkmodem für den drahtlosen Internetzugang über Notebooks und Laptops. Er sieht ähnlich aus wie ein USB-Speicherstick und wird in den USB-Anschluss des Notebooks eingesteckt.

Hier gibt es eine Übersicht über verschiedene Anbieter in Deutschland:

- www.mobilefacts.de/shop/surf-stick/
- www.om-all.de/usb-surfsticks-im-vergleich/
- www.surf-stick-vergleich.de/
- www.plug-n-surf.de/preise/
- www.surfstickvergleich.de/umts-surfstick-anbieter.html
- www.umts-stick.info/?gclid=COLgpLzRnpsCFQNbxwodFV-ytg

Anbieter in USA:

- www.informationweek.com/news/mobility/reviews/showArticle.jhtml?articleI D=208404374

6.2 Bankkonten in beiden Ländern

Kunden sind immer eher geneigt, mit Dienstleistern zu arbeiten, die ihnen die Zusammenarbeit möglichst einfach machen. So wird ein Kunde in Deutschland lieber mit einem Dienstleister zusammenarbeiten, dem er den Rechnungsbetrag wie gewohnt gebührenfrei auf ein inländisches Konto überweisen kann, anstatt eine mit Mehrauf-wand und hohen Gebühren verbundene Auslandsüberweisung vornehmen zu müssen.

US-Kunden sind daran gewöhnt, alle Rechnungen per Scheck zu bezahlen, der in einem Briefumschlag per Post versandt wird. Überweisungen sind in den USA keine gängige Zahlungsmethode.

Deshalb stellt es für Dienstleister einen Wettbewerbsvorteil dar, in beiden Ländern ein Bankkonto zu haben. Dies spart nicht nur dem Kunden, sondern auch dem Dienstleister Zeit und Geld. Das Geld ist schneller auf Ihrem Konto (im anderen Land) und Sie können selbst bestimmen, wann es in die andere Währung umgetauscht werden soll. Wenn der Wechselkurs gerade ungünstig ist, können Sie mit dem Umtauschen warten, bis er wieder gestiegen ist, und so von Wechselkursschwankungen profitieren. Wenn Sie sich dagegen jeden einzelnen Rechnungsbetrag aus dem Ausland überweisen lassen, haben Sie keinerlei Einfluss auf diesen Faktor und Ihr Geld wird immer zum Tageskurs umgetauscht.

6.2.1 Ausländer und/oder nicht in Deutschland Ansässige, die ein Konto in Deutschland eröffnen möchten

1995 wurde vom Zentralen Kreditausschuss der Banken und Sparkassen (ZKA) eine freiwillige Selbstverpflichtung ausgearbeitet, die bis heute gültig ist. Nach dieser Empfehlung des ZKA zum „Girokonto für jedermann" kann jeder ein Girokonto „zur Entgegennahme von Gutschriften, zu Barein- und -auszahlungen und zur Teilnahme am Überweisungsverkehr" einrichten. Auf die Einrichtung eines Kontos besteht jedoch kein Rechtsanspruch.

Bei folgenden Banken ist es im Ausland ansässigen ausländischen bzw. deutschen Kollegen gelungen, ein Konto in Deutschland zu eröffnen:

Deutsche Bank

Hier muss man erst zur Identitätsprüfung seine Unterschrift bei einem deutschen Konsulat oder einer *Deutsche-Bank*-Filiale beglaubigen lassen, eine Beglaubigung von einem Notar wird anscheinend nicht akzeptiert. Laut Angaben eines Übersetzerkollegen kann man in USA die *Deutsche Bank* unter +1-212-250-2500 anrufen und sich mit der *Deutsche-Bank*-Filiale in Frankfurt verbinden lassen.

Postbank und Netbank

Bei der *Postbank* (www.postbank.de) und der *Netbank* (www.netbank.de) soll eine Kontoeröffnung ebenfalls möglich sein.

Wenn Sie ein Konto bei der *Postbank* haben, können Sie Ihre Euros per Online-Banking entweder auf Ihr US-Konto überweisen oder sich einen Auslandsscheck in US-Dollar per Post senden lassen und diesen dann gebührenfrei auf Ihrem US-Konto gutschreiben lassen. Eine Überweisung bis 12.500 Euro kostet ungefähr zwischen 15 und 20 Euro Gebühren, da bei Auslandsüberweisungen immer auch noch zwischengeschaltete Banken Gebühren erheben. Ein Dollar-Auslandsscheck bis 12.500 Euro dagegen kostet insgesamt nur 8 Euro Gebühren.

Man sollte sich zwecks der konkreten Voraussetzungen zur Eröffnung eines Kontos unbedingt erst bei der entsprechenden Bank erkundigen. Mögliche Anforderungen sind eine beglaubigte Unterschrift, Nachweis des ausländischen Wohnsitzes durch

z. B. Strom- oder Wasserrechnung und Angabe einer ausländischen Steuernummer, z. B. US Social Security Number, zu steuerlichen Zwecken.

Gegebenenfalls kann man versuchen, die Bank zur Einrichtung eines Guthabenkontos zu bewegen, indem man einen schriftlichen Antrag mit Verweis auf die oben erwähnte ZKA-Empfehlung stellt.

6.2.2 Ohne US Social Security Number ein Konto in USA eröffnen

Leider kann man bei den meisten Banken in USA ohne Social Security Number (SSN) kein Konto eröffnen. Die *Bank of America* scheint hier eine Ausnahme zu sein, aber laut den Erfahrungen von Personen, die dies versucht haben, hängt die Entscheidung wohl von der jeweiligen Filiale ab.

Laut dem *Code of Federal Regulations, Title 31 CFR § 103.34* muss eine Bank zum Eröffnen eines Kontos nach der Social Security Number (SSN) fragen, muss diese aber nicht in das Formular 1099, mit dem sie dem IRS die Zinseinkünfte meldet, an den IRS weiterleiten. Sie muss auf diesem Formular nur mit Unterschrift bestätigen, dass sie nach der SSN gefragt hat.

Und genau auf diese Regelung scheint sich die *Bank of America* zu berufen, wenn sie Konten ohne SSN eröffnet. Viele Bankangestellte scheinen diese Ausnahmeregelung aber nicht zu kennen, weshalb sie oft die Eröffnung eines Kontos ohne SSN ablehnen. Bei meinen Recherchen diesbezüglich habe ich den Eindruck gewonnen, dass die Eröffnung eines Bankkontos ohne SSN im Großraum Los Angeles problemloser zu sein scheint als in anderen Gegenden der USA.

Tipp: Wählen Sie möglichst eine Bank, die für eingehende Auslandsüberweisungen keine Gebühren nimmt. Wenn Sie dann Geld von Ihrem deutschen Konto überweisen, geben Sie an, dass der Empfänger die Kosten tragen soll. So brauchen Sie nur die Gebühren der zwischengeschalteten Bank zu zahlen, es fallen jedoch keine Gebühren Ihrer eigenen Bank(en) an.

Laut Angaben von Kollegen kann man ohne SSN ebenfalls bei folgenden Banken ein Konto eröffnen:

EverBank

www.everbank.com/001Checking.aspx

Vorgehensweise zur Eröffnung eines Kontos: Das Formular www.everbank.com/documents/applications/eb_PersonalBanking.pdf herunterladen und ausfüllen. Dieses Formular zusammen mit dem ersten Einzahlungsbetrag, einer Farbkopie des Reisepasses, einem Nachweis der Wohnadresse und dem Formular W-8BEN, das unter www.irs.gov heruntergeladen werden kann, an die Bank senden. Separat wird ein *Bank Reference Letter* (Empfehlungsschreiben) von einer Bank des Heimatlandes, bei der man ein Konto hat, verlangt, das direkt von der Bank an die *EverBank* gesendet werden muss.

Man kann auch ein *foreign currency account* eröffnen, für das eine Gebühr erhoben wird.

Webster Bank

www.websterbank.com/servlets/com.websterbank.servlets.Login

Die Kollegin, die hier ein Konto eingerichtet hat, hat dies jedoch vor Ort in Connecticut getan.

Wenn man dann ein US-Konto hat, kann man sich entweder den Rechnungsbetrag vom Kunden als US-Dollar-Scheck per Post schicken lassen und ihn anschließend selbst an die Bank senden oder den Kunden anweisen, den Scheck direkt an die Bank zu senden. Dieser wird dann gebührenfrei auf dem Konto gutgeschrieben.

7 Fazit

Dank der neuen technischen Möglichkeiten sind Deutschland und die USA trotz großer geografischer Entfernung enger zusammengerückt, was eine interkontinentale Geschäftstätigkeit erheblich erleichtert. Wer diese Möglichkeiten richtig einsetzt, kann die Entfernung zwischen beiden Kontinenten virtuell verringern und sich so einen Wettbewerbsvorteil verschaffen.

Bibliografie

American Translators Association (ATA) – Informationen und Daten: www.atanet.org

ATA Bylaws: www.atanet.org/membership/bylaws.php

ATA German Language Division (GLD): www.ata-divisions.org/GLD/

Bundesverband der Übersetzer und Dolmetscher (BDÜ) – Informationen und Daten: www.bdue.de

Code of Federal Regulations, Title 31 CFR § 103.34 Additional records to be made and retained by banks: www.fdic.gov/regulations/laws/rules/8000-1600.html

Empfehlung des Zentralen Kreditausschusses (ZKA) zum Girokonto für jedermann: www.zka-online.de/zka/zahlungsverkehr/girokonto-fuer-jedermann/zka-empfehlung.html und www.zka-online.de/zka/zahlungsverkehr/girokonto-fuer-jedermann.html

Building international networks.
How language services providers can make globalisation work for them

Ralf Lemster

Ralf Lemster Financial Translations GmbH

ralf@lemstergroup.de

Joining forces to tackle the global market

Language services providers (LSPs) have been feeling the direct impact of globalisation for numerous years. Many LSPs have succeeded in growing their business across borders. Yet most freelance translators perceive globalisation as a threat that subjects them to enormous competitive pressures.

This article analyses motivations and background of cross-border cooperation. Starting from an assessment of the status quo, we will look at options for launching your own international network, taking into account drivers of success and risk factors. Although our focus is on translation services, the concepts outlined are generally also applicable to interpreters and other providers of language services.

Motives for (international) cooperation

During the last decade, translations have evolved into a truly global marketplace where common language combinations are offered virtually around the clock. The resulting fierce competition is a challenge for any freelancer. This is true in particular for those living in regions with relatively high cost of living. A factor that is often missed is that globalisation holds manifold opportunities: besides the clearly larger potential to target customers, chances are also available in cooperating with colleagues across all time zones.

Specialise to differentiate yourself

To be successful in this highly competitive market environment, independent LSPs must differentiate themselves from their competitors. By specialising on a clearly defined and logical selection of subjects, providers can distinguish their offering from the mass of competitors, enhancing their attractiveness to potential customers. Disintermedation is another key aspect. To turn linguistic services into a commercially viable business, providers must work as directly with the end customer as possible. In contrast, a chain of intermediaries leaves only a marginal income for the last unit in the chain. This requires presenting a professional and credible profile to the (potential) customer, in order to compete against large, globally active service businesses: a very tall job for a lone freelancer – but perfectly realistic for a team of experts with complementary skills. It is interesting to note that such a team of specialists can often meet customer requirements more precisely and professionally than large 'do-it-all' companies.

Diversifying the business

Working together in a team, freelancers can offer services that they could not sustainably render on their own. A team can extend the business horizon, both in terms of project size and regarding the language combinations and/or subjects covered. A frequent side effect is a diversification of the customer base and the range of projects executed. Very simply, a larger reach will reduce dependency upon individual customers.

The concept of teamwork per se is not a new achievement. In fact, personal networks existed long before the advent of the internet – but these networks were usually restricted to local cooperation. Using state-of-the-art communication technology, freelancers can extend their reach beyond borders – way beyond, in fact. Global collaboration is no longer a privilege available to large conglomerates. Building small networks on a global scale is perfectly viable.

Building the network...

There are virtually countless options for designing networks – ranging from a pure marketing cooperation to project-specific collaboration or even a joint market presence.

Key aspects for building a team are:

- the team structure
- ('peer-to-peer' network or centralised management);
- planned size and scope (professional focus, subject areas);
- geographical reach and target customers; and
- market presence and marketing strategy.

...structuring the team, positioning it on the market...

At the outset, each team must decide whether to opt for a central entity managing the collaboration, or for a 'peer-to-peer' network where every participant has identical rights and responsibilities. The key benefit of centralised management is the clearer definition of tasks and duties. As a consequence, the central entity will need to claim a larger share of total income. All parties involved must agree with this imbalance. In a centrally managed network, the central entity must guarantee a sound business approach and credit quality.

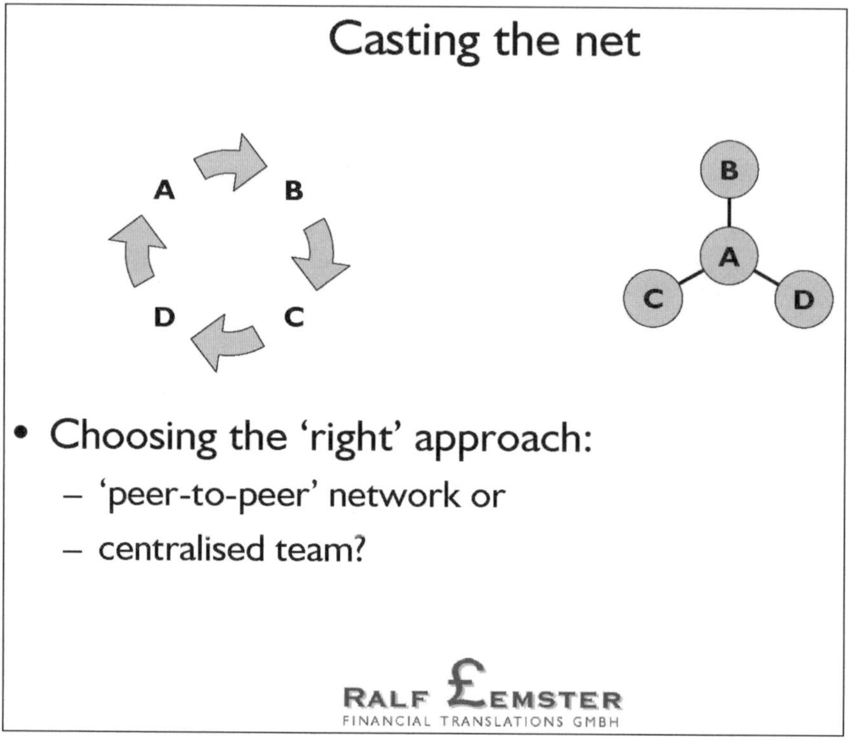

Figure 1: Alternative team structures

The main advantage of a peer-to-peer network is that it is easier to implement than a centrally managed structure. The even distribution of rights and duties is also often considered a general advantage. It must be noted, however, that this even distribution may lead to conflicts where the contributions of individual participants differ. In principle, distributing and allocating income may prove to be a breaking point in a peer-to-peer network; hence, profit-sharing should be agreed upon at the outset.

Once the fundamental issues have been clarified, the team needs to position itself in the market, creating visibility – for potential team members, but particularly for target customers. Besides established online marketing techniques such as search engine optimisation or banner advertising, team members may want to participate in online discussion forums, or attend professional events related to the subject areas the team focuses on. Done properly, such visibility in the (real and virtual) public domain will provide the team with a professional and credible market image.

Smooth collaboration across countries and regions need not be a problem, provided that the technical infrastructure used serves the purpose. There is no need for free-lancers to establish their own IT support department for this purpose, thanks to a wide choice of attractively priced tools available.

Casting the net

	Pros	Cons
Peer-to-peer network	Easy to implement Same rights and duties Shared risk exposure	Measurement of individual contributions can be difficult Management challenges Tax issues
Centralised team	Clear division of responsibilities (even across time zones) Transparent assignment of benefits (transfer pricing)	Contractual issues Central entity assumes economic risk

RALF £EMSTER
FINANCIAL TRANSLATIONS GMBH

Figure 2: Pros and cons of peer-to-peer vs. centralised team structures

... and maintaining the network

Quality assurance is a key aspect for freelance work and team cooperation. Where the scope of the network goes beyond merely passing on recommendations (e.g. in the case of a marketing cooperation), the team must define processes and responsibilities for assuring quality. Even though such processes tend to be easier to implement in a centrally managed network, they are just as feasible in a peer-to-peer structure.

The technical infrastructure used is crucially important, particular in cross-border cooperation: simply using (unencrypted) e-mail is generally insufficient. Besides the security risks involved, even smaller teams can hardly cope with the complexity of trying to manage project status and responsibilities using e-mail only. The good news is that there is a wide range of low-cost – yet sufficiently secure – communication platforms, such as web-based 'data rooms', discussion forums or terminology platforms.

Work in progress

Communications infrastructure	Pros	Cons
Unencrypted e-mail	Easy to implement Easy to use (no additional efforts req'd.)	Unsecure Risk of sending messages to unintended recipients
E-mail plus encryption (e.g. PGP)	Secure Same technical platform as unencrypted e-mail	Encryption solutions hard to implement with customers License costs
Dedicated web platform (online file manager)	Project-specific authorisation Embedded encryption (no separate software required)	Development/maintenance costs

RALF £EMSTER
FINANCIAL TRANSLATIONS GMBH

Figure 3: Communications infrastructure – options

Besides technical security, legal safety must also be ensured when working together across borders. Different legal systems need to be harmonised, for example. Besides differences in contract and tax law, cost structures and profitability of the various team members may be affected by differing social security systems. In other words, a job that is profitable for a freelancer based in the UK is not necessarily commercially attractive for a colleague domiciled in France. Other differences include the treatment of liability risks, typically regarding breaches of confidentiality agreements, or with respect to insider trading rules.

To provide long-term benefits for everyone involved, the network must be sustainably more valuable – for each of its members – than the sum of its parts. In other words, each member must experience the benefits of collaboration, compared to working on his or her own. This is by no means a foregone conclusion – but it works.

Avoiding trouble

Despite the clear overweight of positive aspects, working together with others inevitably involves risks (which we can only cover by way of example here). This is particularly relevant for networks spread across a wide geographical range where the team members may be working in different time zones, making communications difficult at times.

Minimising risks at the outset

Again, the key aspect is quality assurance (QA): if the team's services are found to be substandard, this may damage the reputation of all team members, regardless of who was actually at fault. Simply implementing QA processes is not enough. Team members must be chosen carefully before they join, as having to iron out defective work is generally not a viable option. In a centrally-managed network, the selection of collaborates is somewhat easier – in a peer-to-peer network, it is a good idea to define relevant standards ex ante.

Efficient communications within the entire team – making sure that questions and issues are actively raised, at an early stage, and discussed amongst members – are crucial to maintaining high quality standards.

Depending on the content process, legal issues may go beyond civil law (e.g. liabilities and powers of representation) to include criminal law, for example, where confidential information is passed on to unauthorised third parties (which would constitute a breach of insider rules of the German Securities Trading Act). The careful selection of team members is crucially important against this background.

Managing payments

Handling cash flows is another important issue. As end customers will hardly be prepared to split payments for services rendered amongst team members, the team must have clear rules for passing on payments. In a centrally managed network, the central entity's creditworthiness must be assured, whereas a peer-to-peer network needs to agree on how to proceed in the event of payment delays or customer defaults.

Joining forces for a stronger market position

A team that prepares its collaboration well, carefully selecting its members, setting up suitable mechanisms for quality assurance, payments, etc., and actively explores its target market can gain a strong position. Provided that the issues summarised above are under control, there is nothing to stop the team from working together efficiently.

Andere Länder, andere Sitten! Interkulturelle Kompetenz als strategischer Erfolgsfaktor

Arno Giovannini

SemioticTransfer GmbH, Baden, Schweiz

arno.giovannini@semiotictransfer.ch

Abstract

Worauf müssen Sie sich einstellen, wenn Sie Ihr neuer Geschäftspartner in São Paulo, Peking oder Paris am Flughafen abholt? Wie kommen Sie endlich zum Geschäftsabschluss mit dem Vertreter der Metallfabrik in Brasilien?

Andere Länder, andere Sitten! Immer mehr mittelständische Unternehmen begeben sich aufs Parkett internationaler Märkte und erleben oft Schiffbruch.

Internationalisierung, Globalisierung, Lokalisierung. Andere Länder und Kulturen sind nur 'einen Mausklick' entfernt. Englisch als „Lingua franca" genügt im internationalen Business nicht.

Das Erschließen fremdkultureller Absatzmärkte erfordert einen permanenten Aufbau der interkulturellen Kompetenz. Beispielsweise in den Themenbereichen: Zeiterleben, Raumerleben, Denkmuster, Sprachverhalten, nichtverbale Kommunikation, Wertesystem, Symbole, Verhaltensmuster, soziale Gruppierungen, Hierarchien und Machtdistanz, Projektorganisationen, informelle vs. formelle Businesskulturen usw.

Die Aussage «Andere Länder, andere Sitten!» bezieht sich nicht nur auf Unterschiede zu Ländern aus weiter Ferne, sondern auch auf subtile Unterschiede im Denken, Handeln und Fühlen zwischen Nachbarländern oder auch Regionen im eigenen Land.

So erfahren beispielsweise deutsche Geschäftsleute in der Schweiz, und umgekehrt in Deutschland tätige Schweizer, dass es trotz gemeinsamer Sprache offensichtlich noch mehr Türen und Hürden im gegenseitigen Verständnis gibt. Die Art und Weise, wie Schweizer und Deutsche Geschäfte abwickeln, Projekte strukturieren oder zum Konsens gelangen, ist unterschiedlich. Deutsche und Schweizer haben beispielsweise unterschiedliche Konsenskulturen.

Der Vortrag bietet Hintergrundinformationen sowie anwendbare Praxistipps.

Existenzgründung – erfolgreich am Markt bestehen

Finding and keeping direct clients

Chris Durban

Freelance translator, Paris (SFT, ATA, ITI)

chris.durban@gmail.com

Introduction

France's national association of professional translators (SFT) began offering workshops on setting up as a freelance and building a direct clientele a half-dozen years ago. The aim was to provide up-to-date information to newcomers, encouraging those with a promising profile to give it a go in the best possible conditions, while discouraging dilettantes. The SFT program has been a clear success, with four or five sessions offered each year in as many cities.

I teach on that course, and also co-write the "Fire Ant & Worker Bee" advice column in the online Translation Journal, which regularly fields questions on how to link up with promising clients.

So the tips in today's session draw on both the SFT course and on FA&WB, plus a variety of talks I have given at prior colloquia, not to mention my own practice as a freelance translator specializing in for-publication corporate texts for demanding clients in France.

But first a warning...

Years ago ATA's Neil Inglis defined the "poverty cult" as the situation prevailing "when [translators] indulge in wailing and gnashing of teeth about disrespect and poor translator visibility, while throwing in the towel and doing nothing themselves to correct the situation."

Mr. Inglis went on to describe poverty cult members as those who complain bitterly about foolish clients and media depictions of translators, while never making the effort to correct those erroneous perceptions – thus becoming "participants in their own self-destruction."

His comments resonate with me, for I have observed the same would-be sophisticated cynicism and gloom on endless translator forums, in far too many academic publications, and in translator get-togethers. The leitmotif? That the deck is stacked against freelancers – struggling and noble, but ultimately doomed. Losers through *la force des choses*.

No later than June 2009, participants at an SFT training day assured me that "big companies don't want anything to do with freelance translators; they work exclusively with agencies."

I was happy to disabuse them, correcting the misinformation they had picked up on a commercial platform populated by, well, poverty cultists.

It was in fact easy to do so, by citing examples of demanding corporate clients that work only with known entities: freelance translators with whom they have built up a strong rapport and a history of successful translation projects. Skilled professionals whom these demanding businesses know they can trust not to slither down the slippery slope and off the precipice of subcontracting and sub-subcontracting.

So today's presentation will continue in that vein. The poverty cult has no place here.

My aim, further, is that attendees leave with at least four ideas they can deploy immediately once back at the wordface. And in so doing ratchet up their intellectual satisfaction, self-esteem and income in this most stimulating of professions.

...and a dilemma

As our colleague Steve Dyson has pointed out, there is no single statement about translation that holds true everywhere, at all times – which is no doubt why so many "client education" materials are so unwieldy, and clients so confused. Yet for the professional translator building her practice, educating all the ignorant clients out there is essential; if not, buyers will continue to make poor choices, succumbing to smoke and mirrors rather than opting for solutions likely to net them the sparkling texts they want.

By the same token, there is not a single translation market, rather a multitude of segments – some infinitely more attractive than others.

The translator's first challenge, then, is to analyze her own particular skills and identify markets where these are in demand, before connecting up with clients and their concerns. At which point *speaking their language* – in every sense of the word, and regardless of the segment concerned – is critical.

Misperceptions

At this point, it is obvious to some observers, including myself, that translators' perceptions of "the market" more often than not reflect bad habits, zero business sense, and wild fantasizing about client motivations.

To find and keep direct clients, translators must be weaned off these misperceptions. And experience shows that nothing is more effective than the Authentic Client Statement.

Let us take three examples:

1. "We are manufacturers, not linguists. We would like to be able to trust suppliers in your industry [the language industry], but we have observed first-hand that there are no guarantees despite the lofty declarations made in all those four-color brochures. It is very frustrating."

2. "Our experience with translation suppliers (both freelance and agencies) has been mixed. We have learned to be very wary of any supplier who claims to be able to translate anything, in any language. And we've learned that you can never delegate the entire project; you have to keep an eye on things."

3. "The translation unit at the Ministry of Finance expects its outside suppliers to provide a direct email and phone number, which means we rarely work with translation agencies. We prefer suppliers who specialize in one or several language combinations and who specialize, too, in a very small number of subject areas – even micro-subject areas. It is obviously an advantage if they are at ease with standard office software, but ISO certification is in no way a selection criterion."

The first quote comes from the head of communications at a major listed company in Paris. The second is an SME in a large provincial town. The third is from the head of the French Ministry of Finance translation unit.

How very instructive they are, not least in highlighting the "F" word (frustration at poorly executed work and the sheer powerlessness of non-native-speakerhood). We learn, too, that for good clients (and even potentially good clients) price is not all that important, contrary to a widely held "truth" voiced on translator forums.

Roll up your sleeves

From these initial points come the following concrete tips for practicing translators seeking to up their game and build a direct clientele.

(These tips will be accompanied by relevant examples at the BDÜ conference, and a PowerPoint presentation will be made available to all attendees.)

1. Don't wait for your ideal clients to find you: identify attractive candidates up front and stalk them.

2. Don't tell them about your diplomas.

3. Don't tell clients about *how* you work (CAT tools, dictionaries, etc.); focus instead on *what you can do* for their business.

4. Don't overwhelm them with information when you pitch. Listen.

5. Don't advertise that you work at cheap (or even "reasonable") rates (unless you are looking for clients who pay very little).

6. Actively seek texts that are challenging, even very challenging – the greater the risk, the greater the scope for gain.

7. Read what your clients read, and hang out where your clients hang out.

8. If you have enough work, raise your prices – starting with the next new client (the existing ones know your pain threshold).

9. Having identified promising new clients, use the free trial offer to establish contact.

10. Focus on developing your target-language writing skills (and work only into your native language).

11. By all means invest in technology, but keep in mind that over-use of CAT tools can be bad for your professional health (and that there are many many many areas where these tools will be counterproductive).

Existenzgründung im Zeitalter der Globalisierung

Michelle White

*Dipl.-Soziologin; Baur Technische Fachübersetzungen, Essen
Lehrbeauftragte Fachhochschule Köln und Universität Heidelberg,
Mitglied DGS Deutsche Gesellschaft für Soziologie*

Michelle.White@t-online.de

1   Einleitung

Die Globalisierung hat den Übersetzungsmarkt – und damit auch die Bedingungen für den Markteintritt von Übersetzern, die als freiberufliche Übersetzer eine Existenz gründen wollen – drastisch verändert.

Ich möchte hier insbesondere die folgenden vier Aspekte nennen:

- Übersetzen bedeutet heute mehr denn je **Fach**übersetzen. Dies ist vor allem zwei Faktoren geschuldet: zum einen der exorbitanten Zunahme des Wissens der Menschheit und der damit einhergehenden immer weiteren Ausdifferenzierung von Fachgebieten. Zum anderen haben Unternehmen im Zuge der Globalisierung enorme Summen in die fremdsprachliche Ausbildung von Mitarbeitern investiert, und auch im Bildungssystem spielt die Mehrsprachigkeit zu Recht eine große Rolle. Dies ist verbunden mit der Erwartung, dass zumindest in der quasi als Lingua franca verwendeten Sprache Englisch und in gewissem Maß auch in Französisch und Spanisch die „normale" Geschäftsabwicklung in der Regel direkt in der Fremdsprache stattfinden kann – auch wenn es im wirklichen Leben häufig so ist, dass die so in der Fremdsprache abgefassten Texte alles andere als sprachlich richtig sind und fremdsprachliche Texte oft nur teilweise richtig verstanden werden. Was in diesen Sprachen an Übersetzungsaufträgen nach außen vergeben wird, sind daher meist eher schwierige **Fach**texte oder Texte, an die besondere Anforderungen gestellt werden, wie z.b. Veröffentlichungsreife. Hinzu kommt, dass häufig Texte aus früheren Projekten „recycelt" werden und dem Übersetzer dann oft nur neu hinzugefügte Fragmente vorliegen, deren richtiges Verständnis als Grundvoraussetzung jeder Übersetzung ein hohes Maß an Orientierungsvermögen im jeweiligen Fachgebiet erfordert.

- Das Wirtschaftsleben insgesamt ist heute von einer früher ungekannten **Schnelligkeit** geprägt. Und: Wenn bei internationalen Transaktionen oder Firmenübernahmen quasi „auf Knopfdruck" Milliarden von Euros um die Welt gejagt werden können, dann spielt es für die Unternehmenslenker keine Rolle, dass für die Übersetzung von umfangreichen Unterlagen oder Vertragswerken eine gewisse Zeit benötigt wird. In vielen Fällen müssen Übersetzungsdienstleister heute sehr große Leistungsumfänge in kürzester Zeit bewältigen.

- Die Unternehmen geben den **Kostendruck**, dem sie sich im internationalen Wettbewerb ausgesetzt sehen, an ihre eigenen Auftragnehmer weiter – so auch an Übersetzungsdienstleister. Das drückt sich nicht nur in dem uns allen bekannten Druck auf die Honorare aus, sondern schlägt sich auch darin nieder, dass Unternehmen alle von ihnen benötigten Übersetzungsdienstleistungen zunehmend *„aus einer Hand"* einkaufen und damit internen Verwaltungsaufwand minimieren und durch größere Volumina geringere Preise erzielen wollen.

- In den siebziger und achtziger Jahren war es „Standard", dass Hochschulabsolventen zunächst in einen Sprachendienst von Unternehmen eintraten, bevor sie sich dann später möglicherweise selbstständig machten. Dort arbeiteten sie sich zunächst unter Anleitung erfahrener Kollegen in ihr Fachgebiet ein und lernten all das praktische Handwerkszeug, das es zur Berufsausübung braucht – das die Hochschulen wenn überhaupt nur sehr eingeschränkt vermitteln können. Im Zuge der fortschreitenden Globalisierung und des „Outsourcing" wurden Sprachendienste in Unternehmen über viele Jahre hinweg zunehmend abgebaut, in einigen Fällen reduziert bis zu einer Art „Facheinkaufsabteilungen mit angeschlossener Qualitätssicherung oder -prüfung".

Wer sich heute selbstständig macht, muss dies häufig direkt von der Hochschule weg tun, da nicht ausreichend freie Stellen in qualifizierten Sprachendiensten oder Übersetzungsunternehmen zur Verfügung stehen.

2 Was bedeuten diese vier Aspekte der Globalisierung für Existenzgründer?

2.1 Spezialisierung für ein klares Profil

Das Thema Spezialisierung wird von Existenzgründern häufig fehlinterpretiert. In meinen Lehrveranstaltungen erfahre ich oft, dass sie der Ansicht sind, eine Spezialisierung auf ein Fachgebiet könnten sie sich „nicht leisten", sondern müssten vielmehr „alles machen, was kommt", wobei eigentlich das Gegenteil richtig ist, denn

- Spezialisierung richtet die Akquisitionsarbeit dahingehend aus, dass kunden-gruppenspezifische Akquisition betrieben werden kann. Mit Ingenieuren muss anders geredet werden als mit Rechtsanwälten oder Sozialwissenschaftlern.

- Spezialisierung bedeutet nicht Einschränkung. Niemand hindert einen daran, auch „Blumen links und rechts des Weges zu pflücken" – solange man sich sicher ist, den Anforderungen seiner Kunden gerecht zu werden.

- Spezialisierung kann am Anfang nach außen hin auch als „Interessensschwer-punkt" vermittelt werden, bis wirklich nennenswerte Spezialkenntnis-se/Erfahrungen/Referenzen auf dem jeweiligen Fachgebiet vorliegen.

- Gezielte Weiterbildung – Unerlässlich ist es, sich z.B. durch das Studieren von Fachtexten in den jeweiligen Arbeitssprachen fachliches Rüstzeug anzu-eignen und sich mit dem branchenspezifischen Duktus vertraut zu machen. Auch eine universitäre Weiterbildung könnte in Betracht gezogen werden: Absolvierung eines Bachelor- und/oder Masterstudiums bietet eine solide Grundlage, sich auf hohem Niveau Fachkenntnisse anzueignen und ist auch in der Akquise von Fachübersetzungsaufträgen ein sehr starkes Argument und eine Möglichkeit, sich von Mitbewerbern abzuheben.

- „Technik" oder „Wirtschaft" als Fachgebiet ist heute angesichts der immer weiter fortschreitenden Differenzierung von Fachgebieten keine wirkliche Spezialisierung mehr, da es sich um reine Oberbegriffe handelt. Wer sich zum Beispiel für „Technik" interessiert, der sollte sich genauer die Unterfachgebie-te, die interessant sind, erschließen, um ein Profil zu erhalten, da Technik ein allgemein gefasster Begriff ist und somit wenig aussagekräftig ist.

- Wer sich auf dem jeweiligen Fachgebiet Fachwissen aneignet, wird von sei-nen Kunden leichter als „ihresgleichen" anerkannt – d.h. als gleichwertiger Gesprächspartner, nicht als „Externer" oder „notwendiges Übel".

2.2 Große Auftragsvolumina in kurzer Zeit erfolgreich bearbeiten

Um auch größere Auftragsvolumina mit relativ kurzen Lieferfristen bearbeiten zu können,

- bedarf es unbedingt eines **Netzwerks** mit Kollegen

- bedarf es Kollegen, die Korrektur lesen, da häufig nicht die Zeit bleibt, die eigentlich erforderlich wäre, den nötigen „Abstand" zur eigenen Arbeit zu gewinnen, um die eigenen Fehler noch erkennen zu können.

- bedarf es einer Spezialisierung, denn nur wer sich auf ein Fachgebiet speziali-siert und auf diesem auch terminologisch „zu Hause ist" – d.h. nicht jeder zweite Fachbegriff nachgeschlagen und erstmals durchdacht werden muss – kann **schnell** und „treffsicher" genug arbeiten, um enge Lieferfristen zu hal-ten.

2.3 Kostendruck

Spezialisierung und die damit verbundene inhaltliche und stilistische Vertrautheit mit den bearbeiteten Texten verbessert auch die Verdienstsituation, da Übersetzer in der Regel nicht danach bezahlt werden, wie lange sie an einer Arbeit sitzen, sondern nach Anzahl der Zeilen, die sie produziert haben.

Das Streben der Auftraggeber, alles *„aus einer Hand zu bekommen"*, erfordert den Aufbau eines Netzwerks über das

- verschiedene Sprachen abgedeckt werden können, d.h. nicht nur die eigenen Arbeitssprachen,

- angrenzende oder mit dem eigenen Fachgebiet verbundene Aufträge abgewickelt werden können – so gehen z.b. im Anlagenbau technische Übersetzungen häufig auch mit umfangreichen Vertragsübersetzungen einher,

- auch andere Textsorten bearbeitet werden können. Wenn ein Kunde mit Ihren Übersetzungen z. B. von Spezifikationen zufrieden ist, wird er früher oder später vielleicht fragen, ob Sie nicht auch Imagebroschüren, Unterlagen aus dem Marketing oder Publikationen für ihn übersetzen können. Wenn das nicht „Ihr Ding" ist, dann sollte ein Kollege aus dem Netzwerk zur Verfügung stehen, dessen Ding das ist.

2.4 Wissen und Erfahrung teilen

Zusammenarbeit im Netzwerk mit andern Kollegen muss heute teilweise die Einarbeitung ersetzen, die früher in Sprachendiensten stattfand.

- In der Zusammenarbeit mit Kollegen – z.B. beim gezielten Korrekturlesen – Kritik üben können und selbst lernen.

- Erfahrung austauschen, z.B. in virtuellen Netzwerken qualifizierter Kollegen, wie in „MeinBDÜ".

- Wissensteilung mit anderen qualifizierten Kollegen aus dem Netzwerk.

3 Unternehmerische Basiskompetenz

Die Globalisierung fordert Übersetzer heute mehr denn je nicht nur in fachlicher, sondern auch in **unternehmerischer** Hinsicht.

Dem tragen verschiedene Hochschulen dadurch Rechnung, dass sie in ihre Lehrpläne Module zur Vermittlung unternehmerischer Basiskompetenz aufgenommen haben.

Hochschulabsolventen sind fachlich sehr gut ausgebildet, dennoch fehlt ihnen die Basis für betriebswirtschaftliches Denken und Handeln. Als Lehrbeauftragte für „Unternehmerische Basiskompetenz" beobachte ich häufig, dass Studierende das Angebot gern nutzen und das Gespräch suchen, um Fragen zum Fach, der Berufsfindung oder Existenzgründung zu klären.

Aber was genau ist mit unternehmerischer Basiskompetenz gemeint? In einem Satz wäre umgangssprachlich zu behaupten: ein Rundumschlag um das Unternehmertum als Freiberufler. Dies umfasst insbesondere auch für Existenzgründer wichtige Themen wie z.B. rechtliche Grundlagen der Berufsausübung, Unterschied Freiberufler/Gewerbetreibender, Unternehmensformen, Akquisition, Angebote als Visitenkarte, nachhaltige Kalkulation, Auftragsabwicklung.

Als erster Teil sind die **rechtlichen Grundlagen der Berufsausübung** Bestandteil. Hier sind u.a. Themen wie Verträge und Haftungsgrundlagen, Verträge (Werkvertrag/Dienstvertrag), Versicherungen wichtig.

Der zweite Teil umfasst das Thema **Steuern und Buchhaltung**. Hier werden Themen behandelt wie Abgrenzung Freier Beruf/Gewerbe, „Wo melde ich meine selbstständige Tätigkeit an?", „Wie erstelle ich eine Einnahmen-Überschuss-Rechnung?", Grundlagen zum Thema Steuern, Umsatzsteuerberechnung ja oder nein? Umsatzsteuer/Vorsteuer, Umsatzsteuerberechnung ins Ausland (heutzutage von besonderer Bedeutung, da viele Übersetzer Kunden im Ausland haben).

Der dritte Teil behandelt das Thema **betriebswirtschaftliche Kalkulation**. Der Existenzgründer muss den Markt, den er sich erschließen will, kennen. Was viele vernachlässigen, ist, dass sie auch ihren eigenen Marktwert kennen müssen, wenn sie am Markt antreten. Wichtig ist dabei zu ermitteln, was man selbst an Umsatz im Monat benötigt, daraus lässt sich schnell der Stundensatz, der benötigt wird, errechnen. Wenn dieser ermittelt ist, kann der Existenzgründer schnell seinen Zeilenpreis ermitteln, sofern er mittels Stundenzettel oder Zeiterfassungsprogramm herausgefunden hat, wie viele Zeilen er in einer Stunde produziert. Wobei hier wichtig ist zu erwähnen, dass keine Reduzierung auf reine Zeilenarbeit stattfinden soll, sondern derartiges Vorgehen als Grundlage dient, seine Arbeitszeit und -weise einschätzen zu lernen und so besser kalkulieren zu können. Denn auf dieser Grundlage lassen sich Aufträge schnell und übersichtlich kalkulieren.

Auftragskalkulation, Angebotserstellung und Akquisition sind weitere wichtige Elemente der unternehmerischen Basiskompetenz. Denn ohne vernünftige und zielgruppenorientierte (siehe Spezialisierung) Akquisition wird der Existenzgründer in der Regel Schwierigkeiten haben, langfristig von seinem Geschäft leben zu können. Viele unterschätzen die Erstellung und Abgabe eines Angebotes, das ihre Visitenkarte nach außen ist. Was nützen schönes Briefpapier, Visitenkarten und Flyer, wenn das Angebot nicht durchdacht und für den Kunden transparent nachvollziehbar ist, insbesondere hinsichtlich Leistungsdefinition und Preisbildung? Wer in der Lage ist, ein professionelles und aussagekräftiges Angebot abzugeben, hat seinen Mitbewerbern schon einiges voraus.

Die **Auftragsabwicklung** stellt den Abwicklungspart der unternehmerischen Basiskompetenz dar. Dabei geht es um Projektabwicklung und Management von Aufträgen, Rechnungslegung (was gehört auf eine Rechnung) und Mahnwesen.

4 Fazit

Aus meiner Lehrerfahrung im Fach Unternehmerische Basiskompetenz und als Referentin für Existenzgründerseminare spielen m. E. insbesondere vier Faktoren eine wesentliche Rolle, um langfristig einen erfolgreichen Markteintritt zu schaffen:

1. Spezialisierung
2. Aneignung von Fachkenntnissen und Weiterbildung

3. Netzwerk aufbauen

4. Unternehmerische Kompetenz entwickeln.

Existenzgründer müssen verstehen, dass sie nach allen Seiten offen agieren müssen, um sich ihrer Zielgruppe zu nähern. Neben all dem anderen ist für den erfolgreichen Marktantritt ein professioneller Stil als Geschäftsmann/-frau unerlässlich.

Mit vielen Chancen und Risiken stellt die Globalisierung Existenzgründer mehr denn je vor eine große Herausforderung, die es zu bewältigen gilt.

„Wie erzielt man als Freelance-Übersetzer einen höheren Preis?"

Mats Wiman

Betriebswirt, freiberuflicher Übersetzer (Proz.com), Skog, Schweden

MatsWiman@swipnet.se

Abstract

Er werden Faktoren und Strategien vorgestellt, die wichtig sind, um sich auf einem sehr wettbewerbsgeprägten Markt zu behaupten, und wie man Werkzeuge und Strategien verwendet, um Kunden von der "Weisheit" fernzuhalten, dass man immer nach dem 'billigsten' Übersetzer suchen sollte.

Wie schafft man Vertrauen und Zuversicht bei Kunden, und wie vermeidet man die üblichen Fallgruben beim Verhandeln?

Der Vortrag ist eine verbesserte Version des Vortrages "Earning higher rates?", mehrmals gehalten bei ProZ.com-Konferenzen, diesmal auf Deutsch.

Die vorgetragenen Argumente stellen kein genaues Rezept oder eine Patentmethode dar, sondern fungieren als Checkliste zur Gedankenanregung sowohl für Anfänger als auch für Erfahrene und Gewiefte.

Sprachdienstleistungen in Institutionen

Der kommunale Fremdsprachendienst der Landeshauptstadt Stuttgart – Aufgaben und neue Herausforderungen

Martina Fritz

Diplom-Übersetzerin und staatlich geprüfte Dolmetscherin, Landeshauptstadt Stuttgart, Fremdsprachendienst L/OB-PRE

Martina.Fritz@stuttgart.de

Abstract

Stuttgart ist die Landeshauptstadt von Baden-Württemberg. Mit circa 600.000 Einwohnern ist Stuttgart gleichzeitig Zentrum einer der führenden Wirtschaftsregionen Europas und seit Jahrzehnten Anziehungspunkt für Menschen aus aller Welt: Bürger aus über 160 Staaten leben in der Stadt, mehr als 100 Sprachen werden hier gesprochen.

In Zeiten der zunehmenden Internationalisierung müssen sich auch Kommunalverwaltungen nach innen und in ihrer Außendarstellung mehr und mehr mehrsprachig präsentieren und positionieren. Dies sind wichtige, weiche Standortfaktoren. Kommunalverwaltungen und ihre gewählten Repräsentanten sind daneben zunehmend in internationale Partnerschaften, Projekte, Netzwerke und Gremien eingebunden.

Der kommunale Fremdsprachendienst spiegelt in seiner Querschnittsfunktion für die Stadtverwaltung diese Entwicklung wider.

Von einem, beim zentralen Verwaltungsamt angesiedelten Übersetzungs- und Dolmetscherdienst begann mit der Verlagerung des Fremdsprachendienstes in das Büro des Oberbürgermeisters vor mehr als einem Jahrzehnt eine Aufgabenweiterentwicklung, die noch nicht abgeschlossen ist. Die bisherigen Aufgabenschwerpunkte werden zunehmend ergänzt durch neue Anforderungen, u.a. als Vergabe- und Qualitätssicherungsstelle, als Koordinatorin für das Community Interpreting sowie als fachliche Instanz für den Aufbau einer Corporate Language. In Zukunft wird daher der kommunale Fremdsprachendienst in noch höherem Maß zum wichtigen Bindeglied zwischen den städtischen Ämtern mit sehr unterschiedlichen Aufgabenstellungen und freiberuflichen Sprachdienstleistern.

The present and the future of translation at the Bundesbank

Michael Dear

Deutsche Bundesbank, Frankfurt am Main

Michael.Dear@bundesbank.de

Abstract

In my remarks, I will introduce the Bundesbank's Language Services and explain its activities in the context of the Bundesbank's dual role as a central bank in Europe and a German public sector institution.

I will discuss the tools and workflows with which we manage our translation projects and assure the quality of our work and also list some of the training measures on which we send our staff to keep them fully prepared for the challenges of the job. This part of the talk will also include a presentation of our Elektronische Auftragsverwaltung (EAV) translation management system, which was developed entirely in-house.

In closing, despite the near-impossibility of predicting the future (as has been driven home by recent events on the financial markets), I will venture a tentative glimpse into the future and how we at the Bundesbank intend to "interpret" it.

Is outsourcing the answer?

Dr. Peter Hards

Acting Head of Language Service, European Patent Office

phards@epo.org

1 The EPO language service

Since the European Patent Organisation is an international institution (with currently 35 member states), it is not surprising that the European Patent Office should have had a Language Service from the day it was established in 1977. What may be more surprising is that, despite the EPO's growth to 6 700 or so staff members, only 40 work in the Language Service and fewer than 30 of them are translators (the rest deal with interpreting and administration). The Language Service accounts for a mere

0.5% of the EPO's annual budget. There are various reasons for this. Firstly, the Language Service is, mercifully, not responsible for translating the 150 000 patent applications the EPO receives every year. That is the task of the patent applicant or his legal representative. Secondly, unlike the EU of which it is not part, the EPO only has three official languages (English, French and German). Thirdly, the number of staff needed to translate a document does not depend on the number of its potential readers.

2   To outsource or not to outsource

The cold winds of change have nevertheless also battered the EPO's small Language Service. As far back as 2005, the EPO Vice-President responsible for the Language Service asked us to draw up a study on outsourcing with a view to making greater use of freelance translators. Unsurprisingly, the study established that outsourcing was less expensive, costing about half as much as in-house work. This figure was disputed at the time, however, because it was felt to be virtually impossible to assess the overhead in-house costs involved in outsourcing: negotiating contracts and rates, formatting documents on their return, liaising with authors, answering freelance translators' queries, revision, etc. Nevertheless, it has to be accepted that outsourcing costs are probably lower, particularly for an international organisation with attractive remuneration benefits.

As a result of the study, EPO management decreed that, as a way of cutting costs, more translation work should be outsourced in future. It was originally planned in 2006 to issue an invitation to tender for a framework agreement with a translation agency that would administer at least some of the work outsourced, providing its own quality control system and handling financial matters. This was thought to be a suitable way of avoiding exceeding the current annual budget ceilings per translator and translation agency for contracts placed without an invitation to tender. The idea of a framework agreement was finally not pursued for a number of reasons. One of the main ones was that we would then lose control of the outsourcing operation. We would lose touch with our individual freelance translators, no longer be able to select who should translate particular texts and find it difficult to maintain quality levels. Nor did the amount of material involved seem to warrant a full-scale framework agreement. Instead we decided to increase the size and range of our freelance panel. It must be said, however, that this pragmatic solution has not been welcomed by the Finance Department, who continue to prefer invitations to tender as a more orthodox way of implementing our Financial Regulations.

However, the idea of greater outsourcing itself was kept up and it was eventually decided in 2007 to impose a five-year road map on the Language Service, according to which we would cease to recruit permanent staff once the three translation sections had reached a reduced number of translators, largely through natural wastage (7 English, 9 French, 9 German). This meant a loss of two permanent posts in each section. It was accepted that this was the maximum cut we could agree to while maintaining the Language Service's viability, but it has nevertheless presented us with a number of logistical and linguistic challenges which we are endeavouring to meet as efficiently as possible.

3   How to cope with an unpopular road map

Outsourcing has always been part of the Language Service's work and we normally outsource about 25% of our workload. Indeed, we have only been able to keep the Language Service's size down, despite the EPO's massive expansion, by calling on freelance translators, particularly during peak periods. Similarly, we have always been cost-conscious, long before the current financial constraints were imposed. Whilst we appreciate the need for flexibility in the rates we pay for particular types of job, we are naturally keen to keep outsourcing costs down to a reasonable level. Our aim has been to build up a close relationship with individual freelance translators in specific subject fields and to give them feedback in the form of revision. For non-official languages, in particular, we also use translation agencies. Here too we value long-term relationships, but we are sometimes reluctant to revise agency translations, because we cannot normally choose the translator ourselves and cannot therefore guarantee that the translator we provide feedback to will translate our next job on the same subject. The main challenge presented by our road map is how to increase the proportion of outsourced work without sacrificing quality and overstretching our in-house resources. I shall outline below the ways we are trying to tackle this new situation in a creative and positive way.

3.1 Intensive feedback

Our primary form of feedback to freelance translators is through revision. The translators are usually very appreciative and learn from this feedback. We also offer our services in replying to translators' queries. The plan now is to intensify this relationship with our panel of freelance translators and integrate them more into the EPO culture. This applies in particular to our individual translators, but we also hope to forge closer ties with translation agencies, particularly local ones in the Munich area and those specialising in patents and patent-related material, legal documents and finance, as well as non-official languages such as Japanese, Korean and Chinese.

3.2 Technical support

A key area for expanding our outsourcing operations is the provision of technical tools. Our French terminologist also performs the function of applications manager and is therefore primarily responsible for developing these tools. We already enable our regular freelance translators to access our archive of Administrative Council documents, and we would like to extend such access to other types of documentation. We have also prepared Notes on House Style in our three official languages, which we have made available on the intranet to all EPO staff and in written form to our freelance panel.

Extract from the German Section's Notes on House Style (*Stilfibel*):

Zehn Gebote

1. Gebot: Drücken Sie sich einfach aus.
2. Gebot: Seien Sie präzise.
3. Gebot: Schreiben Sie prägnant.

4. Gebot: Konstruieren Sie logisch.

5. Gebot: Vermeiden Sie Passivkonstruktionen.

6. Gebot: Verzichten Sie auf Nominalstil.

7. Gebot: Verfahren Sie konsequent.

8. Gebot: Zitieren Sie korrekt.

9. Gebot: Sparen Sie mit Abkürzungen.

10. Gebot: Präsentieren Sie Ihre Texte in leserlicher Form.

Similarly, our in-house team of terminologists have built up a trilingual database using Trados MultiTerm, which now contains over 17 000 EPO-related terms. The database is available not only to our in-house translators but also to all EPO staff via the intranet, though not unfortunately to the public for copyright reasons. One of our top priorities is to make the database available in some form to our freelance panel. The EPO's data security firewall is proving a particularly stubborn obstacle, but we hope to have this service up and running by the end of the year. Ensuring correct use of EPO terminology will help our freelance translators achieve an acceptable level of quality without extensive revision. We also use Trados Workbench for suitable texts with sufficient repetition, and we plan to incorporate our translation memories into the suite of tools we offer our freelance translators. But, since many of our documents do not lend themselves to working segment-by-segment as in Workbench, we have recently also acquired MultiCorpora's multilingual search product MultiTrans. Here translations are aligned with the original for search purposes as whole documents after translation. We are still at the trial stage, but hope that this will be a further tool of particular use to our freelance panel.

One aspect of technology that we do not yet plan to offer our freelance translators is machine translation. Despite recent advances in this area, particularly in the statistics-based systems as opposed to the semantics-based ones, we are not yet convinced that machine translation is of much use for translating most of our documents. Where it is already being used is in providing gists, particularly of documents in Asian languages, for our patent examiners. On the basis of the gist they can request a translation of the entire document from us, which we normally outsource. The introduction of machine translation has helped to meet an increasing need among examiners for information about Japanese, Chinese and Korean patents in particular, without significantly increasing the Language Service's workload. When the estimated cost of a translation is very high, we ask the examiner if he really needs the full translation, or whether extracts would not be sufficient. This can save the Office several thousand euros on very long documents. The availability of gisting through machine translation is another reason why the Language Service has been able to stay small, despite the dramatic rise in the number of examiners over the last three decades. Several machine translation projects are under way concurrently at the EPO. The Language Service plays an observer role in them as a way of keeping abreast of technological developments.

3.3 In-house placements

Another way of training freelance translators is to invite them to spend one or two months with us on a temporary placement. This is clearly not always possible with experienced translators who have an existing client base to keep happy, but it lends itself to relative newcomers who show particular potential. We have already welcomed several translators on temporary placements with some success. Following their placement with us, they can go on to become regulars on our freelance panel. I should add that, with our small numbers, we only have limited capacity to implement this measure. The German section, for example, has no need at present for more freelance translators. It already has ten experienced and trained freelance translators on its books.

3.4 Temporary in-house contracts

One of the main reasons for cutting back on permanent staff is to reduce the EPO's long-term pension and health-care liabilities. Temporary contracts offer a way of employing staff for a reasonable length of time without incurring such liabilities. This has been seen by some within the EPO as a way of getting round the road map, but we have argued that such contracts offer a chance to give freelance translators intensive training in EPO documents and terminology. For the past year or so, for example, a local freelance translator has been coming in one day a week to do English terminology work. After an open competition, that person has now been appointed as a full-time translator/terminologist on a temporary contract with effect from 1 July. Similarly, we hope to appoint a French translator on a two-year contract in 2010.

3.5 Relations with freelance panel

Apart from our intensive feedback through revision and consultation, we also plan to arrange an annual get-together with our local translators and agencies in the Munich area as a way of putting faces to names and building up trust and communication. Experience has shown us that personal contact with freelance translators goes a long way to establishing fruitful long-term co-operation.

4   Measures to boost the language service's standing

4.1 Client surveys

In 2008, the Language Service organised its first client survey among EPO staff and the delegations on the Administrative Council and its subordinate committees. The aim was to gauge how our work is assessed by the requesters and draw conclusions on how to organise it in future. The response rate of about 40% was relatively high and the level of satisfaction (over 90%) was gratifying. However, the number of outsourced jobs commented on by the survey respondents was too small to draw conclusions about their comparative satisfaction with in-house and freelance translations. We do not wish to stretch the patience of our clients, but may repeat the questionnaire exercise some time in the future to focus on this aspect.

4.2 Advertising

In July this year, an article on the Language Service was published in our EPO Gazette. This was a good platform for advertising our services, including our terminology database. The client survey showed that only 25% of the respondents knew that the database existed, although 80% of those who did found it useful. It also enabled us to explain how requesters of translations should proceed to obtain the best possible result:

• Minimise the number of amendments after submitting a translation request

• Set realistic but genuine deadlines

• Provide whatever background information and material is available

These requirements are particularly important in the case of freelance translations, where the translator is working at one remove from the requester. We hope that, by making our services better known within the EPO and explaining our requirements, the status of the Language Service will be enhanced and our value to the Office will be better appreciated, not only by our regular clients who depend on us, but also by the staff and management as a whole.

5 The sequel to the road map

I have tried to show above how the EPO's Language Service is coping with the financial constraints that have led to its complement being reduced by two permanent posts per section over a period of five years. The precondition for our accepting this cutback was that the in-house translation sections should not fall below a critical size. Otherwise, we would cease to be viable as a source of in-house expertise and gradually be reduced to the role of an outsourcing post-box. Having obtained recognition of that position, we are now endeavouring to come to terms with the new situation by intensifying our relations with the freelance world, providing technical tools and integrating our freelance translators into our working environment. Our five-year road map runs until 2012. No-one is able to predict what the macroeconomic situation will look like at the end of that period. For all we know, the winds of change may have blown back in the direction of in-house work and permanent staff by then, the cold *mistral* being replaced by the warm *Föhn*, so to speak. It may have been established that outsourcing is not after all the answer, or at least not the entire answer. But whatever happens, we hope that the outsourcing measures we are taking during the road-map period will stand us in good stead as the Language Service accompanies the EPO through its next thirty years.

Translation services taken to the extreme

Josep Bonet

Head of Informatics Unit
European Commission Directorate-General for Translation

josep.bonet-heras@ec.europa.eu

1 DGT's unparalleled translation workload

In the European Union, language policy is the responsibility of the 27 Member states. The EU does not have a common language policy, meaning that the EU institutions only play a supporting role in this field, based on the principle of subsidiarity. The 15th of April 1958 was, and still very much is, a milestone in the history of the European Commission's Directorate-General for Translation (DGT[2]). On that day, (EEC) Council Regulation N° 1 determining the languages to be used by the European Economic Community was adopted.

From the modest beginning of these early days with about 25 translators working in the then four official languages to the actual level of some 1 750 linguists and 600 support staff handling 23 official languages, it has been a long and interesting journey, never short of challenges and difficulties. It was through successfully facing challenges like the "Big Bang", when the number of EU translation languages almost doubled overnight following the 2004 enlargement, that DGT has become the largest institutional translation service in the world and an inspiring model for many. And the beat goes on... with even more challenging issues like a steady increase in workload by 5% annually, bearing in mind that already an estimated 2 million pages have been translated in 2008, and presumably more official languages to be integrated in the future.

2 Translate once and (almost) never again

Within this continuously evolving context, especially during the last two decades, the translator's work has gradually shifted from a mere linguistic approach to an ever more technically skilled one. In fact the role of the translator today is not only to translate the document at hand but also to provide the resources for saving costs and avoiding the fatigue of repeating the effort, particularly when taxpayer money is at stake.

---

[2] http://ec.europa.eu/dgs/translation/index_en.htm

Already since the mid-70's pioneering relational and terminological databases began to be used by the EC. The evolution of the market supported and influenced by research in that domain over the last 30 years have greatly improved reusability of previously translated sentences. This resulted in a real economic benefit for both translation service providers and users. In the European Commission large integrated workflow environments have been built around *"Euramis"*, the homegrown centre piece of the translation recycling architecture. The Euramis corpora contain more than 200 millions sentences in all 23 EU official languages (some 50 millions on the source side and 150 millions on the target side) and they are used simultaneously by thousands of users, both at the Commission and in other EU institutions.

3 Workflow automation

Workflow automation requires standardised and streamlined use of tools and genuine data sharing in order to function properly and improve the effectiveness and efficiency of the work of both translators and managers and the quality and consistency in a service-oriented architecture. Another purpose of automation is to allow a supporting operational infrastructure like DGT to integrate smoothly into the working patterns of its clients, i.e. other Directorates-General of the European Commission, which have constraining political agendas.

The complex DGT workflow system (Figure 1) includes administrative backbone features such as electronic transmission of translation requests from clients to DGT (*Poetry*), electronic management of requests within the DGT (*Suivi*), a document server (*DGTVista*) and a translation management tool coupled with an electronic archiving system (*Dossier Manager*).

As far as proper translation work is concerned, a wide array of tools is available. A central translation memory at DGT (*Euramis*) is integrated with automatic pre-processing of relevant reusable information as well as the Commission's own machine translation system (*ECMT*) which fills the segments where no match is found in translation memories and databases of European law such as EUR-LEX/CELEX. The system also includes an alignment editor for Euramis (*Pedit*) and a software for the local management of data retrieved from the central Euramis memory (currently *SDL Trados Translator's Workbench* and *TagEditor*).

Additional tools that help the translator find information are also available like the metasearch tool *Quest*, which is querying simultaneously more than 30 terminological databases, or *MultiDoc,* a tool for managing reference links.

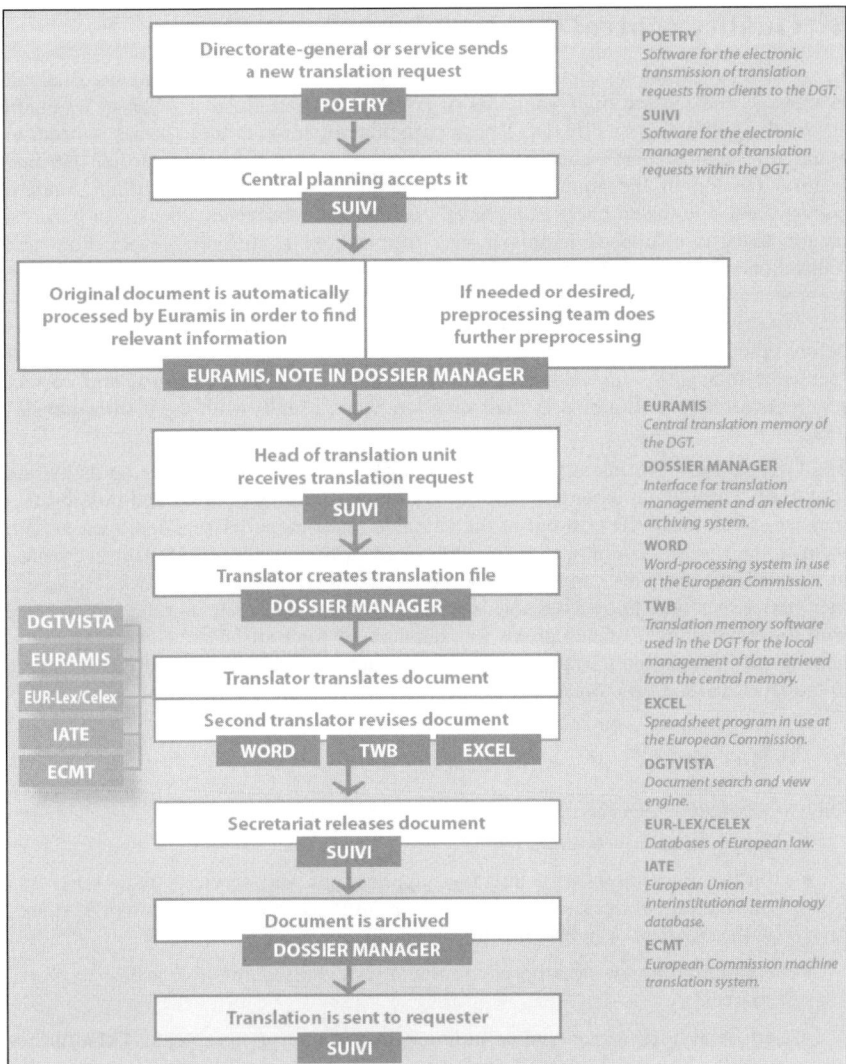

Fig. 1: Translation workflow in the European Commission.

4 Quality control and training

Large-scale multilingual translation resources with multiple entry points are difficult to manage and require high standards of consistency and global control to maintain across-the-board data quality. DGT pays particular attention to these issues in order to avoid that redundancies and errors lingering in the resources jeopardize optimal quality. On top of the automated quality control mechanisms including standard conventions, automated checks on "Save", automated consistency checks for consolidation, there is also considerable human intervention at different levels. For each translation request raw alignments that may result from the automatic retrieval during preprocessing of the original are checked by assistants before they reach the translator. After the translator completes his/her work, assistants run a list of quality checks before uploading the local translation memory into Euramis. There is also a number of "sentence managers" for each language who have the right to control and correct segments directly in Euramis in their own language, usually with input from translators.

The DGT is also devoting significant investment to continuously improving its human resources. Through an extensive offer of continuing training courses and possibilities translators can make the best out of the valuable multilingual assets deployed to help them in their work. Training is at the very heart of the question of cost-effectiveness in translation. The tools cannot reduce the overall workload on their own. However, their extensive and knowledgeable use is important to create a more interesting working environment and improve job satisfaction for translators, since they avoid unnecessary translation and processing. This results in improved quantity and quality of the DGT translation output.

5 What next?

Future development efforts will be focused primarily on:

- further workflow automation;
- further integration with language applications and services, with other EU translation services, with web content and document management systems, with statistical or hybrid machine translation systems;
- creation of a new desktop environment providing an intuitive access to all resources;
- artificial intelligence applied to linguistic resources (subsentence TMs, further tagging, etc.).

DGT also has a permanent "Language Technology Watch" (LTW) activity which consists in identifying global developments in the area of language applications, so that it can efficiently and effectively meet the challenges resulting from global technological changes in the area of language applications.

6 Conclusions

By creating in 2007 a special portfolio for multilingualism, the Commission wanted to materialize with a powerful and symbolic act its determination to bet on languages as both an invaluable human asset and a prevailing communication tool. In this context, DGT plays an essential role contributing to establishing a link between the EU and its citizens in their own language.

DGT has to tackle this challenge for a growing number of documents in 23 languages and to ensure at the same time high quality of service and output, improving continuously its efficiency and customer-orientation. Therefore DGT has no other possibility than taking translation services to the extreme and even beyond, by making use of the best technologies available, adapting them to the needs of its translators, who are its main asset.

Bibliography

Translation tools and workflow, European Commission 2008,
  http://ec.europa.eu/dgs/translation/bookshelf/tools_and_workflow_en.pdf

Translating for a multilingual community, European Commission 2009,
  http://ec.europa.eu/dgs/translation/bookshelf/brochure_en.pdf

Workshops und Podiumsdiskussionen

Globalization, translation/interpretation and conflict transformation

Chidubem Akinyede

Freelance Translator, Lagos, Nigeria

chidubemakinyede@yahoo.fr

Workshop

The world has undoubtedly become a global village with one (formal or informal) business or another to interact with one another, in a greater magnitude or dimension than ever before. With over 6 billion people speaking about 6,912 languages and many more dialects, there are sometimes misunderstandings, which ultimately lead to conflicts. The conflicts vary, from minor ones to major catastrophes. However, with translation and interpretation, nay effective communication, there should be better understanding and greater tolerance.

The immediate aim of this workshop is:

- To actively involve participants in a discussion on globalization, conflict for what it really is and its implication, elicit the role of translators and interpreters and its effect on conflict, which should lead to its eventual transformation.

The general aim would be:

- For participants to understand the role that translators and interpreters have to play in conflict transformation for effective international interaction and relative global peace.

This workshop will be delivered in English via a PowerPoint presentation, possibly with film clips as well, with the use of a projector.

Main considerations: globalization; translation; interpretation; conflict; effective communication; conflict transformation.

Die Übersetzungsdienstleistung für Endkunden: Solider Mannschaftssport oder genialer Alleingang?

Stephanie Wätjen

Moderatorin

Roland Hoffmann

1. Vorsitzender des BDÜ Landesverbandes Bayern; Freier Übersetzer

Heike Leinhäuser

Präsidentin des QSD, Berufsverband der Qualitätssprachendienste Deutschlands; Leinhäuser und Partner

Terence Oliver

Freier Übersetzer

Ilona Wallberg

Siemens AG

Podiumsdiskussion

Die gute Zusammenarbeit zwischen Übersetzern und Übersetzungsdienstleistern, bei denen Letztere gegenüber dem Endkunden für das Produkt Übersetzung im Sinne der Norm DIN EN 15038 haften, ist von fundamentaler Bedeutung für eine erfolgreiche Ausführung von Übersetzungsprojekten.

Dieser Grundsatz entstammt dem Prolog aus dem jüngst von BDÜ und QSD gemeinsam herausgegebenen Leitfaden zur Zusammenarbeit von Übersetzern und Übersetzungsdienstleistern. Was sich nach einer grundsoliden Einstellung und Common Sense anhört, entspricht in vielen Fällen leider nicht der Realität. Dennoch liegt die Zukunft der Übersetzungsbranche im reibungslosen Zusammenspiel aller Marktfaktoren.

In der Podiumsdiskussion werden Vertreter der freiberuflich tätigen Übersetzer (vorw. Direktkunden – vorw. Agenturkunden), der Übersetzungsunternehmen (klein bis mittel – groß) und last but not least ein Übersetzungskunde eine aktuelle Bestandsaufnahme der Marktsituation wagen. Das Auditorium soll dabei stark einbezogen werden.

Die Diskussion hat folgende Schwerpunkte:

1. Welche Bedürfnisse haben die Kunden?
2. Wie wird die ideale Qualität für Übersetzungsdienstleistungen erbracht?
3. Wie lässt sich in der Branche die Spreu vom Weizen trennen?
4. Welche konkreten Vorschläge gibt es zur Verbesserung der Marktsituation?

Die Diskussion soll kritisch die Faktoren herausarbeiten, die als „Sand im Getriebe" des Übersetzungsmarktes identifiziert werden können, und verdeutlichen, dass eine reibungslose Kooperation aller Beteiligten eines der wichtigsten Fundamente für die Übersetzungsbranche der Zukunft sein wird.

II. Neue Berufsprofile, neue Perspektiven

Neue und veränderte Berufsprofile für Übersetzer

A new professional profile: the translator-terminologist. New skills for an enlarged service portfolio

Silvia Cerrella Bauer

Financial Operations Manager, Euroscript Switzerland AG

silvia.cerrella-bauer@euroscript.ch

Taking into account the increasing pressure on translation rates and the growing competition in a globalised translation market, language industry professionals ought to acquire new skills to keep and acquire new clients. There is an ever wider range of professions to be filled nowadays in the language industry globally, and the translator may at a given point in his career, either by necessity or by choice, envisage building up knowledge in one or more subject fields directly or indirectly related to his core business, such as interpreting, localisation, PR editing, technical writing, linguistics, CAT tools, CAT training, translation training, project management, vendor management, etc. Terminology management is a possible value-adding service for professional translators by virtue of its strong connection to translation.

This paper highlights the scope and potential of a new professional profile: the „translator-terminologist". It gives practical hints on how such professionals can provide terminology (management) services, thus diversifying and enriching their service offering. The paper especially addresses single language vendors (SLVs) working independently and interested in terminology management. Professional translators employed by a language services provider (multilingual language vendor, MLV), or in an in-house language services department within an organisation will also find useful hints on possible cooperation models with SLVs in the field of terminology management.

1 The translator-terminologist as a new professional profile

1.1 Task portfolio

The translator may decide to become a „translator-terminologist" and market his services for strategic reasons: his client portfolio or the new clients he is aiming to acquire have a real need for terminology (management) services. The more he builds upon his knowledge in this field and puts it to use with an enlarged service offering, the higher the benefit for his client, and therefore the higher the chances of getting more assignments.

A translator-terminologist is in a position to provide translation services, terminology (management) services and/or a combination of both. He can provide terminology services that are not linked to a specific translation order, sporadically or regularly to specific clients, and apply specific skills according to different business scenarios with his end clients.

When he has the „terminologist's hat" on, the translator-terminologist service portfolio can include one or more of the tasks below:

- gathering, searching for, revising and/or defining single technical terms in one or more of his working languages (incl. his mother tongue).

- making available a multilingual terminology collection in one or more of his working languages (incl. his mother tongue) or in various other languages (by outsourcing to other professionals the term search/review/definition in the languages for which he does not have the relevant language competencies). This can either be a one-off task (e.g. preparing terminology for a specific domain or project) or a recurrent task. The terminology collection can be delivered in a variety of formats. Clients may also require that the terminology collection as a product complies with specific corporate identity/design guidelines.

- managing (or co-managing) the development of a client's terminology database (TDB). This task may involve setting up terminology workflows and/or modelling TDBs from scratch, making changes in the TDB settings (interface, definition, data filters, output formats etc.), importing and/or exporting terminological data, updating term-related data and/or terminological entries, etc.

The above-mentioned tasks require a whole set of technical, coordination and even managerial skills. It is up to the translator-terminologist to decide whether to concentrate on the purely productive and/or the organisational tasks.

There are a number of additional value-added activities related to terminology management, such as training and support services pertaining to the use and maintenance of TDBs, assessment and testing tools supporting terminology work (terminology management systems, TMSs), consultancy services within the framework of product-naming processes, systematic and selective terminological research and classification by subject field, documentation research, sorting and organising systems of concepts and terms, term coinage, drawing up and implementing terminology management policies, etc. Based on experience, it is assumed that such compiling, planning, advisory and training activities are less likely to be requested of the translator-terminologist by his clients and combined with a regular translation activity. Therefore these are not taken into consideration within the framework of this paper.

1.2 Required skills

In order to guarantee professional multilingual terminology management services successfully, the translator-terminologist already has the necessary language competencies through his translation activities (practical experience) and background (education). This high degree of expertise allows for supplying terminology services in the translator's target language and at least one of the translator's working languages (source languages) in his field(s) of specialisation. Full command of text and terminological research techniques using all kind of document and/or electronic resources is also a matter of course.

Yet, as stated under 1.1 *Task portfolio*, a set of additional hard and soft skills are to be acquired (according to: www.iim.fh-koeln.de/radt/Dokumente/RaDT_Berufsprofil_ englisch.pdf.), such as:

Hard skills

- knowledge of the principles and methods of terminology work
- knowledge of best practices for terminology work (process setup, quality assurance, choice of prescriptive or descriptive approaches)
- knowledge of terminology data exchange formats and standards
- proficiency in the use of TMSs

Soft skills

- project management competence (time and organisation management, cost efficiency)
- negotiation skills and assertiveness
- planning and organisational competence
- communicative competence

The Brussels declaration for international cooperation in terminology (within the framework of the First Terminology Summit held in Brussels in 2002) called upon national and international bodies in order to „render compulsory the discipline of terminology and language for specific purposes in all translation curricula and encourage its introduction in all disciplines, in particular those of a scientific and technical nature." Many efforts have been deployed since then and, currently, many of the above-mentioned aspects, especially the hard skills, are covered in various translation bachelor or master programmes offered in most universities and universities of applied sciences in Europe. Some of them even offer web-based distance learning courses. Moreover, these institutions and a number of private bodies offer short-term continuous education programmes (also online) and courses geared to gain practical insight into terminology management methods, tools and processes.

Many language services providers and organisations in Europe also provide internships for junior translator professionals wishing to acquire practical knowledge in the field of terminology. Manufacturers of TMSs propose regular user training in the form of classic presence sessions or remote sessions (webinars), some of them even free of charge.

1.3 Required infrastructure

As far as the infrastructure for ensuring terminology services is concerned, the translator-terminologist can envisage a manual mode of operation using the standard MS Office applications only if he decides to restrict his terminology-related service portfolio to the provision of

- individual technical terms (and equivalents) either as a one-off task or as a recurrent task, though totally dissociated from a given terminology workflow;

- more or less comprehensive monolingual or multilingual glossaries in a list/spreadsheet format.

Specific computer-assisted terminology tools, e.g TMSs, should be used when it comes to recurrent terminology-related services involving more than one person – with or without the client's participation in the terminology processing chain – and when the translator-terminologist's contribution to the development of a terminology collection is not to remain dissociated from a higher-level terminology management workflow, either at his or at his client's end.

TMSs are commercially available as part of translation memory systems or as stand-alones. Some of the core advantages provided by TMSa are:

- capability to allow the set-up of one or more monolingual, bilingual or multilingual terminology databases (TDBs) that can be accessible wherever needed through appropriate server-based solutions

- data exchange capabilities (if the software applies general industry standards)

- data import/export capabilities (with filter functions for selecting/excluding data)

- collaborative work between several translator-terminologists (and user groups at the client's end) on a real-time basis

- terminology capture during the translation process directly in the environment of the translation memory system

- easy and rapid update of terminological data

- low error rate through automated or semi-automated data entry and validation

By using TMSs, the translator-terminologist can consequently be a fully integrated link in the terminology output chain or even be the individual managing the entire process and be ready to cover a much wider range of terminology service scenarios.

The translator-terminologist is in principle free to choose his infrastructure and working methods according to the scope of the terminology (management) services he intends to offer. In many cases though, the client may prescribe the terminology tool that the translator-terminologist has to use. A free licence may be provided to him to deliver his output or he may be obliged to purchase one in order to receive assignments. In any event, the translator-terminologist has to take the relevant training measures to become proficient in the use of such tools.

2 Strategic implications of terminology management

In business, it makes good sense to remain flexible and open to new opportunities, and to diversify the service offering. This is especially true in times of crisis or economic slowdown for both sides of the language services supply chain, the buyers (clients) and the providers (SLVs, MLVs) of language services.

Terminology management is increasingly gaining strategic importance for all stakeholders in the language industry for reasons such as:

- the increasing specialisation in all fields of knowledge and the subsequent higher complexity of the specialised business jargon
- the high rate of innovation driving the need for ever more differentiated specialist vocabulary
- the difficulties in the dialogue between experts and laymen and among experts of one and the same discipline
- the growing need for localising global content in many different languages
- the need for a precise and unambiguous technical language in order to avoid risk of distortions in communication and thus of competitive disadvantages and extra costs caused by vocabulary errors
- the need for prompt and efficient information retrieval and processing

Ultimately, organisations doing business globally but not managing terminology centrally and consistently are exposed to major risks (liability claims due to communication errors, loss of image and of market opportunities due to poor branding, delays in product releases, etc.), whereas translator-terminologists who include terminology in their service offering develop an alternative business opportunity and a professional challenge. So, why not go ahead and fill the niche?

3 Benefits of terminology for the translator-terminologist

3.1 Benefits related to the translator-terminologist's main processes

Terminology management increases productivity and quality

Professionally managed terminology helps organisations to promote their corporate language, ensure unequivocal communication with their staff, partners and stakeholders, and underpin information management processes. Finally, terminology management leads to an increase of productivity and quality for organisations. What is true for them is equally true for the translator-terminologist.

Having a term in one or several source languages and its equivalent in the translator-terminologist's target language means reducing time for term research. The time the translator-terminologist needs to invest for the one-time term entry in the TDB that he should maintain for his client is written off as soon as he encounters the same term in a new translation order. And this is also true even if he decides (which is mostly recommended) to enter the source of the term as well.

By so doing, he ensures consistent output which is an important factor when it comes to assessing translation quality (and customer satisfaction). Translation memories alone are not reliable enough for this purpose since they may contain terminology inconsistencies or even incorrect terms, despite all efforts devoted to avoiding them. Whenever the client gives terminological feedback in a format unsuitable for automatic import in the translation memory, the translator-terminologist usually does not take time to correct the individual segments in the translation memory containing the relevant term (data maintenance) „after the fact". Instead, an update of the TDB or of a simple spreadsheet (glossary or bilingual dictionary managed in a standard MS Office format) means a time investment of only a few seconds. In return, reliable data are available for future use.

Arguably, even if the translator-terminologist were to fail to sell his terminology services „upstream" to a given client, performing terminology work is never lost time. Furthermore, practitioners have reported having sold such services „downstream" at no extra effort!

3.2 Benefits related to the translator-terminologist's business opportunities

Terminology services boost client acquisition and client loyalty

Certain buyers of translation services may indeed require terminological knowledge when it comes to assigning particular projects, or pick only suppliers offering terminology services.

Given the trends towards full or partial outsourcing observed in the language services supply chain in recent years, new business niches can be filled profitably. The table below (next page) illustrates some prospective buyers of terminology services and the most likely outsourcing scenarios.

Outsourced TM services \ Prospective buyers of TM services	Private organisations in the manufacturing (industrial production/design, high-tech, engineering, software etc.) and life sciences sector, typically outsourcing language services
Researching and collecting single terms in one target language (e.g. as a by-product of a translation order)	✓
Researching and collecting single terms or lists of terms in one or several languages within the framework of a specific project (e.g. terminology pertaining to a specific product or service)	✓
Revision of terms/term collections and/or processing terminology entries by adding specific data (e.g. when no internal specialist at the client has the competencies in the relevant languages)	✓
Extracting monolingual or bilingual terminological data in specific language pairs (generally when no internal specialist at the client has the competencies in the relevant languages)	✓ e.g. on the basis of bilingual documents (specifying the terms in the source language for which an equivalent is to be found)
Other value-added TM services: • TM training • performing TDB checks (e.g. adding missing equivalents in term entries) • creating client-tailored databases • creating client CD-compliant glossaries/ dictionaries • creating/writing terminology specifications for client projects • advisory TM services (e.g. terminology process setup, TDB structure, assessing/sorting/importing available terminological data, choice/testing of terminology tools) • TDB administration (e.g. creating user profiles, data filters, database definitions, data layouts; recording and making available TM-related statistics)	✓ e.g. mixed outsourcing to single translator-terminologists and MLVs

Figure 1: Most likely outsourcing scenarios of terminology services according to the prospective buyer groups

Private organisations in the retail and B2B sectors (e.g. banking & finance, public transport, sports, food, non-food etc.) with an in-house language services department (partial outsourcing of language services)	Public sector organisations (e.g. international organisations, NGOs, national public admini-stration) with an in-house language services department	MLVs
✓ e.g. for feeding the corporate TDB with terminological data from translation projects outsourced to external translator-terminologists	✓	✓
✓	✓	✓
		✓ e.g. provision of terms, term equivalents, definitions, additional data (e.g. context sentences, notes, cross-references) according to a given timeframe and a set of rules (data model, language conven-tions etc.)
✓ e.g. on the basis of bilingual data stored in translation memories (for feeding the corporate TDB with terminological data from translation projects outsourced to external translator-terminologists)		✓
		✓ e.g. if the translator-terminologist is acquainted with MLV in-house processes and client requirements or if he works online/in-house at the MLV on a project basis

The content of the table is based on real-life situations reported by practitioners representing different prospective buyer groups based in Switzerland and Germany. These services are provided either as a subproduct of a translation project or irrespective of the provision of translations. Practitioners reported repeatedly on the trends below:

- The more specialised clients are, the higher the expectations in terms of terminological skills (professional terminology training apart from a standard translation background) and infrastructure required (use of specific tools, compliance with specific IT architecture, terminological data format).

- The more frequently clients outsource translations, the higher the chances of receiving assignments for terminology services. This is also true (1) for MLVs assigning their client projects completely (or mainly) to external vendors, and (2) for translator-terminologists providing regular services to an MLV as „dedicated" resources for a specific MLV's end client.

- One is more likely to get terminology assignments from organisations in the private sector, especially from those in the manufacturing and life sciences sector. Reasons: need for product translation/localisation in a very large number of languages due to liability issues. For translation cost reasons, these organisations aim for a high degree of standardisation of their deliverables at the source (authoring), use state-of-the-art content management tools and typically have an in-house technical writing team (documentation department), which in many cases interacts directly with the translation services vendors.

- When terminology services represent a by-product within the framework of translation orders, they are generally remunerated on an hourly basis, as a separate position in the purchase order. This model applies for instance to individual term research, delivery of lists of terms (generally equivalents) with or without supplementary terminological data, or revision of terminological data. This can be justified as the time devoted to term research can vary enormously from language to language.

- Whenever terminology services are supplied independently from translations (e.g. terminology extraction and delivery of term candidates, delivery of larger volumes of terminological data in the form of terminology entries within an extended period of time), lump sums or a fee per individual entry are usually agreed upon in advance.

Terminology services help meeting industry standards and new market demands

According to the European Standard EN 15038:2006 „Translation Services – Service Requirements", translation services providers (TSPs) – regardless of their size – must comply with certain procedures when carrying out their projects. Terminology management represents an effective measure for initiating and monitoring consistency throughout the translation project, as translation quality cannot be assured without unambiguous, correct and consistent terminology. Hence, EN 15038 states in its Annex E („Non-exhaustive list of added value services") the creation/management of terminology databases and terminology concordance as services that can be optionally offered to the client whenever no specific terminology is available for a given project.

EN 15038 is setting foot in the language industry, especially among translation companies based in Europe and worldwide, who are getting the certification to face competition and strengthen their market position. Compliance with the standard means also the ability to perform terminology management tasks, either systematically or selectively, within the translation workflow or as a separate task. Although SLVs in Europe do not generally consider getting an EN 15038 certification yet, their ability to perform professional terminology management will undoubtedly enlarge their chances of reaching a wider range of client target groups, and – last but not least – meet future market demands.

4 Conclusions

Terminology and terminology management are intrinsically linked to the overall management of global content and information processes and are a core quality assuring component of translation and localisation processes. They are thus of pivotal significance to successful product and service marketing internationally. The whole language industry services chain is impacted by the need for successful product localisation that terminology management efficiently supports.

In the ever increasing competition on the translation market, having terminological skills and/or offering terminology services can be an asset for acquiring new clients, building client loyalty, complying with industry standards and, last but not least, can increase translation quality and productivity at the translator-terminologist's end.

Terminology services are going to become a must-have of any service proposal and website entry of any freelance translator-terminologist. The more complex the subject matter at hand, the higher the need for terminology knowledge will be. Knowing little about it will no longer be an option as the „localisation maturity" (DePalma, 2004) – capability of understanding and implementing localisation-oriented processes and enforcing localisation-friendly practices – of buyers of translation services progressively grows in future. Moreover, the more advanced in terms of their localisation maturity the prospects will be, the more chances the translator-terminologist will have to successfully market and sell terminology services.

Bibliography

CERRELLA BAUER, S. (2009): „Professional Corporate Terminology Management: Tips and Tricks for a Successful Introduction", in: www.gala-global.org/GALAxy-article-professional_corporate_terminology_management _tips_and_tricks_for_a_successful_introduction-9835.html

CERRELLA BAUER, S. (2007): „Enquête sur la rémunération et la propriété des travaux de traduction et de terminologie réalisés sur mandat et à l'aide d'outils de traduction assistée par ordinateur", in: www.fit-europe.org/vault/barcelone/ Cerrella.pdf

CERRELLA BAUER, S. (2005): „Terminology as an asset for knowledge sharing and transfer in a learning organisation – A case study", in: Journal of the International Institute for Terminology Research (IITF), vol. 16 2005, Vasa and Kolding (DK).

DePalma, D. (2004): „Localization maturity model" , in: www.commonsenseadvisory.com/research/report_view.php?id=35

RaDT, Council for German Language Terminology (2004): „Professional profile for terminologists", in: www.iim.fh-koeln.de/radt/Dokumente/RaDT_Berufsprofil_englisch.pdf

SAUBERER, G. (2009): „The European Standard EN 15038:2006 for micro-enterprises (OPEs)", in: Presentation at the Translation World Toronto 2009, Termnet

Proceedings of the Computerm meeting in Zurich, Computerm (network of language professionals providing terminology services at Swiss companies) (2002)

Contributions on the subject of outsourcing of terminology services by renowned practitioners based in Switzerland, Germany and Luxemburg (2009)

La post-édition : l'avenir incontournable du traducteur ?

Anne-Marie Robert

SFT (Société française des traducteurs)

tilt.communications@wanadoo.fr

1 Fondements de la post-édition

La post-édition est intrinsèquement liée à la traduction automatique (TA). Les moteurs de traduction automatique produisent des transcriptions linguistiques qui s'apparentent à un mot à mot livré à l'état brut, n'ayant rien en commun avec une traduction professionnelle effectuée par un être humain. Même si la machine n'est pas en mesure de se substituer à l'homme dans l'activité traductionnelle, les intelligences artificielles font l'objet de recherches poussées et des progrès ne cessent d'être réalisés dans le domaine de la traduction automatique. La création d'un système de traduction automatique suffisamment performant pour donner des résultats acceptables représente un enjeu économique de taille. Pour l'heure, il n'est pas encore véritablement question de traduction automatique en tant que telle, mais plutôt de prétraduction automatique dans le sens de « premier jet effectué par une machine ».

Cette prétraduction automatique est omniprésente sur Internet sous forme de services gratuits : moteur disponible sur la page d'accueil de la plupart des fournisseurs d'accès à Internet, Google Traduction, le tout nouveau Microsoft Bing Translator, etc. Les moteurs de traduction automatique n'ont toutefois pas pour prétention de remplacer des traducteurs professionnels, les uns et les uns ne se faisant d'ailleurs pas fondamentalement concurrence. Seul un moteur de traduction automatique est capable de produire la prétraduction mot à mot d'un texte en une fraction de seconde et seul un traducteur professionnel est capable de produire la réflexion nécessaire pour assurer la qualité et l'intelligibilité d'une traduction. Dès lors, pourquoi ne pas concilier les deux en fournissant une base prétraduite automatiquement, qui soit ensuite revue et corrigée par un être humain ? D'où la naissance d'une nouvelle activité et d'une nouvelle spécialisation : la post-édition.

2 Définition de la post-édition

La post-édition désigne l'activité qui consiste à repasser derrière un texte prétraduit automatiquement pour le rendre humainement intelligible. Le langagier chargé d'effectuer cet exercice, à savoir le post-éditeur, a donc pour tâche de *réviser, modifier, corriger, remanier et relire* ce texte brut.

Les termes « post-édition », « post-éditeur » et « post-éditer » sont respectivement les calques des termes anglais « post-editing », « post-editor » et « to post-edit » (le verbe

« to edit » signifiant « réviser » dans un contexte traductionnel et « modifier » dans un contexte informatique).

3   Contexte de la post-édition

Les progrès réalisés dans le domaine de la traduction automatique et l'émergence de la post-édition sont essentiellement dus à l'*augmentation du volume de traduction* qui s'explique par plusieurs phénomènes :

- Mondialisation des échanges
- Développement fulgurant d'Internet, du commerce électronique et des sites Web
- Élargissement de l'Union européenne et politique multilinguiste (27 États membres, 23 langues officielles)
- Obligation légale de traduire certains types de documents (loi Toubon en France)
- Société de l'information reposant sur la communication à l'échelle internationale
- Multiplication des fusions/rachats/acquisitions avec constitution de multinationales et de grands groupes internationaux

Dans ce contexte, la post-édition a pour objectif d'*augmenter la productivité pour répondre aux nouveaux besoins du marché*. En d'autres termes, *traduire plus, plus vite et moins cher* en faisant intervenir des machines en premier lieu, puis des post-éditeurs pour assurer une qualité humaine en second lieu.

Les acteurs de la post-édition sont multiples :

- *Grands comptes et multinationales* amenés à gérer d'énormes volumes de traduction dans un grand nombre de combinaisons linguistiques
- *Grandes institutions internationales* comme l'Union européenne qui lance régulièrement des appels d'offre concernant des travaux de post-édition pour couvrir ses énormes volumes de traduction
- *Éditeurs et fournisseurs d'outils* adaptés aux besoins spécifiques de la post-édition
- Agences de traduction et de localisation proposant des services de post-édition
- *Post-éditeurs*, à savoir terminologues, traducteurs, réviseurs et linguistes-développeurs qui participent en tant que langagiers à cette activité récente

4   Post-édition brute

La post-édition brute consiste à réviser, modifier, corriger, remanier et relire *directement* le texte produit à l'état brut par un moteur de traduction automatique. Dans le cadre de documents informels à usage interne (circulaires, e-mails et rapports, par exemple), cette post-édition brute peut être effectuée par des assistants multilingues en vue d'aider à leur compréhension dans les grandes lignes. Dans le cadre de documents officiels destinés à être publiés, un traducteur professionnel peut légitimement se poser la question de l'utilité de la prétraduction automatique de ce type de document. Un traducteur professionnel ne serait-il en effet pas capable de produire un meilleur résultat plus rapidement qu'un post-éditeur ? Ce type de post-édition n'est toutefois sans aucune mesure avec la post-édition évoluée.

5 Post-édition évoluée

La post-édition évoluée consiste à réviser, modifier, corriger, remanier et relire le texte produit par un *processus qui associe diverses technologies de TA et de TAO*.

La TAO (Traduction Assistée par Ordinateur) entre donc en jeu. Elle désigne tous les outils informatiques mis à la disposition des professionnels de la traduction pour leur faciliter la tâche et n'a rien à voir avec la traduction automatique en tant que telle.

L'imbrication TA-TAO permet d'associer les éléments suivants :

- Des mémoires de traduction (stockant des couples de phrases traduites par des traducteurs)
- Des bases de données terminologiques
- Des systèmes de traduction automatique avec règles

Certaines agences de traduction et de localisation possèdent un *service Recherche et développement chargé de mettre au point des processus complexes mettant en œuvre ces diverses technologies*, et pas seulement la traduction automatique. Tout en étant encore loin d'être acceptable (tout en l'étant toutefois de plus en plus), le texte à post-éditer produit par ce type de processus est donc beaucoup plus intelligible que dans le cadre de la post-édition brute. Ce qui tend à faciliter et à accélérer le travail du post-éditeur lequel est, contrairement à la post-édition brute, amené à effectuer quatre types d'exercices :

- Il *révise* les phrases issues de la mémoire de traduction préalablement traduites par des traducteurs (remontées de mémoire à 100 %).
- Il *met à jour* les phrases bénéficiant de remontées de mémoire partielles de la mémoire de traduction (de 75 % à 99 %).
- Il *post-édite* les phrases ne bénéficiant pas de remontées de mémoire totales ou partielles qui ont été produites par des moteurs de traduction automatique.
- Il harmonise, coordonne et articule le tout.

Ces agences de traduction et de localisation restent très discrètes, voire secrètes, sur les recherches qu'elles effectuent dans ce domaine, chacune cherchant à développer et à améliorer des *processus de haute technologie dans un contexte où les enjeux économiques sont énormes*. La post-édition évoluée ne date d'ailleurs pas d'hier : l'éditeur de progiciel de gestion intégré SAP s'est associé à une grande agence de localisation en 2000 pour lancer un projet pilote visant à assurer la post-édition de ses documentations électronique et papier, à traiter un énorme volume dans des délais inférieurs à ceux traditionnellement pratiqués en traduction et à accélérer la mise sur le marché de ses produits

Même si un traducteur professionnel ne peut que rester dubitatif devant la traduction automatique et la post-édition brute, la post-édition évoluée propose quant à elle de véritables avancées. Il s'agit d'*associer des outils et des savoir-faire*, de *combiner traduction automatique, mémoires de traduction et traduction humaine*.

6   Mode de fonctionnement de la post-édition

Pour aider le post-éditeur, les phrases à post-éditer sont clairement identifiées lors du processus post-éditionnel (« MT! » ou « Machine Translation », par exemple, s'affichent à l'écran). Trois cas de figure se présentent généralement au post-éditeur :

- La phrase est correcte et acceptable et ne nécessite pas de post-édition :
- This command removes the Server01 and Server02 remote computers from the domain to which they were joined. (Source)
- Cette commande supprime les ordinateurs distants Server01 et Server02 du domaine auquel ils ont été joints. (prétraitement/cible)
- La phrase est partiellement correcte/partiellement erronée et nécessite une post-édition :
- Current logged on user's credentials (source)
- Le courant se connecté sur les informations d'identification de l'utilisateur (prétraitement)
- Informations d'identification de l'utilisateur actuellement connecté (cible)
- La phrase est totalement incorrecte et erronée et doit être intégralement (re)traduite :
- This topic assumes that you understand creating and using controls and styles and the basics of control customization. (source)
- Cette rubrique suppose que vous comprend des contrôles créant et utilisant et des styles et l'essentiel de personnalisation de contrôle. (prétraitement)
- Cette rubrique part du principe que vous maîtrisez la création et l'utilisation des contrôles et des styles, ainsi que les concepts de base de la personnalisation des contrôles. (cible)

Les problèmes les plus fréquents répertoriés en post-édition de l'anglais vers le français sont les suivants :

- Termes inconnus, absents des bases de données terminologiques générales et propres au projet
- Phrases longues
- Erreurs dans le texte source (fautes d'orthographe, erreurs de grammaire, syntaxe incorrecte ou mots manquants)
- Ordre des mots
- Structures passives
- Tournures idiomatiques

- Style informel
- Majuscules et minuscules
- Ponctuation incorrecte
- Omission de mots facultatifs (« that », « which », « who », par exemple)
- Abréviations, sigles et troncations

La post-édition ne consiste pas à traduire puisqu'une prétraduction sert de base au travail à effectuer, ni à réviser puisqu'il ne s'agit pas d'une traduction mais d'une prétraduction. *La post-édition ne consiste pas à tout retraduire, ni à tout réécrire, ni à rajouter des corrections stylistiques inutiles.* Pour être efficace, le post-éditeur doit même partir du principe que, dans certains cas, le lecteur peut tolérer un certain niveau de « langage artificiel » à partir du moment où le texte reste intelligible, exact et grammaticalement correct. Il appartient alors au post-éditeur de *gommer les défectuosités et de corriger les défauts* suivants :

- Erreurs de grammaire et de syntaxe : mauvais accords (genre, nombre ou conjugaison), ordre des mots entraînant des problèmes de grammaire, etc.
- Fautes d'orthographe et erreurs de ponctuation : accents manquants, mauvaise accentuation, problèmes de majuscules et de minuscules, absence de ponctuation, etc.
- Défauts structurels : contresens, faux-sens, non-sens, terminologie projet non respectée, etc.

Dans ces conditions, la post-édition ne s'applique pas à tous les types de documents. Les documents hautement rédactionnels ou à structure très libre ne sont donc pas concernés. La littérature, la poésie, le marketing et l'édition en général sont donc des genres non post-éditables. Les documents à dominante technique obéissant à des règles précises aux niveaux terminologique, syntaxique et structurel (parfois poussées à l'extrême dans certaines industries où il est question de « langues contrôlées ») sont, quant à eux, parfaitement post-éditables.

7 2009 : la post-édition à l'honneur

Le marché de la traduction s'oriente résolument vers la post-édition. Pour preuve, trois récents choix technologiques d'acteurs majeurs de l'informatique associée à la traduction vont dans le sens d'un renforcement de la post-édition :

- En janvier 2009, l'éditeur de logiciel de traduction automatique Systran passe un accord avec l'éditeur de logiciel de TAO Multicorpora. En mai 2009, Systran lance Enterprise Server 7, un nouveau moteur hybride alliant traduction automatique et mémoires de traduction, l'objectif étant d'améliorer en permanence les résultats du moteur de traduction automatique et de concilier qualité traductionnelle avec capacités à traiter d'énormes volumes.
- En 2008, l'éditeur de logiciels de TAO SDL Trados introduit une version bêta d'un moteur de traduction automatique dans sa version SDL Trados 2007 Suite. En juin 2009, SDL Trados lance son tout nouveau produit, SDL Trados Studio 2009, qui intègre un moteur de traduction automatique. En d'autres

termes, les traducteurs qui utilisent les produits SDL Trados sont dorénavant en mesure d'exploiter un moteur de traduction automatique dans leur processus traductionnel, ce qui inclut forcément une part de post-édition dans le traitement des documents.

• En juin 2009, Google lance sur le Web une version bêta de Google Translation Toolkit qui associe moteur de traduction automatique, mémoires de traduction et bases de données terminologiques. L'utilisateur est invité à améliorer en permanence le moteur de traduction automatique en « corrigeant les traductions automatiques dans un éditeur convivial » et à partager ses propres mémoires de traduction en « collaborant avec d'autres traducteurs », ce qui ne va pas sans poser des problèmes de confidentialité à l'heure où la traduction collaborative fait par ailleurs scandale auprès des traducteurs professionnels. Google Translation Toolkit n'est donc pas un simple moteur de traduction automatique sur le Web, car il s'appuie sur la TAO pour améliorer son contenu via un éditeur et selon un mode de travail collaboratif humain.

Ces trois outils ont deux points communs : ils associent tous TA et TAO en amont et impliquent une activité de post-édition humaine en aval.

8   La post-édition nouvelle génération : vers un nouveau modèle de travail pour le traducteur professionnel indépendant

Le développement et la mise en œuvre de processus technologiques complexes associant TA et TAO étaient jusqu'à présent réservés à de grandes agences de traduction et de localisation ou à de grandes institutions internationales comme l'Union européenne. Or les derniers produits lancés sur le marché en 2009 mettent à la disposition du traducteur des outils intégrés spécifiquement conçus pour lui permettre de post-éditer des documents et donc de couvrir plus rapidement de plus gros volumes (le post-éditeur est censé post-éditer au moins 3500 mots par jour contre environ 2000 en traduction, ce qui permet de traiter 30 000 mots supplémentaires par mois et par personne).

Grâce à ces nouveaux outils, le traducteur professionnel indépendant est donc aujourd'hui techniquement en mesure de mettre en place son propre processus post-éditionnel en recyclant des traductions humaines (remontées de mémoires de traduction), en exploitant des bases de données terminologiques, en utilisant des fonctionnalités de TAO (alignement, recherche contextuelle, reconnaissance terminologique, travail collaboratif en réseau, détection automatique d'incohérences, etc.), en prétraduisant automatiquement les phrases ne bénéficiant pas de remontées de mémoires de traduction et... en post-éditant le tout. Sa productivité ne pourra qu'augmenter pour mieux répondre aux besoins du marché dans certains secteurs d'activités (traduire plus et plus vite pour accélérer la mise sur le marché de certains produits impliquant d'énormes volumes de traduction), tout en assurant une qualité professionnelle humaine. Rien ne l'empêche par ailleurs d'appliquer ce système à tout projet, quelle qu'en soit la taille, en tant que processus intégré. Une véritable révolution dans le métier pour qui saura/voudra se lancer dans ce nouveau modèle de travail, dans un contexte ultra informatisé hautement technologique.

9   Questionnements futurs

Pour faire face aux nouveaux besoins du marché, à la nouvelle donne mondiale et aux avancées technologiques, le métier de traducteur n'est-il pas condamné à disparaître à moyen/long terme au profit du métier de post-éditeur ? Notre profession, qui a subi de profondes mutations dans son mode d'exercice au cours de ces dernières années (informatique, télécommunications, Internet, outils de TAO, moteurs de recherche, etc.), échappera-t-elle à cette ultime révolution ? À l'ère de l'ingénierie linguistique, le traducteur en tant que tel existe-t-il encore ou n'est-il pas plutôt devenu un « ingénieur en communication multilingue et multimédia » (dixit Daniel Gouadec) ? La post-édition ÉVOLUÉE n'est-elle pas préférable à la traduction automatique seule, à la post-édition brute ou encore au monolinguisme imposé sans traduction ?

Quoi qu'il en soit, l'intervention humaine, même réduite, restera toujours nécessaire pour comprendre et retranscrire les subtilités du langage humain. Il appartient maintenant au traducteur de savoir évoluer et faire des choix : pourquoi ne pas envisager une reconversion complémentaire (et salutaire à long terme ?) dans la post-édition en exploitant les outils informatiques proposés et en mettant en place de nouveaux processus ? Un véritable défi à relever en perspective !

Webographie

Cet article a essentiellement été rédigé sur la base de mon expérience personnelle auprès de clients dont la documentation, les processus et les outils sont propriétaires et confidentiels. Les éditeurs d'outils cités dans cet article sont par ailleurs tous présents sur le Web.

No Future? – Die Zukunft des Wissenschaftsübersetzens

Janet Carter-Sigglow

Zentralbibliothek, Forschungszentrum Jülich GmbH

j.carter-sigglow@fz-juelich.de

1 Einleitung – No Future?

Viele Übersetzerkollegen befürchten, dass ihre Expertise nicht mehr gefragt sein wird, weil in der wissenschaftlichen Community Englisch als Lingua franca gilt, so dass Fachübersetzungen ins Englische und aus dem Englischen überflüssig werden könnten. Wir im Sprachendienst des Forschungszentrums Jülich teilen diese Bedenken nicht. Unsere Antwort darauf ist, dass man seine Kompetenzen zukunftsorientiert einbringen muss.

Besonders von deutschen Wissenschaftlern wird häufig nicht nur vorausgesetzt, dass sie englische Fachtexte mühelos verstehen, sondern dass sie solche Texte auch fehlerfrei produzieren können. Als Sprachmittler wissen wir, dass diese Vorstellung völlig realitätsfern ist. Unsere Aufgaben bestehen nach wie vor, wir müssen uns aber als Übersetzer neu positionieren und unsere Dienstleistungen in entsprechender Form einbringen.

Im Laufe der letzten Jahre haben wir die ermutigende Erfahrung gemacht, dass die Nachfrage nach unseren Diensten durchaus gestiegen ist. Im wissenschaftlichen Bereich reicht das berühmte „Quantum Englisch" (Carter-Sigglow 2008, 59-62) nicht aus. Die Sprache von Texten verschiedenster Art sowohl auf Englisch als auch auf Deutsch muss nicht nur formal korrekt, sondern auch den unterschiedlichen Zielgruppen entsprechend gestaltet sein. Und hier bringen wir unsere Expertise ein.

2 Forschungszentrum Jülich und das wissenschaftliche Übersetzen

Unsere Arbeitsumgebung am Forschungszentrum Jülich ist einmalig. Eingebettet in den ehemaligen Stetternicher Staatsforst am Rande der historischen Kleinstadt strahlt das Forschungszentrum die Atmosphäre einer ländlichen Idylle aus. Das Bild täuscht: Hier hat die Zukunft bereits angefangen.

2.1 Porträt des Forschungszentrums Jülich

An einer der größten multidisziplinären Forschungseinrichtungen Europas beschäftigen sich 1250 Wissenschaftler (von insgesamt 4428 Angestellten) mit zukunftsorientierten Themen wie der Brennstoffzelle als Antrieb für mobile und stationäre Anwendungen, mit Computer-Simulationen zur Vorhersage des Klimawandels oder

der Magnetresonanztomographie zur Erkennung von Demenzkrankheiten im Frühstadium. Laut Leitbild des Forschungszentrums ist Zukunft unsere Aufgabe, und dieser Herausforderung muss sich auch der Sprachendienst stellen.

Im Gegensatz zu einer Industriefirma produziert das Forschungszentrum nicht, oder höchstens in Zusammenarbeit mit externen Partnern und Lizenznehmern. In Jülich wird Wissen geschaffen und verbreitet. Unsere Aufgabe als Sprachendienst ist es, in diesem Prozess Hilfe bei der sprachlichen Darstellung zu leisten.

Anders als beim technischen Übersetzen haben wir weniger mit der Beschreibung von Anlagen oder der Rezeptur von pharmazeutischen Erzeugnissen zu tun. Jülicher Wissenschaftler stellen ihre Versuche dar und ziehen neue Erkenntnisse daraus. Konventionell endet jede Abhandlung mit der Aussicht auf weitere Forschungsarbeiten. So lange ausreichende Finanzmittel angeworben werden können, hört die Wissenschaft nie auf. Jede Erkenntnis bereitet den Weg für neue Entdeckungen.

2.2 Der Sprachendienst

Der Sprachendienst ist in die Zentralbibliothek des Forschungszentrums integriert. Als große wissenschaftliche Spezialbibliothek versteht sich die Zentralbibliothek als Informations- und Kommunikationszentrum für das Forschungszentrum. Diese Dienstleistungspalette wird vom Sprachendienst ergänzt. Zur Zentralbibliothek gehört auch der Eigenverlag des Forschungszentrums. Jülicher Wissenschaftler profitieren von der unmittelbaren Einbindung des Sprachendienstes in diesen Veröffentlichungsprozess. Daher verstehen wir unsere Arbeit als Teil eines größeren Prozesses zur Verbreitung von wissenschaftlichen Ergebnissen weltweit.

Seit mehreren Jahren werden interne Sprachendienste abgebaut und Übersetzungsarbeiten an Freiberufler vergeben. Im Zeitalter der Translation Memories ist Zugang zur hauseigenen Terminologie kein großes Problem mehr. Der Sprachendienst des Forschungszentrums besteht seit fast 40 Jahren und ist immer klein gewesen. Im „vortechnologischen" Zeitalter bestand das Team aus zwei Übersetzern und zwei Fremdsprachenkorrespondentinnen. Jetzt beim Einsatz der elektronischen Tools bewältigen drei Übersetzerinnen die Aufträge. Deutsch, Englisch und Französisch gehörten schon immer zu den Arbeitssprachen; vor zwei Jahren wurde die Palette um Spanisch erweitert.

Aus Sicht des Sprachendienstes könnte das Team weiterwachsen; die Nachfrage ist vorhanden. Allerdings muss kein Mitarbeiter des Forschungszentrums unsere Dienstleistungen in Anspruch nehmen, obwohl jeder nach Genehmigung durch den Institutsleiter einen Auftrag bei uns einreichen darf. Die Zahlen aus dem Jahre 2008 vermitteln einen Eindruck von unseren Leistungen: insgesamt 5164 Seiten, davon 1743 Seiten Übersetzungen aus dem Deutschen ins Englische und 2985 Seiten redaktionelle Bearbeitung von englischen Texten.

2.3 In-house-Dienstleister

Der besondere Wert des Sprachendienstes liegt darin, dass wir die Arbeit des gesamten Forschungszentrums kennen. Wenn in einem Artikel aus dem Bereich der Demenzforschung ein massenspektrometrisches Verfahren zur Untersuchung von

Metallablagerungen in Gehirnzellen erwähnt wird, ist uns die Methode aus der chemischen Analyse bekannt. Multidisziplinarität wird in Jülich großgeschrieben, und daher ist ein interner Sprachendienst von Vorteil. Unsere Stärke liegt in der Vielfalt der Themen, die wir bearbeiten können.

Auch unsere Flexibilität hilft, unseren Fortbestand zu sichern. Auf Anfrage vertonen wir Filme, dolmetschen bei Präsentationen in der Zentralbibliothek, bieten Englisch für Azubis an, beraten bei der Anschaffung von elektronischen Wörterbüchern für das campusweite Intranet oder übersetzen die Speisekarte für das Casino (unsere Kantine). Wir sind auch jederzeit für eine persönliche Sprachberatung erreichbar.

Durch unseren auch Externen zugänglichen Internet-Auftritt zeigen wir Präsenz. Auch beim Tag der offenen Tür sind wir dabei: Unser Beitrag heißt „Your Personal Translator: Mensch oder Maschine?". Da treten wir mit unserem Fachwissen und unseren elektronischen Tools gegen gängige Übersetzungsprogramme aus dem Internet an. Wir geben uns jetzt schon siegessicher.

Das Ziel dieser Fachtagung „Übersetzen in die Zukunft" – das Schärfen des Übersetzerprofils – ist auch unser Ziel. Ohne ein professionelles und selbstbewusstes Auftreten können wir in der Umgebung am Forschungszentrum Jülich nicht bestehen. Wir zeigen uns als Fachleute für Fachleute.

3 Bandbreite unserer Dienstleistungen

Die Bandbreite unserer Arbeiten ergibt sich aus den Forschungsthemen in Jülich. Im Leitbild des Forschungszentrums werden die Themen ganz plakativ zusammengefasst:

„Wir forschen an umfassenden Lösungen für die großen gesellschaftlichen Herausforderungen der Zukunft in den drei Bereichen Gesundheit, Energie und Umwelt sowie Informationstechnologie und schaffen hierzu Grundlagen für zukünftige Schlüsseltechnologien." (Forschungszentrum Jülich 2009)

Diese Thematik findet in vielen unterschiedlichen Formen Ausdruck: im klassischen Forschungsartikel, in der Tagungspräsentation, in der populärwissenschaftlichen Darstellung, im Förderantrag, im Jahresbericht und zunehmend auch auf der Website. Jede dieser Formen birgt ihre Besonderheiten, die der Übersetzer bei seinem Ansatz berücksichtigen muss.

3.1 Das große Geld: Förderanträge

Obwohl das Forschungszentrum eine staatliche Wissenschaftseinrichtung ist (die zwei Partner der GmbH sind die Bundesrepublik Deutschland zu 90 % und das Land Nordrhein-Westfalen zu 10 %), sind die Wissenschaftler immer mehr darauf angewiesen, Drittmittel für ihre Forschung einzuwerben, sei es von der Europäischen Union, von deutschen Stellen oder von der Industrie. Diese Tatsache bestimmt unter anderem auch unsere Arbeit, so dass wir uns nicht nur mit der Bearbeitung von klassischen wissenschaftlichen Abhandlungen beschäftigen, sondern auch mit der ansprechenden Präsentation von Forschungsvorhaben, um Finanzmittel zu erhalten, und mit Berichten, die anschließend die sachgerechte Verwendung dieser Mittel belegen sollen.

Die oft gelobte und ebenso oft gescholtene Sprachvielfalt bei der EU gilt de facto in der Wissenschaft nicht. Theoretisch können Förderanträge in anderen Sprachen eingereicht werden, solche Vorhaben werden aber von internationalen Gremien begutachtet, die sich grundsätzlich des Englischen bedienen. Die Arbeit, die hinter einem vielleicht 20-seitigen Antrag auf Fördergelder in z. T. Millionenhöhe steckt, ist nicht zu unterschätzen, und wir leisten unseren Beitrag beim Übersetzen bzw. Redigieren der Texte. Die ersten Sätze entscheiden darüber, ob der Antrag überhaupt in die engere Auswahl kommt, wobei einige Auswüchse durchaus skurril anmuten:

> „... *the bizarre complexity that scientists find themselves faced with when applying for grants through the EU Framework Programme – such as the requirement to explain the gender relevance of research on single-cell organisms, ...*"
> *(Nature 2009, 622)*

In solchen Fällen beruhigen wir die Gemüter und schlagen eine treffende Formulierung vor.

3.2 Deutsch-deutsche Beziehungen

Bei Anträgen und Berichten für deutsche Stellen wiederum müssen die Dokumente auf Deutsch verfasst sein. Bei Wissenschaftlern setzt man Englischkenntnisse voraus, bei Politikern nicht unbedingt. Manchmal ergibt sich die bizarre Situation, dass wir von deutschen Muttersprachlern auf Englisch verfasste Berichte ins Deutsche übersetzen müssen. In einigen Fällen müssen wir sogar die englischen Vorlagen zuerst redigieren und können erst anschließend den Text übersetzen!

Diese Aufgabe ist nicht trivial, da die Verfasser teilweise nur die englische Terminologie kennen. Hierzu müssen wir nicht nur die Fachterminologie recherchieren, sondern wir müssen auch beurteilen können, ob man überhaupt einen deutschen Begriff verwenden soll. Bei der Brennstoffzelle z.B. werden die aus mehreren Zellen zusammengefügten Aggregate auch auf Deutsch „stacks" genannt. Eine deutsche Entsprechung „Zellstapel" existiert, ist aber nicht geläufig, obwohl Deutschland durchaus eine führende Rolle in der Brennstoffzellenforschung spielt und man annehmen könnte, dass deutsche Terminologie in deutschen Labors benutzt wird.

Als Übersetzer im Wissenschaftsbetrieb müssen wir unsere muttersprachliche Kompetenz und unsere Erfahrung mit wissenschaftlicher Kommunikation einsetzen, um wissenschaftliche Konzepte an die verschiedenen Zielgruppen effektiv zu vermitteln.

4. Redaktionsarbeit

Kurioserweise werden reine Forschungsartikel immer seltener übersetzt. Wie in *Nature* vor ein paar Jahren fast beiläufig festgestellt wurde, „it is now accepted that all high-quality papers are published in English" (King 2004, 623). Daher haben Wissenschaftler keine anderen Vorlagen und schreiben immer häufiger selbst auf Englisch. Hier eröffnet sich ein großes Betätigungsfeld für Sprachmittler. Bei der sprachlichen Redaktion setzen wir Fertigkeiten ein, die wir durch das Übersetzen von themenverwandten Texten erworben haben. Dieses Zusammenspiel von Übersetzung und Redaktion ist für unsere Arbeit sehr fruchtbar.

4.1 Deutsch als Fremdsprache

Diese redaktionellen Kompetenzen sind besonders in einem Forschungszentrum gefragt, das jedes Jahr über 500 Gastwissenschaftler aus mehr als 60 Ländern willkommen heißt. Einige der Gäste bleiben nur wenige Wochen und Monate und haben überhaupt keine Gelegenheit, Deutsch zu lernen.

Dazu kommt, dass einige Arbeiten von Autoren verfasst werden, deren Muttersprache wir nicht mächtig sind. Da uns die Themen und die Terminologie hinter den Texten aus unseren anderen Aufgaben bekannt sind, können wir uns an eine Korrektur heranwagen. Heute werden wissenschaftliche Papers selten von einem einzelnen Autor geschrieben, so dass in den meisten Fällen ein Koautor mit Deutsch als Muttersprache an Bord ist, der – zusammen mit dem Erstautor – uns den Sachverhalt erläutern kann.

4.2 Learning by doing

Diese Aufgaben müssen wir pragmatisch angehen. Als Grundprinzip folgen wir Kohl's Cardinal Rule of Global English: „Don't make any change that will sound unnatural to native speakers of English". (Schaffer 2008, 19)

Bei dieser Redaktionsarbeit haben wir aber lange nach Unterstützung in Form von Fortbildung gesucht. Die Suche hat sich als äußerst schwierig gestaltet, da Kurse entweder den technischen Redakteur ODER den Übersetzer ansprechen. Dann hat meine Kollegin Hazel Rochford das Mediterranean Editors and Translators Meeting entdeckt. Wie der Name besagt, sind wir nicht die primäre Zielgruppe dieser Veranstaltung, aber deren Mission-Statement trifft genau auf uns zu: „Mediterranean Editors & Translators (MET) is a forum for translators and editors who work mainly into or with English." (MET 2009).

Wie so oft in unserem Beruf muss man sich flexibel zeigen. Die Themen dieser Veranstaltung sind für uns äußerst relevant, und dieses Jahr zeigen wir selber Flagge mit einem Beitrag von Hazel Rochford „Publish or Perish: The Role of In-House Language Services in Scientific Publishing". Dieser Beitrag ist ein weiterer Beleg für unsere Bemühungen, das Profil des Sprachendienstes zu schärfen und auch mit anderen Kollegen in Kontakt zu treten.

4.3 Stellenwert der Redaktionsarbeiten

In der heutigen Zeit verzichten immer mehr Fachzeitschriften auf Lektoren. Bei Peer-reviewed-Journals genügt der Hinweis des Gutachters, der nicht unbedingt Englisch als Muttersprache sprechen muss: „English awkward – rephrase" oder „needs severe pruning by a native speaker" und der Artikel kommt zurück. Oft werden Beiträge aus Einrichtungen in Ländern, in denen Englisch keine Verkehrssprache ist, unfair behandelt. Dieses Thema ist vor einigen Jahren in der Zeitschrift *Nature* behandelt worden, und ein Korrespondent aus Indien gibt sich resigniert:

> *"This (rejection of manuscripts) taught us to aim for a higher standard than average for papers published in such journals and to accept with stoic equanimity what may have been unfair rejection of a paper." (Umakantha 1997: 764).*

Aufgabe des Sprachendienstes ist es zu verhindern, dass unsere Kollegen aus Jülich ähnliche Erfahrungen machen. Und unsere Dienste werden von den Wissenschaftlern anerkannt, wie Prof. Dr. Hans Peter Peters von der Programmgruppe Mensch, Umwelt, Technik in einer persönlichen Mitteilung darstellt:

> *„Wir hatten [das Manuskript] ... eingereicht – aus Zeitgründen, ohne es durch Sie editieren zu lassen – und nun haben wir ein positives Feedback, allerdings mit kritischen Bemerkungen zu Sprachqualität. ... Aus dem Reviewer-Response ersehen Sie, wie wichtig Ihre Arbeit für uns ist und dass sie maßgeblich dazu beiträgt, unseren Nachteil gegenüber englischsprachigen „Konkurrenten" zu kompensieren. "*

Ich hätte es selber nicht besser formulieren können.

5 Populärwissenschaft

Auch in Zukunft werden viele Texte aus dem Deutschen ins Englische übersetzt; nur die Art dieser Texte hat sich gewandelt. Heute wird viel Wert auf die Kommunikation wissenschaftlicher Erkenntnisse an ein breites Publikum gelegt – die so genannte Populärwissenschaft. Die Wissenschaft braucht Rückhalt in der Öffentlichkeit und muss daher Laien in geeigneter Weise über ihre Errungenschaften informieren. Diese Übersetzungen verlangen nicht nur technisches Verständnis, sondern auch ausgefeilte Formulierungskünste.

Prof. Dr. Hans Peter Peters, Soziologe und Journalist am Forschungszentrum Jülich, fasst diese Symbiose in einer persönlichen Mitteilung zusammen:

> *„Es wird immer deutlicher, dass Wissenschaft in den Medien nicht nur eine Sache der „Aufklärung" und Information der Bevölkerung ist, sondern eine wichtige Rolle für die gesellschaftlich-politische Wirksamkeit der Wissenschaft spielt. "*

Das ist eine zukunftsorientierte Aufgabe für uns.

5.1 Unternehmenskommunikation

Bei der Öffentlichkeitsarbeit am Forschungszentrum Jülich spielen Broschüren zu den Hauptforschungsthemen eine gewichtige Rolle. Sie sind in erster Linie für die deutsche Öffentlichkeit gedacht, erscheinen aber häufig auch in einer englischsprachigen Ausgabe. Da das Layout in beiden Versionen identisch sein muss, kann man nicht einfach eine englische Broschüre erstellen. Hier sind unsere übersetzerischen Fähigkeiten gefragt, und auch ein Lokalisierungsansatz, da die Themen ursprünglich ein deutsches und kein internationales Publikum ansprechen sollen. Manchmal müssen wir auch Aufklärungsarbeit leisten.

Zum Beispiel sind Windenergieanlagen (zu Deutsch „Windräder") international nicht so verbreitet und deutscher (weißer) Spargel auch nicht. Daher hat es wenig Sinn, auf Englisch von einer „Verspargelung der Landschaft" zu sprechen, obwohl das Bild auf Deutsch natürlich sehr prägnant ist. Der Gegenvorschlag „wind turbines mushrooming all over the place" wurde nur widerwillig angenommen. Autoren klammern sich manchmal an ihre eigene Sprache – daher gehören zur Kompetenz eines Übersetzers auch Überredungskünste.

Auch in diesem Bereich haben wir Unterstützung durch Fortbildung gesucht, und meine Kollegin Regina Zimmermann hat es beim Seminar „Journalistisches Schreiben für Übersetzer" gefunden, angeboten von der Graduate School Rhein Neckar in Mannheim. In gewissem Sinne schreiben wir die Texte neu – gerade in der Populärwissenschaft. Hierbei sind unsere Kenntnisse der gesamten Bandbreite wissenschaftlicher Arbeiten in Jülich von Vorteil. Hinzu kommt, dass wir die Zielgruppe der gebildeten Laien vertreten und daher in der Lage sind zu beurteilen, ob die Thematik verständlich dargestellt worden ist. Hier können wir eine ganz andere Art der Kompetenz einbringen.

5.2 Ziel des populärwissenschaftlichen Übersetzens

Ein Nachruf auf einen ehemaligen Chefredakteur des britischen Wissenschaftsjournals *Nature*, der pikanterweise im amerikanischen Rivalen *Science* kürzlich erschien, beschreibt die Situation bei wissenschaftlichen und noch mehr bei populärwissenschaftlichen Veröffentlichungen sehr treffend:

> *„Scientific ideas are exciting, yet the scientific literature is far from lively. John Maddox's achievement was to sidestep the drabness of scientific writing by emphasizing the ideas that thrived beneath the leaden prose. [...] He recognized that the dry format of the scientific article could not be greatly changed but that the excitement of scientific ideas could be conveyed by other kinds of articles. " (Wade 2009: 1028).*

Unsere Aufgabe ist es, die Prosa etwas aufzuhellen ohne die wissenschaftlichen Ideen zu verfälschen.

6 Verhältnis zu den Wissenschaftlern

Wie oben bereits dargestellt, pflegen wir ein partnerschaftliches Verhältnis zu unseren Kunden, die ja gleichzeitig in den meisten Fällen die Autoren sind. Hier haben wir durchaus die Möglichkeit, auf die Gestaltung des Textes Einfluss zu nehmen. In manchen Fällen wird der deutsche Text überhaupt nicht veröffentlicht und einzig die Übersetzung ist maßgeblich. Wenn eine Formulierung unklar ist oder eine Zahlenangabe widersprüchlich, brauchen wir nicht lange zu rätseln, wir rufen an und klären die Aussage des Textes in einem Gespräch.

Wir versuchen auf die Wünsche der Autoren einzugehen, in Hinblick auf Sprachebene, Rechtschreibung oder Terminologie, und wir bieten Kunden immer die Möglichkeit, ihre Übersetzung oder Korrektur mit uns persönlich zu besprechen.

6.1 Wahrnehmung des Sprachendienstes

Ich habe bereits das Selbstverständnis des Übersetzers als Experte erwähnt, und uns war es auch wichtig zu erfahren, was Wissenschaftler von uns halten. Dazu hatten wir kürzlich auch Gelegenheit bei einem von uns in Jülich veranstalteten Workshop – „CAT Reloaded" – zum Thema Einsatz von elektronischen Tools im Übersetzeralltag. Im Übrigen ist der Workshop ein weiteres Beispiel für unsere Bemühungen, Kontakte mit anderen Übersetzern und Sprachendiensten zu knüpfen.

In einem gemeinsamen Beitrag über die Zusammenarbeit zwischen Übersetzern und Wissenschaftlern am Forschungszentrum von Hazel Rochford und Dr. Bernd Emonts (Institut für Energieforschung – Brennstoffzellen) stellte Dr. Emonts seine Anforderungen an den Sprachendienst dar.

Sehr anschaulich erläuterte er seine Einteilung der Übersetzungen / Redaktionsarbeiten in Low Level (kurze Textbausteine, partielle Eigenübersetzungen, Abbildungen beschriften), Medium Level (Pressemitteilungen, Webseiten, Abstracts) und High Level (lange wissenschaftliche Veröffentlichungen, Projektanträge). Das Übersetzerpublikum war hingegen der Ansicht, dass bei den sprachlichen Schwierigkeiten nicht die Länge des Textes maßgeblich ist. U.a. ist es einfacher, eine ganze wissenschaftliche Veröffentlichung zu übersetzen als eine isolierte Bildunterschrift – manchmal sogar ohne Bild!

Diese Erfahrung zeigt, wie wichtig es ist, mit den Auftraggebern zu kommunizieren und voneinander zu lernen. Wir versuchen auch unsere Arbeitsweise transparent zu machen, manchmal im wahrsten Sinne des Wortes: Wir hatten einmal sogar einen Stand mit einem „gläsernen Übersetzer" um die Mittagszeit im Casino aufgebaut. Da haben wir unsere Arbeitsweise für das ganze Forschungszentrum vorgeführt – zum allgemeinen Staunen.

6.2 Von Fachleuten für Fachleute

Der Übersetzer muss sich in dieser anspruchsvollen Umgebung seiner Sache sicher sein und darf sich nicht einschüchtern lassen. Unsere Dienste werden gefragt, wenn die sprachlichen Aufgaben für andere zu diffizil sind. Alle unsere Arbeiten – sowohl Übersetzungen als auch redaktionelle Arbeiten – werden in irgendeiner Form veröffentlicht – in internationalen Fachzeitschriften, auf der Website des Forschungszentrums oder auf Visitenkarten, in internen Rundschreiben und in Hochglanz-Broschüren, in EU-Anträgen oder Pressemitteilungen.

Es spielt überhaupt keine Rolle, wenn behauptet wird, dass eine gewisse englische Konstruktion in internationalen Forscherkreisen völlig unbekannt sei; trotzdem findet z. B. nach einem negativen Adverb am Satzanfang im Englischen eine Inversion von Subjekt und Verb statt: „Only three years ago did I realize that...". Allerdings muss man auch mögliche Varianten kennen und akzeptieren und darf seine sprachlichen Vorurteile nicht ausleben, z. B. hinsichtlich der britischen oder amerikanischen Rechtschreibung.

7 Kompetenz für die Zukunft

So lautet das Motto des Forschungszentrums Jülich – es sollte aber auch das Motto jedes Sprachendienstleisters sein. Als erfahrene Übersetzer sind wir für die Zukunft gewappnet, wir müssen uns aber nicht davor scheuen, diese Expertise auch bewusst öffentlich darzustellen. Auf lange Sicht sehe ich die Zukunft des Wissenschaftsübersetzens als gleichberechtigten Partner im Prozess des wissenschaftlichen Publizierens. Forschen findet heute nicht im Elfenbeinturm statt, sondern Wissenschaftler müssen mit anderen Antragstellern um öffentliche Fördermittel konkurrieren. In diesem

Wettbewerb haben wir unseren Platz, um gute wissenschaftliche Ergebnisse transparent und ansprechend zu vermitteln.

In einem kürzlich erschienenen Interview äußert sich Christoph Waltz, frisch gekürter Hauptdarsteller bei den Filmfestspielen in Cannes, über seine Rolle in Quentin Tarantinos Film „Inglourious Basterds" (da wäre eine sprachliche Redaktion bitter nötig!) ganz in meinem Sinne:

> „„„Wenn Tarantino sage, der SS-Offizier Landa [von Waltz dargestellt] sei ein linguistisches Genie, sagten alle immer „jaja, der spricht vier Sprachen", spottet Waltz. „Ich habe die ärgsten Idioten gesehen, die sieben Sprachen sprechen. Als wäre Mehrsprachigkeit schon linguistische Genialität. Die Frage ist; was macht der mit Sprache? Sprache schafft eine Welt."" (Lehnartz 2009: 71)

Dieser Frage müssen wir uns in Zukunft auch immer wieder stellen und auch die passende Antwort finden.

Bibliographie

Abbott, Alison (2009): „Europe's parliamentary priorities", in *Nature* 459, S. 622-623.

Carter-Sigglow, Janet (2009): „Ein Quantum Englisch", in: *MDÜ* 2, S. 57-60.

Forschungszentrum Jülich GmbH (2009): www.fz-juelich.de

King, David A. (2004): „The scientific impact of nations", in: *Nature* 430, S. 311-316.

Lehnartz, Sascha (2009): „Der unverhoffte Superstar von Cannes", in: *Welt am Sonntag* Nr. 21, 24. Mai, S. 71.

Mediterranean Editors & Translators (2009): www.metmeetings.org

Schaffer, Deborah (2008): Review of „The Global English Style Guide", in: *Multi-Lingual* Juli/August, S.19.

Umakantha, N. (1997): „Beyond the language barrier", in: *Nature* 385, S. 764.

Wade, Nicholas (2009): „John Maddox (1925-2009)", in: *Science* 324, S. 1028.

Neue und veränderte Berufsprofile für Dolmetscher

Sprachen als Konferenzsprachen im 21. Jahrhundert: Paradigmenwechsel?

Dr. Jacquy Neff

Freiberuflicher Konferenzdolmetscher (AIIC);
Dozent am Fachbereich Angewandte Sprach- und Kulturwissenschaft
der Johannes Gutenberg-Universität Mainz in Germersheim

neff.translations@t-online.de

Abstract

Der Topos „Sprachen als internationale Konferenzsprachen" ist sowohl in der Soziolinguistik als auch in der Dolmetschwissenschaft eine noch weitgehend unerforschte Domäne. Ausgehend von den Ursprüngen des Konferenzdolmetschens Ende des 19. Jahrhunderts bis zu einer noch nie dagewesenen Blütezeit in der 2. Hälfte des 20. Jahrhunderts, frägt der Vortrag nach dem derzeitigen Stand unterschiedlicher Sprachen als Konferenzsprachen, untersucht insbesondere die deutsche Sprache relativ zu den anderen Konferenzsprachen und zeigt eine mögliche Entwicklungsperspektive auf.

Ausgehend von einer weltweiten Befragung von 2.800 AIIC-Konferenzdolmetschern in den Jahren 2004 bis 2007, betrachtet der Autor unterschiedliche Parameter zur Bestimmung der Stellung von Sprachen als Konferenzsprachen: geografische Verteilung (26 Länder), sektorielle Verbreitung (5 Sektoren), marktrelevante Daten (Stratifizierung und Typologisierung von Konferenzveranstaltern, Markteinteilung, Auftragspotenzial für Konferenzdolmetscher), sprachspezifische Aspekte (Sprachenangebot in Aktiv- und Passivsprachen, Sprachkombinationen) sowie der neuartige Ansatz der sprachpaarbezogenen Prävalenz von Konferenzsprachen. Eine prospektive Sicht der Entwicklungsmöglichkeiten einzelner Sprachen und Sprachpaaren für die erste Hälfte 21. Jahrhunderts rundet das Bild ab.

New professional profiles for linguistic mediation: Community interpreting

Clara Pignataro

Conference Interpreter – Researcher and Interpreter Trainer
Iulm University, Milan, Italy

clara.pignataro@iulm.it

La diversité des origines, des langues, des expressions culturelles est de plus en plus présente dans notre vie quotidienne et dans nos métiers. Parfois, l'Étranger dérange, mais nous aimons trouver, avec des musiques ou des objets venus d'ailleurs, dans le métissage des pratiques et des goûts, la source renouvelée de plaisirs partagés et d'inventivité. Ainsi dialoguent les cultures, entre hostilité et hospitalité (www.culture.gouv.fr/culture).

1   Introduction

The paper presents the initial results of a preliminary study aimed at exploring the role of "community interpreting" in the health sector in the region of Lombardy (Italy). The purpose is to understand how multilingual situations are managed in a multicultural setting outside the conference room. Until a decade ago the only interpreting activities deemed worthy of scientific research were simultaneous and consecutive translation, the two principal modes of conference interpreting. Important geopolitical and cultural changes, including mass migrations and globalization, have enormously increased the importance of other forms of oral linguistic mediation. Three main issues will be presented: a general overview on immigration in Italy; a description of the skills and roles of linguistic mediators, as defined by the operators themselves, on the basis of our questionnaires and interviews. The last part contains open questions concerning training issues.

2   The empirical work: methodology

The study is based on the perceptions and opinions reported by those who work in the field, the interpreters/mediators to whom we administered the questionnaire in order to have their direct feedback and perception about their professional role. A questionnaire was distributed in the Region of Lombardy to hospitals, associations of linguistic mediators and conference interpreters as well, with the aim of surveying professional status, working conditions, perceptions of the role, skills required and codes of conduct. Data are still being collected and analysed, but a profile has already emerged. Respondents were asked to provide details about working languages, language proficiency, qualifications, training, working conditions, mode of interpreting and code of ethics. The questions were a mix of multiple choice and open-ended.

3 Migration in Italy: an overview

Globalization has enormously contributed to expanding the horizons of our experience, multiplying ethnic and cultural diversity: the number of languages spoken in Europe is continuously increasing, as are ethnic and religious traditions present in the territory. Diversity and cohesion: this is what characterizes Europe today (www.eurocult.org). In the past 20 years, Italy has become an attractive destination for an increasing number of immigrants (Geraci, 2008). It is estimated that 4 million foreigners are present in Italy and that ¼ of the entire foreign population present in the Italian territory resides in the Region of Lombardy, where one person out of ten is a foreigner. The average yearly influx is 442,000 immigrants, totally unexpected, as noted by the demographer Antonio Golini, in his article in the Corriere della Sera, dated April 28, 2009. Given the soaring number of immigrants and the consequent increase in non-Italian speaking population in Italy, interlinguistic mediators are becoming more and more necessary in various social settings, like schools, hospitals, immigration offices and in legal settings as well, such as police stations and courts. As stated by the European Parliament in 2006 in the decision no. 1983: *"All European citizens and all those living in the European Union on a termporary or permanent basis, should have the opportunity to take part in the intercultural dialogue and fully accomplish themselves in a society made of diversity, pluralism, solidarity and dynamism, not only in Europe but worldwide"*. The migrants have a nearly constant need to communicate with Italian institutions in order to understand and make full use of the opportunities and services available to them (Rudvin 2003). The concept of intercultural mediation, intended as an instrument that facilitates the integration of foreigners and enhances diversity, was introduced for the first time in our national legislation by Laws 36 and 40/98 which guarantee linguistic support for ethnic minorities (Russo, 2004). Hospitals are the service most widely used by immigrant families (National Health Service Decree n. 3184) and it is in this context that the most challenging communication difficulties arise, creating linguistic and cultural misunderstandings not only for users but also for hospital staff: linguistic barriers create inequalities in access to health-care services, which seriously impacts on patients, leading to misdiagnoses, errors and misunderstandings (Chiarenza 2008). Until the 1970's and 80's, when the first waves of immigrants arrived, Italy had always been a country of emigration: immigration was seen as a new and probably temporary phenomenon, and there were no infrastructures to cope with the linguistic and cultural needs of both local administrators and the immigrants. The first initiatives to provide some sort of linguistic mediation were taken by private charity institutions (Caritas) and local NGOs, with an assistance-based and multicultural approach (Rudvin 2003). Since the very beginning the mediators have performed a very significant service, of great value to both the host community and the migrants. The importance of this role is also recognized by CNEL – the agency for the coordination of policies for the social integration of migrants – that defines the mediator as follows: *"...the idea of acting as a "bridge" between different cultures, facilitating the growth of an intercultural exchange, has always been promoted and developed by intercultural mediators"*. The CNEL training program defines the role as *"an agent who plays an active role in the process of integration between foreigners and institutions of the host country, both public and private, without replacing the former or the latter, with the aim of facilitating relations between subjects of different cultures"* (Rome, 8 April, 2009).

4   Cultural mediation: Official recognition of the profession

In English-speaking countries community-based interpreting is more commonly used. The term coined by the Federation of Interpreters and Translators (FIT) refers to interpreting, paid or voluntary, where interpreters work in a normal, everyday setting in the community (Harris 2000:4). Possible settings include health-care facilities, education, social services, legal and businesses. In Italy the discipline is a new one and the nomenclature varies broadly: there is lack of consensus about the use and definition of this term among scholars (Rudvin 2003). *"Cultural mediator", "cultural-linguistic mediator", "expert in mediation":* the variety of definitions illustrate the fragmentation and the lack of standardisation of the different profiles defined by local agencies. In this study we will adopt the definition proposed by UNESCO, that is the *intercultural mediator*, in order to represent "*the Italian approach to integration as it has progressively developed in intercultural terms, intended to promote a dialogue and exchange between different cultures and in line with the indications formulated by UNESCO in 1980"* (UNESCO 1980). The professional role has existed since the 60's in Australia, Canada, the US and the UK, but it is only recently that in Italy the Interpreting Studies' scholars have realized that the field has expanded to include an area other than conference interpreting. As Garzone points out: "*it is surprising that interpreting activities outside the conference room attract limited attention, although in terms of volumes of services required and rendered they are not less important than conference interpreting*" (2003: 15). Our investigation is especially focussed on the importance of so-called "cross-cultural competence" which ranks high in the feedback of our respondents as a priority admission criterion for training and professionalization and on the assumption that "*communication is affected by different aspects of the context, including cultural expectations, social relations and the purpose of communication*" (Bowe, H./ Martin Kylie 2007: 3). Regarding this issue, we basically relied on reports from those working in the field (mediators/interpreters, service providers and service users), who face the situation firsthand, on a daily basis. Data are still being analysed, but general impressions are already evident. First of all, from the surveys and interviews we carried out, it seems that two distinct figures can be outlined: the *cultural and linguistic mediator,* that is to say the *migrant who works as an interpreter* and the *interpreter working for public services* who is a University graduate (Russo 2004). There are characteristics that distinguish interpreting according to the domain where it is performed (conference, business, medical, immigration office) and the nomenclature may be different, but the essence of the task does not vary substantially. Apart from the "labels" we may want to use, it is more productive to investigate on a deeper level. Our assumption is twofold: that any interpreter dealing with an interlinguistic situation is also a "mediator", in the sense that he or she favours interaction and communication, creating a bridge between cultures; and that whatever definition we may decide to adopt, this form of interpreting is more clearly defined by the context were it occurs (Rudvin

2003). Because it is subject to continuous modifications, it will be up to the market to find the right "label", our task is to monitor market needs and try to meet them.

5   Cultural competence and cultural-competent hospitals

According to Favaro's definition (2001), the *cultural mediator* creates contacts between different worlds and through his communication and cross-cultural competence helps to avoid and resolve conflicts. The mediator is needed in those situations where different cultures have to communicate (hospitals, immigration offices, schools, courts). From our interviews and questionnaires, it is clear that, as well as linguistic competence and knowledge of specific terminology, the interesting aspect of cultural mediation is the *intercultural dialogue,* or the possibility of creating "bridges" between different cultures that permit communication. According to Katerina Stenou (Unesco) the notion of dialogue refers not only to the act of speaking with each other but to establishing a discourse and an exchange with the other and for the other. This is the spirit that animates the work of the Association Les Cultures Onlus, founded in Lecco (Italy) in 1993, working as a workshop of international culture. Their aim is to promote an idea of society that includes diversity, based on a peaceful coexistence and respect for differences. They promote several activities of solidarity with the south of the world, work to defend human rights and protection of different cultures. They have also created a linguistic and *cultural mediation service* for the education and health-care sectors, to meet the ever growing needs of public and private institutions. The association collaborates with qualified cultural mediators who act as linguistic and cross-cultural bridges between migrants and Italian health-care staff. In November 2003, Les Cultures signed an agreement with the "Azienda Ospedaliera di Lecco" in the field of Mediazione Linguistico Culturale (Cross-cultural Linguistic Mediation). The Association "Les Cultures" defines the cross-cultural linguistic mediator as follows: " a *person who, in addition to acting as a translator, also functions as a bridge between the local culture and that of the foreigner. The role involves acting as interface between the hospital/medical institution and the patient, interpreting the needs of the latter, often expressed informally, in order to allow the medical personnel to provide effective treatment while at the same time explaining to the patient how the health-care structure operates, thus making the interaction constructive".* In this definition, it is interesting to note that the role of *interface* is assigned to the mediator, with a great deal of responsibilities, in terms of linguistic and cultural competences. The mediators working for the Association Les Cultures are all foreigners and they share with the patient not only the same language but also the same culture and experience, this can be positive for communication but also detrimental in the sense that it may engender empathy and personal involvement. The importance of this topic is also highlighted in a document published by the Association La Nostra Famiglia – IRCCS E.Medea, within the framework of a project named C.I.A.O (**C**onoscenza **I**ncontro **A**ccoglienza **O**pportunità. Mediazione in rete per superare le barriere linguistiche e culturali. Knowledge Meeting Welcoming Opportunity. Mediation network to overcome linguistic and cultural barriers) that involves linguistic mediators. In their reports it is clearly stated that when the mediator is a professional there are several plusses that impact positively on the communicative interaction, like specific cultural training; experience and capability to create relationships with different participants in the interaction; as well as neutrality and a more organised and more structured intervention with the health-care institution. The document of the project also states that employing a professional mediator also has minuses, such as unsustainable costs and long time before the arrival of the mediator/interpreter. Medical staff are convinced that non-professional foreign mediators can better understand the need of the users, due to the fact that he/she may have shared the same experience as a migrant, but there are several areas mentioned as weak points: lack of neutrality due to a high emotional involvement, and the fact that the presence of a non-professional requires more efforts in terms of job and staff organization, as well as less knowledge of hospital procedures, which may prove detrimental both to patients and doctors. Heather Bowe and Kylie Martin explain very well the importance of being culturally competent in the text *Communication Across Culture* (2007). In the medical setting, where the patient and doctor encounter relies heavily on sequences of questions and answers, intercultural communication is particularly relevant: different cultural and social norms shape the way questions and answers are framed. An awareness of possible differences not only facilitates the translation work but also enables the interpreter/mediator not to be surprised about differences when working with/for people belonging to different ethnic and cultural groups (Bowe 2007: 6). A culturally competent mediator not only shares the same linguistic code but also understands the world that a specific language represents: non-verbal communication, cultural codes, variation of terms according to ethnic groups, different perceptions of the concepts of health, maternity, pain. For instance, the physiotherapist or logopedist is unknown in certain cultures, and the perception of disability may vary from culture to culture (Association "La Nostra Famiglia Eugenio Medea" 2008). Language is a reflection of the culture it "speaks" and any verbal interaction implies sharing a common knowledge of the same world (Rudvin 2003). There are huge differences in standard languages, described as "nativised": that is to say those languages that have been semantically and grammatically adapted to their new culture, like English on the Indian subcontinent and in central Africa. This adaptation creates a new and richer language that reflects the world and vision of India and Africa rather than the UK or the US (Garzone 2003). Therefore, interpreting without knowing the cultural context would mean missing the cultural referents that characterise a specific variety of English. Decoding the linguistic codes during a communication, interpreting the "non-spoken" of a patient in order to avoid "misunderstandings" that would lead to frustration in the patients and that may foster feelings of hostility and aggressiveness; supporting the doctor in the creation of a positive therapeutic triangle (les Cultures Onlus). The essence of interpreting, regardless of the context where it occurs, was brilliantly described by Herbert (1952) when he wrote that a good interpreter has the task to reproduce the same effect that the speaker would have produced if the interpreter were not there. Reproducing the same effect does not simply mean finding linguistic equivalents, but coming to terms with differences in cultures, striking a balance between the idea in the source text and the original and reformulating the same idea in a language that uses different instruments to express that same idea (Rudvin 2003). The participatory role of the intercultural mediator/interpreter with his/her culture, sensibility, creativity and common sense is at stake when it comes to solving lexical problems concerning so-called culture-specific terms or expressions pertaining to social culture, organisations, customs, ideas, gestures and habits (Newmark 1981: 71-83). In essence, what Larson maintained with respect to translation, perfectly applies to liaison interpreting and linguistic mediation: *for an effective transfer of the text, the translator must be well acquainted with both the source and receptor language and culture* (Larson 1984:425). Along with cultural competence, respondents also highlighted confidentiality, advocacy as essential elements for an ideal code of conduct.

6 Training: inborn aptitudes and teachable skills

I am in complete agreement with Agostino who maintained that no one can teach anything to anyone else but we do have a chance to make some signs resonate from the outside that may echo in some individuals, but only in those where an aptitude already exists. Aptitude tests and aptitude skills in the interpreting field are a widely investigated topic and further research would also be productive in the field of linguistic mediation or community interpreting.

The professionalisation of community interpreting has been delayed – as Garzone points out (2003: 13) – even though the need to train specialised professionals has been widely recognized, and was also clearly expressed in our survey.

In the light of the many job openings for professional mediators, universities provide training in "Scienze della mediazione linguistica" (Sciences of linguistic mediation): a 3-year first-level university degree extensively described in Russo (2004). The former Scuola Superiore per Interpreti e Traduttori (School for Interpreters and Translators) has been renamed Schools for Linguistic Mediators, as dictated by the Ministerial Decree no. 38, 10 January, 2002 (www.miur.it). The Ministero del Lavoro, della Salute e delle Politiche Sociali has also launched a project to train linguistic and cultural mediators (www.ministerosalute.it) and this is further evidence of the rising awareness about the importance of professionalisation of linguistic mediation.

The "tools of the trade" for a linguistic mediator go beyond linguistic expertise and terminological knowledge: interaction, communication and cultural competence can no longer be ignored in the training programmes. The interpreter-mediated encounter is a "communicative *pas de trois*" – as Wadensjo (1998: 10, 12) describes it – where interpersonal sensitivity, openness towards others, and the inclination to listen to others make a difference in the *triadic exchange*. The "hard skills", such as linguistic proficiency, competence in interpreting techniques and terminology acquisition are essential prerequisites for a mediator and they are "teachable", whereas the "soft skills", that is to say those inclinations and personality traits that determine the sensitivity of the mediator (like interpersonal sensitivity and openness towards others) require a different state of the mind and a strong capacity for listening to others, and they should already be present before training starts. Therefore, future initiatives in the training sector should cover: dialogue interpreting techniques, such as consecutive and chuchotage, memory training, role-playing to simulate different settings and specific terminology but also intercultural communication. Considering that linguistic mediation is not simply a matter of linguistic proficiency, cooperation with other departments is very valuable in order to provide good socio-cultural and intercultural skills.

7 Conclusions

In Italy, as elsewhere, the increasing social complexity deriving from the presence of people from other cultures and ethnic groups has made it necessary for health-care workers to develop a new cultural awareness. This requires putting aside closed, parochial attitudes and opening up to cultural diversity, in order to help those who speak different languages and express different needs. Cultures are dynamic entities and any attempt to circumscribe them in a definition would risk to miss the essence and the complexity of their nature. The same holds true for the *interlinguistic mediator,* an extremely powerful interface, whose understanding of the verbal and non-verbal communication can contribute to the outcome of the encounter. Understanding market needs and providing a flexible solution in terms of human resources is the challenge of the universities.

Bibliography

Bancroft, M. (2005). The interpreter's world tour: An environmental scan of standards of practice for interpreters. Woodland Hills, CA: The California Endowment.

Chiarenza, A. (2008). "Intercultural Mediation". (Online) www.mfheu.net (accessed 20 June 2009).

CNEL (2009). (online) www.edscuola.it/archivio/scuole/mediatoreltercult.pdf (accessed 5 giugno 2009)

Favaro, G. (2001). I Mediatori linguistici e culturali nella scuola, in : Quaderni dell'interculturalità n. 20. Bologna: EMI.

Garzone, G. (2003). "From Conference Interpreting to Dialogue Interpreting", in: Domain-Specific English and Language Mediation in Professional and Institutional Settings. Milano: Arcipelago Edizioni.

Geraci, S. (2008). "Evoluzione del fenomeno migratorio in Italia e impatto sulle politiche sanitarie" in : Qualità dei servizi sanitari in un contesto pluriculturale. (Online). http//ausl.re.it (accessed April 2009).

Goffman, E. (1981). Forms of Talk. Oxford: Blackwell.

Harris, B. (2000). Foreword. Community Interpreting Stage Two, in : The Critical Link 2: Interpreters in the Community. Ed. By R.P. Roberts, S.E Carr, D. Abraham and A. Dufour, Amsterdam-Philadelphia, John Benjamins, p. 1-5.

Herbert, J. (1952). Le Manuel de l'Interprète. Génève: Georg.

La Nostra Famiglia. (Online). www.lanostrafamiglia.it (accessed May 2009).

Larson, M. (1984). Meaning-Based Translation: a Guide to Cross-Language Equivalence.Lanham, MD: University Press of America.

Les Cultures. (Online) www.lescultures.it (accessed May 2009).

Merlini, R. (2009). Seeking asylum and seeking identity in a mediated encounter, in: Interpreting 11:1, p. 57-92. John Benjamins Publishing Company.

Miur. (Online). http//universe.miur.it/mediat-lingue.html. (accessed Aprile 2009).

Newmark, P. (1981). Approaches to Translation. Oxford: Pergamon Press.

Rudvin, M. (2003). Interpreting for Public Services: some Institutional, Professional and Intercultural Aspects, in : Domain-Specific English and Language Mediation in Professional and Institutional Settings. Milano: Arcipelago Edizioni.

Russo, M.C. (2004). "Community Interpreter, Liaison Interpreter, ad hoc Interpreter, Intercultural Mediator…What kind of curriculum for such a multifaceted profession?" in: Professionalization of Interpreting in the Community, International Conference Critical Link 4. Stockholm, Sweden.

Valero-Garces, C., Martin, A. (anno). Crossing Borders in Community Interpreting, Definitions and Dilemmas. John Benjamins Publishing Company: Amsterdam/Philadelphia.

Wadensjo, C. (1998). Interpreting as Interaction. London and New York: Longman.

Wadensjo, C. (1993). "The Double Role of a Dialogue Interpreter" in : Pochhacker, Franz and Shlensinger, Miriam (eds.), The Interpreting Studies Reader, Routledge, London, p. 355-370.

Öffentliche Arbeit- und Auftraggeber für Dolmetscher

Dolmetschen im Auswärtigen Amt

Annelie Lehnhardt

Auswärtiges Amt, Berlin
Leiterin des Dolmetschdienstes

105-1@diplo.de

Abstract

In dem Vortrag wird erläutert, wie der Dolmetschdienst des Auswärtigen Amts strukturiert ist, welche Auftraggeber ihn in Anspruch nehmen und in welchen Bereichen die ca. 170 Dolmetscherinnen und Dolmetscher in der Berliner Zentrale und an den Auslandsvertretungen weltweit eingesetzt werden. Anhand von praktischen Beispielen werden die für das Auswärtige Amt spezifischen Termine und Einsatzarten auf höchster politischer Ebene dargestellt. Zum Abschluss soll beleuchtet werden, welche Anforderungen sprachlicher, fachlicher, intellektueller, physischer und psychischer Art sich daraus an die Dolmetscherinnen und Dolmetscher des Auswärtigen Amts ergeben.

Ressortübergreifender Dolmetscheinsatz für die Bundesregierung

Anne Jacobs-Schleithoff

Spanischdolmetscherin, Bundesministerium für
Wirtschaft und Technologie (BMWi)

anne.jacobs@bmwi.bund.de

Abstract

Im Zuge der Globalisierung nehmen die Auslandskontakte der Bundesministerien, der sogenannten Fachressorts, zu. Der Bedarf an Verdolmetschungen und Übersetzungen bleibt entgegen allen Annahmen konstant. Neben der klassischen Beschäftigung im Auswärtigen Dienst gibt es eine Vielzahl von Arbeitsplätzen für Dolmetscher und Übersetzer, die als Fachkollegen in den obersten Bundesbehörden und Ministerien tätig sind. Für Regierungsdolmetscher und -übersetzer ergibt sich ein spezielles Anforderungsprofil, um ressortübergreifend tätig zu sein. Ähnlichkeiten und Unterschiede zur Tätigkeit des Freiberuflers werden in dem Vortrag herausgearbeitet. Alle Spielarten des Dolmetschens kommen beim sogenannten Amtsdolmetscher zum Einsatz (Sim, Kons, Flüster, Hybridformen), und es sind oftmals Mischarbeitsplätze, an denen sowohl gedolmetscht als auch übersetzt wird. Welche Konflikte, Grenzsituationen und Abhängigkeiten erlebt der Behördendolmetscher? Anhand von konkreten Fallbeispielen geht der Vortrag auf spezielle Herausforderungen eines globalisierten Marktes für die Dolmetsch- und Übersetzungspraxis am Fallbeispiel des Bundesministeriums für Wirtschaft und Technologie ein.

Qualitätssicherung im Dolmetscherdienst des EPA

Ute Kirstein

Dipl.-Dolmetscherin (AIIC), Dipl.-Übersetzerin,
Leiterin des Dolmetscherdienstes des EPA

ukirstein@epo.org

1 Der Dolmetscherdienst des EPA

Das Europäische Patentamt beschäftigt keine fest angestellten Dolmetscher, sondern rekrutiert ausschließlich freiberuflich tätige Konferenzdolmetscher, die in mündlichen Verhandlungen, Beschwerdeverfahren, Fachkonferenzen und den Sitzungen des Verwaltungsrats und der wichtigsten Ausschüsse simultan aus den Amtssprachen Deutsch, Englisch und Französisch in ihre jeweilige Muttersprache dolmetschen. Abgesehen von den drei Amtssprachen besteht im Rahmen der internationalen Zusammenarbeit zunehmend Bedarf an den Sprachrichtungen Japanisch-Koreanisch-Chinesisch-Englisch.

Gegenwärtig rekrutiert der Dolmetscherdienst aus einem Pool von ca. 140 regelmäßig für das EPA tätigen Kollegen aus ganz Europa.

2 Hintergrund der Einführung eines Qualitätssicherungssystems

Die Einführung eines Qualitätssicherungssystems im Dolmetscherdienst des EPA stellte insofern eine Besonderheit dar, als ausschließlich Freiberufler rekrutiert werden und es bis 2005 kein strukturiertes System zur Einschätzung und Sicherung der Qualität gab, wie dies in anderen internationalen Organisationen üblich ist.

Um einen Ansatz zu finden, wurden daher, ausgehend von der vom Amt veranlassten „Organisationsstudie Dolmetscher Service", umfassende Informationen darüber zusammengetragen, wie eine Qualitätssicherung bzw. -beurteilung in vergleichbaren internationalen Organisationen und Institutionen, aber auch großen Firmen durchgeführt wird, die zahlreiche Freiberufler beschäftigen.

Im Ergebnis war festzustellen, dass es sich bei den meisten institutionalisierten Systemen eher um „Top-down"-Systeme handelt, die eine entsprechend dokumentierte Kontrolle durch festangestellte Dolmetscher vorsehen.

Systeme dieser Art schienen allerdings nicht sinnvoll auf einen Dolmetscherdienst wie den des EPA übertragbar, da, wie gesagt, alle Kollegen Freiberufler sind und sämtliche Verhandlungen und Konferenzen hochspezifische rechtlich-technisch-wissenschaftliche Themen zum Gegenstand haben und darüber hinaus die Beherrschung der patentrechtlichen Terminologie voraussetzen, so dass eine entsprechende

Leistungsbeurteilung durch „amtsfremde" Kollegen kaum bzw. nur mit unverhältnismäßig hohem Aufwand durchführbar wäre.

Eine Beurteilung der Simultanleistung und des professionellen Verhaltens eines Dolmetschers ist schließlich nur möglich, wenn man mit dem Kollegen in der Kabine als Mitglied des Teams arbeitet, da nur auf diese Weise Schwierigkeitsgrad der Sitzung und außergewöhnliche Umstände „aus erster Hand" beurteilt werden können.

Das Ziel bei der Ausarbeitung eines auf diese speziellen Gegebenheiten zugeschnittenen Systems war daher in erster Linie die Umsetzung nachvollziehbarer, akzeptabler und transparenter Maßnahmen zur Qualitätssicherung.

Das Gewicht liegt dabei nicht auf einer „Kontrolle", sondern

- erstens darauf, eine möglichst hohe Qualität zu gewährleisten,

- zweitens, festzustellen, in welcher Hinsicht Verbesserungsbedarf besteht, und

- drittens, den Dolmetscher zu sensibilisieren, auch regelmäßig eine Art Selbstbewertung durchzuführen.

Obwohl die Qualität der Dolmetschleistung im EPA im Durchschnitt sehr hoch ist, gibt es immer Verbesserungsbedarf, und selbst bei langjährigen Berufspraktikern schleicht sich gelegentlich ein „laisser-aller" ein, das den Grundregeln professionellen Verhaltens entgegensteht.

Es wird dabei grundsätzlich zwischen Dolmetschern unterschieden, die bereits seit Jahren für das EPA tätig sind und somit über hinreichende Erfahrung im Hinblick auf die Art der Dolmetschereinsätze und die spezielle Terminologie verfügen, die es zu beherrschen gilt, und neu rekrutierten Kollegen, die sich erst einarbeiten müssen.

Weiterhin muss ein Qualitätssicherungssystem sowohl die Beurteilung der Leistung des Dolmetschers (Output) als auch die Abwägung, inwieweit die notwendigen Voraussetzungen zur Erbringung einer Leistung von hoher Qualität erfüllt sind (Input), umfassen.

Qualität im Hinblick auf die Arbeit des Dolmetschers bezieht sich dabei nicht allein auf die in der Kabine erbrachte Dolmetschleistung, sondern umfasst - als weitere wichtige Eckpfeiler effizienter und verlässlicher Arbeit - auch das Verhalten dem „Kunden" (z.B. der Kammer und den Parteien) gegenüber und die Teamfähigkeit (sog. Sozialkompetenz).

3 Struktur des EPA-Systems zur Qualitätssicherung

Das EPA-Qualitätssicherungssystem wurde vor dem Hintergrund der oben angesprochenen Überlegungen strukturiert.

Die Grundlage muss dabei immer eine Definition der Aspekte sein, die bei der Beurteilung jedweder Qualität zu erfassen sind:

3.1 Input

Welche Voraussetzungen müssen erfüllt sein, um eine gute Leistung erbringen zu können:

- Wurde ausreichendes Vorbereitungsmaterial zur Verfügung gestellt?
- Wie ist die Redequalität (schnell, abgelesen, schwer verständlicher Nicht-muttersprachler, spricht der Redner ins Mikrophon?)?
- Arbeitet die technische Anlage störungsfrei?
- Wie ist der Teamgeist in der Kabine?

3.2 Output

Dolmetschleistung in der Kabine

1) Inhalt

- Vollständigkeit
- Genauigkeit
- Klare Vermittlung der Botschaft (auch bei schwierigen Rednern)
- Auslassungen
- Sinnfehler (contresens, faux amis)

2) Rhetorische Fähigkeiten

- Sprachniveau
- Stil / Wortwahl
- Terminologie
- Grammatik
- Bringt der Dolmetscher die Sätze zu Ende
- Macht der Dolmetscher falsche Satzpausen
- Wie viele „Ähs" schleichen sich in die Verdolmetschung ein

3) „Interpreting Skills"

- Beherrschung passiver Sprachen
- „Synchronicity"
- Stimme
- Überzeugungskraft (keine zögernde Vortragsweise)
- Fähigkeit, auch unter Stress ruhig zu bleiben („sang-froid")
- Fähigkeit, Sätze auch zu vollenden, wenn der Redner sie wiederholt „hängen" lässt
- Strukturierung der Verdolmetschung
- Konzentration

- Fähigkeit, sich vom Redner zu lösen (Dolmetscher „klebt nicht am Wort")
- Fähigkeit, „mitzudenken" (z.B. bei falscher Jahreszahl des Redners)

4) Professionelles Verhalten

- Vorbereitung
- Pünktlichkeit
- Dolmetscher als Sprachmittler (Verhalten im „Hintergrund")
- Höflichkeit dem „Kunden" gegenüber
- Teamgeist: Verhalten Kollegen gegenüber, Abwesenheit während arbeitsfreier Zeiten

Um eine möglichst faire und objektive Qualitätssicherung durchführen zu können, wird pro Kabine ein Team aus vier Kollegen, die seit langem für das EPA tätig sind, eingesetzt („Quality Assurance Panel - QAP)". Es handelt sich dabei um ein Team erfahrener und qualifizierter Kollegen, die alle drei Amtssprachen beherrschen, in ihrem Verhalten den Kunden und den Teammitgliedern gegenüber professionell handeln und der Rekrutierung und Einarbeitung neuer Kollegen positiv gegenübersteh en.

Ein aus drei bis vier Kollegen bestehendes Team überprüfender Kollegen wurde eingesetzt, um größere Objektivität zu gewährleisten und um die Verantwortung „auf mehrere Schultern" zu verteilen, was auch für das Team selbst positiv ist.

Jeder Kollege arbeitet nacheinander mit mindestens drei der vier Teammitglieder seiner Muttersprache zusammen.

Sobald ein Kollege mit allen Mitgliedern zusammengearbeitet hat, wird auf der Grundlage der Einzelbeurteilungen und deren Erörterung mit den beurteilenden Dolmetschern ein Gesamtbericht erstellt. Dieser wird dem beurteilten Kollegen in einem Feedback-Gespräch ausgehändigt, in dem erforderliche Verbesserungen aufgezeigt, Anregungen gegeben, aber auch positive Kritik geäußert werden soll. Es wird nie direkt nach einer Sitzung ein Feedback gegeben, da dies immer nur einer Teilbeurteilung gleichkäme und damit unterschiedliche Sitzungsbedingungen und Schwierigkeiten nicht berücksichtigt würden.

Die Grundlage für die Leistungsbeurteilung bilden genau definierte „Kriterien zur Beurteilung der Qualität von Dolmetschleistungen".

Die Einhaltung solch professioneller Standards sollte für die meisten Kollegen ohnehin eine Selbstverständlichkeit sein, und diese sollen auch der Selbstbewertung dienen und eine Art Früherkennung bestehender Mängel ermöglichen.

Neu rekrutierte Dolmetscher arbeiten ungefähr die ersten sechs bis zwölf Monate ihrer Tätigkeit beim EPA ausschließlich mit erfahrenen Kollegen zusammen, die sie in dieser Zeit auch bei der Vorbereitung verstärkt beraten und unterstützen. Erst dann erfolgt eine Beurteilung durch die QAP-Kollegen dahingehend, ob sich der neue Kollege für eine Tätigkeit beim EPA eignet oder nicht.

Selbstverständlich unterziehen sich auch die Mitglieder des QAP selbst einer kritischen Bewertung. Dies geschieht in einem direkten „Peer Review".

Alle Kollegen erhalten uneingeschränkt Gelegenheit, sich dazu zu äußern, ob und wenn ja, welche Maßnahmen erforderlich sind, um Mängel zu beseitigen, die sie an der Erbringung einer entsprechenden qualitativen Leistung hindern.

Das oben beschriebene System ist als ganzheitliches System zur Sicherung der Qualität im Dolmetschprozess zu sehen, dessen Erfolg in hohem Maß davon abhängt, welchen Beitrag der einzelne Dolmetscher bereit ist, zu leisten.

Hinweis:

Die Begriffe „der Dolmetscher" und „der Kollege" im Text sind neutral zu sehen und beziehen sich sowohl auf Dolmetscherinnen und Kolleginnen als auch auf Dolmetscher und Kollegen.

Workshops und Podiumsdiskussionen

Dolmetscher/innen und Übersetzer/innen als Experten für Interkulturelle Kommunikation in Unternehmen und auf dem freien Markt

Carina Turbon

Ct-Cultra culture at work, Bergneustadt

carina.turbon@t-online.de

Workshop

Die Erweiterung des Berufsbildes der Dolmetscher/innen und Übersetzer/innen als Experten für Interkulturelle Kommunikation ist nahe liegend.

Doch was braucht es, um sich guten Gewissens als „interkulturell kompetent" bezeichnen zu können und wie lässt sich gegenüber einem Kunden die Erweiterung des Berufsbildes begründen?

Der Workshop behandelt zwei Seiten einer Medaille:

- Wie können Dolmetscher/innen und Übersetzer/innen ihre interkulturelle Kompetenz bewerten und systematisch weiterentwickeln?

- Wie können Dolmetscher/innen und Übersetzer/innen ihre interkulturelle Kompetenz als Alleinstellungsmerkmal am Markt nutzen und Kunden davon überzeugen?

Der Workshop orientiert sich eng an den Bedürfnissen und Interessen der Teilnehmenden. Der Modebegriff „Interkulturelle Kompetenz" wird im Hinblick auf den aktuellen Forschungsstand definiert, die Arten und Qualitätsmerkmale von interkulturellen Trainings werden vorgestellt und Möglichkeiten aufgezeigt, wie Dolmetscher/innen und Übersetzer/innen ihre erworbene IK-Kompetenz systematisch erweitern, gezielt anwenden und zu einem Produkt entwickeln können. Methodisch wird mit einem Mix aus Trainerinput (Kurzvortrag) sowie praktischem Erfahren (kurze Übungssequenz) gearbeitet.

Ehrenamtliches Dolmetschen und Übersetzen / Volunteer translating and interpreting

Tim Slater

Technischer Übersetzer und Dolmetscher, Augsburg

TranSlater@compuserve.com

Workshop

Viele DolmetscherInnen und ÜbersetzerInnen sind bereit, gelegentlich ihre Dienste unentgeltlich für das Gemeinwohl der einen oder anderen zur Verfügung zu stellen, und entsprechende Organisationen und Gruppen brauchen oft Hilfe bzw. Beratung. Die Vernetzung zwischen den zwei Seiten ist aber mangelhaft.

Wir wollen darüber sprechen, wie diese Zusammenarbeit verbessert werden kann, und z.B.:

- Wie kann man sicherstellen, dass Sprachmittler nicht umsonst arbeiten, aber andere Dienstleister normal bezahlt werden?

- Wie kann man solche Nutzergruppen beraten, damit sie solche Hilfe am sinnvollsten und effektivsten nutzen können?

Ich persönlich habe Erfahrung im Übersetzen und Dolmetschen für die Friedensbewegung, aber die Probleme dürften auch auf ganz anderen Gebieten ähnlich sein.

Many interpreters and translators are willing to do occasional pro bono volunteer work, and relevant organizations and groups often need help or advice. But the networking of these two parties is unsatisfactory.

We will discuss how such collaboration can be improved, and topics such as:

- How can one ensure that we are not working for free, while other service providers are being paid normal fees?

- How can such groups be counselled on how to use this assistance most effectively and usefully?

My experience is in translating and interpreting for the peace movement, but the problems are presumably much the same in quite different fields, as well.

III. Neue Herausforderungen beim Übersetzen

Automatisierung in der Qualitätssicherung – Geheimnis- und Datenschutz

Möglichkeiten und Grenzen der computergestützten Qualitätssicherung im Übersetzungsprozess

Prof. Dr. Uwe Reinke

Fachhochschule Köln,
Institut für Translation und Mehrsprachige Kommunikation

uwe.reinke@fh-koeln.de

1 Qualitätssicherung im Übersetzungsprozess

Die Qualität von Übersetzungen spielt in der Praxis eine zentrale Rolle – zumindest wenn man der Werbung von Übersetzungsdienstleistern Glauben schenken darf. Doch Qualitätssicherung beim Übersetzen ist zeit- und kostenintensiv und steht somit im Widerspruch zu immer schnelleren Innovationszyklen, gleichzeitiger Auslieferung neuer Produkte auf allen Zielmärkten („SimShip"), zunehmendem Kostensenkungs-druck und anderen Zwängen.

Sowohl die Anbieter von Translation-Memory-Systemen (TM) als auch die Entwick-ler spezieller Qualitätssicherungswerkzeuge versprechen, dieses Dilemma zu lösen: „Effizienteres, produktiveres und konsistenteres Übersetzen, deutliche Kostensenkung durch drastisch reduzierten Lektoratsaufwand, objektive und zuverlässige Evaluierung von Übersetzungsqualität, mehr Qualität und mehr Quantität" – so oder ähnlich lauten die Verheißungen der Hersteller.

Nach der Klärung einiger relevanter Grundbegriffe des Qualitätsmanagements und deren Anwendung auf den Übersetzungsprozess soll im Folgenden der Frage nachge-gangen werden, wo die Möglichkeiten und Grenzen der zurzeit am Markt verfügbaren Werkzeuge zur computergestützten Qualitätssicherung von Übersetzungen tatsächlich liegen. Dabei werden die verschiedenen Ansätze und Methoden vorgestellt und klassifiziert sowie Perspektiven für zukünftige Entwicklungen aufgezeigt.

2 Grundbegriffe des Qualitätsmanagements

2.1 Qualität

Der Begriff *Qualität* bezeichnet die realisierte Beschaffenheit eines materiellen oder immateriellen Gegenstands in Relation zu seiner (für einen bestimmten Zweck) geforderten Beschaffenheit (vgl. Geiger/Kotte 2007: 68). Qualitätsurteile sind also immer relativ zu vorher festgelegten Qualitätsforderungen. Solche Festlegungen können z.b. durch Normen und Standards, durch Hersteller und Dienstleister oder durch Kunden erfolgen. Die Normenreihe DIN EN ISO 9000ff. favorisiert einen stark kunden- und dienstleistungsorientierten Qualitätsbegriff. Qualität wird hier definiert als

> *Vermögen einer Gesamtheit inhärenter Merkmale eines Produkts, Systems oder Prozesses zur Erfüllung von Kundenanforderungen oder solcher anderer interessierter Parteien (Kaminske 2000: 15, zit. nach Budin 2007: 55).*

2.2 Qualitätssicherung vs. Qualitätskontrolle

Bei der Erzeugung von Qualität ist zwischen *Qualitätssicherung* (engl. *quality assurance*) und Qualitätskontrolle (engl. *quality control*) zu unterscheiden:

> *Quality assurance is defined as the steps and processes used to ensure a final quality product, while quality control focuses on the quality of the products produced by the process (Esselink 2000: 146).*

Ziel von Qualitätssicherung im Übersetzungsprozess ist die proaktive Fehlervermeidung. Qualitätssicherung findet daher in allen Phasen des Übersetzungsprozesses statt. Sie umfasst u.a. die Festlegung und Standardisierung von Arbeitsabläufen (Prozesssicherung) sowie die rechtzeitige sprachliche Unterstützung und Beratung aller an der Erbringung der Dienstleistung Übersetzung beteiligten Personen, z.B. durch die Bereitstellung von Stilrichtlinien und Glossaren.

Ziel von Qualitätskontrolle im Übersetzungsprozess ist die Fehlerbehebung durch sorgfältiges Lektorat (Produktkontrolle) sowie die Überwachung der Arbeitsabläufe (Prozesskontrolle). Im Unterschied zur Qualitätssicherung ist Qualitätskontrolle also eher reaktiv und bei umfangreichen Projekten mit vielen Zielsprachen und Dienstleistern zentral kaum noch durchführbar (Irmler/Hartwig 2000

3 Computergestützte Werkzeuge zur Qualitätssicherung, -kontrolle und -messung

3.1 Werkzeuge zur Produktsicherung und -kontrolle

Maschinelles Lektorat

Als *Maschinelles Lektorat* wird die computergestützte Überprüfung der korrekten Anwendung unternehmensspezifischer Terminologien und Stilrichtlinien bezeichnet wie sie z.b. in Redaktionsleitfäden und Unternehmensglossaren festgelegt sind, wobei darüber hinaus natürlich auch Rechtschreibung und allgemeine Grammatik einbezogen werden. Eine derartige Überprüfung kann entweder als klassisches Lektorat nach Abschluss der Erstellung eines (Ausgangs- oder Ziel-) Textes erfolgen oder unmittelbar während der Erstellung der Texte, wobei in letzterem Fall die Bezeichnung *Lektorat* dann unzutreffend ist.

Um eine solche terminologische und stilistische Kontrolle durchführen zu können, müssen die Systeme über ‚linguistisches Wissen' verfügen, d.h. sie müssen Wörter und Sätze morphologisch und syntaktisch analysieren können (Abb. 1). Systeme für das computergestützte Lektorat sind aufgrund des hohen Entwicklungsaufwands bislang nur für wenige Sprachen verfügbar. Die Erstellung der jeweiligen Redaktionsleitfäden kann – je nach Umfang des Leitfadens – sehr aufwändig und somit kostspielig sein. Die derzeit am Markt verfügbaren Programme – acrolinx IQ Suite (acrolinx GmbH, Berlin, www.acrolinx.com) und CLAT (Controlled Language Authoring Technology, IAI, Saarbrücken, www.iai-sb.de) – sind daher zwar sehr leistungsfähig, aber auch sehr teuer und derzeit nur für größere Unternehmen und Dienstleister interessant.

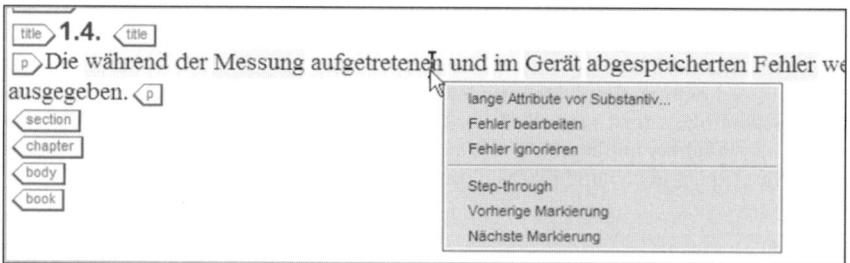

Abb. 1: Stilprüfung mit acrolinx IQ (Quelle: acrolinx GmbH)

Integrierte Qualitätssicherungskomponenten und eigenständige Qualitätssicherungsprogramme

Bereits seit mehreren Jahren stehen einfachere Softwareprodukte zur Qualitätssicherung und -kontrolle sowohl als eigenständige Programme – z.B. ErrorSpy (D.O.G. GmbH, Leonberg, www.dog-gmbh.com) oder QA Distiller (Yamagata Europe, Gent, www.qa-distiller.com) – als auch als integrierte Komponenten von TM-Systemen zur Verfügung. Diese Programme ermöglichen eine schnelle Kontrolle und Behebung typischer formaler Fehler wie z.B. fehlende oder überflüssige Leerzeichen, fehlende, überflüssige oder falsche Layout- und Struktur-Tags, Interpunktionsfehler, Orthographiefehler, fehlerhafte Zahlen, Maßeinheiten sowie Datums- und Zeitangaben. Ferner können Texte auf fehlende Übersetzungen sowie auf inkonsistente Übersetzungen bei identischen Ausgangssätzen geprüft werden.

Außerdem bieten die Tools eine einfache Terminologieprüfung, bei der die in den Übersetzungen verwendete Terminologie mit Wortlisten, Glossaren oder Terminologiedatenbanken verglichen wird. Sie verfügen jedoch nicht über sprachspezifisches ‚linguistisches Wissen‘, so dass syntaktisch-stilistische Prüfungen nur sehr begrenzt möglich sind und die Terminologieprüffunktionen nur bedingt eingesetzt werden können, da diese lediglich auf einem Ähnlichkeitsvergleich der Zeichenketten in den zu prüfenden Texten und den Referenzglossaren und -datenbanken beruhen (siehe das Beispiel in Abb. 2 und 3).

Die Programme werden in der Regel zur Produktkontrolle, also nach der Texterstellung, eingesetzt. Die Qualitätssicherungskomponenten von TM-Systemen können gewöhnlich aber auch interaktiv beim Schreiben verwendet werden.

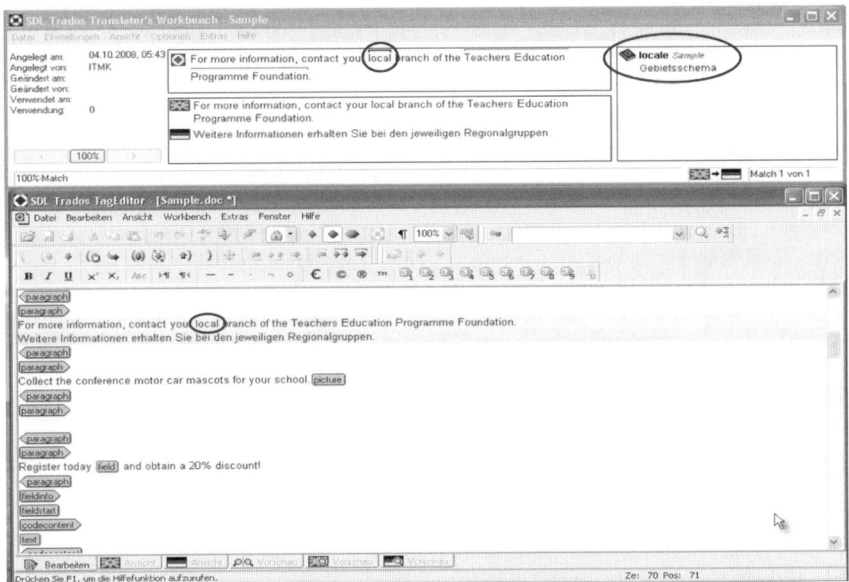

Abb. 2: Fehlerhafte Terminologieerkennung beim Übersetzen bedeutet zugleich …

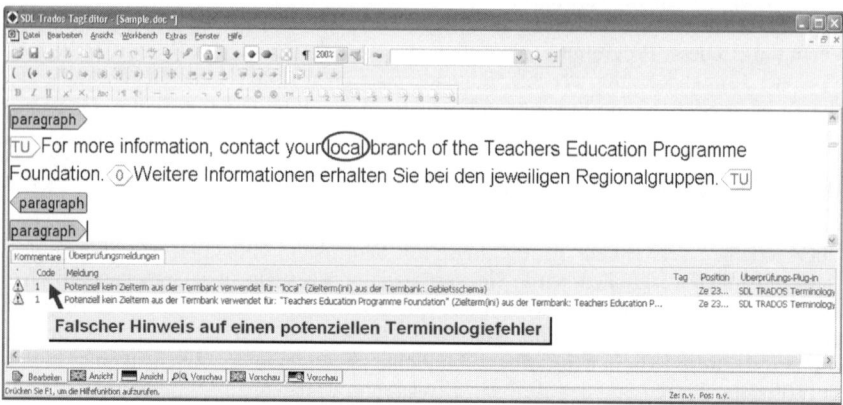

Abb. 3: ... fehlerhafte Terminolgieprüfung beim Lektorat

3.2 Werkzeuge zur Qualtitätsmessung und -bewertung

Neben Werkzeugen für die Suche verschiedener Fehler während oder nach der Erstellung von Texten gibt es auch Tools zur Qualitätsmessung und quantitativen Qualitätsbewertung (z.B. tekom QualiAssistent (Geidel 2007)). Einige Werkzeuge zur Qualitätssicherung und -kontrolle (z.B. ErrorSpy) bieten ebenfalls entsprechende Instrumente.

Die meisten kommerziellen Tools zur Messung von Übersetzungsqualität ermöglichen eine unterschiedliche Gewichtung der einzelnen Fehlertypen, wobei einige Programme und Ansätze fest vorgegebene Gewichtungsfaktoren benutzen, während andere benutzerdefinierte Werte erlauben. Die verwendeten Fehlermetriken unterscheiden sich deutlich in Umfang und Struktur (vgl. Reinke 2008). Eher ‚minimalistische' Konzepte versuchen, mit wenigen Fehlertypen auszukommen und listen diese lediglich auf, während andere Ansätze eine sehr viel größere Anzahl von Fehlertypen definieren und diese z.T. in verschiedene Fehlerklassen zusammenfassen. So beschränkt sich die amerikanische Norm SAE J2450 beispielsweise auf sieben Fehlertypen (SAE 2001). Demgegenüber verwendet das Evaluierungswerkzeug BlackJack (ITR Ltd., London, www.itrblackjack.com) 21 Fehlertypen (Abb. 4).

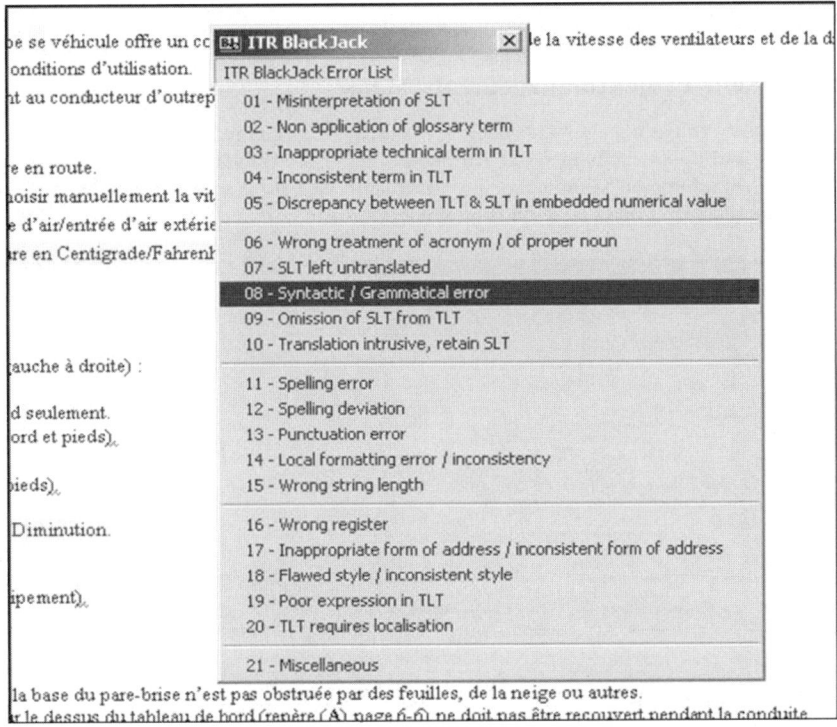

Abb. 4: Fehlerannotation mit ITR BlackJack (aus Onlinehilfe zu BlackJack)

Eine Beziehung zwischen den Ursachen und den Auswirkungen von Fehlern stellt eine bei DaimlerChrysler Language Services entwickelte Fehlertypologie her. Auf diese Weise entsteht eine sehr differenzierte zweidimensionale Matrix, bei der gleiche Fehlertypen je nach Ursache unterschiedlich stark gewichtet werden können. So kann z.b. ein orthografischer Fehler, bei dem es sich lediglich um einen formalen Fehler handelt, sehr viel schwächer bewertet werden als ein orthografischer Fehler, der zu einer Sinnentstellung führt (vgl. Mertin 2006).

3.3 Werkzeuge zur Prozesssicherung und -kontrolle

Zur Planung, Sicherung und Kontrolle von Übersetzungsabläufen nutzen Sprachdienstleister häufig die Funktionen universeller Projektmanagementsysteme oder setzen Eigenentwicklungen ein. Daneben bieten die Hersteller von TM-Systemen z.T. eigenständige Übersetzungsmanagementlösungen an (z.B. SDL TeamWorks) oder integrieren Übersetzungsmanagementkomponenten in ihre TM-Systeme (z.B. Across und SDL Synergy). Neben den TM-System-Herstellern bieten ferner einige Unternehmen systemunabhängige translationsspezifische Projektmanagementprogramme zur Verwaltung von Übersetzungs-, Lokalisierungs- und Dolmetschprojekten an, die am Markt zunehmend Verbreitung finden (z.B. LTC Worx oder Plunet BusinessManager).

Universelle Projektmanagementsysteme

Universelle Projektmanagementsysteme wie MS Project unterstützen vor allem die Planung und Überwachung von Terminen und Arbeitsabläufen. Die Anpassung solcher Programme an komplexere Projektabläufe ist häufig sehr aufwändig. Abb. 5 zeigt eine mit MS Project erstellte Projektvorgangsliste.

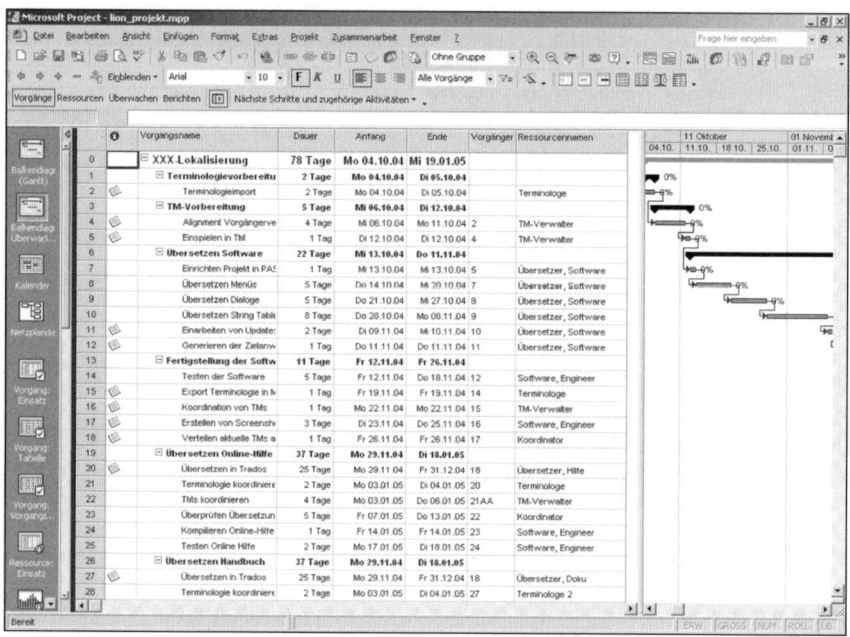

Abb. 5: Projektvorgangsliste mit Gantt-Diagramm in MS Project

Übersetzungsbezogene Ressourcen wie TM- und Terminologiedatenbanken lassen sich nicht ohne Weiteres einbinden, so dass auch Angebotserstellung und Rechnungsstellung nur mit größerem Aufwand automatisiert werden können.

Projektmanagementsysteme und -komponenten der Anbieter von Translation-Memory-Systemen

Schwerpunkt dieser Werkzeuge sind die Verwaltung von Übersetzungsressourcen (Datenressourcen: Translation Memorys, Terminologiedatenbanken, Dokumente, Grafiken etc.; Humanressourcen: Daten von Übersetzern, Lektoren, Dolmetschern etc.) sowie die Steuerung und Kontrolle übersetzungsspezifischer Arbeitsabläufe, wie sie z.B. in der DIN EN 15038 festgelegt sind (Abb. 6). Eine Anpassung an individuelle Übersetzungsabläufe ist dabei jedoch nicht bei allen Systemen möglich. Ebenso lassen sich Datenressourcen anderer TM-Systeme gewöhnlich nicht direkt einbinden.

Im Unterschied zu universellen Projektmanagementtools verfügen diese Werkzeuge in der Regel auch nicht über typische Planungsfunktionen (Erstellung von Projektvorgangslisten, -strukturplänen u.Ä.). Angebotserstellung und Rechnungsstellung werden in der Regel nicht unterstützt.

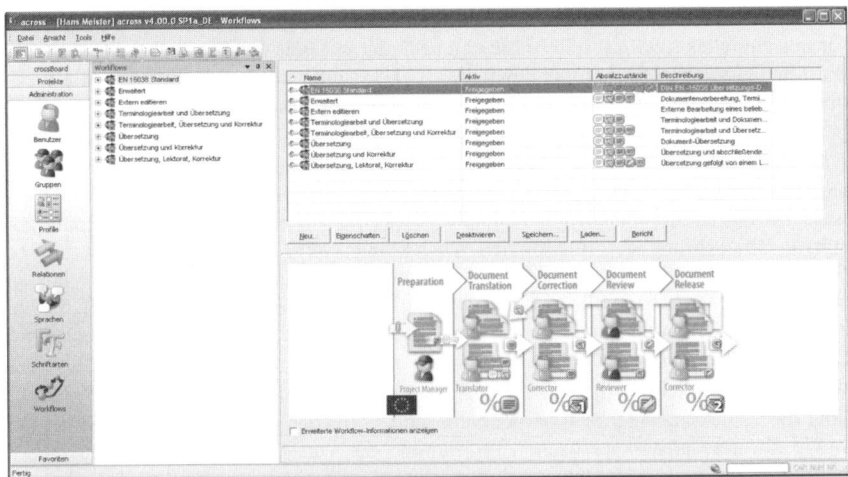

Abb. 6: Festlegung von Arbeitsabläufen in Across

Translationsspezifische Projektmanagementsoftware ohne Bindung an ein TM-System

Programme wie LTC Worx oder Plunet BusinessManager unterstützen vor allem die Planung und Überwachung von Terminen, den Versand und Empfang von Dateien sowie die Erstellung von Angeboten und Rechnungen. Wie die Systeme der TM-Anbieter verfügen sie in der Regel ebenfalls nicht über die typischen Planungsfunktionen universeller Projektmanagementsysteme.

Zumindest die leistungsfähigen Systeme können an individuelle, kunden- oder auftragsspezifische Übersetzungsabläufe angepasst werden. Datenressourcen verschiedener TM-Systeme lassen sich in zunehmendem Maße einbinden. So können häufig die Daten der statistischen Analysen verschiedener TM-Systeme für Kalkulation und Abrechnung weiterverwendet werden.

4 Fazit

Eine formale Qualitätssicherung und -kontrolle, die weitestgehend ohne ‚linguistisches Wissen' auskommt, ist mit vergleichsweise preiswerten Einzelwerkzeugen sowie mit den Qualitätssicherungskomponenten von TM-Systemen möglich.

Die Prüfung der Einhaltung unternehmensspezifischer Stilregeln erfordert demgegenüber umfangreicheres sprachspezifisches ‚linguistisches Wissen'. Systeme für das sogenannte maschinelle Lektorat sind daher bislang nur für wenige Sprachen verfügbar und (noch) sehr teuer.

Ähnliches gilt für eine leistungsfähige und zuverlässige Terminologieprüfung. Auch sie erfordert sprachspezifisches ‚linguistisches Wissen', um Wortartenmehrdeutigkeiten zu bewältigen und morphologisch unterschiedliche Formen desselben Wortes zu erkennen. Im Vergleich zu den aufwändigen Terminologieprüfverfahren der Systeme für maschinelles Lektorat liefern die eigenständigen Tools zur Qualitätssicherung und die Qualitätssicherungskomponenten der TM-Systeme eher unbefriedigende Ergebnisse mit einem hohen Anteil an falsch oder nicht erkannten Fehlern.

Werkzeuge zur computergestützten Qualitätssicherung und -kontrolle des Produkts *Übersetzung* lassen sich vor allem für die formale Qualitätssicherung einsetzen und sind bei der Überprüfung großer Textmengen ein gutes Hilfsmittel, um eine Vorauswahl für ein stichprobenartiges manuelles Lektorat zu treffen. An eine computergestützte Überprüfung der inhaltlichen Korrektheit von Texten ist in kommerziellen Systemen demgegenüber derzeit und auch mittelfristig nicht zu denken. Zu hoffen bleibt, dass Werkzeuge für das maschinelle Lektorat, wie acrolinx und CLAT, in Zukunft deutlich preiswerter werden und somit nicht nur großen Unternehmen und Sprachdienstleistern vorbehalten bleiben.

Im Hinblick auf Werkzeuge zur Prozesssicherung bleibt abzuwarten, welche Entwicklung die Projektmanagementkomponenten und -tools der Anbieter von TM-Systemen sowie die translationsspezifischen Programme der von TM-Systemen unabhängigen Hersteller wie LTC oder Plunet nehmen werden, und ob ein großer Teil der Übersetzungsdienstleister auch in Zukunft mit universellen Projektmanagementprogrammen oder Eigenentwicklungen arbeiten wird. Bei den TM-Systemen sollten Funktionen zur Erstellung kunden- und auftragsspezifischer Arbeitsabläufe jedenfalls nicht den teuren Client/Server-Anwendungen vorbehalten bleiben. Auch für Freiberufler, die in Teams und für unterschiedliche Kunden arbeiten, sind solche Funktionen von Interesse.

Bibliographie

ASTM (2006). *ASTM F 2575 – Standard Guide to Quality Assurance in Translation.* West Conshohocken (PA), USA: ASTM International.

Budin, Gerhard (2007). Entwicklung internationaler Normen im Bereich der Translationsqualität bei ISO/TC 37, In: Schmitt, Peter A.; Jüngst, Heike E. (Hrsg.), S. 54-65.

De Sutter, Natalie (2005). Automated translation quality control, in: *Communicator: The quarterly journal of the ISTC*, Summer 2005, S. 22-25.

Esselink, Bert (2000). *A Practical Guide to Localization.* Amsterdam / Philadelphia: John Benjamins.

Geidel, Michael (2007). „Neuer QualiAssistent unter der Lupe", in: *technische kommunikation*, 1/2007, S. 36ff.

Geiger, Walter / Kotte, Willi (2005). *Handbuch Qualität: Grundlagen und Elemente des Qualitätsmanagements: Systeme – Perspektiven.* Wiesbaden: Vieweg+Teubner.

Gerasimov, Andrei (2007). *Review of Translation Quality Assurance Software,* in: MultiLingual, Januar/Februar 2007.

Irmler, Ulrike / Hartwig, Doris (2000). „Sprachliche Qualität im lokalisierten Softwareprodukt: Kriterien und Vorgehensweisen der Qualitätssicherung", in: Schmitz, Klaus-Dirk / Wahle, Kirsten (Hrsg.). *Softwarelokalisierung.* Tübingen: Stauffenburg, S. 89-100.

Kaminske, Gerd (2000). Qualitätsmanagement, in: Hennig, Jörg / Tjarks-Sobhani, Marita (Hrsg.). *Qualitätssicherung von technischer Dokumentation.* Lübeck: Schmidt-Römhild, S. 11-25.

Kingscott, Geoffrey (2007). Translation quality assessment, in: Schmitt, Peter A. / Jüngst, Heike E. (Hrsg.), S. 317-325.

Kurz, Christopher (2007). Translation Quality Management at SDL International, in: Schmitt, Peter A. / Jüngst, Heike E. (Hrsg.), S. 344-350.

Mertin, Elvira (2006). *Prozessorientiertes Qualitätsmanagement im Dienstleistungsbereich Übersetzen.* Frankfurt am Main et al.: Peter Lang.

Reinke, Uwe (2008). „Some reflections on using TM systems for creating learner translator corpora", in: Dimitriu, Rodica / Freigang, Karl-Heinz: *Translation Technology in Translation Classes.* Iaşi: Institutul European, S. 133-148

SAE (2001). *SAE J2450 – Translation Quality Metric.* Warrendale (USA): Society of Automotive Engineers

Schmitt, Peter A. / Jüngst, Heike E. (Hrsg.) (2007). *Translationsqualität.* Frankfurt am Main et al.: Peter Lang.

Vollmar, Gabriele (2007). Damit die Qualität nicht in der Übersetzungsflut untergeht. Ein Modell für eine pragmatische Qualitätssicherung bei Übersetzungsprojekten, in: Schmitt, Peter A. / Jüngst, Heike E. (Hrsg.), 626-633.

Zerfass, Angelika (2007). Terminologieprüfung, in: *eDITion,* 2/2007, S. 18-20.

Challenges of automation in translation quality management

Dr. François Massion

Geschäftsführer D.O.G. Dokumentation ohne Grenzen GmbH

francois.massion@dog-gmbh.de

1 Summary

In view of the increasing volumes of documents and of the number of languages required, the need to automate the quality assurance process for translations has risen sharply. At large companies or institutions hundreds or even thousands of pages are churned out daily in 20 and more languages. Most are still produced by human translators working with CAT systems (computer-aided Translation, CAT). Some are already produced with machine translation technologies. Quite often these organizations must deliver high-quality translations within a very tight delivery schedule. Often, time and budget do not allow for a meticulous check of all quality aspects. This sounds like squaring the circle.

Automated quality control is the solution. It is by no means a replacement for the work of a reviser. But it can relieve him from tedious tasks and create more capacity for quality assurance.

2 Current situation and needs

Several factors have led in the last decade to a substantial increase in the volume of translated documentation. The globalization of the world economy is coupled with the need to exchange information and documentation in all languages. The widening of the EU and the enforcement of regulations such as the Machinery Directive 98/37/EC has had a strong impact on the demand for translations.

As more and more players enter the global marketplace, the pace of innovation accelerates. It takes now much lesser time than before to create and market a new product and the related documentation needs to be updated in much shorter time periods. In addition, many companies develop a wider variety of products to meet the individual needs of their customers. This all results in a significant increase in the demand for high-quality translations in all major business languages.

At the same time competition has forced companies to control costs and look for cost-saving measures and technologies. The same holds true for institutions or associations which cannot count on unlimited budgets.

The challenge is thus to produce more multilingual documentation at much lower costs and without delay. This is why content management technologies (CMS) have known so much success recently. These technologies manage information units and combine them to create various documentations for different products and audiences.

The same content is reused in several documents and combined with other content which is possibly written by different authors at different periods of time. There is thus a need to improve the quality and consistency of the source content in order to ensure the publication via CMS of high quality and consistent documents. So far there are several technologies on the market which help achieve this goal. In addition guidelines for authors, terminology management systems and the use of controlled language contribute to the creation of consistent source documents.

On the translation side translation memory technologies help deal with the increased volumes by reusing existing translations and integrating terminology modules. Without them it wouldn't have been possible to cope with the overall demand for translations. Some large companies and institutions have gone further and combine CAT technologies with machine translation (MT) technologies to further reduce costs or simply be able to translate large volumes of information in a timely manner.

Due to their mode of operation, these technologies present some dangers despite all positive aspects they offer. They save small units (segments, phrases) with no or little context. Their segmentation rules can in some case lead to the saving of partial phrases which may for linguistic reasons be associated with the wrong segment in the target language. The fuzzy match function can sometimes induce the translator to confirm a wrong translation, transforming it into a correct match for the next reuse.

There is therefore a need to check accurately the quality of the translation before releasing a final version. The problem is, however, that it would just take too much time and be too costly to check all documents line by line. A reviser can check on average about 8,000 – 10,000 words per day. The costs of reviewing all translations based on an hourly rate of 50 Euro/$ would thus amount to 0.05 cents per word. In addition reviewers would be needed for 20 or more languages. Beside the cost factor there is a time factor. Many publications are needed within a short period of time. Some documents have to be submitted at a fixed date.

In view of this the current practice in several companies has been to make a thorough check only for certain types of documents and to do a superficial or spot check on the remaining translations.

Another weakness of the current practice in many companies and institutions is the fact that no or little substantiated feedback is given to translators. It is just too time-consuming to create error reports documenting precisely what was wrongly translated. This is, however, a necessity if the aim is to educate the translator and thus achieve better quality translations in the long run.

Since 2003 there is a software solution for computer-aided quality assurance of translations. The first independent product on the market, ErrorSpy has been followed by a few other products, either as stand-alone applications or as add-ons to existing translation memory technologies.

3 Quality checks

What can be expected from the automation of quality assurance for translations? First we need to have a clear view of the possibilities and limitations of computer-aided quality assurance technologies. There are areas in which such technologies perform better than human revisers and other areas where this is inversely the case. Every time a purely formal check is required, computer-aided systems perform better because they can perform the task extremely fast at the press of a button and do not overlook any words or sentences. This is the case for example for the following types of checks:

- Terminology check: Check if the approved terminology has been used consistently.

- Consistency check: Check if the same sentences are translated the same way.

- Numbers check: Check if numbers and the format of numbers are correct (e.g. 1,23 → 1.23).

- Completeness check: Check if everything has been translated.

- Tag check: Check if tags have been deleted or damaged or if the tag order is unchanged.

- Typography check: Check if the correct typography is used in the target language.

Other categories of checks such as the context-dependant selection of the right terminology or the recognition of mistranslations require human intelligence and can therefore only be performed successfully by revisers.

There is of course a grey area between intelligent and unintelligent checks and as algorithms and statistical data improve, computer-aided quality assurance technologies will learn to recognize sophisticated errors more reliably.

4   Workflows with automated quality assurance

Computer-aided quality assurance systems can either be used ad hoc to expedite the quality assurance of a translation project or they can be part of a comprehensive quality management system. Such systems may have basically 3 complementary components:

1. Interactive and computer-aided quality assurance of projects
2. Automated quality assurance of projects
3. Monitoring and evaluation of consolidated quality results

Interactive and computer-aided quality assurance of projects is not the subject of this article. Basically, the quality assurance software generates a list of possible errors and the reviser goes one by one through this list of errors and decides individually on their status as genuine error or wrong error message. Via a fine tuning of the configuration of checks and a learning function, the initial number of wrongly reported errors can be reduced significantly. In addition a reviser or translation project manager can use interactive quality assurance to generate a report with comments and questions to be sent back to the translator for further processing.

Automated quality assurance can be implemented at the various milestones of a project. Some possible milestones are:

- Checking the quality of translation memories or project memories before the translation starts.
- Checking the quality of the translation when it is completed.
- Checking the quality of the translation when it has been reviewed by a reviser.

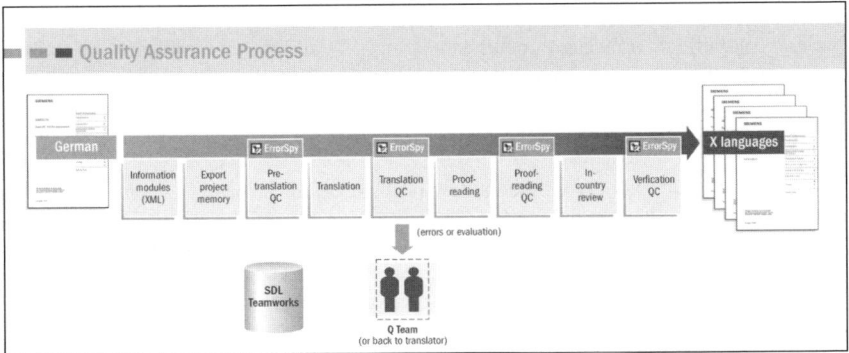

Fig. 1: Example of automated quality assurance workflow at Siemens

The checks are performed with standard configurations in order to ensure consistency and reproducibility of results. In order to enable workflow systems to take certain actions (sending an automated message, returning the translation to the translator etc.) the automated quality check should not only produce a list of errors but should also be able to generate some metrics. Depending on the number of error points and on the way thresholds have been defined, the system will be able to take appropriate actions. This functionality is supported by ErrorSpy which uses a system of number of errors combined with a weighting factor for each error category. This type of metrics is borrowed from the SAE J2450 quality metrics on translations.

5   Implementing automatic corrections

Automatic corrections are a "hot" topic for linguists. A language is a sophisticated living organism with a highly complex system of rules … and exceptions. Automatic corrections can in many cases improve the existing translation for the worse.

Automatic corrections should thus be used very scarcely and only in situations where the decision is unambiguous. There are, however, unequivocal situations as e.g. some typographical corrections, some corrections of numbers or some corrections of consistency errors. If e.g. one variant of a translation occurs 5 times and the other 2 times, the rule may be that the most frequent variant is chosen. With regard to terminology corrections ErrorSpy has implemented an option for the correction of tagged or marked terms as it may be the case with user interface elements. Let's take for example the German verb "beenden". As a normal verb in a sentence it may be translated with various English verbs such as "to complete", "to close", "to finish", etc. As a UI expression it is generally translated with "exit" (a program). As such it doesn't need to be conjugated and can quite safely be automatically replaced. This function is particularly useful when the user documentation is translated while programmers are still making last changes to the program. The prerequisite for automated corrections is that they are logged and can always be undone.

The philosophy behind automatic corrections is that even if they can only apply to a small portion of reported errors, it is still better to correct automatically 5 or 10% of the errors than to correct none of these errors. The advantage is still substantial when the daily volume of translated documents is high. In addition the tools can be trained and learn from wrong or right decisions on reported errors.

6   Quality monitoring

At the end of 2008 D.O.G. released a new product called ErrorSpy Quality Suite. It is so far a unique product on the market for the monitoring and the evaluation of consolidated quality results. For each translation project a quality evaluation report is generated and saved in a database. This report contains general administrative data and metrics about the number of errors and error points for different error categories. This is the reservoir from which a variety of assessments can be generated such as:

- Average quality by period
- Average quality by supplier
- Average quality by language
- Most frequent types of errors

Based on this information the Quality Manager can look at the areas where action is needed, keep track of the efficiency of his decisions and better identify the causes of quality problems.

7   Perspective & goals

A great deal of progress has been achieved since ErrorSpy was first released in 2003. It is now possible to check automatically or interactively large volumes of translations, to relieve revisers of routine tasks and put them in a position to focus on errors of understanding. It is possible to generate error reports at the press of a button and to evaluate the quality of translation in an objective and reproducible way. In addition individual quality results can be consolidated and analyzed to help manage the quality of an organization, a department and/or suppliers over longer periods of time.

There are still interesting and demanding challenges ahead. One is to add progressively linguistic intelligence to the quality checks in order to further reduce the noise level in reported errors and to improve the efficiency of term recognition ("Sie haben gut zusammengearbeitet" → Term: "zusammenarbeiten"). The next challenge is to improve the learning function by enabling the software to recognize automatically some patterns in the reported errors.

Additional challenges are the integration of quality assurance software in various platforms and environments to enable virtual workgroups scattered around the globe to produce together high-quality multilingual documentation.

With the increased use of machine translation technologies another challenge will be measuring of the quality of machine translation output, especially in cases where a combination of CAT and MT technologies is used to translate documents.

Last but not least a challenge will be the definition of commonly accepted metric standards and methods for the evaluation of human and machine translation.

Geheimnisschutz und Datenschutz im globalisierten Übersetzungsmarkt

Manuel Cebulla

LL.M. (BDÜ, BvD)
G & C Datenschutzpartner Uwe Göritz und Manuel Cebulla GbR

cebulla@guc-dsp.de

1 Einleitung

Die Zahl international operierender Übersetzungsunternehmen wächst, Übersetzungsleistungen werden vermehrt weltweit eingekauft und verkauft, die Übersetzer arbeiten in virtuellen Teams über Staatengrenzen hinweg und der zunehmende Einsatz von speziellen Datenverarbeitungsprogrammen erleichtert dies erheblich. Damit stellen sich für alle am Übersetzungsprozess Beteiligten neue Herausforderungen. Fragen des Schutzes von Privat- und Unternehmensgeheimnissen sowie des Datenschutzes wurden bislang indes nur allenfalls am Rande in die Planung sowie in die technische und organisatorische Umsetzung mit einbezogen.

2 Was gilt es zu schützen und warum?

Übersetzer kommen mit den unterschiedlichsten Informationen ihrer Kunden oder Dritter in Berührung. Besonders schützenswerte Güter sind private Geheimnisse, d.h. Informationen aus dem privaten Lebens- und Persönlichkeitsbereich, Betriebs- und Geschäftsgeheimnisse sowie Staatsgeheimnisse.

Gleichermaßen gilt es, das allgemeine Persönlichkeitsrecht zu achten. Zu diesem Zwecke gibt es den Datenschutz, der der Verhinderung missbräuchlicher Verwendung der Daten natürlicher Personen dient. In Sonderbereichen wie dem Sozial- und dem Postrecht umfasst der Datenschutz auch Daten von juristischen Personen.

2.1 Schutz durch das Strafrecht

Damit diese Geheimnisse nicht öffentlich gemacht werden, sieht das Strafrecht entsprechende Sanktionen vor, geregelt in den §§ 93 ff. StGB für Staatsgeheimnisse und in § 203 StGB und anderen Normen für Privat- und Unternehmensgeheimnisse. Eine Strafbarkeit kann schon dann gegeben sein, wenn man ein Geheimnis fahrlässig an einen Unbefugten gelangen lässt oder einem Dritten ungewollt die Möglichkeit der Kenntnisnahme verschafft (ausführlich: Cebulla 2007).

Bei berufsspezifischer Zusammenarbeit mit Kollegen wie der Weitergabe der Übersetzung zum Korrekturlesen liegt in der Regel noch keine Offenbarung im Sinne des Strafrechts vor, sofern es sich um namentlich bekannte oder mit dem Übersetzer persönlich verbundene Personen handelt und diese die Informationen ihrerseits nicht an Andere weitergeben.

2.2 Schutz durch das Datenschutzrecht

Anders im Datenschutzrecht: Dort kann eine Ahndbarkeit bereits gegeben sein, wenn die personenbezogenen Daten auch nur an eine beliebige andere Person weitergegeben werden oder die Einsichtnahme oder des Abrufen von Daten durch einen Dritten ermöglicht wird.

Neben dem Schutz der personenbezogenen Daten durch die Ordnungswidrigkeiten- und Straftatbestände der §§ 43, 44 Bundesdatenschutzgesetz eröffnet das Datenschutzrecht den in ihren Rechten verletzten Betroffenen die Möglichkeit, vom Verletzer Schadensersatz zu fordern. Zudem kann die zuständige Aufsichtsbehörde die weitere Datenverarbeitung untersagen.

2.3 Weiterer zivilrechtlicher Schutz

Schadensersatz- und Unterlassungsansprüche können sich auch dann ergeben, wenn der Sprachmittler gegen einzelvertraglich vereinbarte oder im Rahmen von Allgemeinen Geschäftsbedingungen in den Vertrag einbezogene Geheimhaltungspflichten verstößt.

Zudem gilt ganz allgemeinen – auch ohne explizite Nennung im Vertrag – gemäß § 241 BGB, dass jeder Vertragspartner zur Rücksicht auf die Rechte, Rechtsgüter und Interessen des anderen Vertragspartners verpflichtet ist. Zu diesen Rücksichtnahmepflichten gehört auch der Schutz von Geheimnissen. Bei der Verletzung der Pflicht zu Verschwiegenheit und Geheimhaltung kann nach § 280 BGB ein Anspruch auf Schadensersatz geltend gemacht werden.

Eine Schadensersatzpflicht kann sich auch nach § 823 BGB aus unerlaubter Handlung ergeben, wenn eine Person in ihrem allgemeinen Persönlichkeitsrecht verletzt wird oder Unternehmen z.B. im Bereich von Patenten geschädigt werden.

2.4 Schutz durch Berufsrecht, Standesrecht und Normen

Verschwiegenheitspflichten für Sprachmittler und Sorgfaltspflichten im Umgang mit den ihnen anvertrauten Texten finden sich in den Dolmetschergesetzen einiger Bundesländer für öffentlich bestellte, allgemein beeidigte und ermächtigte Sprachmittler.

Für die Mitglieder des BDÜ schreibt die Berufs- und Ehrenordnung (BDÜ 2007, § 5) eine Verschwiegenheitspflicht vor, die sich auf alles erstreckt, was ihnen in Ausübung ihrer Berufe anvertraut worden oder ihnen bei Gelegenheit der Berufsausübung bekannt geworden ist, wobei diese Pflichten auch über die Beendigung des Auftragsverhältnisses hinaus und auch gegenüber demjenigen bestehen, dem die betreffende Tatsache bereits von anderer Seite mitgeteilt worden ist.

Die seit August 2006 nicht mehr geltende DIN Norm 2345 widmete einen eigenen Punkt der Geheimhaltung. Die aktuelle DIN EN 15038 bleibt dahinter zurück. Vom Übersetzungsdienstleister wird im Rahmen der „technischen Ressourcen" verlangt, dass er „die für die ordnungsgemäße Ausführung von Übersetzungsprojekten erforderlichen technischen Einrichtungen einschließlich des sicheren und vertraulichen Handlings, der Speicherung, Bereitstellung, Archivierung und Entsorgung von Dokumenten und Daten" sicherstellen muss (DIN 2006, Punkt 3.3 a).

3 Bedrohungen

Sowohl personenbezogene Daten als auch Geheimnisse unterschiedlichster Art sind wie die gesamte bei Sprachmittlern zum Einsatz kommende Informations- und Kommunikationstechnologie vielfältigen Gefahren ausgesetzt. Neben den üblichen kriminellen Angriffen mit Schadprogrammen, gegen die sich jeder Computernutzer schützen muss, stellen Sprachmittler ein interessantes Ziel für indirekte Wirtschaftsspionage und Konkurrenzausspähung dar.

Wirtschaftsspionage ist die staatlich gelenkte oder gestützte, von ausländischen Nachrichtendiensten ausgehende Ausforschung von Wirtschaftsunternehmen. Der Bundesverfassungsschutz nennt beispielhaft russische und chinesische Geheimdienste (BfV 2008, S. 10). Mit den ausspionierten Informationen werden Unternehmen des eigenen Landes mit Know-how versorgt oder mit Informationen zu aktuellen Teilnahmen an Ausschreibungen. Konkurrenzausspähung hingegen ist die Ausforschung eines Unternehmens durch einen Wettbewerber.

Ein weiterer Bereich, in dem Übersetzer anhand der vielen von ihnen verarbeiteten personenbezogenen Daten Ziel von Ausspähung sein können, ist der sogenannte Identitätsdiebstahl. Unter Benutzung fremder persönlicher Angaben werden Straftaten begangen. Diese Art der Gefährdung steigt laut Bundesamt für Sicherheit in der Informationstechnik derzeit erheblich (BSI 2009, S. 28).

In diesem Zusammenhang ist auch das Social Engineering zu nennen: Entweder werden Übersetzer – ohne es zu bemerken – über Angelegenheiten ihrer Übersetzungskunden ausgehorcht, oder die bei Übersetzern unbefugt erlangten personenbezogenen oder geschäftlichen Daten können genutzt werden für Social-Engineering-

Angriffe auf Mitarbeiter von Wirtschaftsunternehmen, Forschungsinstitutionen oder staatlichen Stellen.

Bedrohungen können sich auch an anderer Stelle ergeben. Bestimmte Multifunktions-geräte – also Geräte mit Drucker, Fax, Scanner in einem –, senden unbemerkt Daten an Server. Anwender von Standardsoftware oder Übersetzungssoftware wissen nicht, was diese Programme neben den gewünschten Funktionalitäten auf den Rechnern treiben und an wen sie welche Daten weitergeben.

Suchmaschinenbetreiber oder ungebetene Mitleser der Rechercheaktivitäten können sich anhand der vom Übersetzer eingegebenen Suchbegriffe ein Bild davon machen, in welchem Bereich oder gar für welchen Kunden der Übersetzer gerade übersetzt.

Dass es heutzutage ein Leichtes ist, E-Mails mitzulesen oder Trojaner zum Ausspähen von Daten einzusetzen, dessen sollten sich Übersetzer immer bewusst sein. Aber auch ohne kriminelle Eingriffe kann es für den Kunden und damit auch für den Übersetzer folgenreich sein, wenn Telefaxe oder E-Mails an die falsche Adresse geschickt werden, wenn Kundeninformationen beim lauten Handytelefonat im Zug öffentlich gemacht werden, gedruckte Texte ungeschreddert im Hausmüll landen etc.

Bezüglich aller hier genannten Bedrohungen bedarf es in der Übersetzungsbranche gesteigerter Sensibilität und Achtsamkeit und angemessener technischer und organisa-torischer Maßnahmen, um die Vertraulichkeit, Integrität und Verfügbarkeit der Daten bzw. Informationen zu gewährleisten.

4   Aktuelle Lage in der Sprachmittlungsbranche

Die aktuelle Lage in der Sprachmittlungsbranche sieht indes wohl anders aus: Über-setzungen liegen unverschlüsselt auf Rechnern. Mit denselben Rechnern wird im Internet gesurft. Die Schutzmaßnahmen sind mäßig. Übersetzungen werden per unverschlüsselter E-Mail hin- und hergeschickt, größere Dateien über fremde FTP-Server. Daten werden zumeist auch unverschlüsselt auf USB-Sticks, Laptops, CD-ROMs umhergetragen und gehen in der Übersetzungsbranche sicherlich genauso häufig verloren wie in anderen Bereichen.

Eine neue Entwicklung ist, dass nicht nur Tausende von E-Mails mitsamt den ange-hängten Ausgangstexten und Übersetzungen auf Servern irgendwo auf der Welt schlummern und auch Backups auf externe Server ausgelagert werden, sondern dass Übersetzer immer häufiger online mit externen Programmen arbeiten. Dadurch wird es für die Übersetzer zunehmend unmöglich, Herr über die ihnen anvertrauten Daten zu bleiben.

Es ist an der Zeit, dass auch die Hersteller von Übersetzungssoftware dem Thema Geheimnis- und Datenschutz einen seiner Wichtigkeit entsprechenden Platz zuweisen. Ich stehe hier gerne beratend zur Verfügung.

Neben dem erforderlichen technischen Schutz der Daten ist gerade in Anbetracht der Globalisierung der Übersetzungsbranche eine weitere Frage von zentraler Bedeutung: Dürfen Ausgangstexte und Übersetzungen über staatliche Grenzen hinweg transferiert werden?

5 Datenschutzrechtliche Betrachtung

Hier soll nicht die Rechtslage für innerdeutsche Übersetzungsprozesse erörtert werden. Nur soviel: Ohne eine erlaubende oder verpflichtende Rechtsgrundlage oder die informierte, bewusste Einwilligung des Betroffenen, die in der Regel schriftlich erteilt werden muss, dürfen Übersetzungsdienstleister, d.h. Übersetzer oder Übersetzungsbüros nicht mit den Daten Anderer umgehen.

Unter den Umgang mit personenbezogenen Daten fällt auch die Übermittlung von Daten, d.h. das Bekanntgeben gespeicherter oder durch Datenverarbeitung gewonnener personenbezogener Daten an einen Dritten. Auch hierfür bedarf es einer Rechtsgrundlage oder Einwilligung.

Der Umgang der Übersetzer mit personenbezogenen Daten in den Ausgangs- und Zieltexten ist als Auftragsdatenverarbeitung anzusehen. Bei der Verarbeitung von Daten im Auftrag sieht § 11 BDSG – sofern bestimmte Voraussetzungen von Auftraggeber und Auftragnehmer erfüllt sind – eine Erleichterung insofern vor, als dass die Weitergabe von Daten zwischen Auftraggeber und Auftragnehmer keine Übermittlung im datenschutzrechtlichen Sinne darstellt und somit in der Regel eher unproblematisch ist.

5.1 Datenweitergabe innerhalb des Europäischen Wirtschaftsraumes

Sowohl bei der Übermittlung an Dritte als auch im Falle der Auftragsdatenverarbeitung ist die Weitergabe von Daten an Personen oder Stellen in Vertragsstaaten des Europäischen Wirtschaftsraumes (EWR) – das sind die Mitgliedstaaten der Europäischen Union sowie Liechtenstein und Norwegen – grundsätzlich uneingeschränkt möglich, da davon ausgegangen wird, dass in diesen Staaten ein einheitlich hohes datenschutzrechtliches Niveau herrscht. Die Zulässigkeit der Weitergabe richtet sich nach den auch innerhalb Deutschlands geltenden Regeln.

Eine für Übersetzer relevante Ausnahme ergibt sich aus § 4b BDSG: Handelt es sich um Übersetzungen im Auftrag von Sicherheits- oder Strafverfolgungsbehörden im EWR-Ausland, so wird die Weitergabe der Texte immer wie eine Übermittlung in Drittstaaten gehandhabt.

5.2 Datenweitergabe in Drittstaaten

Die Übermittlung von Daten in Staaten außerhalb des EWR (Drittstaaten) muss grundsätzlich unterbleiben, soweit der Betroffene ein schutzwürdiges Interesse am Ausschluss der Übermittlung hat.

Das ist insbesondere dann der Fall, wenn im Zielland ein angemessenes Datenschutzniveau nicht gewährleistet ist, wovon grundsätzlich bei allen Drittstaaten ausgegangen wird. Für einige Drittländer hat die EU-Kommission indes festgestellt, dass dort ein angemessenes Datenschutzniveau besteht, das sind z.B. Kanada und die Schweiz. Die USA gelten hingegen als unsicheres Drittland. Allerdings sind solche Stellen in den USA taugliche Empfänger von Datenübermittlungen, die sich den „Safe Harbor Principles" angeschlossen haben.

Für Übermittlungen in Drittländer, die nicht von der EU-Kommission als sicher eingestuft worden sind bzw. an Stellen oder Personen in den USA, die nicht die Safe Harbor Principles einhalten, gilt, dass die Daten nur übermittelt werden können, wenn die übermittelnde Stelle sicherstellt (z.B. vertraglich oder bei Filialen durch verbindliche Unternehmensregelungen), dass die Empfänger ein angemessenes Datenschutzniveau einhalten.

Bei der Auftragsdatenverarbeitung im Drittland geht das Datenschutzrecht davon aus, dass die Privilegierung, die die Auftragsdatenverarbeitung innerhalb des EWR bietet, bei der Datenweitergabe in Drittländer nicht greift, sodass der in der EU beheimatete Auftraggeber in jedem Fall die Zulässigkeit der Weitergabe durch besondere Maßnahmen beispielsweise vertraglicher Art herstellen muss.

Sitzt indes der Auftraggeber im Drittland und die Daten werden in der EU bzw. im EWR verarbeitet und dann ins Drittland zurückgegeben, dann ist die Weitergabe vom Auftragnehmer an den Auftraggeber hingegen keine Übermittlung. Allerdings ist der Auftragnehmer für die von ihm durchgeführte Datenverarbeitung verantwortlich, während normalerweise die Verantwortung bei der Auftragsdatenverarbeitung beim Auftraggeber liegt.

Den Auftragnehmer trifft in diesem Falle die Pflicht zur materiellen Plausibilitätsprüfung bezüglich seines Umgangs mit den Daten des Auftraggebers. Verarbeitungen, die eindeutig gegen den deutschen Ordre public verstoßen (z. B. bei Menschenrechtsverletzungen), sind unzulässig, auch wenn die Daten keinerlei Bezug zu EU oder EWR aufweisen. Auf eine solche Unvereinbarkeit muss der Auftragnehmer den Auftraggeber hinweisen und gegebenenfalls die Datenschutzaufsichtsbehörde einschalten und widrigstenfalls die weitere Ausführung des Auftrages einstellen.

Daten können ohne eine besondere Rechtsgrundlage oder besondere Maßnahmen auch dann an andere Stellen im EWR-Ausland oder in Drittstaaten weitergegeben oder übermittelt werden, wenn der Betroffene (das ist die Person, deren Daten betroffen sind) zuvor in die Weitergabe eingewilligt hat. Dann muss er aber hinreichend über Empfänger, Zielland und etwaige Risiken wie den möglichen Zugriff durch dortige Behörden informiert werden.

6 Lösungsvorschläge

Übersetzungsdienstleister (Sprachmittler und Übersetzungsagenturen) müssen die Grundprinzipien des Datenschutzes beachten: Kein Umgang mit fremden Daten ohne eine Rechtsgrundlage oder eine gesetzeskonforme Einwilligung des Betroffenen; keine Verwendung der Daten zu anderen Zwecken als der Anfertigung der Übersetzung; keine unbefugte Weitergabe an Andere; Schutz von Daten vor Verletzung der Vertraulichkeit (ausführlicher: Cebulla 2008). Zu beachten ist auch der wichtige Grundsatz der Datenvermeidung: Es dürfen nur die Daten gespeichert werden, die wirklich für die Zweckerfüllung erforderlich sind; Daten, die nicht mehr erforderlich sind, müssen gelöscht werden.

Da die Anfertigung von Übersetzungen im Auftrag (also nicht durch eigene Angestellte) Auftragsdatenverarbeitung ist, müssen die diesbezüglichen gesetzlichen Regelungen eingehalten werden. Dazu gehört die sorgfältige Auswahl und Kontrolle der

Auftragnehmer und die schriftliche Fixierung der Anforderungen bzw. Maßnahmen für den Datenschutz.

Bei der Auftragsdatenverarbeitung über die Grenzen des EWR hinweg – das ist auch dann der Fall, wenn ein Server in einem Nicht-EWR-Staat zur Speicherung oder als Plattform genutzt wird, auf der Übersetzungsprogramme laufen – , sind die oben angedeuteten Besonderheiten zu beachten.

Personenbezogene Daten und andere schützenswerte Geheimnisse sollten immer sicher verschlüsselt sein. Dasselbe gilt auch für Daten auf mobilen Speichermedien und beim Versand per Internet. Es ist davon abzuraten, die Verschlüsselungsprogramme zu verwenden, die von den Anbietern stammen, bei denen man Daten speichert oder deren Übersetzungswerkzeuge man verwendet. Denn man kann nicht davon ausgehen, dass sie keine „werksseitig eingebaute Hintertür" für den Anbieter selbst oder für einen Dritten haben.

Wenn Übersetzer die Ausgangstexte unverschlüsselt erhalten und ihre Übersetzungen auch unverschlüsselt an die Kunden senden, sollten sie vertraglich vereinbaren, dass der Auftraggeber den Übersetzer von jeglicher Haftung für alle mit der Übersendung verbundenen Risiken freistellt und der Übersetzer nicht verpflichtet ist, die Übersetzung verschlüsselt an den Auftraggeber zurückzusenden, wenn dieser den Ausgangstext unverschlüsselt an den Übersetzer gesendet hat.

Bei Übersetzungsverträgen mit einer die nationalen Grenzen überschreitenden Komponente muss je nach Fallkonstellation im Einzelfall geprüft werden, ob Verarbeitungs- oder Weitergabeverbote aufgrund ausländischer Rechtsnormen zum Tragen kommen bzw. die Übersetzung oder Übersendung von bestimmten Geheimnissen unzulässig ist. Den ausländischen Auftraggeber trifft hier die Pflicht, den Übersetzer über solche Regelungen in Kenntnis zu setzen. Auch hier sollte zusätzlich vereinbart werden, dass der Auftraggeber den Auftragnehmer von jeder diesbezüglichen Haftung freistellt. Im Gegenzug ist der Auftragnehmer verpflichtet, dem Auftraggeber anzuzeigen, ob, wo und in welcher Weise von ihm Unterauftragnehmer eingesetzt werden.

Zum Schutze von vertraulichen Informationen bietet es sich schließlich an, in die Übersetzungsverträge Vertragsstrafen für nachweisbare Vertraulichkeitsverletzungen aufzunehmen. Sprachmittler sollten es sich allerdings auch selbst zur Pflicht machen, immer auf die Interessen und Rechte ihrer Kunden und der Betroffenen zu achten. Ihre berufsethische Pflicht zur Verschwiegenheit sollten sie möglichst auf alle Tatsachen erstrecken, die ihnen bekannt werden, auch zum eigenen Schutze, da es für sie nicht immer sofort ersichtlich ist, bei welcher Information es sich bereits um ein Geheimnis handelt.

Bibliographie

BDÜ (2007). *Berufs- und Ehrenordnung (Grundsätze des Standesrechts), Fassung vom 27. 10. 2007.* Im Internet unter: www.bdue.de / Wir über uns / Regularien / Berufs- und Ehrenordnung.

BfV Bundesamt für Verfassungsschutz für die Verfassungsschutzbehörden in Bund und Ländern (2008). *Wirtschaftsspionage. Risiko für Ihr Unternehmen.* Köln.

BSI Bundesamt für Sicherheit in der Informationstechnik (2009). *Die Lage der IT-Sicherheit in Deutschland*. Bonn.

Cebulla, M. (2007). *Sprachmittlerstrafrecht. Die Strafrechtliche Verantwortlichkeit der Dolmetscher und Übersetzer*. Berlin: Wissenschaftlicher Verlag Berlin. (Beziehbar über die BDÜ Service GmbH).

Cebulla, M. (2008). *Datenschutz für Übersetzer und Dolmetscher. Solider Schutz vertraulicher Daten*, in: *MDÜ – Fachzeitschrift für Dolmetscher und Übersetzer*, Heft 1 2008, S. 34 – 36.

DIN Deutsches Institut für Normung e.V. (2006). *DIN EN 15038 Übersetzungs-Dienstleistungen – Dienstleistungsanforderungen; Deutsche Fassung EN 15038:2006*.

Übersetzen und Qualitätssicherung, Normung

Kann man Übersetzungsdienstleistungen zertifizieren? LICS®-Zertifizierung zur EN 15038

Klaus Kurre

kurre.de

klaus@kurre.de

Dr. Peter Jonas

Austrian Standards Plus GmbH

peter.jonas@as-plus.at

1 Die Europäische Norm EN 15038

Die 2006 vom Europäischen Komitee für Normung (CEN) angenommene und veröffentlichte Europäische Norm EN 15038 „Übersetzungsdienstleistungen – Dienstleistungsanforderungen" ist die erste regionale Norm zur Festlegung der Anforderungen für die Lieferung von Qualitätsdienstleistungen durch Übersetzungsdienstleister (TSP, Translation Service Provider).

Die Norm legt die Anforderungen an Übersetzungsdienstleister fest, die in Bezug auf personelle und technische Ressourcen, Qualität und Projektmanagement bestehen. Ein wichtiger Teil der Norm befasst sich mit der Beziehung zwischen dem Kunden und dem Übersetzungsdienstleister und fordert vom Übersetzungsdienstleister eine aktive Kommunikation mit dem Kunden, um die Bedürfnisse des Kunden und die aktuellen Parameter des Übersetzungsprojektes (wie Zweck und Zielpublikum der Übersetzung, Lieferfristen, Details usw.) zu ermitteln. Der Übersetzungsdienstleister muss eine Vereinbarung mit dem Kunden treffen, in der die kaufmännischen Dienstleistungsbedingungen des Projektes festgelegt werden. Abschnitt 5, „Arbeitsprozesse für die Erbringung von Übersetzungsdienstleistungen", definiert die Prozesse, denen der Übersetzungsdienstleister zur Durchführung eines Übersetzungsauftrages folgen muss. Ein wesentlicher Punkt in diesem Abschnitt stellt die Anforderung dar, dass Übersetzungen Korrektur gelesen werden müssen, d.h. ihre Eignung für den vereinbarten Zweck muss von einem zweiten Übersetzer geprüft werden, der Quell- und Zieltext miteinander vergleicht.

Mit der Einführung der EN 15038 möchte das CEN Übersetzungsdienstleistern helfen, sich auf Grundlage von formalen Prozessen und Qualität zu differenzieren und Käufer ihrer Dienstleistungen bei der Kaufentscheidung zu unterstützen.

Die Norm gilt für alle Arten von Übersetzungsdienstleistern unabhängig von Struktur und/oder Größe. Es ist wichtig von Anfang an darauf hinzuweisen, dass die EN 15038 auch von Einzelübersetzern angewandt werden kann. Daher ist die Zertifizierung unter bestimmten Voraussetzungen auch für freiberuflich tätige Einzelübersetzer machbar. Die Erfüllung der Norm und Einführung eines zu diesem Zweck erforderlichen Systems wird nicht durch die Tatsache beeinträchtigt, das der Übersetzungsdienstleister eine Einzelperson ist.

2 Warum Zertifizierung?

Die Zertifizierung von Übersetzungsdienstleistern gewinnt für Unternehmen und Endkunden weltweit zunehmend an Bedeutung. Die Kunden fragen verstärkt nach Zertifizierung, um sicherzustellen, dass die erworbene Dienstleistung den Mindestanforderungen entspricht. Dies gilt insbesondere für grenzüberschreitende Transaktionen.

Übersetzungsdienstleister sehen Zertifizierung als zusätzliches Marketingwerkzeug, aber auch als Hilfsmittel, um Ansprüche zu verteidigen, falls sie aufgefordert werden sollten, nachzuweisen, dass ihre Dienstleistungen in Übereinstimmung mit anerkannten Spezifikationen erbracht wurden. Bei Rechtsstreitigkeiten könnten sie aufgefordert werden, zu belegen, dass ihre Dienstleistungen dem Stand der Technik entsprechen.

Die EN 15038 empfiehlt die Konformitätsprüfung und Zertifizierung als Mittel zur Verbesserung der Markttransparenz und Kundenzufriedenheit im Übersetzungssektor. Der Markt der zertifizierten Übersetzungsdienstleister entwickelt sich seit der Veröffentlichung der EN 15038 ständig weiter. Austrian Standards plus Certification GmbH (www.as-plus.at) hat als Zertifizierungsstelle des Österreichischen Normungsinstituts als erster Zertifizierer in Europa ein Zertifizierungsschema eingeführt und zertifiziert seitdem Übersetzungsdienstleister in Österreich und dem Rest der Welt.

3 Language Industry Certification System LICS®

Die EN 15038 wurde mit dem Ziel eingeführt, hochwertige Übersetzungsdienstleistungen, fairen Wettbewerb, verbesserte Transparenz und Qualität für Endkunden zu gewährleisten. Die Publikation der Europäischen Norm hat sowohl in Europa als auch weltweit zu verschiedenen Zertifizierungsmöglichkeiten für Übersetzungsdienstleister geführt.

Um die oben erwähnten Ziele nicht durch Zertifikate verschiedener Zertifizierungsstellen abzuwerten, da jede Zertifizierungsstelle unterschiedliche Bewertungsverfahren und Kriterien angewandt hat, ist ein harmonisiertes Verfahren erforderlich, mit dem sichergestellt sein soll, dass die Zertifizierungsstellen kompatiblen Vorgehensweisen folgen. Harmonisierte Bewertungsverfahren sind Voraussetzung für die gegenseitige Anerkennung der Zertifikate. Die Entwicklung unterschiedlicher Bewertungssysteme und Zertifizierungsmarken führt zu unerwünschter Konkurrenz zwischen den Zertifizierungsstellen und senkt damit das Qualitätsniveau derartiger Zertifizierungen.

Um der Übersetzungsbranche ein einzigartiges Werkzeug für den verlässlichen Nachweis der Qualität ihrer Dienstleistungen zur Verfügung zu stellen, hat das Österreichische Normungsinstitut zusammen mit dem Internationalen Netzwerk für Terminologie (TermNet, www.termnet.org), das so genannte „Language Industry Certification System®" LICS® geschaffen, www.lics-certification.org.

LICS® bietet Übersetzungsdienstleistern auf der ganzen Welt die Möglichkeit zum Erwerb eines weltweit gleichartigen und anerkannten Zertifikats zum Nachweis der EN 15038-Konformität ihrer Übersetzungsdienstleistungen.

LICS® arbeitet mit einem wachsenden Netzwerk lokaler Partner in Europa und dem Rest der Welt zusammen. Es bietet eine Zertifizierung gemäß EN 15038 durch Dritte, die sich insbesondere auch Kleinunternehmen leisten können. LICS® hat mittlerweile Partner und/oder Kunden in Belgien, Großbritannien, Deutschland, Kanada, Bulgarien, Kroatien, der Slowakei und dem arabischen Sprachraum. Es gibt Verhandlungen mit zukünftigen Partnerschaften in Spanien, Irland, China usw.

4 Wie funktioniert LICS®

LICS® ist eine registrierte Marke der Austrian Standards plus GmbH. LICS® bietet dem Markt eine Zertifizierungsmarke für Übersetzungsdienstleister, ein global anerkanntes Markenzeichen verlässlicher Qualitätsdienstleistungen, ein Zertifizierungsschema zur EN 15038, „akkreditierte" lokale Zertifizierungspartner, die Zertifizierungen in einer bestimmten Region durchführen, eine Dokumentation, wie sie zum Umsetzen des Systems erforderlich ist, Schulungsprogramme für Auditoren inklusive Trainingsmaterial und eine Website mit einem umfassenden Register der zertifizierten Dienstleister (z.B. Übersetzungsdienstleister) unter www.lics-certification.org.

LICS® arbeitet mit lokalen Partnern zusammen, die in bestimmten Regionen die tatsächliche Zertifizierung durchführen. Diese Partner werden für Ihre Arbeit von LICS® akkreditiert und einer regelmäßigen Überwachung unterzogen. Die lokalen Partner berichten LICS® über die Ergebnisse der einzelnen Zertifizierungsverfahren und ermöglichen so die Unterhaltung eines zentralen Registers zertifizierter Übersetzungsdienstleister.

4.1 Partnerkategorien

Solche lokalen Partner können überall auf der Welt ansässig sein. Es gibt drei Kategorien lokaler Partner:

- *Zertifizierungsstellen*: Unternehmen, die nachgewiesen haben, dass sie die international anerkannten Anforderungen an Zertifizierungsstellen erfüllen. Zertifizierungsstellen sind für den Zertifizierungsprozess und die Ausstellung der Zertifikate mit dem LICS®-Logo verantwortlich. Sie erhalten eine Lizenz zur Verwendung des LICS®-Zertifizierungsschemas und des LICS®-Logos.

- *Lokale Vertriebspartner*: Dies sind Unternehmen, die die Anforderungen an Zertifizierungsstellen nicht erfüllen. Lokale Vertriebspartner organisieren Zertifizierungen für Kunden mit ihren lokal verfügbaren Auditoren und nehmen die Kunden unter Vertrag. Austrian Standards plus Certification GmbH ist Zertifizierungsstelle für diese Zertifizierungen.

- *Einzelne Auditoren*: Qualifizierte Auditoren, die die Kompetenzvoraussetzungen des anzuwendenden Zertifizierungsschemas erfüllen, können direkt für das österreichische Normungsinstitut arbeiten, das in diesem Fall als Zertifizierungsstelle auftritt. Die Auditoren sind für den Kontakt zum Kunden verantwortlich und organisieren alle für die Konformitätsprüfung erforderlichen Maßnahmen. Die Kunden werden direkt von Austrian Standards plus Certification GmbH unter Vertrag genommen.

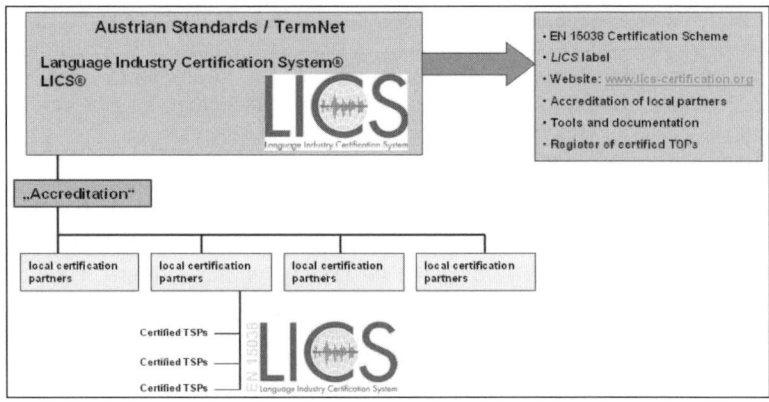

Abb. 1: Die LICS®-Struktur

5 Der LICS®-Zertifizierungsprozess

5.1 Das Zertifizierungsschema

Eines der Hauptziele von LICS® ist die Harmonisierung der Art und Weise, wie Übersetzungsdienstleister von den verschiedenen Zertifizierungsstellen zertifiziert werden. Ein Werkzeug zur Harmonisierung ist das Zertifizierungsschema, d.h. die Prüfverfahren zum Auditieren und Zertifizieren von Übersetzungsdienstleistern gemäß EN 15038. Dieses Zertifizierungsschema definiert das Verfahren zur Auditierung eines Übersetzungsdienstleisters, gibt an, wie der Übersetzungsdienstleister seine Aktivitäten für den Audit zu dokumentieren hat und legt die Kompetenzen der Auditoren fest, die das Audit durchführen, sowie den Intervall der Re-Auditierung.

Um das Urteil des Auditors so objektiv wie möglich gestalten zu können, gibt das Zertifizierungsschema so genannte „Erfüllungskriterien" vor, die die Konformität mit den einzelnen Anforderungen der EN 15038 festlegen.

Schritt 1: Antrag

Alle Übersetzungsdienstleister können unabhängig von Größe und/oder Struktur eine LICS®-Zertifizierung gemäß EN 15038 beantragen. Einer der Vorteile des LICS®-Systems ist die Tatsache, dass es insbesondere für kleine und mittelgroße Unternehmen konzipiert wurde, sodass sich auch Kleinunternehmen und Einzelunternehmer eine Zertifizierung leisten können.

Um eine Zertifizierung zu beantragen, muss der Bewerber einen Antrag einreichen, der den Allgemeinen Bedingungen von LICS® entspricht.

Schritt 2: Dokumentation

Vor der tatsächlichen Durchführung des Audits muss der Übersetzungsdienstleister eine Dokumentation über die zu zertifizierenden Dienstleistungen vorlegen. Diese Dokumentation muss allgemeine Informationen zum Übersetzungsdienstleister wie den Namen des Unternehmens, Anschriften aller Niederlassungen, ein Unternehmensprofil, etwaige Spezialisierungen usw. enthalten. Neben diesen Basisinformationen muss der Übersetzungsdienstleister eine Erklärung zur Erfüllung aller einzelnen Anforderungen der Norm vorlegen. Das LICS®-EN-15038-Zertifizierungsschema hilft dem Übersetzungsdienstleister bei der Erstellung dieser Dokumentation. Die Dokumentation bildet die Grundlage des Audits.

Schritt 3: Das Audit

Mittelpunkt des Zertifizierungsprozesses bildet das Audit, dessen Ziel ist, Nachweise zu sammeln, dass der Übersetzungsdienstleister alle Anforderungen der Norm erfüllt.

Solche Belege sind Gespräche mit der Unternehmensführung, mit Projektleitern und Übersetzern (sofern der Übersetzungsdienstleister mit internen Übersetzern arbeitet) sowie anderen Mitarbeitern, die am Übersetzungsprozess und sonstigen Kundenaktivitäten beteiligt sind. Als weiterer Nachweis dienen Aufzeichnungen jeder Art, wie Aufzeichnungen laufender und abgeschlossener Übersetzungsprojekte, alle Arten der Kommunikation zwischen Kunde und Übersetzungsdienstleister, Datenbanken zu freiberuflichen Übersetzern, die für Übersetzungsaufträge eingesetzt werden usw.

Das Audit wird von einem Lead-Auditor geführt. Der Lead-Auditor ist ein formell qualifizierter Auditor, der eine Ausbildung zur Auditierung erhalten hat, über tiefgreifende Kenntnisse der EN 15038 verfügt und Erfahrungen mit Übersetzungsdienstleistungen hat. Er verwendet eine Checkliste mit Erfüllungskriterien, die als Grundlage für die Beurteilung der Konformität der Dienstleistungen des Übersetzungsdienstleisters dient.

Sollten die Auditergebnisse Punkte zu Tage fördern, die vom Übersetzungsdienstleister zu klären sind, wird der Lead-Auditor zusammen mit dem Antragsteller nach Maßnahmen suchen, die es dem Übersetzungsdienstleister ermöglichen, die Anforderungen zu erfüllen.

Zum Abschluss des Audits wird der Auditor seinen Bericht mit seiner abschließenden Beurteilung und der Empfehlung an den Zertifizierer erstellen, ob ein Zertifikat ausgestellt werden soll oder nicht.

Schritt 4: Ausstellen des Zertifikats

Nach dem Audit sendet der Auditor seinen Report an den zuständigen Zertifizierer, der die endgültige Entscheidung über eine Ausstellung oder Nichtausstellung des Zertifikats trifft. Voraussetzung für die Ausstellung des Zertifikates ist eine positive Beurteilung des Audits. Das Zertifikat gilt über einen Zeitraum von 6 Jahren.

Mit dem Zertifikat erhält der Übersetzungsdienstleister das Recht, das LICS® EN 15038-Konformitätszeichen zu führen (siehe Abbildung 1).

Abb. 2: Das LICS® EN 15038-Konformitätszeichen

5.2 Aufrechterhaltung des Zertifikats

Während der sechsjährigen Laufzeit des Zertifikats werden zur Aufrechterhaltung der Lizenz zur Führung des ausgestellten Zertifikats alle zwei Jahre Re-Audits durchgeführt.

6 Erfolgsgeschichte

Die Zertifizierung nach einer Norm ist für jedes Unternehmen eine Investition in die Zukunft. Die Kosten für eine Zertifizierung müssen also letztendlich durch einen erhöhten Umsatz aufgrund einer gestiegenen Zahl von Kunden ausgeglichen werden. Es gibt klare Hinweise, dass sich eine LICS®-Zertifizierung gemäß EN 15038 fast umgehend für den Übersetzungsdienstleister auszahlt.

Die folgende Abbildung zeigt beispielhaft die prozentuale Entwicklung der tatsächlich beauftragten Anfragen des ersten in Deutschland gemäß EN 15038 zertifizierten Übersetzungsdienstleisters vor der Zertifizierung (2007) und nach der Ausstellung des EN 15038-Zertifikats (2008).

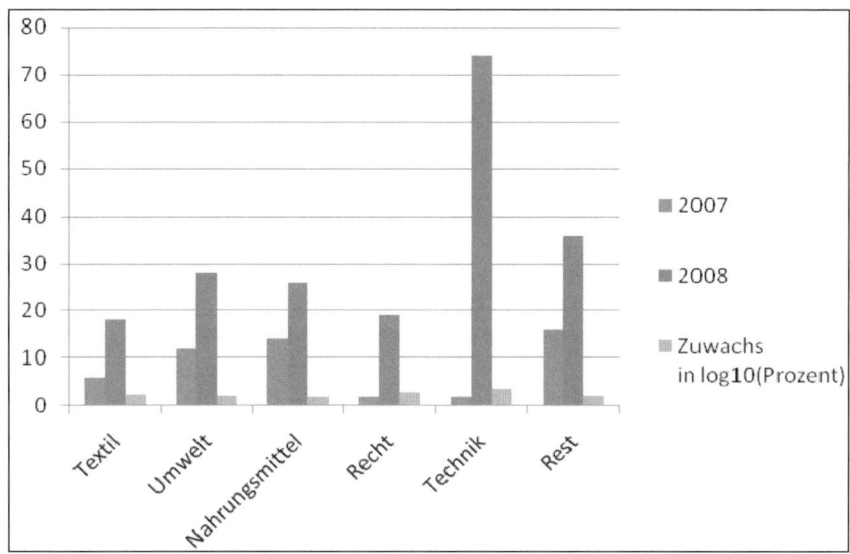

Abb. 3: Aufgrund der LICS®-Zertifizierung realisierte Aufträge im Jahresvergleich 2007 und 2008 (logarithmisch) [Quelle: Frank Publishing GmbH]

In den Bereichen Recht und Technik konnten tatsächlich Beauftragungssteigerungen von 850% bis 3600 % erreicht werden (s.u.). Es hat sich ferner gezeigt, dass die Zertifizierung dem Übersetzungsdienstleister geholfen hat, neben den Umsätzen mit Bestandskunden auch ganz allgemein die Zahl der Kunden zu erhöhen. Hierbei ist festzustellen, dass jetzt Kunden erreicht werden, die ohne Zertifizierung nicht erreicht werden konnten. Diese Neukunden sind hauptsächlich in Österreich und Belgien ansässig.

	2007	2008	Zuwachs in Prozent
Textil	6	18	200
Umwelt	12	28	133
Nahrungsmittel	14	26	86
Recht	2	19	850
Technik	2	74	3600
Rest	16	36	125

Abb. 4: Aufgrund der LICS®-Zertifizierung realisierte Aufträge im Jahresvergleich 2007 und 2008 (prozentual) [Quelle: Frank Publishing GmbH]

Dies belegt, dass die EN 15038 als globales Werkzeug dient, um zuverlässige Geschäftspartner in der Übersetzungsbranche zu finden. Kunden fragen nicht nach Übersetzungsdienstleistern mit Sitz in einem bestimmten Land- sondern suchen nach Sicherheit in der Dienstleistungsqualität in Form einer EN 15038-Zertifizierung.

7 Zusammenfassung

Die Europäische Norm EN 15038 hat ihren Dienstleistungssektor mehr als jede andere Norm im Übersetzungssektor zuvor beeinflusst. Sowohl Übersetzungsdienstleister als auch deren Kunden sind sich dieser Norm verstärkt bewusst und verwenden sie in ihren Geschäften als Werkzeug zur Qualitätssicherung.

Obwohl die EN 15038 keine Norm darstellt, um Einzelübersetzer entsprechend ihren persönlichen Kompetenzen zu zertifizieren, ist eine Zertifizierung gemäß EN 15038 für jede Art von Dienstleister unabhängig von Größe und Struktur möglich.

Das LICS®-Verfahren zur Zertifizierung von Übersetzungsdienstleistern gemäß EN 15038 hat sich in puncto Zuverlässigkeit und Durchführbarkeit nicht nur für große Übersetzungsunternehmen, sondern auch für mittelgroße und kleine Übersetzungsdienstleister sowie Einzelübersetzer als geeignetes Mittel erwiesen.

Worldwide quality standards for translations: Pipe-dream or perspective?

Terence Oliver

Freelance technical translator

olitrans@aol.com

Preamble – Three general remarks:

Firstly, I have to point out that by the time the version in these proceedings is read, it will already be out of date, because the annual meeting of the relevant committee of the International Organization for Standardization (ISO) is due to take place in Bogotá (Colombia) in August. As a result, there should be global developments to report when the paper is presented in September.

Secondly, let me stress that although I am using English for this paper, my work in the field of standardisation has been entirely in Germany and Austria, so I am only really qualified to talk from a German point of view. Having said that, I imagine that in relation to other major standards at global level, my standpoint can be said to be fairly representative of the European approach – if such a thing exists.

Thirdly, it is obvious that in the time available I can only skim the surface, and I would also emphasise that what I am going to say today is a very personal view. It does not necessarily represent the official stance of any association or committee I have worked for in recent years.

Do translators need standards? If so, what kind?

Probably this is not the right question. What we should be asking is: "Who needs what kind of standards relating to translations?" The players involved are of course the client, any intermediaries such as translation companies or agencies, the translator and – in a mostly passive role – the reader or consumer.

Since language is a highly individual and dynamic process, one might be forgiven for arguing that language itself, and hence translation, is essentially not capable of standardisation. Indeed, both the former German process standard DIN 2345 and the current European service standard EN 15038 tacitly skirt round the problem of assessing or standardising what I would call the intrinsic quality of the translation. Instead they focus on the process or service aspects. The thinking is that even if we cannot yet devise standards that will improve the intrinsic quality of the translation, we *can* devise standards which improve the efficiency of virtually everything that is peripheral to the central task of translation. If the translation is unchanged and the handling of the job is improved, this is bound to improve the quality of the service package as a whole.

I have to point out here that in practice, compared with the situation without a standard, the translation does not necessarily remain unchanged: for example, careful third-party revision or the use of translation memory may ensure more consistent use of terminology or phraseology than the individual translator is capable of, but the downside is that such intervention may also lead to more stilted or less attractive results.

Do consumers/readers need standards? Well, maybe not actively – they probably aren't even aware that such standards exist. On the other hand, anything that raises the general quality of the results they read – which they may or may not know are translations – can't be a bad thing.

Do translators need standards? Many probably do – but they don't know it. Depending on where their jobs come from, many individual translators can very likely spend their whole working lives without having to comply with translation standards. Others may work for industries where standardisation is part of everyday life, and here purchasing departments may specify that compliance with a translation standard is a condition for placement of the order. My own view is that anything which raises awareness of potential deficits and potential means of improvement is a good thing – even if the translator does not go so far as to promise full compliance.

Do translation companies and agencies need standards? The best ones probably don't, but they tend to be the ones that follow them in any case and obtain certification. The worst ones certainly do, but as they probably aren't concerned with the quality of the result, but merely with the fact that they have a result of some sort to deliver, they are unlikely to be very worried about compliance with standards anyway.

Do clients need standards? Since many clients don't know what they want in the first place, this is more difficult to answer. On the other hand, the European standard at least has a section on the need to clarify certain details before tackling the job, and an ISO working group is specifically concerned with this aspect. So, if the translation is to be fit for the purpose, anything that makes the players more aware of what exactly they are buying or selling, and of the need to communicate about these aspects, has to be a good thing.

At this point I would briefly like to dispel a common misunderstanding: translation standards are not laws. Translators are not automatically bound to comply with them. But standards can be taken as a basis for contracts, either in individual agreements or by reference in general conditions. If translators sign such agreements, or if they unilaterally declare that they will comply with the standard, then they have undertaken to abide by the requirements of the standard, and they may have to face the consequences of not doing so.

Let me try to put this section in a nutshell: As in any human relationship, communication is crucial. By communication I mean a two-way flow, with both sides listening as well as speaking. Anything that improves communication between the active players has to be a good thing.

By institutionalising such arrangements, standards such as EN 15038 help to raise the quality of translation services. But they can't do it entirely on their own. That is where agreements like those between the Finnish translators' association SKTL and translation companies in Finland, or between BDÜ and QSD in Germany, can play an important role. They may make reference to relevant standards, but since they can be less abstract than standards they can offer concrete examples and breathe life into the standard. Maybe this could be an interesting area for FIT Europe to pursue: comparing such existing agreements and distilling a version on which the whole of Europe could agree.

Is international consensus possible?

Translating is by its nature an international business. Clients and translators frequently work in different countries. Indeed, these days translators can work almost anywhere in the world, regardless of their languages. So, to take the communication and awareness idea a stage further, the ideal situation in the interests of efficient communication between translation players in different countries would be to have an international standard with which all players were familiar in their local language, or maybe the official UN languages, for example. This would simplify the process of negotiation between a client in one country and a translation service provider in another country: The players might agree that the entire standard applied to the job in question, or possibly that a particular clause – uniquely identified by number – did not apply. Or they might want to amplify some aspect that needed special clarification.

With the everyday items institutionalised, the players would be free to concentrate on any unusual aspects peculiar to a specific job. Everybody would know what they were supposed to be doing, and also how and when, and it would be possible to check whether or not they had done it. Of course, the standard would have to avoid detailed commercial or legal stipulations, as these are often confined to individual countries or groups of countries – in other words, it would have to focus solely on the translation service.

This is what has been done in Europe with EN 15038. Between 2003 and 2006, a total of 29 European countries – some of them working from pre-existing national standards, some starting from scratch – reached a consensus on the present standard. There is no denying that the result is a kind of "least common denominator", as the results of negotiation and compromise usually are. But the fact remains that despite differences in culture, legal systems and commercial requirements, the translating profession in those countries found a common basis.

In theory, therefore, EN 15038 should form a suitable starting point for building an international standard. Some countries outside Europe have already adopted it, at least as a basis. To the best of my knowledge, these include Canada, Colombia and Uruguay, for example. In practice, however, even if there were no competition from other major standards, there would still be substantial cultural, legal and commercial differences to overcome. These would be considerably greater at global level than within Europe, but as the saying goes: "Where there's a will, there's a way".

One problem is that there are at least two other major standards out there, created in the USA and in China. The US standard is far more detailed than EN 15038, possibly because there was not nearly so much of a consensus problem within national boundaries as there was in Europe, and it also strays beyond the confines of the core elements of providing translation services. My own impression is that while it provides valuable guidance, it reads more like a manual on translating, and not much like the concentrated, abstract essence that I expect of a true industry standard. Actually, although the US work is widely referred to as a "standard", it is not in fact a true standard and does not claim to be one:

> "This guide offers an organized collection of information and does not recommend a specific course of action. This guide cannot replace education or experience and should be used in conjunction with professional judgment. Not all aspects of this guide can be applicable in all circumstances. This ASTM guide is not intended to represent or replace the standard of care by which the adequacy of a given professional service shall be judged, nor should this guide be applied without consideration of a project's unique aspects. The word 'Standard' in the title of this guide means only that the guide has been approved through the ASTM international consensus process."

And in Section 1.2 it expressly states:

> "This guide is designed to provide a framework for agreement on specifications for translation projects. Within this framework, the participants in a service agreement can define the processes necessary to arrive at a product of desired quality to serve the needs and expectations of the end user."

Thus in the best of all possible worlds, I would like to see an improved and augmented European standard adopted at ISO level, but supported by a manual on practical implementation that embodied the best elements of the US "standard".

I must admit that I am less familiar with the Chinese standard, which seems to be closer in approach to the European standard, but here again we potentially encounter the problem of conflicting cultural, legal and commercial approaches.

A working group at ISO level has produced a comparative analysis of what these three major standards have to say about a dozen key areas. Whether the findings of this analysis will eventually result in the adoption of EN 15038 plus any useful extra elements from the other two, or whether they will simply lead to deadlock or some other form of non-progress, remains to be seen.

Another problem, which to my mind weighs much heavier, is that the further up the standardisation hierarchy you go, the greater is the likelihood that practical work will get bogged down in politics, prestige and even intrigue. In the three years of my involvement in ISO matters I have been thoroughly disillusioned and frustrated by the fact that despite annual meetings in Beijing, Salt Lake City and Moscow (at considerable expense to the individuals involved), virtually no progress has been made towards producing something that will benefit the profession. I sincerely hope the next three years will be more fruitful, but I am convinced this will only happen if some of the people involved at last realise that they are in these bodies for the good of the profession, and not for their own advancement.

How is compliance demonstrated, checked, verified, certified? What pressures and constraints arise from increasing globalisation? What can translators do to protect themselves from unrealistic demands?

There are many other issues such as these that I would like to look at, but as there are four speakers in this session, which restricts us to about twenty minutes each, I reluctantly propose to skip these aspects and move on to a final question which I believe is of crucial importance to the acceptance of standards by translators. And that is:

What can translators' associations do during the making of standards to ensure that standards are realistic and practicable, and to pave the way for their acceptance?

To my mind, one major problem is that many colleagues feel that standards are imposed on them from above and that they have no say in the process. All "top-down" and no "bottom-up". To a large extent this is true: a few experienced stalwarts labour for several years to produce what they think is an acceptable document, and when the draft standard is at last published, the rest of the profession have a mere six months to comment and submit suggestions.

This problem, at least in Germany, is partly due to the confidentiality obligations imposed on the members of the standardisation committee, which prevent them discussing their proposals properly with their colleagues in the association or else-where. I believe there is a need here for the translators' associations to join forces and approach the standardisation body with a view to arriving at more flexible arrange-ments. Maybe a kind of pre-draft disclosure stage could be introduced.

Today all German associations are doing much more to publicise and discuss stan-dards issues. This is good. It would be even better if they could make a point of announcing, publicising and coordinating the comment stage, to ensure that col-leagues have the maximum possible time for informed comment.

Where does this leave us?

Standards are not an end in themselves. They are part of the wider issue of relations between players in the translation business. They should be seen not as a nuisance, but as an opportunity to improve such relations. And they should be welcomed by anyone with an interest in improving service quality. In this spirit, they should be developed and refined at European and global level. Even if the way is long, I believe that the vision of global consensus on quality standards is worth pursuing. We have a great profession. We should stop moaning about lack of status and get our act together on the quality front – we need to show that we know what we are doing and that we can deliver the goods. That way we can make sure that the vision is not condemned to remain a pipe-dream, but becomes a practical perspective.

Bibliography

ASTM International, F 2575-06 *Standard Guide for Quality Assurance in Transla-tion,* June 2006.

DIN EN 15038:2006-08 E, *Translation services – Service requirements.* In: *Normen für Übersetzer und technische Autoren,* G. Herzog & H. Mühlbauer, 2007, Beuth Verlag GmbH, Berlin – Vienna – Zurich. (In addition to the German and English versions of EN 15038, this compilation also contains many other standards of relev-ance to translators in the German-speaking world.)

National Standard of the People's Republic of China, GB/T 19363.1–2003, *Specifica-tion for Translation Service – Part 1: Translation,* 27.11.2003

National Standard of the People's Republic of China, GB/T 19682–2005, *Target text quality requirements for translation services,* 24.03.2005

Von Dienstleistungen, Mehrwertdienstleistungen und professionellem Handeln – Anmerkungen zur europäischen Translationsnorm DIN EN 15038

Jürgen F. Schopp

Universität Tampere (Finnland)
Finnischer Übersetzer- und Dolmetscherverband SKTL

jurgen.schopp@uta.fi

„... der Übersetzer ist ein Textgestalter von Beruf. ",
Justa Holz-Mänttäri (1979: 23)

1 Translatorische Realitäten

Anders als bei staatlich kontrollierten Lehr- und Ausbildungsberufen handelt es sich bei „Übersetzer" bekanntlich um eine ungeschützte Berufsbezeichnung, die sich zulegen kann, wer immer auch sich aufgrund seiner Fremdsprachenkenntnisse dazu berufen fühlt. So ist es nicht unüblich, dass ausländische Akademiker sich in der Zielkultur zunächst einmal als Übersetzer betätigen. Ihrem meist sprachkontrastiven Verständnis vom Übersetzen entsprechend sehen die Translationsprodukte aus, die vielleicht ein genaues Abbild der ausgangssprachlichen Textoberfläche bieten, aber nicht unbedingt als optimales zielsprachliches Kommunikationsmittel taugen.

Ein anderer Fall: Auf studentischen Mailinglisten translatorischer Ausbildungsanstalten werden Übersetzer für anspruchsvolle Aufgaben gesucht –, ausdrücklich *keine* professionellen Übersetzer. Abgesehen davon, dass Studierende translatorischer Curricula nicht mehr als „Semiprofessionelle" angesehen werden sollten, steht hinter Jobangeboten dieser Art in der Regel der Wunsch, die Ausgaben für die translatorische Leistung möglichst gering und die Gewinnspanne möglichst hoch zu halten. Nicht selten handelt es sich bei den Anfragenden um einen sog. „envelope switcher", der sich auf die Vermittlung von Translationsaufträgen spezialisiert hat und ein Netz von translatorischen Zulieferern unterhält, an die er die Aufträge weiterleitet – oft Freischaffende, die die Konkurrenz der auf dem Translationsmarkt tätigen Semiprofessionellen fürchten – ein nicht unwesentlicher Grund für die „Erosion der Honorare" (BDÜ 2008).

Semiprofessionelles Übersetzen liegt vor, wenn nur ausgewählte Aspekte des professionellen translatorischen Handelns praktiziert werden und das eigene Handeln, z.B. das Übersetzen in die B-Arbeitssprache, zu Ungunsten des Gesamtherstellungsprozesses und der Qualität des Endproduktes verabsolutiert wird.

Doch sei hier grundsätzlich die Frage gestellt, ob die professionelle translatorische Praxis selbst wirklich schon alle Kriterien erfüllt, die für einen Beruf im eigentlichen Sinne gelten. Einer der Themenbereiche auf diesem Kongress ist das „Übersetzen von

Textbausteinen ohne Kontext" (BDÜ 2008), genauer vielleicht als „Übersetzen aus dem textuellen Zusammenhang gerissener Textfragmente" zu bezeichnen. Sofern der Kontext durch Einsatz geeigneter Software zur Verfügung steht, macht diese Arbeitsweise der „Schnipselübersetzung" bei bestimmten Auftragstypen durchaus Sinn (Freisler 2009: 35). Bedenklich aber ist, wenn Vertreter des Berufsstandes daraus ein Professionalitätskriterium ableiten wollen, etwa in dem Sinne, ein professioneller Übersetzer müsse die betreffende Fachsprache so gut beherrschen, dass er in der Lage sei, auch kleinste Fragmente ohne Kontext einwandfrei zu übersetzen (z.B. ADÜ Infoblatt 8/2007: 17f). Zugleich zeigt sich hier die gerade für das translatorische Berufsfeld (noch) typische passiv-reagierende Haltung, die expressis verbis in dem Zitat eines Übersetzers deutlich wird, der mir am 2.3.2006 in einer E-Mail schrieb: „Ich meine wir Übersetzer haben immer weniger Einfluss auf das fertige Produkt, leider."

2   EN 15038: Professionalität durch Normierung?

Natürlich haben auch die translatorischen Berufsverbände erkannt, dass das berufliche Handeln der Translatorenzunft noch zu wünschen übrig lässt und dass unter dem Druck der Verhältnisse auf einem immer „enger" werdenden globalen Translationsmarkt der Kampf um Marktanteile nur durch Qualität gewonnen werden kann. Davon zeugen die Bemühungen um Normierung bzw. Standardisierung des Übersetzungsprozesses wie auch die Zusammenschlüsse von Translationsdienstleistenden in Qualitätsnetzwerken und -verbänden.

In Europa haben sich Vertreter von 29 „Translationskulturen" (ein Begriff von Erich Prunč 1997: 99–127) – auf einen gemeinsamen Standard geeinigt, eben die Translationsnorm EN 15038, im deutschsprachigen Raum als DIN EN 15038 vom Deutschen Institut für Normung in Berlin betreut und vom Beuth-Verlag herausgegeben. Die im November 2006 in Kraft getretene Norm ersetzt bisherige nationale Normen wie DIN 2345 und (leider auch) die beiden Önormen D1200 und D1201.

Im Heft 6 des Mitteilungsblattes MDÜ aus dem Jahr 2004, das dem Thema „Qualitätssicherung für Übersetzungsdienstleistungen" gewidmet ist, beschreibt der Obmann des deutschen Normungsausschusses, Enrique López-Ebri, den Werdegang des Normentwurfs sowie die Zielsetzung, die neben den unmittelbaren Zielen, die sich an industriellen Maßstäben wie Vier-Augen-Prinzip, Rückverfolgbarkeit und reproduzierbaren Ergebnissen orientieren, mittelbare Ziele hat wie „...das Vertrauen in die professionelle Leistung unseres Berufes steigern" sowie „... Image und Lobby des Übersetzerberufes auf eine mit anderen Berufen vergleichbare Ebene anheben" (2004: 11). Im gleichen Sinne äußerte sich Manuela Hübner im ITI bulletin: "The new standard has been introduced to improve the quality of translation services throughout Europe and to raise the profile of the translation industry by bringing it into line with other 'standardised' industries and giving it a more professional image." (2007: 13)

Dies kann als Eingeständnis von unmittelbar Beteiligten gewertet werden, dass es sich bei den translatorischen Berufen noch nicht um vollwertige Berufe handelt, m.a.W., dass wesentliche Merkmale eines Berufes wie strukturierte Ausbildung, öffentlich anerkannter Qualifikationsnachweis, Autonomie des Handelns und Know-how-Vorsprung gegenüber dem Kunden auf das Übersetzen (noch) nicht zutreffen.

Prinzipiell ist die Norm zu begrüßen, zeugt sie doch von dem Willen aller Beteiligten auf dem Translationsmarkt, den Status quo zu überwinden und mehr Qualität in den Übersetzungsprozess zu bringen. Ob die Norm in ihrer derzeitigen Fassung allerdings geeignet ist, die gesetzten Ziele zu erreichen, muss in Frage gestellt werden. Da bei dem Entwurf der Norm wie bereits erwähnt 29 europäische Normungsinstitute und Ausschüsse mit Vertretern des Marktes und der Ausbildung beteiligt waren – und das heißt 29 Translationskulturen mit z.T. sehr unterschiedlichen Arbeitsprinzipien und -konventionen –, darf es nicht verwundern, dass dabei ein Kompromiss entstand, der zwar weiter greift als die auf einem veralteten Übersetzungsbegriff basierende und in sich widersprüchliche DIN-Norm 2345, andererseits aber auch Normen wieder außer Kraft gesetzt hat wie die beiden ÖNORMEN D1200 und D1201, die schon wesentlich fortschrittlicher waren als es jetzt die europäische Norm ist.

3 Übersetzen als „Sprachmittlung"?

Offensichtlich in Anknüpfung an den im alten bundesdeutschen Raum gebräuchlichen, von der traditionell orientierten Sprachwissenschaft stammenden Begriff „Sprachmittlung" (Bausch 1980: 797), der im Gegensatz zum Begriff „Translation" der Leipziger Schule stand, bezeichnen sich viele bundesdeutsche ÜbersetzerInnen heute noch als „Sprachmittler" (z.B. BDÜ 2008). Damit stellt sich aber die Frage, welcher Übersetzungsbegriff zugrunde liegt und in welchem Umfang sich das berufliche Selbstverständnis der Übersetzenden darin widerspiegelt.

So ist es nicht weiter verwunderlich, dass auch EN 15038 von dem traditionell engen Übersetzungsbegriff ausgeht und diesen zum Inhalt der (eigentlichen) „Übersetzungsdienstleistung" macht, den sie von „Mehrwertdienstleistung" abgrenzt (EN 15038 2006: 5). Das Problem liegt dabei nicht so sehr in der Verwendung dieser beiden Bezeichnungen, sondern in ihrem Bedeutungsumfang und ihrer gegenseitigen Abgrenzung, da dadurch die gängige Praxis und Auffassung vom Übersetzen als bilinguale Handlung – als „Sprachmittlung" – und dem Übersetzer als „Sprachmittler" festgeschrieben wird, dem translatorischen Berufsfeld aber nicht grundsätzlich die Zuständigkeit für jede Art von inter- und transkulturellem Botschaftstransfer und damit die selbstverständliche Anfertigung unterschiedlicher Translationsprodukte zugesprochen wird, wie es schon Holz-Mänttäri in ihrem „Translatorischen Handeln" gefordert hat, als sie den Übersetzer als Experten für die Herstellung von Texten für den transkulturellen Botschaftstransfer definierte (1984: 27). Hinter dieser Forderung stand die Einsicht, dass Ausgangstexte nicht selten suboptimal konzipiert und formuliert werden. Da die betreffenden Schreiber zwar Experten ihres Fachgebietes sind, aber keine professionellen Texter, sind viele Ausgangstexte defekt und entsprechen nicht den Kommunikationszwecken. Im Klartext heißt dies, dass in der Praxis der transkulturellen Kommunikation eine rein sprachliche Umkodierung des Ausgangstextes oft nicht ausreicht, sondern Änderungen des textlichen Konzepts notwendig sind, wenn die Botschaftsvermittlung im Vordergrund stehen soll.

Daher erhebt sich die Frage, warum in Translationskreisen an dieser „sprachmittelnden" Selbstbeschränkung festgehalten wird bzw. warum man diese immer noch unterstreicht, wie sich z.B. in EN 15038 in der Definition translatorischer Leistungen wie Lokalisierung etc. als „Mehrwertdienstleistung" zeigt, die ja impliziert, dass sich der „eigentliche" translatorische Zuständigkeitsbereich auf die sprachliche Wiedergabe des Ausgangstextes in der Zielsprache beschränkt.

4 Übersetzen – eine Dienstleistung?

Die Auffassung des Übersetzens als Sprachmittlung resultiert konsequenterweise in der Definition des Übersetzens als Dienstleistung. Nicht ausreichend berücksichtigt wird dadurch allerdings, dass bei jeder schriftlichen translatorischen Tätigkeit ein konkretes Produkt entsteht, das selbst wieder Teil von materiellen Produkten ist, von Print- und digitalen Kommunikationsmedien, die als Kommunikationsmittel in transkultureller Kommunikation eingesetzt werden. Was diese Art von Produkten von gewöhnlichen, in der Regel für private und befristete Nutzung erbrachten Dienstleistungen vor allem unterscheidet sind ihre Lebens- bzw. Nutzungsdauer, ihr Öffentlichkeits- bzw. Verbreitungsgrad sowie ihr Material- und Repräsentationswert (Schopp 2005: 269–271). Damit in engem Zusammenhang steht die Bearbeitungsqualität des Translats, die u.a. darüber entscheidet, mit wem der Übersetzer kooperieren muss, um die entsprechende Qualität zu erzielen (vgl. Schopp 2005: 398–406: „Veredlungsstufen").

In Bezug darauf erfüllt die Herstellung eines Translats rechtlich den Sachbestand eines Werkvertrags. Aus diesem folgen Leistungen und Pflichten wie Kostenvoranschlag, Angebotskalkulation, Sachmängelhaftung und Nachbesserungspflicht, aber auch die Nebenpflicht zur Aufklärung und Beratung des Kunden aufgrund des Knowhow-Gefälles zwischen Auftraggeber und Auftragnehmer (vgl. Heuer 2002). Damit aber ist ein wesentlich weiterer Handlungs- und Verantwortungsrahmen gesetzt als es der Fall ist, wenn die translatorische Dienstleistung in erster Linie lediglich als Sprachmittlung fokussiert wird.

Wie üblich wird also auch in der europäischen Translationsnorm EN 15038, schriftliche Translation wie selbstverständlich als Dienstleistung aufgefasst und diese zum Kern- und Ausgangspunkt gemacht. Die Norm soll vom Nordkap bis Sizilien, von Island bis Zypern der Qualitätssicherung und Zertifizierung von Übersetzungsdienstleistungen dienen – basierend auf „Festlegung und Definition von Anforderungen, die für das Erbringen einer qualitativ hochwertigen Dienstleistung durch Übersetzungsdienstleister erforderlich sind" (EN 15038, 2006: 4). Durch Beschreibung und Festlegung der gesamten Dienstleistung, ihrer Arbeitsprozesse und Anforderungen soll Übersetzerinnen und Übersetzern geholfen werden, „den Bedürfnissen des Marktes gerecht zu werden" (ibid.).

Die Definition für die Basisdienstleistung „Übersetzen" lautet: „Schriftliches Übertragen von Informationen von der Ausgangs- in die Zielsprache" (ibid.), d.h. also im Ausgangstext enthaltene Elemente werden zielsprachlich formuliert. Was aber, wenn relevante, wichtige Informationen fehlen? Wenn in der Zielkultur diese Textsorte grundsätzlich anders konzipiert ist oder wenn ganz andere „Informationen" den vom Auftraggeber bzw. Kunden erhofften Effekt beim Adressaten hätten?

Diese Definition zeugt somit von freiwilliger Einschränkung der Translationsbranche auf das „eigentliche Übersetzen" und fokussiert die translatorische Rolle auf den „Sprachmittler", anstatt die Rolle des „Experten für transkulturellen Botschaftstransfer" in Anspruch zu nehmen. Das hat zur Folge, dass translatorische Leistungen wie Adaption, Rewriting, Lokalisierung u.a., die in der Önorm D 1200 als gleichberechtigte translatorische „Transferleistungen" aufgelistet sind, in EN 15038 im Anhang E als „Mehrwertdienstleistung" geführt werden (EN 15038, 2006: 17).

Letzten Endes ist dies wohl darauf zurückzuführen, dass als „Übersetzung" in erster Linie offensichtlich der Formulierungsprozess des Zieltextes gemeint ist. So kommt es zu dem terminologischen Widerspruch, dass sich in der Norm die Benennung „Übersetzung" auf zwei Begriffe bezieht. Als Bestimmungswort im Oberbegriff „5.4 Übersetzungsprozess" (EN 15038, 2006: 11) trägt es eindeutig eine progressivere Bedeutung, nämlich „Herstellung eines transkulturellen Kommunikationsmittels", das bis zu seiner endgültigen Gestalt eine Reihe von unterschiedlichen, aufeinander bezogenen Arbeitsphasen zu durchlaufen hat. Im Unterbegriff „5.4.1 Übersetzung" (ibid.) kommt dann wieder die traditionelle Bedeutung zum Zuge. So wird „Übersetzung" zu einem Teil des „Übersetzungsprozesses" – was doch wohl Grundsätzen terminologischen Arbeitens widerspricht.

Ein weiteres terminologisches Problem bilden – zumindest in der deutschen Fassung von EN 15038 – die im Zusammenhang mit dem Korrekturlesen auftretenden Benennungen (vor allem „Fahnenkorrektur" anstatt „Kundenkorrektur"), die von nicht allzu großer Vertrautheit mit den einzelnen Arbeitsphasen des Gesamtprozesses der Herstellung eines Printmediums zeugen (hierzu Schopp 2007: 70). Besonders bedauerlich ist, dass die bei der Herstellung des zielkulturellen Mediums in der Ausgangs- oder in einer Drittkultur wichtige translatorische Arbeitsphase der Kundenkorrektur terminologisch und inhaltlich nicht ausreichend berücksichtigt wird. So heißt es in der Norm lediglich: „Wenn die Dienstleistungsanforderungen eine Fahnenkorrektur vorsehen, dann muss der Übersetzungsdienstleister sicherstellen, dass eine solche Fahnenkorrektur durchgeführt wird" (EN 15038, 2006: 12).

5 „Mehrwertdienstleistung" – ein unscharfer Begriff

Die Fixierung des Übersetzungsbegriffes auf die sprachliche Umkodierung lässt sich deutlich an dem durch die Norm in das translatorische Handlungsfeld eingeführten Begriff „Mehrwertdienstleistung" demonstrieren, welcher als Ergänzung zur „übersetzerischen Dienstleistung" konzipiert ist.

Als Mehrwertdienstleistungen werden „Dienstleistungen, die vom Übersetzungsdienstleister … zusätzlich zur Übersetzungsdienstleistung erbracht werden können" definiert (EN 15038, 2006: 5). Dadurch sollen Leistungen erfasst und berechenbar gemacht werden, die bisher nicht selten vom Auftraggeber als selbstverständlich vorausgesetzt wurden wie z.B. die typografische Gestaltung des Translats mit DTP-Software oder das Überschreiben der layoutformatierten Ausgangstextdatei mit der Übersetzung. Leistungen dieser Art als Mehrwertdienstleistung zu deklarieren und zu berechnen, ist selbstverständlich voll berechtigt, handelt es sich doch um zusätzliche Arbeitsleistungen, die von translatorischer Seite zusätzliche Kompetenz und zusätzlichen Zeitaufwand voraussetzen und das Translationsprodukt mit zusätzlichen qualitativen Eigenschaften ausstatten.

Doch obwohl die Einführung des Begriffs „Mehrwertdienstleistung" für solche Leistungen prinzipiell zu begrüßen ist, handelt es sich um einen nicht unproblematischen und in seinem Bedeutungsinhalt in der Norm inkonsequent gehandhabten Begriff.

Erstens greift die Norm – wie bereits erwähnt – mit ihrer Auffassung von „übersetzerischer Dienstleistung" enger als das Berufsbild von 1988 mit seiner Liste unterschiedlicher Auftragsformen, u.a. die originale Erstellung von Texten aufgrund von ausgangssprachlichem Material (vgl. BDÜ 2006: [4]); und sie greift wesentlich enger als die ÖNORM D 1200, die wie oben aufgeführt z.b. das Lokalisieren zusammen mit anderen interkulturellen Vertextungsverfahren als gleichberechtigte „Transferleistung" auflistet, während EN 15038 diese aus dem selbstverständlichen translatorischen Aufgabenfeld herausnimmt und ihnen als Mehrwertdienstleistung eine Sonderrolle zuweist.

Zum anderen darf bezweifelt werden, dass Übersetzer – wie es die Norm auf S. 12 fordert – so ohne weiteres in der Lage sind, für bestimmte Mehrwertdienstleistungen das gleiche Qualitätsniveau zu erbringen wie für die translatorische Dienstleistung, z.b. im Bereich DTP, bei der Grafik- und Internetseitengestaltung (wobei der Verdacht nicht unbegründet scheint, dass unter „Gestaltung" hier die konkrete Formatierung gemeint ist, nicht die kreative Formgebung, die in der Regel ja auch eine eigene Ausbildung voraussetzt).

Und schließlich drittens: Ein Teil der aufgeführten Mehrwertdienstleistungen widerspricht eindeutig der Definition von S. 5, d.h. besitzt nicht die den Begriffsinhalt konstituierenden Merkmale, da es sich nicht um „zusätzliche Leistungen zur Übersetzungsdienstleistung" handeln kann wie z.b. „Fachliche Prüfung und/oder [das] Korrekturlesen von Fremdübersetzungen" (EN 15038, 2006: 17).

6   Ein neues Berufsverständnis?

Die Analyse zentraler Begriffe der Norm und ihr Vergleich mit den ÖNORMEN D 1200 und D 1201 zeigt also erstens das noch unterschiedlich weit ausgebildete berufliche Selbstverständnis der ÜbersetzerInnen in den beteiligten Translationskulturen und zweitens die Fokussierung auf die bilinguale Handlung. So erweist sich die Norm als Spiegel einer noch nicht voll professionell handelnden Praxis –, als Spiegel der heterogenen Zusammensetzung des Berufsstandes sowie dessen nicht unproblematischem Berufsverständnis. Dies lässt sich nachweisen an der Definition des beruflichen Handlungsumfangs, an der Beschreibung des Produktionsprozess-Umfanges sowie dem Eingehen auf die Zusammenarbeit mit Berufen, die an der Herstellung des zielkulturellen Endprodukts (als Print- oder elektronisch-digitales Medium) beteiligt sind. Und schließlich – worauf hier nicht näher eingegangen werden kann – an der Definition der beruflichen Kompetenz.

Warum aber fühlt man sich in translatorischen Kreisen nicht prinzipiell zuständig für die Konzipierung und Anfertigung von optimal funktionierenden Kommunikationsmitteln für transkulturelle kommunikative Zwecke? Gerade darin könnte doch ein neues Aufgabenfeld und damit auch ein erweitertes Berufsverständnis liegen? Schließlich würde so ein Weg zum selbstständigen, transkulturellen Kommunikationsberuf beschritten, durch den sich ÜbersetzerInnen vom Makel des „akademisch geschulten Hilfsarbeiters" und unkreativen Befehlsempfängers befreien könnten. Anstelle des „Sprachmittlers" und seinem begrenzten Übersetzungsverständnis, der seine Leistung per Zeichen, Wort, Zeile oder Seite berechnet (Tabelle, Typus 1), müsste der Experte, die Expertin für Konzeption und Herstellung von Kommunikationsmitteln für transkulturelle Kommunikationsaufgaben treten (Tabelle, Typus 2).

Berufskonzept	Translator-Typus 1 (traditionell)	Translator-Typus 2 (zukünftig?)
Grundsätzliches Berufsverständnis	»Sprachmittler«	»transkultureller Kommunikationsexperte«
Expertise; Know-how-Vorsprung	Fremdsprachen- (und -kultur-)Kenntnisse	transkulturelles Kommunikationsdesign
Merkmalsumfang des Begriffs »Übersetzungs-«/ »Translationsprozess«	auf Ausgangstextanalyse basierende Reformulierung des AT mit zielsprachlichen Mitteln	auf Auftragsanalyse basierender umfangreicher Workflow zur Produktion von zielkulturellen Kommunikationsmitteln
Grad der Eingliederung in den medialen Produktionsprozess	gering; eigene bilinguale Leistung fokussierend	hoch; translatorisches Handeln produktionsphasenbewusst & teamorientiert integrierend
Honorarberechnungsgrundlage	Zeichen, Wort, Zeile, Seite (»Wortsklave«, »Tagelöhner«)	statistisch ermittelter zeitlicher Arbeitsaufwand auf Stundenbasis
Standortbestimmung in der Berufsgruppe	solipsistisch; Einzelkämpfermentalität	berufsgruppen-solidarisch; in Netzwerken bzw. virtuellen Teams arbeitend

Der bloße Umstand, dass jemand seinen Lebensunterhalt durch Übersetzen verdient, bedeutet nicht automatisch, dass er/sie wirklich professionell arbeitet – es sei denn, man lässt die Gleichung „in der Praxis = professionell" gelten, wie es ja auch tatsächlich nicht selten vorkommt. Wirklich professionell handelt aber nur, wer entsprechend seiner Ausbildung und seinem Kenntnis- und Fertigkeitsstand, d.h. entsprechend seinem persönlichen beruflichen Kompetenzprofil und Qualifikationsgrad, geeignete Aufgaben im Berufsfeld ausübt und professionelle translatorische Arbeitsprinzipien befolgt.

Sicher wird EN 15038 in vielen europäischen Translationskulturen allmählich zu einer weiteren Professionalisierung führen, wenn man den Umstand „zu einem Ziel unterwegs zu sein" schon als solchen gelten lassen möchte. Erreicht ist das Ziel allerdings noch lange nicht und es ist zu wünschen, dass die nächste Version der Norm mutige Schritte unternimmt auf dem Weg zu einem echten translatorischen Vollberuf, indem weniger die Sprachmittlung als Ausgangs- und Bezugspunkt dient, sondern das Expertentum für die Konzeption und Herstellung transkultureller Kommunikationsmittel.

Bibliographie

Bausch, K.-R. (1980). Sprachmittlung: Übersetzen und Dolmetschen, in: Althaus, H.P. / Henne, H. / Wiegand H.E. (Hrsg.). *Lexikon der Germanistischen Linguistik.* Bd.4. 2. vollst. neu bearb. u. erw. Aufl. Tübingen: Niemeyer. S. 797–802.

BDÜ (Hrsg.) (2006): *Berufsbild Übersetzer, Dolmetscher und andere Fremdsprachenberufe.* Berlin: Bundesverband der Dolmetscher und Übersetzer e.V.

BDÜ (2008): *Übersetzen in die Zukunft.* www.uebersetzen-in-die-zukunft.de/de/020000.php [26.10.2008]

Berufsbild (1988) für Übersetzer, Dolmetscher und verwandte Fremdsprachenberufe. – Sonderdruck aus Mitteilungsblatt für Dolmetscher und Übersetzer 4/34, Juli/August 1988.

DIN 2345 (1999), Übersetzungsaufträge, in: Baxmann-Krafft, E.-M. / Herzog G.: *Normen für Übersetzer und technische Autoren,* 1. Aufl., hrsg.: DIN Deutsches Institut für Normung e.V. Berlin, Wien, Zürich: Beuth.

DIN EN 15038 (2006): *Übersetzungs-Dienstleistungen – Dienstleistungsanforderungen.* Berlin: Beuth.

Freisler, S. (2009): „Kontextinformationen bei Schnipselübersetzungen", in: *MDÜ* 1/2009, S. 33–36.

Heuer, J.-U. (2002): „Werkvertrag", in: *technische kommunikation,* 24. Jhg. 1/2002, S. 38.

Holz-Mänttäri, J. (1979): „Übersetzer müssen texten können", in: *texten + schreiben* Nr. 5, S. 21–23.

Holz-Mänttäri, J. (1984): *Translatorisches Handeln. Theorie und Methode.* Helsinki: Academia Scientiarum Fennica.

Hübner, M. (2007): „The new standard for translation services", in: *ITI bulletin* January-February 2007, S. 13.

López-Ebri, E. (2004): „Europäische Einigung über die Qualitätssicherung und Zertifizierung von Übersetzungsdienstleistungen", in: *MDÜ* 6/2004, S. 10–12.

ÖNORM D 1200 (2000): *Dienstleistungen – Übersetzen und Dolmetschen. Übersetzungsleistungen. Anforderungen an die Dienstleistung und an die Bereitstellung der Dienstleistung.* Hrsg. vom Fachnormenausschuss 239. Wien: Österreichisches Normungsinstitut.

ÖNORM D 1201 (2000): *Dienstleistungen – Übersetzen und Dolmetschen. Übersetzungsleistungen. Übersetzungsverträge.* Hrsg. vom Fachnormenausschuss 239. Wien: Österreichisches Normungsinstitut.

Prunč, E. (1997): „Translationskultur. Versuch einer konstruktiven Kritik des translatorischen Handelns", in: *TextconText,* Vol.11 = NF 1 (1997), S. 99–127.

Schopp, J. F. (2005): *„Gut zum Druck"? – Typographie und Layout im Übersetzungsprozeß.* Tampere: Tampere University Press (= Acta Universitatis Tamperensis 1117).

Schopp, J. F. (2007): „Korrekturlesen – ein translatorisches Stiefkind?" – In: *Lebende Sprachen* Nr. 2/2007, S. 69–74.

Normen für Übersetzungsdienstleister – Anspruch und Wirklichkeit

Manfred Schmitz

Intertext Fremdsprachendienst e.G., Berlin

manfred.schmitz.berlin@t-online.de

Abstract

In dem Beitrag wird zunächst ein Vergleich maßgeblicher Qualitätsnormen vorgenommen, sodann speziell auf die Umsetzung der europäischen Norm DIN EN 15038 eingegangen. Dabei werden vor allem die (organisatorischen und wirtschaftlichen) Probleme beleuchtet, die sich in der Zusammenarbeit von Übersetzungsbüros untereinander und in der Zusammenarbeit zwischen Übersetzungsbüros/Agenturen/ Sprachendiensten und freien Mitarbeitern bei der Anwendung der Norm ergeben. Abschließend werden Möglichkeiten der Messbarkeit von Parametern der Norm DIN EN 15038 erörtert.

Gutes und richtiges Übersetzen und Schreiben

Kommunikation aus einer Hand – übersetzte Marketingtexte

Carsten Mende

RWS Group GmbH, Berlin

projekt@rws-group.de

Abstract

International tätige Unternehmen verfügen weltweit über Standorte und sprechen Kunden auf allen Kontinenten an. Die direkte Ansprache in der jeweiligen Muttersprache ist in Zeiten der Serviceorientierung ein unbedingtes Muss.

Wie können diese Unternehmen eine einheitliche Kommunikation garantieren?

Der Übersetzer stellt mit seiner Übersetzung und Lokalisation ein Bindeglied zwischen der Muttergesellschaft und den auswärtigen Niederlassungen dar. Wie kann er einen funktionierenden Ablauf und Transport der „Message" sicherstellen, ohne im Unternehmen verwurzelt zu sein?

Qualitätskontrolle bei Übersetzungen „kreativer" Texte

Sibel Türker

SKH SprachKontor Hamburg GmbH

st@sprachkontor.de

Jörg Heinemann

SKH SprachKontor Hamburg GmbH

jh@sprachkontor.de

Einleitung

Allgemeines

Kaum eine ÜbersetzerIn, kaum eine Agentur, die nicht behauptet, die von ihr angefertigten oder gelieferten Übersetzungsprodukte würden hohe Qualität bieten. Doch wie ist eine solche hohe Qualität überhaupt zu beurteilen?

Begriffsbestimmung

Als „kreative" Texte bezeichnen wir Gebrauchstexte ohne literarischen Anspruch, die jedoch „zwischen den Zeilen" schöpferische Qualitäten haben. Sie sind ein Mittelding zwischen einerseits rein funktionalen Texten wie Bedienungsanleitungen, Verträgen, Hinweisschildern usw., die im Idealfall ihren Inhalt explizit darstellen, und andererseits „echten" literarischen Texten. Es geht also um journalistische sowie um Marketing-, Werbe- und PR-Texte.

Vorgehen und Aufgabenstellung

Nach dem Modell von Katarina Reiß (1971, nach Schäffner 2005) gehören die hier „kreativ" genannten Texte zum operativen (appellbetonten) Texttyp, bei deren Übersetzung „das Ziel in der Beibehaltung des textimmanenten Appells [bestehe], was durch eine adaptierende Übersetzungsmethode erreicht werden" könne (Schäffner 2005, 111). Wir schließen uns der Forderung nach einer adaptierenden Methode an – wann allerdings kann eine Adaption als gelungen angesehen werden?

Es gibt viele verschiedene Ansätze, allgemein die Güte einer Übersetzung nachvollziehbar zu beurteilen – neben quantitativen meist qualitative, die jedoch zum Teil ebenfalls dem Formalen verhaftet bleiben. Einige dieser Ansätze stellen wir in einem kurzen Überblick dar.

Als Vorbereitung einer Analysemethode stellen wir – ebenfalls im Überblick – zwei Theorien vor, die sich beide auf „Diskurs" beziehen.

Wir gehen hier zuerst von einem allgemeinen Diskursbegriff aus: Der „Ausdruck [hat] die Funktion […], die Herstellung und die gesellschaftliche Unterhaltung von komplexen Wissenssystemen zu bezeichnen" (Ehlich 2000, 162).

Für unsere Zwecke nehmen wir anschließend die gemeinsamen Aspekte der beiden vorgestellten Theorien und schätzen mit deren Hilfe die Qualität von Übersetzungen ein.

Um zu einer solchen Einschätzung zu gelangen, werden wir kein fertiges Verfahren entwickeln, sondern anhand von Beispielen Möglichkeiten zu einer Vorgehensweise vorschlagen. Gerade kreative Texte haben derart vielfältige Funktionen und Wirkungsfelder, dass wir meinen, ein geschlossenes Instrumentarium sei schon vom Ansatz her nicht möglich.

1 Vorhandene Ansätze

1.1 Allgemeines

Es gibt verschiedene Ansätze, *Qualität* bei Übersetzungen nachvollziehbar darzustellen. Dazu gehört indirekt auch, nach welchen Kriterien ÜbersetzerInnen Mitglied in einem Standesverband werden können – nach Ausbildung, Berufserfahrung, Kundenreferenzen usw.

Andere Ansätze gehen vom Projektablauf aus oder vom formalen Ergebnis des Übersetzungsprozesses.

1.2 DIN EN 15038 Übersetzungsdienstleistungen

Norm DIN EN 15038 regelt vor allem das Projektmanagement und die Anforderungen, die an dieses und an die hieran Beteiligten zu stellen sind. Da dies an anderer Stelle (z.B. MDÜ 1/2007, 18–22) ausführlich erläutert wird, gehen wir hier nicht weiter darauf ein.

1.3 Qualitätsmessverfahren J-2450

Das Qualitätsmessverfahren J-2450 der *Society of Automotive Engineers* (SAE) geht auf eine im Herbst 1997 gegründete Arbeitsgruppe mit VertreterInnen verschiedener Automobilkonzerne zurück. Im Oktober 2001 wurde eine Empfehlung zur Vorgehensweise verabschiedet, wie die Qualität von Übersetzungen automobiltechnischer Wartungs- und Reparaturinformationen unabhängig von den beteiligten Sprachen und von der Art des Übersetzungsverfahrens gemessen werden kann.

Bei diesem Bewertungsverfahren werden die Übersetzungen im Nachhinein nach Art und Anzahl etwaiger enthaltener Fehler bewertet, wobei die Fehler unterschiedlich stark gewichtet werden. Die Summe der gewichteten Fehler wird ins Verhältnis zur Textmenge gesetzt, woraus sich ein Fehlerquotient ergibt:

Error type	Num * serious	Num * minor	Category weighted score
Wrong term score	0	0	0
Wrong sense score	0	0	0
Omission score	0	0	0
Grammatical error score	0	4	4
Misspelling score	3	0	3
Punctuation score	0	0	0
Miscellaneous error score	0	1	1
Document score	0.049		

Tabelle 1: Bewertungsmaske, Ausschnitt aus der J-2450-Evaluationswebsite eines Sprachdienstleisters für die Automobilindustrie

1.4 Weitere Ansätze

Als Beispiele dafür, wie Übersetzungen z. B. literarischer Texte bewertet werden können, stellen wir kurz zwei Arbeiten vor.

1.4.1 Maierhofer: Übersetzungsvergleich

In ihrer Diplomarbeit vergleicht Silvia Maierhofer zwei Übersetzungen eines Agatha-Christie-Krimis. An verschiedenen Passagen untersucht und bewertet sie deren zahlreiche Unterschiede. Sie fragt auch danach, wo die ÜbersetzerInnen Informationen hinzugefügt haben.

Als Hinzufügen sieht Maierhofer jedoch auch an, wenn eine Konstruktion mit *Past Perfect – she had had 'flu* – nicht durch die ungewöhnliche deutsche Form „sie hatte Grippe gehabt", sondern durch Partikeln oder Ähnliches („sie hatte eben eine Grippe überstanden" bzw. „sie hatte damals eine Grippe hinter sich") (Maierhofer 2007, 50 f.) ausgedrückt wird.

Eine solche formale Bewertung nähert sich nicht der Funktion des Textes an. Wir halten sie für unsere Zwecke für nicht hilfreich.

1.4.2 Liebel: Bewertung unter anderem von Funktion und Wirkung

Das Analysemodell von Dorothea Liebel (2009), das sie in ihrer Dissertation erarbeitet, geht deutlich über das Formale hinaus. Auch sie betrachtet literarische Übersetzungen, und zwar die des schwedischsprachigen Romans *Vägen till Klockrike* von Harry Martinson ins Deutsche.

Martinsons Schreibstil zeichnet sich durch spontane Wortbildungen aus, die Liebel nicht nur auf Äquivalenz bei Denotation und Konnotation der Übertragungen ins Deutsche prüft. Liebel bewertet außerdem, welche Intention und Wirkung – beides fasst sie unter *Wirkung* zusammen – die Übersetzungen haben. Dies ermöglicht ihr, Übersetzungen breiter zu bewerten und auch zu erkennen, wenn in der Übersetzung stilistisch etwas verloren geht, obwohl die außersprachlichen Bezüge erhalten bleiben (z. B. ebd., 127: stilistisch nähere Übersetzungsvorschläge „schweißkutschierten", „nachtreizbaren").

AT: svettkörda, nattretliga						
ZT: in Schweiß kutschierten, infolge der nächtlichen Stunde reizbaren						
Inv	*Sonder*	*Form*	*Inhalt*		*Funktion*	
	Kult	*Stil*	*Den*	*Kon*	*Inten*	*Wir*
–	*0*	–	+	+	–	–

Tabelle 2: Beispiel für Analyseraster bei Liebel (2009, 127 – Abb. 5; zu den Abkürzungen siehe dort).

Interessant ist hieran, dass die Funktion ins Spiel kommt, zu kurz greift jedoch, dass diese nur auf Wortebene angewendet wird.

2 Theorien zur Diskursanalyse

2.1 Diskursanalyse nach Rehbein und Ehlich

Die *funktional-pragmatische Kommunikationsanalyse* wurde in den 1970er-Jahren von Konrad Ehlich und Jochen Rehbein in der kritischen Auseinandersetzung mit der *speech act theory* nach Austin und Searle begründet. Rehbein und Ehlich vertreten eine Pragmalinguistik, die auf Karl Bühler zurückgeht und bei der die Kategorien „Handlung" bzw. „sprachliches Handeln" eine entscheidende Rolle spielen. Demnach liegen jedem gesellschaftlichen Handeln unter anderem auch sprachliche Handlungsmuster zugrunde, die von den AktantInnen in gesellschaftlichen Prozessen erlernt und verinnerlicht werden. Das Wissen über die diversen sprachlichen Handlungsmuster, wie Wegbeschreibungen, Erzählen oder Arztgespräche, steht jeder einzelnen SprachbenutzerIn zur Verfügung (vgl. Ehlich 1991, 132 ff.). Die *funktionale Pragmatik* versteht unter *sprachlichem Handeln* eine Interaktion zwischen einer SprecherIn und einer HörerIn. Sie geht damit darüber hinaus, Sprache isoliert von ihren BenutzerInnen als ein in sich geschlossenes System zu begreifen.

Der Begriff *Diskurs* wird im funktional-pragmatischen Sinne wie folgt definiert: „[...] zweckbezogen strukturierte Ensembles von Sprechhandlungen, die sprachliche Handlungsmuster zu größeren kommunikativen Einheiten umsetzen." (Schnieders 2005, 55, unter Verweis auf Ehlich 1993, 162) Also stellen jede Sprechsituation, jede sprachliche Handlung und jeder Text einen Diskurs dar, der auf seine Zweckmäßigkeit untersucht werden kann. Denn jedes sprachliche Handeln ist strukturiert und gesteuert durch den Zweck, den es erreichen sollte (vgl. Ehlich/Rehbein 1972, 215; zitiert bei Galinski 2004, 17). So kann eine „funktionale Analyse [...] nur erreicht werden, wenn man die dem sozialen Leben zugrundeliegenden Kräfte und Strukturen herausfindet. Aus ihnen erst lässt sich die Erklärung der an der Oberfläche auftretenden Erscheinungen entwickeln" (ebd.).

Demnach betrachten wir den zur Übersetzung vorliegenden Originaltext als eine Art sprachliches Handeln, das in seinem gesellschaftlichen Kontext nach seinem Zweck zu analysieren ist. Erst wenn die ÜbersetzerIn in ihrem Arbeitsprozess das Original einer funktionalen Analyse unterzogen und den von diesem zu erfüllenden Zweck herausgefunden hat, wird sie in der Lage sein, die Intention des Textes in die Übersetzung einzubringen. Bei diesem Prozess wird sie sicherlich andere Werkzeuge als die der Originalsprache heranziehen müssen, nämlich die, die ihr die Zielsprache bietet.

So kann es notwendig sein, dass das, was in der Ausgangssprache beispielsweise im Konjunktiv ausgedrückt wird, in der Zielsprache etwa mit einer Partikel wiedergegeben werden muss. Das Erfüllen gleicher Funktion durch unterschiedliche Kategorien ist also abhängig vom *Handlungswissen* der ÜbersetzerIn in ihren Arbeitssprachen: Sie übernimmt im Übersetzungsprozess die Rolle der SprecherIn und muss durch ihre Übersetzungskompetenz die bezweckte Hörerrezeption erreichen.

2.2 Kritische Diskursanalyse

Mit *kritischer Diskursanalyse* bezeichnen wir hier eine Gruppe sprachwissenschaftlicher Theorien, wie sie unter anderem Ruth Wodak, Teun van Dijk und Norman Fairclough vertreten (vgl. Chilton 2005, 20 f.).

Nicht alle AutorInnen nennen ihre Form der Diskursanalyse „kritisch"; zur Abgrenzung vom Ansatz Ehlich/Rehbein behalten wir den Begriff aber für diese Gruppe von Ansätzen bei. „Kritisch" bedeutet hier, dass verborgene Strukturen eines Textes offengelegt werden – es geht nicht um den oftmals auch vorhandenen emanzipatorischen Anspruch der AutorInnen.

Kritische DiskursanalytikerInnen gehen über den in der Einleitung genannten Diskursbegriff hinaus: In der Sprache scheint nicht nur die Wirklichkeit auf, sondern sie steht in einer gegenseitigen Beziehung zu dieser und verändert sie auch (vgl. Fairclough 2009, o. S.) Fairclough ist auch der Auffassung, dass Diskurs in heutiger Zeit als Element des gesellschaftlichen Lebens deutlich an Bedeutung gewonnen hat und allgemeine gesellschaftliche Veränderungen oftmals als diskursive Veränderungen ausgelöst und vorangetrieben werden (ebd.). Somit ist zwischen „Text" und „Diskurs" zu unterscheiden (vgl. Pöllabauer 2005, 148): „Texte sind [...] lediglich Teil dieses [sozialen] Interaktionsprozesses." (ebd.)

Texte stehen also nicht unabhängig da, sondern existieren in einem diskursiven Zusammenhang, und zwar nicht nur mit den LeserInnen, sondern auch mit der AutorIn und darüber hinaus mit der gesamten Kommunikationsgemeinschaft (vgl. Strauß/Haß/Harras 1989, 602). So unterliegen Texte auch jeweils den diskursiven Regeln, *was von wem worüber* gesagt werden kann.

Dies gilt insbesondere für „kreative" Texte im hier verwendeten Sinne: Gerade journalistische wie Marketing- und PR-Texte haben zur Aufgabe, gesellschaftlich zu wirken. In bestimmtem Umfang gilt dies sicherlich für alle Texte; aber die diskursive Einbindung ist bei Bedienungsanleitungen weniger auffällig.

Wenn wir vor diesem Hintergrund Übersetzungen auf ihre Qualität prüfen wollen, müssen wir uns also zuerst fragen, ob sie dieselbe diskursive Funktion erfüllen wie der Originaltext.

2.3 Zusammenführung der beiden Ansätze

Vor dem Hintergrund der funktional-pragmatischen Diskursanalyse muss die ÜbersetzerIn über Sprechhandlungswissen verfügen und dieses im Sinne der Intention des Originaltextes in der Zielsprache einsetzen.

Nach der kritischen Diskursanalyse ist es beim Übersetzungsprozess notwendig, den Text auch in seiner diskursiven Einbindung zu übertragen.

Die ÜbersetzerIn sollte unseres Erachtens weder nur die handlungsspezifische Betrachtungsweise des funktional-pragmatischen Ansatzes berücksichtigen noch nur den alleinigen diskursiven Textzusammenhang in Betracht ziehen. Erst wenn sie es schafft, beide Ansätze zusammenzuführen, hat sie eine fruchtbare Basis für den Übersetzungsprozess geschaffen.

Heruntergekocht auf den Alltag bedeutet dies: Für eine gute Übertragung ist es erforderlich, dass der ÜbersetzerIn über den Ausgangstext mehr als bloß seine Textlänge und -sorte usw. bekannt ist. Sie muss wissen, *wer den Text zu welchem Zweck für wen und in welchem Zusammenhang verwendbar* verfasst hat.

Diese Informationen zur Makroebene erhält sie bei der Auftragsannahme vom Auftraggeber. Damit ist sie gut ausgestattet, um den Ausgangstext auch auf der Mikroebene adäquat zu interpretieren.

Was gehört nun zu dieser Mikrointerpretation? Die Antwort darauf ist oberflächlich gesehen banal. Ja, die Mikrointerpretation hängt vom jeweiligen Text ab, für sie gibt es keine Schablone; sie lässt sich aber im Prinzip mit den W-Fragen von oben beschreiben. Und zwar bei jeder einzelnen Übersetzungseinheit – das meinen wir nicht im Sinne eines CAT-Programms, sondern kontinuierlich im gesamten Übersetzungsprozess: *Warum steht dieser Textteil an dieser Stelle und welche Funktion hat er in diesem textuellen Zusammenhang?* Zum Beispiel reicht es nicht zu wissen, dass ich jetzt einen Streikaufruf übersetze und mitreißend formulieren muss, sondern die verschiedenen Absätze darin haben unterschiedliche Aufgaben – sie vermitteln ein Solidaritätsgefühl (identitätsstiftend); informieren über Fakten zum Ablauf und zu rechtlichen Bedingungen; stimmen auf Gehaltsverhandlungen ein, indem die wirtschaftlichen Bedingungen des bestreikten Unternehmens beschrieben werden. Jeder dieser Absätze hat also eine spezifische Funktion, die beim Übersetzungsprozess übertragen werden muss.

Wir demonstrieren im folgenden Kapitel anhand von Beispielen an einzelnen Textabschnitten, was wir mit Mikrointerpretation meinen und wie wir mit ihrer Hilfe die Übersetzungsqualität verbessern.

3 Beispiele

Beispiel 1: TR–DE

Im Rahmen eines Pressespiegels wird für den Schweizer Exporteur des darin be-
schriebenen Gerätes ein Zeitschriftenartikel übersetzt. Der Text besteht aus einer
Headline, einer Subhead, einer Einleitung und dem Fließtext. Der Text beschreibt,
dass ein Gerät zur Minderung von Cellulitis nun auch in der Türkei eingesetzt wird.
Dieses Gerät, und das ist der Foto-Aufhänger des Textes, wird auch vom Popstar
Madonna verwendet. Die Subhead lautet:

Madonna'nın evinde de bu akustik enerji dalgaları var

*(Wörtliche Übersetzung: Auch in Madonnas Haus sind diese akustischen Ener-
giewellen vorhanden)*

Sie wird wie folgt übersetzt:

Akustische Energiewellen in Madonnas Haus

Im Türkischen lenkt der Ausdruck *evinde* (wörtlich: „in ihrem Haus") nicht den Blick
auf den tatsächlichen Ort, sondern auf die prominente Person. Im Deutschen hingegen
drückt „in Madonnas Haus" aus, *wo konkret* sich das im Artikel beschriebene Gerät
befindet. Der Blick wird gar von Madonna weggelenkt.

Die dem Text gerecht werdende Übersetzung lautet daher (für den Kontext samt
Einleitung):

Akustische Energiewellen auch bei Madonna

*Hollywoodstars, Models, die High Society, ja sogar Madonna: Alle Welt spricht
von der „Therapie mit akustischen Wellen", um Cellulitis erfolgreich zu bekämp-
fen. Dieses Verfahren wird seit einigen Jahren in Europa und Amerika angewandt
und ist nun endlich auch in der Türkei verfügbar.*

Beispiel 2: RU–DE

Auch im zweiten Beispiel wird ein Zeitungsartikel übersetzt. Der Auftraggeber ist ein
Unternehmen, das über Mitbewerber in Osteuropa informiert werden will.

Wir beschäftigen uns für diese Mikroanalyse nur mit dem Verb in dem einleitenden
Hauptsatz sowie mit den Übersetzungen zweier Ausdrücke:

Юрий Дробилко рассказал *и о том, что при выдаче техусловий
«Николаевгаз» предлагал* субъектам хозяйствования *купить* кое-какие
*предметы под предлогом того, что они очень необходимы для развития
сетей «Николаевгаза».*

Die Übersetzung lautet:

Jurij Drobilko erzählte *auch darüber, dass bei der Aushändigung der technischen
Dokumentation „Nikolajewgas"* den Wirtschaftssubjekten irgendwelche *Gegenstände zum Kauf anbot, unter dem Vorwand, dass sie sehr notwendig für die Entwicklung der Netze von „Nikolajewgas" sind.*

Schlägt man das Verb *рассказывать* im Wörterbuch nach, trifft man auf eine Bandbreite von möglichen Entsprechungen:

рассказывать: berichten (что-л., о чём-л.); erzählen; hersagen; abspinnen; berichten (что-л., о чем-л.); hersagen (все подряд, от начала до конца); singen und sägen (www.multitran.ru)

Hier muss die ÜbersetzerIn auf ihr Handlungswissen im funktional-pragmatischen Sinne zurückgreifen, um sich für die richtige Entsprechung zu entscheiden. Im Deutschen wird in Zeitungstexten „berichtet", „erläutert", „ausgeführt" usw., aber keineswegs „erzählt"; gerade dieses Verb vermittelt „geringe Glaubwürdigkeit".

Dass das Handlungswissen nicht eingesetzt worden ist, zeigen auch die wörtliche Übersetzung von *субъектам хозяйствования* als „Wirtschaftssubjekte" und das Bemühen, das Indefinitpronomen *кое-какие* ebenfalls zu übersetzen („irgendwelche". Dies ist der Textform nicht angemessen und kann daher schlicht entfallen).

Die angemessene Übersetzung muss also wie folgt lauten:

Jurij Drobilko berichtete schließlich, dass Nikolaevgas bei der Aushändigung der technischen Dokumentation Unternehmern Gegenstände zum Kauf unter dem Vorwand angeboten habe, sie seien notwendig für den Ausbau der Netze von Nikolaevgas.

Beispiel 3: DE–EN

Unter der Rubrik „Personalien" erscheint in der Mitarbeiterzeitschrift des Großunternehmens XX folgende Meldung:

Seit Mitte April hat XX erstmals eine Personalchefin: NN. Schon seit Anfang ihrer beruflichen Laufbahn hat sie mit dem Personalwesen zu tun, denn sie absolvierte parallel zu ihrem Studium eine Ausbildung in einem Großunternehmen in diesem Bereich – und hat es nach eigenem Bekunden nie bereut.

Diese wird zuerst wie folgt übersetzt:

In mid April, XX appointed its first ever personnel manager: NN. Since the beginning of her career she has been involved in Human Resources. She completed her training in this area with a large company while at the same time studying at university – and she admits that she has never regretted her choice of career.

Bei einer textinternen Betrachtung der Übersetzung gelingt es nicht, den Fehler festzustellen: Der Zieltext ist grammatisch und auf der Wortebene richtig. Bei einer Überlegung, was die AutorIn jedoch sagen wollte, wird klar, dass der wesentliche Aspekt verloren gegangen ist: Die Firma XX richtet nicht zum ersten Mal eine Stelle für die Personalleitung ein, sondern die wesentliche Aussage des Textes ist, dass diese Funktion erstmalig von einer Frau übernommen wird. Dies wird in der Übersetzung erst klar, wenn das *-in* ausnahmsweise mitübersetzt wird:

In mid April, XX appointed its first ever female personnel manager: NN. ...

Die „richtige" Nachricht ergibt sich diskursiv: Ein Großunternehmen hat auf jeden Fall eine PersonalchefIn – die Einstellung einer solchen kann daher keine Neuigkeit sein. Das *erstmals* verweist also auf etwas Neues. Dies kann in diesem Satz nur das Geschlecht der PersonalchefIn sein.

Beispiel 4: EN–DE

In diesem Beispiel wird die Website eines Finanzdienstleisters übersetzt. Das Unternehmen bewirbt hier Finanzprodukte für den Gesundheitsbereich und stellt seine Vorteile unter anderem wie folgt dar:

> *At XX YY Financial Services in Europe, we understand the business of financing healthcare. Our global team of professionals truly understands the complexities and challenges of the healthcare industry, bringing a comprehensive set of financial products and services to all players in the sector.*

Die Übersetzung lautet:

> *Wir von XX YY Financial Services in Europa kennen uns mit der Finanzierung im Gesundheitswesen bestens aus. Unser internationales Expertenteam versteht sich auf die Komplexität und die Herausforderungen des Gesundheitssektors und liefert ein umfangreiches Angebot an Finanzprodukten und -dienstleistungen, um wirklich allen branchenspezifischen Bedürfnissen gerecht zu werden.*

Hier sind bei der Verwendung in einem Werbetext folgende Stellen problematisch:

1. In der ersten Hälfte des zweiten Satzes ist das Wesentliche *complexities and challenges*; in der Übersetzung geht durch die Nennung von „Gesundheitssektor" der Fokus jedoch auf diesen Begriff über. Da die Branche jedoch bereits bekannt ist, wird hier etwas wiederholt, wodurch der LeserIn unterstellt wird, sie habe dies seit dem vorangehenden Satz bereits vergessen. Hier kommt also Fachtextwissen zum Zuge: Gerade in Werbetexten wird nicht etwas bereits Bekanntes wiederholt, sondern es wird über das Bekannte etwas Neues gesagt. Diese Regel wird hier verletzt.

2. Es ist nicht nur unnötig, „Gesundheit" in den Komposita zu wiederholen, sondern hier trifft auf der Wortebene dieselbe Art der Kritik zu wie bei 1.

3. Der zweite Satz ist zu lang und umständlich formuliert. Er widerspricht der Textsorte „Marketingtext". Nach der aktuellen Auffassung dürfen bei dieser nur kurze und möglichst nicht verschachtelte Sätze verwendet werden.

3. Die Phrase *in the sector* wird umständlich durch „wirklich allen branchenspezifischen Bedürfnissen" wiedergegeben. Diese nochmalige Einschränkung ist überflüssig – worüber sonst wird hier gesprochen?

Im Proofreading wurde die Übersetzung in folgende Fassung verändert:

> *Wir von XX YY Financial Services Europa verstehen uns auf Finanzierungsdienstleistungen im Gesundheitswesen. Unser globales Expertenteam kennt Zusammenhänge und Herausforderungen der Branche. So bieten wir allen Beteiligten umfassende Finanzprodukte und Dienstleistungen an.*

Es könnte sein, dass diese Finalversion der Übersetzung dahingehend kritisiert wird, sie würde zu stark vom Original abweichen. Allerdings findet eine solche „Abweichung" nur auf der Oberfläche statt. Unter der anfangs genannten Voraussetzung, dass eine Übersetzung jedoch den Ausgangstext in seiner Funktion und diskursiven Einbindung wiedergeben müsse, halten wir diese stark interpretierende Arbeitsweise genau für die erforderliche Methode, um dieses Ziel zu erreichen; wir meinen, dass die übersetzte Version des Marketingtextes an die „Gewohnheiten" der Zielsprache angepasst werden muss – nicht an die einzelnen Wörter.

4 Schluss

Natürlich muss eine Übersetzung auf der Wortebene stimmen, aber dies setzen wir als selbstverständlich voraus. Definieren wir hingegen Qualität einer Übersetzung dadurch, dass der Zieltext dieselbe appellative Funktion und diskursive Einbindung wie der Ausgangstext hat, dann können wir zusammenfassend feststellen, dass die ÜbersetzerIn stets über den Tellerrand des eigentlichen Textes hinausschauen muss. Das Bewusstsein für die Funktion muss in jedem Moment des Übersetzungsprozesses und ebenso kontinuierlich während des Proofreadings vorhanden sein und sich in Satzstellung, Reihenfolge der Sätze, Mitteln für Textbezüge und nicht zuletzt in textsortenspezifischer Zielsprachenverwendung ausdrücken.

Bibliografie

Chilton, P. (2005). Missing links in mainstream CDA – Modules, blends and the critical instinct, in: Wodak, R.; Chilton, P. A. (Hg.). *A new agenda in (critical) discourse analysis: theory, methodology, and interdisciplinary.* Amsterdam: John Benjamins. S. 19–51.

Ehlich, K. (1991). Funktional-pragmatische Kommunikationsanalyse. Ziele und Verfahren, in: Flader, D. (Hg.). *Verbale Interaktion. Studien zur Empirie und Methodologie der Pragmatik.* Stuttgart: Metzler. S. 127–143.

Ehlich, K. (2000). Diskurs, in: Glück, H. (Hg.). *Metzler Lexikon Sprache.* Stuttgart/Weimar: Metzler. S. 162–163.

Ehlich, K. / Rehbein, J. (1972). Zur Konstitution pragmatischer Einheiten in einer Institution: Das Speiserestaurant, in: Wunderlich, D. (Hg.): *Linguistische Pragmatik.* Frankfurt a. M.: Athenäum. S. 209–254.

Fairclough, N. (2009): www.ling.lancs.ac.uk/profiles/263 (Abfrage 2009-05-30).

Galinski, A. (2004). *Zweierlei Perspektiven auf Gespräche.* Linguistik-Server Essen (2009-05-30).

Liebel, D. (2009). *Tageslichtfreude und Buchstabenangst.* Diss. Univ. Umeå.

Maierhofer, S. (2007). *Agatha Christie in neuer Übersetzung.* Diplomarbeit Karl-Franzens-Univ. Graz.

Pöllabauer, S. (2005). *„I don't understand your English, Miss."* – Dolmetschen bei Asylanhörungen. Tübingen: Narr.

Reiß, K. (1971). *Möglichkeiten und Grenzen der Übersetzungskritik.* München: Max Hueber.

SAE J2450 (2009): www.sae.org/technicalcommittees/j2450p1.htm (2009-05-26).

Schäffner, C. (2004). Systematische Übersetzungsdefinitionen (Formal definitions of translations), in: Kittel, H. et al. (Hg.). *Übersetzung – Ein internationales Handbuch zur Übersetzungsforschung.* 1. Tbd. Berlin: de Gruyter. S. 101–117.

Schnieders, G. (2005). *Reklamationsgespräche: eine diskursanalytische Studie.* Tübingen: Gunter Narr.

Strauß, G.; Haß, U.; Harras, G. (1989). *Brisante Wörter: von Agitation bis Zeitgeist.* Berlin: de Gruyter.

Wird dem Übersetzer immer mehr die Feder geführt?

Corinna Schlüter-Ellner

Sprachen & Dolmetscher Institut München/BDÜ

schlueter-ellner@t-online.de

Wenn man als Übersetzer auf eine vorgefertigte Übersetzung zurückgreifen kann, freut man sich über die Arbeitserleichterung. Es kann sich aber auch in eine Last verkehren, wenn es für das zu bearbeitende Original bereits eine Übersetzung gibt, die man dem Zielleser liefern muss, aber nicht zur Hand hat und erst mühsam suchen muss.

Dass der Kunde als Übersetzung genau vorgegebene Formulierungen oder Texte braucht, kann praktische Gründe haben, kann aber auch daher rühren, dass der Kunde vom Recht der Zielkultur zur Verwendung dieser Formulierungen gezwungen wird. Solche Vorgaben werden immer häufiger im Zuge der Globalisierung und des Verbraucherschutzes. Es fragt sich, ob es zur guten Qualität einer Übersetzung gehört, dem Kunden diese Formulierungen exakt zu liefern, ob es also zur Aufgabe des Übersetzers gehört, entsprechende Recherchen anzustellen.

1   Vorgabe bestimmter Übersetzungen aus praktischen Gründen

Bei Zitaten aus literarischen und anderen Kunstwerken, z.B. Bühnenstücken, entspricht es schon lange der Konvention, dass man nicht selbst eine Übersetzung kreiert, sondern sich der bereits veröffentlichten Übertragung bedient (Kautz 2002: 124). Das fordert nicht nur der Respekt vor der künstlerischen Leistung des Autors und seines Übersetzers, sondern dient auch der praktischen Handhabung, etwa wenn der Rezipient sich das ganze Werk in Übersetzung beschaffen will.

Daneben gibt es neuere technische Gesichtspunkte, die bestimmte Formulierungen und entsprechende Übersetzungen erfordern, etwa beim kontrollierten Schreiben in der technischen Dokumentation oder beim Gestalten von Texten im Hinblick auf die

Google-Suche. In diesem technischen Bereich gibt es jedoch sehr viel berufenere Fachleute, so dass ich darauf nicht näher eingehen werde (vgl. Tjarks-Sobhani und Decombe, in Freudenfeld/Nord 2007: 23 u. 41).

2 Rechtlich vorgegebene Übersetzungen

Zur Bewältigung der vielfältigen grenzüberschreitenden Verflechtungen werden immer mehr internationale Absprachen getroffen und mehrsprachige Standardtexte für die Abwicklung des Rechtsverkehrs geschaffen. Damit will man Rechtssicherheit und gleiche Rahmenbedingungen diesseits und jenseits der Grenze schaffen und die Zusammenarbeit zügiger und reibungsloser gestalten. Diese Entwicklung ist nicht nur bei der staatlichen Zusammenarbeit, sondern auch bei der wirtschaftlichen Verflechtung zu beobachten und wird sich im Zuge der Globalisierung weiter verstärken. Auch der Verbraucherschutz bringt es mit sich, dass bestimmte Formulierungen für Hinweise zur Gesundheit, Sicherheit, Rechtslage etc. vorgeschrieben werden, die man zu beachten hat, wenn man grenzüberschreitend liefern oder Leistungen erbringen will.

In diesem Bereich ist dem Kunden möglicherweise nicht mit einer selbst formulierten Übersetzung gedient,

- wenn es für das Original eine Fassung in der Zielsprache gibt, die international verbindlich vereinbart ist oder im Geschäftsverkehr üblicherweise als Referenztext verwendet wird;

- wenn es einen zielsprachigen Paralleltext gibt, der nach dem nationalen Recht des Ziellandes verbindlich ist;

- wenn im Zielland die Verwendung einer bestimmten Terminologie vorgeschrieben ist.

2.1 Mehrsprachige Fassungen desselben Textes

2.1.1 Internationale Abkommen und europäische Rechtsakte

Beim Titel von multi- oder bilateralen Abkommen, von Rechtsakten der Europäischen Gemeinschaften und anderer internationaler Organisationen oder bei Zitaten daraus muss man sich aus folgenden Gründen an die amtliche Fassung in der Zielsprache halten:

Das Recht existiert nur durch die Sprache, so dass man durch divergierende Formulierungen prinzipiell unterschiedliche rechtliche Inhalte zum Leben bringen kann. Damit also internationale Abkommen und Rechtsakte in verschiedenen Sprachfassungen keinen abweichenden Inhalt haben, wird der Wortlaut von den erlassenden Institutionen in mehreren Sprachen amtlich festgelegt. Dazu ist eine genaue und umfangreiche redaktionelle Arbeit unter Berücksichtigung des Sprachgebrauchs in allen beteiligten Ländern erforderlich. Wird z.B. der deutsche Wortlaut geschaffen, so muss die Rechtssprache in Deutschland, Österreich, Schweiz u.a. berücksichtigt werden. Die jeweilige amtliche Übersetzung ist also ein Produkt langwieriger Abstimmungen und Redaktionsarbeiten von Fachleuten auf rechtlichem und sprachlichem Gebiet, um zur optimalen Übereinstimmung zu kommen.

Wenn der amtliche Text zitiert wird und dieses Zitat zu übersetzen ist und der Übersetzer dabei statt zum existierenden amtlichen Wortlaut in der Zielsprache zu einer eigenen Übersetzung greift, so besteht die Gefahr, dass er nicht dieselbe Formulierung trifft und damit von der rechtlichen Bedeutung her etwas Anderes ausdrückt oder zumindest nicht erwünschte Spielräume für eine andere Auslegung dieser Formulierung eröffnet.

In diesem Bereich ist die Verwendung der amtlichen Übersetzung also nicht nur eine Frage der Konvention, sondern der inhaltlichen Genauigkeit und des Vertrauens, das die Zielgruppe der Juristen in die Übersetzungsarbeit haben kann. Der Übersetzer hat hier m.E. keine Wahl, selbst zu übersetzen, es sei denn, er kann mit vertretbarem Aufwand den amtlichen Text in der Zielsprache nicht ermitteln. Dann sollte er seine eigene Übersetzung allerdings mit einem Hinweis in der Fußnote versehen, dass er den amtlichen Text nicht zur Verfügung hatte.

Übrigens spielt auch hier der praktische Aspekt des Auffindens eine Rolle. Nach dem Grundsatz „Ein Blick in das Gesetz erleichtert die Rechtsfindung" neigen Juristen dazu, juristische Regelungen am jeweiligen Quelltext zu überprüfen. Damit sie ihn finden und entscheiden können, ob sie den richtigen Text vor sich haben, muss man ihnen den korrekten Titel liefern, wie er in der amtlichen Fassung in der jeweiligen Sprache festgelegt worden ist. Und das gilt meines Erachtens selbst dann, wenn man sich beim Originalzitat schon nicht um die exakte Formulierung gekümmert hat, was in der Praxis gar nicht so selten vorkommt.

2.1.2 Internationale Regelwerke als Referenzklauseln

Ebenso zu behandeln sind Regelwerke für grenzüberschreitende Geschäfte, die in verschiedenen Sprachfassungen auf internationaler Ebene abgesprochen sind und als Referenzbedingungen zur Verfügung gestellt werden, z.B. kaufmännische Bedingungen wie Incoterms und FIDIC oder Schiedsgerichtsordnungen wie die der ICC.

2.1.3 Grenzüberschreitender Rechtsverkehr mit Standardformularen

Um die grenzüberschreitende Zusammenarbeit von Behörden zu erleichtern, werden in multi- oder bilateralen Abkommen Standardformulare verabredet, die nur noch ausgefüllt, aber kaum noch übersetzt werden müssen. Vor allem die Europäische Union hat durch Verordnungen oder Richtlinien eine Reihe solcher Standardformulare in Kraft gesetzt und führt immer wieder neue ein. Dadurch will man nicht nur Zeit, sondern - zu unserem Leidwesen - auch Übersetzungsaufwand einsparen.

Apostille nach Haager Übereinkommen

Traditionell bekanntes Beispiel ist die Apostille zur Legalisation von Unterschriften nach dem Haager Übereinkommen von 1961. Die Apostille (Text im Anhang zum Übereinkommen) wird einsprachig ausgestellt und muss nach dem Abkommenstext nicht übersetzt werden. In der Praxis wird die Übersetzung häufig trotzdem verlangt. Dann sollte man die offizielle Fassung in der Zielsprache benutzen, um die Wiedererkennung bei den Behörden des Zielstaates zu unterstützen. An sich ist sie aber durch den französischen Hinweis auf das Übereinkommen in der Überschrift gewährleistet, der auf jeden Fall nicht zu übersetzen ist.

Standardisierte Formulare der Europäischen Union

Im Zuge der justiziellen Zusammenarbeit, also dem Bereich, der früher durch Rechtshilfeersuchen bearbeitet wurde, hat die EU für die Einschaltung von Gerichten in einem anderen Mitgliedstaat Formulare mit einem Standardtext in allen Amtssprachen entwickelt, in denen man sich anhand der parallelen Nummerierung zurecht finden kann, ohne eine Übersetzung zu brauchen. Damit will man die Zusammenarbeit insgesamt schneller, reibungsloser und inhaltlich sicherer machen.

Solche mehrsprachigen Standardformulare gibt es im zivilrechtlichen Bereich für die Zustellung von Schriftstücken und die Beweisaufnahme in Gerichtsverfahren, für Ehe- und Kindschaftssachen, Insolvenzverfahren etc., und in Strafsachen gehören dazu beispielsweise der Europäische Haftbefehl und Strafregisterauszüge. Wo man bisher Rechtshilfeersuchen und Scheidungsurteile oder Strafbestimmungen übersetzen musste, füllt man heute also nur noch Formulare aus.

Die Texte der Formulare findet man im Anhang der Rechtsakte, also der Richtlinien und Verordnungen, mit denen das jeweilige Verfahren geregelt wird. Eine Übersicht (Stand 2006) gibt es bei Becher 2007:1131. Masken der Formulare zum Ausfüllen, Übersetzen und Ausdrucken stehen im Internet im Europäischen Gerichtsatlas für Zivilsachen zur Verfügung (http://ec.europa.eu/justice_home/judicialatlascivil/html/index_de.htm).

Da EU-Verordnungen in den Mitgliedstaaten unmittelbar geltendes Recht sind, müssen die zuständigen Gerichte diese Texte verwenden. Wenn man als Übersetzer für diese Stellen arbeitet, muss man statt zu übersetzen also zu diesen Texten greifen und sie an den Stellen vervollständigen, an denen die staatlichen Auftraggeber sie mit Formulierungen ausgefüllt haben, die noch einer Übertragung in die Zielsprache bedürfen, z.B. die Personenbeschreibung beim Europäischen Haftbefehl. Meist bekommt man von den Auftraggebern bei Gericht entsprechende Vorlagen mitgeliefert oder kann danach fragen.

Aussteller der Formulare sind die Gerichte, allerdings sind sie nicht nur – wie Rechtshilfeersuchen – an Gerichte im Ausland adressiert, sondern zum Teil zur Verwendung für Privatleute gedacht, beispielsweise die „Bescheinigung über Entscheidungen in Ehesachen", mit der man nachweisen kann, dass man geschieden ist. Arbeitet der Übersetzer für Privatpersonen, muss er sich zwar nicht an die Formulare halten, es ist aber zu empfehlen, damit sie bei staatlichen Stellen, denen der private Auftraggeber sie vorlegt, als EU-Formular wiedererkannt werden, wodurch sie mehr Vertrauen genießen und das Verfahren auch für den Privatkunden zügiger vor sich geht.

2.2 Zielsprachige Paralleltexte

Beim Verbraucherschutz gibt es auch im nationalen Recht vieler Staaten – sei es auf Veranlassung der EU oder nicht – viele Vorgaben zu konkreten Formulierungen, die auf Verpackungen, bei der Werbung etc. zwecks Aufklärung der Verbraucher verbindlich sind. Diese Formulierungen liegen in der Amtssprache des jeweiligen Staates vor und sind nicht unbedingt als Übersetzung für entsprechende Texte aus einem anderen Land gedacht. Sie können aber als Übersetzung in Frage kommen, wenn sie dieselbe Funktion haben und in demselben Kontext gebraucht werden wie der Ausgangstext. Ob sie sich tatsächlich eignen, lohnt sich zu prüfen, wenn man sich Arbeit sparen will, und muss man prüfen, wenn sie für das Zielland zwingend vorgeschrieben sind.

Einige Beispiele sollen illustrieren, wie vielfältig die Gebiete sind, auf denen man mit konkreten Formulierungen für den Verbraucherschutz rechnen muss, und welche Konsequenzen drohen, wenn man die Vorgaben nicht beachtet, sprich: welche Probleme man dem Kunden mit einer Übersetzung aufladen kann, die nicht den Vorgaben der nationalen Gesetze entspricht.

2.2.1 Informationspflichten und Widerrufsrechte bei Verträgen mit Verbrauchern

Für Informationen, die der Verbraucher bei bestimmten Geschäften im Sinne seiner Sicherheit, Gesundheit oder Unerfahrenheit bei komplizierten Gestaltungen bekommen soll, sind von der EU Standardformulare eingeführt worden, die in allen Amtssprachen vorliegen.

Beispielsweise sieht die Verbraucherkreditrichtlinie 2008/48/EG im Anhang Muster für die **Vorabinformation des Kreditnehmers** vor. Er soll die Angebote in standardisierter Form unterbreitet bekommen, damit er sie besser vergleichen kann, bevor er sich zum Abschluss eines Vertrages entschließt. Mit der Verwendung der Standardformulare stellt die Bank gleichzeitig sicher, dass sie alle Informationen gegeben hat, die nach der Richtlinie verlangt sind.

Ein heikler Bereich im Verbraucherschutz sind **Widerrufsrechte** bei Geschäftsabschlüssen im Internet oder sonstigem Fernabsatz, an der Haustür, beim Timesharing (Teilzeitnutzungsrechte von Ferienwohnungen), bei Verbraucherkredit- und Versicherungsverträgen etc. Solange ein Unternehmer über diese Rechte nicht korrekt in allen Einzelheiten informiert, erlöschen sie für den Verbraucher nicht - so lange bleibt das Geschäft also in der Schwebe. Und wenn der Unternehmer die sog. Widerrufsbelehrung für den Verbraucher nicht exakt in der Weise formuliert, dass sie alle Forderungen der Verbraucherschutzbestimmungen erfüllt, kann er darüber hinaus von seinen Konkurrenten mit kostenpflichtigen Abmahnungen nach Wettbewerbsrecht überzogen werden.

Deshalb gibt es für die Formulierung solcher Belehrungen Muster in den nationalen Rechtsordnungen, mit denen man gegenüber Verbrauchern und Konkurrenten auf der sicheren Seite ist. Allerdings liegen sie natürlich nur in der Amtssprache des jeweiligen Staates vor. In Deutschland gibt es beispielsweise in der BGB-Informationspflichten- Verordnung mehrseitige Vorlagen mit Formulierungsvarianten für alle Widerrufsrechte, die den Verbrauchern im BGB zugesprochen werden.

Das spanischen Timesharing-Gesetz (Art. 9 Abs. 1 Nr. 6 Ley 42/1998) schreibt vor, dass die Artikel 10 bis 12 des Gesetzes über den **Rücktritt** vom Vertrag, das Verbot von Anzahlungen und die Vergabe von Krediten für den Erwerb der Rechte wortwörtlich aus dem Gesetz in den Vertrag zu übernehmen sind.

2.2.2 Kennzeichnung von Produkten und Hinweise in Werbung

- Im Verkaufsprospekt von **Dachhedgefonds** für Privatanleger muss folgender Warnhinweis angebracht sein: „Der Bundesminister der Finanzen warnt: Bei diesem Investmentfonds müssen Anleger bereit und in der Lage sein, Verluste des eingesetzten Kapitals bis hin zum Totalverlust hinzunehmen." (§ 117 Abs. 2 Investitionsmodernisierungsgesetz)

- Bei der Werbung für **Arzneimittel** außerhalb der Fachkreise ist der Text "Zu Risiken und Nebenwirkungen lesen Sie die Packungsbeilage und fragen Sie Ihren Arzt oder Apotheker" gut lesbar und von den übrigen Werbeaussagen deutlich abgesetzt und abgegrenzt anzugeben. (§ 4 Abs. 3 Heilmittelwerbegesetz)

- **Tabakerzeugnisse** dürfen nur mit vorgeschriebenen Warnhinweisen auf der Verpackung in den Verkehr gebracht werden, denen vorangestellt ist: „Die EG-Gesundheitsminister:" und die z.b. lauten: „Rauchen ist tödlich" oder „Rauchen kann tödlich sein" oder „Rauchen fügt Ihnen und den Menschen in Ihrer Umgebung erheblichen Schaden zu".

- Das Mindesthaltbarkeitsdatum, bis zu dem ein **Lebensmittel** seine spezifischen Eigenschaften behält, ist mit den Worten „mindestens haltbar bis zum …" auf der Verpackung anzugeben. (§ 7 Abs. 2 Lebensmittelkennzeichnungsverordnung)

2.3 Verbindliche zielsprachige Terminologie

2.3.1 Verbot von Termini

Das Recht zur Teilzeitnutzung von Ferienimmobilien (Timesharing) darf in Spanien nicht mehr als „multipropiedad" (Multieigentum) oder sonst als „Eigentum" bezeichnet werden, damit dem Interessenten nicht eine Eigentümerstellung vorgegaukelt wird (Art. 1 Nr. 4 Ley 42/1998), die er gar nicht bekommt.

2.3.2 Vorgeschriebene Termini

Das Ziel, die Verbraucher durch Aufklärung zu schützen und zu informieren, verfolgt auch der **französische** Staat mit seiner **Sprachgesetzgebung**. So ist vorgeschrieben:

> *„In der Bezeichnung, dem Angebot, der Aufmachung, der Gebrauchsanweisung oder Bedienungsanleitung, der Beschreibung des Umfangs und den Garantiebedingungen von Gütern, Produkten oder Dienstleistungen sowie in Rechnungen und Quittungen ist die französische Sprache zu benutzen. Dieselben Bestimmungen kommen bei jeder schriftlichen, gesprochenen oder audiovisuellen Werbung zur Anwendung."*
>
> *(Art. 2 Gesetz Nr. 94-665 über den Gebrauch der französischen Sprache, Übersetzung ins Deutsche: www.culture.gouv.fr/culture/dglf/).*

Dadurch verbietet sich nach dem Verständnis des französischen Gesetzgebers die Verwendung von nichtfranzösischen Wörtern, insbesondere von Anglizismen. Wie Gruber (2009: 4) berichtet, werden für staatliche Stellen daher im Gesetzblatt (Journal officiel) verbindliche Termini zur Vermeidung von Anglizismen vorgegeben. Für private Redakteure der o.g. Texte empfiehlt sich die Beachtung dieser vorgegebenen Termini ebenfalls, da sie dann sicher sein können, wirklich französisch zu schreiben und keine Sanktionen von staatlicher Seite zu riskieren. Wenn man als Übersetzer Texte zur Verwendung in Frankreich produziert, stellt sich die Frage, ob man diese vorgegebenen Termini verwenden muss.

3   Pflichten des Übersetzers

Wenn man postuliert, dass dem Kunden ein zielsprachiger Text geliefert werden muss, mit dem dieser im Verwendungsland nicht gegen Verbraucherschutz- und sonstige Vorschriften verstößt, so mutet man dem Übersetzer, wie die gerade aufgezählten Beispiele zeigen, einiges zu.

Dem wissenschaftlichen Anspruch an die Übersetzer, auch als Kulturmittler zu wirken und ihr interkulturelles Knowhow zur Geltung zu bringen, würde dieses Postulat in der Tat entsprechen. Wenn man Übersetzer in ihrer Rolle als Auftragnehmer dazu befragt, hört man ebenfalls, dass sie ihren Kunden diesen Dienst gern erweisen möchten, andererseits wird angesichts der Fülle und der fachlichen Komplexität dessen, was dann zu recherchieren wäre, auch von Überforderung gesprochen.

Juristisch lässt sich die Problematik in die Frage ummünzen, ob die Übersetzung einen Mangel aufweist, wenn der Kunde bei Verwendung des Textes gegen nationales oder europäisches Recht verstoßen würde.

Mangelhaft ist eine Werkleistung (Übersetzung) nach § 633 BGB,

- wenn sie nicht die vertraglich vereinbarte Beschaffenheit hat,
- wenn sie nicht für den vertraglich vorausgesetzten Verwendungszweck geeignet ist oder
- wenn sie für den allgemein vorausgesetzten Gebrauch nicht geeignet ist.

Die vertragliche Leistungsbeschreibung bietet also dem Kunden die Möglichkeit zu verlangen, dass die Übersetzung so beschaffen sein muss, dass man mit der Verwendung nicht gegen Vorschriften verstößt. Ebenso ermöglicht sie dem Übersetzer, sich von der Verantwortung dafür zu entlasten. Wenn man also nicht dafür haften möchte, dass die Übersetzung mit Verbraucher-, Kennzeichnungs- und sonstigen nationalen Bestimmungen des Ziellandes tatsächlich konform ist, sollte man in den jeweiligen Vertrag oder in Allgemeine Geschäftsbedingungen eine entsprechende Klausel aufnehmen.

Ist im Vertrag weder die Beschaffenheit noch die Verwendung der Übersetzung ausdrücklich festgelegt, so könnte sich – wie oben aus dem Gesetz zitiert – die Anforderung, dass sie keinen Rechtsverstoß im Zielland provozieren darf, noch aus dem allgemein üblichen Gebrauch solcher Übersetzungen ergeben. Dazu muss man die Gegebenheiten des Einzelfalls und den Usus in der jeweiligen Branche interpretieren. Zu welchem Ergebnis man bzw. ein Gericht dabei kommen würde, lässt sich nicht allumfassend vorhersagen.

Verschiedene Gesichtspunkte sprechen jedoch meines Erachtens gegen die Annahme, der Rechtsverkehr setze allgemein voraus, dass der Übersetzer die Konformität seiner Übersetzungen mit den Vorschriften im Land der Verwendung zu sichern habe:

- Zu entscheiden, ob der konkrete Fall überhaupt in den Anwendungsbereich der betreffenden Vorschriften fällt und ob alle sonstigen Voraussetzungen erfüllt sind, würde eine rechtliche Prüfung voraussetzen, zu der ein Übersetzer von seiner Ausbildung her nicht unbedingt in der Lage ist und für die ihm das Material fehlt, sofern nicht der zu übersetzende Text zufällig ausreichende Informationen enthält. Diese Arbeit ist m.E. als fachliche Prüfung neben der Übersetzung zu qualifizieren. Nach den Usancen der Übersetzungsbranche, für die man in der Norm DIN EN 15038 einen ersten Anhaltspunkt hat, gehört eine fachliche Prüfung zu den Dienstleistungen, die ausdrücklich vereinbart werden müssen, die also nicht selbstverständlich vorausgesetzt werden (vgl. 5.4.4 EN 15038:2006).

- In vielen Bereichen ist die Recherche, welche Vorschriften bei grenzüberschreitenden Geschäften im Zielland zu beachten sind und wie man das im Einzelnen umsetzt, so kompliziert, dass besondere Exportberatungsfirmen oder -institute zugezogen werden und entsprechend zu bezahlen sind. Ein solcher Aufwand kann unmöglich in der Übersetzungsdienstleistung und der dafür üblichen Vergütung enthalten sein.

- Fragt man Unternehmer, die auf internationaler Ebene Geschäfte machen, ob sie die betreffende rechtliche Absicherung vom Übersetzer erwarten, so bekommt man meist zur Antwort, dass sie sich wegen der Einhaltung von Vorschriften auf ihre Geschäftspartner und Rechtsberater vor Ort, auf ihre Branchenverbände, auf Exportförderungsorganisationen wie die gtai (Germany Trade and Invest) der Bundesregierung, auf die Auslandshandelskammern oder eben auf die oben genannten spezialisierten Dienstleister verlassen.

Es sprechen also einige rechtliche und praktische Umstände dagegen, dass es – bei Fehlen konkreter Vereinbarungen – ein Mangel der Übersetzung sein soll, wenn sie nicht die Gewähr dafür bietet, dass der konkrete Wortlaut in der Zielrechtsordnung gesetzeskonform ist.

Wenn man sich auf einem Gebiet sicher fühlt, kann man dem Kunden diese Dienstleistung natürlich trotzdem anbieten. Will man sich auf diesem Gebiet dagegen nicht in die Haftung begeben, sollte man die Gewähr für die Konformität mit dem ausländischen Recht vertraglich ausschließen.

Wo es nicht um rechtliche Wertungen geht, sondern um das Auffinden existierender mehrsprachiger Fassungen des zu übersetzenden Zitats oder Textes (Ziffern 2.1 und 2.3), dürfte der Rechercheaufwand allerdings zum normalen Leistungsumfang eines professionellen Übersetzers gehören.

Bibliographie

Becher, Herbert (2007): Wörterbuch Recht, Wirtschaft, Politik, Deutsch-Spanisch, München: C.H. Beck

Freudenfeld, Regina/Nord, Britta (Hrsg.) (2007): Professionell kommunizieren –
Neue Berufsfelder-Neue Vermittlungskonzepte, Hildesheim: Olms

Gruber, Joachim (2009): Die französische Sprachgesetzgebung und Texte mit Bezug
zum Internet, in: Lebende Sprachen Heft 1/2009, Berlin: de Gruyter, S. 4

Kautz, Ulrich (2002): Handbuch Didaktik des Übersetzens und Dolmetschens, 2.
Aufl. – München: Iudicium

Wissensmanagement und Arbeiten mit verteilten Teams

Modernes Übersetzen: Spagat zwischen Informationsmanagement und Wissensmanagement

Dr.-Ing. Wolfgang Sturz

Transline Deutschland Dr.-Ing. Sturz GmbH

sturz@sturz-gruppe.de

1 Übersetzen – Kunstgewerbe oder Handwerk?

Übersetzen – ist das eigentlich eine Kunst? Oder handelt es sich um profanes Handwerk? Fragestellungen, bei denen man sich je nach Gesprächspartner gehörig in die Nesseln setzen kann.

Zunächst einmal: Das Übersetzen ist ein sehr alter Beruf. Schon in der Antike gab es Übersetzer, die für die große Politik, aber auch für Handel und Wirtschaft unentbehrlich waren. Wie langweilig wäre die alttestamentliche Geschichte des an den ägyptischen Hof verschleppten Josef ohne die Dolmetscher, mit deren Hilfe er seine eigene Mehrsprachigkeit verschleiern konnte.

Auch in der jüngeren Geschichte spielen Übersetzer immer wieder eine wichtige Rolle. Einer der bekanntesten ist wohl Martin Luther, der als Übersetzer nicht nur ausgesprochen produktiv war, sondern auch die zu seiner Zeit gar nicht vorhandene deutsche Sprache geprägt und damit den Grundstock für unser heutiges Deutsch gelegt hat. Ein wahrer Sprachkünstler, wenn nicht ein Sprachgenie. Auch ein Johann Wolfgang von Goethe, der eigentlich als Dichter bekannt ist, hat übrigens sehr viel übersetzt. Es heißt sogar, dass er mehr Übersetzungen als eigenes Dichtwerk zu Papier gebracht haben soll.

Heute scheinen die übersetzerischen Leistungen dieser großen Vorbilder ein wenig in Vergessenheit geraten zu sein – das Übersetzen ist ein profanes Handwerk geworden. Schlimmer noch: Die Handwerker werden offensichtlich immer öfter durch Heimwerker ersetzt, durch „Do-it-Yourselver", für die es in unserem globalisierten Multi-Kulti-Zeitalter nach einem halben Auslandssemester selbstverständlich ist, die im Beruf benötigten Übersetzungen quasi nebenbei selbst zu erledigen.

Sowieso – so die häufig kolportierte Auffassung – sei der Übersetzerberuf ja vom Aushungern oder gar Aussterben bedroht. Die EDV wird es schon richten, und wer sich Anfang des 21. Jahrhunderts für ein Übersetzerstudium entscheidet muss sich immer öfter die Frage gefallen lassen, ob diese Arbeit vielleicht zwar noch nicht jetzt, aber doch in absehbarer Zukunft nicht in hinreichender Qualität ganz vom Kollegen Computer übernommen werden wird.

2 Der Computer als vollwertiger Übersetzer-Ersatz oder der Computer als Übersetzer-Assistenz?

Tatsache ist: Die EDV-Spezialisten versuchen seit den allerersten Anfängen des IT-Siegeszuges vor etwa 60 Jahren den Computern das Übersetzen beizubringen. Bis heute waren diese Bemühungen – trotz unendlicher Anstrengungen und immenser Investitionen – nicht wirklich erfolgreich.

Dabei ist die Arbeit des Übersetzers heute ohne den Einsatz einer leistungsfähigen EDV gar nicht mehr denkbar. Das Zusammenspiel zwischen Übersetzern und Computern hat sich allerdings – genau betrachtet – recht eigenartig entwickelt. Ganz am Anfang – in den 50er und 60er Jahren, waren die Hoffnungen groß, bald über funktionstüchtige Übersetzungscomputer zu verfügen. Genährt wurde diese Erwartung durch die großen Forschungsetats, die zu Zeiten des kalten Krieges für das Übersetzen zur Verfügung gestellt wurden. Die Amerikaner wollten schließlich unbedingt wissen, was in Russland geschrieben und publiziert wurde – und das war so viel, dass die Humantranslatoren nicht nachgekommen sind. Der ersten Euphorie folgte aber schnell die Ernüchterung. Als dann offensichtlich wurde, dass Sprache sich nicht in regelbasierte Analyse- und Synthesesysteme einpacken lässt, kamen – mit der Einführung der PCs – zunächst einmal sehr einfache Übersetzungshilfen auf den Markt. EDV-gestützte Terminologieverwaltung – das war das Motto der 80er Jahre, das für einen ersten Produktivitäts- und Qualitätsschub führte. Als dann Anfang der 90er Jahre die Rechner billiger wurden und Speicherbedarf keine nennenswerte Rolle mehr gespielt hat, entstand im Böblinger-Sindelfinger Umfeld der IBM die Idee, nicht nur einzelne Begriffe, sondern ganze Sätze mit ihren jeweiligen Übersetzungen in Datenbanken zu verwalten. Dies war die Geburtsstunde der Translation-Memory-Programme. Aus genau diesem personellen Umfeld heraus sind übrigens die drei ersten Vorreiter dieser Werkzeuge entstanden: der Translation Manager von IBM, der nach wenigen Jahren wieder vom Markt genommen wurde, die Workbench von Trados und Transit von der Firma Star.

Damit war aber auch die Rollenverteilung klar. Nicht der Computer übersetzt – das kann er nämlich auch heute noch nicht in hinreichender Qualität – sondern der qualifizierte Humantranslator, der Übersetzer aus Fleisch und Blut. Das Motto: Der Computer sorgt für die Produktivität und unterstützt bei der Sicherstellung der übersetzerischen Konsistenz. Der Mensch behält die Kontrolle.

Dabei sind allerdings schon Abhängigkeiten entstanden, die zu einer Umwälzung der übersetzerischen Tätigkeit geführt haben. Das hat beispielsweise dazu geführt, dass die Generation der Power-Übersetzer, die sich mit einem Diktiergerät vor einen Stapel Ausgangstexte gesetzt haben und bei Leistungen von 50 oder mehr Schreibmaschinenseiten pro Tag manchmal sogar mehrere Schreibkräfte gleichzeitig auslasten konnten, gänzlich ausgestorben ist. Für die Qualität der Übersetzungen war das allerdings vielleicht eher positiv, weil nur ganz wenige dieser Diktat-Übersetzer ihren Beruf so beherrscht haben, dass auch beim Diktieren von hunderten von Seiten die Terminologiekonsistenz gewährleistet werden konnte, ohne dass dazu ein Terminologiesystem zur Verfügung stand.

3 Schnipselübersetzungen – hat man dafür studiert?

Damit kommen wir aber auch schon zu der Kehrseite der zunehmenden Computerassistenz. Bei der Einführung der Translation-Memory-Technologien kam nämlich nicht nur eitel Freude auf. Übersetzer arbeiten heute interaktiv am PC, und dabei werden ihnen 100-%-Matches oder Fuzzy Matches vorgeschlagen. Besonders problematisch war dabei die Tatsache, dass Übersetzer lernen mussten, Vorübersetzungen von Kollegen zu akzeptieren und zu übernehmen. Das stand im krassen Widerspruch zu dem bisherigen Selbstverständnis der Übersetzer, das unter anderem daraus genährt wurde, dass für jede vorgeschlagene Übersetzung immer eine bessere Variante gefunden werden konnte. Diese „künstlerische Freiheit" wurde den Übersetzern durch die Einführung der Match-Technologien genommen. Sie dürfen heute richtige Übersetzungen nicht mehr durch schönere Übersetzungen ersetzen …, wenn sie das doch machen, führt das zu den berüchtigten „matschigen" Translation Memories.

Diese EDV-Programme legen den Übersetzern also ein Korsett an. Mehr noch, Translation Memories erhöhen zwar die Produktivität des Übersetzervorganges – die Übersetzer verkommen aber zunächst einmal, so der erste Eindruck, mehr und mehr zu Schnipselübersetzern, die sich in den allermeisten Fällen nicht mehr mit einem Gesamttext, sondern nur noch mit einzelnen Passagen auseinandersetzen dürfen.

4 Informationsmanagement und Wissensmanagement im Übersetzungsprozess

Was haben diese Ausführungen nun mit den Begriffen Wissensmanagement und Informationsmanagement zu tun? Zunächst sollten diese beiden Begriffe dazu vielleicht einfach einmal definiert werden.

Informationsmanagement ist die Bereitstellung

- der richtigen Information
- in einer verwertbaren Form
- in der erforderlichen Menge
- in der benötigten Qualität
- zum gewünschten Zeitpunkt
- am richtigen Ort
- zu den günstigsten Kosten.

Wissensmanagement hingegen befähigt Sie bzw. das Projektteam,

- Informationen zu finden,
- Informationen richtig zu interpretieren,

- Informationen richtig zu verwenden,
- neue Informationen zu generieren,
- Informationen zu teilen!

Genau betrachtet war das Informationsmanagement schon immer Bestandteil eines jeden Übersetzungsprozesses. Jeder Übersetzer war für die Beschaffung von Terminologie und Referenztexten verantwortlich. Die jüngeren Übersetzer dürften heute kaum in der Lage sein, sich vorzustellen, wie viel akribische Arbeit vor der Einführung des Internets damit einherging. Jeder professionelle Übersetzer hatte in seinem Büro eine möglichst umfassende Sammlung von Prospekten, Fachbüchern, Veröffentlichungen und sonstigen Unterlagen. Damals haben die professionellen Übersetzer Messen besucht, um Terminologie zu sammeln – der Erfolg der Messebesuche bemaß sich an den laufenden Metern Katalogmaterial, die man nach Hause brachte. Heute reduziert sich das Informationsmanagement weitgehend auf das Internet. Vor einem Übersetzungsprojekt wird nach Referenzmaterial und nach Terminologie gegoogelt – das Konzept des Informationsmanagements ist aber gleich geblieben.

Wer heute als Übersetzer Erfolg haben will, muss – vor allem bedingt durch die zunehmende Komplexität der Themen, mit denen man sich auseinandersetzen muss – sein Informationsmanagement 100%ig im Griff haben. Dazu gehört eindeutig mehr als die Fähigkeit, in der Suchmaske von www.google.de einen Suchbegriff einzutragen. Übersetzer müssen eine möglichst große Bandbreite an Suchmaschinen mit dem jeweiligen Vor- und Nachteilen kennen. Sie müssen das verknüpfte Suchen beherrschen. Leider wird den Übersetzern an den Hochschulen nur selten gelehrt, was Boole'sche Verknüpfungen sind. Übersetzer müssen in der Lage sein, ihre Suchergebnisse beispielsweise auf Webseiten aus bestimmten Ländern oder in bestimmten Sprachen einzuschränken. Oft bringt das indirekte Suchen weiter, indem man zum Beispiel die Suchmaschine beauftragt, ausgehend von der Webseite des Übersetzungskunden ähnliche Webseiten zu finden – der Informationsgehalt solcher Recherchen ist oft verblüffend. Und es soll immer noch Übersetzer geben, die den Wert von Wikipedia mit seinen vielen Sprachen nicht kennen oder nicht intensiv genug nutzen.

Kurz und gut: Früher bestand das Informationsmanagement des Übersetzers aus dem mit einer gewissen Sammelleidenschaft gefüllten und natürlich gut organisierten Archiv. Ergänzt wurde das durch ein soziales Netzwerk, das aber auf dem Kommunikationsmedium Telefon und später manchmal auch auf dem Telefaxgerät beruhte. Jeder gute Übersetzer wusste damals um den Wert der gedruckten „Gelben Seiten" aus seinem Zielsprachenland. Dort konnte er Fachleute finden, die oft völlig uneigennützig unschätzbare Unterstützung bei Terminologierecherchen geboten haben.

Informationsmanagement war für Übersetzer also schon immer notwendig – heute ist es aber wichtiger als je zuvor. Warum? Die zu übersetzenden Themen und Fachgebiete werden komplexer und spezialisierter, damit nimmt die terminologische Vielfalt zu. Außerdem bleibt im Zeitalter der Schnipselübersetzungen deutlich weniger Zeit für eine intensive Auseinandersetzung mit dem Text und dem jeweiligen Fachgebiet.

Die modernen Werkzeuge des Informationsmanagements sind dabei sehr vielfältig und beschränken sich nicht auf die bereits erwähnte Suchmaske von Google oder neuerdings Bing. Eigene Datenbanken, Funktionen wie die Konkordanzsuche (es gibt immer noch Übersetzer, die mit Translation Memories arbeiten, aber die Konkordanz-

suche nicht kennen), oder auch die sogenannten „Sozialen Netzwerke" mit Diskussionsforen, in denen oft ein sehr fruchtbarer Gedankenaustausch zu Terminologiefragen
stattfindet – das sind nur einige der vielen Möglichkeiten des modernen Informationsmanagements, die zum Standardrepertoire eines jeden Übersetzers gehören sollten.

Damit wird nun aber auch der Unterschied zwischen Informations- und Wissensmanagement deutlich. Während das Informationsmanagement heute mehr denn je
technologieorientiert ist, kommt es beim Wissensmanagement auf die Befähigung an,
Informationen zu finden und die (manchmal wenigen) Informationen richtig zu
interpretieren und richtig zu verwenden.

5 Der Übersetzer 2.0 – ein anspruchsvolles Anforderungsprofil

Heute scheint alles 2.0 zu sein. Das Internet, aber auch die Unternehmen und sogar
die Politik und der moderne Wahlkampf. Wie wird man aber ein 2.0-Übersetzer? Was
sind 2.0-Übersetzer?

Übersetzer 2.0 sind Informationsmanager:

- Sie beherrschen alle wichtigen Werkzeuge des Informationsmanagements.
- Sie sind in der Lage, aus den vielen Werkzeugen die für ihre Aufgabe richtigen und wichtigen auszuwählen und anzuwenden.

Übersetzer 2.0 sind aber auch Wissensmanager:

- Sie verfügen über die notwendige Metaqualifikation, Informationen zu bewer-
  ten.
- Sie verfügen über die Fähigkeit, Informationen zu verwerten und zu nutzen.
- Sie sind im Umgang und der Verwertung von Informationen kreativ.
- Sie sind bereit, Informationen weiterzugeben bzw. zu teilen.

Und an dieser Stelle treten sowohl im Rückblick als auch in der Vorschau auf zukünftige Entwicklungen einige Trends hervor, die sich in den kommenden Jahren deutlich
verstärken dürften:

- Übersetzer 1.0 sind kreative Sprachkünstler.
- Übersetzer 2.0 sind strukturierte Informationsmager.
- Übersetzer 1.0 sind Einzelkämpfer.
- Übersetzer 2.0 sind Teamplayer, die bereit sind, ihre Informationsbasis zu
  entwickeln, zu nutzen und zu teilen.

Abschließend – und das sollte vielleicht die wichtigste Botschaft sein:

- Übersetzer 1.0 stehen leider im Wettbewerb zu den vielen „Do-it-Yourselvern", die dieser Branche oft den Ruf des Unseriösen geben.
- Übersetzer 2.0 sind so hochspezialisiert, effizient und professionell, dass sich
  der Wettbewerb zu den „Do-it-Yourselvern" ihrer Branche von alleine erledigt.

Managing complex translation projects effectively through virtual spaces: a case study

Dr. Fola Yahaya

Strategic Agenda LLP, Londo

fola.yahaya@strategicagenda.com

1 Introduction

The issues surrounding translation are exemplified further when content needs to be delivered to customers in multiple formats, through multiple distribution channels in geographically dispersed locations. As a result global translation projects often suffer from issues such as:

- poor inter- and intra-staff communication within translation project teams
- lack of automated technology processes to manage, grow and protect translation assets, which put a company's intellectual property at risk
- delays in disseminating centralised terminology militate against content quality and consistency drives
- quality compromise as a result of pressure to deliver content in more languages in reduced time while operating under tighter budgets.

The translation industry has responded with innovations in computer-aided translation software and server-based terminology management, which have improved the ability of disparate teams of translators to produce a consistent output. However, there is much room for improvement in global collaboration processes and technology.

An alternative and effective approach to managing translation workflow for complex translation projects is the use of virtual spaces.

However, this reluctance to outsource holds little sway in an era of aggressive cost cutting and efficiency drives, so organisations are increasingly seeking out LSPs who can offer them the best of both worlds: direct access to experienced translators without the overhead of in-house staff. Innovations in translation technologies and processes in the last 10 years have seen the rapid uptake of translation management software and increasingly globalised translation projects designed to improve the quality of outsourced translation. Coupled with low cost, efficient communication channels translation has truly become a de-coupled industry, with work increasingly being carried out by decentralised and often geographically dispersed translation resources.

A way to effectively manage complex global projects whilst reducing client's fears over losing control through outsourcing is to use a virtual space.

Yet, despite the increased availability of tools and technologies to support translation projects, traditional approaches still dominate the industry. Companies often have unrealistic expectations that translation is simple and that they can outsource their requirements to a third party only to have their expectations dashed when they receive substandard translations carried out using a standard translation life-cycle approach. The traditional translation life cycle involves the following steps:

- document divided into parts
- parts assigned to individual translators
- translators work in isolation
- reviewers consolidate individual sections into a single document ready for client review
- client reviewer assesses and corrects text as necessary
- LSP returns finalised text to client for final sign-off

The problems with this approach include:

- opaqueness - lack of process transparency leaves clients in the dark on translation quality until it is (sometimes) too late
- consolidation of inconsistencies is difficult, even when working from an existing termbase due to different styles and interpretations of translators
- lack of interaction - there is little if any direct interaction between client and translator
- too little too late – too little time and resource are allocated to document revision which means that finalising a file for say publication is squeezed into the end of translation project
- rapid incorporation of changes can be difficult to achieve without a centralised messaging platform

By using a virtual space the project overcame the traditional problems associated with dispersed teams working in isolation. Client can replicate their direct relationship with a translator through a mediated platform. Their anxiety over the quality of the final 'product' is lessened by their interaction with the actual translator working on their project and their ability to shape the translation as it progresses. Thus virtual spaces offer clear benefits to all parties involved: client, LSP and freelance translator.

2   Key findings and lessons learned

The project exemplifies an innovative approach to rapid translation of high volumes of specialised text supported by a virtual space. The key findings of the project case study were that virtual spaces can be a valuable tool for supporting global translation project management. Benefits included:

- increased buy-in: translators feel part of the team rather than hired hands
- interacting with the client review team from the project outset improves the translation/reviewer dynamics and reduces the likelihood of the "not translated by us" syndrome

- a shared sense of responsibility for project success means that both the client and reviewer feel they play an important part in the translation process and in achieving a successful project outcome

- reduced client anxiety over outsourcing their text to third parties – clients enjoy having direct access to translators

- translation can be faster – a centralised messaging system means communicating changes to terminology, etc. is faster and documented

- clear audit trail – sophisticated reporting mechanisms mean that all versions are stored and accessible online and who said what when is captured for later analysis.

Lessons learned

Using virtual spaces effectively is not as simple as setting up a hosted service and hoping for the best. Rather the level of transparency that typifies the majority of collaboration platforms means that client/LSP resource interaction must be carefully managed. Key lessons learned include:

- Ensure freelancers are fully briefed on how to interact with the client if that option is enabled. They represent the public face of your company even though they are often 'guns for hire'. Ensure each freelance project resource undergoes a thorough induction in how to use the virtual space.

- Carefully manage what is posted online. Early drafts may be better managed offline rather than being posted for the client to see. Alternatively have a private 'sandbox' area on your virtual space that will allow your internal resources to post and discuss early drafts. Collaboration spaces are like goldfish bowls where potentially everything is visible so manage permissioning (who can see/do what where and when) carefully.

- Ensure clients are fully briefed on their roles and responsibilities on the translation project. There needs to be an informal service level agreement on how quickly client reviewers can respond to translators' questions (typically 24hrs).

3   The future of global translation management and collaboration

3.1 Greater automation

It is clear that the trend towards increased automation of translation processes will continue unabated. While the holy grail of inputting complex source text, pressing a button and instantly receiving perfect target text will remain a dream for somewhat longer, it will not be long before companies with considerable translation volumes will insist on a level of automated translation in order to improve the three key criteria in the translation equation: cost, time and quality. While cost and time can be measured exactly, quality remains a subjective factor. This is likely to have an impact on how the key actors in the translation equation, clients, LSPs and translators, collaborate in the future in the following ways:

3.2 Greater openness and willingness to share translation assets

As translation workflow and linguistic asset management become standard features, industries will collaborate on an agreed terminology and will be increasingly likely to share translation memories in order to reduce costs. It is likely that translation assets – translation memories and terminology – will be organised by industry domains rather than being limited by company boundaries. This will enable the quick assembly of unified linguistic databases for industrial domains. Clients may create industry-specific virtual spaces for storing translation assets and making them available to translators et al.

3.3 Intelligent customers - companies get smarter about content management

Companies will implement controlled language authoring, machine translation, XML-based publishing and global workflow systems to improve the quality and speed of translation whilst lowering the costs. As companies collaborate on production so will they collaborate to reduce industry-wide translation costs. Expect the emergence of vertical translation organisations[3].

3.4 Social translation: the increased use of crowdsourcing

Wikipedia defines crowdsourcing as "the act of taking a task traditionally performed by an employee or contractor, and outsourcing it to an undefined, generally large group of people, in the form of an open call". In the context of translation of a website this means a client inviting its customers to offer translations of product collateral and content[4].

Mirroring the open source and creative commons philosophy, some organisations, especially in the software development industry, will rely on external user communities to translate their software or catalogues. Francis Tsang, director of globalisation at Adobe Systems Inc. recently stated that:

"Companies like Adobe and Sun Microsystems use naturally emerging crowds with specialist knowledge about products who want more product content in their own languages. This way we can localize product-related content for languages which may not be high priority, but which nevertheless help grow our markets"[5].

---

[3] An example of this is the Translation Automation User Society (TAUS) whose members include companies such as Symantec, Auto-desk, EMC, Cisco, and Hewlett-Packard. TAUS members benchmark their translation processes and share lessons learned. See also Sun Systems use of Worldwide Globalization Centres (WGCs) – http://developers.sun.com/global/technology/translation/

[4] See Crowdsourcing Translation – www.iheni.com/crowdsourcing-translation/

[5] Crowdsourcing at Adobe –
www.translationautomation.com/user-cases/crowdsourcing-at-adobe.html

The increasing use of the "wisdom of crowds" may see companies and organisations making great use of machine translation supported by tightly controlled term bases and translation memories, and then refined by 'crowd translators'[6]. For an organisation such as the UN this might involve sending automatically translated texts for refinement via online communities of practice (e.g. UN internal translators). The question remains as to how to manage this process – marshalling the chatter of many individuals into a coherent viewpoint on how a particular sentence should be optimally translated. For the moment this would seem far more time-consuming and expensive in the long run than assigning the translation to a small translation team.

4 The translator

4.1 The translator is dead – long live the post machine translation editor

Whilst increased machine translation will reduce the time and cost of translation, quality will still be judged in human terms. The future is likely to see the replacement of the traditional role of translator by the role of post machine translation (PMT) editor. Translations will be increasingly based on previous translations or assembled from previously translated segments which will allow rapid and cheap initial translation. The translation management software will automatically carry out quality assurance to check segment consistency, and a final check will be carried by a native speaker to make minor adjustments to the text. Experienced PMT editors will develop a routine to identify and correct these mistakes quickly. This editing will be integrated into a translation project management virtual space or platform so that real-time editing of TM's feed through to a central repository that is accessible by other editors.

Greater use of virtual spaces. Clients will come to expect greater collaboration and transparency during complex translation projects. Clients want to reduce the feeling that outsourcing a translation project is like throwing a boomerang in the dark, by being able to shape the translation process throughout its life cycle. There will thus be an increased demand for virtual spaces where client staff can interact directly with LSP resources.

5 Conclusion

The case study exemplifies an innovative approach to client-LSP collaboration that can improve translation quality. By using a virtual space translation both LSPs and their clients can benefit from:

- more efficient translation asset management – virtual spaces are an effective mechanism for securely sharing translation assets
- improved client relationship management

---

[6] Facebook is another example of a technology company that used crowdsourcing to translate its graphical user interface into over six different languages

- reduction in client anxiety and fears over outsourcing translation projects
- faster translation – all parts of the translation are available to all members of the translation team in real time which allows for faster knowledge dissemination
- improved translation/reviewer dynamics – interacting with the client review team from the project outset improves the translation/reviewer dynamics and reduces the likelihood of the "not translated by us" syndrome, which often occurs as a result of the sometimes competing agendas of in-house and external translators.

Übersetzung interaktiver elektronischer technischer Dokumentation (IETD) im Rahmen großer Rüstungsprojekte – Grundlagen, Probleme und Verfahren

Werner Könne

Bundessprachenamt

wernerkoenne@bundeswehr.org

Einleitung

Die hohe Komplexität moderner Waffensysteme, die damit einhergehende Datenmenge sowie die Gewährleistung von Aktualität und Verfügbarkeit der technischen Dokumentation auch im erweiterten Aufgabenspektrum der Streitkräfte machen es in zunehmendem Maße erforderlich, von der gedruckten technischen Dokumentation mit ihrem aufwändigen Änderungsdienst zu einer elektronischen Form der Dokumentation überzugehen. Diese trägt im Bereich der Bundeswehr die Bezeichnung Elektronische Technische Dokumentation (ETDok) bzw. Interaktive Elektronische Technische Dokumentation (IETD). Häufig findet auch die gleichbedeutende englische Kurzform IETP (Interactive Electronic Technical Publication) Anwendung.

Die aufgabenbezogen und am Geräteaufbruch orientiert modular aufgebaute IETD-Dokumentation ermöglicht die Handhabung großer Datenmengen bei kleinstem Volumen, die direkte Verknüpfung mit anderen DV-Anwendungen, die Bereitstellung zusätzlicher visueller Informationen und eine hohe Aktualität des Datenbestands. Durch die Minimierung des physischen Dokumentationsumfangs werden Transport- und Lagerkapazitäten drastisch verringert und durch den Wegfall des Druckaufwands

Kosten für Erstellung und Änderungsdienst eingespart. Die Einsparpotenziale können jedoch nur dann in vollem Umfang ausgeschöpft werden, wenn die im internationalen Rüstungs- und Industriebereich verwendeten Datenstandards und Informationsstrukturen einheitlich zur Anwendung kommen.

Im Zusammenhang mit der Umstellung der technischen Dokumentation auf IETD ist auch ein anwachsender Übersetzungsbedarf für technische Dokumentation zu verzeichnen. Dies ist u. a. auf zwei Rahmenbedingungen zurückzuführen, und zwar zum einen auf das am 1. Mai 2004 in Deutschland in Kraft getretene Geräte- und Produktsicherheitsgesetz (GPSG) und zum anderen auf die Zunahme multinationaler Rüstungsprojekte mit vereinbarter englischer IETD-Datenbasis.

Nach den Bestimmungen des als Umsetzung einer europäischen Richtlinie in Kraft gesetzten GPSG darf ein Produkt in Deutschland nur dann in den Verkehr gebracht bzw. errichtet und betrieben werden, wenn es so beschaffen ist, dass bei bestimmungsgemäßer Verwendung oder vorhersehbarer Fehlanwendung die Sicherheit und Gesundheit von Verwendern oder Dritten nicht gefährdet werden. Die 9. Verordnung des GPSG, die sog. Maschinenrichtlinie, legt darüber hinaus fest, dass bei Einfuhr in ein bestimmtes Sprachgebiet die Betriebsanleitung in der entsprechenden Sprachfassung beigefügt sein muss.

Gemäß der Verfahrensregelung VWT 200, Arbeitssicherheit, des Bundesamts für Wehrtechnik und Beschaffung (BWB) vom Dezember 2005 für die Bundeswehr ist das GPSG bei der Bedarfsermittlung, Bedarfsdeckung und Nutzung von Produkten grundsätzlich anzuwenden und in Leistungsbeschreibungen die Einhaltung der sicherheitstechnischen Mindeststandards des GPSG festzuschreiben.

Aufgrund dieser Vorgabe muss die technische Dokumentation eines Systems oder Geräts im Grundsatz vollständig in deutscher Sprache vorliegen. Angesichts der Beschaffung zahlreicher Systeme und Komponenten auf dem internationalen Markt mit häufig nur in englischer Sprache vorhandener technischer Dokumentation hat dies einen zunehmenden Übersetzungsbedarf ins Deutsche zur Folge. Umgekehrt ist bei multinationalen Beschaffungsvorhaben, bei denen durch vertragliche Regelungen eine gemeinsame IETD-Datenbasis in englischer Sprache vereinbart wird, wiederum die vermehrte Übersetzung deutscher Datenmodule ins Englische erforderlich. Ein Beispiel hierfür ist die deutsch-italienische Zusammenarbeit beim Beschaffungsvorhaben U-Boot-Klasse 212A mit vertraglich vereinbarter englischer Datenbank.

Grundlagen

ASD SPEC 1000D

Das Ausgangs- und Grundlagendokument für den gesamten konzeptionellen Ansatz und die zugehörigen Strukturfestlegungen der Interaktiven Elektronischen Technischen Dokumentation ist die von der ASD (AeroSpace and Defence Industries Association of Europe) herausgegebene Spezifikation ASD Spec 1000D (kurz S1000D), International Specification for Technical Publications Utilizing a Common Source Database. Diese internationale Spezifikation zur Erstellung technischer Dokumentation unter Verwendung einer einheitlichen CSDB-Datenbank wurde ursprünglich von der AECMA (Association Européenne des Constructeurs de Matériel Aérospatial), einer Interessenorganisation der europäischen Luftfahrtindustrie, erarbeitet.

Zielsetzung der Spezifikation ist es, für multinationale Rüstungsprojekte einen einheitlichen Dokumentationsstandard zu entwickeln, der eine modulare Erstellung der notwendigen Technischen Dokumentation erlaubt. Sie enthält neben den allgemeinen Regeln zur Erstellung technischer Vorschriften auch die Spezifikation über die Einrichtung und den Betrieb einer CSDB-Datenbank sowie die Festlegungen für das zu verwendende Codierungssystem für die Erstellung der Dokumentation.

Eine Dokumentation nach S1000D besteht aus sogenannten Datenmodulen, die ursprünglich unter Verwendung der Auszeichnungssprache SGML, ab Version 1.9 in XML, erzeugt und in der CSDB-Datenbank gespeichert werden. Bei diesen Datenmodulen handelt es sich um Dateien, in denen die für das Untersystem oder die Komponente relevanten Informationen in einer definierten Struktur enthalten sind. Für unterschiedliche Anwendungen der Dokumentation stellt die Spezifikation verschiedene grundlegende Datenmodultypen zur Verfügung, z. B. Beschreibende Datenmodule, die der allgemeinen Beschreibung technischer Sachverhalte dienen, oder Prozedurale Datenmodule zur Beschreibung von Arbeitsabläufen. Die jeweilige Struktur der Datenmodule wird durch eine zugehörige Dokumenttyp-Definition (DTD) festgelegt.

ASD SPEC 2000M

Die ASD Spec 2000M bzw. S2000M wird ebenfalls von der ASD herausgegeben. Sie ist eine international einheitliche Richtlinie für integrierte Verfahren der Materialwirtschaft im Rahmen der Entwicklung und Beschaffung von Wehrmaterial und dessen Nutzung.

ASD STE 100 Simplified Technical English

In den 80er Jahren definierte die AECMA als weiteren Dokumentationsstandard der Luft- und Raumfahrtindustrie das sog. AECMA Simplified English, eine kontrollierte Sprache, bei der das natürliche Englisch für einen bestimmten Zweck auf eine standardisierte Teilmenge begrenzt wird. Mittlerweile trägt das betreffende Regelwerk die Bezeichnung ASD STE 100.

Der Zweck des Simplified English ist es zunächst, Unklarheiten in technischer Dokumentation zu verringern und die Verständlichkeit zu erhöhen. Zielgruppe ist dabei explizit auch der englische Muttersprachler, da das Englische aufgrund seiner internationalen Verbreitung zahlreiche nationale und regionale Ausprägungen angenommen hat. In zweiter Instanz sollen einheitliche Vorgaben auch die Erstellung von technischer Dokumentation erleichtern und deren Übersetzung vereinfachen.

Das Simplified English verfügt über einen festgelegten Wortschatz, bei dem jeder Begriff genau eine Bedeutung hat (kontrolliertes Vokabular). Weiterhin sind nur bestimmte grammatische Formen und eine definierte Syntax zugelassen. Diese Richtlinien sind in Form zahlreicher Schreibregeln zusammengefasst, die u. a. auch Interpunktion und Satzlängen regeln.

Analog zum Simplified English gibt es auch im deutschen Sprachraum für technische Dokumentation Richtlinien für ein „Kontrolliertes Deutsch" (KD). Merkmale dieser fachsprachlichen Variante der natürlichen Sprache sind ebenfalls ein reduzierter Wortschatz einschließlich einer vorgegebenen Fachterminologie sowie die Anwendung eines bestimmten Stils.

Bundeswehrseitige Vorgaben und Spezifikationen

Im Juli 1999 erließ das Bundesverteidigungsministerium das Rahmenkonzept „Elektronische Technische Dokumentation der Bundeswehr", das allgemeine Zielvorstellungen und Richtlinien für die Einführung und Nutzung Elektronischer Technischer Dokumentation in der Bundeswehr vorgibt und Zuständigkeiten regelt. Das Rahmenkonzept beinhaltet neben einer allgemeinen Beschreibung einen fachlichen Teil mit Vorgaben zur Erstellung, Verwaltung, Versorgung und Nutzung von ETDok.

Im November 2002 wurde der „Katalog der Festlegungen, Standards und Verfahren für die Erstellung, Beschaffung, Verwaltung und Nutzung Elektronischer Technischer Dokumentation der Bundeswehr" erlassen. Er dient auf der Basis des Rahmenkonzepts als einheitlicher und verbindlicher Leitfaden für alle Vorhaben- und Nutzungsmanager.

Die Richtlinie für die Datenmodul-Erstellung gemäß AECMA S1000D (Ausgabe 2 vom Oktober 2005) ist verbindlicher „National Style Guide" für die Erstellung von SGML-Datenmodulen im Hinblick auf die Sicherstellung eines bundeswehreinheitlichen Datenbestandes und die ordnungsgemäße Darstellung der Quelldaten durch das IETD-Präsentationssystem der Bw, das IETP-X-Bw. Die Richtlinie enthält ergänzende Angaben und detaillierte Festlegungen zur Anwendung der ASD S1000D bei der Erstellung von IETD für die Bundeswehr. Layout-Details wie Schriftart und Farbe von Text, Zahl der Textspalten usw. sind nicht Thema dieser Richtlinie, sondern werden in Form von Style Sheets für das IETP-X-Bw mit dem Auftraggeber abgestimmt.

Implementierung der IETD-Publikationen

Die technische Realisierung der IETD-Systemkomponenten für die Bundeswehr erfolgt durch die Softwareeinheiten CSDB-Bw (Datenbank) und IETP-X-Bw (Anwendungssoftware). CSDB-Bw ist eine zentrale Datenbank, auf der die von der Industrie gelieferten Datenmodule eines Waffensystems eingestellt werden. Die Softwarekomponente IETP-X-Bw dient zur Anzeige der auf dem IETP-X-Bw-Server eingestellten IETD sowie zur Navigation innerhalb der Publikation.

IETP-X-Bw ist eine webgestützte Anwendung und basiert auf einer Client-Server-Architektur. Auf der Client-Seite ist der Standard-Browser der Bundeswehr (Internet Explorer) erforderlich. Für autarke Einzel-Arbeitsplätze können die Funktionalitäten „Server" und „Client" auf einem PC oder Notebook zusammengefasst werden.

Übersetzungen von Datenmodulen im Rahmen von IETD

Bereitstellung der IETD-Datenmodule

Datenmodule werden auf der Grundlage technischer Ausgangsdokumente erstellt, die in der Regel vom Gerätehersteller geliefert werden. Dabei kann es sich um beschreibende Dokumentation, Betriebsanleitungen, Wartungs- und Instandsetzungsanweisungen, Ersatzteillisten, Teilekataloge u. Ä. handeln.

Die Datenmodulerstellung erfolgt in der Regel bei der Industrie im SGML- bzw. künftig im XML-Format, wobei die einzuhaltenden Konventionen durch die Leistungsbeschreibung vertraglich festgelegt werden. Nach Fertigstellung aller Datenmodule eines kompletten Systems werden die Module als vollständige Publikation in Form eines Datenpakets an den Auftraggeber geliefert. Dieses Datenpaket enthält neben den Datenmodulen im SGML-/XML-Format Grafikdateien sowie Dateien mit DTD-Strukturvorgaben. Nach erfolgter Mitprüfung wird das Datenpaket auf dem IETP-X-Bw-Server in Wilhelmshaven zur Nutzung freigegeben.

Probleme

Bei einem technologischen Großprojekt, das hunderte von Untersystemen und Komponenten von einer großen Anzahl unterschiedlicher Zulieferer umfasst, stellt insbesondere auch für die spätere Übersetzung die Heterogenität des gelieferten Quellenmaterials eines der größten Probleme dar. Dies ist u. a. auf die unterschiedlichen Firmenphilosophien im Hinblick auf Dokumentationserstellung, Materialerhaltungsverfahren, Layout, Art der Kundenansprache usw. zurückzuführen.

Ein weiterer Problembereich ist die Qualität der technischen Redaktion, d. h. inwieweit die Dokumentation durch professionelle technische Redakteure unter Einhaltung marktüblicher bzw. genormter Verfahren und Regelungen gefertigt wird. Ein Beispiel hierfür wäre die korrekte und ausschließliche Verwendung der normgemäßen Sicherheitshinweise „Vorsicht" und „Achtung" mit ihren definierten Inhaltsabgrenzungen gegenüber firmenspezifischen Sprachkonventionen wie „Lebensgefahr" oder „Streng verboten". Zwar gibt es für die Erstellung technischer Dokumentation im Rüstungsbereich eine Reihe verbindlicher Regelwerke (z. B. die M 011, Bestimmungen für das Erarbeiten von Dienstvorschriften mit technischem Inhalt im Materialverantwortungsbereich der Marine), deren Anwendung aber häufig aus finanziellen oder sonstigen Gründen nicht beauftragt wird.

Die rein sprachliche Qualität ist ein weiterer Problempunkt. Dies gilt insbesondere für in englischer Sprache von Nichtmuttersprachlern erstellte Dokumentation, für die mittlerweile im Bundessprachenamt die Sprachklassifizierung „Non-native English" eingeführt ist. Diese Problematik ist in einem Maße angewachsen, dass selbst die EU genötigt war, ein Editoring-Referat einzurichten, um nicht von Muttersprachlern verfasste Texte übersetzbar aufzubereiten.

Terminologie ist ein weiterer kritischer Punkt. Bei einer großen Zahl Zulieferer ist die Inkonsistenz der Terminologie im Grunde vorprogrammiert. Querschnittlich verwendete Teile werden häufig unterschiedlich benannt, z. T. infolge mangelnder Abstimmung zwischen den Herstellern, z. T. aber auch infolge eigentumsrechtlicher oder marktpolitischer Einschränkungen wie z. B. eingetragene Handelsnamen oder patentrechtlich geschützte Bezeichnungen. Diesem Problembereich kann nur durch eine weit im Vorfeld mit den Herstellern abgestimmte Terminologiedatenbank entgegengewirkt werden, wozu aber in der Regel Zeit, Geld und das entsprechende Terminologiebewusstsein fehlen.

Erforderliche technische Voraussetzungen

Für eine Übersetzung von Datenmodulen wird eine Reihe spezieller Programme benötigt, und zwar für die Übersetzung selbst sowie für ergänzende Aufgaben wie Qualitätssicherung, Bildbearbeitung und Endkontrolle. Im Bundessprachenamt werden für diese Aufgaben die nachstehend kurz erläuterten Programme verwendet. Diese Programme sowie weitere u. a für Recherche- oder Terminologiezwecke verwendete Anwendungen sowie die in den einzelnen Bearbeitungsschritten anzuwendenden Verfahren erfordern dabei zwingend eine entsprechend leistungsstarke Rechnerausstattung mit ausreichend hohen Speicherkapazitäten sowie schnelle Netzverbindungen.

Epic Editor

Die Erstellung von Datenmodulen in der Auszeichnungssprache SGML erfolgt mit Hilfe geeigneter Editor-Programme. Für die Datenmodulerstellung im Rahmen des Projekts U212A wird das Programm Epic Editor der Firma Arbortext verwendet, das auch für das BSprA beschafft wurde, um ggf. Änderungen oder Fehlerkorrekturen im Dokument vornehmen zu können. Das seit 1998 angebotene Editor-Programm ist in Aussehen und Funktionsweise mit einer Textverarbeitungssoftware vergleichbar und ermöglicht es, Dokumente aus wiederverwendbaren Komponenten zu erzeugen und Daten aus verknüpften Datenbanken und anderen Datenquellen in Dokumente einzubetten. Der Editor überwacht bei der Eingabe die Gültigkeit der Eingabeelemente.

IsoView

Das bundeswehrweit eingeführte Betrachterprogramm IsoView der Firma Arbortext ermöglicht die Anzeige technischer Grafiken in einer interaktiven elektronischen Umgebung und wird für die Darstellung der auf dem IETP-X-Bw-Server abgelegten Datenmodule und Illustrationen benötigt.

IsoDraw

Arbortext IsoDraw ist ein Grafikprogramm für die Einbindung von grafischen Informationen in technische Dokumente. Es ermöglicht die schnelle und kostengünstige Erstellung hochwertiger technischer Illustrationen z. B. durch automatische Konvertierung von 3D-Konstruktionsdaten in technische Illustrationen. Die verschiedenen Ausgabeformate von IsoDraw gestatten den Einsatz der Grafiken sowohl in gedruckten Handbüchern als auch in interaktiven Dokumenten. Das Programm wird im BSprA dazu verwendet, um bei der Bildbearbeitung eventuell beschädigte Grafikelemente wiederherzustellen.

TRADOS Translator's Workbench

Die seit mehreren Jahren im BSprA verwendete computergestützte Übersetzungssoftware SDL TRADOS Translator's Workbench ist mittlerweile flächendeckend im Sprachendienst eingesetzt. Neben dem Translation-Memory-System (TMS) selbst besteht das Programmpaket aus der Terminologiedatenbank MultiTerm, Filterprogrammen zur Anbindung an Textverarbeitungsprogramme und den sog. Alignment-Tools. Für die Übersetzung von Datenmodulen wird mindestens die TRADOS-Version 7.5 benötigt, da erst ab dieser Version der integrierte TagEditor für die Bearbeitung von SGML- bzw. XML-Texten ausreichend stabil läuft.

MultiTerm

Das Programm MultiTerm als Bestandteil des TRADOS-Softwarepakets fungiert als Schnittstelle für den zentralisierten Terminologiezugriff und gewährleistet durch die Echtzeitverifizierung der Terminologie die Verwendung korrekter und konsistenter Benennungen während des gesamten Übersetzungsprozesses. Die Termini werden in einer zentralen servergestützten Datenbank gespeichert, die zusätzlich Kontextinformationen und Bildmaterial aufnehmen kann. Zugriffsmöglichkeiten gibt es in Form einer Client-Server-Anwendung, über Standard-Webbrowser oder durch Bereitstellung exportierter Daten auf Datenträgern in verschiedenen Formaten und Darstellungsarten.

TagEditor

Der TagEditor ist eine Komponente des SDL-TRADOS-Pakets, die als Bearbeitungsumgebung mit der Translator's Workbench zusammenarbeitet. Der TagEditor unterstützt eine Vielzahl unterschiedlicher Dateitypen (u. a. SGML, XML, Excel, Word), wobei jeweils Inhalt (zu übersetzender Text) und Struktur (Formatierungsinformationen) voneinander getrennt dargestellt werden.

Zugangssoftware für IETP-X-Bw-Server

Für den Zugriff auf den IETP-X-Bw-Nutzungsserver im Rechenzentrum Bw in Wilhelmshaven muss auf den für die Bearbeitung vorgesehenen Arbeitsplatzrechnern die erforderliche Zugangssoftware installiert werden. Auf dem Nutzungsserver sind die ausgangssprachlichen Datenmodule abgelegt und stehen dort zum Abruf über das Intranet Bw bereit. Zugriff auf den Server ist für den Übersetzer zu Referenzzwecken erforderlich, da ihm der für die Bearbeitung im TagEditor vorbereitete Text lediglich als unformatierter Fließtext angezeigt wird. Um Informationen über Struktur, Kontext oder Formatierung des Ausgangstextes zu erhalten, muss er sich an der Textdarstellung der Originalmodule auf dem Nutzungsserver orientieren.

In Ergänzung zum Nutzungsserver wurde im BSprA ein sog. IETP-X-Bw-Bereichsserver aufgesetzt. Damit ist es möglich, fertig übersetzte Datenmodulpakete auf dem Server zur Ansicht hochzuladen, um in einem letzten Prüfgang insbesondere Formatierung und Grafikinhalte auf Übereinstimmung mit dem Original auf dem Nutzungsserver zu kontrollieren.

Übersetzungsvorgang

Vorbereitung der Datenmodule

Das zur Übersetzung gelieferte Datenpaket einer vollständigen Publikation (Infoobjekt) enthält in mehreren Unterordnern sämtliche Datenmodule im SGML- und XML-Format, die Grafikdateien im CGM- oder TIF-Format sowie die sog. DMSL- und ISL-Dateien, in denen in Form von Excel-Tabellenblättern die strukturelle Hierarchie der Datenmodule (DMSL) und der Abbildungen (ISL) aufgelistet ist.

Für eine Übersetzung der Datenmodule mit Hilfe des TagEditors müssen diese im TRADOS-spezifischen zweisprachigen ttx-Dateiformat vorliegen. Die Umwandlung der SGML-/XML-Dateien erfolgt mit Hilfe von Initialisierungsdateien. Für die weitere Bearbeitung wird eine Verzeichnisstruktur angelegt, die eine übersichtliche Darstellung sowie eine sukzessive Abarbeitung der Datenmodule ermöglicht. Diese Verzeichnisstruktur wird bis zur endgültigen Fertigstellung zentral und servergestützt geführt, um jederzeit allen Bearbeitern den Zugriff auf das Verzeichnis zu ermöglichen und die systematische Bearbeitung der Datenmodule zu erleichtern.

Übersetzung und Überprüfung

Für die Übersetzung ist es zweckmäßig, zu Referenzzwecken das Original-Datenmodul auf dem IETP-X-Bw-Nutzungsserver zu öffnen, da ein Originaldokument im eigentlichen Sinne nicht mehr existiert. Für die Bearbeitung des Moduls müssen die Programme Translator's Workbench, TagEditor und MultiTerm sowie ggf. die integrierten Prüfprogramme für Rechtschreibprüfung und Tag-Überprüfung geladen werden. Für den Überprüfungsvorgang gelten im Wesentlichen die gleichen Verfahren und Vorgaben wie für die Übersetzung. Am Überprüferarbeitsplatz wird in der Regel zusätzlich das integrierte Qualitätsprüfprogramm QA Verifier aktiviert und für die gewünschten Prüfmerkmale konfiguriert.

Das Cleanup nach erfolgter Überprüfung wird jeweils für einen kompletten Datenmodulsatz durch gleichzeitige Bearbeitung aller im Unterordner enthaltenen ttx-Dateien durchgeführt. Dabei werden automatisch zielsprachliche sgm-Dateien erzeugt, die denselben Namen wie die ttx-Dateien tragen.

Bildbearbeitung und Endkontrolle

Nach dem Überprüfungsvorgang ist ggf. noch eine Bildbearbeitung erforderlich, bei der Texte von Bildinschriften in die Zielsprache umgesetzt oder auch Bilder aufgrund textlicher Beschränkungen in der Zielsprache größenmäßig angepasst werden.

Für eine letzte Endkontrolle bzw. auch ggf. zu Prüfzwecken während des Übersetzungsprozesses kann das Datenmodul im IETP-X-Bw-Bereichsserver des BSprA zur Ansicht hochgeladen werden. Das Hochladen einer Publikation erfordert mehrere Schritte. Zunächst muss eine Transformation von SGML nach XML erfolgen, anschließend kann das Infoobjekt geladen werden.

Probleme

Im Kontext der Vorbereitung, konkreten Bearbeitung und Verwaltung der IETD-Datenmodule sind vornehmlich zwei Problembereiche zu identifizieren. Dies sind zunächst die technischen Rahmenbedingungen, die durch die Hardware- und Softwareausstattung vorgegeben werden.

Hardwareseitig ist infolge der Zahl der bereits erwähnten Programme sowie der zusätzlich für Recherche, Bürokommunikation und Rechnerbetrieb erforderlichen Anwendungen konstant von einer starken Rechnerauslastung mit hohem Arbeitsspeicherbedarf auszugehen. Da die Dateiablagestruktur darüber hinaus im Bundessprachenamt intern, aber auch zur Einbindung extern dislozierter Mitarbeiter weitestgehend servergestützt ist, sind außerdem schnelle Datenübertragungsverbindungen notwendig. Die Vielzahl der gleichzeitig geöffneten Programme und die Notwendigkeit, den zu übersetzenden Text im Original in seinem strukturellen und inhaltlichen Kontext nachzuvollziehen, macht zusätzlich einen zweiten Monitor erforderlich.

Softwareseitig ermöglichen und unterstützen die genannten Programme zwar alle das Arbeiten mit Datenmodulen, weisen aber auch sämtlich noch zahlreiche Schwächen im Hinblick auf die IETD-Bearbeitung auf. Dies ist z. T. auf Kompatibilitätsprobleme mit Microsoft-Anwendungen oder auch auf Abstimmungsdefizite innerhalb des SDL-Programmpakets zurückzuführen.

Die Probleme im Verfahren und Ablauf konzentrieren sich im Wesentlichen auf den hohen Aufwand bei der Arbeitsvorbereitung, d. h. die Umwandlung der Module in das TRADOS-lesbare Format, die Strukturierung der Ordner für die Abwicklung der Übersetzung, die unterschiedlichen z. T. manuellen Verfahren zur Mitkopplung der abgearbeiteten Datenmodule in den verschiedenen Bearbeitungsphasen sowie die für die Datenmodul-Übersetzung besonders umfangreiche Vorarbeit zur Bereitstellung einer konsistenten Terminologiebasis.

Schlussbemerkungen

Insgesamt besitzt das Konzept der Interaktiven Elektronischen Technischen Dokumentation zahlreiche Vorteile auf der Nutzer- und Materialbewirtschaftungsseite. Die Erstellung der Datenmodule ist relativ aufwändig, wobei sich jedoch hier aufgrund der systematischen und systemübergreifend vergleichbaren Strukturierung von Inhalten und Form mit der Zeit Nutzeffekte ergeben werden. Dies bedingt allerdings, dass seitens der Ausgangsdatenersteller zunehmend die grundsätzlichen Vorgaben der einschlägigen Spezifikationen und Standards Berücksichtigung finden und angewendet werden.

Der Übersetzungsprozess nimmt in diesem Kontext neue Dimensionen an, und zwar sowohl im Hinblick auf die hohen Software- und Hardwareanforderungen in Form neuer anspruchsvoller Programme, leistungsstarker Rechner und schneller Netzverbindungen als auch hinsichtlich des erforderlichen Aufwands während des gesamten Bearbeitungsablaufs. Hier gibt es für die einschlägigen Programmanbieter noch einen deutlichen Nachbesserungsbedarf in puncto Leistungsfähigkeit, Programmoptionen und Zuverlässigkeit. Darüber hinaus gilt es aber auch, auf der Grundlage weiterer

Erfahrungen die Arbeitsabläufe zu optimieren, da die rein quantitativen Arbeitsergebnisse aufgrund der vielen Bearbeitungsschritte noch nicht in einem angemessenen Verhältnis zum getriebenen Aufwand stehen.

Dennoch ist der Einstieg in diese neue Art des Übersetzens unter Nutzung modernster Hilfsmittel eindeutig positiv zu werten. Die Übersetzungen der Datenmodule genügen in gleichem Maße wie die Ausgangsdokumente den Anforderungen an eine zentral verfügbare, aktuelle, umfassend verlinkte, modulare technische Dokumentation und erfüllen damit die IETD-Zielsetzungen der Bundeswehr. Angesichts der Planung der Teilstreitkräfte zur durchgängigen Implementierung der IETD für alle neuen Rüstungsvorhaben erwächst hier ein gewaltiger Bedarf an qualitativ hochwertigen Übersetzungen technischer Dokumentation.

Terminologieschöpfung und -recherche

„Klar gibt es diesen Ausdruck – habe ich doch bei Google gefunden!"

Dr. Anja Rütten

Diplom-Dolmetscherin, Konferenzdolmetscherin
(AIIC, VKD-BDÜ, BDÜ)

ruetten@sprachmanagement.net

1   Gängige Praxis

„Sage ich jetzt wirklich ‚Zeitverwendungserhebung' – oder gibt es da nicht einen ‚deutscheren' Ausdruck? Mal bei Google nachsehen … 116 Treffer. Nicht schlecht. Aber ‚time use survey' hat viel mehr Treffer, 55 200. Mal sehen …" An dieser Stelle greift ein als „schöpferisches Improvisieren" (vor allem bei Dolmetschern) bzw. „gründliches Recherchieren" (bei Dolmetschern und Übersetzern) bekannter, sehr zentraler Prozess, der jedoch nicht Gegenstand der vorliegenden Betrachtungen ist. „ … und ‚Zeitbudgeterhebung'? 5 720 Treffer. Schon besser. Aber ist das jetzt viel oder wenig? Und aus welchen Ländern stammen die Treffer eigentlich?"

2 Differenzierter ist besser

2.1 Trefferzahlen nach Ländern

Wenn es darum geht, anhand von Google Hinweise auf die Verwendungshäufigkeit eines Ausdrucks zu erhalten, bietet Termprofile.com kostenlos Unterstützung. Musste man bisher unzählige Suchanfragen starten und die jeweiligen Trefferzahlen im Gedächtnis behalten, um die Trefferzahlen in unterschiedlichen Ländern vergleichen zu können, ermittelt Termprofile.com jetzt auf einen Blick Trefferzahlen für bis zu drei verschiedene Ausdrücke differenziert in bis zu drei verschiedenen Ländern pro Ausdruck. Hierbei wird die bei Google in der erweiterten Suche angebotene Regionensuche zugrundegelegt. Der Clou: Für die Sprachen Englisch und Spanisch sind die wichtigsten Länder in Gruppen zusammengefasst.

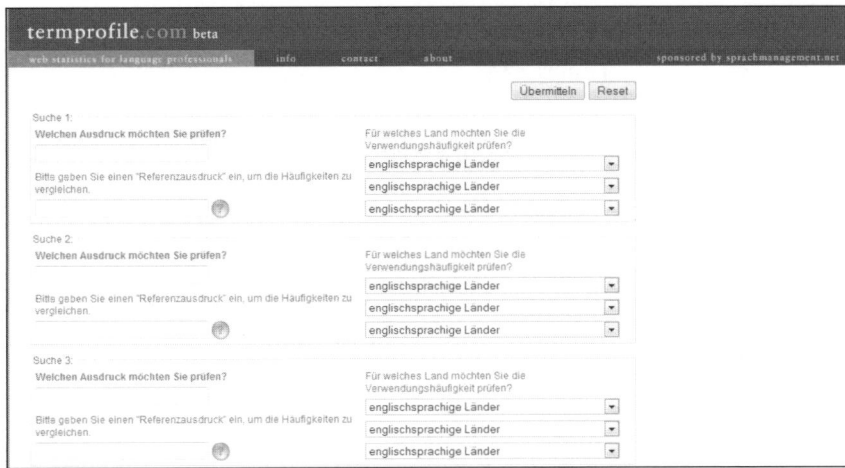

Konkret heißt das: Ist man sich nicht sicher, ob ‚Zeitverwendungserhebung‘ wirklich die richtige Übersetzung für ‚time use survey‘ ist, so kann man in Termprofile.com gleichzeitig die Google-Trefferzahlen für den englischen und den deutschen Ausdruck bzw. zwei mögliche deutsche Ausdrücke ermitteln, und zwar jeweils für drei Länder oder Ländergruppen.

Das Ergebnis sieht folgendermaßen aus:

time use survey			Zeitverwendungserhebung			Zeitbudgeterhebung		
Land	absolute Häufigkeit: Treffer time use survey	relative Häufigkeit: Treffer time use survey / Treffer ...	Land	absolute Häufigkeit: Treffer Zeitverwendungserhebung	relative Häufigkeit: Treffer Zeitverwendung g / Treffer ...	Land	absolute Häufigkeit: Treffer Zeitbudgeterhebung	relative Häufigkeit: Treffer Zeitbudget erhebung / Treffer ...
englisch-sprachige Länder	11100	1:0.000	Deutschland	47		Deutschland	2680	
			Österreich	41		Österreich	109	
Summe	11100	0	Summe	88		Summe	2789	
weltweit	53700	01:00	weltweit	100		weltweit	4080	

Man sieht auf einen Blick, dass ‚Zeitbudgeterhebung' sowohl in Deutschland als auch in Österreich deutlich häufiger verwendet wird als ‚Zeitverwendungserhebung'.

2.2 Relative Verwendungshäufigkeit

Aber was ist, wenn die absoluten Zahlen nicht ganz so eindeutig sprechen? Wenn wir gerne wissen möchten, ob die Trefferzahl in einem kleineren Land verhältnismäßig hoch oder niedrig ist im Vergleich zu einem größeren Land (wobei die Größe sich natürlich auf die Größe der Internetpopulation bezieht)? Dann hilft Termprofile.com, denn hier ist es möglich, den gesuchten Ausdruck ins Verhältnis zu einem anderen, einem Referenzwort der gleichen Sprache zu setzen, das dann gleichsam die Grundgesamtheit darstellt. Dies kann ein ganz allgemeines Wort sein, etwa ‚unter' oder ‚under'. Es kann auch ein etwas spezifischeres Wort sein, etwa ‚money' oder ‚Geld', wenn man einen Begriff wie ‚hedge fund' prüft. Es gilt nur darauf zu achten, dass die Referenzwörter in den verschiedenen Suchen ähnlich verbreitet sind (also nicht ‚und' in der deutschen Suche und ‚money' in der englischsprachigen).

Wenn man nun also ‚time use survey' mit dem Referenzausdruck ‚statistics' sowie ‚Zeitverwendungsherhebung' und ‚Zeitbudgeterhebung' mit dem Referenzausdruck ‚Statistik' prüft, erhält man folgendes Ergebnis:

time use survey			Zeitverwendungserhebung			Zeitbudgeterhebung		
Land	absolute Häufigkeit: Treffer time use survey	relative Häufigkeit: Treffer time use survey / Treffer statistics	Land	absolute Häufigkeit: Treffer Zeitverwendungsheb ung	relative Häufigkeit: Treffer Zeitverwendungserheb ung / Treffer Statistik	Land	absolute Häufigkeit: Treffer Zeitbudget erhebung	relative Häufigkeit: Treffer Zeitbudget erhebung / Treffer Statistik
englisch-sprachige Länder	11300	1:10796	Deutschland	45	1:926667	Deutschland	2680	1:15560
Deutschland	872	1:20872	Österreich	41	1:194390	Österreich	110	1:72455
Österreich	164	1:98177						
Summe	12336	1:11496	Summe	86	1:577558	Summe	2790	1:17803
weltweit	53700	1:10223	weltweit	101	1:1009901	weltweit	4080	1:24755

Betrachtet man die relative Häufigkeit von ‚time use survey' in der zweiten Spalte, so sieht man zunächst, dass der englische Ausdruck in englischsprachigen Ländern einen Wert von ca. 1:11 000 hat, in Deutschland ca. 1:21 000. Je niedriger der Wert hinter dem Doppelpunkt, desto größer die Verwendungshäufigkeit des geprüften Ausdrucks (im Verhältnis zum Referenzausdruck, hier ‚statistics'). Die Werte liegen hier in einer ähnlichen Größenordnung, eventuell ist der englische Ausdruck unter deutschen Statistikern also genauso geläufig wie unter englischsprachigen. Man sieht ferner, dass „Zeitverwendungserhebung" im deutschsprachigen Raum verhältnismäßig deutlich weniger Verwendung findet, die relative Häufigkeit liegt im sechsstelligen Bereich. ‚Zeitbudgeterhebung' allerdings ist mit ca. 1:16 000 relativ noch häufiger als der englische Fachausdruck.

Ein weiteres Beispiel für die relative Verwendungshäufigkeit ist die Frage, wie man das Wort ‚Produktpalette' ins Spanische übersetzen sollte. Wählt man ‚paleta de productos', so stellt man fest, dass in Deutschland 570 Treffer dafür gefunden werden, in den spanischsprachigen Ländern 504. In absoluten Zahlen ist es hier schon auffällig, dass im relativ kleinen Deutschland mehr Treffer für einen spanischen Ausdruck anfallen als im spanischsprachigen Raum, wenn auch die relative Häufigkeit in Deutschland sogar etwas niedriger ist. Wenn man dann noch die relative Häufigkeit von ‚Produktpalette' in Deutschland (1:357) mit der von ‚gama de productos' in den spanischsprachigen Ländern (1:442) vergleicht, wird klar, welches der bessere spanische Ausdruck ist.

Produktpalette			paleta de productos			gama de productos		
Land	absolute Häufigkeit: Treffer Produktpalette	relative Häufigkeit: Treffer Produktpalette / Treffer Produkt	Land	absolute Häufigkeit: Treffer paleta de productos	relative Häufigkeit: Treffer paleta de productos / Treffer producto	Land	absolute Häufigkeit: Treffer gama de productos	relative Häufigkeit: Treffer gama de productos / Treffer producto
Deutschland	1 320 000	1:357	spanischsprachige Länder	504	1:39 286	spanischsprachige Länder	4 000 000	1:5 025
			Spanien	244	1:1 745 902	Spanien	976 000	1:442
			Deutschland	570	1:107 719	Deutschland	52 800	1:1 163
Summe	1 320 000	1:357	Summe	1074	1:75 605	Summe	4 052 800	1:20,110
weltweit	1 730 000	1:821	weltweit	3540	1:0.000	weltweit	2 360 000	1:0.000

3   Nicht alles geht

3.1 Inhaltliche Grenzen

Natürlich ist Google und damit auch Termprofile.com kein Nachschlagewerk und das Internet alles andere als ein 100 % verlässliches Korpus. Es schreibt, wer will und vor allem wie er will. Durch die Identifizierung der Herkunft von Treffern kann man jedoch die Wahrscheinlichkeit der Muttersprachlichkeit deutlich steigern.

Auch ist die Äquivalenz von zwei Ausdrücken in zwei verschiedenen Sprachen natürlich nicht anhand eines ähnlichen webstatistischen Profils („Termprofil") nachweisbar. Äquivalenz ist und bleibt semantisch, es ist immer wichtig, Begriffe im Kontext ihrer Verwendung zu betrachten, um ein Gefühl für ihre Verwendung und Bedeutung zu bekommen. Dennoch können ähnliche Trefferzahlen – und hier vornehmlich die relative Verwendungshäufigkeit – wertvolle Indizien sein, die Äquivalenz untermauern. Sehr unterschiedliche Zahlen hingegen sind oft ein deutliches Warnsignal, das darauf hindeutet, dass es wahrscheinlich passendere Ausdrücke gibt.

Es kann auch durchaus vorkommen, dass zwei äquivalente Begriffe in unterschiedlichen Sprachen sehr unterschiedliche Webstatistiken aufweisen. Hierfür gibt es verschiedene Gründe:

- Die Suche in mehrsprachigen Ländern wie Kanada, Belgien oder der Schweiz verzerrt das Bild.

- Ein Begriff ist in einem bestimmten Sprachraum entstanden, etwa ein deutscher technischer Begriff aus dem Maschinenbau. Dieser ist in Spanien noch gar nicht bekannt, daher wird von Sprachmittlern oder Terminologen ein entsprechender spanischer Terminus eingeführt, der dann zwar mit dem deutschen äquivalent ist, aber (zumindest zu Beginn) weitaus weniger häufig verwendet wird. Auch ist es etwa durch unterschiedliche volkswirtschaftliche oder kulturelle Gegebenheiten so, dass bestimmte Themen unterschiedlich häufig im Internet des jeweiligen Sprachraums behandelt werden. Es gibt beispielsweise nach den Termprofile-Erkenntnissen im deutschsprachigen Web verhältnismäßig mehr Seiten zum Thema Maschinenbau als im spanischsprachigen Web. Diesem Umstand kann man dadurch gerecht werden, dass man auch den – allgemeineren – Referenzausdruck aus dem entsprechenden Fachgebiet wählt.

- Eine Benennung hat in einer Sprache mehrere Bedeutungen, die entsprechende Benennung der anderen Sprache nicht. Das englische ‚well' wird zum Beispiel nie ein ähnliches webstatistisches Profil haben wie das deutsche ‚Brunnen'. Hier hat sich die Verwendung von Kontextwörtern (beispielsweise ‚water') bei der Suche bewährt, um die Treffer einzugrenzen. Solche Kontextwörter werden einfach neben den gesuchten Begriff im gleichen Suchschlitz von Termprofile.com eingetippt.

3.2 Technische Grenzen

Termprofile.com hat nicht nur inhaltliche, sondern auch gewisse technische Grenzen:

- Da eine einzige Termprofile-Anfrage bis zu neun parallele Google-Suchen umfasst, kommt es mitunter vor, dass aufgrund der hohen Belastung nicht alle Zahlen vollständig geliefert werden (es tauchen Nullen im Ergebnisraster auf).

- Da die großen Datenmengen bei Google durch unterschiedliche Server verarbeitet werden, werden die Trefferzahlen für eine identische Anfrage nicht immer 100 % deckungsgleich sein (auch bei Google direkt nicht).

- Termprofile.com führt die Abfragen über eine sogenannte API (Application Programming Interface) von Google durch. Die Zahl solcher Abfragen ist durch Google auf 1000 pro Tag begrenzt. Eine unbegrenzte API wäre eventuell gegen Bezahlung möglich.

- Offensichtlich blockiert die Abfrage über die API bei zu hohen Trefferzahlen, die Suche nach sehr häufigen Wörtern wird sozusagen verweigert (das Ergebnis bei Termprofile ist ‚0'; siehe beispielsweise die weltweite relative Häufigkeit zu ‚gama de productos'). So kann man weltweit oder auch nur in den USA weder nach ‚and' noch nach ‚you' oder ‚with' suchen. ‚Under' hingegen funktioniert. In Deutschland, Großbritannien und allen spanischsprachigen Ländern scheint diese Einschränkung bisher nicht zu greifen.

4   Wie geht es weiter?

Das Arbeiten mit Termprofile.com liefert Übersetzern und Dolmetschern sehr viel differenziertere und aussagekräftigere Daten als die direkte Eingabe in Suchmaschinen. Wenn man regelmäßig mit Termprofile arbeitet, entwickelt man außerdem ein Gefühl für Größenordnungen von Treffern in verschiedenen Sprachen, Fachbereichen usw. Das Tool entwickelt sich regelrecht zum Spielzeug, weil man immer neue Dimensionen und Verhältnisse entdeckt.

Nun geht es darum, aus den Erfahrungen der Nutzer zu lernen und Termprofile weiterzuentwickeln. Einschätzungen zu Vor- und Nachteilen, Verbesserungsvorschläge usw. sind daher immer willkommen. Diplom- bzw. Masterarbeiten etwa in Form von Fallstudien zum Thema Internetstatistik und Terminologie könnten sicher weiteren Aufschluss über dieses allgegenwärtige Thema geben.

Um Termprofile.com auf eine neue Ebene der Professionalität zu heben (etwa mit einer Verfügbarkeit von mehr als 1000 Anfragen pro Tag), werden finanzielle Mittel benötigt, die über die bisherige Privatfinanzierung hinausgehen. Anregungen von interessierten Investoren, Sponsoren und Werbetreibenden werden gerne berücksichtigt.

Wie finde ich die richtigen Worte? Schöpfung neuer und Auswahl guter Terminologie

Prof. Dr. Klaus-Dirk Schmitz

Fachhochschule Köln / Deutscher Terminologie-Tag e.V.

klaus.schmitz@fh-koeln.de

1 Einleitung

Die Auswahl und Festlegung sowie die konsistente und korrekte Verwendung von Fachwörtern (Terminologie) sind Grundvoraussetzungen für eine erfolgreiche (Fach-) Übersetzung. Die Adressatengruppe eines Textes will in einem bestimmten Zielmarkt in ihrer jeweiligen Muttersprache angesprochen werden. Je nach Fachlichkeitsgrad des Textes kann der Anteil der fachspezifischen Terminologie unterschiedlich groß sein. Oft behandeln (übersetzte) Texte innovative Fachgebiete und Themen, bei denen die zu verwendende Terminologie in der Zielsprache (noch) nicht existiert oder etabliert ist. Deshalb muss die Terminologie erst geprägt oder aus existierenden Fachwörtern das am besten geeignete ausgewählt werden, bevor mit dem Übersetzungsprozess begonnen werden kann.

2 Verfahren zur Bildung neuer Benennungen

2.1 Allgemeines

Entstehen neue Begriffe und möchte man innerhalb einer Sprachgemeinschaft über diese neuen Begriffe sprechen und schreiben, so müssen neue Benennungen dafür gebildet werden. Dabei spielt es zunächst keine Rolle, ob diese neuen Begriffe innerhalb der eigenen oder innerhalb einer anderen Sprach- und Kulturgemeinschaft entstehen, Beispielsweise wurde für die Benutzeroberfläche von Microsoft Office 2007 ein neues graphisches Bedienkonzept entwickelt, das in der amerikanischen Version als *„ribbon"* bezeichnet wird. Für die Lokalisierung ins Deutsche musste eine neue deutsche Benennung gefunden werden, da dieses Bedienkonzept bisher noch nicht existierte und deswegen nicht mit einer etablierten Benennung belegt war. Man hat sich für die Benennung „Multifunktionsleiste" entschieden; aber auch andere Benennungen wie „Band" oder „Ribbon" wären möglich gewesen. Im Folgenden werden die lexikalischen Möglichkeiten der Benennungsbildung im Deutschen beschrieben; in vielen anderen Sprachen stehen ähnliche Benennungsbildungsmechanismen zur Verfügung. Es muss noch erwähnt werden, dass sehr häufig die dargestellten Verfahren bei der Bildung neuer Benennungen miteinander kombiniert werden.

2.2 Komposition

Bei der Komposition werden zwei oder mehr selbstständige Wörter zu einer neuen Benennung zusammengeführt. So entstehen neue Komposita, die durch die Verwendung von Bindestrichen übersichtlicher und verständlicher gestaltet oder durch die Verwendung von Fugenelementen leichter sprechbar werden können.

Beispiele: Menüleiste, PowerPoint-Version, Übergangsgeschwindigkeit

Die Bildung von Komposita ist besonders im Deutschen ein sehr häufig angewandtes Verfahren, das allerdings bei der Übersetzung in andere Sprachen, die diesen Bildungsmechanismus nicht kennen oder nicht so häufig anwenden, zu Schwierigkeiten führen kann, da die Beziehungen zwischen den Kompositateilen explizit gemacht werden müssen.

Die Komposition neuer Benennungen in der Fachsprache kann aber auch zur Bildung von Benennungen führen, die aus mehr als einem (zusammengesetzten) Wort bestehen. Diese Mehrwortbenennungen, die übrigens im Englischen und in den romanischen Sprachen sehr viel häufiger auftreten, bereiten automatischen Verfahren zur Extraktion von Terminologie aus Texten besondere Schwierigkeiten.

Beispiele: benutzerdefinierte Bildschirmpräsentation,
getestete Einblendzeiten verwenden

2.3 Derivation und Konversion

Die Derivation beschreibt das Verfahren, bei dem eine neue Benennung durch die Kombination eines Stammwortes mit einem oder mehreren Affixen (Präfixen, Suffixen) entsteht.

Beispiele: Vorlage, Einfügen, Textrichtung, Foliensortierung, Auflösung

Die Derivation ist neben der Komposition das im Deutschen am häufigsten verwendete Verfahren zur Bildung neuer Benennungen. Oft werden auch beide Verfahren kombiniert.

Bei der Konversion, die manchmal auch Nullderivation genannt wird, findet ein Übergang von einer Wortklasse in eine andere statt, ohne dass Affixe hinzukommen.

Beispiele: Layout – layouten, löschen – das Löschen, überlappen – überlappend

Die Konversion vom Verb zum Substantiv und umgekehrt ist gerade im Englischen ein oft verwendetes Mittel der Benennungsbildung.

2.4 Terminologisierung

Terminologisierung bezeichnet das Benennungsbildungsverfahren, bei dem eine Benennung eines Begriffs aus der Gemeinsprache als Benennung für einen Begriff in einem Fachgebiet verwendet wird. Vereinfacht kann man die Terminologisierung als den Übergang eines Wortes zu einer Benennung beschreiben. Das Verfahren der Terminologisierung wird häufig mit Verfahren der Komposition und Derivation kombiniert.

Beispiele: Lineal, Fenster, Folie, Textfeld, Kopf- und Fußzeile

Bei der Terminologisierung wird sehr oft das Prinzip der Metaphorik oder der Metonymie eingesetzt; siehe hierzu 3.3 Transparenz und Motivation.

Von Umterminologisierung spricht man, wenn die Benennung nicht aus der Gemeinsprache sondern aus einer anderen Fachsprache (eines anderen Fachgebiets) übernommen wird.

2.5 Entlehnung

Ein leider viel zu häufig angewandtes Verfahren der Benennungsbildung ist die Entlehnung, bei der eine Benennung aus einer Sprache als Benennung für einen Begriff in einer anderen Sprache übernommen wird. Auch wenn die Entlehnung aus dem Englischen im Deutschen gerade heute ein sehr beliebtes und oft verwendetes Mittel zur Schöpfung neuer Benennungen ist, sollte bedacht werden, dass besonders bei diesem Verfahren die Transparenz einer Benennung (siehe 3.3) nicht immer gegeben ist.

Beispiele: Zoom, Frame, ClipArt, Add-in, Folienmaster

Besonders kritisch sind so genannte Scheinentlehnungen, bei denen es so aussieht, als wäre eine Benennung aus einer anderen Sprache übernommen worden, wobei aber die Benennung in der Ausgangssprache nicht oder in einer anderen Bedeutung existiert (z.B. *Handy* oder *Friseur*).

2.6 Kürzung

Die Kürzung von Benennungen ist in der Fachsprache sehr üblich, führt aber nicht in allen Fällen wirklich zu neuen Begriffsbezeichnungen.

Beispiele: Info, Tabstopp, AutoText, USB-Schnittstelle

Über die unterschiedlichen Arten der Kürzung von Benennungen informiert ausführlich die DIN 2340.

2.7 Urschöpfung

Die vollständige Neubildung von Benennungen ohne Nutzung der oben beschriebenen Benennungsbildungsverfahren (2.2 – 2.6) ist – außer bei Produkt- und Unternehmensnamen – sehr selten, auch weil die Transparenz von Benennungen (siehe 3.3) sehr selten gegeben ist. Man könnte die Benennung „*simsen*" für das Senden von Kurznachrichten mittels Mobiltelefonen als Urschöpfung bezeichnen, aber auch als eine Kombination von Entlehnung (*short message service*), Kürzung (*SMS*), Konversion (*smsen*) und Anpassung an die Sprechbarkeit. Ähnlich verhält es sich mit der Benennung „*googeln*" für die Suche im Internet.

3 Anforderungen an Benennungen

3.1 Allgemeines

Sowohl bei der Schöpfung neuer Benennung nach den in Abschnitt 2 aufgeführten Mechanismen als auch bei der Auswahl von vorhandenen Benennungen sind unterschiedliche Anforderungen an bestimmte Eigenschaften der Benennungen zu berücksichtigen. Der letztgenannte Fall ist typisch für die präskriptive Terminologiearbeit, bei der beispielsweise innerhalb eines Normungsgremiums, eines Unternehmens, einer Produktlinie oder für einen bestimmten Text eine von mehreren möglichen Benennungen für denselben Begriff als bevorzugte Benennung ausgewählt werden muss.

Die im Folgenden dargestellten Anforderungen an Benennungen beschreiben sinnvolle und notwendige Eigenschaften von Benennungen. Oft können aber nicht alle Anforderungen gleichzeitig erfüllt werden, da sich bestimmte Eigenschaften gegenseitig ausschließen. So kann etwa die Benennung für einen sehr komplexen Begriff sehr lang werden und damit dem Prinzip der sprachlichen Ökonomie widersprechen, wenn sie gleichzeitig transparent und treffend sein soll.

3.2 Genauigkeit und Eineindeutigkeit

Unter Genauigkeit und Eineindeutigkeit wird verstanden, dass eine Benennung genau einen Begriff bezeichnet. Damit soll vermieden werden, dass es mehrere Benennungen für denselben Begriff gibt (keine Synonymie) und dass eine Benennung nicht mehrere unterschiedliche Begriffe bezeichnen kann (keine Homonymie). Dieses Ziel sollte zumindest innerhalb eines Fachgebietes, aber auch innerhalb eines Unternehmens, einer Produktlinie oder eines Textes erreicht werden, um Missverständnisse zu vermeiden und die Effizienz der fachsprachlichen Kommunikation sicherzustellen. Ein Nachfrage des Textrezipienten oder Kommunikationspartner, ob beispielsweise „*Eingabetaste*" und „*Return-Taste*" dieselbe Taste auf der Tastatur bezeichnet und damit denselben Begriff repräsentiert, sollte unbedingt vermieden werden.

Es soll noch darauf hingewiesen werden, dass die in 2.4 beschriebene Terminologisierung bzw. Umterminologisierung als typisches und oft angewandtes Verfahren der Benennungsbildung prinzipiell dazu führt, dass Mehrdeutigkeiten entstehen und die Genauigkeit einer bestimmten Benennung verringert wird. Allerdings geschieht dies nur gesamtsprachlich betrachtet und die Eineindeutigkeit einer Benennung innerhalb eines Fachgebietes wird dadurch nicht negativ beeinflusst.

3.3 Transparenz und Motivation

Von Transparenz oder Motivation bei Benennungen spricht man, wenn die Merkmale des Begriffs in der Benennung „durchscheinen" und man leicht den Begriff hinter der Benennung ohne Definition und Erklärung erfassen kann. Transparente und motivierte Benennungen sind vor allem durch Komposition und Derivation gebildet.

Man unterscheidet bei der Motivation die morphologische, die semantische und die phonetische Motivation.

Bei der morphologischen Motivation ergibt sich der Inhalt des repräsentierten Begriffs direkt aus den Bestandteilen der Benennung.

Beispiele: Bildschirmpräsentation, Zwischenablage, Fehlermeldung,
serielle Schnittstelle

Bei der semantischen Motivation werden die Bestandteile einer Benennung im übertragenen Sinn verwendet. Besonders Benennungsbildungsverfahren wie die Terminologisierung führen oft zu einer semantischen Motivation.

Beispiele: Kopfzeile, Fensterrahmen, Maus, Computervirus, infizierte Datei

Eine phonetische Motivation findet man in den Fachsprachen sehr selten. Eventuell kann man Benennungen wie *„klicken"* oder *„zippen"* als lautmalerische Benennung bezeichnen, die aber erst nach einer Entlehnung aus dem Englischen entstanden sind.

Besonders bei der Entlehnung von semantisch motivierten Benennungen aus anderen Sprachen (und Kulturen) muss sichergestellt werden, dass der Mechanismus der Bedeutungsübertragung beim Übergang in eine andere Kultur noch transparent bleibt. So wird etwa das Bild hinter der Benennung *„Firewall"* in vielen Sprachen nicht richtig als „Mauer zum Schutz vor Feuer" sondern als „Mauer aus Feuer" verstanden, da in diesen Kulturen keine Brandschutzmauern verwendet werden.

Ein weiteres Phänomen kann die Transparenz von Benennungen gerade bei Komposita im Deutschen (und Englischen) einschränken. Oft werden die Beziehungen zwischen den morphologisch oder semantisch motivierten Teilen eines Kompositums nicht klar. Bekannte Beispiele hierfür sind die Benennungen *„Schweineschnitzel"*, *„Jägerschnitzel"* und *„Kinderschnitzel"*. Auch Mehrdeutigkeiten bei vielgliedrigen Komposita können durch unterschiedliche Interpretation der Motivation entstehen; so bezeichnet die Benennung *„Schrankwand"* sowohl die Rückwand eines Schrankes als auch einen wandbreiten Schrank. Oft kann die Setzung eines Bindestriches zur Verdeutlichung beitragen, wie etwa bei *„Mädchen-Handelsschule"* oder bei *„Gummi-Schuhsohle"* vs. *„Gummischuh-Sohle"*.

3.4 Angemessenheit

Unter Angemessenheit werden unterschiedliche Eigenschaften von Benennungen verstanden. So soll eine angemessene Benennung dem Leser vertraut und geläufig sein, keine Verwirrung oder Unsicherheit erzeugen und auch keine negativen Konnotationen haben. Angemessene Benennungen sind auch geschlechtsneutral, politisch korrekt und nicht diskriminierend. Aus der Gemeinsprache sind bekannte Beispiele die Ersetzung des *„Mohrenkopfes"* durch den *„Schokokuss"*, die Verwendung von *„Vertrauensperson"* statt *„Vertrauensmann"* oder der Versuch *„Unkraut"* durch *„Wildkraut"* zu ersetzen.

Beispiele: Fehler im Anwendungsprogramm (statt Anwenderfehler)
barrierefreier Zugang (statt behindertengerechter Zugang)
Bedienoberfläche (statt Bediener- oder Benutzeroberfläche)
Client-Server-Architektur (statt Master-Slave-Architektur)
Entwickler-Handbuch (statt Programmier-Bibel)

3.5 Ableitbarkeit

Ableitbarkeit ist eine Anforderung an Benennungen, die vor allem der weiteren Bildung neuer Benennungen nach dem Prinzip der Derivation oder Konversion (siehe 2.3) dient. Ableitbarkeit wird vor allem für englische, aber auch für deutsche Benennungen gewünscht, da in diesen Sprachen häufig von diesen Benennungsbildungsmechanismen Gebrauch gemacht wird. Die Benennung *„Semantik"* ist beispielsweise dem bedeutungsgleichen Synonym *„Bedeutungslehre"* unter dem Aspekt der leichteren Ableitbarkeit vorzuziehen (*semantisch, Semantiker* etc.), auch wenn *„Bedeutungslehre"* eine höhere Transparenz aufweist.

3.6 Sprachliche Ökonomie

Versucht man Benennungen für komplexe Begriffe möglichst transparent und genau zu bilden, wird oft das Prinzip der sprachlichen Ökonomie oder Knappheit verletzt. Hoffmann (1985) nennt hier als extremes Beispiel die Benennung *„Ultrakurzwellenüberreichweitenfernsehrichtfunkverbindung"*, die zwar sehr transparent ist, in der fachsprachlichen Verwendungspraxis aber schnell zu einer Kürzung (siehe 2.6) führen wird. In diesem Sinne sollte bei einer neuen Benennung immer auch die sprachliche Ökonomie bedacht werden.

Beispiel: Termbank statt Terminologie-Datenbank-System

3.7 Sprachliche Korrektheit und Sprechbarkeit

Es ist eigentlich selbstverständlich, dass neue Benennungen den grammatischen, besonders den morphologischen und phonetischen Regeln der jeweiligen Sprache folgen müssen. Viele neue Benennungen entsprechen aber bzgl. der Verwendung von Leerzeichen, Apostrophen, Groß-/Kleinschreibung und Bindestrichen nicht immer den gültigen Rechtschreib- und Grammatikregeln. So werden oft Binnenmajuskeln (*„TerminologieSystem"*), falsche Leerzeichen (*„Karosserie Rohbau"*) und falsche Apostrophe (*„Susi's Frisiersalon"*) verwendet oder ein Fugen-S mit einem Bindestrich (*„Übersetzungs-Dienstleistungen"*) kombiniert.

Beispiele: USB-Schnittstelle (nicht USB Schnittstelle)
Betriebssystem Microsoft Windows (nicht Microsoft Windows-Betriebssystem)
Translation-Memory-System (nicht Translation Memory System)

Auch bei der Übernahme von Benennungen aus anderen Sprachen (siehe 2.5), heute vorwiegend aus dem Englischen, ist darauf zu achten, dass die sprachliche Korrektheit nicht negativ beeinflusst wird. So haben viele Entlehnungen schon den Weg in das grammatische System der deutschen Sprache vollzogen und verhalten sich sprachlich korrekt, wie etwa *„Keks"* (aus dem englischen *„cakes"*). Bei anderen Benennungen wie etwa *„update"* oder *„input"* ist vor allem die Bildung flektierter Formen noch nicht etabliert und erzeugt ein Gefühl der sprachlichen Inkorrektheit (z.B. *„upgedatet"* oder *„upgedated", „inputten"*).

Bei der Bildung von Mehrwortbenennungen ist besonders im Deutschen darauf zu achten, dass etablierte grammatische Konventionen nicht verletzt werden. So spezifiziert ein Adjektiv in der Regel den bedeutungstragenden, d.h. letzten Teil eines Kompositums; Mehrwortbenennungen wie *„fünfköpfiger Familienvater"* oder *„gemischte Obsttorte"* sind demnach grammatisch (und logisch) inkorrekt.

Werden neue Benennungen gebildet, so ist auch auf deren Sprechbarkeit zu achten. Dies betrifft zunächst die Nutzung von Fugenelementen bei Komposita (*„Arbeitsbereich"* statt *„Arbeitbereich"*), um eine leichte Sprechbarkeit zu unterstützen. Auch bei der Entlehnung aus anderen Sprachen muss bedacht werden, dass nicht alle phonetischen Elemente der Ausgangssprache im Deutschen gebräuchlich sind und von der Mehrzahl der Sprecher richtig ausgesprochen werden kann; so hat eine irische Brauerei ihr Bier außerhalb des englischen Sprachraums nicht *„Smithwick's"* sondern *„Kilkenny"* genannt.

3.8 Bevorzugung der eigenen Muttersprache

Auch wenn die Entlehnung aus anderen Sprachen (siehe 2.5) ein seit langem und sehr häufig verwendetes Verfahren der Benennungsbildung ist, so muss doch berücksichtigt werden, dass Transparenz, Sprechbarkeit und sprachliche Korrektheit – vor allem bei Nutzern, die keinerlei Kenntnisse der Ausgangssprache haben – sehr leiden. Die Forderung nach einer Bevorzugung der eigenen Muttersprache hat nichts mit Sprachpurismus und Nationalismus zu tun; sie führt einfach nur dazu, dass Benennungen in der Muttersprache leichter verständlich und leichter nutzbar sind.

Beispiele: *aktualisieren statt updaten*
                Startseite statt Homepage
                Eingabe und eingeben statt Input und inputten
                Zwischenablage statt Clipboard
                Multifunktionsleiste statt Ribbon

3.9 Sonstige Anforderungen

Neben den genannten Anforderungen an Benennungen werden in der Literatur auch weitere genannt, die hier nur kurz beleuchtet werden sollen.

Die **Konsistenz** von Benennungen bezieht sich auf zwei unterschiedliche Anforderungen. Zum einen sollen natürlich Benennungen innerhalb eines Dokumentes konsistent verwendet werden; auch wenn dies keine Eigenschaft einer einzelnen Benennung ist, so wird doch eine konsistente Verwendung durch die Forderung nach Genauigkeit und Eineindeutigkeit (siehe 3.2) unterstützt. Zum anderen bedeutet die Forderung nach Konsistenz, dass bei der Neubildung einer Benennung die Bildungskriterien verwandter Benennungen berücksichtigt und analog angewandt werden sollen. Wird etwa ein neuer Typ eines Computer-Bildschirmes entwickelt und alle anderen, bereits existierenden Bildschirmtypen sind als Komposita mit dem Bestandteil *„Bildschirm"* benannt, sollte die Benennung für den neuen Begriff nicht als Bestandteil *„Monitor"* enthalten.

Soll unter mehreren Benennungen eine Auswahl für eine bevorzugte Benennung getroffen werden, etwa im Rahmen der Festlegung einer Unternehmenssprache, so sollte man neben den oben genannten Kriterien auch die **Verbreitung** der bereits existierenden Benennungen berücksichtigen. Bereits etablierte und gebräuchliche

Benennungen lassen sich leichter durchsetzen und verwenden als selten benutzte und wenig bekannte Benennungen.

Ebenfalls muss bei der Auswahl von Benennungen die **Gesetzes- und Normenkonformität** bedacht werden. Auch wenn nach den oben genannten Kriterien eine geeignetere Benennung gefunden wird, so muss doch der in Gesetzen, Vorschriften und Normen festgelegten Benennung der Vorzug gegeben werden, um rechtliche Konsequenzen auszuschließen.

Oft wird gefordert, dass bei der Benennungsbildung der Aspekt der **Internationalität** zu berücksichtigen sei, damit eine leichtere Verständlichkeit von Benennungen über Sprachgrenzen hinweg unterstützt wird. Meist betrifft das die Verwendung von etablierten Affixen lateinischen oder griechischen Ursprungs wie „*auto-*", „*inter-*" oder „*sub-*". Allerdings sollte das Streben nach Internationalität nicht der Transparenz oder sprachlichen Korrektheit von Benennungen zuwiderlaufen.

4 Fazit

In diesem Beitrag wurden unterschiedliche Verfahren für die Bildung neuer Benennungen sowie Anforderungen an Benennungen aufgeführt, die bei der Schöpfung und Auswahl von Benennungen zu berücksichtigen sind. Wie erwähnt lassen sich nicht immer alle Kriterien gleichzeitig erfüllen; es ist im Einzelfall zu entscheiden, welchen Aspekten bei Konflikten der Vorzug zu geben ist.

Auch wenn versucht wurde, in diesem Beitrag alle wesentlichen Verfahren der Benennungsbildung und Benennungsauswahl systematisch zusammenzustellen und zu beschreiben, so können doch nicht alle Aspekte in der notwendigen Ausführlichkeit behandelt werden. Für die intensivere Beschäftigung mit der Thematik sei auf die im Literaturverzeichnis angeführten relevanten terminologischen Grundsatznormen, grammatischen und terminologischen Standardwerke sowie weitere Veröffentlichungen verwiesen.

Bibliographie

Arntz, R. / Picht, H. / Mayer, F. (2009). Einführung in die Terminologiearbeit. Hildesheim: Olms.

DIN 2330 (1993). *Begriffe und Benennungen: Allgemeine Grundsätze.* Berlin: Beuth.

DIN 2332 (1988). *Benennen international übereinstimmender Begriffe.* Berlin: Beuth.

DIN 2340 (2007). *Kurzformen für Benennungen und Namen.* Berlin: Beuth.

Donalies, E. (2007). *Basiswissen Deutsche Wortbildung.* Tübingen: UTB.

Eichinger, L. M. (1994). *Deutsche Wortbildung: Eine Einführung.* Heidelberg: Groos.

Hoffmann, L. (1985). *Kommunikationsmittel Fachsprache: Eine Einführung.* Tübingen: Narr.

ISO 704 (2000). *Terminology work - Principles and methods.* Genf: ISO.

Schmitz, K.-D. (2008). Was ein Wort bedeutet, kann ein Satz nicht sagen - Zur Bedeutung der Terminologiearbeit für die Technische Kommunikation, in: *DokuDialog Westfalen*, Dortmund/Paderborn: tecteam/mediaprint, p. 24-27.

Schmitz, K.-D. (2008). Zur Begrifflichkeit von Terminologie in Softwareoberflächen, in: Krings, H. P., Mayer, F. (Hrsg.): *Sprachenvielfalt im Kontext von Fachkommunikation, Übersetzung und Fremdsprachenunterricht. Für Reiner Arntz zum 65. Geburtstag.* Berlin: Frank & Timme, p. 267-275.

Schmitz, K.-D (2007). Indeterminacy of terms and icons in software localization, in: Antia, B. (Ed.): *Indeterminacy in LSP and Terminology. Studies in Honour of Heribert Picht.* Amsterdam/Philadelphia: John Benjamins, p. 49-58.

Terminologiemanagement

Terminologiemanagement im Bereich der technischen Übersetzung

Sébastien Desautel

Mechatronikingenieur
Leiter des Terminologiemanagements
Document Service Center GmbH

s.desautel@dsc-translation.de

1 Terminologiemanagement

Terminologiemanagement (oder Terminologiearbeit) ist die Erstellung kundenspezifischer Terminologiedatenbanken und besteht aus vier Hauptphasen:

- die Extraktion von Termini in einer Quellsprache anhand der Quelldokumente,
- die Terminologierecherche für eine oder mehrere Zielsprachen,
- die Prüfung/Genehmigung der Ergebnisse,
- die Erstellung von Datenbanken bzw. die Pflege der Datenbanken.

Die Terminologiearbeit ist der erste Schritt des Übersetzungsprozesses. Terminologiedatenbanken gewährleisten die Konsistenz innerhalb der übersetzten Dokumente und ermöglichen es, auch Übersetzer in einem Projekt einzusetzen, die keine Spezialisten in dem Fachgebiet sind. Zielsetzung ist letztlich die Erarbeitung eines Kundenwörterbuches.

1.1 Die Terminologiedatenbank

Eine Terminologiedatenbank besteht aus mehreren Einträgen. Ein Eintrag stellt ein Konzept bzw. eine Idee dar: den „Begriff". Er wird für jede relevante Sprache mit einer Bezeichnung versehen: dem Terminus (pl. Termini), der aus mehreren Wörtern bestehen kann. Gegebenenfalls werden Synonyme, des Weiteren Definitionen, die Quelle, Name des Terminologen, Status des Terminus etc. für die Begriffe und Termini eingetragen. Für den jeweiligen Kunden und gegebenenfalls für das einzelne Projekt wird eine Datenbank erstellt. Die Datenbank dient dann als Wörterbuch für die Übersetzung der Dokumente des entsprechenden Kunden.

1.2 Die Extraktion

Die Extraktion erfolgt rechnergestützt oder manuell. Die heutigen Softwaretools ermöglichen die Extraktion von Termini aus Quelldokumenten, nachdem der Anwender Parameter wie Wortanzahl pro Terminus und Anzahl der gesamten extrahierten Termini angegeben hat. Das Ergebnis ist leider nicht immer zufriedenstellend, da nach „mathematischen Gesichtspunkten" extrahiert wird, zum Beispiel je nachdem, wie häufig ein Wort vorkommt. Die Liste schließt oft wichtigere Termini aus, die für die Übersetzung relevant wären. Dies hat zur Folge, dass der Übersetzer die komplette Terminologierecherche während der Übersetzung durchführen muss, obwohl diese von einem Fachmann hätte besser gemacht werden können. Darüber hinaus muss die rechnergestützte automatische Extraktion anschließend manuell bereinigt werden, da immer auch unwichtige Termini mitextrahiert werden, die zum Grundvokabular der Zielsprache gehören und nicht in eine Terminologiedatenbank aufgenommen werden sollten. Diese nachträgliche Arbeit kostet viel Zeit und der Anwender kann schwer, ohne Kontext, eine sinnvolle Auswahl vornehmen.

Obwohl die manuelle Extraktion auf dem ersten Blick mehr Zeit benötigt als die rechnergestützte, ist sie eine sehr effiziente Methode zur Termextraktion. Der „Extrahierer" muss dabei die Quelldokumente vollständig lesen. Er markiert nach und nach jeden Terminus, der unbekannt oder spezifisch erscheint. Der Vorteil dabei ist, dass der „Extrahierer" besser beurteilen kann, ob ein Terminus für die Terminologie relevant ist oder nicht, weil er im textlichen Kontext arbeitet. Darüber hinaus erfährt er viel über das Thema an sich und kann dadurch bei der Terminologierecherche klarer unterscheiden, welcher Terminus in der Zielsprache der geeignetere ist. Dieser Lerneffekt sollte nicht unterschätzt werden.

Nach Abschluss dieses Arbeitsschrittes können die Termini in einer Tabelle zusammengefasst und eventuell noch in Gruppen unterteilt werden, so zum Beispiel nach kundenspezifischen Marken- und Eigennamen, Produktbezeichnungen, Komponenten- und Teilbezeichnungen, marketingspezifischen Besonderheiten, allgemeinen technischen Termini bis hin zu Stellungsbezeichnungen und internen Diensten.

Noch effizienter wird die Extraktionsarbeit, wenn der Kunde zwischenzeitlich das Ergebnis selbst analysiert. Um die Terminologierecherche zu vereinfachen, fasst er Synonyme zusammen, weist auf nicht zu verwendende Termini hin und markiert nicht zu übersetzende Termini. Eine solche Analyse ermöglicht dem Kunden, seine eigene Quellterminologie zu prüfen bzw. anzupassen.

1.3 Die Terminologierecherche

Die Terminologierecherche wird häufig mit dem Übersetzungsprozess in Zusammenhang gebracht. Sie muss hingegen vom eigentlichen Übersetzungsprozess getrennt werden, weil es sich keinesfalls nur um eine Übersetzung handelt: Es wird nach Äquivalenten in der Zielsprache gesucht. Äquivalente sind Bezeichnungen von ein und demselben Begriff in verschiedenen Sprachen. Die Äquivalente können gefunden werden, indem man eine Definition, ein Bild, eine Erklärung oder einen Kontext analysiert und vergleicht. Der Zielterminus kann somit als Übersetzung des Quellterminus für ein Übersetzungsprojekt verwendet werden; Quell- und Zielterminus können demnach in einem Eintrag der Datenbank zusammengefasst werden.

Selbstverständlich werden für diese Aufgaben Wörterbücher oder allgemeine Terminologiedatenbanken verwendet. Deren Einträge dienen als Hinweise, und es muss geprüft werden, ob eine Äquivalenz im Kontext des bearbeiteten Dokumentes besteht.

Dies erfolgt aus verschiedenen Gründen nur bedingt: Quelltermini können mehrere Homonyme haben, die nicht in einem Wörterbuch behandelt wurden. Das heißt, sie haben im Kontext eine andere Bedeutung als im Wörterbuch. Auch können Quelltermini vom Verfasser im Text so verwendet werden, dass sie etwas bezeichnen, was mit ihrer üblichen Bedeutung wenig zu tun hat. Dies passiert zum Beispiel, wenn die Redaktion nicht von Muttersprachlern durchgeführt wurde (u.a. in internationalen Konzernen, in denen es eine Konzernsprache gibt, die von allen Mitarbeitern verwendet werden soll). Der Wortschatz der Redakteure ist dabei unter Umständen geringer als der eines Muttersprachlers und dementsprechend der Text nicht so präzise, wie es erforderlich wäre. Deshalb sind für diese Arbeiten Bilder, Glossare oder das Anschauen des Produktes an sich als auch ein Kundenbesuch sehr hilfreich. Der Hinweis auf die Muttersprache des Redakteurs kann ein guter Hinweis für den Seniorterminologen sein, um zu verstehen, wie augenscheinlich seltsame Begriffsbezeichnungen zustande kommen konnten.

Die beste Quelle für die Terminologierecherche sind Dokumente (Publikationen, Normen, Fachbücher, Fachzeitschriften), die in der Zielsprache geschrieben wurden, vorzugshalber von Spezialisten, Dokumente von Konkurrenzunternehmen (Betriebsanleitungen, Patente), eventuell fachspezifischen Foren, um übliche Bezeichnungen zu finden. Übersetzte Dokumente von Konkurrenten hingegen sollten als Quelle mit Vorsicht verwendet werden, da die Terminologie nicht immer allgemein gültig ist. Die Qualität wäre dann nicht gewährleistet.

1.4 Die Prüfung/Genehmigung

Die Prüfung bzw. die Genehmigung der Arbeit des Terminologen sollte am besten vom Kunden selbst erfolgen, denn er verfügt über das fachliche Wissen. Er kann beurteilen, ob die vorgeschlagenen Äquivalente präzise, ausreichend, unspezifisch oder gar falsch sind. Manchmal möchte der Kunde eine bestimmte interne Sprache öffentlich verwenden, deren Terminologie nirgendwo zu finden ist. Da es sich teilweise um persönliche stilistische Vorlieben des Kunden handelt, sollte die Verantwortung der Terminologie in der Verantwortung des Kunden bleiben. Die Terminologen helfen mit ihrer Erfahrung und sprachlichen Kompetenz, eine gewisse Vorarbeit zu leisten. Die Prüfung wäre dann für den Kunden die einzige, aber sehr wichtige Aufgabe.

Die Gegenprüfung der durch den Kunden geänderten Termini sollte dennoch ein weiteres Mal vom Terminologen vorgenommen werden, damit sich der Kreis schließt und etwaige falsche Korrekturen erkannt werden können. Terminologen haben eine bestimmte Erfahrung mit Übersetzungen und Terminologie und können erkennen, ob ein korrigiertes Wort unter Umständen wieder geändert werden muss. Gründe dafür können eine ungeeignete Schreibweise (z. B. Groß- oder Kleinschreibung) sein oder ein potentielles Missverständnis seitens des Übersetzers. Erst wenn sich beide Seiten einig sind, kann die Pflege der Datenbank beginnen.

1.5 Die Pflege

Wenn die Terminologie geprüft und genehmigt wurde, steht sie für den Übersetzungsprozess zur Verfügung: als Merkblatt, Tabelle oder normgerechte Termdatenbank (TBX-kompatibel). Sie wird dazu führen, dass sich der Übersetzungsprozess beschleunigt, weil der Übersetzer weniger Zeit für die Recherche verwenden muss, und sich stattdessen auf die eigentliche Aufgabe konzentrieren kann: das Übersetzen. Darüber hinaus kann so auch die terminologische Konsistenz besser und effektiver gewahrt werden. Mehrere Softwaretools ermöglichen eine automatische Terminologieerkennung und schlagen in Echtzeit die Zieltermini vor. Bei der weiteren Zusammenarbeit mit dem Kunden wird die Datenbank sukzessiv erweitert.

Dennoch sollte man sich im Klaren darüber sein, dass Termini im Laufe der weiteren Zusammenarbeit auch Änderungen unterworfen sein können. Gründe dafür können sein:

- Neue Quelltermini kollidieren in der Zielsprache mit vorhandenen.
- Im Lektorat bzw. Korrektorat fallen Missverständnisse in der Übersetzung auf.
- Der Kunde stellt In-country-Korrekturen zur Verfügung und zweifelt die verwendete Terminologie an.

Hierbei stellt sich dann die Frage, inwieweit neue Einträge hinzugefügt werden oder vorhandene korrigiert bzw. mit neuen Definitionen, Synonymen und eventuell verbotenen Zieltermini versehen werden müssen.

Die Datenbanken sollten so strukturiert sein, dass sie während des Übersetzungsprozesses optimal genutzt werden können. Das heißt auch, sie sollten nicht mit zu vielen Informationen überfrachtet sein, damit der Übersetzer schnell und sicher erkennen kann, wie er einen Terminus zu verwenden hat.

2 Das Verfahren

Mehrere Vorgehensweisen sind möglich, wobei man immer die Wünsche und das Budget des Kunden berücksichtigen muss.

Der Kunde prüft die Terminologie

In diesem Fall muss abgesprochen werden, inwieweit die Vorbereitungsarbeit erfolgen soll. Braucht der Kunde nur eine automatische Extraktion? Soll die Terminologierecherche oberflächlich erfolgen oder in die Tiefe gehen? Soll die Terminologie erst nach der ersten Übersetzung und dem Kundenkorrektorat erstellt werden?

Die Extraktion kann leicht durch Juniorübersetzer erfolgen, da hierfür keine fachspezifischen Vorkenntnisse explizit notwendig sind. Die Extraktion ist dann quantitativ umfangreicher und die Datenbank kompletter.

Die Terminologierecherche könnte von einem Übersetzer (der „Extrahierer" wäre von Vorteil) oder von einem Seniorterminologen/Übersetzer durchgeführt werden. Dies muss allerdings der Kunde entscheiden, weil es eine Zeit- und Kostenfrage ist. Für eine oberflächliche Prüfung fallen dem Kunden zwar weniger Kosten an als für eine umfassende Bearbeitung der Terminologie, allerdings vereinfacht und verkürzt letztere die Prüfung seitens des Kunden.

In einem Fall, bei dem der Kunde schon diverse Dokumente hat übersetzen lassen, könnte man auf Basis der extrahierten Quellterminologie die entsprechenden Übersetzungen im Kunden-Translation-Memory aufsuchen und eine Liste erstellen. Nach der Prüfung dieser Terminologieliste kann zusätzlich eine Pflege des Translation-Memorys vereinbart werden.

Der Kunde prüft die Terminologie nicht

Kunden, die keine Niederlassung im Land der Zielsprache haben, und keinen Mitarbeiter, der die Quell- und Zielsprache beherrscht, werden die Terminologie nicht prüfen können. Wenn der Kunde jedoch hohe Qualitätsansprüche an seine Terminologie hat, wird der Übersetzungsdienstleister einen Fachspezialisten einsetzen müssen, der die Prüfung durchführt. Darüber hinaus benötigt man einen guten Terminologen, der die Vorschläge nach dem Vier-Augen-Prinzip validiert. Solche Verfahren sind in der Regel mit hohen Kosten verbunden. Die Qualität der Terminologie ist stark abhängig von der Erfahrung des Prüfers. Optimalerweise verfügt der Terminologe über sehr gute Sprachfähigkeiten in der Quellsprache und gute technische Kenntnisse. Die Prüfer brauchen vor allem ausgeprägte technische Kenntnisse in der Zielsprache. Ein weiterer Parameter der Qualität liegt in der Dokumentation, die für die Terminologiearbeit vom Kunden geliefert wird. Die Terminologierecherche ist umso einfacher, je mehr Dokumente zur Verfügung gestellt werden, vor allem Fotos, Schemata und Glossare.

Manche Kunden sind sich der Bedeutung der Terminologie nicht bewusst und lassen deshalb keine Terminologiedatenbank erstellen. Für den Übersetzungsprozess ist sie jedoch außerordentlich wichtig, weil sie die Qualität erhöht und die Kosten reduzieren kann. Daher sollte man versuchen, den Kunden davon zu überzeugen, zumindest ein Minimum an Terminologiearbeit in den Aufträgen einzuschließen. Das wäre eine einfache Extraktion mit anschließender Terminologierecherche durch einen Junior-Terminologen/Übersetzer und die regelmäßige Pflege mit Hilfe der Übersetzer- und Korrektoren-Feedbacks, möglicherweise auch durch ein Feedback des Kunden. Dadurch wird der fundamentale Grundsatz bei der Übersetzung technischer Inhalte unterstützt: die Konsistenz, d.h. die Verwendung von einem einzigen Terminus pro Begriff (also keine Synonyme oder Varianten, weil man diese zum Beispiel schöner findet). Eine Terminologie wird, unabhängig von ihrer Qualität, auf jeden Fall einen positiven Einfluss auf die Konsistenz einer Übersetzung haben. Die nachträgliche Pflege zur Korrektur eines Terminus kann durch einfaches Suchen/Ersetzen erfolgen.

In jedem Fall ist die Wahl der Mitarbeiter entscheidend für die Qualität des Ergebnisses. Deshalb sollte die Qualifikation der Mitarbeiter in der Verhandlung mit dem Kunden festgelegt werden. Der Kunde und der Dienstleister sollten sich auf ein bestimmtes Qualitätsniveau einigen. Diese Transparenz vermeidet falsche Erwartungen und der Kunde kann selbst entscheiden, welchen Wert die Qualität für ihn hat und er ist es auch, der hierfür die Verantwortung trägt.

3. Kommunikation als Voraussetzung für gute Zusammenarbeit

Das Terminologiemanagement ist eine wichtige Schnittstelle zwischen dem Kunden und dem Übersetzungsdienstleister. Eine enge Zusammenarbeit mit sehr viel Klarheit und Transparenz ist an dieser Stelle sehr wichtig. Das alte Modell von verschiedenen Abteilungen in einer gleichen Firma, die zusammen eng kooperieren, existiert fast nicht mehr. Dennoch besteht nach wie vor die Notwendigkeit der Kooperation. Der Übersetzungsdienstleister verfügt über die Übersetzungserfahrung, die Grundlage für die Einschätzung einer Terminologiearbeit ist. Er ist dabei der Experte. Der Kunde braucht seinerseits genügend Raum, um zu erklären, was ihm wichtig ist, was seine Ansprüche sind. Dass die Terminologiearbeit insbesondere für die technische Dokumentation äußerst wichtig ist, steht außer Frage. Die Frage wäre, welche Form der Terminologiearbeit für beide Seiten die optimalste bzw. effizienteste ist.

Die Terminologiearbeit gewährleistet Konsistenz sowohl in der Zielsprache als auch in der Quellsprache. Sie erleichtert die Arbeit des Übersetzers zeitlich, aber auch geistig. Sie verbessert die Lesbarkeit der Dokumente und verringert den Aufwand für Lektorat und Korrektorat. Letztendlich kann der Kunde nur davon profitieren.

Die Rolle des Übersetzungsdienstleisters ist, dies dem Kunden zu vermitteln. Die Kommunikationsfähigkeit wird hierbei von allen Beteiligten sehr stark geforderet. Eine gute und direkte Verständigung erzeugt Vertrauen und Vertrauen ist die Basis für eine gute und effiziente Zusammenarbeit. Es geht also nicht nur um die Qualität der Dokumente, sondern auch um die Qualität der Arbeitsbeziehungen und des Arbeitsumfeldes.

Praktische Schritte hin zum zentralen Terminologiemanagement

Wolfgang Zenk

Acolada GmbH, Nürnberg

w.zenk@acolada.de

Diana Brändle

Freiberufliche Dipl.-Übersetzerin, Dolmetscherin und Terminologin

db@dbterm.de

Abstract

Der Stellenwert der Terminologie hat sich gewandelt. Das hängt damit zusammen, dass Terminologie aus der Rolle des Wortpaar-Lieferanten für die Übersetzung entwachsen ist. Terminologie wird heute in vielerlei Kontexten und von unterschiedlichen Zielgruppen und Anwendungen genutzt. Um zu vermeiden, dass für jede neue Anwendung oder für einzelne Nutzergruppen „eigene" und sich überschneidende Terminologie-Datenbestände entstehen, ist eine Zentralisierung der Terminologie im Unternehmen notwendig. Nur so lässt sich Mehraufwand für die Verwaltung der Terminologie verhindern und terminologische Einheitlichkeit und sprachliche Klarheit gewährleisten.

Für die neue „Produktivität" in der Terminologiearbeit fehlen vielfach die Regeln, wie verschiedene „Spieler" zusammenspielen und wie verschiedene Datenpools zusammenpassen. Auf Basis von Projekterfahrungen soll Antwort auf folgende Fragen gegeben werden:

- Ist es sinnvoller, Unternehmensterminologie in einer oder mehreren Termbanken zu verwalten?

- Welche Regeln sollten bestehen, wenn nicht alle an einer Termbank arbeiten können?

- Wo sind die Fallstricke, wenn man sich dazu entscheidet, mehrere Terminologie-Datenbestände zusammenzuführen und zu vereinheitlichen?

Gerade dort, wo eine Mehrfachnutzung der Terminologie angestrebt wird, existiert bereits Terminologie, bzw. existieren sogar häufig mehrere Terminologie-Datenbestände. Von der Zusammenführung zahlreicher Terminologiequellen, den Strategien hierfür, den Erfahrungen und den Lehren handelt der Praxisteil des Vortrags.

Die neuen Aufgaben der Terminologie

„Gute" Terminologie wird heute nicht nur beim Übersetzen, sondern an vielen weiteren Stellen benötigt: in der Konstruktion / Entwicklung, der technischen Redaktion, im Produktinformationsmanagement, Marketing, Personalwesen in den ausländischen Niederlassungen, im Trainingsbereich, beim Kundendienst, im Support, als Arbeitshilfe bei der fremdsprachigen Korrespondenz usw.

Ebenso vielfältig ist die Nutzung von Terminologie: als Intranet-basiertes Unternehmenswörterbuch, als Terminologiedatenbank für Übersetzer und Technische Redakteure, als integraler Bestandteil bei der Überprüfung von Texten mit Hilfe von Autorensystemen oder zur Integration in maschinelle Übersetzungssysteme.

Die Vielzahl von Benutzergruppen und Anwendungsbereichen stellt ganz unterschiedliche Anforderungen an die Unternehmensterminologie: vom Nachschlagewerk zur Begriffsklärung, als integrierbare Termbank beim Übersetzen, als Basiswerkzeug bei Terminologie-Einhaltungsprüfung u.a.m.

Um alle diese Aufgaben leisten zu können, muss die Terminologie jeweils passend bereitgestellt werden. Passend bedeutet dabei sicherzustellen, dass Benutzer auf die jeweils benötigte Terminologie zugreifen können und dass die Terminologie auch die jeweils benötigten Informationen enthält. Passend machen und bereitstellen geschieht am einfachsten, wenn die Terminologie von einer Stelle kommt: einem zentralen Terminologiemanagementsystem.

Vom verteilten zum zentralen Terminologiemanagement

Der Beginn der Terminologiearbeit ist selten strategisch geplant: Meist entsteht eine recht bunte Inselwelt. In den meisten Unternehmen liegt Terminologie in irgendeiner Form bereits vor: als Word-Glossar, in gemeinsamen oder individuell erstellten Excel-Listen, in einem Terminologiemanagementsystem oder am häufigsten in mehreren Formen gleichzeitig. Daneben entsteht Terminologie auch extern bei Übersetzungsdienstleistern, die Terminologie auch begleitend zu Projekten erstellen, bei Niederlassungen, Zulieferern etc.

Die bunte Inselwelt mag für einen einzelnen Prozess ausreichend sein; wenn jedoch neue Aufgaben hinzukommen, entsteht häufig Chaos. Neue Aufgaben oder Prozesse erfordern neue Schnittstellen. Wer die Terminologie in einer bunten Inselwelt pflegt, kann diese neuen Schnittstellen gar nicht bereitstellen. Auch macht es eine Vielzahl von Terminologiequellen nahezu unmöglich, einheitliche Strukturen und Qualitätsstandards zu etablieren.

Der Weg zum zentralen Terminologiemanagement ist also zuallererst der Weg durch das Chaos, der irgendwann zu einer zentral verwalteten und für alle verfügbaren wie verbindlichen Unternehmensterminologie führt.

Eine oder mehrere Termbanken?

Es gibt mehr gute Gründe für nur eine Termbank als für mehrere Termbanken. Es gibt dagegen nur in Ausnahmefällen Gründe für viele Termbanken.

Eine Termbank bedeutet: Es gibt nur eine Quelle, aus der alle Benutzer, Schnittstellen und Anwendungen bedient werden. Dies erfordert Offenheit des Systems, also eine integrationsfreudige Anwendung. Zugleich erfordert es gute Selektionsmöglichkeiten: Daten müssen sich filtern und in Teilbeständen bereitstellen lassen für bestimmte Anwendungen, Projekte, Benutzer, Prozesse. Auf der Eintragsebene bringt dies vermutlich zusätzliche Datenfelder mit sich, um alle notwendigen Selektionen durchführen zu können. Zusätzliche Pflichtfelder bedeuten auch mehr Bearbeitungs-aufwand pro Eintrag. Dies muss gegen die Alternativen (mehrere Termbanken) abgewogen werden.

Mehrere Termbanken bedeutet: Vor Aufnahme jeden Eintrags ist zu entscheiden, in welche Termbank der Eintrag aufgenommen wird. Egal, ob projekt-, kunden- oder fachbereichsorientierte Datenbankorganisation: Abgrenzungsprobleme sind hier vorprogrammiert, die im Einzelfall dazu führen, dass Benennungen z.B. in einer Übersetzung nicht berücksichtigt werden, weil die Datenbank, in der sie gespeichert sind, nicht durchsucht wird. Auf der Plusseite stehen die einfachere Datenbankstruk-tur, die einfacher zu bestimmenden Kompetenzen für Zugang und Pflege und der geringere Pflegeaufwand pro Eintrag.

Wo immer es – vor allem systemseitig – möglich ist, sollte einer zentralen Termbank der Vorzug gegeben werden. Hier wird das Single-Source-Prinzip, das sich in der technischen Redaktion erfolgreich durchgesetzt hat, verwirklicht und macht die Nutzung der Terminologie-Datenbank für neue Anwendungen viel leichter.

Eine Termbank, viele Nutzer: die goldenen Regeln der Zusammenarbeit.

Welche Regeln sollten bestehen, wenn nicht alle an einer Termbank arbeiten können?

Eine Standardlösung oder einen Standardprozess für eine verteilte Terminologiearbeit gibt es nicht. Wohl aber Beispiele aus der Praxis, die funktionieren, und Empfehlun-gen, wie die Bearbeitung organisiert werden kann.

Jede Praxislösung muss sich natürlich in einen Unternehmenskontext einpassen. Einflussfaktoren:

- Die Tool-Landschaft (Welches Terminologiewerkzeug wird eingesetzt und welche Prozesse bietet es an?)
- Die Terminologiepolitik (Wer darf Termini erstellen/ändern? Wie erfolgen Freigaben?)
- Die technischen Gegebenheiten (Bestehen überhaupt Zugriffsmöglichkeiten auf interne Server/Datenbanken durch externe Bearbeiter der Terminologie?)
- Die Inhalte und Sprachen, die der Einzelne bearbeitet.

Ausgangspunkt für verteilte Prozesse sollte ein Terminologieleitfaden sein: Er definiert die Prozesse, die für die Terminologiebearbeitung gelten. Er legt auch die

Inhaltsstruktur der Termeinträge fest und stellt ggf. Templates bzw. Datenbank- und Eingabemodelle zur Verfügung. Zielsetzung ist es, Einträge, die außerhalb der zentralen Terminologiedatenbank erstellt wurden, entweder automatisch, zumindest aber ohne aufwändige manuelle Nacharbeit integrieren zu können.

Inhalt der Prozessdefinition im Terminologieleitfaden:

- Wie wird Terminologie an Externe (Übersetzer oder Niederlassungen) bereitgestellt? Wie kommen neue Vorschläge für neue Termini von diesen zurück ins Unternehmen, wer verifiziert diese und wie erfolgt die Übernahme in die Datenbank? Wie, wann, an und durch wen wird die Datenbank in aktualisierter Form wieder bereitgestellt?

- Grundstruktur des Terminologieeintrages, Pflichtfelder und optionale Felder.

- Templates, Datenbank- und Eingabemodelle sind bezogen auf das konkrete Werkzeug, mit dem die Terminologie erstellt wird.

Mögliche Workflows:

- Externe Mitarbeiter erhalten nur lesenden Zugriff auf die Terminologie: Sie können Termini beantragen, nicht aber selbst Einträge erstellen oder ändern. Die Spannbreite von Lösungen reicht hier vom einfachen Mail-Mechanismus bis hin zu Software-Produkten, mit denen vollständig strukturierte Einträge erstellt werden, die dann automatisch in die zentrale Terminbank und in definierte Freigabeprozesse münden.

- Externe arbeiten mit einem lokalen Terminologiemanagementsystem: Bei Verwendung vorgegebener Datenbank- und Eingabemodelle ist eine spätere Synchronisierung mit einem zentralen Terminologiemanagementsystem weitgehend automatisch möglich. Damit Externe nur Einträge anlegen, die in der zentralen Termbank noch nicht vorhanden sind, sollte eine Projektterminologie oder ein Export aus der zentralen Termbank zur Verfügung stehen.

- Konvertierung aus anderen Tools: Werkzeuge wie Excel können ebenfalls eingesetzt werden, erfordern jedoch eine Konvertierung. Bei Einhaltung der Regeln des Terminologieleitfadens (bzw. eines Excel-Templates) lassen sich Prozesse auch hier teilautomatisieren und ein Standardprozess etablieren.

Terminologiequellen zusammenführen – praktische Erfahrungen

Vom Konzept zur Praxis

Am Anfang stehen der Wunsch nach Vereinheitlichung oder auch ganz praktische Erfordernisse, Daten zentral bereitstellen zu können. Der Weg dahin erfordert ein fundiertes Konzept, das in einer Konzeptionsphase erarbeitet wird.

In der Konzeptionsphase werden Bestände analysiert, Beteiligte festgelegt, Workflows definiert und die einzelnen Schritte nach Priorität, Zeitplan und Budget geplant. Wenn das Ziel klar ist und die Möglichkeiten der Umsetzung geprüft wurden, kann die Realisierungsphase und damit die Zusammenführung von Beständen starten.

Während in der Konzeptionsphase repräsentative Daten gesichtet werden, um Struktur, Mengengerüst und mögliche Workflows zu ermitteln, steht die Gesamtheit aller Daten häufig erst in der Realisierungsphase zur Verfügung. Erst jetzt wird häufig sichtbar, dass repräsentativ nicht ganz repräsentativ ist, sondern dass es eine ganze Bandbreite von Strukturen gibt, selbst wenn sie aus der gleichen Quelle kommen. Solcherlei Überraschungen sind nicht selten, sondern eher schon die Regel.

Was sind das für Überraschungen, die einen meist ambitionierten Zeitplan schnell ins Wanken bringen?

• Die Anzahl der Datenquellen ist möglicherweise größer als ursprünglich beschrieben.

• Obgleich Datenbestände mit dem gleichen Terminologiemanagement-System erstellt wurden, unterscheiden sie sich dennoch: für die einzelnen Datenbanken bestehen unterschiedliche Datenbankdefinitionen und / oder die Datenbestände wurden mit unterschiedlichen Datenbankversionen erstellt. Das verhindert eine direkte Synchronisierung bzw. wirft es direkt die Frage nach der Kompatibilität von Datenbankversionen und Exportformaten auf.

• Die Organisation der Termdaten – multilingual und bilingual – ist recht bunt gemischt. Mehrsprachige Terminologiedatenbanken erscheinen dann neben sprachpaarbezogenen (z. B. Deutsch–Englisch, Deutsch–Französisch, Deutsch–Spanisch, Englisch–Deutsch–Chinesisch etc.). Wenn aus den Termbanken nur einzelne Informationen übernommen werden sollen, kann dies dazu führen, dass erhebliche Vorarbeit zu leisten ist, bevor eine Zusammenführung gestartet werden kann. Andernfalls würde eine Vielzahl von Dubletten erzeugt, die in der Folge aufwändig manuell zu bereinigen wären.

• Gerade wenn Office-Formate (Word, Excel) berücksichtigt werden, sind überlappende, mehrfach erfasste Informationen – also eine Vielzahl von Dubletten – vorprogrammiert. Auch hier werden vorbereitende Arbeiten oder Zwischenschritte nötig, um manuelle Nacharbeiten nach Möglichkeit zu vermeiden.

• Ein häufiges Problem: Je nach Terminologiequelle und -system werden Groß- und Kleinschreibung, Umlaute und Sonderzeichen inkonsistent verwendet. Die Zeichenproblematik stellt sich verstärkt, wenn unterschiedliche Zeichensätze und Zeichenkodierungen auftreten. Gerade Benennungen, die in Versalien aus Drittsystemen in eine Terminologiedatenbank übernommen werden, müssen vor einer Zusammenführung zwingend bereinigt werden, um eine Vielzahl von Varianten zu verhindern. Spätestens hier versagen Standardmechanismen – ab hier muss Intelligenz in Form von Programmierung vor der Synchronisierung von Datenbanken erfolgen.

• Fehlende Informationen: Es kommt häufig vor, dass z. B. Status- oder Quellenangaben, Artikelnummern oder andere Felder, die für eine zentrale Unternehmensterminologie wichtig sind, fehlen. Diese müssen dann vor oder auch nach der Zusammenführung ergänzt werden.

• Falsche Zuordnung zu Datenfeldern: Mitunter sind in Feldern wie „Note" oder „Bemerkung" tatsächlich Definitionen oder Kontextbeispiele enthalten. Sofern möglich, müssen solche Informationen an die richtige Stelle „verschoben" werden. Auch hier ist wieder Intelligenz nötig. Die notwendige Logik ergibt sich erst aus dem Kontext.

- Vereinheitlichung von Werten: bei der Anlage unterschiedlicher Terminologie-Datenbestände werden nicht nur Felder, sondern auch Wertemengen / Picklisten jeweils neu konfiguriert. Das führt dazu, dass Feldbezeichner und Werte konsolidiert werden müssen. Das Feld-Wertpaar „Status: 1" aus Termbank 1 ist äquivalent zu „Zuverlässigkeit: vorzugsweise" aus Termbank 2. In der neuen zentralen Termbank soll das Feld „Status: preferred" heißen. Auch hier sind also Vorarbeiten erforderlich.

- Änderungen in der Struktur: Terminologie-Datenbestände können durchaus unterschiedliche Strukturen aufweisen. Die gilt es bei der Überführung ebenso zu beseitigen. So müssen Felder wie Fachgebiet schon einmal „verschoben" werden auf dem Weg von der Quelle zum Ziel, der zentralen Datenbank. Wichtig dabei ist wieder zu prüfen, ob durch die „Verschiebung" nicht ungewollt neue Dopplungen entstehen.

Wie weit kommt man mit den Standardwerkzeugen oder: wo scheitert die Zusammenführung mit den Bordmitteln von Terminologiewerkzeugen?

Die von den Tool-Anbietern mitgelieferten Standardwerkzeuge zur Zusammenführung von Terminologie-Datenbeständen sind für bestimmte Aufgaben bei der Zusammenführung von Datenbeständen völlig ausreichend. Gleichwohl muss man in der Konzeptionsphase klar definieren, welche Aufgaben tatsächlich bei der Zusammenführung zu leisten sind.

Zusammenführung von Datenbeständen wird häufig als Oberbegriff verstanden, der nicht nur das Verschmelzen mehrerer Datenbestände zu einem einzigen umfasst, sondern zugleich auch eine Harmonisierung von Strukturen und Inhalten. Harmonisierung umfasst also viel mehr, denn sie meint auch:

- Vereinheitlichen hinsichtlich einer gemeinsamen Datenstruktur und zulässigen Werten in Picklisten

- Einheitliche Regeln anwenden, speziell für Groß-/Kleinschreibung

- Anreichern mit zusätzlichen, implizit oder explizit enthaltenen Informationen

- Löschen von unnötigem Ballast

- Vermeiden von doppelten Informationen in Einträgen durch „blindes" Zusammenführen und Vermeiden von Dubletten

Wenn Harmonisierung und nicht nur Zusammenführen gemeint ist, sind die Standardwerkzeuge der Tool-Anbieter nicht ausreichend. Regeln für die Harmonisierung sind nicht generalisiert, sondern erfordern eine Einzelfallbetrachtung und somit auch eine Einzelfallbehandlung.

In jedem Fall sind eine genaue Planung und eine sorgfältige Analyse möglichst aller Datenbestände erforderlich, um sich nicht hinsichtlich Zeit- und Aufwandsschätzungen zu „vergaloppieren".

Wenn die Zusammenführung von Daten scheitert, dann häufig deshalb, weil die Komplexität der Daten, uneinheitliche Strukturen oder Änderungsbedarf nicht frühzeitig erkannt wurden. Gerät ein Projekt erst mal in eine solche Schieflage, lohnt es sich, ggf. völlig neu anzusetzen. Da vielfach eine harmonisierte Terminologie das Ziel ist, ist eine neutrale, extern erstellte Analyse ein sinnvoller erster Schritt. Steht einmal das Gerüst in Form einer abgestimmten Matrix für die Bereinigung bzw. Anpassung der Bestände, können die nächsten Schritte vor und ggs. nach der Zusammenführung nach „Drehbuch" erfolgen.

In wieweit helfen Standards?

Der wichtigste Standard für den Austausch von Terminologiedaten ist TBX. Das TermBase eXchange Format hat sich als Standard weitgehend durchgesetzt und wird inzwischen von den wichtigsten Tool-Herstellern unterstützt.

In wieweit hilft TBX aber, um unterschiedliche Datenbestände zusammenzubringen?

Auf den ersten Blick ist es gute und sinnvolle Idee, alle Quellen in einem einheitlichen Format wie TBX abzuspeichern und dann zusammenfassen zu können. Allerdings lehrt der Blick unter die „Motorhaube" von Terminologiemanagementsystemen, dass TBX nicht gleich TBX ist. Die TBX-Unterstützung wirkt noch nicht ausgereift, ähnlich wie dies auch bei TMX für den TM-Austausch lange Zeit der Fall war. Spätestens wenn man sich mit Terminologiedaten aus Office-Systemen beschäftigt, tun sich Fragezeichen auf. Ein „Speichern unter" im TBX-Format wird man in Word oder Excel vergeblich suchen.

Auch beim nächsten Schritt: „Wie bringe ich meine TBX-Dateien zusammen?" ist Fehlanzeige. Frei verfügbare Werkzeuge, die es ermöglichen TBX-Dateien zusammenzufassen, gibt es derzeit noch nicht. So ist man wieder auf die Synchronisierungsfunktionen der einzelnen Terminologiemanagementsysteme und deren TBX-Importfunktionen angewiesen. Auch hier, wie auch bei der Vereinheitlichung von Datenfeldbezeichnern, lauern noch allerlei Fallstricke, die nur durch eine genaue Analyse im Vorfeld und bei Bedarf durch Datenbereinigung und -pflege mit Hilfe von programmierten Routinen umgangen werden können

So stellt TBX leider nur auf den ersten Blick eine wirkliche Hilfe dar. Solange die Werkzeuge drumherum aber fehlen, bietet es noch keine Arbeitserleichterung.

Fazit

Der Aufbau eines zentralen Terminologiemanagements ist machbar, selbst wenn die Terminologie in unterschiedlichsten Formaten, Quellen, Sprachen oder Datenstrukturen vorliegt.

Die wichtigsten Schritte sind:

- Werden Sie sich über Ihre Ziele klar: handelt es sich um eine Zusammenführung oder um eine Harmonisierung von Datenbeständen?

- Analysieren Sie genau alle vorhandenen Bestände unter Angabe ihrer Zuverlässigkeit und ihrer Priorität

- Stellen Sie kritische Fragen an die eigene Terminologie:

- wie zuverlässig und konsistent sind Ihre Bestände wirklich?

- soll in der zentralen Termbank erkennbar sein, aus welchem Bestand der Terminus bzw. Eintrag ursprünglich stammte?

- welche Felder sollen wie übernommen werden (Fachgebiet = Subject)?

- gibt es globale Änderungswünsche?

- sind die Schreibweisen korrekt?

- Definieren Sie vorab eine – unter Umständen neue – Datenbankstruktur, die den Anforderungen an ein zentrales Terminologiemanagementsystem gerecht wird

- Schauen Sie nicht nur nach hinten (die vorliegenden Terminologiedatenbestände), sondern auch nach vorn: Was sind die Anforderungen aller Beteiligten bezüglich Inhalt, Form, Bereitstellungsart? Welche Anwendungen/ Schnittstellen müssen vorliegen?

- Erstellen Sie einen Projektplan mit Zeitplan, Budget, Beteiligten

- Dokumentieren Sie den Prozess

Ist eine zentrale Unternehmensterminologie erst einmal verfügbar, sollte den Benutzern unbedingt die Möglichkeit eingeräumt werden, ihr Feedback zu geben. Denn Terminologie ist ein Unternehmenswert, der für alle im Unternehmen extrem nützlich ist, der aber auch vom Input und dem Know-how Einzelner lebt und wächst.

Ein zentrales Terminologiemanagement gehört an sich ins Zentrum eines Unternehmens, denn es bestimmt die Qualität der Unternehmenssprache maßgeblich, garantiert Einheitlichkeit und Konsistenz und damit in der Summe eine gelungene internationale Unternehmenskommunikation.

A dictionary publisher's proposal for meeting translators' current linguistic resource needs

Marie-Jeanne Derouin

Langenscheidt KG/Langenscheidt Fachverlag, München

marie-jeanne.derouin@langenscheidt.de

Dr. André Le Meur

Consultant for terminology management, Rennes, France

andre.lemeur@uhb.fr

1   The challenge

Times are changing for translators and for dictionary publishers: new needs, new media and especially the increasing role of the Internet have changed the relationship between translators and publishers. Our dictionaries are no longer translators' sole companions, and they now meet only a small part of their needs. The Internet is the most widely used resource and consequently dictionary publishers need to review their product and marketing strategies if they wish once again to play a significant role as content providers for translators.

The challenge is a big one, especially in view of the current economic downturn which is forcing all of us to set priorities and to consider very carefully the efficiency of our workflow and the price-performance ratio of the tools we use. Considering translators' current practices and our data portfolio, we have good reason to believe that dictionary publishers could offer professional translators the reliable linguistic resources they need. This will require a "transformation" in our approach, geared towards addressing the following major challenges by providing:

- a large amount of regularly updated bilingual and multilingual dictionary data in general and specialist language on all possible media used by translators including print and electronic devices
- a greater range of information, for example term definitions, contextualized examples, references to standards and pragmatic information specific to terms, in addition to the possible translations in the target language
- reliable dictionary data based on validated sources and compiled by experts in the various subject areas and in lexicography
- easy access to these data either in print form or on electronic devices, online or offline, and with a fair pricing policy.

To this end, we have adopted a step-by-step strategy over the course of the past few years which will be described in this paper. The main requirements in terms of data management, cooperation with other language providers and product definitions have already been met. Nevertheless this is still a "work in progress" and a new relationship between publishers and language professionals needs to be developed. Although there are a lot of commonalities between general language dictionaries and specialist dictionaries in this area, this paper will focus mainly on the latter.

2   A new generation of dictionaries

2.1 A unique source for a wide variety of dictionaries

Because of the multiplicity of dictionary types in both print and electronic formats, together with the competition from freely available dictionaries on the Internet, publishers have had to find ways of creating different types of dictionaries based on a single-source data manuscript. Some dictionary publishers such as Langenscheidt have now also become content providers for a wide range of electronic devices and increasingly also the Internet. For this to be possible, it has been necessary to develop a strict DTD (document type definition) in accordance with the ISO 1951 standard, allowing import and export of data, data extraction for concise editions and extensive data manipulation in order to produce offline and online dictionary versions and ultimately also to integrate them into other language tools.

The standardization of dictionary products is beneficial for dictionary publishers. New market demands require new dictionary products and dictionary users need global language solutions. The interoperability of data saves time and cuts costs which is extremely important as dictionary prices have to be kept low because of the increasing development of free Internet products and consequently of price consciousness among dictionary users. Data homogeneity is also a prerequisite for a diversified dictionary programme – it ensures stylistic consistency across the different products in a series and therefore promotes user-friendliness. While standardization may not be as indispensable as in other branches of industry, conformity to an ISO Standard will improve quality assurance and contribute to a better appreciation of dictionary products. In view of the above, Langenscheidt Fachverlag was pleased to be the first publisher to be awarded the DIN Prize for best practice in 2008.

2.2 Print dictionaries for professional use in 2009

Traditionally, bilingual print dictionaries have been the tools mostly widely used by translators. In the last decade they have lost their dominant position as electronic dictionaries have become more and more popular. There are three main reasons why users have started to turn away from print dictionaries: limited content, lack of frequent updating and the inability to integrate them with translators' electronic equipment. For about five years it has seemed likely that they could completely disappear from translators' desks. Consequently, in many fields updated data content has only been available in electronic format and fewer and fewer large specialist dictionaries have been published in print form.

Market research indicates that at least 20% of translators would be prepared to buy bilingual specialist print dictionaries providing they are regularly updated and provide more content than before. Moreover, a combined search in print and electronic dictionaries would probably be kinder on translators' eyes!

Print-on-demand (PoD) publishing has made huge strides in recent years, both from the technical and marketing point of view. The physical appearance of the books can now compete with traditional dictionaries. Efficient data management means that it is now possible to provide users with an annually updated print version of every dictionary available on electronic devices. Terms such as 2nd or 3rd revised edition will soon be a thing of the past and will be replaced by 2009 or 2010 edition etc. People who prefer to use books will no longer find themselves at a disadvantage compared to those who prefer electronic formats!

The first Langenscheidt PoD editions were published this summer. They can be ordered from booksellers, our online shop and Amazon and are sent free of charge to the user's address within a week. If the products are well received on the market, subscription systems will be introduced in order to implement an attractive price policy.

Figure 1: Example of PoD cover

Anmerkung zur Print-on-Demand-Ausgabe 2009

Liebe Nutzerin, lieber Nutzer,

Sie haben sich für die aktuelle Print-on-Demand-Ausgabe des Fachwörterbuchs "..." entschieden. Diese basiert auf der letzten Bearbeitung der elektronischen Ausgabe, die jährlich um den neuesten Wortschatz erweitert wird. Sie halten somit auch im Printbereich das aktuellste Werk in Händen. Zu Ihrer Information wurden die Vorworte der vorhergehenden Print-Ausgaben hier nochmals mit aufgenommen.

Der Verlag

Figure 2: Explanatory text from the preface of a PoD dictionary

Semi-bilingual specialist dictionaries or "definitions dictionaries" provide users with translations and term definitions in both language directions. These products were developed in cooperation with other publishers who already work on such dictionaries or with institutions such as UEFA for football terminology. As there are still limits on the size of print dictionaries, this model is suited to "narrow" specialist fields. This type of pocket dictionary can be regularly updated.

Bezugsgruppe *f* - reference group
Personengruppe, die ein Individuum nachahmen möchte, bzw. deren Werte, Lebensstil oder Sozialschicht und wirtschaftliche Lage. Werbungmuss hier in ihren Werbemitteilungen die Wünsche und Motivation der Zielperson aufgreifen, nicht die reale Situation Gruppe, mit der eine andere Gruppe verglichen wird.

Figure 3: German Headword-German Definition- English translation

---

reference group - Bezugsgruppe *f*
The group of people which an individual attempts to imitate or whose values, lifestyle or social and economic class he aspires to have. In order to achieve the implication of the target public, the advertisement usually uses a representation of the reference group in its messages rather than that to which the target actually belongs, reflecting, in that way, his aspirations and desires rather than his real situation.

Figure 4: English Headword-English Definition- German translation

2.3 Electronic dictionaries as personal download, Intranet solutions, multiuser licences

Specialist dictionaries on CD-ROM or e-dictionaries have enjoyed great popularity over the last decade. The different publishers have all developed their own series which means that users have quite a lot of compatibility problems if they wish to consult dictionaries from different publishers. Because of their enhanced functionality and annual updates, they have now overtaken printed editions among language professionals. However, publishers' decision to put user-friendliness before a high degree of security meant that piracy soon made this tool unprofitable.

Multiuser licenses are aimed at companies and institutions. Intranet solutions are available in B2B. Download copies for PC, PDAs smartphones, palmtops and Windows mobile, Simian and Blackberry can be ordered from publishers' websites and now appear to offer a more promising solution. A wide range of general language and business dictionaries developed in cooperation with handheld providers are also on sale.

Nevertheless, the market for CD-ROM dictionaries for language professionals is declining in favour of online solutions.

3 Integrated bilingual specialist dictionaries in translation memory systems

The number of specialized translation titles is steadily increasing especially in the technical, economic and legal fields. At the same time, the companies and institutions responsible for the majority of orders are having to cut costs and in many cases the budget for language communication is subject to very strict controls. As a consequence, a lot of simple and repetitive translation tasks are performed by non-professionals or translation software whereas professional translators are given the most difficult texts to translate while also being required to keep their rates down if they wish to continue receiving work. As such, they have to optimize their workflow and are therefore on the lookout for time-saving tools and strategies.

3.1 Terminology management and translation memory providers (TMS)

have equipped professional translators with valuable translation management tools which enable them to compile their own dictionaries and store their validated translated text segments for reuse in future translations. These tools are regularly improved in new user-friendlier versions. In order to meet the growing demand for an efficient global translation tool solution, TMS providers and specialist bilingual dictionary publishers have decided to propose a unique tool which will allow translators to reuse their stored data and offer easy and quick access to specialist terminology that they have not previously translated and therefore need. This unique tool – translation memory with "à la carte" integrated specialist dictionaries – will save time-consuming Internet research.

3.2 LexTerm: a methodology for transforming lemma-oriented data into concept-oriented terminological entries

One of the main challenges for dictionary publishers has been to convert thousands of lemma-oriented lexicographical data from bilingual specialist dictionaries into concept-oriented terminological data to be integrated into the translator's workbench.

The tools for converting ("lemma-oriented") dictionary entries into ("concept-oriented") terminological entries are based on lexicographical and terminological ISO standards: ISO 1951 for dictionaries and ISO 16642 for terminology. This method relies on breaking down polysemic structures into a set of data categories that can be recombined into monosemic entries compatible with most of the terminology management engines on the market. Details can be found in [Le Meur, Derouin 2006][7].

---

[7] André Le Meur, Marie-Jeanne Derouin (2006), Lemma-oriented dictionaries, concept-oriented terminology and translation memories, in: LREC 2006 proceedings

3.3 The products

As a result of these efforts, the first 5 Langenscheidt English-German/German-English specialist dictionaries on Technical Engineering and Applied Sciences, Electrical Engineering & Electronics, Architecture and Construction, Business & Banking and Chemistry are now available for Across Systems. Depending on the translators' expertise more dictionaries will be added to provide German TMS users with the largest collection of validated and annually updated specialist bilingual dictionaries in Europe.

The following example screenshot shows a user-friendly interface. The unknown specialist terms in the user's language are marked in the partly translated text. On the right-hand side of the display, different possible translations are suggested with reference to the source, subject field, and semantic and pragmatic information. The user needs only to select one of them and it will be inserted automatically into the translated text.

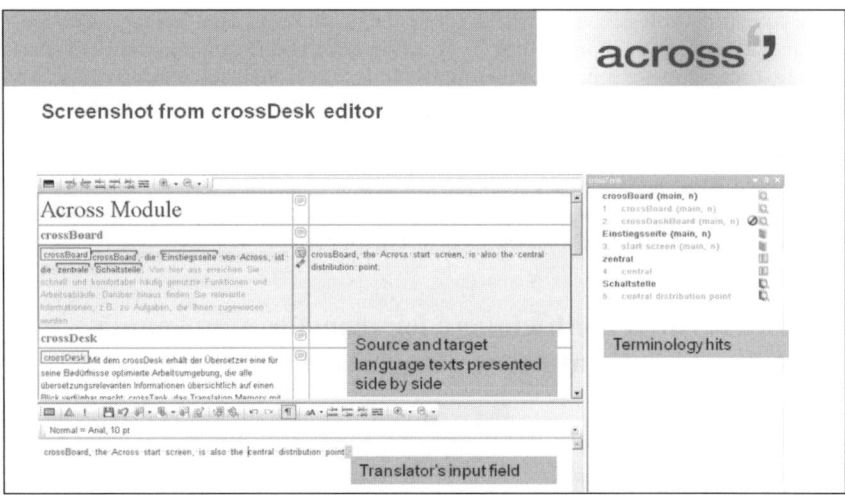

Figure 5: Example screenshot Editor crossDesk (Across Systems)

4 Publishers' dictionaries online

Providers of free dictionary data on the Internet have strongly impacted translators' relationship with dictionary publishers. Quite apart from the financial considerations, which should not be underestimated, translators use Internet resources because they provide content not found in publishers' products: a wealth of up-to-date terms, multilingual text corpora, terminological definitions, and translations in numerous languages etc.

In order to compete with these free Internet resources, dictionary publishers' portals need to be very ambitious, offering a wide variety of products and services over and above the specialist dictionaries, capitalizing on the reliability of the resources and allowing easy access to them. We believe that professional users and especially translators would appreciate such a proposition and be prepared to pay a reasonable price for it, as long as it saved them time and they could trust the information provided. This is in our opinion the only prerequisite for successful online marketing.

Such a plan requires a major financial commitment and usually takes longer than originally intended. Therefore, Langenscheidt's specialist dictionary range has hitherto been licensed to dictionary content providers' portals such as Babylon.

4.1 A future dictionary publisher's online portal

should have a section specifically devoted to language professionals and offer a platform not only for in-house dictionary products but also for those of partner publishers on both a free and a subscription basis. It should also address translators worldwide and therefore be international with language combinations from and into English.

Moreover it should offer a variety of terminological products which could complement specialist dictionaries. This means cooperating with terminology providers in institutions and industry. The dictionary and the terminological data would have to be compatible to ensure that it is implemented successfully.

4.2 The cooperation project with universities

aims to offer translators the resources of terminology papers produced by terminology students in a wide range of specialist fields. A validation procedure will ensure the reliability of the data which should set it apart from free Internet language resources.

For many years now, universities have been accumulating valuable student work describing very specific language for special purposes. These data could be of great help to translators because they not only offer an in-depth study of the concepts of a domain but also provide the non-specialist in that domain with "conceptual networks" showing how these concepts interact, which is an efficient means of understanding the logic behind the terms. Unfortunately, at the moment these data are produced and stored in various formats and on various media, which restricts their dissemination and updating. As all of them are based on the same principles and method defined in the ISO standards, it is possible to define a generic XML model onto which they can be mapped.

4.3 MemoTerm is an XML data model

dedicated to terminology as it is practised in terminology courses at university level in many European countries.

Figure 6 shows an example of an entry produced with Trados Multiterm and published as a pdf document.

Figure 7 shows the same example after conversion to MemoTerm indicating how it can be displayed in HTML.

digitale Kompaktkamera, f
Note: Es gibt keine eindeutige Klassifikation von unterschiedlichen
                     Kameratypen. Daher kann es vorkommen, dass ein und dasselbe
                     Modell bei unterschiedlichen Referenzquellen unterschiedlich
                     benannt wird. Der Vollständigkeit halber werden hier alle gefundenen
                     Benennungen aufgelistet, die gleiche Kameraeigenschaften für die
                     jeweilige Kategorie erwähnen. Auf eine Unterteilung in Megapixel-
                     Klassen wird hier aufgrund der immer seltener werdenden
                     Verwendung dieser verzichtet.
Kompaktkamera, f
kleinere Kompaktkamera, f
größere Kompaktkamera, f
Expl: "Die Mehrzahl der digitalen Kameras gehört in die Kategorie
                     "Kompaktkameras". [...] Der überwiegende Teil der Kameras ist mit
                     einem Zoomobjektiv ausgestattet, wobei die Brennweite in einem
                     dreifachen oder größeren Bereich verstellbar ist. [...] Die manuelle
                     Scharfeinstellung kann nützlich sein, bei einfacheren Modellen fehlt
                     diese Möglichkeit jedoch häufig". (Scheibel, Josef/Scheibel, Robert
                     (2005): Fotos digital. Basiswissen aktuell. Gilching: vfv Verlag: 15.)
Hyper: Digitalkamera
Cohypo: All-In-One-Kamera; digitale Spiegelreflexkamera
°fotocamera digitale compatta, f
Note: Dato che non esiste una classificazione univoca per i vari modelli di
                     fotocamere digitali, è possibile trovare per lo stesso tipo di
                     fotocamera differenti denominazioni. Per completezza, in questo
                     glossario verranno elencate tutte le varianti trovate che presentano le
                     stesse o simili caratteristiche. Una classificazione in base ai
                     Megapixel non verrà effettuata in quanto questa suddivisione sta via
                     via scomparendo.
°fotocamera compatta, f
°compatta, f
°fotocamera entry-level, f
°compatta point and shoot, f
Expl: "L'offerta delle compatte "point and shoot" è molto varia, sia per quel
                     che riguarda l'estetica sia per le funzioni in dotazione alle fotocamere.
                     Le fotocamere di questo tipo, completamente automatiche sia per

Figure 6

Has for hypernym : fotocamera digitale

digitale Kompaktkamera , f   fotocamera digitale compatta , f
kleinere Kompaktkamera , f   fotocamera entry-level , f
größere Kompaktkamera , f   compatta point and shoot , f
Es gibt keine eindeutige Klassifikation von unterschiedlichen
Kameratypen. Daher kann es vorkommen, dass ein und
dasselbe Modell bei unterschiedlichen Referenzquellen
unterschiedlich benannt wird. Der Vollständigkeit halber
werden hier alle gefundenen Benennungen aufgelistet, die
gleiche Kameraeigenschaften für die jeweilige Kategorie
erwähnen. Auf eine Unterteilung in Megapixel-Klassen wird
hier aufgrund der immer seltener werdenden Verwendung
dieser verzichtet. [Scheibel, Joseph Giuseppe, Branca,
Giovanni : 2005 , p.15]

Has for co-hyponym : fotocamera compatta di fascia media

Has for co-hyponym : fotocamera reflex digitale

Figure 7: A terminological entry in a pdf document (Graz university)

The following example (Figure 8) is a MemoTerm view of data from the CATS system (Leipzig University).

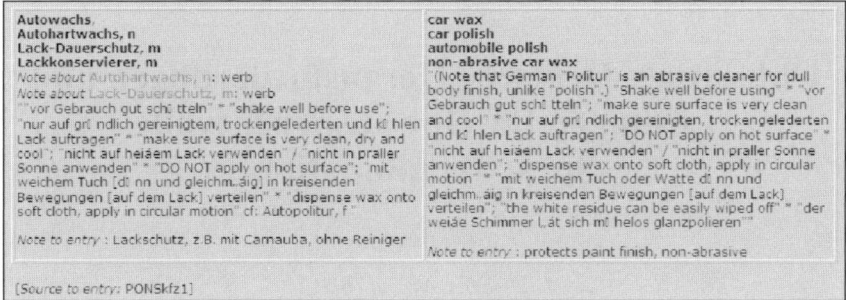

Figure 8

Collecting data on an authoring server offers the possibility of sharing common editing procedures and common references (thesauruses, classification schemes and ontologies). It should facilitate checking of semantic networks consistency by the editors, detection of homographs, and validation by experts, while also providing users with access to a large range of subject fields and better navigation through the semantic relationships.

5 The future role of dictionary publishers in the globalized interpreting and translation world

In our opinion, this tremendous evolution in the product typology will add a new dimension to the relationship between the two parties. In the future, access to validated dictionary and terminology data will be achieved through a platform for collaborative networking. Translators and other language professionals such as interpreters, technical writers and terminologists could be both users and contributors or validators in order to expand the resources generated by dictionary authors and provide a useful alternative to the plethora of heterogeneous Internet dictionaries and terminological databases by offering reliable data that can be used for professional translation. A new fair business model between translators and publishers in the service of translation quality will hopefully allow dictionary publishers to provide an appropriate response to translators' needs in the future.

Bibliography

ISO 1951 Standard (2007). *Presentation/representation of entries in dictionaries* (2007). Berlin: Beuth Verlag

André Le Meur, Marie-Jeanne Derouin (2006), *Lemma-oriented dictionaries, concept-oriented terminology and translation memories*, in: LREC 2006 proceedings

Probleme distanter Sprachen

Chinesisch–Deutsch: Herausforderungen und Lösungen für eine anspruchsvolle Sprachkombination

Iris Kleinophorst

Dipl.-Übersetzerin (BDÜ)

iris.kleinophorst@web.de

„Wow, du kannst Chinesisch. Da bist du als Übersetzerin ja sicher gut im Geschäft!"

Das ist die Standardreaktion, wenn ich meine Sprachkombinationen Englisch, Chinesisch, Französisch erwähne. Weise ich dann darauf hin, dass ich eher selten Aufträge für Chinesischübersetzungen bekomme, sind die meisten Leute überrascht. Erkläre ich aber, dass mir viele Aufträge für Chinesischübersetzungen entgehen, weil Auftraggeber den von mir als qualifizierter Chinesischübersetzerin geforderten Preis nicht bezahlen wollen, nicken sie verständnisvoll. Ein Bekannter, der selbst als Freiberufler im IT-Bereich arbeitet, sagte neulich sogar wörtlich: „Bei Übersetzungen ist die Qualität doch nicht wichtig"!

Damit brachte er eines der Probleme, mit denen sich Dolmetscher und insbesondere Übersetzer heutzutage immer häufiger konfrontiert sehen, auf den Punkt: Für viele Auftraggeber spielt die Qualität einer Übersetzung gegenüber dem Preis eine untergeordnete Rolle.

„Wir haben da einen chinesischen Werkstudenten, der macht uns unsere Übersetzungen nebenbei."

Oder: „Meine chinesischen Angestellten übersetzen mir das, was ich brauche, mal eben ins Englische. Das reicht mir dann", so Firmenvertreter, die ich fragte, wer ihre Chinesischübersetzungen erledige. Dass die Qualität dabei auf der Strecke bleibt, war beiden klar. Hauptsache der Preis ist niedrig. Damit sehen sich auch Sprachmittler mit Chinesischkenntnissen einer Entwicklung ausgesetzt, die in anderen Sprachen bereits sehr viel früher eingesetzt hat: ein rapider Preisverfall für Sprachdienstleistungen. Dafür ging sie bei Chinesisch sehr viel schneller vonstatten. Noch vor einigen Jahren waren für Chinesischübersetzungen Preise üblich, die das Doppelte bis Dreifache der Zeilenpreise gängiger Sprachkombinationen betrugen. Inzwischen hat die Globalisierung auch uns erreicht: Die Menge an deutschen Muttersprachlern mit Chinesisch-kenntnissen (auf unterschiedlichsten Niveaus) hat enorm zugenommen. Zudem haben immer mehr Chinesen die Möglichkeit und auch die finanziellen Mittel für einen längeren Aufenthalt in Deutschland. Hinzu kommt die elektronische Entwicklung: Internetkontakte mit asiatischen Ländern und auch der Austausch umfangreicher Dateien stellen im Zeitalter von Unicode und DSL kein Problem mehr dar.

Leider sehen viele Auftraggeber nur den Preisvorteil, ohne zu bedenken, welche Nachteile die möglichst billige Erledigung von Sprachdienstleistungen mit sich bringt. Übersetzungen ins Deutsche, die von chinesischen Muttersprachlern entweder hier in Deutschland oder sogar in Asien kostengünstig erledigt werden, weisen in der Regel gravierende Mängel bei der Sprachgestaltung auf. Von mangelnder Sorgfalt beim Layout der Texte gar nicht zu reden. Teilweise sind die Übersetzungen sogar so schlecht, dass man sich doch der qualifizierten deutschen Muttersprachler erinnert und diese den Text überarbeiten lässt. Dadurch werden die Übersetzungen dann teurer, als wenn man gleich einen qualifizierten muttersprachlichen Übersetzer beauftragt hätte. Ähnliches gilt bei der Vergabe von Sprachdienstleistungen an deutsche Muttersprach-ler, die eben keine ausgebildeten Sprachmittler sind. Beherrscht jemand zwei oder mehr Sprachen leidlich bis gut, heißt dies nicht, dass derjenige auch fähig ist, einen Text aus einer Sprache in eine andere zu übersetzen. Noch gravierender wirkt sich dies bei Dolmetschaufträgen aus. Eine schlechte Übersetzung ist leicht zu erkennen und kann in der Regel überarbeitet werden. Mängel bei der Dolmetschleistung sind für den Kunden hingegen nicht offensichtlich. Und Fehler und Probleme, die durch falsches Dolmetschen entstehen, lassen sich nicht so einfach überarbeiten wie eine Übersetzung.

„Bitte senden Sie mir ein Angebot für den angehängten chinesischen Text. Liefertermin der Übersetzung morgen Mittag."

So ein typischer E-Mail-Text einer Anfrage. Damit steht man bei chinesischen Texten vor dem ersten Problem: der Kalkulation. Bei englischen oder französischen Texten ist es meistens ein Leichtes, Wörter und Zeichen und damit Standardzeilen zu zählen. In der Regel lässt sich auch der Schwierigkeitsgrad beim Darüberlesen bestimmen. Ein erfahrener Übersetzer oder eine erfahrene Übersetzerin kann damit den Zeitauf-wand ganz gut abschätzen und hat eine gute Grundlage für eine realistische Kalkula-tion.

Bei zu übersetzenden chinesischen Texten handelt es sich jedoch oft um eingescannte Texte, die als PDF geliefert werden oder, schlimmer noch, um Faxe, die nachträglich eingescannt wurden. Da bleibt einem dann nichts weiter übrig, als die Zeichen von Hand durchzuzählen und aufgrund von hoffentlich schon vorliegenden Erfahrungs-werten grob zu überschlagen, welcher Aufwand da auf einen zukommt und welchen Preis man anbieten soll. Fehlen die Erfahrungswerte, bleibt einem nichts anderes übrig, als einige Zeilen als Probe zu übersetzen und dann auf dem Text hochzurech-nen. Meistens führt dies dazu, dass man bereits viel Zeit in die Kalkulation investiert, dem Kunden ein ordentliches und realistisches Angebot schickt und dann als Antwort bekommt: „Vielen Dank, aber der Auftrag wurde bereits an einen billigeren Anbieter vergeben." Solche Anbieter haben dann entweder keine Erfahrungswerte, was ihren Zeitaufwand betrifft. Oder übernehmen Aufträge zu jedem Preis. Möglicherweise sind sie finanziell auch so abgesichert, dass eine wirtschaftliche Kalkulation für sie keine Rolle spielt.

Bekommt man den Auftrag fast schon wider Erwarten, beginnt die eigentliche Herausforderung. Eine Terminvorgabe wie die oben genannte führt meistens zu viel Stress. Viele Auftraggeber sind sich nämlich nicht bewusst, dass eine Seite chinesischen Textes drei bis vier Seiten an deutschem Text entsprechen kann. Allein dadurch fällt für die Übersetzung eines chinesischen Textes ein größerer Zeitaufwand an als dies bei vergleichbaren englischen oder französischen Texten der Fall ist.

Ein weiterer Zeitfaktor bei der Übersetzung chinesischer Zeichen ist der Aufwand für die Zeichenrecherche. Ein englisches Wort finde ich im Wörterbuch problemlos in der alphabetischen Auflistung. Bei einem chinesischen Zeichen, dessen Aussprache unbekannt ist, muss zuerst die Strichzahl des bestimmenden Elements, des Radikals, ermittelt werden. Hat man das Radikal in der nach Strichzahlen geordneten Radikalliste gefunden, wird auf eine weitere Liste verwiesen, in der alle Zeichen, die das jeweilige Radikal enthalten, wiederum nach Strichzahlen aufgeführt sind. Also muss nun die Strichzahl der übrigen Elemente des Zeichens ermittelt werden. Mit Hilfe dieser Reststrichzahl findet man den Seitenverweis auf den eigentlichen Wörterbucheintrag und damit auch die Aussprache. Die Aussprache benötigt man zudem, um ein Wort elektronisch nachzuschlagen. Diese (notwendige!) Vorgehensweise stellt schon bei gut lesbaren Texten einen erheblichen Zeitaufwand dar. Handelt es sich bei der Vorlage um einen Scan oder schwieriger noch ein gescanntes Fax, vervielfacht sich der Zeitaufwand entsprechend. Bei europäischen Sprachen kann die schlechte Lesbarkeit einzelner Wörter bei PDFs minderer Qualität in der Regel über den Kontext gelöst werden. Bei den hochkomplexen chinesischen Zeichen, bei denen einzelne Zeichenkomponenten bedeutungsrelevant sind, ist dies nur mit erheblichem Zusatzaufwand möglich.

Selbst bei Texten, die elektronisch vorliegen, gestaltet sich die Recherche sehr schwierig. Dort ist es zwar möglich, die Aussprache und teilweise auch Bedeutung einzelner Zeichen direkt über Kopieren des Zeichens und Einfügen in Online-Wörterbucher schnell zu ermitteln. Die Grundbedeutung einzelner Zeichen hilft aber nicht weiter, da es sich meistens um Zeichenkombinationen mit Wortbedeutungen handelt. Die gängigsten dieser „Wörter" sind zwar in Wörterbüchern zu finden. Allerdings entwickelt sich die chinesische Sprache derart schnell, dass Neologismen selbst für chinesische Muttersprachler und natürlich für Nichtmuttersprachler ein großes Problem darstellen. Dies betrifft insbesondere Fachsprachen wie Wirtschaft, Technik oder Recht. Zuverlässige Quellen für Fachvokabular fehlen also. Zumal die Entwicklung solcher Neologismen nicht unbedingt einem standardisierten Ablauf folgen. So gibt es zum Beispiel in Taiwan wenig Bestrebungen, Fachvokabular zu standardisieren. Viele Universitäten und Institutionen basteln sich dort ihr eigenes Vokabular, und Fachwörterbücher existieren kaum. Und selbst wenn solche Quellen in der Form von Fachwörterbüchern in China oder Taiwan existieren, ist es hier in Deutschland nahezu ausgeschlossen, die Titel zu finden, geschweige denn die Bücher zu bestellen. Die Suche nach dem deutschen Pendant komplizierter Fachausdrücke gestaltet sich dadurch sehr schwierig.

Ein weiteres typisches Problem der chinesischen Sprache ist die Verwendung von Redewendungen und blumigen Metaphern selbst in Fachtexten. Dabei bestehen die Schwierigkeiten zum einen darin, die Bedeutung der Redewendungen und Metaphern zu recherchieren. Zum anderen müssen diese dann in einer Form ins Deutsche übertragen werden, die sowohl der Bedeutung der Metapher wie auch dem Sprachstil des Fachtextes gerecht wird. Dies stellt erhebliche Anforderungen an die Leistung des Sprachmittlers, insbesondere des Dolmetschers, der ja noch weniger Zeit hat, Recherche zu betreiben und am Text zu feilen.

Auch Zahlen als spezifisch chinesisches Problem sollten nicht unterschätzt werden. Während die deutsche Sprache hohe Werte in regelmäßigen Zehnerpotenzen wie Eintausend, Zehntausend, Hunderttausend etc. aufführt, werden im Chinesischen alle Zehnerpotenzen zwischen Zehntausend und einhundert Millionen als Vielfaches von Zehntausend gerechnet. Die deutsche Zahl „1.000.000" wird im Chinesischen dementsprechend als „einhundert (mal) Zehntausend" ausgedrückt. Die Umrechnung von Zahlen erfordert beim Übersetzen also große Sorgfalt. Noch komplizierter gestaltet sich die Umrechnung beim Dolmetschen, wo der Dolmetscher diese Umrechnungsleistung innerhalb von Sekunden vollbringen muss. Doch auch bei der Übersetzung von in arabischen Ziffern ausgedrückten Zahlen muss man diese genau prüfen und an die unterschiedlichen Schreibweisen (Punkt statt Komma und umgekehrt im angelsächsischen Sprachraum und damit auch bei Ziffern in chinesischen Texten) anpassen. Die ebenfalls schon vorgekommene Forderung von Auftraggebern, Ziffern bei der Übersetzung nicht abzurechnen, ist daher strikt abzulehnen.

„Wenn jemand eine Fremdsprache übersetzt, spielt es doch keine Rolle, welche. Chinesischübersetzer können doch genauso gut Chinesisch wie Englischübersetzer Englisch. Das rechtfertigt doch keine höheren Preise."

Diese Aussage haben so oder so ähnlich die meisten Sprachmittler für Chinesisch schon einmal zu hören bekommen. Und sich geärgert. Denn der höhere Aufwand, den das Erlernen und auch Erhalten einer Sprache wie Chinesisch bedeutet, wird dabei vollkommen missachtet. Hätte ich anstelle von Chinesisch „nur" einen Abschluss in Englisch und Französisch, wäre mein Studium um ein Wesentliches kürzer und leichter gewesen. Und ich wäre heute wirtschaftlich vermutlich mindestens ebenso erfolgreich wie ich es mit der Sprachkombination Chinesisch-Deutsch bin. So aber haben meine Mitstreiter und ich uns durch ein Studium gekämpft, dessen Wochenstundenzahl erheblich über der anderer Sprachkombinationen lag. Das Gleiche gilt für die Vor- und Nachbereitungszeit der verschiedenen Lehrveranstaltungen, die bei Chinesisch den Zeitaufwand für andere Sprachen weit übertraf. Und das berücksichtigt noch nicht den mentalen Aufwand für das Erlernen einer so komplexen Sprache wie Chinesisch.

Ein verlängertes Studium mit erhöhtem Zeitaufwand bedeutet natürlich auch einen höheren finanziellen Aufwand. Dazu kommt der Aufwand für die Asienaufenthalte, die für den Spracherwerb unerlässlich sind. Für Dolmetscher ist die Situation noch komplizierter: In Deutschland gibt es gegenwärtig eine einzige Ausbildungsstätte, die einen Abschluss zum Chinesischdolmetscher anbietet. Lange existiert sie noch nicht. Und die Kurse finden nur bei einer ausreichenden Anzahl an Interessenten statt. Um eine Qualifikation als Chinesischdolmetscher zu erwerben, muss man also meistens im Ausland studieren. Mit einem entsprechend höheren finanziellen Aufwand.

Auch nach Abschluss des Studiums erfordert es einen höheren Aufwand, die chinesischen Sprachkenntnisse zu pflegen und auf dem Laufenden zu halten. Englische Filme zeigt inzwischen jedes Kino irgendwann einmal. Chinesische Filme im Original laufen allenfalls einmal alle paar Jahre im Kulturfernsehen, und dann zu absurden Sendezeiten. Hat man nicht die Möglichkeit, regelmäßig nach Asien zu fliegen und sich vor Ort einzudecken, ist der Erwerb chinesischer Bücher, Filme oder CDs nur schwer möglich. Und ist man nicht zufällig mit einem chinesischen Ehepartner verheiratet, wird das aktive Sprechen schnell zum Problem. Chinesisch wird auf deutschen Straßen nun mal nicht so häufig gesprochen wie Englisch.

Der Aufwand für die Qualifizierung geht aber natürlich über den reinen Spracherwerb hinaus. Ohne tiefgehendes interkulturelles Verständnis ist eine mündliche oder schriftliche Übertragung zwischen der chinesischen und der deutschen Sprache unmöglich. Ein solches interkulturelles Verständnis erwirbt nur, wer sich wirklich intensiv mit der anderen Kultur auseinandersetzt. Dies erfordert viel Zeit und Geld. Auch dieser Aufwand muss berücksichtigt werden.

„Wir suchen einen Mitarbeiter auf 400-Euro-Basis. Relevanter Studienabschluss und chinesische Sprachkenntnisse erforderlich."

Zu einem solchen Preis muss sich hoffentlich niemand verkaufen, der den Aufwand für eine Qualifizierung als Sprachmittler für Chinesisch betrieben hat. Leider wird es für Neueinsteiger immer schwieriger, die Preise zu erzielen, die für erfahrene Kollegen selbstverständlich sind. Was können wir als Sprachmittler im Bereich Chinesisch aber tun, um unsere qualitativ hochwertige Arbeit zu wirtschaftlichen Preisen zu verkaufen?

Tauschen Sie sich mit anderen Chinesischsprachmittlern aus, vernetzen Sie sich. Das hilft Ihnen, ein Gespür dafür zu bekommen, welche Preise realistisch und wirtschaftlich zugleich sind. Zudem ergeben sich so immer wieder Möglichkeiten zur Zusammenarbeit. Angebote gibt es hierfür verschiedene. So ist im internen Diskussionsforum des BDÜ vor einem Jahr eine Chinesischgruppe entstanden, in der sich Chinesischübersetzer und -dolmetscher aus allen Ecken Deutschlands und darüber hinaus austauschen. Inzwischen haben auch die ersten Treffen stattgefunden. Weitere sind geplant. Der Austausch mit den Kollegen, die vor den gleichen Problemen stehen, hilft sehr bei einer realistischen Einschätzung der eigenen Situation. Und langfristig kann dies vielleicht dazu führen, dass bei Auftraggebern das Bewusstsein für hochqualitative Chinesischübersetzungen und -dolmetschleistungen steigt. Wichtig ist in diesem Zusammenhang auch die Teilnahme an den in Zukunft jährlich stattfindenden Honorarumfragen des BDÜ. Die Ergebnisse dieser Umfragen stellen einen guten Anhaltspunkt für Marktpreise dar. Und können eventuell einmal gegenüber Kunden als Argumentationsbasis dienen.

In Ihren Kundenbeziehungen sollten Qualitätsmerkmale wie Termintreue, qualitativ hochwertige Arbeit, Einhaltung von Vereinbarungen in Bezug auf Verschwiegenheit oder ähnliche Anforderungen des Kunden selbstverständlich sein. Deshalb ist es nicht sinnvoll, solche Profileigenschaften extra zu betonen. Berufen Sie sich lieber auf Fähigkeiten, die Sie von anderen Sprachmittlern unterscheiden. Zusatzqualifikationen, die den Anforderungen des Kunden entgegenkommen, sind immer von Vorteil. Dazu gehören Kenntnisse in Fachgebieten wie Wirtschaft, Recht oder Technik. Erwerben Sie zusätzliche Kenntnisse oder bauen Sie die Kenntnisse aus, die Sie in solchen Bereichen haben und schaffen Sie sich Nischen, die Sie für Kunden aus diesen Nischenbereichen interessant machen. Berufen Sie sich auch auf andere Fähigkeiten, die beim Übersetzen der chinesischen Sprache eine große Rolle spielen. Recherchekompetenz ist hier ganz wichtig. Da wie bereits erwähnt Fachwörterbücher großenteils fehlen, müssen Sie sich ihre Kenntnisse auf andere Weise erarbeiten. Umfassende Recherchen im Internet und anderen zur Verfügung stehenden Quellen spielen dabei eine große Rolle. Machen Sie dem Kunden deutlich, wie vorteilhaft eine kompetente Recherche für die Sprachdienstleistung und damit für sein Image ist. Pflegen Sie Ihre Sprachkenntnisse aktiv und sehen Sie auch dies als wichtige Qualifikation für Ihre Arbeit als Sprachmittler.

„Nicht jeder, der Chinesisch spricht, ist automatisch ein guter Übersetzer geschweige denn Dolmetscher."

Wie können Sie als Auftraggeber die Qualität Ihres Übersetzungs- oder Dolmetschauftrags bei einer angemessenen Bezahlung erreichen? Zunächst gilt, was für alle Übersetzungs- und Dolmetschaufträge gelten sollte:

Suchen Sie nach qualifizierten Sprachmittlern. Lassen Sie sich dafür ausreichend Zeit. Eine gute Anlaufstelle für die Suche nach qualifizierten Sprachmittlern ist die Webseite des BDÜ, des Bundes der Dolmetscher und Übersetzer in Deutschland e. V. Dort können Sie gezielt nach Übersetzern suchen, die in ihre Muttersprache übersetzen. Auch Dolmetscher und Spezialisten für verschiedene Fachbereiche finden Sie dort. Und da alle BDÜ-Mitglieder ihre Qualifikation im Sprachmittlerbereich nachweisen müssen, können Sie sicher sein, dass die dort gefunden Sprachmittler über die erforderliche Qualifikation verfügen.

Sollten Sie eine Agentur mit der Organisation Ihrer Aufträge beauftragen, stellen Sie sicher, dass das Büro bestimmte Kriterien erfüllt. So sollten für die Bearbeitung bestimmter Fachgebiete immer Fachübersetzer zum Einsatz kommen. Die Agentur sollte das Vier-Augen-Prinzip erfüllen: Alle erledigten Übersetzungen sollten von einem zweiten Übersetzer Korrektur gelesen werden. Je nach Auftrag sollte die Agentur Translation-Memory-Tools einsetzen, um die sprachliche Konsistenz sowohl des aktuellen Auftrags wie eventueller Folgeaufträge wahren zu können. Und auch

Terminologieverwaltung sollte dem Unternehmen wichtig sein, um qualitativ hochwertige Sprachdienstleistungen zu liefern.

Stellen Sie keine unmöglichen Anforderungen, die sich negativ auf die Qualität auswirken! Wenn Sie eine Agentur mit der Übersetzung eines 150 Seiten umfassenden Dokuments beauftragen, der Liefertermin aber so knapp ist, dass ein Übersetzer das alleine nicht schafft, wird die Agentur das Dokument aufteilen. Im günstigsten Fall bleibt genug Zeit für einen Korrekturleser, alles durchzulesen und die gröbsten terminologischen Abweichungen zwischen den Übersetzungen einzelner Teile anzupassen. Im schlimmsten Fall liest sich jemand in der Agentur, der weder die Ausgangssprache kann noch sich im Fachgebiet auskennt, den Zieltext durch und vergleicht, ob alle Zahlen übereinstimmen. Wenn er sie denn überhaupt lesen kann.

Da dies in der Regel bei Chinesisch nicht der Fall ist, sollten Sie mit Chinesischaufträgen immer Personen beauftragen, die über die erforderlichen Sprachkenntnisse verfügen. Vergeben Sie Aufträge nicht an den billigsten, sondern an den kompetentesten Anbieter. Geschriebene und gesprochene Texte gehören zu den Visitenkarten eines Unternehmens. Machen Sie bei solchen Visitenkarten keine Abstriche bei der Qualität!

„Der Bedarf ist da, nur die Nachfrage fehlt."

lautete die Reaktion einer Kollegin auf eine Anfrage, bei der ein lächerlich geringer Zeilenpreis geboten wurde. Der Auftrag war innerhalb kürzester Zeit vergeben. Über die Qualität dieser Übersetzung wurde leider nichts bekannt.

Warum tun wir Chinesischübersetzer und -dolmetscher es uns an, in einem Bereich zu arbeiten, in dem nur mit Mühen ein wirtschaftliches Arbeiten möglich ist, in dem aus Preisgründen mit schlechter Qualität vorliebgenommen wird und bei dem die Anerkennung unserer Fähigkeiten offensichtlich nur eine geringe Rolle spielt?

Weil wir viel Zeit und Geld in die Qualifikation gesteckt haben. Weil uns die Sprache interessiert. Weil wir uns für die entsprechenden Länder und Kulturen interessieren. Weil die Situation doch bestimmt auch mal wieder besser wird. Und weil wir für uns den Anspruch vertreten, qualitativ hochwertige Sprachdienstleistungen in einer anspruchsvollen Sprachkombination zu liefern.

Sprachtechnologie für übersetzungsgerechtes Schreiben am Beispiel Deutsch, Englisch, Japanisch

Dr. Melanie Siegel

acrolinx GmbH

melanie.siegel@acrolinx.com

1 Einleitung

Die meisten von uns haben schon extrem schlechte Anleitungen gesehen, wie sie auch in Internet-Foren, Büchern und Zeitschriften kursieren. So wie solche Beispiele auf der einen Seite lustig sind, haben Sie doch auf der anderen Seite oft ernsthafte Folgen:

- Die Übersetzung wird in hohem Maße erschwert, weil die Texte zum Teil unverständlich, zum Teil von erheblicher Ambiguität sind.

- Die Kosten für Support steigen, wenn Kunden erst nachfragen müssen, wie ein Gerät bedient wird.

- Die juristischen Folgekosten können erheblich sein, wenn durch falsche Bedienung Geräte kaputtgehen.

- Schließlich können bei falscher Bedienung aufgrund schlechter Anleitungen sogar Menschen zu Schaden kommen.

Es bedeutet eine hohe Anforderung für den Autor, einen guten instruktiven Text zu schreiben, zumal wenn dieser Text auch noch in einer Fremdsprache geschrieben werden muss. Die Übersetzungsaufgabe dabei auch noch im Blick zu behalten, erfordert hohe Qualifikation.

Wir bei acrolinx haben uns zur Aufgabe gesetzt, Wege zu finden, wie linguistisch basierte Software den Prozess des Schreibens technischer Dokumentation unterstützen kann.

Dabei haben wir einerseits die Schwierigkeiten im Blick, die japanische und deutsche Autoren (und andere Nichtmuttersprachler des Englischen) beim Schreiben englischer Texte haben. Besonders japanische Autoren haben mit Schwierigkeiten zu kämpfen, weil sie hochkomplexe Ideen in einer Sprache ausdrücken müssen, die von Informationsstandpunkt her sehr unterschiedlich zu ihrer Muttersprache ist.

Andererseits untersuchen wir technische Dokumentation, die von Autoren in ihrer Muttersprache geschrieben wird. Obwohl hier die fremdsprachliche Komponente entfällt, ist doch auch erhebliches Verbesserungspotential vorhanden. Das Ziel ist hier, Dokumente verständlich, konsistent und übersetzungsgerecht zu schreiben.

Der fundamentale Ansatz in der Entwicklung linguistisch basierter Software ist, dass gute linguistische Software auf Datenmaterial basiert und sich an den konkreten Zielen der besseren Dokumentation orientiert.

2 Autorenunterstützung für englische technische Dokumentation

Die Qualität technischer Dokumentation wird maßgeblich durch diese Faktoren bestimmt:

- Korrektheit von Rechtschreibung und Grammatik
- Verständlichkeit
- Lesbarkeit
- Konsistenz
- Übersetzbarkeit
- Terminologie

Für die Qualitätssicherung dieser Faktoren bieten wir Unterstützung in den Bereichen Rechtschreibung, Grammatik, Schreibstil, Terminologie und Konsistenz in der Formulierung an.

2.1 Autorenunterstüzung für englische Rechtschreibung

Dieselben Rechtschreibregeln gelten für alle Autoren, die Englisch schreiben. Allerdings gibt es verschiedene Varianten des Englischen (die europäische und die US-amerikanische Variante), wofür die unterstützende Software angepasst sein muss. Wichtig ist hier Konsistenz: Die Entscheidung für eine Variante muss immer bewusst gefällt und konsistent geprüft werden.

Gute linguistisch basierte Software für die Rechtschreibprüfung sucht gezielt nach Fehlern und bietet dafür Verbesserungsvorschläge an. Welche Fehler in den untersuchten Texten prominent sind, das ist abhängig von der Domäne: Der Gebrauch von Wörtern differiert in unterschiedlichen Domänen, so dass unterschiedliche Fehler prominent sind. Jede Domäne wird daher am besten abgedeckt, wenn eine präzise Analyse großer Datenmengen vorausgeht.

Für Autoren, die nicht in ihrer Muttersprache schreiben, kommt dazu, dass die Fehler, die sie machen, nach der Beschaffenheit ihrer Muttersprache variieren. Um diese Fehler zu finden und zu kategorisieren, haben wir englischsprachige technische Dokumente von japanischen Muttersprachlern analysiert:

- Das Schriftsystem und damit die Zuordnung von der Orthographie zum Laut unterliegen grundsätzlich anderen Regeln im Japanischen als im Englischen oder Deutschen. Dies führt zu besonderen Schwierigkeiten bei der Rechtschreibung, z. B. bei „deviaton", „communicaion".

- Das Japanische hat keinen „r"-Laut. Fehler in der technischen Dokumentation waren z. B. „accurary", „nealy".

- Das Japanische hat keine Vorkommen von „st" oder „xp" in Wörtern. Fehler waren z. B. „exeposed", „assitance".

- Das Japanische kennt keine Leerzeichen zwischen Wörtern, was besonders schwierig bei zusammengesetzten Nomen im Englischen ist. Ein Fehler war z. B. „step wise"

Diese Beispiele machen deutlich, dass die Struktur der Muttersprache schon bei der Rechtschreibprüfung einbezogen werden muss.

2.2 Autorenunterstützung für englische Grammatik

Grammatikregeln gelten für alle Sprecher einer Sprache gleichermaßen, egal, in welchem Kontext sie sich befinden oder welches ihre Muttersprache ist. Eine gute Autorenunterstützung sucht jedoch gezielt nach Grammatikfehlern und gibt Vorschläge zur Verbesserung. Daher ist auch hier eine Datenanalyse unerlässlich. Die grammatischen Strukturen unterscheiden sich zum Teil erheblich in unterschiedlichen Domänen (z.B. Marketing-Texte oder Benutzeranleitungen) und damit auch die Fehler, die auftreten. Bei nichtmuttersprachlichen Autoren kommt hinzu, dass die grammatische Struktur der Muttersprache eine erhebliche Rolle dabei spielt, welche Fehler überhaupt auftreten und mit welcher Frequenz.

Auch dies stellen wir am Beispiel japanischer Muttersprachler dar, die Englisch schreiben:

- Im Japanischen gibt es keine Numerus-Information. Daher kommt es besonders häufig zu Fehlern in der Numerus-Kongruenz, wie in diesen Beispielen: „Be sure to supply power to *a* control and *an* expansion *units* from a single power supply." – "Always replace them with *a* new *ones*."

- Das Konzept der Subjekt-Verb-Kongruenz im Japanischen bezieht sich auf andere Information als im Englischen, nämlich auf die soziale Beziehung zwischen den Interaktanten. Es ist daher kein Wunder, dass es zu Kongruenz-Fehlern kommt: „Check if instructions are programmed in such a way that a *scan* never *finish*."

- Besondere Schwierigkeiten haben japanische Muttersprachler mit Artikeln. Das liegt daran, dass die japanische Sprache keine Artikel kennt, so dass der Umgang mit Artikeln im Zweitsprachenerwerb erst mühsam erlernt werden muss. So finden sich in den Texten viele Verletzungen der Regel zum Gebrauch von „a" und „an", wie in „a isolating transformer" oder „an program". Artikel werden zu oft oder zu selten gesetzt, wie in „Move the both guides".

- Das Japanische kennt nicht den Unterschied zwischen zählbaren und unzählbaren Nomen. Das führt einerseits zu Problemen bei der Auswahl der Artikel. Andererseits führt dieser konzeptionelle Unterschied in der Sprache zu Problemen bei der Unterscheidung von den Wörtern „amount" und „number", wie in den folgenden Beispielen: „number of simultaneous input", „number of connection is one".

- Das Japanische hat nur sehr wenige unregelmäßige Verben, im Gegensatz zum Englischen. Die Flexion der unregelmäßigen Verben ist für alle Nichtmuttersprachler des Englischen problematisch: „IP can be automatically *get*".

- Im Japanischen ist es möglich – oft die bessere Schreibweise – Subjekt und Objekt auszulassen, wenn die Referenzen bekannt sind. Z.B. ist *„ikimashita"* (gegangen) ein perfekter japanischer Satz, wenn im Kontext bekannt ist, wer wohin gegangen ist. Diese Möglichkeit gibt es aber im Englischen nicht, was bei Japanern zu folgenden Fehlern geführt hat: *„It also enables to transfer the programs", „Using this function enables to take samplings"*.

Wir haben den „Hiroshima English Learners Corpus" (Hiroshima University) auf grammatische Fehler analysiert, um die Fehlerverteilung zu untersuchen:

Kongruenz	245 (25.8%)
Artikel	126 (13.3%)
Verbform	256 (27%)
Verwechslung von Wörtern (Semantik)	192 (20.2%)
Valenz	17 (1.8%)
Wortstellung	113 (11.9%)

2.3 Autorenunterstützung für den Schreibstil englischer technischer Dokumentation

Stilrichtlinien können für unterschiedliche Anwendungszwecke ganz unterschiedlich sein. Guter Schreibstil bedeutet etwas ganz anderes für unterschiedliche Texttypen, wie z.B. Technische Dokumentation und Pressemitteilungen. Auch verschiedene Domänen (hier z.B. Software-Beschreibungen oder Maschinenanleitungen) erfordern oft die Einhaltung unterschiedlicher Richtlinien. Schließlich ist der Schreibstil auch sehr davon abhängig, wer die Zielgruppe für den Text ist, z.B. Endbenutzer eines Haushaltsgeräts oder Heizungsmonteure.

Auch wenn Texttyp, Domäne und Zielgruppe bestimmt und die Stilrichtlinien definiert sind, ist doch auch hier wieder die Muttersprache des Autors mitbestimmend. Wir deutschen Muttersprachler tendieren z.B. zu langen und komplexen Sätzen. Zu komplexe Sätze sind jedoch einerseits im Englischen generell und andererseits in der technischen Dokumentation nicht sinnvoll. Daher gilt die Stilrichtlinie zwar generell, aber bei deutschen Muttersprachlern muss besonders darauf geprüft werden.

Stilrichtlinien für die englische technische Dokumentation betreffen die Bereiche Einfachheit, Konsistenz, Korrektheit, Ansprache. Für japanische Muttersprachler sind einige Regeln besonders relevant:

- *Direktheit in der Ansprache, Benutzung des Imperativs in Handlungsanweisungen*: Japanische Autoren vermeiden die direkte Ansprache und direkte Anweisungen, da dies in der japanischen Sprache nicht angemessen ist. Daher finden sich Handlungsanweisungen wie *„However, it is recommended to take measures", „you should generate a copy".*

- *Lesbarkeit und Übersetzbarkeit, Vermeidung von "this", "that" "these" ohne Nomen*: Im Japanischen gibt es, wie oben schon erwähnt, keine Artikel. Allerdings gibt es Entsprechungen von *"this", "that" "these"*, nämlich *„kore", „sore", „korera"*, die aber nicht mit Nomen auftreten können. Daher ist die stilgerechte Formulierung für japanische Muttersprachler auch hier besonders schwierig. Wir fanden Formulierungen wie *„Once this is done, specific marks can be measured as substitute marks."*

- *Lesbarkeit und Übersetzbarkeit, Gebrauch von Artikeln:* Der Gebrauch von Artikeln im Englischen ist oft keine Frage der Grammatik, sondern des Schreibstils. Die Stilregel für den Gebrauch von Artikeln wurde besonders für japanische Muttersprachler angepasst. Ein Beispiel aus dem Korpus: *„When VSC calibration is active, the device displays a calibration fault code."*

- *Lesbarkeit und Übersetzbarkeit, Auswahl von Artikeln:* Die Auswahl der richtigen Artikel im Englischen ist auch abhängig von der Zählbarkeit von nominalen Entitäten, wie bereits oben erwähnt. Das Konzept der Zählbarkeit ist nicht Teil der japanischen Sprache. Dazu gehören Regeln wie:
  o Do not use *a/an/many* with uncountable nouns.
  o Do not use *some/any* with countable nouns in singular.
  o Do not use *much* with countable nouns.
  o Use an article with countable nouns in singular

- *Ansprache des Lesers, Vermeidung von „ 's":* Den richtigen Ton zu treffen in der technischen Dokumentation einer Fremdsprache ist immer schwierig, weil die Auswahl des richtigen Tons anderen sprachlichen Merkmalen unterliegt. Für die englische technische Dokumentation gilt z.B., dass Possessivangaben mit „'s" vermieden werden sollen. In unseren Daten von japanischen Muttersprachlern fanden wir viele Beispiele dafür, unter anderen *„Unit 's current consumption table".*

2.4 Autorenunterstützung für die Terminologie englischer technischer Dokumentation

Geprüfte, einheitliche Terminologie ist eine Grundvoraussetzung für konsistente technische Dokumentation. Diese Konsistenz ist erforderlich, um Dokumente übersetzen zu können, aber auch, um in Dokumenten suchen zu können. Dazu kommt der Wiedererkennungswert von Produktnamen bei Endverbrauchern. Idealerweise gibt es eine Benennung mit einer Bedeutung und einer Übersetzung pro Sprache in einer Domäne. In der Analyse von Dokumenten (von Muttersprachlern und Nichtmuttersprachlern gleichermaßen) finden wir verschiedenerlei Varianten, wie z.B.:

- web server – web-server
- upload protection – upload-protection
- timeout – time out

- Reset – ReSet

- sub station – sub-station

Um konsistente Terminologie zu gewährleisten, werden die Texte auf Varianten geprüft. Eine Termdatenbank der Domäne oder des Benutzers liegt zugrunde, in der Vorzugsbenennungen enthalten sind. Wenn eine Vorzugsbenennung beispielsweise „*timeout*" ist, so werden falsche Varianten davon automatisch erkannt. Außerdem können in der Termdatenbank gesperrte Benennungen und Übersetzungen gespeichert werden. Eine automatische Prüfung unterstützt den Autor dabei, konsistent zu formulieren.

2.5 Autorenunterstützung für die Formulierungskonsistenz englischer technischer Dokumentation

Wenn große Mengen technischer Dokumentation produziert werden, so geschieht das oft über Jahre. In den meisten Fällen sind viele verschiedene Autoren beteiligt. Das führt dazu, dass derselbe Sachverhalt auf viele verschiedene Arten beschrieben wird. Ein Beispiel aus unseren Dokumenten:

- Congratulations on acquiring your new wearable digital audio player

- Congratulations, you have acquired your new wearable digital audio player!

- Dear Customer, congratulations on purchasing the new wearable digital audio player!

Neben der mangelnden Konsistenz haben technische Redaktionen hier auch ein finanzielles Problem: Jeder dieser Sätze muss neu übersetzt werden.

Die Autorenunterstützung von acrolinx unterstützt die Formulierungskonsistenz in der technischen Redaktion. Eine Datenanalyse zeigt auf, welche Inkonsistenzen sich in den vergangenen Jahren eingeschlichen haben. Die Redaktion legt fest, welche Formulierungsmuster künftig dafür verwendet werden sollen. In der Prüfung werden schließlich die gefundenen und weitere Varianten der Formulierungsmuster erkannt, markiert, dann werden dem Autor die Formulierungsmuster zur Ersetzung vorgeschlagen.

3 Autorenunterstützung für japanische technische Dokumentation

Bei der Entwicklung einer Autorenunterstützung für japanische technische Dokumentation gab es zunächst drei grundlegende Unterschiede der japanischen Sprache zu den europäischen Sprachen zu beachten.

Erstens hat das Japanische drei Arten von Schriftzeichen: Hiragana, Katakana und Kanji. Das zugrundeliegende Konzept keines dieser Schriftzeichenarten ist direkt mit lateinischen Buchstaben vergleichbar. Hiragana und Katakana sind Silbenschriften, während Kanji Schriftzeichen sind, die semantische Einheiten ausdrücken. Kanji werden für Wörter gebraucht, die Bedeutung tragen, Hiragana für Funktionswörter und Katakana für nichtjapanische Wörter. Dazu kommt, dass auch lateinische Buchstaben und arabische Zahlen verwendet werden.

Zum Beispiel: ロビンが本を読んだ。*Dieser Satz enthält Hiragana, Katakana und Kanji:* ロビン *(Katakana),* が *(Hiragana),* 本*(Kanji),* を*(Hiragana),* 読*(Kanji),* んだ*(Hiragana),* 。*(Satzendepunkt).*

Die Identifizierung dieser Schriftzeichen ist entscheidend für die Prüfung von Rechtschreibung, Grammatik, Stil und Terminologie, denn Regeln referieren auf verschiedene Schriftzeichenarten: Katakana-Wörter sind meistens Fremdwörter oder Namen und daher – zusammen mit Kanji – gute Kandidaten für die Termextraktion. Rechtschreibung für Katakana und Hiragana ist dem Konzept der Rechtschreibung für das Englische und Deutsche recht ähnlich. Rechtschreibung für Kanji beinhaltet den Gebrauch eines Schriftzeichens im richtigen Kontext. Eine Stilregel überwacht die richtige Verteilung von Hiragana und Kanji, damit der Text für den Adressaten maximal verständlich ist.

Zweitens ist die Segmentierung des Textes bereits eine Herausforderung für Software, die sich mit der japanischen Sprache befasst: Geschriebenes Japanisch hat keine Leerzeichen zwischen den Wörtern und anderen Satzelementen, so dass Segmentierung substantiell komplexer als für die europäischen Sprachen ist.

Drittens hat die japanische Sprache andere morphologische Information als die europäischen Sprachen. Japanische Nomen haben keine Information über Numerus und Genus. Stattdessen flektieren Sie, um die soziale Beziehung zwischen den Interaktanten auszudrücken. Z. B. bedeutet das japanische Wort „*hon*" „*Buch*" oder „*Bücher*", je nach Kontext. Wenn aber das Buch jemandem gehört, den der Sprecher sozial höhergestellt einstuft, so bekommt es das Präfix „*go*".

Verben flektieren nach Tempus, Modus und wieder sozialer Beziehung, aber nicht nach Person, wie im Englischen oder Deutschen. Das Verb „*yomu*" wird zu „*yomimasu*", wenn der Adressat nicht in einer persönlichen Beziehung zum Sprecher steht.

3.1 Autorenunterstützung für japanische Rechtschreibung

Gute Rechtschreib-Prüfsysteme basieren auf zwei Strategien:

Die erste Strategie basiert auf einem umfangreichen Lexikon mit morphologischer Analyse. Wörter, die nicht in diesem Lexikon enthalten sind, sind potentielle Rechtschreibfehler. Diese Strategie garantiert einen hohen *Recall* – viele falsch geschriebene Wörter werden gefunden. Auf der anderen Seite ist die *Präzision* stark davon abhängig, wie gut das Lexikon zur Domäne passt und wie umfangreich es ist. Die Erkennung von Namen und die Anbindung an die Terminologie mit spezifischen Wörtern sind von großer Bedeutung, um nicht zu viele Falschalarme zu bekommen.

Die zweite Strategie ist die Definition von Fehlern. Dazu gehören eine Liste von potentiellen Fehlern und deren Korrekturen sowie eine Menge von Regeln, die Rechtschreibfehler definieren. Bei dieser Strategie ist die Präzision hoch, denn Fehler werden direkt kodiert. Der Recall ist abhängig davon, ob ausreichend Fehlerdefinitionen vorliegen.

Diese grundlegenden Strategien werden auch für die Prüfung des Japanischen miteinander kombiniert. So gibt es ein großes Lexikon mit morphologischer Information, das mit der benutzerspezifischen Terminologie verknüpft ist. Eine Regel sucht unbekannte Wörter und präsentiert sie dem Autor, wie das auch für die europäischen Sprachen geschieht. Allerdings wird der Effekt dieses Mechanismus vom japanischen Sprachsystem gemindert. Unbekannte Wörter können Schreibfehler von Katakana- oder Hiragana-Wörtern sein. Weil aber das Japanische viele Homonyme und Kurzwörter enthält, sind unbekannte Hiragana-Wörter selten. In den meisten Fällen findet sich ein Homonym im Lexikon. Unbekannte Katakana-Wörter sind oft Namen und daher eher Kandidaten für die Terminologie als Rechtschreibfehler. Kanji-Wörter sind selten unbekannt, weil sie vom Autor mit einem Textverarbeitungsprogramm eingefügt werden, das auch lexikalisch basiert ist.

Die Rechtschreibkorrektur des Japanischen basiert daher viel mehr auf der zweiten Strategie, den Regeln für Fehler. Dafür ist intensive Korpusarbeit notwendig. Die japanischen Rechtschreibfehler haben oft mit dem Schriftzeichensystem selbst zu tun, zum Beispiel der Gebrauch von Kanji, wenn Hiragana gebraucht werden sollten.

Anders als im Englischen und Deutschen spielen also in der japanischen Rechtschreibprüfung die Fehlerregeln eine große Rolle. Ein typischer Fehler im Japanischen ist der Gebrauch eines Kanji im falschen Kontext. Der Autor schreibt zunächst ein Wort in Hiragana und drückt eine Taste. Das Textverarbeitungssystem schlägt dem Autor eine Liste von möglichen Kanji für diesen Hiragana-String vor, aus dem der Autor unter Umständen ein falsches Kanji auswählt. Das Zeichen ist nicht falsch, aber im speziellen Kontext falsch eingesetzt. Z. B. stehen unterschiedliche Kanji für „atsui" zur Verfügung, die „heiß (Wetter)" oder „fett" bedeuten. Die einzige Möglichkeit, diese Fehler zu lokalisieren, ist, große Mengen von Daten zu analysieren und Kontexte zu isolieren, in denen der Autor die falschen Kanji gewählt hat.

3.2 Autorenunterstützung für japanische Grammatik

Die Entwicklung einer Autorenunterstützung für die japanische Grammatik basiert auf umfangreichen Datenanalysen. Bei der Entwicklung für das Englische hat sich gezeigt, dass nur auf diese Weise die Fehler gefunden werden, die im täglichen Schreiben tatsächlich auftreten.

Um eine Möglichkeit zu haben, große Mengen japanischer Daten effizient zu analysieren, nutzen wir das acrolinx Micro-Clustering. Dieser Mechanismus stellt Sätze mit ähnlichen Formulierungen zusammen. Die Ergebnisse zeigen auf, wo Formulierungsvarianten aufgrund von grammatischen Variationen bestehen. Z. B. zeigte das Micro-Clustering häufig auftretende Verwechslungen zwischen Verb-Endungen wie "reru – rareru", "seru – saseru" und "teru – teiru" in den technischen Dokumenten. So fanden wir u. a. die folgende Variante:

- juuden shite *iru* baai wa ...
- juuden shite *ru* baai wa ...

    (*Im Falle des Aufladens...*)

Geschriebene Sprache erfordert die Verwendung der ersten Variante.

Als Ergebnis stellten wir Grammatikregeln für die korrekte Verwendung von Verb-Endungen auf.

Andere Grammatikregeln beziehen sich z. B. auf Verbargumente. Zwar sind die meisten Verbargumente im Japanischen optional und können im jeweiligen Kontext weggelassen werden, es gibt jedoch einige wenige Ausnahmen.

3.3 Autorenunterstützung für japanischen Stil

Stilregeln für die japanische technische Dokumentation haben dieselben Ziele wie Stilregeln für englische oder deutsche technische Dokumentation: Konsistenz und Übersetzbarkeit. Für die Aufstellung japanischer Stilregeln haben wir verschiedene Informationsquellen:

- *Erfahrungen mit der Aufstellung englischer, deutscher und französischer Stilregeln.* Z.B. gilt für alle Sprachen, dass Umgangssprache vermieden werden soll. Welche umgangssprachlichen Ausdrücke jedoch im Japanischen vorkommen, das musste eine Datenanalyse klären.

- *Datenanalyse und Micro-Clustering.* Wie auch bei der Aufstellung von Grammatikregeln geben unterschiedliche Formulierungsmuster auch Hinweise für die Aufstellung von Stilregeln, die für die technische Dokumentation wirklich relevant sind.

- *Stilrichtlinien japanischer Firmen.* Japanische Firmen haben ebenso Redaktionshandbücher wie europäische oder amerikanische Firmen auch. Die sprachlichen Richtlinien dieser Redaktionshandbücher sind eine wichtige Informationsquelle dafür, was in technischen Redaktionen tatsächlich redigiert wird.

- *Informationen des JTCA.* Die Japan Technical Communicators Association (JTCA, http://www.jtca.org/) veranstaltet regelmäßige Symposien und gibt Informationsmaterial zu technischer Dokumentation.

3.4 Autorenunterstützung für die Terminologie japanischer technischer Dokumentation

Terminologieprüfung ist eine Prüfung auf konsistente Benennung. Die Datenbank für Terminologie ist multilingual und daher direkt für japanische Terminologie verwendbar. Terminologieprüfung prüft jedoch nicht nur Benennungen, die in der Datenbank als gesperrt markiert sind, sondern sucht auch automatisch nach inkonsistenten Varianten von Termen in der Datenbank.

Für das Japanische gibt es zwei Schlüsselfunktionen in der Termprüfung, die wiederum mit der Struktur der japanischen Schriftsprache zusammenhängen.

Erstens werden inkonsistent geschriebene Katakana identifiziert. Weil Katakana-Wörter Namen oder Fremdwörter sind, gibt es oft keinen Konsens über ihre Schreibweise. Z.B. kann ein japanischer Autor den Namen „Siegel" als "シゲル", "シーゲル", "ジゲル" oder "ジーゲル" schreiben. Welche Varianten in den Dokumentationen tatsächlich vorkommen, das stellt die Datenanalyse fest. In der Termbank entscheidet sich die technische Redaktion für eine bevorzugte Benennung. Varianten dieser Benennung findet die Termprüfung in künftigen Dokumenten.

Zweitens hilft die Terminologieprüfung bei der konsistenten Verwendung von Kanji. Im Japanischen kann jedes Kanji auch in der Silbenschrift Hiragana geschrieben werden, was zu einiger Variation in den Schreibweisen führen kann. Einerseits muss der technische Redakteur allzu unbekannte Kanji vermeiden, damit der Text auch für Nichtfachleute lesbar bleibt. Andererseits wirkt die zu häufige Verwendung von Hiragana unprofessionell auf den Leser.

Der richtige Weg, den Gebrauch von Kanji und Hiragana optimal an die Zielgruppe anzupassen, wird von einer Termdatenbank mit Termprüfung unterstützt.

4   Zusammenfassung

Übersetzungsgerechtes Schreiben mit Toolunterstützung ist ein wirkungsvolles Mittel, Übersetzungsprozesse und insbesondere maschinelle Übersetzung effizienter zu gestalten. Linguistisch basierte Autorenunterstützung für die technische Redaktion ist für Muttersprachler wie für Nichtmuttersprachler gleichfalls relevant, muss in ihrer Ausprägung jedoch auf die spezifischen Probleme der Sprachen eingehen. Besondere Herausforderungen ergeben sich dabei für Japanisch, unter dem Aspekt der japanischen Autoren, die Englisch schreiben, wie auch unter dem Aspekt der japanisch geschriebenen Texte.

Essentiell ist dabei, dass die linguistische Software auf Phänomenen und Problemen basiert, die in tatsächlich in Dokumenten vorkommen. Dazu kommt die Einbeziehung von Stilrichtlinien und Terminologien der Anwender, aber auch von internationalen Standards.

Die Vielfalt der deutschen Rechtssprachen aus italienischer Sicht – eine Herausforderung für Übersetzer und Dolmetscher

Fabio Proia

Libera Università degli Studi „San Pio V", Rom
Facoltà di Interpretariato e Traduzione

fabio.proia@luspio.it

Einleitung

Die Übersetzung juristischer Texte stellt für ÜbersetzerInnen und DolmetscherInnen, die im Folgenden einfachheitshalber als Translatoren bezeichnet werden, eine große Herausforderung dar. Eine korrekte Rechtsübersetzung setzt bekanntlich einerseits vertiefte sprachlich-übersetzerische Kompetenz voraus, fundierte juristische Ausbildung andererseits. Da Rechtstranslatoren allerdings nicht immer über eine solche Doppelqualifikation verfügen, sind sie verstärkt auf zuverlässige und hoch spezialisierte Hilfsmittel angewiesen. Das gilt umso mehr, wenn eine Sprache sozusagen in verschiedenen nationalen Rechtsordnungen „lebt", wie das bei der deutschen Sprache der Fall ist.

Dieser komplexe Sachverhalt erfordert je nach Zweck und Adressat der Übersetzung unterschiedliche translatorische Strategien und setzt den bewussten Rückgriff auf einschlägige Quellen, Nachschlagewerke und Datenbanken voraus. Rechts- und Übersetzungswissenschaftler beschäftigen sich zwar seit Jahren mit der Vielfalt der deutschen Rechtssprachen, doch eine diesbezügliche Evaluierung der Instrumente, die Translatoren in ihrer Berufspraxis behilflich sind, ist bis jetzt kaum erfolgt. Dieser Beitrag möchte nach einer Bestandaufnahme der deutschen Rechtssprachen am Beispiel der Sprachenkombination Italienisch-Deutsch einen ersten Einblick in die Rolle gewähren, die aktuell Lexikografie, Terminographie und juristische Fachverlage im Hinblick auf die translatorische Tätigkeit spielen.

1   Eine Sprache für viele Rechtsordnungen

Die Verwendung des Deutschen als Rechtssprache umfasst die Rechtsordnungen der Bundesrepublik Deutschland, der Republik Österreich, der Schweizerischen Eidgenossenschaft, des Fürstentums Liechtenstein, der italienischen Autonomen Provinz Bozen-Südtirol, der EU und der Deutschsprachigen Gemeinschaft des Königreichs Belgien. Wie mehrfach von der einschlägigen Literatur hervorgehoben wurde, ist die Landschaft der deutschen Rechtssprachen sehr vielfältig, wenn man das Bezugsrechtssystem berücksichtigt (Wiesmann 2004:117 ff.). Es lohnt sich, hier einen kurzen Überblick über die unterschiedliche Stellung der vorhandenen deutschen Rechtssprachen zu geben.

1.1 Einsprachige Rechtsordnungen

Neben lokal anerkannten Minderheitensprachen, auf die hier nicht eingegangen werden kann, ist Deutsch Amts- und Gerichtssprache auf nationaler Ebene in den folgenden Staaten:

- **Bundesrepublik Deutschland**

    Das bei weitem bevölkerungsreichste deutschsprachige Land ist die Bundesrepublik Deutschland. Ihre Amts- und Gerichtssprache ist Deutsch (s. § 23, VwVfg und § 184 GVG). Aus der Tatsache, dass die BRD jahrzehntelang auch das einzige deutschsprachige EU-Mitglied war, resultiert noch immer seine dominante Rolle in der Rechtssprache der EU.

- **Fürstentum Liechtenstein**

    Gemäß Art. 6 der Verfassung ist die deutsche Sprache die Staats- und Amtssprache Liechtensteins. Die Übernahme österreichischer und schweizerischer Rechtsvorschriften hat dazu geführt, dass Rechtsordnung und -terminologie des Fürstentums sehr stark von denen der beiden Nachbarstaaten beeinflusst sind (Jacometti 2008:154).

- **Republik Österreich**

    Deutsch ist die Muttersprache der Bevölkerungsmehrheit und daher laut Artikel 8, Abs.1 des Bundes-Verfassungsgesetzes Staatssprache der Republik Österreich.

1.2 Zweisprachige Rechtsordnungen

Bei zweisprachigen Rechtsordnungen ist der Terminologievergleich leicht durchführbar, zumal die unmittelbar vom Gesetzgeber selbst normierte Rechtsterminologie durch effektive terminologische Hilfsmittel zur Verfügung gestellt und verbindlich gemacht werden kann (s. 3.).

- **Autonome Provinz Bozen-Südtirol (Italien)**

    Die Einführung des Deutschen als Amts- und Gerichtssprache in der italienischen Autonomen Provinz Bozen-Südtirol wurde erstmals 1972 im Zweiten Autonomiestatut (Dekret des Präsidenten der Republik vom 31. August 1972, Nr.670, Art.100) festgelegt. Deutsch und Italienisch waren damals allerdings noch nicht völlig gleichgestellt, denn „in den Akten mit Gesetzeskraft und immer dann, wenn dieses Statut eine zweisprachige Fassung vorsieht, ist der italienische Wortlaut maßgebend" (Art.99). Dazu kam es erst Ende der 1980er Jahre, als Durchführungsbestimmungen den Gebrauch der deutschen Sprache im Verkehr des Bürgers mit der öffentlichen Verwaltung und in gerichtlichen Verfahren genauer regelten und als unabdingbare Pflicht vorsahen (Zanon 2008:52).

1.3 Mehrsprachige Rechtsordnungen

Bei mehrsprachigen Rechtsordnungen liegt ebenfalls die normierende Festlegung der Rechtsterminologie in der Regel nahe, was die Arbeit des Translators einerseits einengt, andererseits jedoch erleichtert (s. 3.).

* **Deutschsprachige Gemeinschaft des Königreichs Belgien**

    In Belgien zählt Deutsch neben Französisch und Niederländisch zu den Landessprachen, obwohl es nur für die an der Grenze zur BRD verbreitete Deutschsprachige Gemeinschaft (DG) von Bedeutung ist. Föderale Gesetze und Erlasse kommen im Rahmen einer offiziellen Koredaktion auf Französisch und Niederländisch zustande und gelten in beiden Sprachfassungen als gleichwertig. Nur Gesetzestexte, die die DG betreffen, werden ins Deutsche übersetzt und anschließend im Belgischen Staatsblatt veröffentlicht (Megale 2008:48f.).

* **Europäische Union**

    Die EU-deutsche Rechtssprache ist eine der 23 Amtssprachen, in denen die EU ihr eigenes supranationales Rechtssystem ausdrückt. Als die Bundesrepublik Deutschland das einzige deutschsprachige EU-Mitglied war, bestand jahrzehntelang bei der deutschen Formulierung von Rechtshandlungen keine Gefahr, dass bestimmte Begriffe in anderen deutschsprachigen Mitgliedstaaten unterschiedliche Bedeutungen haben könnten. Diese Situation änderte sich jedoch mit dem Beitritt Österreichs, sowie durch die Entstehung einer deutschen Rechtssprache in Belgien und Südtirol. Diese neue Lage veranlasste die EU, im Jahre 2000 Richtlinien für die redaktionelle Qualität der Gemeinschaftsrechtsakte festzulegen und im „Gemeinsamen Leitfaden des Europäischen Parlaments, des Rates und der Kommission für Personen, die in den Gemeinschaftsorganen an der Abfassung von Rechtstexten mitwirken" u.a. Folgendes zu bestimmen:

    „Ausdrücke und Wendungen – besonders juristische Begriffe, aber nicht nur diese – dürfen nicht zu stark an die Sprache oder das Rechtssystem des Verfassers gebunden sein [...]." (5.3.)

    „Bei juristischen Fachausdrücken sollte auf Begriffe verzichtet werden, die zu eng an die nationalen Rechtsordnungen gebunden sind." (5.3.2.)

    Das hat die Entstehung einer EU-deutschen Rechtssprache gefördert, die es möglichst eindeutig von anderen deutschen Rechtssprachen zu unterscheiden gilt.

* **Schweizerische Eidgenossenschaft**

    Nach der Bundesverfassung besitzt die Schweiz vier offizielle Landessprachen: Deutsch, Französisch, Italienisch und Rätoromanisch (Art.4). Amtssprachen sind jedoch nur die ersten drei, da das Rätoromanische nur „im Verkehr mit Personen rätoromanischer Sprache [...] Amtssprache des Bundes" ist (Art.70). Bundesgesetze und -verordnungen werden in den drei Amtssprachen veröffentlicht, und diese drei Fassungen sind in gleicher Weise verbindlich (Megale 2008:48).

1.4 Mögliche Übersetzungssituationen

Bei einer Übersetzung aus dem Italienischen ins Deutsche können sich drei unterschiedliche Übersetzungssituationen ergeben, auf die nachfolgend eingegangen wird.

- Die Translation erfolgt innerhalb ein und desselben nationalen Rechtssystems, d.h. Ausgangs- und Zieltext haben dieselbe Bezugsrechtordnung. Dies ist der Fall, wenn etwa ein italienischer Rechtstext für einen Südtiroler Adressaten ins Deutsche übersetzt wird. Die gleiche Konstellation ergibt sich, wenn die Translation die schweizerisch-italienische und die schweizerisch-deutsche Rechtssprache betrifft. In beiden Fällen, die eine lokale bzw. nationale Dimension kennzeichnen, kann der Translator auf eine normierte Rechtsterminologie zurückgreifen, da ihm einschlägige zweisprachige Rechtsquellen zur Verfügung stehen (s. 3.1., 3.2.).

- Die Translation erfolgt innerhalb ein und desselben supranationalen Rechtssystems, wie dies beim EU-Recht der Fall ist. Geht es um die Übersetzung eines Rechtstextes aus der EU-italienischen in die EU-deutsche Rechtssprache, so kann man von der vollständigen Äquivalenz jedes Zielterminus ausgehen, wenn man die vorhandenen terminologischen Vorgaben berücksichtigt und supranational ausgerichtete Hilfsmittel zu Rate zieht (s. 3.3.).

- Die Translation erfolgt zwischen zwei Rechtssystemen. Dies ist der häufigste Fall und kann theoretisch zu folgenden Kombinationen führen:

Italienische ▶	• bundesdeutsche • liechtensteinische • österreichische • schweizerisch-deutsche • belgisch-deutsche	Rechtssprache

Die Anfertigung solcher Übersetzungen weist oft einen hohen Schwierigkeitsgrad auf, da der Translator auf seine Kenntnisse allein angewiesen ist, um Ausgangs- und Zielrechtstermini jeweils in ihrem Äquivalenzverhältnis zu beurteilen.

2 Lexikographie

Gedruckte und elektronische zweisprachige Wörterbücher zählen zu den unentbehrlichen Hilfsmitteln eines Translators. Während konventionelle Wörterbücher seinen Bedürfnissen jedoch kaum gerecht werden, können zweisprachige Rechtswörterbücher ein nützliches Hilfsmittel sein, wenn sie einige Bedingungen erfüllen:

- sie müssen u.a. darauf hinweisen, dass die Übersetzungsvorschläge nicht immer völlige Äquivalente der Begriffe des Ausgangsrechtssystems sind;

- sie müssen anhand von Zitaten auf den Kontext der ausgangs- und zielsprachigen Termini hinweisen, damit der Benutzer über ihren Äquivalenzgrad entscheiden kann (De Groot 2008:7).

Im Hinblick auf den daraus resultierenden Vorteil für den Translator kann man die Rechtswörterbücher, die gegenwärtig für das Sprachenpaar IT-DE im Handel erhältlich und im Anhang 1 aufgelistet sind, auf die Probe stellen. Es sei betont, dass es dabei ausschließlich um den Nutzungswert des Nachschlagewerks geht.

Die meisten Werke schlagen für italienische Rechtstermini Entsprechungen vor, die jeweils in unterschiedlichen deutschsprachigen Rechtssystemen gelten. Solche rechtsordnungsübergreifende Wörterbücher halten sich nicht ans Prinzip des „Übersetzens von Rechtssystem nach Rechtssystem" (De Groot 2008:2, Sacco 2000:126). Im Gegensatz dazu engen rechtsordnungsspezifische Wörterbücher ihr Blickfeld bewusst ein, da sie die Rechtssprache eines bestimmten Rechtssystems als einzige Zielsprache wählen.

2.1 Rechtsordnungsübergreifende Wörterbücher

Einige Wörterbücher greifen auf zielsprachliche Äquivalente zurück, die aus verschiedenen deutschsprachigen Rechtsordnungen stammen. Dadurch versuchen sie, der breiten Palette der möglichen Kombinationen zwischen Rechtssystemen und Rechtssprachen gerecht zu werden, doch leider ist dieses Ziel zum Scheitern verurteilt, wenn sie ihrem Benutzer allzu dürftige Hinweise geben. In dieser Kategorie unterscheidet man zwei Untergruppen: ob ein Wörterbuch auf die Gesamtheit der Rechtszweige oder auf ein spezielles Gebiet ausgerichtet ist.

2.1.1 Allgemeine Hilfsmittel

Gegenwärtig sind für das Sprachenpaar IT-DE folgende Rechtswörterbücher im Handel erhältlich:

- Grundwortschatz der Rechtssprache (BL)
- Rechtsitalienisch. Deutsch-italienisches und italienisch-deutsches Rechtswörterbuch für jedermann (KÖ)
- Wörterbuch der Rechts- und Wirtschaftssprache (CB)
- Wörterbuch für Recht und Wirtschaft (TSHM)

Diese Werke werden von De Groot als Wörterlisten bezeichnet, da ihre Übersetzungsvorschläge mit keinen bzw. spärlichen Erläuterungen gegeben werden: dadurch stellen sie sich als völlige Äquivalente vor und erwecken beim Translator den falschen Eindruck einer gewissen Beliebigkeit (De Groot 2008:9). Für das italienische „permesso di soggiorno" werden beispielsweise jeweils folgende Termini vorgeschlagen:

BL	Aufenthaltsgenehmigung
CB	Aufenthaltserlaubnis, Aufenthaltsgenehmigung
KÖ	Aufenthaltserlaubnis, Aufenthaltsgenehmigung
TSHM	Aufenthaltsbewilligung; Aufenthaltserlaubnis; Aufenthaltsgenehmigung; Zuzugsgenehmigung

2.1.2 Themenspezifische Hilfsmittel

Unter den Wörterbüchern, die Termini aus mehreren Rechtssystemen als Übersetzungsvorschläge geben, sind auch welche, die sich auf einen speziellen Themenbereich beschränken. Sie wenden sich hauptsächlich an Juristen und Fachübersetzer, die vertiefte Kenntnisse in einem Rechtszweig haben oder haben wollen und veranlassen zu einer stärkeren sprachlichen bzw. übersetzerischen Spezialisierung. Es handelt sich dabei um Hilfsmittel, die den Vergleich zwischen den Rechtssystemen in Italien, Deutschland, Österreich und der Schweiz im jeweiligen Bereich unterstützen:

- Terminologisches Wörterbuch zum Schuldrecht
- Terminologisches Wörterbuch zum Gesellschaftsrecht
- Terminologisches Wörterbuch zum Vertragsrecht

2.2 Rechtsordnungsspezifische Wörterbücher

Einen wesentlich höheren Nutzungswert haben Wörterbücher, die die Rechtssprache eines bestimmten Rechtssystems als einzige Zielsprache wählen und sämtliche Termini, die zu anderen deutschsprachigen Rechtsordnungen gehören, außer Acht lassen. Musterbeispiele dieser Kategorie sind folgende terminologische Wörterbücher:

- TermLeg 1.0, Vertragsrecht: Ein terminologischer Vergleich
- TermLeg 2.0, Arbeitsrecht: Ein terminologischer Vergleich
- Terminologisches Wörterbuch zum Hochschulwesen Italien-Österreich

Diese Hilfsmittel haben das Ziel, im jeweiligen Rechtszweig inhaltliche, formale und sprachliche Unterschiede zwischen österreichischer und italienischer Rechtsordnung zu überwinden.

Besonders erwähnenswert sind zwei Wörterbücher, die in der für Juristen und Translatoren idealen Rahmenbedingung entstanden sind, wenn nämlich Ausgangs- und Zielsprache sich auf dasselbe Rechtssystem beziehen, wie dies in Südtirol der Fall ist:

- Terminologisches Wörterbuch zur Südtiroler Rechts- und Verwaltungssprache
- Terminologisches Wörterbuch zum Tätigkeitsbereich des Ministeriums für Inneres

Zu dem jeweiligen Themenbereich enthalten beide Werke Rechtstermini, die aus dem Festlegungs- bzw. Normierungsprozess der in Südtirol zu verwendenden Rechtssprache hervorgegangen sind.

3   Terminologiedatenbanken

Den herkömmlichen gedruckten Wörterbüchern gegenüber haben elektronische Terminologiedatenbanken Vorteile, die dem Benutzer bekanntlich einen flexibleren Datenzugriff ermöglichen. Der größte Vorteil dieser elektronischen Hilfsmittel ist jedoch ihr hoher Grad an Flexibilität und Dynamik: Im Recht sehr häufige Aktualisierungen sind viel einfacher und kostengünstiger zu handhaben als bei Druckwerken.

Im Folgenden sind die wichtigsten öffentlich zugänglichen Terminologiedatenbanken angeführt, die einem Translator hilfreich sein können.

3.1 Südtirol – BISTRO

www.eurac.edu/bistro.htm

Seit 1994 sind von der Paritätischen Terminologiekommission zusammen mit dem Institut für Fachkommunikation und Mehrsprachigkeit der EURAC Bozen über 50.000 Termini erarbeitet und ins kostenlose Online-Informationssystem BISTRO eingefügt worden. Von großem Nutzen erweisen sich die Abkürzungen, die auf das Bezugsrechtssystem hinweisen (Lyding/Ties 2008:76).

3.2 Schweiz – TERMDAT

www.termdat.ch

TERMDAT, die seit März 2009 im Internet frei zugängliche Datenbank der Schweizerischen Bundesverwaltung, enthält die schweizerische Rechts- und Verwaltungsterminologie in den vier Landessprachen und in Englisch. Die Termini stammen überwiegend aus schweizerischen Gesetzestexten.

3.3 EU – IATE

http://iate.europa.eu

Die Entwicklung der gemeinsamen Terminologiedatenbank der EU-Organe und -Einrichtungen begann Anfang 2000. Die zunächst für den internen Gebrauch bestimmte Datenbank ist seit Juni 2007 frei über das Internet zugänglich. Ende 2007 umfasste IATE etwa 1,5 Millionen Konzepte, 8,7 Millionen Benennungen und 0,5 Millionen Abkürzungen. Der Bestand umfasst die 23 EU-Amtssprachen (Riem 2008).

3.4 Österreich – Innsbrucker Termbank Online

http://webapp.uibk.ac.at/terminologie/trm_start.html

Diese Datenbank umfasste 2008 insgesamt über 25.000 zwei- oder mehrsprachige Einträge zu verschiedenen Themen, u.a. auch „Recht", in Deutsch und einer oder mehreren Fremdsprachen (EN, FR, IT, ES). Der Fachbereich „Recht" berücksichtigt in der Sprachenkombination IT>DE drei Rechtsgebiete: Kündigungsschutz, Gesellschafts- und Erbrecht.

3.5 Belgien

Für die belgisch-deutsche Rechtsterminologie kann man auf zwei dreisprachige Terminologiedatenbanken (DE, FR, NE) zurückgreifen:

- SEMAMDY

  www.ca.mdy.be/DE/semamdy.asp

  ist erstellt worden, um den Wortschatz zu vereinheitlichen, der bei der offiziellen Übersetzung von Gesetzes- und Verordnungstexten ins Deutsche verwendet wird.

- DEBETERM

  www.ca.mdy.be/DE/debeterm.asp

  ist aus den Arbeiten des Ausschusses für die deutsche Rechtsterminologie hervorgegangen.

4   Der Beitrag der juristischen Fachverlage

In den letzten beiden Jahrzehnten hat der Rechtsverkehr zwischen Italien und den deutschsprachigen Ländern kontinuierlich zugenommen und so zu einer Steigerung der Nachfrage nach juristischen Übersetzungen geführt. Das mag mit ein Grund gewesen sein, weshalb anerkannte juristische Fachverlage wie Beck und Athesia einige für die italienische Rechtsordnung grundlegende Quellen, wie etwa das Zivil-, Straf- und Handelsrecht, ins Deutsche übersetzt und veröffentlicht haben. Hierbei handelt es sich in der Regel um zweisprachige Ausgaben in gedruckter Form, die links den italienischen Originaltext und rechts die deutsche Übersetzung präsentieren.

Diese Texte werden in der praktischen Übersetzungsarbeit zu unentbehrlichen Hilfsmitteln, denn ihre Übersetzungsvorschläge sind, anders als bei den meisten Rechtswörterbüchern, im Kontext eingebettet und bieten somit Informationen über Rechtsgebiet, Kollokation und kontextuellen Gebrauch des zu übersetzenden Terminus.

Die deutschsprachigen Ausgaben der jeweiligen italienischen Gesetzbücher dürfen allerdings nicht unkritisch zu Rate gezogen werden, da sie im Normalfall für einen bestimmten Adressaten bzw. für den praktischen Gebrauch in einer Rechtsordnung gedacht sind. Da hier eine detaillierte Überprüfung sämtlicher Übersetzungen nicht möglich ist, sei diese Hinweisbenutzung am Beispiel des italienischen Codice Civile veranschaulicht (für Titel und Abkürzungen s. Anhang 2).

Das grundlegende Gesetzbuch für das italienische Privatrecht ist sowohl bei bundesdeutschen als auch bei Südtiroler Verlagen in deutscher Übersetzung erschienen. Der 1965 bei de Gruyter als einsprachige Ausgabe herausgegebenen deutschen Übersetzung (CCBE) folgte 2007 bei Beck die erste zweisprachige Ausgabe des Codice (CCPA), die vom Standpunkt des Translators moderner und viel nützlicher ist, da die synoptische Darstellung das Verständnis des Originaltextes erleichtert und zugleich einen Übersetzungsvorschlag bietet.

In Südtirol ist die Übersetzung des Codice Civile ins Deutsche unter ganz anderen Bedingungen und aus anderen Beweggründen zustande gekommen: Die Übersetzung italienischer Rechtsquellen war nämlich unabdingbare Voraussetzung für den Aufbau einer deutschen Rechtssprache sowie für die Umsetzung des Gleichstellungsprinzips zwischen der italienischen und der deutschen Sprache. Zweck der Übersetzung war also nicht die Erschließung des Ausgangstextes, sondern die Erstellung eines deutschen Gesetzestextes, der innerhalb des gleichen Rechtssystems (des italienischen) Gültigkeit erlangen sollte.

Die zweisprachige Ausgabe des Codice Civile erschien 1987 im Athesia Verlag und liegt seit 2004 in der vierten Auflage vor. Anregungen zur Verbesserung einiger syntaktischer und morphologischer Ungereimtheiten (Soffritti 1995), die teilweise auf eine zu starke Interferenz mit der Ausgangssprache zurückzuführen waren, wurden vor allem in der dritten Auflage (2000) aufgegriffen.

Von großem Nutzen, wenngleich in einer umgekehrten Perspektive, sind ferner die italienischen Übersetzungen von deutschsprachigen Gesetzbüchern. Sie fördern bei Translatoren den Rechtsvergleich und tragen entscheidend zu einer besseren Kenntnis der Ausgangs- und Zielrechtssysteme bei. Erwähnenswert sind hier die bei CEDAM bzw. Beck/Giuffrè veröffentlichten zweisprachigen Ausgaben des bundesdeutschen Strafgesetzbuchs (Il Codice Penale Tedesco, 2003) und des BGB (Il Codice Civile Tedesco, 2005).

Im Bereich der juristischen Translation ist der Nutzungswert eines zweisprachigen Hilfsmittels gleich welcher Art also von einer wesentlichen Voraussetzung abhängig: Werden die Ausgangs- und Zieltermini verschiedenen Rechtsordnungen entnommen, müssen dem Benutzer eindeutige Hinweise hinsichtlich ihrer Zugehörigkeit zu einem Rechtsbereich und einer Rechtsordnung gegeben werden. Wie oben ansatzweise aufgezeigt, geht das Streben nach Vollständigkeit oft auf Kosten der Genauigkeit und Zuverlässigkeit. Hilfsmittel wie Datenbanken und terminologische Wörterbücher, die für ein beschränktes Rechtgebiet erschöpfende Zusatzinformationen zu jedem Terminus anbieten, ermöglichen dagegen einen produktiven Rechtsvergleich und eine adäquate Translation aus einer Rechtssprache in die andere.

Anhang 1

Im Handel erhältliche zweisprachige Rechtswörterbücher (DE-IT)

- Grundwortschatz der Rechtssprache, DE-IT/IT-DE, von E. Brandt und V. Lori. Neuwied u.a.: Luchterhand, 1997
- Rechtsitalienisch. Deutsch-italienisches und italienisch-deutsches Rechtswörterbuch für jedermann, von G. Köbler. München: Vahlen, 2. Aufl., 2004
- Terminologisches Wörterbuch zum Gesellschaftsrecht. München: Beck, 2002
- Terminologisches Wörterbuch zum Hochschulwesen Italien-Österreich. Bozen: Raetia, 2000
- Terminologisches Wörterbuch zum Schuldrecht. München: Beck, 2001
- *Terminologisches Wörterbuch zum Tätigkeitsbereich des Ministeriums für Inneres, hg. von L. Lentini und F. Mayer. B*ozen: EURAC, 2001
- Terminologisches Wörterbuch zum Vertragsrecht. München: Beck, 2003
- *Terminologisches Wörterbuch zur Südtiroler Rechts- und Verwaltungssprache, hg. von F. Mayer. Bozen: EURAC, 1998*
- TermLeg 1.0 Vertragsrecht: Ein terminologischer Vergleich Italienisch – Deutsch, hg. von P. Sandrini. Innsbruck: Studia-Verlag (CD-ROM), 2001

- TermLeg 2.0 – Arbeitsrecht: Ein terminologischer Vergleich Italienisch – Deutsch, hg. von P. Sandrini. Innsbruck: Studia-Verlag (CD-ROM), 2002
- Wörterbuch der Rechts- und Wirtschaftssprache, von G. Conte u. H. Boss. München: Beck, 5. Aufl., Teil I IT-DE, 2001; 6. Aufl., Teil II DE-IT, 2003
- Wörterbuch für Recht und Wirtschaft, von H. Troike Strambaci und E.G. Helffrich Mariani. München: Beck, 2. Aufl., Teil I DE-IT, 1997; Teil II IT-DE, 1999

Anhang 2

Veröffentlichte Gesetzbücher in zweisprachiger Ausgabe (DE-IT)

	BRD	**Südtirol**
IT▶DE	CCBE	ITZP
	CCPA	ITKO
		ITST
		ITZG
		ITSP
		NGIZ
DE▶IT	CPVI	
	CCTP	

Legende:

CCBE	Italienisches Zivilgesetzbuch 1942: nebst Einführungs-, Durchführungs- und Übergangsvorschriften, von H.J. Becher. Berlin: de Gruyter, 2. Aufl., 1968
CCPA	Das italienische Zivilgesetzbuch, hg. von S. Patti. München: Beck, 2007
CCTP	Codice Civile Tedesco, a cura di S. Patti. Milano: Giuffrè, 2005
CPVI	Il Codice Penale Tedesco. Padova: CEDAM, 2. Aufl., 2003
ITKO	Das neue italienische Gesetz über Konkurs und andere Insolvenzverfahren. Bozen: Athesia, 2006
ITSP	Italienische Strafprozessordnung. Bozen: Athesia, 1991
ITST	Italienisches Strafgesetzbuch. Bozen: Athesia, 1995
ITZG	Italienisches Zivilgesetzbuch. Bozen: Athesia, 4. überarb. Aufl., 2004
ITZP	Italienische Zivilprozessordnung. Bozen: Athesia, 1996
NGIZ	Nebengesetze zum Italienischen Zivilgesetzbuch. Bozen: Athesia, 1993

Bibliographie

Monographien

Groot, G.-R. de/van Laer, C.J-P. (2008). The Quality of Legal Dictionaries: An Assessment, Maastricht Faculty of Law Working Paper 2008/6. Maastricht: UM

Megale, F. (2008). Teorie della traduzione giuridica. Fra diritto comparato e Translation Studies. Napoli: Editoriale Scientifica.

Wiesmann, E. (2004). Rechtsübersetzung und Hilfsmittel zur Translation. Tübingen: Narr.

Aufsätze in Sammelbänden

Jacometti, V. (2008). Il linguaggio giuridico tedesco, in: Pozzo, B./Timoteo, M. (eds.). Europa e linguaggi giuridici. Milano: Giuffrè, S. 123-184

Lyding, V./Ties, I. (2008). Computerlinguistische Anwendungen zur Nutzung normierter terminologischer Daten, in: Chiocchetti, E./Voltmer, L. (eds.). Normierung, Harmonisierung und Sprachplanung, Tagungsband. Bozen: EURAC, S. 75-95.

Riem, A. (2008). IATE. Die Terminologiedatenbank der EU, in: Mayer, F./Schmitz, K.-D. (eds.). Terminologie und Fachkommunikation. München/Köln: DTT, S. 93-100.

Soffritti, M. (1995). Il codice civile in versione originale e in traduzione tedesca: problemi di linguistica contrastiva e di analisi testuale, in: Arntz, R. (ed.). La traduzione. Nuovi approcci tra teoria e pratica. Napoli: Cuen, S. 109-135.

Zanon, H. (2008). Zur Problematik der Entwicklung einer deutschen Rechtssprache in Südtirol, in: Chiocchetti, E./Voltmer, L. (eds.). Normierung, Harmonisierung und Sprachplanung, Tagungsband. Bozen: EURAC, S. 49-59.

Aufsätze in Zeitschriften

Sacco, R. (2000): „Lingua e diritto", in: Ars Interpretandi, Annuario di ermeneutica giuridica, S. 117-134.

Workshops und Podiumsdiskussionen

Was ist Qualität – und wer soll sie bezahlen? Kriterien und Verfahren zur Qualitätssicherung im Übersetzungsgeschäft am Beispiel der Automobilindustrie.

Gabriele Sauberer

International Network for Terminology (TermNet)
Internationales Terminologienetz (TermNet)
Réseau international de terminologie (TermNet)

gsauberer@termnet.org

Workshop

1 Prozess- und Produktqualität

Im Übersetzungsgeschäft hat sich weitgehend die Unterscheidung in Prozess- und Produktqualität durchgesetzt. Ob die Qualität kreativer Leistungen überhaupt messbar sei, wird kaum mehr in Frage gestellt, sondern als gegeben anerkannt. Die Kriterien zur Bewertung von Qualität werden zunehmend in Form von internationalen Normen und Standards erarbeitet.

Die entsprechenden Verfahren zur Kontrolle und Sicherung der in diesen Normen als aktueller „Stand der Technik" beschriebenen Qualitätskriterien werden in Zertifizierungsschemen dargestellt.

Ob ein Dienstleister oder ein Produkt diese Anforderungen erfüllt, wird durch einen unabhängigen Dritten festgestellt. Die reine Absichts- oder Selbsterklärung des Dienstleisters ist immer problematisch, da sie zu unklaren rechtlichen Situationen führen kann (siehe unten, Produkthaftung und Abschnitt 3).

Als unabhängiger Dritter fungiert ein geprüfter, akkreditierter Zertifizierer, der dem Dienstleister nach erfolgreichem Audit ein Konformitäts- oder Prüfzertifikat ausstellt, das die Qualität der Übersetzung bzw. Übersetzungsdienstleistung bescheinigt. Im Beitrag von Peter Jonas und Klaus Kurre werden im vorliegenden Tagungsband die wesentlichen Aspekte internationaler Zertifizierung in der Sprachindustrie vorgestellt.

Versuchte man in früheren nationalen Normen, sowohl die Prozess- als auch die Produktqualität in einer einzigen Norm abzudecken, geht der Trend derzeit in Richtung separater Behandlung von Übersetzungsdienstleistungs- und Textqualität. In China sind die beiden entsprechenden nationalen Normen bereits vor einigen Jahren erschienen (siehe Abschnitte 2.1 und 2.2.). Auf Europäischer Normungsebene wird Übersetzen hingegen zurzeit vorrangig als Dienstleistung definiert und bewertet, besonders seit Einführung der Europäischen Norm EN 15038 im Jahr 2006, die auch als Basis des neuen kanadischen Standards diente (siehe unten, 2.1).

1.1 Automobilindustrie und Produkthaftung

Die Qualität der Übersetzung selbst, d.h. die Textqualität, wird in erster Linie nach dem Muster der Industrienorm SAE J2450 gemessen. Diese Qualitätsmetrik für Übersetzungen hat ihren Ursprung bekanntlich in der US-amerikanischen Automobilindustrie, mit Schwerpunkt auf Wartungs- und Reparaturinformationen. Zur Lokalisierung und Weiterentwicklung des Qualitätsmessverfahrens wurde auch eine europäische Taskforce gegründet. Informationen dazu sind auf der Webseite www.sae.org/standardsdev/j2450p1.htm veröffentlicht.

Die Bedienungsanleitung eines Fahrzeugs ist Teil des Produkts und somit zu einem wesentlichen Faktor der Produkthaftung geworden. Diese technische Dokumentation ist nicht mehr „Service-Literatur" im Sinn von Wartungs- und Reparaturinformationen von Technikern für Techniker, sondern geschrieben von technischen Redakteur/innen für die Autofahrer/innen als Endnutzer/innen.

Die Automobilindustrie eignet sich gut als Beispiel für Kriterien und Verfahren zur Qualitätssicherung im Übersetzungsgeschäft. Durch Auslagerungen, komplexe Prozesse und die Globalisierung bei der Herstellung von Fahrzeugen haben wir es mit gesteigertem Bedarf an Qualitätssicherung zu tun.

Umso mehr, als Produkthaftung einen besonderen Stellenwert auch und gerade in der Automobilbranche bekommen hat. Ende 2008 wurde die Mitschuld von Volvo an einem tödlichen Unfall in Frankreich bestätigt: Knapp zehn Jahre nach dem Unfall, bei dem zwei Schulkinder im Elsass ums Leben kamen, hat ein Berufungsgericht die Strafe für den schwedischen Autobauer Volvo bestätigt. Das Gericht in Colmar befand im Dezember 2008, dass Volvo – wie in erster Instanz festgelegt – wegen fahrlässiger Tötung und Körperverletzung eine Strafe von 200.000 Euro zahlen müsse. Zu dem Unfall kam es, weil die Bremsen eines Volvo 850 nicht funktionierten. Schwierigkeiten bei dem Bremssystem seien dem Hersteller bekannt gewesen, trotzdem habe man nicht reagiert.

Quellen:

- *www.123recht.net/Urteil-gegen-Volvo-wegen-toumldlichen-Unfalls-in-Frankreich-bestaumltigt-__a36077.html*

- *www.welt.de/motor/article1618021/Volvo_hat_Mitschuld_am_Tod_zweier_Kinder.html*

- *www.auto-motor-und-sport.de/news/frankreich-prozess-um-volvo-bremsen-729134.html*

Zudem wird in Fachkreisen häufig betont, dass Volvo in der Bedienungsanleitung und deren französischer Übersetzung nicht erwähnt hätte, wie man sich beim Ausfall eines

Bremskraftverstärkers verhalten muss. Diese Auslassung wäre von den französischen Richtern ebenfalls als Indiz für die Mitschuld von Volvo bewertet worden. Dafür ließ sich für den vorliegenden Beitrag jedoch keine Quellenangabe finden. Im Workshop werden die Fakten, Konsequenzen und Mutmaßungen im „Fall Volvo" mit Vertreter/innen der Übersetzungs- und Automobilbranchen diskutiert werden. Für die Verifizierung oder Falsifizierung dieser Einschätzung ist in jedem Fall die Einsicht in das vollständige französische Gerichtsurteil erforderlich.

In Deutschland ist seit dem 1. Januar 1990 im Produkthaftungsgesetz (ProdHaftG) die europäische Richtlinie 85/374/EWG umgesetzt und unmittelbar gültig als nationales Gesetz. § 1 Abs. 1 Satz 1 des ProdHaftG lautet: „Wird durch einen Fehler eines Produktes jemand getötet, sein Körper oder seine Gesundheit verletzt oder eine Sache beschädigt, so ist der Hersteller des Produktes verpflichtet, dem Geschädigten den daraus entstehenden Schaden zu ersetzen."

Ein Fehler liegt z.B. dann vor, wenn das Produkt nicht die Sicherheit bietet, mit der „auf Grund seiner Darbietung gerechnet werden kann". Diese „Darbietung" inkludiert nicht nur Kataloge, Produktbeschreibungen oder Verpackungen, sondern auch Gebrauchs- und Bedienungsanleitungen.

2   Welche Standards sind für die Übersetzungsbranche relevant?

Nicht nur die Automobilindustrie steht beim Übersetzen technischer Dokumentation vor neuen Herausforderungen. Es ist allerdings sicher kein Zufall, dass zwei herausragende Publikationen zur Qualitätssicherung im Übersetzungsgeschäft von Übersetzer/innen und Terminologen aus der Automobilbranche stammen:

Elvira Mertin hat mit ihrem Buch „Prozessorientiertes Qualitätsmanagement im Dienstleistungsbereich Übersetzen" einen wertvollen und umfassenden Beitrag zum Thema vorgelegt (Mertin 2006) und Jean-Marc Dalla-Zuanna verdankt die Branche ein aktuelles Terminologiewörterbuch Kraftfahrzeugtechnik auf Deutsch und Französisch, das zweifellos entscheidend zur Qualitätssicherung von Übersetzungen technischer Literatur und der Bedienungsanleitungen beiträgt (Dalla-Zuanna 2009).

Für beide Arten der Übersetzungsqualität fehlen internationalen ISO-Normen. Für die Bestimmung der Prozessqualität liegen Normen und Richtlinien einzelner Länder und Regionen vor. Im Bereich der Textqualität gehen die Initiativen zur Qualitätskontrolle hingegen vor allem von einzelnen Industrien aus, siehe 2.2.

2.1   Qualität der Prozesse: Übersetzen als Dienstleistung

Hier ist unter anderem interessant, dass in der europäischen und kanadischen Norm von Anfang an die Zertifizierung von Übersetzungsdienstleistern angestrebt wurde (siehe EN 15038:2006 (D), Einleitung, Seite 4: „Basierend auf dieser Norm sind Konformitätsbewertung und Zertifizierung vorgesehen."), während dies in der chinesische Norm und in der US-amerikanischen Richtlinie offengelassen wird.

International gesehen sind folgende Standards für Übersetzungsdienstleistungen und -dienstleister relevant:

- Europa: Translation services – service requirements (EN 15038:2006);
- Canada: Translation Services (CAN/CGSB-131.10-2008), weitgehend basierend auf der Europäischen Norm EN 15038;
- China: Specification for translation service – Part 1: Translation 翻译服务规范 第1部分:笔译 (GB/T 19363.1-2003);
- USA: Standard Guide for Quality Assurance in Translation (ASTM F2575-06);

Für die Automobilindustrie sind bei der Kontrolle und Sicherung der Prozessqualität neben der ISO 9000-Familie vor allem die EN 15038 relevant. Das wichtigste Verfahren zur Qualitätsevaluierung wird von der SAE J 2450 abgeleitet, siehe 2.2.

Die Europäische Norm EN 15038:2006 „Übersetzungs-Dienstleistungen – Dienstleistungsanforderungen" folgt in hohem Maße der Logik der ISO 9001:2008 „Qualitätsmanagementsysteme – Anforderungen".

Das bedeutet unter anderem, dass nicht wenige Aspekte der allgemeinen Qualitätsmanagement-Anforderungen für die Übersetzungsbranche adaptiert und konkretisiert werden. Auf den Punkt gebracht sagt die ISO 9001 dem Dienstleister, dass er oder sie ein – allgemeines – System für Qualitätsmanagement implementieren soll, während die EN 15038 sagt, was – konkret – er oder sie für die Qualitätssicherung der Übersetzungsdienstleistung tun soll. Und zwar entsprechend der Größe des Unternehmens, das auch ein branchentypisches Einpersonenunternehmen (EPU) sein kann.

Die wichtigsten Gemeinsamkeiten und Unterschiede zwischen EN 15038 und ISO 9001 sind in den folgenden beiden Illustrationen zusammengefasst, die aus der LICS®-EN 15038-Auditorenausbildung stammen:

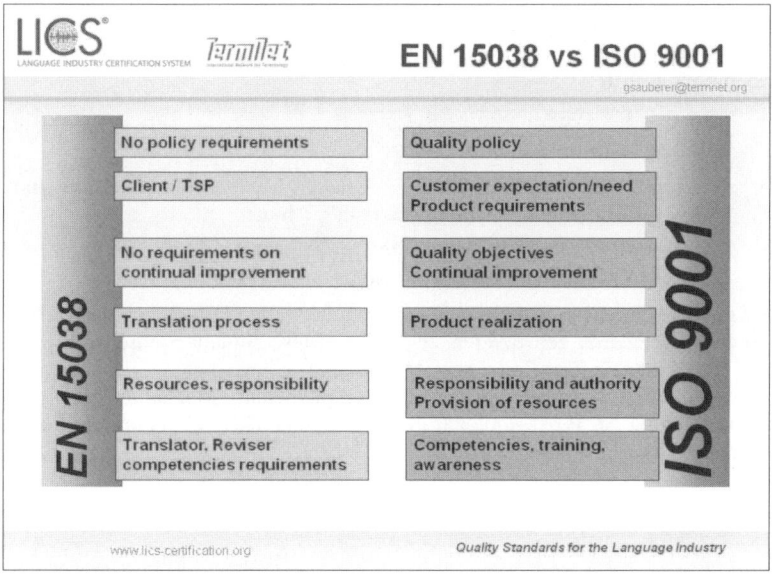

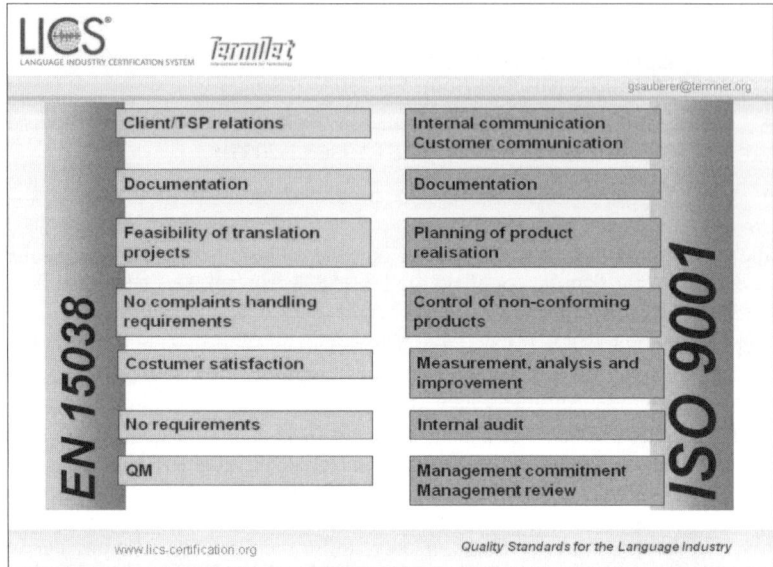

In Indien sind die marktführenden Übersetzungsdienstleister häufig ISO 9001-zertifiziert, was die Auditierung und Zertifizierung nach EN 15038 erleichtert.

2.2 Qualität des Textes: Die Übersetzung als Produkt

Wie erwähnt geht hier die Qualitätskontrolle und Qualitätssicherung vor allem von einzelnen Industrien aus, mit Ausnahme der chinesischen Norm, die zwei Jahre nach Erscheinen der „Specification for translation service" Anforderungen an die Qualität des Zieltextes auflistet.

- China: GB/T 19682-2005 – 翻译服务译文质量要求 – Target text quality requirements for translation services
- Automobilindustrie: SAE-J2450 – Quality Metric of Automotive Industry (www.sae.org/technicalcommittees/j2450p1.htm)
- Lokalisierungsindustrie: LISA QA model: **Multiple localization quality metrics** (www.lisa.org/LISA-QA-Model-3-1.124.0.html).

Bisher gab es keine Möglichkeit, sich durch unabhängige Dritte nach diesen Normen und Industriestandards zertifizieren zu lassen. Diese Situation wird sich in Kürze ändern, internationale Zertifizierungsschemen sind in Ausarbeitung. Die Bestimmung der Textqualität ist unseres Erachtens eine komplementäre Maßnahme zur Erfassung und Verbesserung der Prozessqualität im Allgemeinen (ISO 9001) und im Speziellen (z.B. EN 15038).

3 Wer bezahlt für Übersetzungsqualität?

Wie bisher werden – und sollen – auch in Zukunft alle Anspruchsgruppen der Übersetzungsbranche Ihren Beitrag zur Qualitätssicherung leisten:

Im Rahmen technischer Komitees werden die entsprechenden Normen erarbeitet, und zwar von Branchenvertreter/innen gemeinsam mit Arbeitnehmer- und Arbeitgebervertretern, Konsumentenschutz, Nutzern, NPOs/NGOs und der Öffentlichkeit.

Kunden sind auch und gerade in Krisenzeiten bereit, für Qualität zu bezahlen, und Dienstleister werden auch weiterhin in die Zertifizierung durch anerkannte Zertifizierer investieren und ihre Produkte und Prozesse verbessern.

Irreführend und problematisch erscheint uns hingegen die reine Selbsterklärung, als Übersetzungsdienstleister nach der EN 15038 zu arbeiten. Daran ändert auch eine kostenpflichtige Registrierung bei bekannten Organisationen wie z.b. DIN CERTCO nichts, denn „Es handelt sich bei der Registrierung um eine eigenverantwortlich abgegebene Konformitätserklärung des Übersetzers mit den Anforderungen der Europäischen Norm."

Quelle:
www.dincertco.de/de/produkte_und_leistungen/registrierungen/uebersetzungsdienstle ister/index.html

Sowohl die Übersetzungsdienstleister selbst als auch deren Kunden könnten hier irrtümlich glauben, es liege echte Zertifizierung vor. Bei Rechtsstreitigkeiten und Produkthaftungsfällen kann es hier sehr leicht für alle Parteien zu bösen Überraschungen in juristisch-finanzieller Hinsicht kommen.

Die Kosten für eine echte EN 15038-Zertifizierung sind recht unterschiedlich. International gesehen nimmt die Zertifizierungsplattform LICS® auch in preislicher Hinsicht eine kunden- und branchenorientierte Marktführerschaft ein. Nähere Informationen, Ansprechpartner und ein Register von EN 15038-zertifizierten Übersetzungsdienstleistern weltweit finden sich unter www.lics-certification.org.

3.1 Die Inhalte des interaktiven Workshops zu Thema 3: Neue Herausforderungen beim Übersetzen

Der Workshop trägt denselben Titel wie der vorliegende Beitrag: Was ist Qualität – und wer soll sie bezahlen? Kriterien und Verfahren zur Qualitätssicherung im Übersetzungsgeschäft am Beispiel der Automobilindustrie.

Interaktiv und in Form von moderierten Diskussionen setzt sich der Workshop mit den Erfahrungen und Fallbeispielen der Teilnehmenden auseinander. In erster Linie werden folgenden Fragen behandelt:

Wie kann Qualität von Übersetzungen gewährleistet und kontrolliert werden? Was können Auftraggeber und Übersetzungsdienstleister dazu beitragen – und wer soll dafür wie viel bezahlen? Welche Kriterien und Verfahren zur Qualitätssicherung gibt es und welche kommen wo zur Anwendung?

Produkthaftung und ihre juristisch-finanziellen Folgen werden als „heißes Thema" auch in Europa und besonders für die Automobilindustrie diskutiert: Die Verantwortung für Fehler und Auslassungen in übersetzten technischen und anwendergerichteten Dokumenten kann nicht ausgelagert werden, sie liegt bei den Herstellern. tätskontrolle ist daher das Gebot der Stunde. Auch und gerade bei stagnierenden Absatzzahlen und einbrechenden Märkten in der Automobilindustrie.

Die Zusammenfassung der Ergebnisse des Workshops wird auf der Webseite von TermNet unter www.termnet.org/deutsch/veranstaltungen/index.php veröffentlicht.

Bibliographie

Dalla-Zuanna, J.-M. (2009). Fachwörterbuch Kraftfahrzeugtechnik Französisch – Dictionnaire de la technique automobile. Deutsch-Französisch/Französisch-Deutsch; Allemand-Français, Français-Allemand. Langenscheidt

Jonas, P. (2008). Can translation services be certified? – The LICS® approach on certification of the EN 15038, in: Proceedings of the FIT 2008 World Congress, Shanghai, China

Mertin, E. (2006). Prozessorientiertes Qualitätsmanagement im Dienstleistungsbereich Übersetzen. Frankfurt: Peter Lang

Working according to the cross-check principle („Vier-Augen-Prinzip"): What does it mean and how does it work?

Dr. phil. Karen Leube

Freelance translator and translator trainer;
School of Applied Linguistics and Cultural Studies
(Fachbereich Angewandte Sprach- und Kulturwissenschaft [FASK]
at the University of Mainz in Germersheim

kleube@uni-mainz.de

Workshop

Since the introduction of DIN EN 15038, numerous discussions have taken place regarding the technical and legal side of the quality assurance process. When it comes to the actual revision work, however, expectations are not always clear.

This workshop aims to find out what the translation market expects of revisors, targeting all members of the revision process, from members of company translation departments, translation agency owners and staff, to the freelancers in the field who do the revision work, as well as seasoned revisor-translator teams. Does revision work call for simply ensuring correctness and completeness, or does it involve in-depth editing and stylistic reworking? Is the ideal revisor a fellow translator or an expert in the subject area? Another native speaker of the target language or rather a native speaker of the source language? Is it important for the revisor to live in the country in which the text will be used? How much work should the revision entail? When does revision stop and retranslating begin?

The workshop will begin with a look at typical revision scenarios. In the second part of the session, participants will be asked to do an actual revision job (German-English or English-German) in accordance with a specific brief.

Das Beste aus den Normen

Kornelia Meyer

Dolmetscherin und Übersetzerin, DGQ-Auditorin,
Geschäftsführerin der MeDok GmbH Technische
Dokumentation, Mitglied im BDÜ und bei der DGQ

kornelia.meyer@medok.de

Workshop

Im professionellen Übersetzungsbereich entscheiden über die Qualität einer Übersetzung die Bedingungen, unter denen sie entsteht, d.h. wie viel Zeit und Geld hat der Übersetzer zur Verfügung und nach welchen Kriterien wurde der Übersetzer ausgesucht. Diese Bedingungen gilt es, festzuhalten, d.h. zu dokumentieren. Die Mittel der Wahl zu diesem Zweck sind Qualitätsnormen.

Immer und für alle Bereiche trifft die DIN EN ISO 9001 zu, jedoch hält die Mehrheit der Einzelübersetzer die kurz ISO genannte Norm für überdimensioniert und nicht passend.

Aus diesem Grund – und damit die Übersetzer auch eine Norm haben, auf die sie sich beziehen können – wurden die nationalen Normen DIN 2345 in Deutschland, und ON 1200 in Österreich geschaffen, nachfolgend kurz die DIN genannt. Zum ersten Mal wurden die Dinge, um die es beim Übersetzungsauftrag geht, benannt und eine Standardlösung vorgeschlagen, wobei immer die Vereinbarung mit dem Kunden Vorrang hatte.

Seither hat sich ein Bewusstsein eingestellt, dass Übersetzungsarbeit mehr ist als nur „Tippen Sie das mal in Englisch".

Diese beiden nationalen Normen sind abgelöst worden von einer europäischen Variante, der DIN EN 15038, nachfolgend kurz EN genannt.

Eigentlich als Weiterentwicklung gedacht, geht die EN einen Sonderweg, d.h. in die aufeinander aufbauenden Normen DIN und ISO passt die EN nicht hinein, und zwar aus folgendem Grund:

In der EN ist nur ein einziger Prozess für Übersetzungsdienstleistungen beschrieben, der zudem nicht von einem Freiberufler alleine durchgeführt werden kann. Es wird suggeriert, dass nur ein Büro, das mehrere Übersetzer beschäftigt, die Norm einhalten und damit qualitätsgesicherte Übersetzungen liefern könne. Zudem sind Zuständigkeit und Verantwortung nicht klar geregelt, was eine unabdingbare Voraussetzung z.B. in der ISO darstellt, um Qualität zu sichern.

Die Verbände, viele Übersetzungsagenturen und Einzelübersetzer interpretieren daher die Norm schon fast beliebig dahingehend, dass das sogenannte Vier-Augen-Prinzip, das in der Norm als Muss-Bestimmung enthalten ist, nur bei ausdrücklicher Vereinbarung mit dem Kunden durchgeführt werden müsse. Die Konformitätserklärung in Form einer Registrierung bei DIN CERTCO würde nur bedeuten, dass man in der Lage wäre, nach Norm zu arbeiten, jedoch nicht immer danach arbeiten müsse. Die DIN CERTCO-Registrierung bedeutet aber vielmehr, dass man immer nach Norm arbeitet und, wenn man es nicht tut, den Kunden darauf hinweisen muss.

Das Durcheinander ist groß, und aus diesem Grund sollte die Übersetzerbranche, auch die Einzelübersetzer, bevorzugt die ISO anwenden. Diese Norm ist keineswegs nicht geeignet für Einzelübersetzer, auch wenn es nur eine Zertifizierung gibt und keine Registrierung.

Der große Unterschied ist, dass bei einer Zertifizierung (egal ob nach ISO oder nach der EN) ein Handbuch hergestellt werden muss. Bei der Registrierung bei DIN CERTCO wird dieses nicht benötigt.

Die Frage ist nicht: Was muss ich alles tun, um die Forderungen der ISO zu erfüllen? Sondern: Was tue ich jetzt schon, da ich mein Geschäft professionell betreibe, was die Forderungen der ISO erfüllt? Wer sich damit befasst, erkennt, dass er zu mindestens genauso viel Forderungen der ISO wie der EN erfüllt.

Ein großer Vorteil ist bei der ISO dann noch, dass die Prozesse, und zwar alle vorkommenden, in die Norm passen. D.h. je nach Kundenwunsch, Anforderungen und Bedingungen sind alle Übersetzungsaufgaben abgedeckt, und kein Übersetzer muss sich sagen lassen, er würde es halt nicht schaffen, die EN anzuwenden, wenn er es anders macht, als dort beschrieben.

Ein weiterer Vorteil ist die Anerkennung der ISO in Industrie und Wirtschaft. Sowohl die nationalen Normen als auch die EN sind zwar vordergründig auf die Bedürfnisse der Übersetzer zugeschnitten, der Bekanntheitsgrad jedoch und die Wirkung auf die Auftraggeber ist bei den Übersetzernormen auf die Branchen-Insider beschränkt.

Bei einer Zertifizierung nach ISO 9001, die auch für Einzelübersetzer erschwinglich ist, profitiert der Zertifizierte von der mittlerweile jahrzehntelangen Erfolgsgeschichte dieser Norm. Es bleibt zu bezweifeln, dass die EN etwas Vergleichbares vor sich hat.

Für viele Einzelübersetzer kommt eine Zertifizierung nicht in Frage: bestenfalls eine Registrierung bei DIN CERTCO scheint vom Aufwand her vertretbar. Das könnte sich jedoch als Falle herausstellen, denn bei der Registrierung erklärt man, dass man die EN IMMER anwendet und bei Nichtanwendung den Auftraggeber informieren muss. Bisher hat sich nur noch kein Auftraggeber betrogen gefühlt und den Dienstleister belangt, der trotz Konformitätserklärung die Bestimmungen der Norm nicht eingehalten hat. Eine wettbewerbsrechtliche Verfolgung durch einen Branchenkollegen ist schwierig, wenn man keine „Täuschung" der Kunden nachweisen kann.

Aus diesem Grund ist eine Zertifizierung nach der EN eleganter, denn man kann zum einen den Geltungsbereich definieren und damit einschränken, wie es die bisher nach der EN zertifizierten Unternehmen getan haben (siehe www.tuev-sued.de/industrie_konsumprodukte/zertifikatsdatenbank). Die meisten bestimmen den „Redaktionsprozess Übersetzungen" (8) zum Gegenstand der Zertifizierung oder „Übersetzungsdienstleistung" mit einer genauen Angabe der betroffenen Fachgebiete (4).

Was den Umkehrschluss zulässt: Nur ein bestimmter Prozess, der noch dazu die Redaktion betrifft, ist zertifiziert, konform mit der EN zu sein. Ebenso unterliegen nicht genannte Fachgebiete nicht der Überwachung. Das bedeutet, die zertifizierten Unternehmen machen entweder mehr als nur die Übersetzung oder bearbeiten nur bestimmte Übersetzungen gemäß Norm.

Wohingegen ein Einzelübersetzer, der bei DIN CERTCO registriert ist und dort in der Liste steht, erklärt, dass er IMMER ALLE Übersetzungen normkonform herstellt (siehe: www.dincertco.de/de/produkte_und_leistungen/registrierungen/uebersetzungsdienstleister/din_registrierte_uebersetzungsdienstleister.html)

Der Ausweg aus dem Dilemma: Eine Registrierung bei DIN CERTCO nach der EN ist nicht anzuraten. Wenn jedoch eine Zertifizierung nicht in Frage kommt, dann ist es sinnvoll, eine Eigenerklärung nach ISO 9001 abzugeben. Denn alle Kollegen, die gut mit der „alten" DIN 2345 zurechtkamen, haben, was die Prozesse angeht, den halben Weg zur ISO 9001 bereits zurückgelegt. Wohingegen die Anwendung der EN eine Änderung der Prozesse darstellt.

Eine Weiterentwicklung besteht darin, sinnvoll die eigene Arbeitsweise zu dokumentieren und dabei die ISO 9001 als Referenz heranzuziehen, so dass auf diese Weise früher oder später das erforderliche Handbuch für die Zertifizierung von ganz alleine entsteht und die Zertifizierung im Bedarfsfall von heute auf morgen durchgeführt werden kann.

Bei der Beschreibung und Festlegung der Prozesse im eigenen Geschäftsbetrieb ist es in jedem Fall angeraten, sich an den speziell für die Branche ausgearbeiteten Standard, den die EN darstellt, „anzulehnen". Denn zweifellos gibt es eine Reihe von Regelungen und Bestimmungen, die für die Arbeit des Übersetzers sehr hilfreich sind.

Das ist z.B. der Prozessansatz bei der DIN EN ISO 9001 und das Management von Übersetzungsprojekten bei der DIN EN 15038. Dabei schadet es nicht, nach wie vor sinnvolle Regelungen aus den nicht mehr gültigen nationalen Normen zu kennen, z.B. die Einbeziehung der Auftraggeber bei der DIN 2345 und die Differenzierung der Transferleistungen bei der ÖNorm 1200.

Dabei gilt wieder: Alles was die „Best Practices" ausmacht, bedeutet eine Erfüllung der Forderungen der ISO.

Im Workshop werden die Dokumente vorgestellt, die die Prozesse beschreiben und die für ein Handbuch erforderlich sind. Ebenso gibt es einen Überblick über die Kosten für Registrierung, Zertifizierung nach DIN EN 15038 und DIN EN ISO 9001.

IATE – Die Terminologiedatenbank der EU

Andreas Riem

Dipl.-Übersetzer, Europäische Kommission, Übersetzungsdienst, Brüssel, Belgien

Andreas.Riem@ec.europa.eu

Workshop

1 IATE Public

Die Terminologiedatenbank IATE ist seit 2007 unter http://iate.europa.eu kostenfrei und ohne Passwort über das Internet abrufbar. Ursprünglich war die Datenbank für den internen Gebrauch durch die Mitarbeiter der EU-Institutionen entwickelt worden. Ab 2006 wurde eine besondere Schnittstelle für externe Nutzer geschaffen. Die öffentlich zugängliche Version heißt *IATE Public*. Der Inhalt von *IATE Public* deckt sich fast völlig mit demjenigen der internen Version, lediglich die nicht validierten Einträge erscheinen nicht.

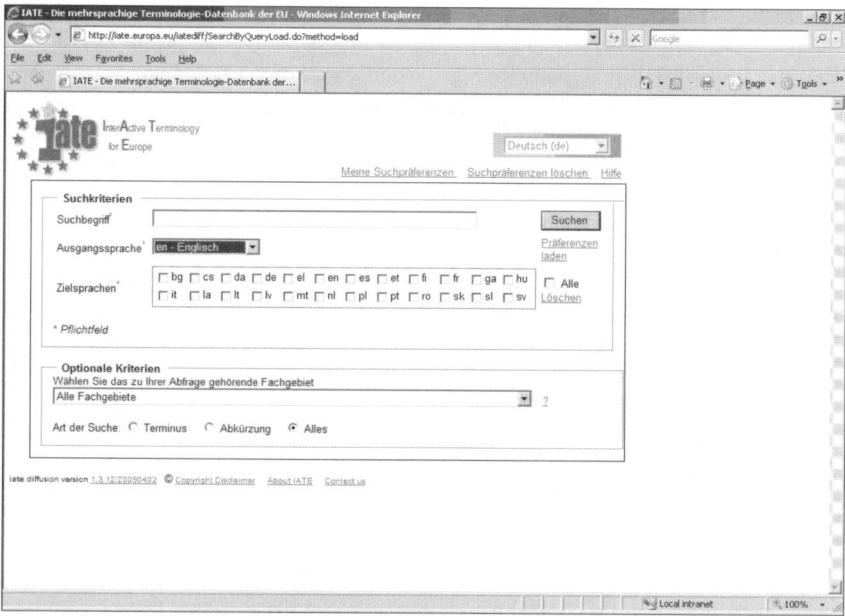

Abb. 1: Die Einstiegsseite von IATE Public

2 Entstehung

IATE steht für *Inter-Active Terminology for Europe* und ist die gemeinsame Terminologiedatenbank der Organe und Einrichtungen der Europäischen Union. IATE ist das Ergebnis einer Fusion aller damals bestehenden Datenbanken, also von *Eurodicautom* (Kommission), *TIS* (Rat), *Euterpe* (Europäisches Parlament), *EUROTERMS* (Übersetzungszentrum), *CDTERM* (Rechnungshof) sowie des Bestandes der übrigen Partner des IATE-Projekts, bei der allerdings jede Institution Eigentümerin ihrer eigenen Einträge mit allen damit verbundenen Rechten bleibt. Während früher die verschiedenen Übersetzungsdienste ihre Terminologie unabhängig voneinander verwalteten, was zu beträchtlicher Doppelarbeit und zu zahlreichen terminologischen Divergenzen führte, macht die Struktur von IATE eine zentrale Koordinierung der Terminologiearbeit erforderlich. Die dringendste praktische Aufgabe ist die Konsolidierung des Bestandes, denn der zentrale Zugriff auf die Terminologiebestände aller Organe und Einrichtungen der EU hatte einen starken Anstieg der Zahl der Mehrfacheinträge zur Folge. Wenn man bedenkt, dass schon die getrennten Datenbanken nicht wenige Dubletten enthielten, ist es nicht verwunderlich, dass sich dieses Problem infolge der Fusion noch verschärft hat, insbesondere für die dienstälteren Amtssprachen. Dieses Problem erfordert die gemeinsame Anstrengung aller am IATE-Projekt Beteiligten und werden auf zwei Ebenen angegangen, intern und interinstitutionell. Die neueren Sprachen (am stärksten betroffen sind die seit 2004 hinzugekommenen Amtssprachen) sehen sich mit dem umgekehrten Problem konfrontiert, da sie nur über einen sehr begrenzten terminologischen Grundstock verfügen und erst wenig Gelegenheit hatten, EU-spezifische Benennungen zu prägen, und folglich zahlreiche Äquivalenzlücken aufweisen.

3 Aktueller Bestand

Zurzeit umfasst IATE etwa

- 1,5 Millionen Begriffe
- 8,4 Millionen Benennungen (ohne Abkürzungen)
- 0,5 Millionen Abkürzungen

Der Bestand deckt die 23 EU-Amtssprachen sowie Latein und einige weitere Sprachen ab:

Sprache	Anzahl Termini	Sprache	Anzahl Termini
BG	8.630	LA	69.222
CS	24.878	LT	34.610
DA	605.108	LV	16.698
DE	1.197.527	MT	8.024
EL	519.393	NL	699.171
EN	1.478.738	PL	31.442

Sprache	Anzahl Termini	Sprache	Anzahl Termini
ES	624.973	PT	529.540
ET	20.311	RO	9.523
FI	323.913	SK	24.840
FR	1.507.108	SL	21.558
GA	9.856	SV	313.128
HU	30.009	Sonstige	24.364
IT	826.985		

Der weitaus größte Teil der Daten (rund 80%) gehört der Kommission. Aus den Zahlen wird ersichtlich, dass die Einträge sehr ungleich auf die verschiedenen Sprachen verteilt sind. Den höchsten Bestand weisen die drei Verfahrenssprachen (Englisch, Französisch, Deutsch) auf, die Präsenz der übrigen Sprachen hängt hauptsächlich von der Dauer der EU-Mitgliedschaft des betreffenden Landes ab. Momentan liegt sogar Latein noch weit vor den Sprachen der Länder, die ab 2004 beigetreten sind.

4 Datenstruktur

Eine IATE-Karteikarte ist in drei Ebenen unterteilt:

Die oberste Ebene, der sog. Language Independent Level (LIL), enthält alle sprachunabhängigen Informationen, d. h. diejenigen Informationen, die sich auf das Konzept als Ganzes beziehen. Hierzu zählen insbesondere die Nummer der Karteikarte, der Sachgebietscode, die Kollektion, zu der die Karteikarte gehört, und das Land, in dem das Konzept seinen Ursprung hat. Eventuelle Querverweise auf andere Karteikarten haben hier ebenso ihren Platz wie das Datum des Eintrags und der Name des Autors. Dieser hat beim Anlegen einer Karteikarte unter anderem die sog. *problem language* zu wählen: Damit ist die Sprache gemeint, die ihn zu diesem Eintrag veranlasst hat, also in der Regel die Sprache des Ausgangsterminus. Ferner besteht schon auf dieser Ebene die Möglichkeit, in freien Textfeldern Anmerkungen hinzuzufügen.

Die mittlere Ebene ist die Sprachebene (Language Level (LL)). Auf ihr finden sich diejenigen Informationen, die zur Beschreibung eines Begriffs in einer bestimmten Sprache erforderlich sind, und zwar die Definition mit Quellenangabe und eventuellen Anmerkungen. Falls keine Definition vorhanden ist, kann diese Ebene beim Anlegen eines Eintrags komplett übersprungen werden. Bei der Abfrage erscheinen die betreffenden Felder in diesem Fall leer.

Auf der unteren Ebene (Term Level (TL)) findet man schließlich die nach Sprachen geordneten Benennungen neben Quellenangaben, Anmerkungen und Kontextbeispielen. Die Benennungen können in verschiedene Kategorien (einfache Termini, Abkürzungen, Phrasen, Formeln und Kurzbezeichnungen) eingeteilt werden. Ferner besteht die Möglichkeit der Kennzeichnung als Vorzugsbenennung, zulässige, veraltete und missbilligte Benennung. Weitere Abstufungsmöglichkeiten bieten der Zuverlässigkeitscode und der Vertraulichkeitscode. Zahlreiche Felder sind für pragmatische

Zusatzinformationen vorgesehen, welche die Stilebene, den regionalen Gebrauch und die Grammatik betreffen. Orthographische Varianten können in einem Extrafeld („Lookup Forms') untergebracht werden, ohne als sichtbare Synonyme zu erscheinen.

Beim Anlegen einer Karteikarte folgt man den drei Ebenen nach einem festen Schema von oben nach unten. Sobald der Language Independent Level (LIL) vollständig ausgefüllt ist, vergibt das System eine Nummer, mit der später nach dem Eintrag gesucht werden kann. Alle administrativen Angaben wie Datum und Autor werden automatisch hinzugefügt. Der Sachgebietscode muss hingegen manuell eingegeben werden. Er basiert auf der Eurovoc-Klassifikation und lässt bis zu drei Ebenen zu. Der Zuverlässigkeitscode spiegelt das Stadium der Validierung wider: Die beiden höchsten Stufen („reliable' und „very reliable') sind den von Muttersprachlern validierten Benennungen vorbehalten.

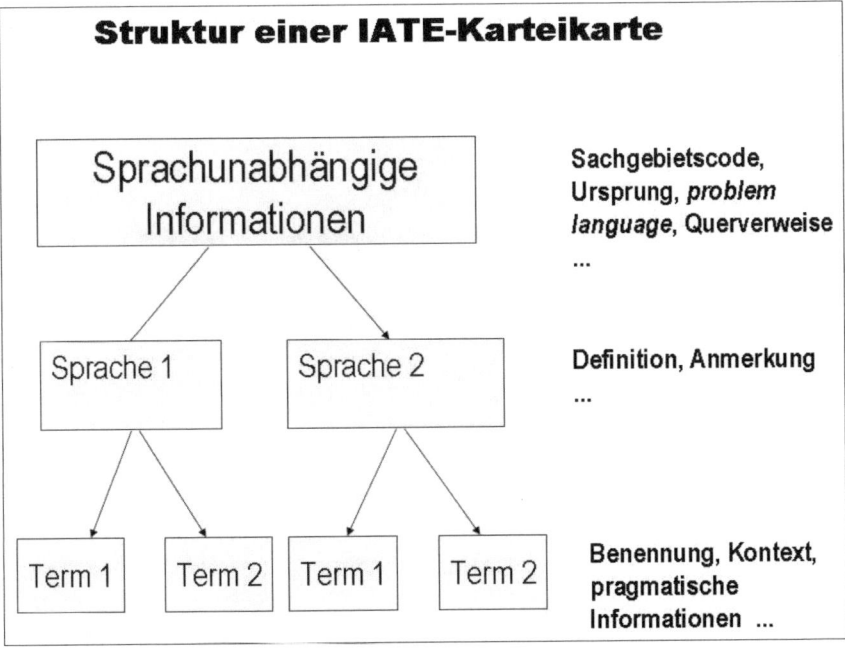

Abb. 2: Datenstruktur

5   Beispiele

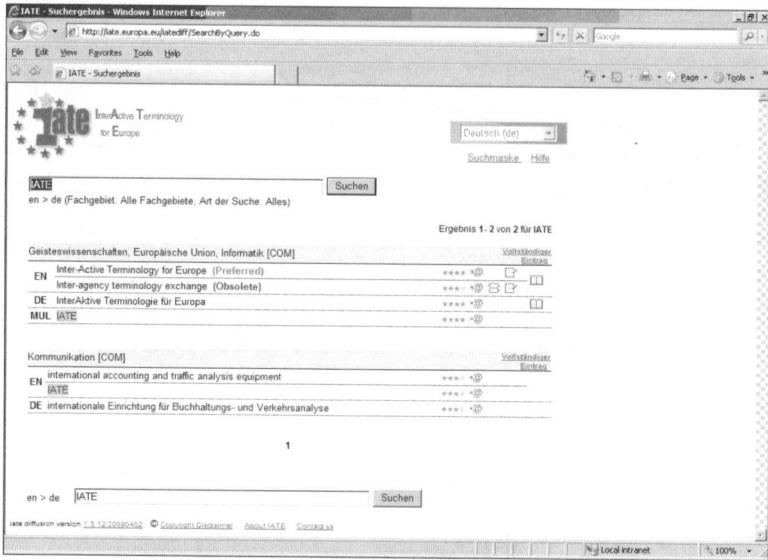

Abb. 3: Trefferliste mit dem Suchwort „IATE" (EN-DE)

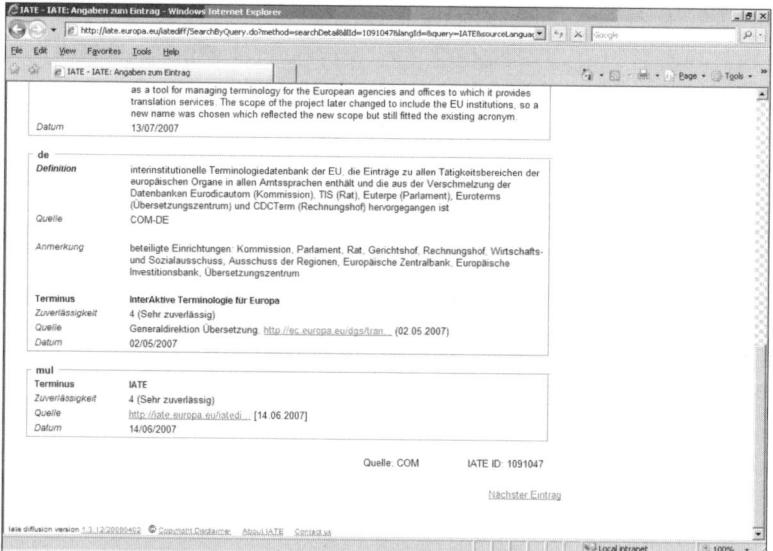

Abb. 4: vollständiger Eintrag zu „IATE" (DE)

IV. Neue Herausforderungen beim Dolmetschen

Konferenzdolmetschen

Oser un pronostic pour l'interprétation simultanée. Test d'aptitude à la simultanée : conception, étude pilote, évaluation

Dr. phil. Catherine Chabasse

Dipl.-Dolmetscherin (VKD-BDÜ)
Johannes Gutenberg-Universität Mainz,
Fachbereich Angewandte Sprach- und Kulturwissenschaft,
Arbeitsbereich Deutsch/Interkulturelle Germanistik

chabasse@uni-mainz.de

1 Pourquoi un test d'aptitude à l'interprétation simultanée ?

Suite à la déclaration de Bologne, les universités allemandes ont introduit le système Bachelor et Master pour un grand nombre de cursus, dont l'interprétation de conférence, qui est ainsi devenu un cursus post-gradué requérant un examen d'aptitude avant l'inscription. Les universités allemandes se sont alors vues dans l'obligation de concevoir un test d'aptitude à l'interprétation.

Les universités francophones et anglophones pratiquent ce type de test depuis des décennies mais ceux-ci sont surtout axés sur l'interprétation consécutive (IC). Cependant, la traductologie donne matière à penser que la simultanée et la consécutive font appel à des processus cognitifs différents. Il est donc important d'inclure dans un test d'aptitude des épreuves permettant de tester également l'aptitude à l'interprétation simultanée (IS). En outre, une approche pluridisciplinaire permet de conforter les hypothèses développées.

2 Une approche pluridisciplinaire

Un test d'aptitude a pour fonction de mesurer le potentiel d'un candidat et de permettre un pronostic quant à son évolution, objectif que poursuivent également les chercheurs, pédagogues et psychologues, qui se penchent sur le thème des dons, du talent et de l'intelligence.

En termes de théories de l'intelligence, on peut identifier, schématiquement, deux courants. L'un considère que l'intelligence se compose de deux facteurs (théorie bifactorielle : Spearman 1932, Cattel 1973) : le facteur g (*general factor*) qui participe à toutes les opérations cognitives et un certain nombre de facteurs s (*special factors*) qui sont mobilisés pour des opérations spécifiques. La deuxième école part du principe que l'intelligence est un système multifactoriel non hiérarchique, composé de plusieurs facteurs indépendants les uns des autres (Thurstone 1938, Guilford 1965, Meili 1981, Gardner 1991).

Dans son modèle multifactoriel, Thurstone suppose l'existence de neuf aptitudes mentales primaires qui se combinent différemment en nombre et en intensité selon les besoins. Cinq d'entre elles sont sollicitées par l'opération cognitive complexe qu'est l'IS :

- *Verbal Comprehension* : capacité à saisir le sens et les structures logiques
- *Word Fluency* : production verbale par association plus que par contenu
- *Memory* : mémoire à court terme
- *Reasoning* : raisonnement logique, inductif et déductif
- *Perceptual Speed* : capacité à sélectionner les éléments nécessaires à la compréhension
- *Speed of closure* : capacité à structurer et à former des ensembles
- *Flexibility of Closure* : flexibilité, capacité à remodeler et à restructurer à partir d'éléments connus

Cette théorie de l'intelligence multifactorielle est à la base de différents modèles de talent (*giftedness*). Pour Renzulli (1978), le talent repose sur l'interaction de trois éléments : aptitude intellectuelle supérieure à la moyenne, forte volonté d'atteindre son objectif (*task commitment*) et créativité ; Mönks (1992) y ajoute le rôle de l'environnement social ; Wieczerkowski/Wagner (1985 :113) intègrent des catégories (talent intellectuel, artistique, psychomoteur, social), des traits de personnalité (ténacité, ambition, stabilité émotionnelle etc.) et des modes de pensée (pensée divergente, flexibilité etc.) ; Heller et al. (1994 :19) introduit des éléments de personnalité non cognitifs (*nicht-kognitive Persönlichkeitsmerkmale*) que Gagné (2000 :68) nomme *intrapersonnal catalysts* dans son modèle (*Differentiated Model of Giftedness and Talent DMGT*).

Cependant, ces modèles ne concernent que les enfants. Il y manque les compétences, c'est-à-dire les connaissances acquises, qui représentent un élément majeur dans le contexte d'une formation universitaire. C'est pourquoi il semble préférable d'utiliser le terme d'aptitude car il permet d'inclure les compétences cognitives dont on peut espérer que de jeunes adultes qui aspirent à des études universitaires les possèdent.

Ainsi, le concept d'aptitude peut être défini comme la somme des talents (capacité cognitives + éléments de personnalité cognitifs et non cognitifs) et des compétences cognitives (Chabasse 2009).

3   Modèle d'aptitude à l'interprétation simultanée

Le traitement de la parole en situation d'IS se différencie de celui qui prévaut en situation de communication normale sans intermédiaire (*ungemittelte Kommunika-*

tion) (Kohn/Kalina 1996 : 123) du fait de la quasi-simultanéité des multiples opérations, souvent contradictoires, qu'exerce l'interprète de conférence, ce qui requiert une forte concentration et cause un stress important :

- compréhension du texte dans la langue de départ : l'interprète doit former un modèle mental dans la langue de départ à partir d'un nombre suffisant d'éléments (*chunks*) qu'il doit stocker dans sa mémoire de travail avant de pouvoir commencer sa production verbale,

- or, afin de disposer de suffisamment de capacités pour assurer une production verbale de qualité, l'interprète doit décharger sa mémoire de travail le plus rapidement possible. Les opérations de compréhension et de production de la parole se superposent et risquent de créer des interférences linguistiques menant à des erreurs syntactiques, lexicales, idiomatiques etc.

- pour les prévenir, l'interprète doit effectuer un contrôle permanent de sa production verbale (*monitoring*), ce qui occupe une partie de ses ressources cognitives dont il ne dispose plus pour interpréter (Gernsbacher/Faust 1991, Gile 1995).

Afin de pouvoir assurer parallèlement ces opérations simultanées, l'interprète a recours à diverses stratégies qui lui facilitent la compréhension (inférence, anticipation, segmentation etc.), la production verbale ou la cohérence (compression ou expansion) (Kalina 1998 :115-119).

Ces stratégies requièrent des capacités spécifiques qui ne sont pas exclusivement de nature linguistique. Elles sont représentées dans le modèle qui suit : les compétences cognitives nécessaires à l'apprentissage de l'IS sont situées dans la colonne de gauche: maîtrise de la langue maternelle (langue A) et de la (ou des) langue(s) étrangère(s) (langue B ou C), compétences interculturelles et culture générale ainsi que les capacités cognitives : fluidité, intelligence verbale, logique, mémoire et rapidité.

La colonne de droite énumère les éléments non cognitifs de la personnalité : la motivation comprenant la volonté d'entreprendre cette formation et la ténacité permettant de la mener à bien, le *self-management*, c'est-à-dire la gestion de ses propres capacités : concentration et gestion du stress, dont nous verrons plus loin qu'il s'agit d'un aspect essentiel pour l'aptitude à l'IS, et enfin les éléments non cognitifs de la personnalité : la flexibilité, le sens de la communication, l'assurance et l'esprit d'équipe, en d'autres termes, les *soft skills*.

En-dessous de ces deux colonnes, se trouvent trois flèches, deux vers le haut figurant les évènements qui peuvent se produire au cours de la formation dans la vie personnelle des étudiants ainsi que le rôle de l'environnement qui peuvent avoir un impact positif ou négatif sur leurs aptitudes, la troisième, partant des aptitudes pour mener au développement systématique de compétences d'expert, visualise le travail qui devra être effectué par les étudiants et sans lequel aucune aptitude, si grande soit-elle, ne mènera au résultat escompté.

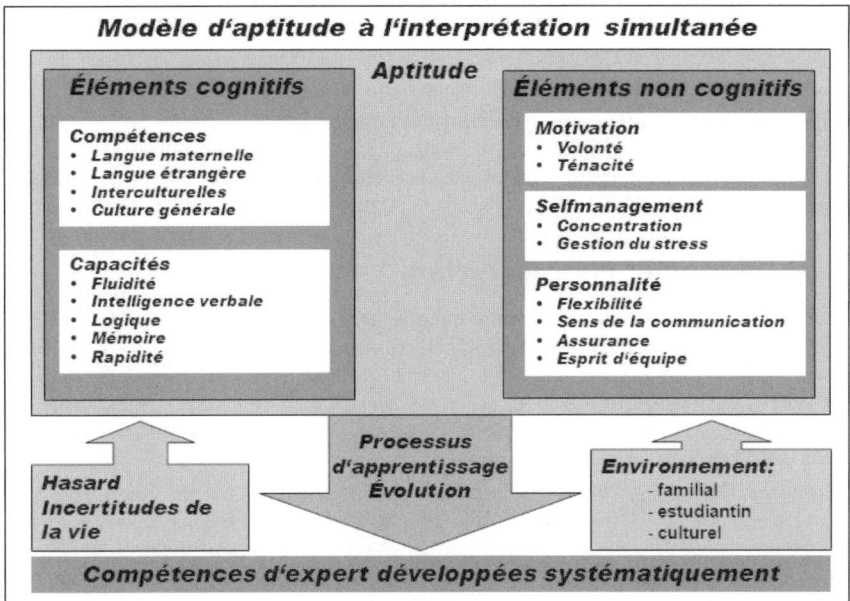

Figure 1 : Modèle d'aptitude à l'IS (Chabasse 2009)

Cet article se concentrera sur deux éléments de ce modèle : la gestion du stress et la concentration dont il a été dit qu'ils sont inhérents à l'IS.

4   La gestion du stress

Le stress est une réaction biologique extrême qui est déclenchée par la perception d'un déséquilibre entre les réactions qui seraient nécessaires pour répondre à une sollicitation et les possibilités personnelles disponibles, qu'elles soient réelles ou supposées (Semmer 1980 :489). Étant donné que la perception de l'écart mentionné dépend directement de la gestion des capacités propres, le stress est une réaction individuelle. Ce qui peut être perçu comme agent de stress par l'un, peut ne pas l'être par un autre, ce qui est considéré comme stressant aujourd'hui, peut ne pas l'être demain.

Cependant, le stress peut également influencer positivement l'efficacité, jusqu'à un certain point. Une fois ce point dépassé, il y a rupture, le stress devient négatif, l'efficacité se détériore (Linneweh 2002 :35). Cooper identifie quatre catégories de stress chez les interprètes de conférence (Cooper et al. 1982) :

- les facteurs externes (température dans la cabine, mauvaise vue sur les ora-teurs etc.)
- les facteurs intrinsèques (élocution rapide des orateurs, voyages fréquents etc.)

- les facteurs intra-personnels (manque d'esprit d'équipe, concurrence entre les collègues etc.)
- l'interface vie professionnelle et vie familiale.

S'il est possible d'influencer certains de ces facteurs (par exemple en choisissant d'habiter une métropole pour éviter les longs déplacements), d'autres sont inévitables. Le stress fait partie intégrante de cette profession. Il doit donc être inclus dans un test d'aptitude.

5 Attention et concentration

L'attention définit la perception automatique de ce qui nous entoure, alors que la concentration nous permet le traitement sélectif des stimuli que nous avons perçus. La concentration n'est pas un processus automatique, elle demande la mobilisation de ressources cognitives (Schmidt-Atzert et al. 2004). Plus la mémoire à long terme est structurée, plus nous disposons de schémas cognitifs et plus la sélection des informations pertinentes est rapide.

Parmi les différentes formes d'attention (Schmidt-Atzert et al. 2004), le type d'attention mobilisée pour l'IS est l'attention sélective. En situation normale, l'attention sélective est soit focalisée, soit partagée : l'attention sélective inhibe les informations inutiles pour ne traiter que les informations pertinentes, alors que l'attention partagée permet de traiter parallèlement plusieurs informations. On peut supposer que l'IS requiert une combinaison des deux : une attention sélective à la fois partagée et focalisée. Comme ce type d'attention n'est généralement pas nécessaire dans la vie quotidienne, on peut supposer que personne n'en dispose de façon innée. Elle doit être formée. Il est donc nécessaire, dans un contexte de test d'aptitude à l'IS, d'inclure cet aspect en terme de potentiel.

6 Résultats de l'étude empirique

Le test d'aptitude a été mis à l'essai sur un échantillon de 25 étudiantes de trois universités allemandes, en novembre/décembre 2006. L'objectif de cette étude était d'analyser la corrélation existant entre les résultats du test et ceux de l'examen de fin de semestre, constitué d'une épreuve de simultanée (3 minutes B-A) et de deux épreuves de consécutive (3 minutes respectivement B-A et A-B).

Afin de s'assurer que les compétences testées sont bien celles qui sont nécessaires à l'exercice de cette activité, huit interprètes de conférence professionnelles ont accepté de se soumettre au même test pour servir de population de référence.

Le test était composé de trois parties :

- **Compétences linguistiques langue A et langue B**

  Elles ne sont certes pas spécifiques à l'IS (elles sont tout aussi importantes, par exemple, pour la formation de traducteurs ou de professeurs de langue), cependant les langues étant l'outil de l'interprète, l'absence de qualification dans ce domaine conduirait automatiquement à l'échec de la formation, indépendamment de l'aptitude cognitive du candidat. Il est donc indispensable de couvrir ce volet.

- **Capacités cognitives :**

  Les étudiantes étant toutes de langue maternelle allemande, les tests ont été puisés dans le *WILDE-Intelligenz-Test* (Jäger / Althoff 1994), un des tests de structure de l'intelligence les plus reconnus en Allemagne.

- **Élément non cognitifs :**

  Concentration : Les exercices se sont inspirés des exercices proposés par Kurz (1996 :109-114). Il s'agit d'exercices de *Shadowing* cognitif : l'étudiant est en cabine d'interprétation, il entend une phrase qu'il doit répéter après avoir répondu si oui ou non la phrase est exacte, ou bien une question à laquelle il doit répondre, tout en écoutant la phrase suivante. Les phrases sont très simples, y répondre n'exige pas de connaissances spécifiques. Il s'agit en effet d'exclure qu'une mauvaise réponse soit due à l'ignorance et non pas à un problème de traitement cognitif.

Le shadowing cognitif se compose de quatre types de test :

(1) phrase déclaratives A-A, B-B :

   « L'Espagne et la France ont une frontière commune. – Oui, l'Espagne et la France ont une frontière commune ».

(2) questions fermées A-A-, B-B :

   « Les autobus à Paris sont-ils gratuits ? – Non, les autobus à Paris ne sont pas gratuits ou bien Non, les autobus à Paris sont payants ».

(3) questions ouvertes A-A, B-B :

   « Pourquoi beaucoup de malades vont-ils à Lourdes ? – Ils espèrent qu'un miracle va les guérir ».

(4) Questions ouvertes avec changement de langue B-A et A-B :

   „Pourquoi certaines personnes évitent-elles les chats ? – Viele Leute mögen keine Katzen, weil sie allergisch dagegen sind. "

Les exercices A-A sont classés dans la catégorie « concentration », les exercices B-B dans la catégorie « concentration et fluidité dans la langue étrangère » et les exercices B-A et A-B dans la catégorie « concentration avec changement de langue ».

Il s'est avéré que le dernier type d'exercice comprenant un changement de langue était le plus sélectif. Il est cependant nécessaire de garder les exercices de *shadowing* précédents, sans toutefois les noter, afin de permettre une progression car une partie des candidats venant de cursus non traductologiques, ils n'ont aucune expérience de ce genre d'activités. Ils doivent donc pouvoir se familiariser avec l'exercice qui leur est demandé.

L'étude empirique a permis de constater que l'une des principales raisons de l'échec à l'examen de fin de semestre est un manque de compétences dans la langue B, que la logique n'est pas un critère de sélection, que l'intelligence verbale est, certes, un critère mais uniquement en combinaison avec d'autres éléments et que les facteurs décisifs se trouvent dans la catégorie « concentration » et tout particulièrement « concentration avec changement de langue », c'est-à-dire les qualités qui sont testées par l'exercice 4.

7 Quelques profils caractéristiques

Le champ gris foncé représente la moyenne des interprètes professionnels, le gris clair la moyenne des étudiantes et la ligne noire les résultats individuels de l'étudiante concernée.

Bon profil malgré une certaine faiblesse dans la langue B

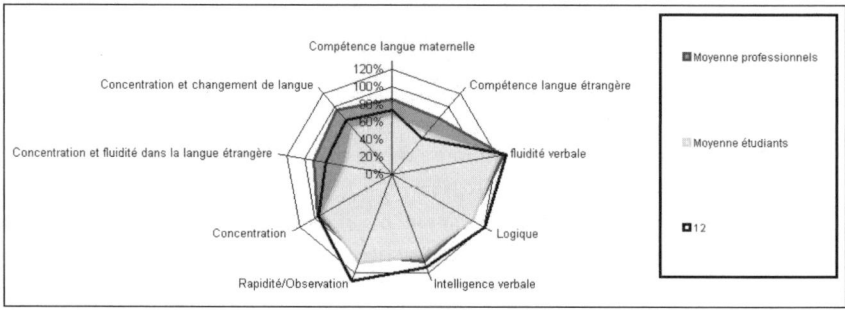

Figure 2

La légère faiblesse dans la langue B de cette étudiante est compensée par le score obtenu dans les tests « concentration et fluidité dans la langue B » et « concentration avec changement de langue ». On est en droit de supposer qu'elle a de bonnes chances de réussir ses études, il est cependant nécessaire qu'elle remédie auparavant à ses lacunes linguistiques, par exemple par un séjour à l'étranger.

Grave déficit en langue B

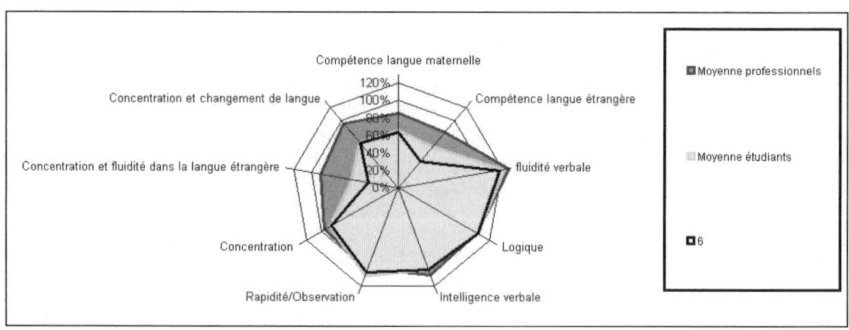

Figure 3

Ce profil présente de grandes lacunes dans la langue B qui influent tellement sur les résultats des épreuves de concentration qu'il est impossible de dire s'il y a véritablement déficience dans ce domaine. Indépendamment de cela, les compétences linguistiques de cette étudiante sont insuffisantes pour lui permettre d'entamer des études d'interprétation avec un tant soit peu de chances de les réussir.

Déficit en langue A

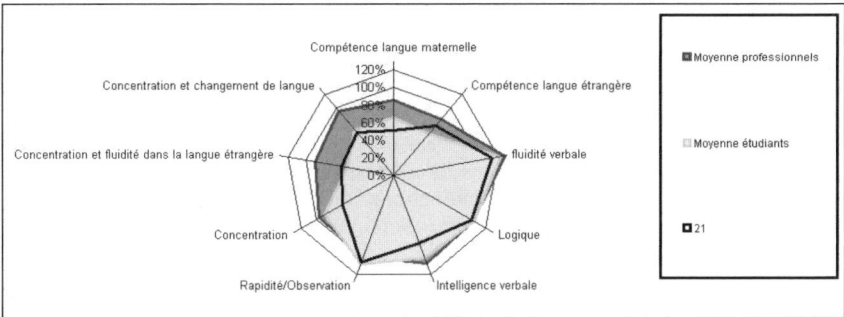

Figure 4

Ce profil est problématique car il présente plusieurs déficits dans le domaine linguistique qui risquent de se cumuler. On constate que la compétence en langue A, la fluidité et l'intelligence verbale sont inférieures à la moyenne. En outre, la faiblesse en langue A se reflète également dans les résultats des épreuves de concentration, y compris la concentration avec changement de langue. Le pronostic est donc défavorable.

Déficit en concentration

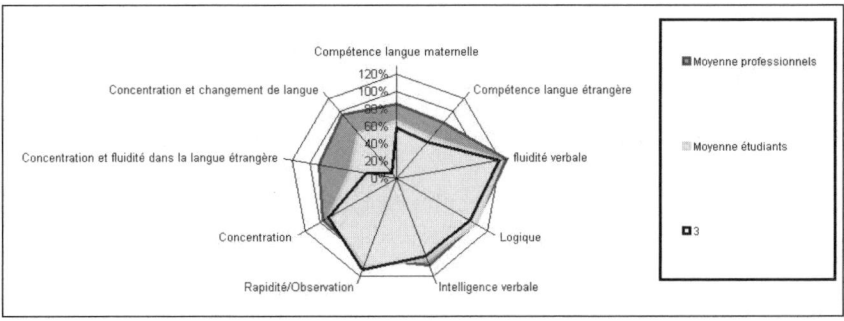

Figure 5

Ce profil entraine également un pronostic défavorable. La compétence linguistique, tant dans la langue A que dans la langue B, ainsi que l'intelligence verbale sont inférieures à la moyenne. De plus, les résultats du test « concentration et fluidité dans la langue étrangère » sont très faibles et ceux du test « concentration avec changement de langue » quasiment nuls.

8 Conclusions

L'étude pilote a montré qu'il n'existe pas UN indicateur unique pour démontrer l'aptitude à l'IS mais qu'il est nécessaire de prendre en compte plusieurs facteurs qui, selon leur intensité et leur combinaison, peuvent permettre à un jury d'oser un pronostic. Il n'est donc pas possible de se contenter de tester UNE capacité pour pouvoir prédire de manière fiable si un candidat réussira ou non ses études d'interprète. Pour qu'un jury soit en état de prendre une décision fondée, il est indispensable qu'il se fasse une image la plus complète possible du candidat en prenant en considération toutes ses compétences, capacités cognitives ainsi que les éléments non cognitifs de sa personnalité. Un test d'aptitude devra être composé de plusieurs épreuves qui devront être interprétées globalement.

Il s'est cependant avéré que la concentration et, en particulier, la concentration avec changement de langue, est un bon indicateur, à condition qu'elle soit combinée avec une bonne compétence en langue A et B.

En outre, ce test est un bon instrument diagnostique car il permet d'établir un bilan détaillé des forces et des faiblesses des étudiants qui permettra de leur indiquer avec précision où mettre l'accent dans leur travail.

Une partie de ce test a été mis à l'essai à l'université de Mayence/Germersheim pour l'examen d'entrée aux études de Master en été 2008. Il sera possible, au cours des années, en suivant le parcours des étudiants admis, d'adapter le test et de l'élargir à d'autres langues. Pour ce faire, un groupe de travail plurilingue s'est mis en place en été 2009.

Bibliographie

Cattel, Raymond Bernard (1973): Die empirische Erforschung der Persönlichkeit. Weinheim, Basel

Chabasse, Catherine (2009): Gibt es eine Begabung für das Simultandolmetschen? Erstellung eines Dolmetscheignungstests mit Schwerpunkt Simultandolmetschen. Berlin

Cooper, Cary L. /Davies, Rachel /Tung, Rosalie (1982): Interpreting Stress: Sources of Job Stress among Conference Interpreters. In: Multilingua 1/2. Berlin

Gagné, Françoys (2000): Understanding the Complex of Talent Development Through DMGT- Based Analysis. In: Heller, Kurt/ Mönks, Franz J./ Sternberg, Robert J./Subotnik, Rena F. (Ed.) (2000): International Handbook of Giftedness and Talent. Amsterdam, Lausanne, New York, Oxford, Shannon, Singapore, Tokyo, 67-79

Gardner, Howard (1991): Abschied vom IQ. Die Rahmentheorie der vielfachen Intelligenz. Stuttgart

Gernsbacher, Morton. Ann/ Faust, Mark (1991): The Role of Suppression in Sentence Comprehension. In: Simpson, G.B. (Ed.): Understanding Word and Sentence, North-Holland, 97-128

Gile, D. (1995): Basic Concepts and Models for Interpreter and Translator Training. Amsterdam, Philadelphia

Guilford, Joy Paul (1965): Persönlichkeit. Weinheim, Bergstraße

Heller, Kurt A./Perleth, Christopher /Hany, Ernst A. (1994): Hochbegabung - ein lange Zeit vernachlässigtes Forschungsthema. In: Einsichten - Forschung an der Ludwig-Maximilians-Universität München, Vol. 3, No. 1, 18-22

Jäger, Adolf Otto/Althoff, Klaus (1994): Der WILDE-Intelligenz-Test. Ein Struktur-diagnostikum. Göttingen, Bern, Toronto, Seattle

Kalina, Sylvia (1998): Strategische Prozesse beim Dolmetschen. Theoretische Grundlagen, empirische Fallstudien, didaktische Konsequenzen. Tübingen

Kohn, Kurt/Kalina, Sylvia (1996): The Strategic Dimension of Interpreting. Meta 41/1, 118-138

Kurz, Ingrid (1996): Simultandolmetschen als Gegenstand der interdisziplinären Forschung. Wien

Linneweh, Klaus. (2002): Stresskompetenz. Der erfolgreiche Umgang mit Belastungssituationen in Beruf und Alltag. Weinheim, Basel

Meili, Richard (1981): Struktur der Intelligenz. Bern, Stuttgart, Wien

Mönks, Franz J. (1992): Ein interaktionales Modell der Hochbegabung. In: Hany, Ernst A. /Nickel, Horst (Hrsg.) : Begabung und Hochbegabung, Theoretische Konzepte – Empirische Befunde – Praktische Konsequenzen. Bern, Göttingen, Toronto, Seattle, 17-23

Renzulli, Joseph S. (1978): What Makes Giftedness: Reexamining a Definition. Phi Delta Kapan 60(3), 180-184

Schmidt-Atzert, Lothar/Büttner, Gerhard/Bühner, Markus (2004): Theoretische Aspekte von Aufmerksamkeits-/Konzentrationsdiagnostik. In: Büttner, G. und Schmidt-Atzert, L. (Hrsg.): Diagnostik von Konzentration und Aufmerksamkeit. Jahrbuch der pädagogisch-psychologischen Diagnostik. Tests und Trends. Neue Folge Bd. 3. Göttingen, Bern, Seattle, Oxford, Prag, 3-22

Semmer, Norbert (1980): Streß. In: Asanger, Roland/Wenninger, Gerd (Hrsg.): Handwörterbuch der Psychologie. Weinheim. 486-493

Spearman, Charles (1932): The Abilities of Man. London

Thurstone, Louis, Leon (1938): Primary Mental Abilities. Chicago

Wieczerkowski, Wilhelm / Wagner, Harald (1985): Diagnostik von Hochbegabung. In: Jäger, Reinhold / Horn, Ralf / Ingenkamp, Karlheinz (Hrsg.) (1985): Tests und Trends 4. Jahrbuch der Pädagogischen Diagnostik. Weinheim, Basel, 109-134

Hinter den Kulissen: Dolmetschen für Kunst und Kultur

Lilian-Astrid Geese

VKD BDÜ, AIIC

liageese@comunicada.de

Als ich zum ersten Mal auf einer Bühne stand, war ich drei Jahre alt. Ich war ein Zirkuskind in Paul Burkhards Operette *Das Feuerwerk*, einer Inszenierung des Kölner Theaters, dessen Direktor mein Vater damals war. Es war keine Sprechrolle. Ich musste nur einer Artistin einen Ball zuwerfen, und sie warf ihn dann zurück.

Dieses Bild kommt mir heute noch manchmal in den Sinn, wenn ich auf einer Bühne meinen Part spiele. Doch heute habe ich eine Sprechrolle. Künstler werfen mir die Bälle zu, ich spiele sie ins Publikum weiter. Ich bin ihre Dolmetscherin.

Premierenfieber

Mein beruflicher Schwerpunkt ist die Welt der Kunst und Kultur, eine Branche, in der es manchmal an Geld, nie jedoch an Herausforderungen mangelt. Wie diese gestaltet sind, soll im Folgenden mit Blick auf die spezifischen Veranstaltungsformen dieses Marktsegments betrachtet werden. Im Gegensatz zu wissenschaftlichen Symposien und Kongressen, die in allen Sparten den Alltag einer Dolmetscherin ausmachen, geht es hier um Lesungen, literarische Kolloquien, Filmprojekte, Theatertage, Konzertabende, Ausstellungsführungen, Kuratoren- und Künstlersymposien sowie die großen Events: Buchmessen, Literatur- und Filmfestivals, Biennalen und andere Kunstschauen. Die Praxisbeispiele verdanke ich meinen Geschäftspartnern in der Kreativbranche, insbesondere: Haus der Kulturen der Welt, documenta Kassel, kunstwerke / berlin biennale, Literarisches Colloquium Berlin, Internationales Literaturfestival Berlin, Buchmesse Frankfurt und Leipzig, HAU Hebbel am Ufer, Schaubühne am Lehniner Platz, Berliner Ensemble, Volksbühne am Rosa-Luxemburg-Platz, Akademie der Künste, Typo Berlin, Staatliche Museen zu Berlin, Stiftung Schloss Neuhardenberg, Berliner Festspiele und ZDF.

Konferenzen und Tagungen in thematisch verwandten Bereichen – Design, Typographie, Mode, Architektur, Garten- und Landschaftsplanung, Museales, Archäologie, Gedenkstätten, Philosophie, Kulturwissenschaft – bleiben dagegen unberücksichtigt. Sie sind Teil des Brot- und Butter-Geschäfts jeder Konferenzdolmetscherin[8], das grundsätzlich alle Fachgebiete umfasst. Die gegenseitige Befruchtung der Genres an den Schnittstellen von Kunst und Wissenschaft soll dabei natürlich nicht geleugnet werden: Referenzen für eine Politikertagung zur Globalisierung wären Frantz Fanon, Homi Bhabha oder Edouard Glissant. Archivare, die sich auf einem technischen

---

[8] Die weibliche Form meint die Männer mit.

Seminar über die Digitalisierung unterhalten, zitieren vielleicht Walter Benjamin und das *Kunstwerk im Zeitalter seiner technischen Reproduzierbarkeit*. Der Eröffnungs-redner einer Tagung über Leichtstahl im Autobau ist möglicherweise ein enthusiasti-scher Anhänger von Adornos *Konstruktion des Ästhetischen*. Dennoch: Aus interpre-interpretatorischer Perspektive unterscheiden sich bei allgemeinen wissenschaftlichen Tagungen die Themen, nicht die Methode: Wir ringen um Redemanuskripte und PowerPoints, hoffen auf kohärente und in akzeptablem Tempo vortragende Rednerin-nen, wenig Vorleser, viele Freisprecher, und meist sitzen wir in der Kabine.

In der anderen Welt – der Kunst – gelten oft besondere Bedingungen, von der Vorbe-reitung der Veranstaltung bis zu dem Moment, in dem der Vorhang fällt. Von jener anderen Welt soll im Folgenden die Rede sein.

Schnöder Mammon, schöner Schein

Dolmetschen für die schönen, schrägen, modernen, musealen, aufregenden, anregen-den, lauten und leisen Künste operiert mit anderen Prämissen als denen, die unseren Beruf in den übrigen Szenen prägen. Erwartet werden, hier wie dort, Kompetenz, Engagement, Leidenschaft. Gefragt ist überdies Präsenz und erlaubt ist das Unkon-ventionelle. Professionalität ist ein Muss. Aber das graue Kostüm kann im Schrank bleiben und das „kleine Schwarze" darf, selbst beim Dinner für konservative Mäzene oder kunstsponsernde Banker, mit extravaganten Creolen und neonschriller Boa aufgepeppt werden. In einem Ambiente, in dem der Handkuss und die Zigarettenspit-ze überlebt haben, gilt: *À chacun(e) son goût!*

Beginnen wir den Trip hinter die Kulissen jedoch wesentlich weniger glamourös mit einer strikt materiellen Frage: Ist Kunst finanziell eine interessante Branche für Dolmetscherinnen? Meine These lautet: durchaus, und heute mehr denn je. Schon die Römer boten *panem et circensis*, weil sie wussten, dass man Menschen nicht nur ausbeuten darf. Die Arenen und Stadien unserer Zeit füllen sich dank der Ikonen der Eventkultur, Massenspektakel sind ein lukratives Geschäft. Je schwächer die Wirt-schaft, desto überzeugter die Entscheider, dass das Divertimento eine sinnvolle Investition ist. Darüber hinaus sind weder die Suche nach Werten noch der gern genannte Paradigmenwechsel ohne Kunst denkbar. *Crossover* und *Fusion* sind die Schlagworte der Stunde. Der Blick über den Tellerrand ist global, also international. Da braucht man Dolmetscherinnen. Die Kulturbranche ist – vom Megadimensionalen abgesehen – natürlich keine reiche Branche. Der Vorteil in konjunkturschwachen Zeiten und vor allem in der 2009 hochaktuellen Krise: Dolmetscherinnen in diesem Marktsegment sind knappe Kassen und eine gewisse Flexibilität beim Aushandeln der Honorare gewöhnt. Auch unbare Leistungen werden geboten und akzeptiert: Sponso-ren-Logo und Link zur eigenen Website im PR-Material für die Veranstaltung, Gästekarten für die Show/Lesung/Performance, Kataloge, Merchandising-Produkte, Transfer im VIP-Shuttle und natürlich die *Credits*, von denen später noch die Rede sein wird. Gleichgültig aber, wie die materielle Lage sich darstellt: In der Kunst- und Kulturbranche werden Kreativität und Können gewürdigt – und vergütet. Die viel-leicht fast perfekte Synthese – von Inspiration, Professionalität und Geld – hat allerdings ihren Preis.

Der *Special Effect* ist die Norm

Mindestens ebenso wichtig wie das Monetäre sind die Arbeitsbedingungen. Prägend für das Engagement in Kunst und Kultur, im Theater, Kino, Konzertsaal und Fernsehstudio, sind ungewöhnliche Arbeitszeiten, enorme Exponiertheit, manchmal „unmögliche" Arbeitsplätze und nicht selten wenig Ruhe. Dafür viele aufgeregte Zuständige, denen oft alle am Set wichtig sind – außer der Dolmetscherin. Gefordert ist der ganze Mensch, so platt das klingen mag.

Konkret: Wenn andere sich am Freitagnachmittag dem Wochenende nähern oder dieses am Sonntagvormittag genießen, sitzt, wer in Sachen Kultur unterwegs ist, oft in der Kabine oder mit dem Notizblock neben einem zu dolmetschenden Gast. Wenn andere gegen Mitternacht überlegen, ob es Zeit für süße Träume ist, beginnt eine letzte Lesung oder ein After-Show-Talk auf der Bühne. Doch die Uhr ist nicht das einzige Außergewöhnliche in der kreativen und Kultur fördernden Industrie. In meiner Anekdotendatei finden sich:

- Die Kabine, die in einer ehemaligen Lagerhalle im Hafen auf einem wackeligen Podest in luftiger Höhe stand und nur über eine reichlich staubige und ziemlich steile Bauleiter zu erreichen war. Der Gestalter der Location fand das schick. Die Dolmetscherinnen im Team waren froh, an diesem Tag nicht im Rock zur Arbeit gekommen zu sein.

- Die israelische Autorin und ich – diesmal beide im eher kurzen Rock – auf Barhockern auf einem leicht erhöhten Podium. Die Veranstalter wollten es „relaxed". Sie waren allerdings auch nicht diejenigen, die souverän balancierend und mit Notizblöckchen, Kuli, Mikrofon (nicht Headset, sondern „Keule"!) und Seltersfläschchen jonglierend arbeiten mussten.

- Die Dolmetschkabine für die Live-Schalte der Abendnachrichten auf der Wiese vor dem von Christo und Jeanne-Claude verhüllten Reichstag, umstanden von neugierigen Menschenmassen und bekrabbelt von Mücken und Käfern. Zum Glück ohne Regen!

Richtig gute Nerven erforderte 1998 eine Veranstaltung mit Salman Rushdie und Günter Grass in der Berliner Akademie der Künste. Ayatollah Khomeini hatte im Februar 1989 eine Fatwa gegen den berühmten indischen Autor der *Satanischen Verse* ausgesprochen[9]. An jenem Abend, auf der Bühne zwischen den beiden prominenten Schriftstellern sitzend, hoffte ich nicht nur aus prinzipiellen Erwägungen, niemand würde einen Mordanschlag versuchen.

Bei diesen in vielfacher Hinsicht herausragenden Begegnungen können auch Technik und Akustik immer wieder zu Stolpersteinen werden. Beim Mitschnitt für TV oder DVD und beim Internet-Streaming ist kaum ein Tontechniker davon zu überzeugen, dass man mit den zarten B&O-Kopfhörern (Bang & Olufsen A8) so viel schöner hört: Dann muss es wegen der Klangqualität das Headset sein – selbst wenn es ein schraubstockähnliches Modell ist. Steht man auf den „Brettern, die die Welt bedeuten", empfiehlt es sich, mit den Saaltechnikern vor Veranstaltungsbeginn die Bühnenakus-

---

[9] Khomeinis Fatwa wurde übrigens nie zurückgenommen. Dies könne nur derjenige, so die iranische Regierung 1998, der sie verhängt hat. Khomeini starb im Juni 1989.

tik durchzusprechen. Wenn nur der Saal beschallt wird, hört man auf der Bühne nichts – vielleicht noch den Autor, neben dem man sitzt, aber schon nicht mehr die Moderatorin, die Fragen an ihn richtet.

Klug ist, wer weiß, wie Theatersäle ausgeleuchtet werden. Voll Vorfreude ging ich neben meinem Dramatikeridol Harold Pinter anlässlich einer Preisverleihung auf die Bühne des Berliner Ensembles – und blickte in gleißendes Weiß, das mir aus dem Zuschauerraum entgegengrellte. Nur schemenhaft sah ich dort Menschen, und plötzlich wusste ich, was „Lampenfieber" tatsächlich bedeutet. Anders als Schauspieler, die den Blickkontakt mit dem Publikum während der Vorstellung weder brauchen noch wollen, sucht die Dolmetscherin die Gesichter der Zuhörerinnen, möchte Bestätigung, freundliches Lächeln, Interesse erkennen.

Eigene „Technik" und mitunter Körpereinsatz sind gefragt, wenn es gilt, VIPs bei Massenveranstaltungen zu begleiten, beispielsweise einen Präsidenten als Ehrengast der documenta. Hier zeigt sich, ob man den subtilen Kampf gegen die Security gewinnen und dem mächtigen Staatsmann näher sein kann als die Einmeterfünfundneunzig-Jungs mit dem Knöpfchen im Ohr – und die aggressiv drängelnde Journalistenmeute.

Dolmetschen für Kunst und Kultur, so viel dürfte deutlich geworden sein, ist also weit mehr als leserliche Notizen und schöne Worte. Dolmetschen in diesem Genre ist, wie das Leben, eine einzige Herausforderung.

Methoden und die Grenzen der Kompetenzen

Eine Herausforderung – auch was die Arbeitsweise angeht. Anders als bei Business Meetings oder Fachtagungen ist das Motto bei Kulturveranstaltungen nicht *time is money*. Bei Autorengesprächen und Lesungen, Publikumsrunden nach der Vorstellung im Theater oder Kino, Führungen mit Kuratorinnen durch ihre Ausstellung und Pressekonferenzen ist konsekutives Dolmetschen daher oft der Modus der Wahl. Vom Exponiertsein und vom Balanceakt war bereits die Rede. Daneben stellt sich häufig noch ein anderes Problem: die Zähmung der „Hier kann doch jeder Englisch!"– Fraktion, die besonders im deutschen Publikum recht stark ist. Internationale, meist bilinguale Communities, die bei anderssprachigen Veranstaltungen – Spanisch, Französisch, Italienisch – oft einen Großteil der Zuhörer stellen, zeigen interessanterweise weitaus weniger Hybris. Die ungeduldigen Skeptiker zu fesseln, damit auch die Zuhörer die Veranstaltung genießen, denen es schwerer fällt, von Muttersprachlern oder eben Nichtmuttersprachlern gesprochenes Englisch zu verstehen, erfordert Können, Charme und manchmal geradezu diplomatisches Geschick. Vor einigen Jahren waren sich bei einer Talk-Runde weder die Diskutanten Tariq Ali, Peter Schneider und Eliot Weinberger neben mir auf dem Podium einig, ob ich dolmetschen solle, noch der Saal. Der Veranstalter insistierte am Bühnenrand. Jemand rief: „Abstimmen!". Erst zögerlich, dann nachdrücklich hoben sich viele Hände für eine Verdolmetschung. … Am Ende war es ein spannendes Gespräch und ein gelungener Abend. Wenngleich es eine Menge Selbstbewusstsein erfordert, zunächst gegen so manch trotziges Gesicht im Saal anreden zu müssen, bis man alle davon überzeugt hat, dass Zweisprachigkeit nicht die Debatte kaputt macht – jedenfalls nicht, wenn Profis ran dürfen. Angesichts der oft zum Dolmetschen angeheuerten Nichtprofis

– Literaturwissenschaftlerinnen, Lektoren, Übersetzerinnen, sonstige Sprachkundige – ist die Skepsis allerdings auch verständlich: lieber nicht jedes Wort verstehen, als störendes Gestammel. Da müssen wir – Profis, Berufsverbände – noch Überzeugungsarbeit leisten!

Dazu eine Zwischenbemerkung zu den Grenzen der Kompetenzen: Nur routinierte Moderatoren beherrschen die Doppelrolle des Gesprächspartners und Dolmetschers in einer Person. Einige Rundfunkkollegen sind versiert, weil sie in ihren Sendungen häufig beide Funktionen erfüllen müssen. Diese wissen dann übrigens oft mehr als andere zu schätzen, wenn sie für eine öffentliche Debatte eine Dolmetscherin mit „an Bord" haben. Umgekehrt sollten Dolmetscherinnen, es sei denn, sie arbeiteten sonst auch als Sprecherinnen, den Vortrag von literarischen und lyrischen Texten professionellen Schauspielern überlassen. Wer für eine Lesung Eintritt bezahlt, hat auch Anspruch auf gute Vorleser! Dabei gilt natürlich auch hier: Keine Pauschalisierung: Es gibt Übersetzerinnen, die auch gut dolmetschen können, es gibt Moderatoren, die sehr gekonnt zweisprachig moderieren, es gibt Dolmetscher, die exzellente Vorleser sind.

Eine weitere Herausforderung sind Künstler, die sich gar nicht gern in der Öffentlichkeit und mit gesprochenen Worten verkaufen. Ihr expressives Medium sind ihre Bilder, ihre Bücher, ihre Musik. Natürlich begegnen mir auch die Stars der Szene – Isabel Allende, Paolo Coelho, Doris Lessing, Henning Mankell, Margaret Atwood, Jonathan Franzen, Wole Soyinka, Spike Lee, Jeff Koons und einige mehr – deren Esprit auf der Bühne für die Dolmetscherin die pure Lust ist. Doch nicht jeder, der faszinierend schreibt, malt oder komponiert, ist automatisch ein begnadeter Redner oder gar, ganz im Trend der Zeit, zugleich Entertainer. Natürlich stellt sich das Problem des mäßig begabten Rhetorikers in unserem Beruf als ein grundsätzliches. Aber Arm an Arm auf der Bühne, im trauten Trio mit der Moderatorin, ist die atmosphärische Wirkung zu langer oder zu kurzer Antworten nicht zu unterschätzen: „Erzählen Sie uns doch, was Sie zu diesem Buch inspirierte." – „My wife." Wer könnte da dem flehenden Blick der Gastgeber widerstehen und nicht leise flüsternd nachfragen: „You mean, when you first met her?" oder irgendwas, damit der prominente Gesprächspartner noch ein wenig zulegt. Das ist dann doch mehr, als man in einer solchen Situation in der Kabine tun würde, wo man vermutlich eher grinsend das Notebook zuklappt und – bei gedrückter Räuspertaste – der Kollegin zuflüstert: „Ich pack schon mal. Ich glaub, wir sind gleich durch."

Damit wird jedoch zugleich deutlich, was sich in der Vorbereitung von Dolmetschengagements in Kunst und Kultur von anderen Aufträgen unterscheidet: Der Kampf um die PowerPoints entfällt. Bei Lesungen oder anderen Kulturevents finden diese – außer vielleicht im Rahmen einer Pecha-Kucha-Inszenierung – noch keinen Einsatz. Allerdings steht im Vorfeld die Lektüre mindestens des jüngsten Werkes der Autorin beziehungsweise des Textes, aus dem gelesen wird. Man liest das Original, weil es authentischer ist, aber für das Gespräch in jedem Fall auch die Version, die für das Publikum vorgetragen wird: Hermione heißt beim deutschen Harry Potter Hermine, und man will ja niemanden verwirren, indem man plötzlich von einem ganz andere Mädchen spricht. Oder selbst irritiert sein, weil die Schauspielerin auf der Bühne von anderen Personen redet, als man sie erinnert. Ich habe mir angewöhnt, auf der hinteren Umschlagseite der Bücher die Namen aller Protagonisten (in den für mich relevanten Sprachen) zu notieren, und in welcher Beziehung sie zueinander stehen. Daneben liest man natürlich auch Verlags-PR, die Biografie(n) der jeweiligen Künstlerin und Informationen über das Land, aus dem sie kommt oder über das sie schreibt[10]. Man produziert eine Titelliste und hört vielleicht das eine oder andere online verfügbare Interview. Atmosphärisch und zur Klärung letzter offener Fragen wichtig ist das Vorgespräch mit Künstlerin und Moderatorin. Das ist nicht selten auch der Moment, die Nervosität aller Beteiligten abzubauen und genau den Mix zwischen guter Stimmung, Entspannung und Spannung hinzubekommen, der später den Funken zwischen den Protagonisten auf der Bühne und dem Publikum überspringen lässt.

Parallelen der Genres

Das hier zu den Lesungen Gesagte gilt analog für Gespräche mit Dramatikern, Regisseurinnen, Dramaturgen und Schauspielerinnen im Theater, und für die Filme, die man – zusammen mit ihren Protagonisten und Macherinnen – nach der Vorführung mit dem Publikum und/oder der Presse diskutiert.

Ein ganz anderer Bereich ist die Arbeit für Kino oder Fernsehen am Set. Mein erstes Dokumentarfilmprojekt – *Che Guevara – Der Mythos lebt,* gedreht 1998 für den WDR in Bolivien und Cuba – bot gleich die komplette Bandbreite dolmetscherischer Einsatzmöglichkeiten:

- Produktionsvorbereitung: Recherchesupport, Screening fremdsprachiger Texte, Erstellung von Abstracts für Regisseur und Produzent;

- am Set / vor Ort: Organisation, Drehgenehmigungen, Kontakte, Vorgespräche, Interviews, Auswertung der O-Töne;

- Postproduktion: Sichten, Übersetzung der O-Töne, Support beim Schnitt, Sprachcoaching für die Sprecher, Untertitelung.

Der Blick hinter die Kulissen ist bei Filmarbeiten im Grunde die Fortschreibung dessen, was Dolmetscherinnen theoretisch ohnehin ständig tun müssen: sich in diverse Themen einarbeiten, sich in andere Kontexte hineinversetzen. Hier wird man zum Mitglied der Crew und verinnerlicht die notwendigen Tricks einer anderen Branche: immer der Kamera nah sein, ohne ins Bild zu geraten; immer so stehen, dass der Interviewpartner beim Antworten in die Kamera blickt; und zur Not bei den Tonaufnahmen assistieren, wenn der Tonmann krank wird, aber kein teurer Drehtag ungenutzt verstreichen darf.

Turbulent und bunt ist auch der Bereich Bildende Kunst. Neben analysierenden Panels sind kommentierte Ausstellungsführungen mit Künstlern oder Kuratoren eine der Haupttätigkeiten. Natürlich hat die Dolmetscherin, die das interessierte Publikum und den kompetenten Guide durch die Ausstellung begleitet, die Exponate vorab gesehen und den Katalog studiert und kann selbst einiges zur Künstlerin, zur Installation, zum Oeuvre insgesamt sagen. Die Vorbereitungszeit ist meist ausreichend; Ausstellungen, zumal die großen, haben einen langen Vorlauf. Die Schwierigkeiten

---

[10] Ressourcenauswahl: www.wikipedia.org, www.kulturportal.de, www.perlentaucher.de, www.theaterderzeit.de

bei der Mitarbeit an so schönen Projekten wie documenta, berlin biennale oder MoMA in Berlin, bestehen hier eher a) in der Akustik (Ausstellungshallen sind der denkbar schlechteste Ort, um zu hören, was jemand sagt und sich dann selbst Gehör zu verschaffen) und b) in der Tatsache, dass das Publikum gern vergisst, dass die Dolmetscherin zum Dolmetschen da ist und nicht unbedingt die Person, die lange, ergänzende Erläuterungen zu diesem oder jenem Werk machen kann. Dies gilt umso weniger, wenn die Kuratorin bereits zum nächsten Objekt weiter gezogen ist. Ein Sonderfall sind VIP-Führungen. Aber vom Kampf mit der Security war ja bereits oben die Rede.

Die Affinität von Sprachkünstlerinnen und Kunst

Kurz vor Schluss dieser kleinen Tour d'Horizon soll es noch um einen Aspekt gehen, der bei näherer Betrachtung so ungewöhnlich nicht daherkommt: die Nähe von Kunstschaffen und Sprachmittlung. Nicht nur, dass erwiesenermaßen viele Dolmetscherinnen musikalisch sind und nicht wenige selbst Instrumente spielen oder singen. Es gibt unter uns auch Schriftsteller, Malerinnen und Schauspielerinnen.

Umgekehrt ist auch unsere Arbeit für Künstler inspirierend. In einer aus der Sicht der Dolmetscherin faszinierenden Umkehrung von Ort und Rolle spielt Christoph Kellers Installation *The Interpreters* mit der inhärenten Bedeutung des Übersetzens und Interpretierens.[11] Keller führte Gespräche mit Dolmetschern über das Dolmetschen, die er dann simultan dolmetschen ließ. Der Ausstellungsbesucher sitzt in einer Dolmetschkabine und lauscht über Kopfhörer der Verdolmetschung des Gesprächs, zu dem er auf einem Videobildschirm vor der Kabine das Bild sieht. Für die Manifesta7 inszenierte Hannah Hurtzig die Projektion eines simultan ins Italienische gedolmetschten Vortrags des Literatur- und Kulturwissenschaftlers Joseph Vogl über das Zaudern.[12]

Eher kritisch erwähnt werden sollen die Werke der Belletristik, in denen Dolmetscher eine mehr oder weniger tragende Rolle spielen, die allerdings mit unserem realen beruflichen Leben nur marginal zu tun haben und häufig Klischees bedienen[13]. Beispiele hierfür sind die legendäre Dolmetschszene in Xavier Marias *Mein Herz so weiß*, der Ich-Erzähler in Mario Vargas Llosas' *La niña mala* oder Bruno Salvador in John le Carrés *The Mission Song*.

Unter dem Aspekt der Realitätstreue zu unserem Beruf gelungener ist der Thriller *Die Dolmetscherin* mit Nicole Kidman, für den Regisseur Sidney Pollack als erster Filmemacher überhaupt die Erlaubnis erhielt, am Originalschauplatz im Hauptsitz der Vereinten Nationen in New York zu drehen. Hier gelang es übrigens, dank der Intervention des BDÜ, den deutschen Verleih davon zu überzeugen, dass der Film

---

[11] *The Interpreters*, zuletzt gezeigt 2009 in der Shedhalle, Zürich: www.shedhalle.ch. Christoph Keller, Berlin: www.christophkeller.com.

[12] *Night Lesson*, eine Produktion der Mobile Academy für Manifesta7 in Trento/Italien, 2008: www.mobileacademy-berlin.com/englisch/2008/ nightless01.html. Literaturhinweis: Joseph Vogl, *Über das Zaudern*, Verlag Diaphanes, 2007.

[13] Vgl. Dörte Andres, *Dolmetscher als literarische Figuren. Von Identitätsverlust, Dilettantismus und Verrat*. Verlag Martin Meidenbauer, 2008

„Die Dolmetscherin" und nicht „Die Übersetzerin" heißen muss, obwohl man dort der Meinung war, „Die Übersetzerin" klänge schöner.

Nur Mühsal der Ebenen?

Fassen wir zusammen: Dolmetschen für Kunst und Kultur bedeutet weniger oder schwieriger auszuhandelndes Honorar, mehr Stress, Arbeit abends, nachts und/oder am Wochenende, kapriziöse Stars, ein anspruchsvolles Publikum und viele konsekutive Gigs. Lohnt das denn?

Die Antwort lautet: Unbedingt! Erstens: Was wäre das Leben, ohne die ständige Herausforderung? Und zweitens: Wo sonst bereitet man sich auf die Arbeit vor, indem man Romane, Lyrik und Essays liest, ins Kino und Theater geht, Ausstellungen besucht und sich der Lektüre prächtiger Kataloge widmet, die überdies im Laufe der Jahre eine beeindruckende Kollektion in der eigenen Bibliothek ergeben? Wo sonst tummelt man sich Backstage? Wo sonst steht man auf der Bühne, ist den Menschen ganz nah, deren künstlerische Arbeit man bewundert oder die einen bewegt? Trinkt mit ihnen Espresso beim Briefing und Wein nach der Show? Ist ihre Stimme, wählt ihre Worte – in einer anderen Sprache, aber genauso mitreißend, unterhaltsam, provozierend? Wo sonst bekommt man, neben dem Honorar, Applaus und Rosen am Ende der Vorstellung? Wo sonst wird man von Fremden im Park angesprochen, weil sie einen auf der Bühne oder in der Kabine sahen?

Die Werbewirksamkeit der Engagements in dieser Szene ist in der Tat nicht zu unterschätzen: Man bekommt konsequent seine Credits, wird namentlich genannt und ins Programm gedruckt.[14] Vertreter von Verlagen und Agenturen lassen sich Visitenkarten geben. Veranstalter empfehlen einen gern weiter.

Für den Enthusiasmus, die Intuition und die Leidenschaft, die Menschen, deren Profession und Obsession die Kunst ist, auch von ihrer Dolmetscherin erwarten, bekommt man also viel zurück. Die Zeit, die man verbringt, um sich mit der Terminologie des Musiktheaters, der Filmproduktion, der Bildenden Künste und all der anderen Bereiche in dieser schönsten aller Welten vertraut zu machen, wird einem generös entschädigt. Nicht zuletzt, weil man immer wieder auf – virtuelle – Reisen geht und in Bildern und Worten neue Länder und Kontinente entdeckt. Weil man selbst das lebenslange Lernen lebt und zugleich dazu beiträgt, dass kluge Gedanken und schöne Ideen vermittelt werden.

Da Capo und Coda

Damals, im Theater in Köln, war ich mächtig stolz, wenn es am Ende der Vorstellung Applaus gab. Und erleichtert, wenn ich wieder einen Abend hinter mir hatte, an dem mir der Ball nicht über die Rampe in den Saal rollte. Heute lasse ich ihn rollen und hole ihn dann zurück. Und freue mich immer noch über den Applaus. Für die Künstler, deren Stimme und Worte ich eine Weile sein darf, und auch für mich. Ein schöner

---

[14] Beispiele für *best practice:* HKW, HAU und Schaubühne nennen bei allen Veranstaltung die Dolmetscherinnen namentlich oder zumindest das Team. Das ilb hat die Kategorie „Dolmetscher" mit Kurzbios der am Festival beteiligten Kollegen in die Website integriert.

Beruf, denke mir dann. Ideal für neugierige Sprachbegabte mit guten Nerven. Ein Job, bei dem man hinter die Kulissen schauen kann. Und selbst Teil der Show ist.

Konferenzdolmetschen und Community Interpreting: Schritte zu einer Partnerschaft

Prof. Dr. phil. Ursula Gross-Dinter

Hochschule für Angewandte Sprachen / Fachhochschule des SDI

gross-dinter@sdi-muenchen.de

1 Zwei Welten des Dolmetschens?

In vielen Typologien von Dolmetscharten, wie sie sich in der einschlägigen Literatur finden (u.a. Feldweg 1996:25ff; Kalina 2001:51, 2002:170; Matyssek 1989:7; Pöchhacker 2000:33), werden Konferenzdolmetschen (KD) und andere Formen des Dolmetschens unterschieden. Letztere werden gelegentlich englisch als *Non-Conference Interpreting* oder *NCI* bzw. deutsch als Nicht-Konferenzdolmetschen oder NKD bezeichnet. Für das NKD wiederum finden sich Termini wie Besprechungs-, Betreuungs-, Gesprächs-, Verhandlungs- oder Dialogdolmetschen, welche die Art der Interaktion bezeichnen; oder es werden explizit bestimmte Settings wie das Community Interpreting (CI) bzw. Public Service Interpreting (PSI), das Gerichts- und Polizeidolmetschen oder das Geschäftsdolmetschen vom KD abgegrenzt.

Sind KD und NKD nun zwei völlig getrennte Welten? Und gilt dies insbesondere für den hier im Mittelpunkt stehenden Teilbereich des NKD, das CI?

Man kann sich dieser Frage mit einer Betrachtung der Praxis, aber auch durch eine Analyse der Entwicklung der Dolmetschwissenschaft nähern.

1.1 Ein Blick in die Praxis

Durch die Zuwanderungsströme in die Industriegesellschaften hat sich in den letzten Jahrzehnten ein wachsender Dolmetschbedarf in den Settings des CI (bei Behörden, im Krankenhaus, in der Psychotherapie, in der Schule, in Beratungs- und Betreuungs-einrichtungen) ergeben. Sieht man sich die derzeitige Praxis im deutschsprachigen Raum an, stellt man allerdings fest, dass das CI hier im Vergleich zum KD ein noch deutlich niedrigeres Ansehen genießt. Trotz zunehmender Bemühungen um Profes-sionalisierung z.B. durch die Schaffung eigener Studienangebote, Qualifizierungskur-se, Fortbildungsprogramme und Zertifizierungen (vgl. *MDÜ* 5/07) werden Aufgaben im Bereich des CI in vielen Fällen noch immer von Laien, oft von Verwandten,

Kindern oder gar Reinigungskräften übernommen. (Pöchhacker/Kadric 1999) Der Teufelskreis aus kaum vorhandener Ausbildung, niedriger Vergütung (die wiederum eine Investition in Ausbildung nicht sinnvoll erscheinen lässt), mangelndem Prestige und fehlendem Bewusstsein für die Notwendigkeit qualifizierter Leistungen seitens der Nachfrager scheint nach wie vor nur schwer zu durchbrechen zu sein.

Konferenzdolmetscher wiederum sind eher selten als Community-Dolmetscher tätig, was angesichts der mageren Honorare für solche Einsätze auch nicht weiter verwundern kann. Manche sehen sich vielleicht gar als eine Art „boothed gentry" (Viaggio, zit. in Amato/Mead 2002:297), halten sich für Tätigkeiten im Bereich des CI für überqualifiziert und blicken möglicherweise auf die nicht an Hochschulen oder gar nicht ausgebildeten „anderen" Sprachmittler geringschätzig herab. Für Community-Dolmetscher ist umgekehrt das KD oft eine völlig fremde Welt, zu der sie keinen Zugang haben.

Es scheint also in der Praxis tatsächlich so etwas wie eine „erste Welt" des KD und eine „dritte Welt" des CI zu geben (Pöchhacker 2000:125), zwei getrennte Welten, die kaum miteinander in Berührung kommen und sich wenig oder überhaupt nicht kennen.

1.2 Ein Blick in die Dolmetschwissenschaft

Es ist vor diesem Hintergrund sicher auch für Praktiker aufschlussreich, den Blick der Dolmetschwissenschaft auf diese „zwei Welten" kennenzulernen.

Betrachtet man Zahl und Thematik dolmetschwissenschaftlicher Publikationen, stellt man fest, dass die Forschung in ihren Anfängen stark von den Fragestellungen des KD beherrscht wird und das Gerichtsdolmetschen mit wenigen, das CI mit noch weniger Beiträgen vertreten ist (vgl. Pöchhacker 1995:24). Ab den 1990er Jahren etablieren sich dann jedoch ausgehend von klassischen Einwanderungsländern wie Australien, Kanada, den USA, Großbritannien, aber auch Schweden und Israel immer mehr Studien zum NKD. Internationale Tagungen wie z.B. die Reihe der *Critical Link*-Konferenzen zum Dolmetschen in Justiz, Medizin und sozialen Einrichtungen erzielen große Aufmerksamkeit, und das NKD ist immer stärker an prominenter Stelle in renommierten Fachzeitschriften wie *Target, The Translator, Interpreting* oder auch *MDÜ* (Hefte 2/02 und 5/07) vertreten. Selbst die Online-Zeitschrift des Internationalen Verbandes der Konferenzdolmetscher AIIC *Communicate* veröffentlicht seit dem Jahr 2000 immer wieder auch Artikel zum Thema CI oder Gerichtsdolmetschen.

Zwar widmen sich diese Publikationen zunächst noch mehrheitlich praxisorientierten Fragestellungen wie Ausbildung, Standards, berufsständischer Organisation, Akkreditierung und Berufsethik. Die immer zahlreicher werdenden empirischen Forschungsvorhaben in NKD-Settings weiten aber den Blick für Bedingungen und Prozesse und zeitigen Erkenntnisse, die für jede Form des Dolmetschens aufschlussreich sind.

1.2.1 Erkenntnisse aus der NKD-Forschung

Einen entscheidenden Anstoß zu dieser Entwicklung gibt Wadensjö (1998) mit ihrer Arbeit zu den interaktiven Prozessen zwischen den Partnern (einschließlich des Dolmetschers) in der *Face-to-face*-Kommunikation (*Interpreting as Interaction*). Ihre

Erkenntnisse zur Doppelfunktion des Dolmetschers als Text Reproduzierendem und Gesprächsmanager in einer triadischen Situation bereiten den Weg zu weiteren Forschungen in diesem neuen, von Pöchhacker (2004:78f; 2007:17) als *DI Paradigm (discourse and interaction paradigm)* bezeichneten Forschungsparadigma. Beziehen sich Wadensjös Beobachtungen ebenso wie die von Roy (2000) zur Sprecherwechselorganisation in einem von einem Gebärdendolmetscher gemittelten Gespräch noch auf typische CI-Situationen (Einwanderungsbehörde, Arzt-Patienten- bzw. Lehrer-Lerner-Kommunikation), so bewegt sich Birgit Apfelbaum (u.a. 2004) mit ihren Beobachtungen zur gedolmetschten technischen Fachkommunikation schon in die Richtung dessen, was man als konferenzähnliches Setting und durchaus auch als Einsatzgebiet eines professionellen Konferenzdolmetschers bezeichnen würde. Die Dolmetschwissenschaft als interdisziplinäre Wissenschaft greift so auf Methoden und Wissen aus bisher in der KD-Forschung wenig beachteten Disziplinen wie der interaktionalen Soziolinguistik und der Konversationsanalyse zurück und eröffnet damit neue Horizonte. Vor allem aber sind es die starke Beachtung kulturbedingter Faktoren wie auch die Infragestellung präskriptiver, auf einem idealen Rollenbild beruhender Vorstellungen von der Funktion des Dolmetschers und die Betonung der Bedeutung des gesamten situativen Kontextes in der CI-Forschung, die der KD-Forschung neue Impulse geben. Die Besonderheiten der Kommunikation in Institutionen mit ihren vorgeprägten Handlungsschemata, der Einfluss von Rollen und Status der Kommunikationspartner, von kultur- und wissensbedingten Unterschieden und vor allem die Frage der Rolle des Dolmetschers im Spannungsfeld zwischen unbeteiligtem Mittler und Vermittler zwischen Sprachen und Kulturen rücken ins Zentrum der Aufmerksamkeit.

Vor diesem Hintergrund misst Rudvin (2006:30) der CI-Forschung für die zukünftige Entwicklung der Dolmetschwissenschaft eine entscheidende Bedeutung bei:

> *"I would go so far as to say that CI has had – or rather is in the process of having – a significant impact on the direction IS [Interpreting Studies] will take in the future, both in its epistemological basis and for what concerns research methodologies. Thus one might say that CI is prising open the reified boundaries of IS, forcing it to take on board macro-structural aspects relating to the wider social and cultural context, thus greatly enriching the discipline."*

1.2.2 Öffnung der KD-Forschung

Die Forschung zum KD verfolgt lange Zeit schwerpunktmäßig eher kognitionspsychologische und psycholinguistische Ansätze; Fragen wie die der Informationsverarbeitung oder der Aufmerksamkeitsverteilung stehen im Vordergrund. In jüngerer Zeit wird nun aber von vielen Wissenschaftlern (und gleichzeitig Praktikern) eine integrative Sichtweise angestrebt (z.B. Kalina 2001, 2002; Pöchhacker 2001), und ursprünglich aus dem KD kommende Autoren verweisen auf die wertvollen Anstöße durch das NKD. Unterschiede und Gemeinsamkeiten zwischen allen und innerhalb aller Settings werden differenziert und in gegenseitigem Respekt betrachtet. Betont werden nicht die Trennlinien, sondern die Realisierungen des Dolmetschens werden als Kontinuum gesehen: Dazu Kalina:

"I therefore think that we should give up regarding CI and NCI as two strictly separate fields of interpreting with specific characteristics typical of each, as CI and some types of NCI have many shared characteristics while differences exist even within the NCI sector." (2002:173)

Die Notwendigkeit, die Besonderheiten und Anforderungen jeder einzelnen Situation zu erkennen und jeweils adäquat zu handeln, treten ins Bewusstsein. Die Beschäftigung mit dem situativen Kontext wird zum zentralen „Bindeglied[...] zwischen den auf das Konferenzdolmetschen bzw. das Gesprächsdolmetschen ausgerichteten Forschungssträngen in der Dolmetschwissenschaft". (Pöchhacker 2003:180) Die mit der adäquaten Einschätzung der spezifischen Anforderungen der jeweiligen Situation unmittelbar zusammenhängende Frage der Dolmetschqualität - fraglos eine der Schlüsselfragen der Dolmetschwissenschaft und der Dolmetschpraxis (Kutz 2004:779) - ist ein weiteres verbindendes Thema. Normen und Rollenbilder wie die absolute Neutralität des Dolmetschers, seine Funktion als unbeteiligtes „Sprachrohr", seine „Unsichtbarkeit" werden immer häufiger auch für das KD hinterfragt (vgl. z.B. Angelelli 2004, Diriker 2004), Einstellungen und Verhalten werden weniger normativ vorgegeben, als vielmehr in ihrer tatsächlichen Ausprägung in der Praxis deskriptiv erfasst, die Bedeutung der Situation und der Interaktion aller am Kommunikationsereignis Beteiligten rückt immer mehr in den Mittelpunkt des Interesses. Geht man von einer für alle Formen des professionellen Dolmetschens gleichen zentralen Grundkompetenz aus, so lassen sich darüber hinaus für dialogische Dolmetschsituationen, unabhängig davon, ob es sich um das Dolmetschen in Diplomatie, Politik oder Wirtschaft, in der wissenschaftlich-technischen Kommunikation oder in CI-Settings handelt, Beschreibungen entwickeln, anhand derer Lernende über spezifische Anforderungen reflektieren, situationsadäquate Entscheidungen treffen (d.h. translatorisch handeln) und diese Leistungen selbst evaluieren bzw. von anderen evaluieren lassen können. (Gross-Dinter 2007, 2009)

2 Ein Brückenschlag in der Lehre

Dass und wie solche dolmetschwissenschaftlichen Entwicklungen in die Dolmetschdidaktik einfließen und auf diesem Weg wiederum positiv auf die Praxis zurückwirken können, soll nun anhand eines konkreten Ausbildungsangebots aufgezeigt werden.

An der *Hochschule für Angewandte Sprachen / Fachhochschule des SDI* in München, die mit dem Wintersemester 2007/08 ihren Betrieb aufgenommen hat, wurde schon in der Phase der Konzeption der Studiengänge beschlossen, einen Beitrag zur Annäherung von KD und NKD zu leisten und im viersemestrigen Masterstudiengang Konferenzdolmetschen auch je einen Kurs in CI und Gerichtsdolmetschen anzubieten. Die Zielsetzung war dabei eine zweifache: Auf der einen Seite sollten den Studierenden für ihre spätere Berufspraxis ergänzende Möglichkeiten eröffnet werden; auf der anderen Seite sollten aber vor allem angehende Konferenzdolmetscher für die hohen Anforderungen des NKD sensibilisiert, ihre Hochachtung geweckt und so ein Beitrag zur Überbrückung der Kluft auch in der Kollegenschaft geleistet werden.

2.1 Das Konzept der Hochschule für Angewandte Sprachen des SDI

Das Konzept der 30 Unterrichtsstunden umfassenden Lehrveranstaltung sieht je zur Hälfte einen Seminarteil mit der Vermittlung der theoretischen Hintergründe und praktische Übungen mit Rollenspielen mit Beteiligung von zwei Dozenten pro Sprachenpaar vor. Für einen einführenden Gastvortrag konnte dankenswerterweise die Geschäftsführerin des *Bayerischen Zentrums für Transkulturelle Medizin* gewonnen werden, die Dozenten und Studierenden über die Arbeit ihres Dienstes, die nachgefragten Sprachen, die Besonderheiten der interkulturellen Kommunikation beim Dolmetschen bei Behörden, sozialen Diensten und im Gesundheitswesen sowie die – erfolgreichen – Bemühungen ihres Zentrums um eine gezielte Qualifikation der eingesetzten Laiendolmetscher berichtet. Im weiteren Verlauf des Semesters werden Theorie- und Praxisunterricht jeweils zeitlich so koordiniert, dass direkte Bezüge hergestellt werden können. Im Seminarteil werden auf der Grundlage der einschlägigen Literatur in Dozentenvorträgen, Studierendenreferaten und Erfahrungsberichten die folgenden Aspekte behandelt: Klärung des Begriffs CI, Profil des Community-Dolmetschers, Risiken und Konsequenzen mangelnder Professionalität, Besonderheiten der Kommunikation in Institutionen, asymmetrische Kommunikationssituationen, indirekte Sprechakte in stark hierarchisierten ritualisierten Handlungsgefügen, institutionenabhängige soziale Rolle des Community-Dolmetschers, potenzielle Rollenkonflikte, Neutralität als kontrovers diskutiertes Thema, emotionale Distanz und psychosoziales Stressmanagement, CI im Krankenhaus (Onkologie, Anamnese- und Aufklärungsgespräch, Erschließung medizinischer Termini mittels Entschlüsselung über griechische und lateinische Affixe) und Diskursform „polizeiliche Vernehmung" (in Vorwegnahme und zur Entlastung der im folgenden Semester angebotenen Lehrveranstaltung zum Gerichtsdolmetschen). In den praktischen Übungen werden folgende Situationen simuliert: Personenstandssachen (Beratung über Ehevertrag, Niederlassungerlaubnis), Schuldnerberatung, Verbraucherinsolvenzverfahren, Rentenauskunft, Auskunft über und Beantragung von Sozialleistungen, Probleme älterer Migranten (Betreuungsangebote, kultursensible Pflege), Schulberatung, Arztbesuch, Krankenhausdolmetschen, Polizeidolmetschen (Strafanzeige wegen Diebstahls mit Beschuldigten- und Zeugenvernehmung, Abfassung des Protokolls, Hinweise auf die Phasen des Strafverfahrens).

2.2 Erkenntnisse der Studierenden

Natürlich können in einem Semester nicht sämtliche möglichen Situationen erfasst und geübt werden. Dass es anhand exemplarischer Darstellungen, Diskussionen und Übungen aber wohl gut gelingt, die Studierenden für die hohen Anforderungen des CI zu sensibilisieren und vor allem auch dem Entstehen einer Mauer in den Köpfen zukünftiger Konferenzdolmetscher vorzubeugen, beweist das Ergebnis einer kleinen Umfrage, die nach Abschluss des Semesters unter den jeweils sieben Teilnehmern des ersten und zweiten Jahrgangs des MA durchgeführt wurde.

Alle bestätigten, dass sie durch den Kurs für die Besonderheiten – Unterschiede wie Gemeinsamkeiten – von CI und KD sensibilisiert worden waren; den meisten (zwei

Ausnahmen) waren diese vorher nicht bewusst. Als wesentliche Aspekte nannten die Studierenden insbesondere die Problematik der Neutralität, der emotionalen Distanz zum Klienten in einer Situation persönlicher Nähe, die hohe psychische Belastung und die sich daraus ergebende Notwendigkeit einer ausreichenden Stressbewältigung und adäquater Abgrenzungsstrategien. Aufgefallen waren auch die oft schwierigen Arbeitsbedingungen (Nachteinsätze, kein professionelles Umfeld), die Statusdifferenz und das Wissensgefälle zwischen den Gesprächspartnern und das sich daraus häufig ergebende Erfordernis einer Registeranpassung. Hervorgehoben wurden die notwendige interkulturelle Kompetenz sowie die Fähigkeit des Dolmetschers, als einfühlsame Bezugs- und Vertrauensperson sowie als Gesprächsmanager in dialogischen Situationen zu agieren. Unter den Gemeinsamkeiten betonten alle, dass es sich in beiden Settings um anspruchsvolles Dolmetschen handle; fast alle wiesen auf die überall unabdingbare sorgfältige fachliche Vorbereitung und ein gezieltes Wissensmanagement sowie auf gute Fremdsprachenkenntnisse und die Genauigkeit der Verdolmetschung hin. Ein hohes Maß an Flexibilität und das richtige Gleichgewicht zwischen Engagement für die Sache und nicht zu großer persönlicher Involvierung wurden als verbindendes Element erkannt. CI wurde als genauso anstrengend und schwierig wie KD gewertet. Sehr aufschlussreich ist auch die Erkenntnis, „dass man nicht unbedingt ein guter Community Interpreter sein muss, nur weil man in der Kabine unschlagbar ist".

Ein besonders erfreuliches Ergebnis ist, dass mit Ausnahme einer eher zurückhaltenden Antwort alle Studierenden bestätigten, sie würden in Zukunft gerne („selbstverständlich", „meine ethische Pflicht") auch im Bereich des CI Aufträge annehmen, den nur im Bereich des CI tätigen Sprachmittlern mit Hochachtung begegnen und diese Haltung auch gegenüber Kollegen aus der Riege der Konferenzdolmetscher vertreten. Sehr wichtig erscheint hier der Hinweis, dass die emotionalen Anforderungen als Herausforderung und der Kurs als echter Erkenntnisgewinn gesehen wurden: „Ich bin dankbar, diese Erfahrung gemacht haben zu dürfen."

3 Auf dem Weg zur Partnerschaft: Geben und Nehmen

Dass das KD von den Erkenntnissen aus Wissenschaft und Praxis des NKD profitieren kann, wurde in den bisherigen Ausführungen deutlich. Umgekehrt können Community-Dolmetscher aus traditionell in KD-Studiengängen vermitteltem Wissen und Können Nutzen ziehen. Beispielhaft seien hier Recherchetechniken und Terminologieverwaltung, Strategien im Umgang mit dem Kunden (z.B. mit Blick auf das Aushandeln der Interaktionsbedingungen oder des Aufgabenumfangs) oder die in CI-Situationen regelmäßig gefragte Technik des simultanen Flüsterdolmetschens genannt.

3.1 Notationstechnik für Community-Dolmetscher

Vor allem darf auch die Notationstechnik für das Konsekutivdolmetschen als ein Bereich gelten, in dem Community-Dolmetscher im KD entwickelte Fertigkeiten für sich einsetzen können. Auch Community-Dolmetscher sind immer wieder in der

Situation, längere zusammenhängende Äußerungen rezipieren und reproduzieren zu müssen (z.b. bei Dienstbesprechungen, Personalschulungen in Sozialeinrichtungen, psychiatrischen Untersuchungen, psychotherapeutischen Gesprächen). Der Annahme, für das CI sei keine Beherrschung einer professionellen Notationstechnik erforderlich, kann daher keineswegs generell zugestimmt werden. Vielmehr trägt das Notieren nicht nur selbstverständlich zu Vollständigkeit, Genauigkeit und Flüssigkeit der Wiedergabe bei; darüber hinaus erhöht es die Glaubwürdigkeit des Dolmetschers als professionell Handelndem. (Schweda-Nicholson 1990:138) Wird beispielsweise die Technik des Notierens von Wiederaufnahmen und logischen Verknüpfungen im Text beherrscht oder können Nebensequenzen (Rückfragen, ergänzende Erläuterungen usw.) zugelassen werden, weil die Notationstechnik es ermöglicht, den „roten Faden wiederzufinden", so kann das auch im CI nur von größtem Nutzen sein. Allerdings sollte die Technik flexibel den jeweiligen Gegebenheiten der *Face-to-face-Interaktion* angepasst werden. Wirklich hilfreich ist sie auch nur dann, wenn sie automatisiert ist und damit den in Gesprächssituationen so wichtigen Blickkontakt nicht behindert. Schulungen von Laiendolmetschern sollten den genannten Aspekten Aufmerksamkeit schenken. Eigens für Community-Dolmetscher entwickelte Anleitungen wie beispielsweise die von Heimerl (2007), die ihre in einer KD-Ausbildung erlernte Technik anpasst, sind ein gutes Beispiel für einen solchen Transfer.

3.2 Fazit

Die hier geschilderte Initiative im MA Konferenzdolmetschen an der *Hochschule für Angewandte Sprachen* ist sicher nur ein kleiner Beitrag zur Bewältigung einer großen Herausforderung. Aber wenn es nach und nach gelingt, in den Köpfen einiger zukünftiger Dolmetscher Barrieren erst gar nicht entstehen zu lassen und sie dadurch vielleicht zu Multiplikatoren zu machen, so darf man mit diesem Ergebnis wohl ganz zufrieden sein.

Bibliographie

Amato, A. / Mead, P. (2002). Interpreting in the 21st Century: What lies Ahead. Summary of the Closing Panel Discussion, in: Garzone, G. / Viezzi, M. (eds.). *Interpreting in the 21st Century. Challenges and Opportunities. Selected Papers from the 1st Forlì Conference on Interpreting Studies, 9-11 November 2000.* Amsterdam/Philadelphia: John Benjamins, S. 295-301.

Angelelli, C. (2004). *Revisiting the Interpreter's Role. A study of conference, court, and medical interpreters in Canada, Mexico, and the United States.* Amsterdam/Philadelphia: John Benjamins.

Apfelbaum, B. (2004). *Gesprächsdynamik in Dolmetsch-Interaktionen. Eine empirische Untersuchung von Situationen internationaler Fachkommunikation unter besonderer Berücksichtigung der Arbeitssprachen Deutsch, Englisch, Französisch und Spanisch.* Radolfzell: Verlag für Gesprächsforschung.

Diriker, E. (2004). *De-/Re-Contextualizing Conference Interpreting. Interpreters in the Ivory Tower?* Amsterdam/Philadelphia: John Benjamins.

Feldweg, E. (1996). *Der Konferenzdolmetscher im internationalen Kommunikationsprozeß.* Heidelberg: Julius Groos.

Gross-Dinter, U. (2007). Portfolio für das bilaterale Konsekutivdolmetschen – ein Instrument der Verbesserung von Unterrichts- und Lernqualität, in: Schmitt, P. A. / Jüngst, H. (Hrsg.). Translationsqualität. (= Leipziger Studien zur angewandten Linguistik und Translatologie, Band V). Frankfurt a. M.: Peter Lang, S. 222-236.

Gross-Dinter, U. (2009). *Portfolio für das bilaterale Konsekutivdolmetschen. Translationswissenschaftliche und pädagogische Grundlegung, Entwicklung und Erprobung eines didaktischen Konzepts.* München: Europäischer Universitätsverlag.

Heimerl-Moggan, K. / John, I. V. (2007). *Note-taking for Public Service Interpreters.* Timperley: Interp-Right Training Consultancy Ltd.

Kalina, S. (2001). Zur Professionalisierung beim Dolmetschen. Vorschläge für Forschung und Lehre, in: Kelletat, A. F. (Hrsg.). *Dolmetschen. Beiträge aus Forschung, Lehre und Praxis.* Frankfurt a.M.: Peter Lang, S. 51-64.

Kalina, S. (2002). „Interpreters as Professionals", in: *Across Languages and Cultures* 3(2), S. 169-187.

Kutz, W. (2004). Zum Gegenstand der Translatologie aus dolmetschwissenschaftlicher Sicht, in: Fleischmann, E. / Schmitt, P. A. / Wotjak, G. (Hrsg.). *Translationskompetenz. Tagungsberichte der LICTRA (Leipzig International Conference on Translation Studies), 4.-6.10.2001.* Tübingen: Stauffenburg, S. 763-784.

Matyssek, H. (1989). *Handbuch der Notizentechnik für Dolmetscher. Ein Weg zur sprachunabhängigen Notation. Teil 1 und Teil 2.* Heidelberg: Julius Groos.

Pöchhacker, F. (1995). "Writings and Research on Interpreting: A Bibliographic Analysis", in: *The Interpreters' Newsletter* 6, S. 17-31.

Pöchhacker, F. (2000). *Dolmetschen. Konzeptuelle Grundlagen und deskriptive Untersuchungen.* Tübingen: Stauffenburg.

Pöchhacker, F. (2001). „Quality Assessment in Conference and Community Interpreting", in: *Meta* XLVI (2), S. 410-425.

Pöchhacker, F. (2003). Situationsanalyse und Dolmetschen, in: Nord, B. / Schmitt, P. A. (Hrsg.). *Traducta Navis. Festschrift zum 60. Geburtstag von Christiane Nord.* Tübingen: Stauffenburg, S. 165-181.

Pöchhacker, F. (2004). *Introducing Interpreting Studies.* London/New York: Routledge.

Pöchhacker, F. (2007). Critical linking up. Kinship and convergence in interpreting studies, in: Wadensjö, C. / Englund Dimitrova, B. / Nilsson, A.-L. (eds.). *The Critical Link 4. Professionalisation of interpreting in the community. Selected papers from the 4th International Conference on Interpreting in Legal, Health and Social Service Settings, Stockholm, Sweden, 20-23 May 2004.* Amsterdam/Philadelphia: John Benjamins, S.11-23.

Pöchhacker, F. / Kadric, M. (1999). "The Hospital Cleaner as Healthcare Interpreter. A Case Study", in: *The Translator* 5:2 (special issue on dialogue interpreting), S. 161-178.

Roy, Cynthia B (2000). *Interpreting as a Discourse Process.* New York/Oxford: Oxford University Press.

Rudvin, Mette (2006). The cultural turn in Community Interpreting. A brief analysis of epistemological developments in Community Interpreting literature in the light of paradigm changes in the humanities, in: Hertog, E. / van der Veer, B.. *Taking Stock: Research and Methodology in Community Interpreting.* (=Linguistica Antverpiensia, New Series, 5/2006), S. 21-41.

Schweda-Nicholson, N. (1990). Consecutive Note-Taking for Community Interpretation, in: Bowen, D. / Bowen, M. (eds). *Interpreting – Yesterday, Today, and Tomorrow.* Birmingham: SUNY, S. 136-145.

Wadensjö, C. (1998). *Interpreting as Interaction.* London/New York: Longman.

Dolmetschen aus unterschiedlicher Perspektive

Was Dolmetschnotizen über die Form des Konsekutivdolmetschens verraten

Prof. Dr. phil. Barbara Ahrens

Diplom-Dolmetscherin,
Fachhochschule Köln, Institut für Translation und
Mehrsprachige Kommunikation (ITMK)

barbara.ahrens@fh-koeln.de

Vorbemerkung

Der vorliegende Beitrag beruht auf Beobachtungen, die die Verfasserin im Rahmen ihrer Tätigkeit als freiberufliche Konferenzdolmetscherin und als Dozentin an diversen Hochschulen im In- und Ausland sowie bei verbandsinternen und -externen Fortbildungsangeboten gemacht hat. Ihr Dank gilt allen Kolleginnen, Kollegen und Studierenden, die in persönlichen Gesprächen, durch die Beantwortung von Fragen sowie das Überlassen ihrer Dolmetschblöcke zur Entstehung dieses Artikels beigetragen haben.

Im Folgenden werden sämtliche Personenbezeichnungen aus Gründen der Übersichtlichkeit und besseren Lesbarkeit in inkludierender Form verwendet.

1 Einführung

Beim klassischen Konsekutivdolmetschen denkt man sofort an offizielle Anlässe, Tischreden und das diplomatische Parkett, so wie es von praktizierenden Konferenzdolmetschern, Ausbildern und Dolmetschwissenschaftlern im Laufe des 20. Jahrhunderts immer wieder beschrieben wurde (u.a. Herbert 1952, van Hoof 1962, Seleskovitch 1968). Diese Form des Dolmetschens wird häufig als die „Königsdisziplin" des Konferenzdolmetschens angesehen (van Hoof 1962: 32; Henderson 1976: 108), gilt es dabei doch, mehr oder weniger lange Abschnitte formeller Reden unmittelbar nach den Ausführungen des ausgangssprachlichen Redners in der Zielsprache wiederzugeben (AIIC 2009a). Dadurch werden nicht nur hohe Anforderungen an die Gedächtnis- und Konzentrationsleistung des Dolmetschers gestellt, sondern aufgrund seiner unmittelbaren physischen Präsenz im Konferenzgeschehen auch seine rhetorischen und kommunikativen Fähigkeiten in besonderem Maße gefordert.

Seit seinem ersten Einsatz im großen Stil bei den Nürnberger Prozessen hat sich das Simultandolmetschen im internationalen Konferenzgeschehen immer mehr durchgesetzt, da es insbesondere im Falle von mehr als zweisprachigen Konferenzen Zeit spart (Albl-Mikasa 2007: 12). Sitzungen im Rahmen multilingualer internationaler Organisationen wie der UNO oder der EU wären ohne Simultandolmetscher gar nicht durchführbar (Europäische Kommission 2009a). Dennoch legen institutionelle Arbeitgeber – also internationale Organisationen, Ministerien und nachgeordnete Behörden – ebenso wie Ausbildungsinstitute weiterhin großen Wert auf eine gute Konsekutivkompetenz. Dies zeigt sich einerseits in den Testverfahren, andererseits auch in den Studienverlaufsplänen und Prüfungsordnungen der einschlägigen Ausbildungsstätten (u.a. Europäische Kommission 2009b, FH Köln). Dies mag nicht zuletzt daran liegen, dass die beim Konsekutivdolmetschen zu beobachtenden Abläufe Aufschluss über die Analyse-, Abstraktions-, Speicherungs- und Wiedergabekompetenzen des Dolmetschers geben.

Die Dominanz des Simultandolmetschens zeigt sich nicht zuletzt auch darin, dass auf Fragen zur Auftragslage und Verteilung der Dolmetschmodi praktizierende Konferenzdolmetscher immer wieder antworten, dass sie hauptsächlich simultan arbeiten, was in manchen Fällen sogar dazu führt, dass Konsekutivaufträge wegen mangelnder Übung gar nicht erst angenommen werden (auch Kalina 1998: 25).

2 Konsekutivdolmetschen – (k)eine vergessene Kunst?!

Trotz der Dominanz des Simultandolmetschens auf dem Dolmetschmarkt und den nur noch in spezifischen Settings vorkommenden, „hochoffiziellen" Konsekutiveinsätzen mit Grußworten, Tischreden oder auch Laudationes behauptet sich dieser ältere Dolmetschmodus dennoch auf allen Ebenen des Dolmetschmarktes. In den letzten Jahren lässt sich sogar eine Art „Renaissance" des Konsekutivdolmetschens feststellen, wobei die Gründe ganz unterschiedlicher Natur sind:

- Zunahme von Sitzungen mit nur zwei Arbeitssprachen,
- größere Sprachenvielfalt, insbesondere vermehrter Bedarf an den so genannten „kleinen" Sprachen,
- Kostendruck und
- Settings, in denen keine Kabine zum Einsatz kommen kann (Platzgründe, Abhörsicherheit, Tradition etc.).

Es ist also davon auszugehen, dass das Konsekutivdolmetschen auch in Zukunft ein auf dem Markt nachgefragter Dolmetschmodus bleiben wird (Gillies 2005: 3). Daher ist es in der Ausbildung von Konferenzdolmetschern auch weiterhin unverzichtbar, wobei jedoch eventuell eine Anpassung der Lehr- und Prüfungsmodalitäten erforderlich werden wird.

3 Notizentechnik

Wie bereits erwähnt, stellt das Konsekutivdolmetschen hohe Anforderungen an die Gedächtnisleistung des Dolmetschers. Um sein Gedächtnis nicht zu überlasten bzw. um den Abruf der im Gedächtnis gespeicherten Inhalte zu gewährleisten, bedient sich der Dolmetscher seiner Dolmetschnotizen. Bei ihnen handelt es sich nicht um einen „Gedächtnisersatz", sondern um ein Hilfsmittel des Dolmetschers.

Auch wenn immer wieder die Individualität der Notizentechnik postuliert wird, gibt es doch gewisse Prinzipien und Systematika, die sich in allen einschlägigen Notizentechnik-Lehrbüchern finden (für eine ausführliche Darstellung seien u.a. Rozan 1956, Matyssek 1989, Gillies 2005 empfohlen). Dazu gehören die Notation von logischen Verbindungen, die Abgrenzung von Sinnschritten, Tempusmarkierungen und Verneinungen sowie die einrückende und vertikal ausgerichtete Schreibweise auf dem Dolmetschblock. Auch bieten alle gängigen Lehrbücher Anregungen für Abkürzungsverfahren sowie für die Verwendung und Entwicklung von Zeichen und Symbolen (Ahrens 2005). Diese Prinzipien lassen sich in der Regel auf den Blöcken von Studierenden und praktizierenden Dolmetschern erkennen. Die geforderte Individualität des jeweiligen Systems liegt eher in der Mischung der beim Notieren verwendeten Wörter, Symbole, Abkürzungen sowie Sprach- und Schriftsysteme, da diese auf der persönlichen Disposition und Neigung des einzelnen Dolmetschers beruhen.

4 Daten

In den folgenden Kapiteln sollen anhand von Beispielen aus der Konsekutivpraxis die Unterschiede im Notat in verschiedenen Dolmetschsituationen beschrieben werden.

4.1 Klassisches Konsekutivdolmetschen

Bei den folgenden Abbildungen handelt es sich um die ersten zwei Blockseiten einer bei einer Artenschutzkonferenz in den 1990er Jahren notierten Rede. Man kann also von einer klassischen Konsekutivsituation ausgehen.

Sehr deutlich werden hier im Notat die in Abschnitt 3 des vorliegenden Beitrags kurz dargestellten Prinzipien der Notizentechnik: Sinnschritte werden durch kurze horizontale Linien abgegrenzt, Handlungsträger (Abb. 1: „I") und logische Verbindungen sowie textuelle Strukturierungselemente (Abb. 1: „1.)" etc.) finden sich am linken Seitenrand, Tempus- und Verneinungsmarkierungen sowie die Verkettung von Elementen durch Verbindungslinien sind eindeutig feststellbar (Abb. 1). Auch die in der Notizentechnik-Literatur immer beschriebene Mischung aus Abkürzungen, Symbolen und Wörtern ist klar erkennbar.

4.2 Gesprächs- bzw. Verhandlungssituation

Die folgenden Abbildungen stammen aus ein und derselben Gesprächs- bzw. Verhandlungsdolmetschsituation aus dem Bereich Landwirtschaft aus den letzten Jahren. Der analysierte Dolmetschblock umfasst 50 Seiten. Die im Folgenden angegebenen Seitenzahlen beziehen sich auf die tatsächlichen Blockseiten im Notat.

Während sich auf Seite 7 im Gesprächsnotat zunächst dieselben Charakteristika wie die oben anhand des klassischen Konsekutivnotats beschriebenen (Handlungsträger, logische Verbindungen, Sinnschrittabgrenzung, Verneinungen, Tempusmarkierungen, vertikale Schreibweise und Einrücken) feststellen lassen, findet sich ein erster Unterschied in Bezug auf die Quantität der Elemente auf dem Block: Sie ist hier auch in einem längeren Redebeitrag eines der Verhandlungspartner wesentlich höher als bei der klassischen durchgehenden Rede. Darüber hinaus werden sehr viel mehr Wörter verwendet, teilweise sogar komplett ausgeschrieben (Abb. 3: „crisis centre", „we transposed ' RiLi"). Auf der darauf folgenden Seite 8 enden diese längeren Ausführungen oben, was durch den horizontalen Strich über die gesamte Blockbreite gekennzeichnet wird. Auch die Durchstreichung des gesamten Sinnschrittes sowie der beiden auf derselben Seite folgenden ebenfalls durch über die Blockbreite gezogene Striche abgesetzten kurzen Redebeiträge ist auffällig. Für sie gilt außerdem auch die zur Verwendung von Wörtern gemachte Feststellung.

Im Gegensatz zu den sehr „orthodox" – im Sinne von redenartig – notierten Seiten 7 und 8 des Gesprächsnotats zeichnen sich die hier abgebildeten Seiten 34 und 45 durch eine scheinbare Durchbrechung notizentechnischer Prinzipien und Systematika aus. Die abgegrenzten Einheiten reichen nicht mehr unbedingt über die gesamte Block-breite, sodass der dadurch entstehende Platz durch einen weiteren Redebeitrag genutzt wird (Abb. 5 und 6). Auffällig ist, dass logische Verbindungen trotz der Verteilung der Redebeiträge auf dem Block links oben in einem Abschnitt notiert werden (Abb. 5: „da", „desh."). Wie auch schon auf den Seiten 7 und 8 des Blocks finden sich hier ebenfalls mehr Wörter und die Durchstreichung des gesamten Abschnitts. Eine Besonderheit dieser beiden Seiten ist weiterhin, dass teilweise nur ein Wort in einem Abschnitt steht (Abb. 6: „Diagn fähig", „2001"), was auf einen schnellen Sprecher- und damit Turnwechsel im Gesprächs- bzw. Verhandlungsverlauf hindeutet.

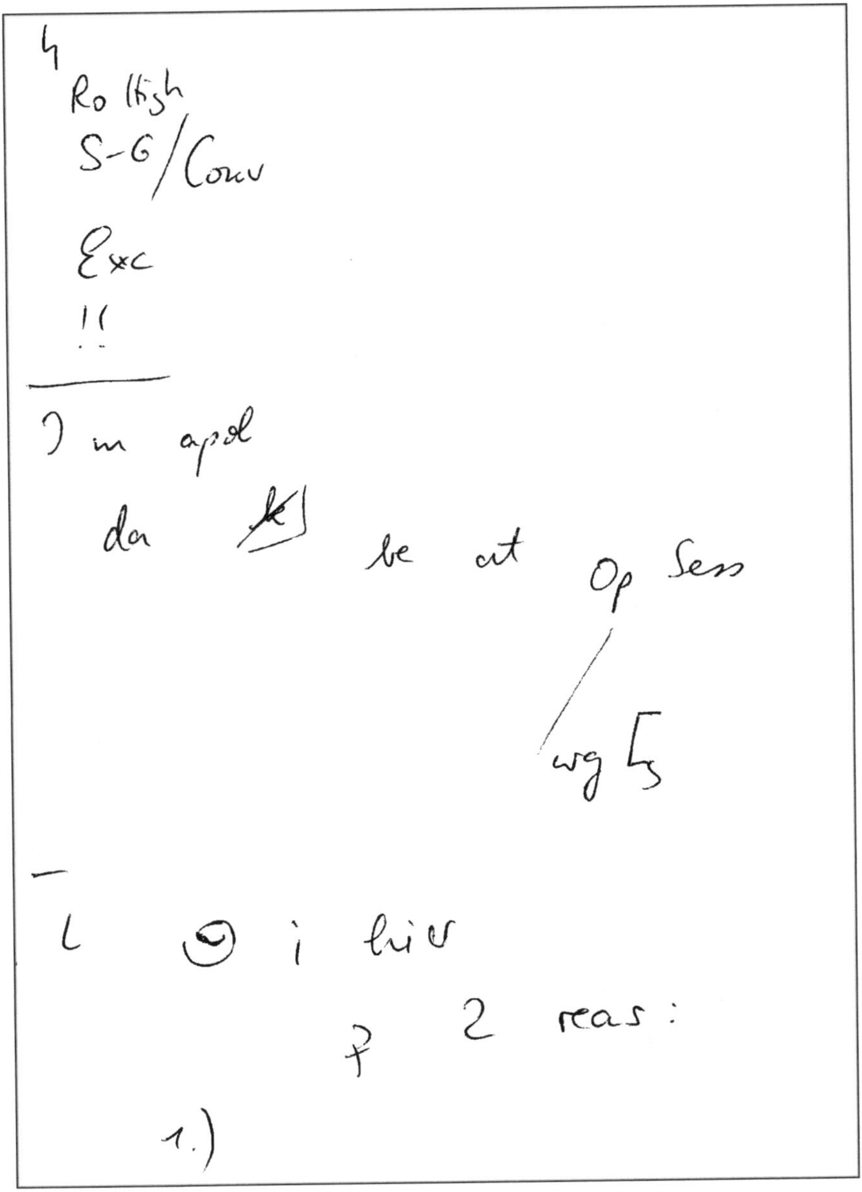

Abb. 1: Konsekutivnotat Seite 1

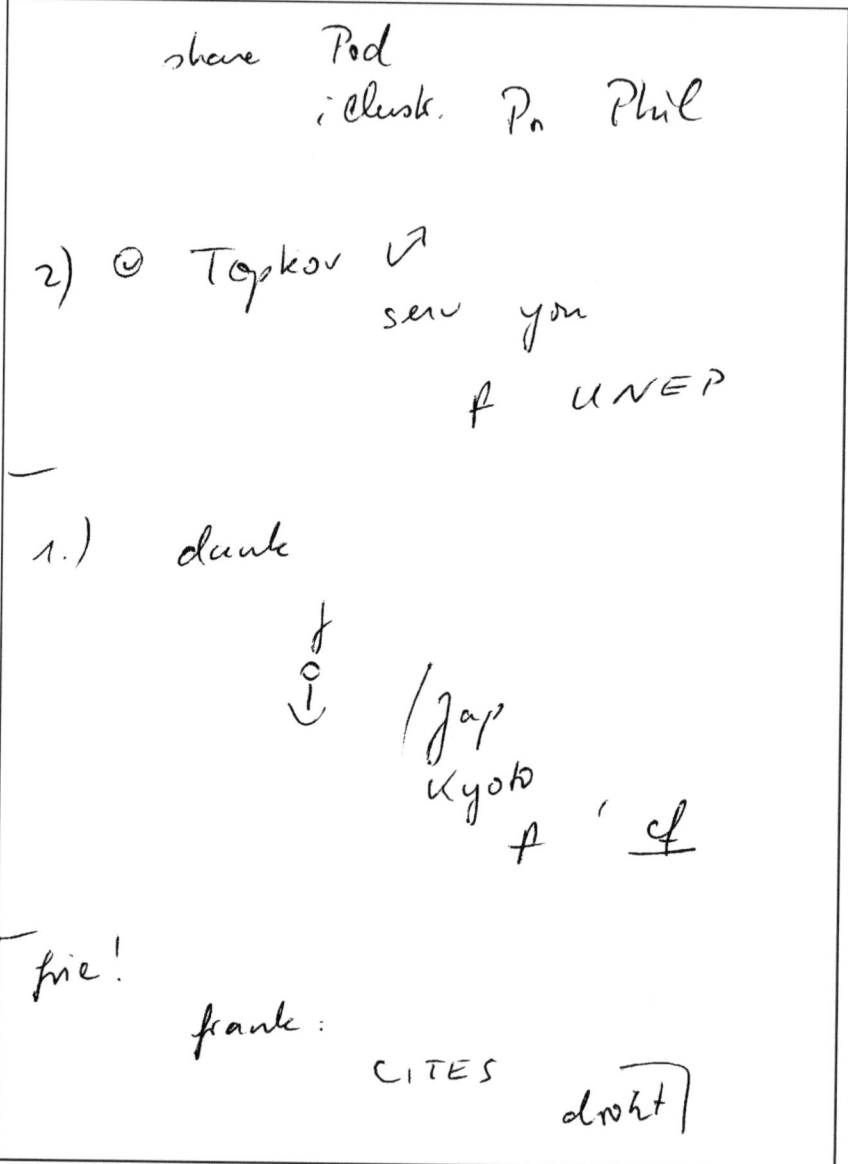

Abb. 2: Konsekutivnotat Seite 2

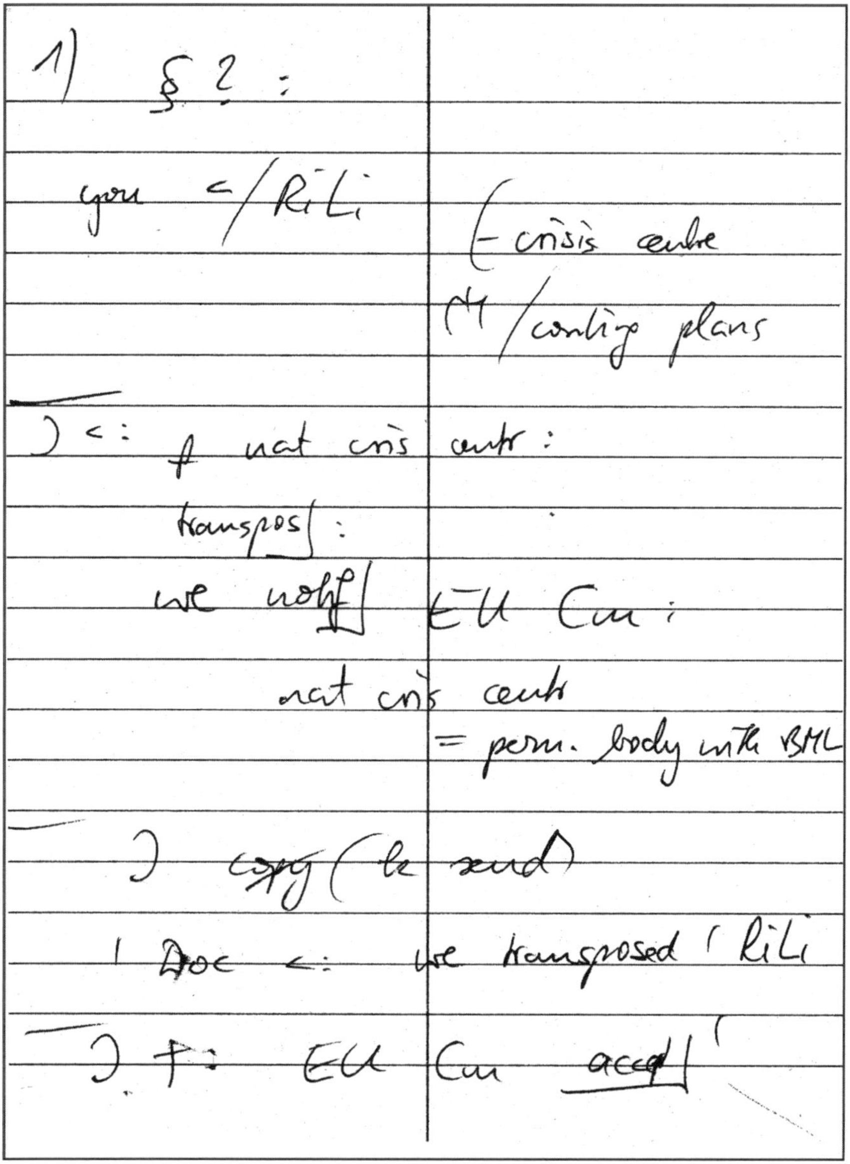

Abb. 3: Gesprächsnotat Seite 7

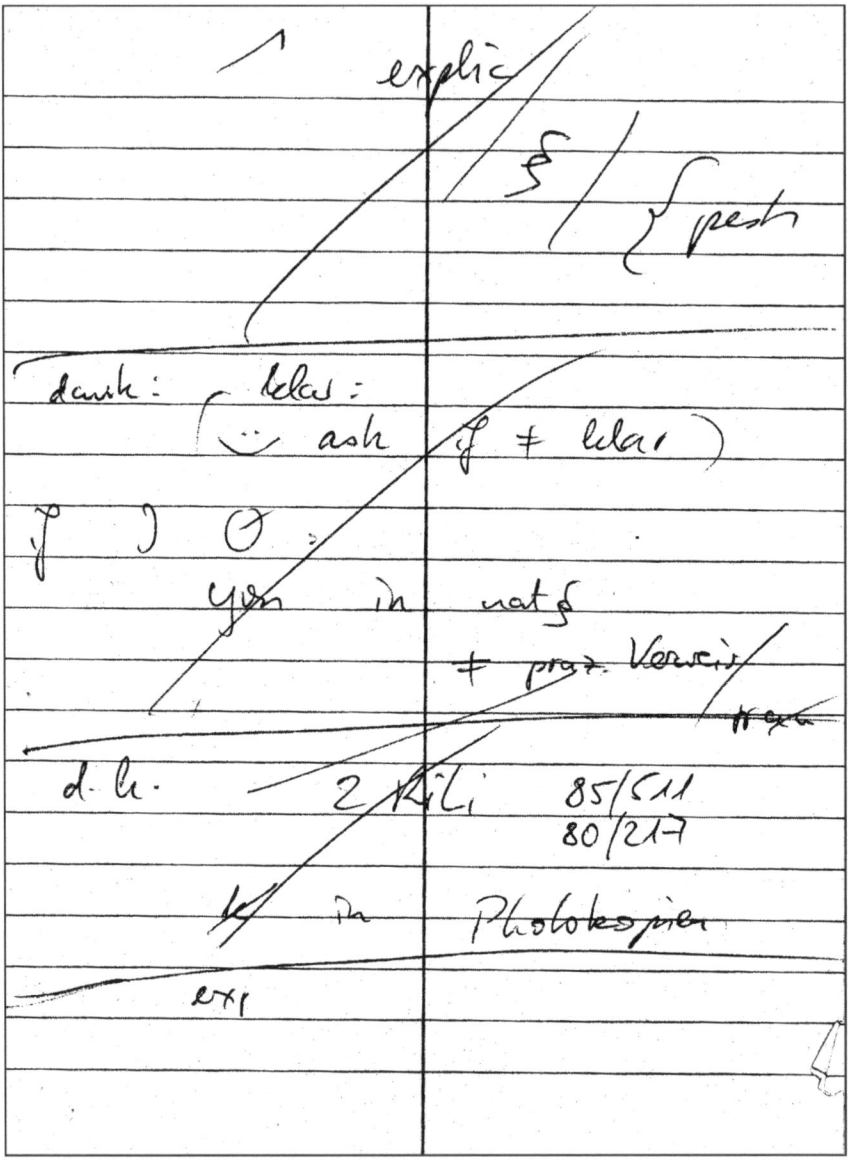

Abb. 4: Gesprächsnotat Seite 8

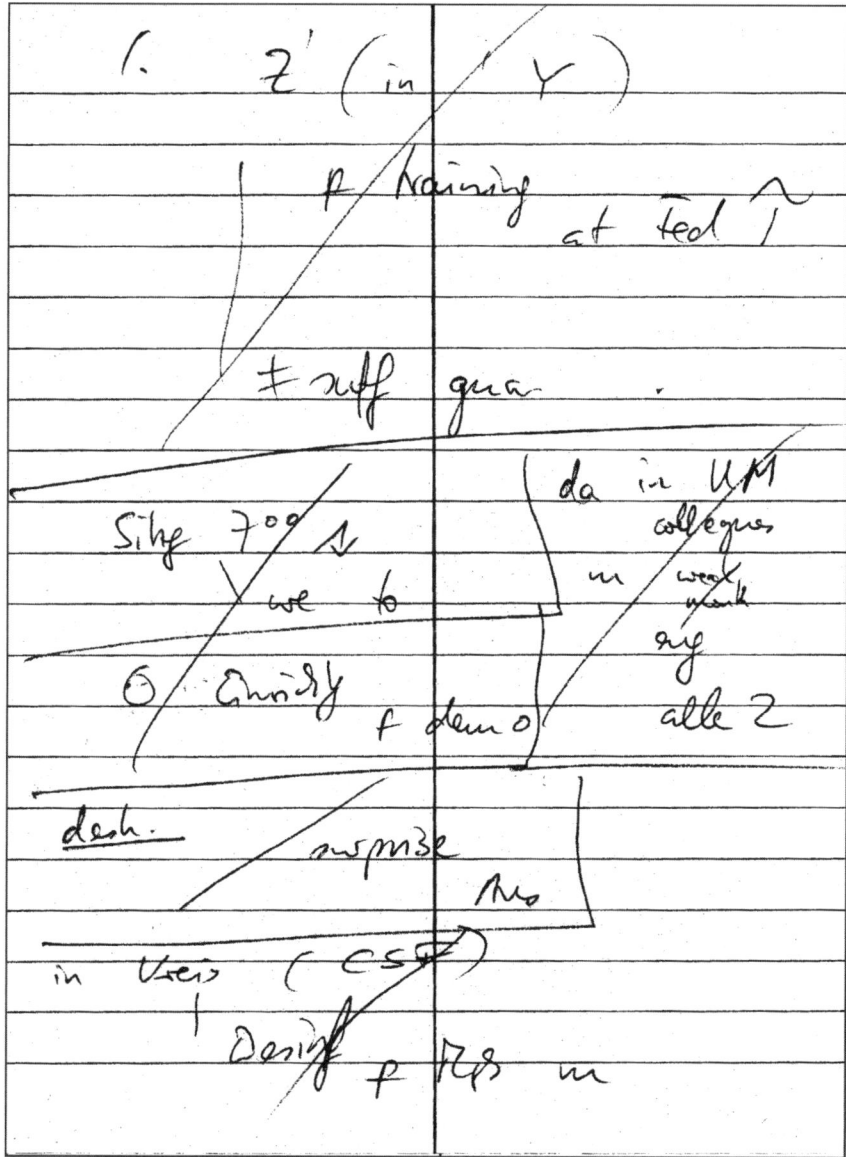

Abb. 5: Gesprächsnotat Seite 34

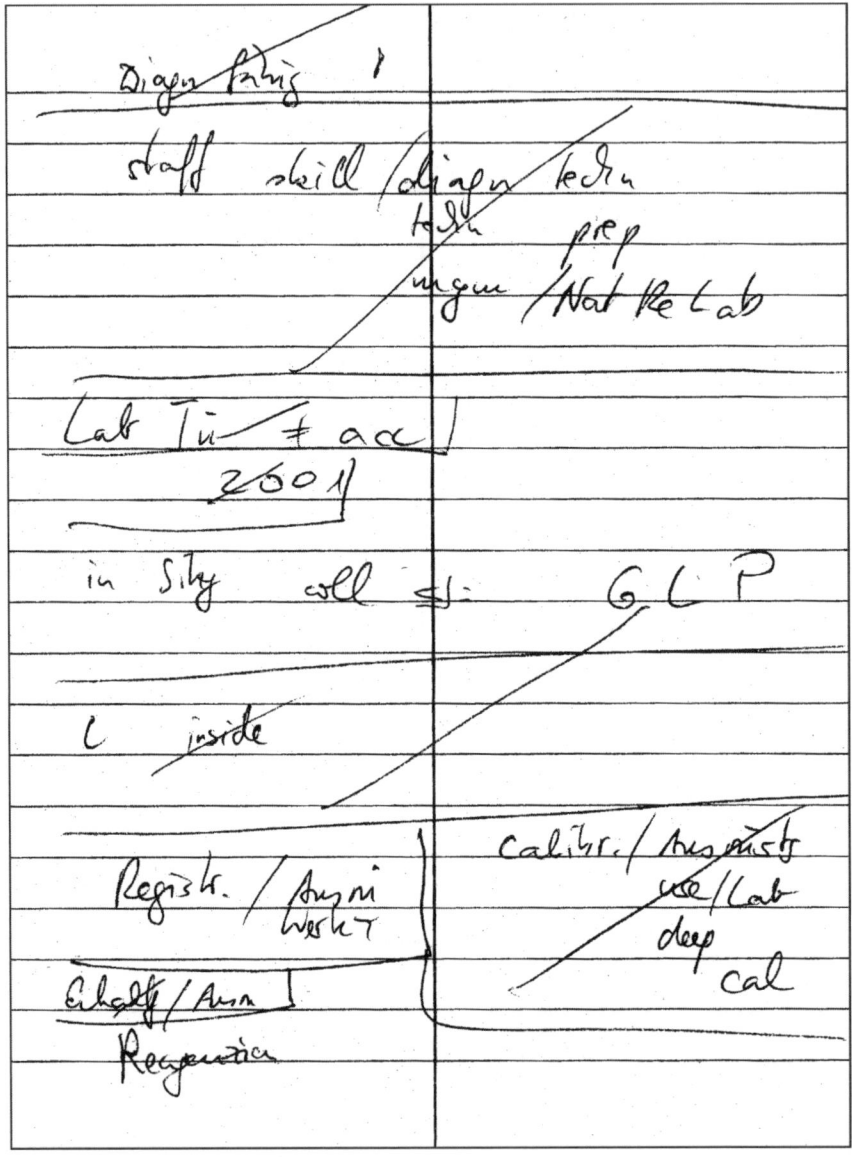

Abb. 6: Gesprächsnotat S. 45

4.3 Diskussion der Daten

Die auf den 6 ausgewählten Blockseiten des Datenmaterials festgestellten Auffällig-
keiten korrelieren eindeutig mit der konsekutiven Dolmetschsituation, in der sie
entstanden sind.

Während in längeren Redebeiträgen – sei es nun in Form einer klassischen Rede
(Abb. 1 und 2), sei es in längeren Ausführungen (Abb. 3) in einer Verhandlung oder
einem Gespräch – die Notizen die für die Notation beim Dolmetschen allgemein
geltenden Prinzipien erfüllen, verändert sich das Erscheinungsbild der Notizen auf
dem Block mit zunehmender Verkürzung der Redebeiträge im Laufe eines Gesprächs
oder einer Verhandlung. Zum einen werden in der Gesprächssituation mehr Wörter
(Abb. 3 und 4) bis hin zu ausschließlich Wörtern aufgeschrieben (Abb. 5 und 6). Das
könnte daran liegen, dass gerade in Verhandlungen häufig der vollständige Wortlaut
von Bedeutung ist. Da Dolmetschen im Allgemeinen aber keine wortlaut-, sondern
inhaltsbasierte Tätigkeit ist, wird in Situationen mit Wortlauterfordernis auch in der
Notation dieser Anforderung offensichtlich Rechnung getragen. Dies wurde von den
dazu befragten Dolmetschern im Rahmen der Analyse der Daten auch bestätigt.

Zum anderen machen die Abgrenzungen der Redebeiträge den Gesprächsverlauf
deutlich: Wird in der klassischen Redesituation für den Beginn einer weiteren längeren Rede eher eine neue Blockseite verwendet, werden in der Gesprächssituation die
Einlassungen der einzelnen Sprecher durch deutliche Striche über die gesamte
Blockbreite vollständig voneinander abgegrenzt (Abb. 4), bei kurzen Turns endet
dieser sogar manchmal unmittelbar hinter dem Wort (Abb. 5 und 6), wobei jedoch
auch hier die vollständige Abgrenzung durch Linien gegenüber den vorangegangenen
und den nachfolgenden Notizen gegeben ist, um so eine sinnentstellende Verknüpfung
separater Abschnitte zu vermeiden. Darüber hinaus dient die auch nur in den schnell
aufeinanderfolgenden Turns festzustellende Durchstreichung der Notizen eines
Abschnitts nach erfolgter Verdolmetschung und vor Beginn des nächsten Gesprächs-
beitrags ebenfalls dazu, die bereits gedolmetschten Redeabschnitte zu kennzeichnen.
Im vorliegenden Datenmaterial konnte auf sämtlichen Blöcken aus Gesprächs- bzw.
Verhandlungssituationen festgestellt werden, dass in Phasen längerer Einlassungen
nicht alle einzelnen Sinnschritte desselben Turns durchgestrichen wurden, sondern
immer nur der letzte, um so das Ende des gesamten Turns eindeutig zu markieren
(Abb. 3 und 4). Es scheint sich also um eine Strategie zur Wahrung der Eindeutigkeit
des Notats und der damit verbundenen Verdolmetschung zu handeln.

Interessant ist in diesem Zusammenhang außerdem, dass die eindeutige Position
logischer Verbindungen, die als unabdingbar für eine zuverlässige Notizentechnik
angesehen werden (Ahrens 2005: 12), auch in den kurzen Turns beibehalten wird: auf
der linken Seite des Abschnitts, häufig durch Einrücken abgesetzt (Abb. 5), wodurch
eine schnelle und eindeutige Erfassung in der Abrufphase der konsekutiven
Dolmetschleistung gewährleistet wird. Die Notizen spiegeln somit klar die verinner-
lichte Dolmetschtechnik zur Wahrung der Argumentationsstruktur und damit des
inhaltlichen Fokus des Redners wider.

5   Schlussfolgerungen

Zusammenfassend lassen die hier vorgestellten Beobachtungen zur Entwicklung des Konsekutivmarktes sowie die Analyse der Dolmetschblöcke aus unterschiedlichen Konsekutivsituationen folgende Schlussfolgerungen für die Dolmetschdiktatik und -praxis zu:

- Konsekutivdolmetschen ist keine vergessene Kunst, sondern weiterhin ein unverzichtbarer Dolmetschmodus, der wieder zunehmend nachgefragt wird, auch wenn sich die Settings für seinen Einsatz verändern.

- In der Ausbildung von Konferenzdolmetschern sollten die Veränderungen der Settings berücksichtigt werden. Konsekutivdolmetschen längerer Reden zum Training der Analyse- und Abstraktionsfähigkeit sowie des sprachlich-stilistischen Ausdrucks muss weiterhin Bestandteil des Curriculums von Dolmetschstudiengängen sein. Darüber hinaus sollten aber auch häufiger Gesprächs- und Verhandlungssituationen trainiert werden, um die dort teilweise geltenden Anforderungen an den Wortlaut und die Wahrung der Gesprächs-dynamik zu erlernen. Gesteigert werden können die Anforderungen durch thematische Komplexität, einen kontroversen und/oder formalen Charakter des Gesprächs, das Tempo des Turntakings oder auch die Verwendung techni-scher Hilfsmittel wie Präsentationen, Videos etc., um so die Praxisnähe und Marktorientiertheit der Ausbildung zu gewährleisten.

- In Bezug auf die Notizentechnik sollte weiterhin auf die Vermittlung der übli-chen Prinzipien und Systematika geachtet werden. Jedoch sollten auch die in Gesprächs- und Verhandlungssituationen vorkommenden Besonderheiten des Notierens angesprochen und geübt werden. Hier könnte vor allem ein Aus-tausch zwischen Verhandlungs- oder auch Besprechungsdolmetschern – wie sie teilweise in Behörden genannt werden – und Konferenzdolmetschern sinn-voll sein, um die im jeweiligen Modus vorherrschenden Bedingungen sowie Tipps und Tricks zu lernen.

Bibliographie

Ahrens, B. (2005): „Rozan and Matyssek: Are they really that different? A Compara-tive Synopsis of Two Classic Note-Taking Schools", in: *Forum. International Jour-nal of Interpretation and Translation* 3.2, S. 1-15.

AIIC – Association Internationale des Interprètes de Conférence (2009a). *Glossary: Consecutive Interpreting.* www.aiic.net/glossary/default.cfm?ID=103&letter=C (zu-letzt aufgerufen am 18.06.2009).

AIIC – Association Internationale des Interprètes de Conférence (2009b). *Glossary: Note-Taking.* www.aiic.net/glossary/default.cfm?ID=133&letter=N (zuletzt aufge-rufen am 18.06.2009).

Albl-Mikasa, M. (2007). *Notationssprache und Notizentext. Ein kognitiv-linguistisches Modell für das Konsekutivdolmetschen.* Tübingen: Narr.

Europäische Kommission, Generaldirektion Dolmetschen (2009a). http://scic.ec. europa.eu/europa/jcms/j_8/home (zuletzt aufgerufen am 18.06.2009).

Europäische Kommission, Generaldirektion Dolmetschen (2009b). *Testing Times: EU Institutions' Interpreter Test*. DVD. Brüssel: VideoSCIC production.

FH Köln (2009). *Allgemeine Informationen zum MA Konferenzdolmetschen*. www.f03.fh-koeln.de/fakultaet/itmk/studium/nationale-studiengaenge/ma-konferenzdolmetschen/index.html (zuletzt aufgerufen am 28.06.2009).

Gillies, A. (2005). *Note-taking for Consecutive Interpreting: A Short Course*. Manchester: St. Jerome.

Henderson, J. A. (1976): „Note-Taking for Consecutive Interpreting", in: *Babel* 22.3, S. 107-116.

Herbert, J. (1952). *Manuel de l'interprète: Comment on devient interprète de conférence*. Genf: Georg.

Hoof, H. van (1962). *Théorie et pratique de l'interprétation*. München: Hueber.

Kalina, S. (1998). *Strategische Prozesse beim Dolmetschen: Theoretische Grundlagen, empirische Fallstudien, didaktische Konsequenzen*. Tübingen: Narr.

Matyssek, H. (1989). *Handbuch der Notizentechnik für Dolmetscher: Ein Weg zur sprachunabhängigen Notation*. 2 Bände. Heidelberg: Groos.

Rozan, J.-F. (1956). *La prise de notes en interprétation consécutive*. Genf: Georg.

Seleskovitch, D. (1968). *L'interprète dans les conférences internationales: Problèmes de langage et de communication*. Paris: Minard.

Multidimensionale Studie der erlebten Erwartungen von Usern in einer gedolmetschten Gerichtsverhandlung

Tina Paulsen Christensen

Aarhus School of Business, University of Aarhus, Aarhus

tpc@asb.dk

Abstract

Die meisten Dolmetscher betrachten wahrscheinlich Professionalismus als das alles überragende Ziel der Dolmetschtätigkeit und fühlen sich bei der Ausführung ihrer Tätigkeit der Qualitätssicherung stets verpflichtet. Es ist daher problematisch, dass weder unter den Dolmetschern selbst noch in Forschungskreisen darüber Einigkeit besteht, was eigentlich unter Qualität zu verstehen ist.

Diese Studie baut auf der Annahme auf, dass das Community Interpreting (und somit auch das Gerichtsdolmetschen) im Sinne einer Serviceleistung vorwiegend als ein interaktiver Prozess aufzufassen ist, bei dem Qualität mit erfolgreicher Kommunikation gleichzusetzen ist. Dies bedeutet wiederum, dass der Grad des Erfolgs/ Misserfolgs von Seiten der an der gedolmetschten Kommunikation teilnehmenden Parteien subjektiv zu bewerten ist.

Dieser Vortrag präsentiert die Ergebnisse einer qualitativen Befragung zu den Erwartungen, die die User von Gerichtsdolmetschern in einer authentischen dänischen Gerichtsverhandlung an den beteiligten Dolmetscher stellen. Die Studie verfolgt einen multidimensionalen Ansatz, der die erlebten Erwartungen von allen an der Interaktion beteiligten Personen (dem Angeklagten, dem Richter, dem Verteidiger, dem Vertreter der Anklagebehörde und dem deutschsprachigen Zeugen) berücksichtigt. Mittels Fragebögen sind diese Kommunikationsteilnehmer gebeten worden, ihre Erwartungen darzustellen und gleichzeitig die Leistung des Dolmetschers zu bewerten. Integrierter Bestandteil der Studie ist ferner die Frage, inwieweit die Erwartungen des Dolmetschers über die User-Erwartungen mit den tatsächlichen Erwartungen der User übereinstimmen.

Ziel dieses Beitrags ist es, den (auch angehenden) Gerichtsdolmetschern eine tragfähige, empirische Grundlage zur Verfügung zu stellen, auf der sie ihre alltäglichen Dolmetschentscheidungen basieren können, anstatt intuitiv zu handeln.

Community interpreting and ethnic communities – Using minority children as "convenient tools" in public service interpreting

Dr. Iris Guske

Director of the Fachakademie für Fremdsprachenberufe, Kempten

iris.guske@online.de

Abstract

A recent seminar by the British Economic and Social Research Council and the first ever international conference on that topic in Manchester in March 2005 showed that language brokering by children is a widespread activity which takes place around the world every day, yet goes largely unacknowledged in spite of its importance for the basic functioning of migrant families.

As children are often the first to master the adopted country's language, they are faced with the task of acting as language mediators with regard to their families' administrative, economic, and social needs in a total reversal of normal family roles.

While instances of successful language and culture brokering certainly bolster an adolescent's self-esteem, children often perceive these tasks as a burden, especially when the stakes are high and a situation requires mediation skills that are beyond their linguistic, cognitive and emotional capabilities.

The aim of the study which I carried out in Germany in 2003/04 was to find out if such tasks put second-generation immigrants under pressures unknown by their host-culture peers, whether they consequently gravitated towards their ethnic peers, and how the cross-pressure situations thus experienced impacted on the development of the self.

Results show that native youths are often perceived as immature, so that a sense of belonging is predominantly provided by the social reference group of their ethnic peers. This is characterised by processes of selecting and rejecting values from either culture, and culminates in the establishment of a distinct, third, identity.

Awareness should be raised among migrants and host-society authorities that parentification might pose major developmental problems if minority youths are not relieved of (some of) the potential burdens of language and culture brokering. In this context the benefits and drawbacks of community interpreting services offered to minorities in Great Britain and Germany are discussed.

Medical translation and interpreting

Dolmetschen im medizinischen Bereich oder: die Hoffnung stirbt zuletzt

Dr. Dörte Andres

Johannes Gutenberg-Universität Mainz/FASK Germersheim

doerte.andres@t-online.de

Abstract

Vermischung und Vermengung durch Globalisierung, Massenmigration und steigende Mobilität sind nicht mehr zu übersehen, auch nicht der dadurch immer größer werdende Bedarf an Personen, die als Mittlerinnen und Mittler in den entstehenden Zwischenräumen fungieren. Gebärdensprachdolmetschen, Dolmetschen im medizinischen, sozialen und juristischen Bereich sowie Dolmetschen in Krisengebieten haben in den letzten 15 Jahren in der Welt erheblich an Bedeutung gewonnen und rücken zunehmend in das Blickfeld von Gesellschaft und Politik. Doch während das Konferenzdolmetschen durch seine Internationalität und Professionalität hohes Ansehen genießt, ist vor allem das Fachdolmetschen im Sozial-, Gesundheits- und Rechtswesen weiterhin durch einen Mangel an angemessenen Ausbildungs- und Akkreditierungsmöglichkeiten, inakzeptable Bezahlung und mangelnde Anerkennung gekennzeichnet. Der Vortrag behandelt den Stand der Forschung, den Bedarf an DolmetscherInnen, die erforderlichen Kompetenzen und vorhandene sowie geplante Ausbildungsmöglichkeiten.

Remote interpreter services in healthcare, a shift of paradigm in the United States

Oscar Arocha

M.M. – Director, Interpreter & Guest Support Services
Boston Medical Center, Boston, Massachusetts

osarocha@comcast.net

Abstract

Under pressure from regulatory agencies and government departments such as the Department of Public Health and the Department of Justice, hospitals have been increasingly developing medical interpreter service programs. Although they started by providing these services in person, hospitals are increasingly offering *remote* interpreting. The systems in place today require hospital funding as administrative costs are not covered by private nor government-supported health insurance. The need to provide interpreter services ubiquitously 24 hours a day in a large number of languages is making program administrators rely more and more on *remote* interpreting.

The two main modalities are: 1) over the phone (OPI), 2) video medical interpreting (VMI). This is shifting the general belief in some hospitals that medical interpreting in person is to be offered as the primary option in healthcare settings. Depending on the specifics of the situation, hospitals are realizing that not having an interpreter in the exam room will not necessarily generate a negative experience to patients. Timeliness, preference, access, availability and cost are all factors that weigh into the decisions of which modality to use.

This presentation will focus on how Boston Medical Center's Interpreter Service Department, the first in the United States to staff medical interpreters, went from having a small program to being the largest in the country, relying at first on primarily on-site interpreter staff, then developing a large OPI operation, and ultimately pioneering VMI. It will discuss the operational challenges that led to the adoption of new technology and the strategies to leverage a more efficient multisystem program which allowed BMC to provide 200,000 interpreter requests in 2008.

Kulturelle Aspekte bei der Übersetzung von medizinischen Texten

Susanne Geercken

Dipl.-Übersetzerin

susanne.geercken@pfizer.com

Abstract

Medizinische Texte werden oft als weitestgehend „kulturell neutral" eingestuft, da die Anatomie und Physiologie des menschlichen Körpers auf der ganzen Welt gleich ist. Diese Annahme wird noch gefördert durch die weltweite Rolle des Englischen als „Lingua franca" in der medizinischen Kommunikation.

Bei näherer Betrachtung wird jedoch deutlich, dass selbst in den kulturell relativ ähnlichen „westlichen" Ländern unterschiedliche historische und sprachliche Einflüsse zu kulturspezifischen Betrachtungsweisen medizinischer Sachverhalte geführt haben. In meinem Vortrag werde ich auf eine Reihe solcher kultureller Unterschiede eingehen.

Die – oft subtilen – kulturell bedingten Unterschiede stellen eine besondere Herausforderung für den Übersetzer dar. Anhand von kurzen Textbeispielen aus dem anglo-amerikanischen Sprachraum werde ich einige Kulturspezifika in medizinischen Texten vorstellen und Probleme und Lösungsmöglichkeiten bei deren Übersetzung ins Deutsche diskutieren.

Medical interpreter certification - A new global credential for a new specialization

Izabel Arocha

M.Ed., President of the International Medical Interpreters Association (IMIA), Boston, USA

iarocha@imiaweb.org

Presents as proceedings for this presentation:

Breaking the language barrier: *Health care quality, efficiency and savings through professional medical interpretation by Louis F. Provenzano, Jr.*

Introduction

The growing linguistic diversity of the United States is having a dramatic impact on the delivery of essential social services, particularly health care services. Each day, thousands of patients arrive at hospitals, urgent care centers and primary care medical offices, and before their temperature is taken or their blood pressure is gauged, they face a potentially devastating barrier that could affect the quality of care they receive, the outcome of their visit, and their future health. These patients have limited English proficiency (LEP), defined as speaking English less than very well or not at all, and the language barrier they face has a detrimental effect on their care and overall health.

Here is an example of the scenario that LEP patients encounter: an individual arrives at a hospital with shooting pain in the abdomen, but is unable to tell physicians and nurses what he is experiencing, or how it relates to his personal medical history.

He tries to explain his symptoms, but his description is misunderstood, leading to a delay in treatment and unnecessary tests.

For those with limited English skills, this hypothetical example is all too real. Hospitals and medical centers offer medical interpretation services in order to avoid the type of situation described above ("interpretation" is the spoken form of language translation). In fact, any facility that receives federal funds is required by law to provide access to competent language services, but the reality is that some offer medical interpretation services in name only, relying on untrained administrative staff or a patient's family members – even young children – to help with communication. While medical interpretation by trained, qualified professionals has a documented positive impact on health care efficiency and effectiveness, it is simply not consistently available.

The reasons why quality interpretation services are not readily available are varied, but almost always involve the question of cost and responsibility for payment. Private insurers do not generally reimburse for language services, and only a handful of states provide Medicaid reimbursement. Medicare does not provide coverage. In addition, there are no national standards that define competent medical interpretation although many professionals and organizations are working toward the goal of national certification including standards for training, testing and on-going education. There is perhaps no greater step that can be taken to improve health outcomes for LEP patients, reduce unnecessary medical costs as they relate to these patients, and standardize the availability and quality of medical interpretation, than to provide reimbursement for language access services. This white paper examines the growing impact of language diversity, the role of quality medical interpretation, and the importance of reimbursement for language services by Medicaid, Medicare and private insurers.

The changing linguistic landscape

Statistics clearly demonstrate that the ethnic and linguistic make-up of the United States is changing rapidly. Across the country, in urban and rural areas, an increasing number of languages are spoken by a growing number of residents. According to U.S. Census data, over 47 million people in the country speak a language other than English at home, and nearly 24 million are considered LEP. The number of foreign-born individuals in the country has now reached an all-time high of 38.1 million, according to the Census Bureau's 2007 American Community Survey.1 The Bureau has also predicted that minorities will comprise the majority of the country's population by 2042, with the demographic shift being driven by greater diversity and increases in immigration. Census information also clearly maps the rate and nature of linguistic change. Between 1990 and 2000, for instance, the percentage of American residents speaking a language other than English at home rose from 13.8 percent to 17.8 percent, and the LEP population increased from 6.1 percent to 8.1 percent. In addition, evidence shows that LEP speakers come from all age and income groups. Today, more than 176 languages and various dialects are spoken across the country. Languages once considered rare in certain parts of the U.S. are now heard more frequently. For example, in Arlington, Virginia, there is a need for Krio language interpreters; Krio is the language of Sierra Leone, Africa. Denver needs Karen speakers; Karen is spoken in Myanmar. In the Seattle area, interpreters are needed for Oromo, a language of Ethiopia. In Phoenix, Dari is spoken; Dari is a language of Afghanistan. The linguistic diversity trend is predicted to continue, with marked effects on many key social functions, from the operation of the judiciary to the delivery of emergency services. Perhaps no other segment of our economy, however, is experiencing as dramatic an impact as the health care arena.

The impact of language on health care and the role of Title VI

In hospital emergency rooms and urgent care clinics, the reality of our nation's linguistic situation is perhaps most notable and obvious. As more LEP patients arrive for care and consultation, there is a vital need for high quality medical interpretation and translation to ensure that diagnoses and treatments can be delivered quickly and accurately. Patients arriving for care must be able to communicate their symptoms, medical histories, and the circumstances of their illness to their care givers, and without quality interpretation, they simply cannot do so. While the effect is clear in emergency settings, it is also obvious in other medical circumstances, including regular physician visits and outpatient testing.

As health care administrators are well aware in the United States, Title VI of the Civil Rights Act has long required those who receive federal funding to provide the same level of access to services for limited English speaking patients as they do for those who speak English. This requirement represents a protection against discrimination based on national origin. An Executive Order "Improving Access to Services for Persons with Limited English Proficiency," issued in 2000,4 attempted to clarify and strengthen the language access implications of Title VI, but it has left gaps in structure and enforcement. Without guidance or consistent enforcement, hospitals and other medical facilities have responded to the federal language access requirement in dramatically different ways, with some offering in-house interpreters combined with over-the-phone language interpreting services, and others offering much less. Even among those with formal interpreting services, the level of quality varies greatly.

Given the growing LEP population and the widening inconsistency in patient communication, state and federal requirements that govern how hospitals communicate with a diverse patient population are certain to become more stringent and strictly enforced in years to come. In fact, many new laws and regulations have already come into effect in recent years. In California, for instance, a 2003 law that took effect on January 1, 2009 requires all health plans to offer the same access to language services as enrollees in government plans. Hawaii requires language services in all state programs, with the mandate that oral and written interpreting must be provided to LEP individuals. Similarly, the State of Maryland requires the provision of oral language assistance by hospitals and agencies receiving federal funds. And in Washington, a State Cultural Competence requirement mandates cultural competency training for physicians. In New York, regulations require hospitals to develop language assistance programs to ensure "meaningful access" to medical services, as well as accommodation for all patients who require language assistance.

More legislative and regulatory changes are on the horizon. Federal and state legislation has been proposed to extend language access requirements to all health care organizations, and to define more carefully the nature and content of these programs. Washington, California, New Jersey and New Mexico are all considering or have implemented cultural competency requirements. While federal and state lawmakers and regulators work to implement new requirements, The Joint Commission has undertaken a comprehensive research project that provides important support for government action on a number of fronts. The study, entitled *Hospitals, Language, and Culture: A Snapshot of the Nation*, investigates how hospitals offer care to diverse populations, and clearly demonstrates the challenges that hospitals face as well as the need for financial support. At the same time, The Joint Commission has added a language services component to its assessment criteria.

The importance of providing medical interpretation

As mentioned, while most medical care givers are required to provide language access services, the manner in which they do so is widely inconsistent. Many medical facilities have formal medical interpretation programs, but many others are less formal. Anecdotal evidence shows that facilities often rely on family members of patients to provide medical interpretation; others rely on untrained administrative staff. The consequences of this approach can be deadly - and costly.

Statistics show that language is a major factor in cases of misdiagnosis and instances of poor treatment at hospitals, and delays in service or access to preventive care. Medical error in general is a troubling issue, but patients with limited English proficiency are almost twice as likely to suffer adverse events in U.S. hospitals, resulting in temporary harm or death, according to a pilot study by The Joint Commission entitled *Language Proficiency and Adverse Events in U.S. Hospitals*.6

In addition, LEP patients are more likely to report poor health, defer medical care, leave hospitals against medical advice, miss follow-up appointments and experience complications from medications.7 Whether LEP patients are delaying care because they expect to face a difficult medical encounter due to language issues, or whether they are receiving substandard care due to miscommunication and delays caused by language gaps, the end result is the same: language barriers are clearly resulting in the unequal delivery of medical care, and in physical harm.

Language barriers: Personal stories

Take the high-profile case of William Ramirez. Twenty years ago, paramedics in Miami defined his word "intoxicado" as "high on drugs" instead of "food poisoning." His care was delayed as a result of a series of related emergency room miscommunications, and now a quadriplegic, he has been awarded a $71 million malpractice settlement. Other cases are equally tragic. A three year-old girl arrived at an emergency room with her parents. The girl suffered from abdominal pain, but this was not clearly communicated to medical staff, delaying a diagnosis of appendicitis, resulting in a 30-day hospitalization, and infections. While the toll on the health and well-being of LEP patients is disconcerting, there is also a financial toll on health care organizations, and state and federal agencies. Language barriers can result in inefficient and therefore more expensive care. Often, without proper medical interpretation, care givers cannot accurately gauge the symptoms or medical histories of their patients, and therefore must perform additional, costly tests and otherwise unnecessary invasive procedures. These costs are ultimately born by patients and insurers, including Medicaid and Medicare.

Providing quality, trained medical interpreters can therefore not only improve medical outcomes, it can save health care dollars by ensuring faster results, fewer unnecessary medical procedures, and reduced legal expenses. By making LEP patients more comfortable with health care encounters, interpretation can also encourage preventive care and overall improved health care habits. According to studies, patients with limited English skills who are provided with interpreters "make more outpatient visits, receive and fill more prescriptions, do not differ from English-proficient patients in test costs or receipt of intravenous hydration, have outcomes among those with diabetes that are superior or equivalent to those of English-proficient patients, and have high satisfaction with care."8 Medical interpreters are an essential link between LEP patients and needed care.

The role of the trained medical interpreter

Nationally, there are more than 41,000 trained interpreters, many of whom work in the health care field in more than 176 languages. An interpreter who is specially trained in medical interpretation has a deeper knowledge of medical issues and terminology, understands privacy issues surrounding HIPAA, and has a clear under- standing of the role that interpreters play in the relay of information between medical staff and patients. Medical facilities can employ the services of professional interpre- ters in a variety or combination of ways:

1. *In-House Staff Interpreters*: Facilities can employ trained bilingual clinical staff and bilingual employees who are dedicated to providing medical inter- pretation.

2. *Independent Contractors*: Facilities may engage individuals who are contrac- tors who provide interpretation on an as needed or part-time basis.

3. *Telephone Interpretation Services*: Facilities may contract with telephone in- terpretation services that provide on-call interpretation in any language via a three-way call, typically involving a dual handset used by the patient and medical staff, with the interpreter on the line remotely.

4. *Video Interpretation Services:* Facilities may supplement their language ser- vices offerings with video interpretation, a service used primarily for the deaf and hard of hearing.

Whether relying on in-house staff or telephone and video interpretation services, medical providers can only be assured of quality and accuracy if they employ inter- preters that are trained and tested. Since standards for training and certification generally are not in place, as discussed in the next section, facilities must make special efforts to gauge the quality of the services they employ.

The need for reimbursement for language access services

Medical and social research studies, along with accepted legal interpretations, are clear on three important matters:

1. Medical providers receiving any federal funds have a legal responsibility to provide language access services.

2. Language barriers lead to inefficient care and poor outcomes for those with limited English skills.

3. Trained medical interpreters can help improve outcomes, which in turn results in better care and reduced medical expenses.

Given the facts and data, it is reasonable to assume that all medical providers would provide quality medical interpretation according to an agreed-upon set of standards, and on a consistent basis. But because there is no clear funding to accompany the Title VI requirement, and because there are no specific guidelines or standards set for medical providers, medical interpretation is in fact not consistently available.

The state of reimbursement today

Many incidents of miscommunication in hospitals, emergency rooms and doctor's offices could be avoided if state and federal health agencies, along with private insurers, paid for qualified or certified medical interpreters to be available for those with limited English skills. Facing budgetary restrictions, medical facilities often make decisions regarding the depth and breadth of their language access services based on a quick and anecdotal assessment of general needs: hospitals that see a high number of Spanish-speaking patients, for instance, may decide to hire a trained in-house Spanish interpreter staff, while hospitals that see fewer such patients may rely on untrained staff who may or may not be truly competent interpreters. For languages that are spoken less frequently at a given medical facility, administrators may simply believe that it is more cost-effective to rely on a patient's family members.

Ultimately, LEP patients may receive different kinds of interpretation assistance, and therefore a different quality of care, depending upon what hospital or physician they visit, what the local population of limited English speakers might be, and the extent of that facility's language assistance program. The decision regarding the type of interpretation services that a medical facility will provide is driven most clearly by cost, and so, by offering reimbursement for interpretation according to set standards, Medicaid, Medicare, and private insurers can not only solve a financial problem, they can improve medical outcomes and efficiency in the long run.

Under Medicaid and CHIP (Children's Health Insurance Program), states can pay for interpretation services, and they will be eligible for federal matching funds of up to 75 percent. Currently, 12 states and the District of Columbia have implemented programs to utilize these federal matching funds, and these states have developed mechanisms for reimbursement, along with qualifications and standards for interpretation and translation services that are eligible.9 States that authorize Medicaid reimbursement are able to take a significant step toward improving care for their Medicaid popula-tions. At the same time, states can keep their health care institutions in top working order, by easing the financial challenge that LEP patients pose to hospitals and other medical facilities. Federal matching funds ensure that states can achieve these goals in a way that is cost-effective for their own fiscal health.

Available data suggest that private insurers do not generally provide reimbursement for language services, although some, like Kaiser Permanente and Group Health Cooperative, provide a level of direct interpretation services for their members. Like Medicaid, however, private insurers can encourage better health care decisions, improve outcomes and reduce unnecessary tests and procedures, and therefore costs, by agreeing to reimburse for language services. In fact, the argument in favor of Medicare, Medicaid and private insurance coverage for language interpretation is very similar to the argument for coverage of preventive care, something that insurance companies are beginning to actively promote and embrace. Communication with medical providers is the first rule of preventive care, since communication can lead to better outcomes and prevent mistakes, all while making patients feel comfortable enough to seek care at the first sign of trouble. Language assistance, like preventive care, saves money and lives in the long run.

Reimbursement as the first step toward universally available, quality medical interpretation

The federal government does not set clear guidelines for states that opt to accept matching funds to provide Medicaid reimbursement for language services. Just as the federal government requires hospitals and other entities that receive federal funds to provide language access, but does not provide thorough guidelines on how this should be accomplished, the federal CHIP Reauthorization Act of 2009 provides funds for Medicaid reimbursement for language services, but leaves it to the states to determine the methodology. In some cases, policy makers have expressed concern regarding standards of eligibility for interpretation and translation providers. They have asked, rightly, how to determine the qualifications of interpreters, the quality of interpreting services, and how to ensure ongoing quality monitoring. If interpreters are to be reimbursed by Medicaid for services in the same way that medical testing facilities are reimbursed for their services, how can state officials be certain that the interpreters, whether working in-house or by means of a telephone interpretation service, are qualified?

By giving states latitude to develop the method for reimbursement, the federal government has provided them with an opportunity to ensure quality, but it has also created the strong possibility that standards will vary greatly from state to state, causing confusion for interpreters. States that offer Medicaid reimbursement must develop a method for structuring their payments and in doing so can develop regulations that specify standards of eligibility and quality for medical interpreters and translators.

In developing these standards, states will find an abundance of data and information on the issue of quality and standards, since many language interpretation professionals have been working to develop certification programs for medical interpreters. In fact, across the health care interpretation profession, the issue of developing a program of certification, including training, testing and continuing education, has been a priority for many years. A certified medical interpreter, like a licensed nurse, certified medical technician or certified medical assistant would demonstrate measurable skills, appropriate understanding of medical terminology, and an ongoing commitment to their profession.

Recently, the International Medical Interpreters Association (IMIA) and Language Line Services signed an agreement to join forces in an effort to work toward swift implementation of a national medical certification program. This unified effort is aimed at achieving a consistent methodology that will ensure the quality of language services in every state. If adopted, national certification will bring clear and tested procedures for measuring the overall quality of a facility's language services offerings. It also promises to aid a more streamlined process of hiring, compensating, and verifying the up-to-date credentials of medical interpreters. With national certification, Medicare, Medicaid and private insurers will have a clear path toward setting universal quality and eligibility standards for the reimbursement of medical interpreters.

Today, only Washington State has implemented a program of certification. And so, in the absence of national certification, states are left to create regulatory standards for quality interpretation as they implement Medicaid reimbursement for translation and interpretation. In this way, they can ensure that they will pay for services that are verifiably valuable and achieve the desired outcomes of efficient and effective care.

Conclusion

Today, the doors of our nation's medical facilities are opening to a changing world defined by cultural and linguistic diversity. With more than 24 million U.S. residents having limited English proficiency, nearly every emergency room, urgent care clinic, hospital admitting department and physician's office in the nation will experience first-hand the way in which language barriers can delay care, create confusion and errors, and strain budgets. While Title VI requires equal access to care and the provision of language assistance services, widespread inconsistency in the way that this requirement is implemented has led to a serious disparity in care between those who speak English very well and those who do not.

Evidence clearly demonstrates that trained, qualified medical interpreters make the delivery of health care more efficient and effective for LEP patients. But while Medicare, Medicaid and private insurers reimburse for a variety of medical services that are deemed essential, they do not consistently reimburse for language assistance services. Twelve states and the District of Columbia do offer Medicaid reimbursement for interpretation services, but in order for health care delivery to be truly consistent, reimbursement must become the standard. The federal government should provide payment for medical interpretation for Medicare patients. All states must offer Medicaid and CHIP reimbursement for language services, and federal matching funds make this approach very cost-effective. Private insurers must also recognize the clear benefits of medical interpretation to both patients and the bottom line.

For patients with limited English skills, language services can be as important as medical diagnostic equipment, such as an MRI. Only with good communication can patients explain their symptoms, elaborate on their medical histories, and understand the care that is being offered. Like an MRI, accurate communication can lead to efficient diagnoses and effective treatment. Language access is also closely related to preventive care for LEP patients – making them comfortable with the services they receive, encouraging them to seek care early and continue with medications, and helping to avoid errors and future complications.

Breaking the language barrier white paper

Ensuring quality is a critical part of the equation when it comes to laws and regulations related to language access. Reimbursement for language services by Medicare, Medicaid, and private insurers is one of the most important social and health issues facing policy makers today, as it involves not only questions related to determining just how vital medical interpretation is, but also questions related to determining what constitutes successful, quality interpretation. States that allow Medicaid reimbursement for interpretation and translation, for instance, have wide authority to determine who is eligible to receive payment and what quality standards should apply to their work. Many state and federal policy makers and organizations are working to implement programs of certification for medical interpreters. States should demand a comprehensive, national approach to the issue of quality in language services, but until a truly national certification program is in place, they can greatly accelerate the move toward quality medical interpretation through the Medicaid reimbursement process. Reimbursement will not only require standards of eligibility, it will lead to an entirely higher standard of quality by allowing more medical facilities to improve their approach to language services. Given the evidence and data, this consistency and quality must be the goal.

Bibliography

U.S. Census Bureau, "American Community Survey," www.census.gov/acs/www/index.html.

L. Ku and G. Flores, "Pay Now or Pay Later: Providing Interpreter Services in Health Care," *Health Affairs*, Volume 24, No. 2 (2005).

Source: LanguageTrak® by Language Line Services.

Presidential Executive Order 13166, "Improving Access to Services for Persons with Limited English Proficiency," *Federal Register* 65, no. 159 (2000).

The Joint Commission, the California Endowment, "Hospitals, Language and Culture: A Snapshot of the Nation," www.jointcommission.org/NR/rdonlyres/E64E5E89-5734-4D1D-BB4D-C4ACD4BF8BD3/0/hlc_paper.pdf (2007).

Chandrika Divi, Richard G. Koss, Stephen P. Schmaltz and Jerod M. Loeb, "Language Proficiency and Adverse Events in U.S. Hospitals: A Pilot Study, *International Journal for Quality in Health Care* (April, 2007)

Ku and Flores, "Pay Now or Pay Later: Providing Interpreter Services in Health Care," *Health Affairs*, Volume 24, No. 2 (2005): p. 436.

Ku and Flores, "Pay Now or Pay Later: Providing Interpreter Services in Health Care," *Health Affairs*, Volume 24, No. 2 (2005): p. 437.

"Medicaid and SCHIP Reimbursement Models for Language Services," National Health Law Program (2007).

Ku and Flores, "Pay Now or Pay Later: Providing Interpreter Services in Health Care," *Health Affairs*, Volume 24, No. 2 (2005): p. 438.

Workshops und Podiumsdiskussionen

Quality assurance in simultaneous interpreting

Werner Kittel

Freiberuflicher Konferenzdolmetscher, Castrop-Rauxel

wernerkittel@hotmail.com

Workshop

1. This workshop will provide current and future conference interpreters with an opportunity to discuss "Quality" in simultaneous interpreting in an informal yet informed setting and to examine examples of "Best Practice".

   - What does quality mean and how do we define it?
   - How do we achieve quality?
   - How is quality perceived by the customer?
   - Do we have external guidelines on quality?

2. The presenter will show the results of a mini-survey on the definition of quality among British interpreters and compare these with a survey of the workshop participants.

3. Which quality model do we follow? How do we compare with other service providers in terms of quality?

4. Presentation of a case scenario. Discussion of quality from the customer perspective.

5. Current research outcomes on tools (objective criteria) to assess quality in simultaneous interpreting and their potential consequences.

Challenges and Pitfalls of Interpreting during Depositions

Barbara M. Müller-Grant

Mueller Translations, Wiesbaden

translations@mgrant.de

Workshop

This workshop is intended to help participants ask the right questions prior to interpreting depositions. In this workshop, I will cover some of the reasons for and the various types of depositions. We will also take a look at "players", including the court reporter. How can you prepare for a deposition? What is the purpose of "discovery"? What are some of the pitfalls for the interpreter(s) or the checker? What does a typical assignment look like?

V. Neue Technologien

Technologie und Dolmetschen

Dolmetschen im Wandel – neue Technologien als Chance oder Risiko

Prof. Dr. phil. Sylvia Kalina

*Institut für Translation und Mehrsprachige Kommunikation (ITMK)
an der Fachhochschule Köln; Diplom-Dolmetscherin*

Sylvia.Kalina@fh-koeln.de

1 Einleitung

Seit vor ca. 60 Jahren die internationale Kommunikationslandschaft durch den Einsatz der Technik des Simultandolmetschens und der hierfür erforderlichen Technologie revolutioniert wurde, arbeiten Simultandolmetscher[15] in Kabinen zu zweit oder zu dritt von einer oder mehreren Ausgangssprachen in ihre Zielsprache oder hin und her zwischen zwei Sprachen.

Auf den ersten Blick könnte man meinen, dass im Vergleich mit den Entwicklungen im Bereich des Übersetzens das Dolmetschen seit den immer wieder zitierten Anfängen (Nürnberger Prozesse) im Wesentlichen unverändert geblieben sei. Daran ist richtig, dass Konsekutivdolmetscher in der Tat noch immer ihr Gedächtnis strapazieren und/oder mittels handschriftlicher Notizen festhalten, was sie anschließend in einer anderen Sprache wiedergeben. Richtig ist auch, dass Dolmetschen nach wie vor durch eine enorme Konzentrationsleistung und exzellente Kenntnisse der Sprachen und Fachgebiete überhaupt erst möglich wird. Das Berufsprofil Dolmetscher umfasst allerdings inzwischen mehr Arten des Dolmetschens; Gerichtsdolmetschen und Dolmetschen bei Behörden oder in der medizinischen Beratung haben an Bedeutung hinzugewonnen.

Und auch beim Konferenzdolmetschen sind einige wesentliche Veränderungen festzustellen. Nicht alle sind rein technischer Natur. Zunächst fällt auf, dass die heute im Simultan- oder Konsekutivmodus arbeitenden Konferenzdolmetscher nach einem Hochschulstudium wissen, was sie eigentlich tun, wenn sie dolmetschen; sie beherrschen Vorbereitungs- und Einarbeitungsmethoden sowie die Technik der Kabinen, die ihnen inzwischen einiges abverlangt. Die Wissenschaft hat sich sehr darum bemüht, zu erklären, wie eine Dolmetschleistung zustande kommt. Zahlreiche Strategien oder

---

[15] In diesem Artikel wird durchgehend das generische Maskulinum verwendet; mit allen anderen Personenbezeichnungen wird der Einheitlichkeit halber ebenso verfahren.

Techniken sind beschrieben und empirisch untermauert worden (vgl. Kalina 1998). Doch auch die Abläufe auf Konferenzen haben sich verändert, und diese Veränderungen haben sich auch auf die Arbeit des Dolmetschers ausgewirkt. Im Folgenden sollen einige dieser Veränderungen näher beleuchtet werden.

2 „English only" – und ohne Dolmetscher

Neue Technologien, Globalisierung und Internet haben dazu geführt, dass die Dominanz der englischen Sprache immer mehr Bereiche erfasst. Dies gilt in besonderem Maße für internationale Kontakte und Kommunikation.

Zunächst ist festzustellen, dass angesichts der zunehmenden Verwendung von Englisch als Konferenzsprache die Benachteiligung nicht englisch sprechender Vortragender zu einem immer größeren Problem wird. Konferenzteilnehmer, die nicht in englischer Sprache vortragen wollen oder können, verzichten auf Vortrag oder gar auf die Teilnahme an der Konferenz. Dass es erhebliche Abstriche am Kommunikationserfolg geben muss, wenn Konferenzteilnehmer sich nicht in ihrer Muttersprache ausdrücken können, ist wissenschaftlich nachgewiesen, aber in der Praxis wird diese Erkenntnis, oft aus Kostengründen, nicht umgesetzt. In der EU wird hingegen Sprachenvielfalt praktiziert, was zwar häufig für technische Probleme sorgt, was bei 23 Sprachen, also über 500 Dolmetschrichtungen, nicht verwundert, doch der Umstand, dass auf vielen EU-Konferenzen in viele Sprachen gedolmetscht wird, zeigt, dass auch eine solche Herausforderung gemeistert werden kann.

Auf der anderen Seite ist in der Konferenzpraxis immer wieder zu erleben, dass Unternehmen bei großen Konferenzen für ihre Kunden den eigenen Angestellten untersagen, von der für die Kunden angebotenen Verdolmetschung aus dem Englischen Gebrauch zu machen; die Präsentationen müssen generell in der sogenannten *corporate language* gehalten werden. Für das Dolmetschen insgesamt und für die Bedeutung anderer Sprachen in der internationalen Kommunikation ist dies eine Gefahr.

3 Vorbereitung mit IT: das grenzenlose Informationsangebot

Betrachtet man, welche Rolle neue Technologien im Ablauf eines Dolmetschauftrages spielen, so fällt zunächst auf, dass sich sowohl die Auftragsakquise als auch die Wege der Beschaffung von Vorbereitungsmaterial stark verändert haben. Anfragen gehen per Mail an zahllose Dolmetscher mit dem Ziel, den billigsten Anbieter zu finden; Verträge enthalten oft keine Angaben über die technische Ausstattung und gehen meist äußerst kurzfristig ein, und Vorbereitungsmaterial ist im Internet zu recherchieren oder kommt auf elektronischen Speichermedien daher.

In der Vorbereitungsphase werden die Veränderungen, die durch die Entwicklung neuer Technologien eingetreten sind, besonders deutlich; das Thema ist oft größtenteils selbst zu recherchieren, dafür stehen im Internet bzw. auf den Websites der Auftraggeber Dokumente nicht nur zum Lesen, sondern auch als Audio- und Videodokumente zur Verfügung. Dazu befragt der Dolmetscher die verschiedensten Datenbanken, benutzt elektronische Wörterbücher, erstellt Glossare in dem Programm, das ihm die besten Funktionalitäten bietet, fügt bei Bedarf erarbeitete Lösungen in die elektronischen Manuskript- oder PowerPoint-Vorlagen ein, und all das auf dem Laptop, der ihn auch im Einsatz begleitet.

Präsentationen im Medienmix können leichter an die Dolmetscher weitergeleitet werden als die früher angeforderten und oft nicht gelieferten Manuskripte. Allerdings gibt es nach wie vor Redner, die ihre Dolmetscher am liebsten mit Überraschungen konfrontieren, doch ist es für Dolmetscher heute möglich, sich auch von diesen Zeitgenossen und ihren Vorlieben auf der Basis der Flut von Informationen aus dem Internet ein Profil zu erstellen, was den Überraschungseffekt abschwächen hilft. Die Aufgabe des Dolmetschers ist es nun, aus der Flut der verfügbaren Informationen die richtigen auszuwählen, um sich gezielt vorbereiten zu können.

4 Technologie in Konferenz und Kabine

4.1 Die Kabine als elektronischer Arbeitsplatz

Die technische Ausstattung der Kabinen (aktuelle Kabinennormen: ISO 4043 und DIN 56924) wird in der Regel von Technikern des Konferenztechnikproviders überprüft. Diese weisen ggf. die Dolmetscher auch in Bedienbesonderheiten ein. Inzwischen gibt es Großsysteme mit bis zu 32 Sprachkanälen und bis zu fünf Relaiskanälen, die gleichzeitig nutzbar sind. Wenn allerdings mehr und mehr Konferenztechniker eingespart werden, führt dies zu Risiken für die Kommunikation allgemein und erschwert den Einsatz der Dolmetscher.

Zu den eigentlichen Dolmetschaufgaben sind technische Funktionen hinzugekommen, die der Dolmetscher in seinem Einsatz zu beachten hat, wie die Verantwortung für den Wechsel von Kanälen, komplexe Relaisschaltungen, bei denen die Gefahr besteht, dass eine Kabine sich nicht wieder aus dem Relais ausschaltet, etc., aber auch die gleichzeitige Bedienung von Rechnern, Videoprogrammen oder anderen audiovisuellen Einspielungen. Allein die Displays der Dolmetschpulte weisen immer mehr Informationen auf. Früher gab es ein rotes und ein grünes Lämpchen für das ein- bzw. abgeschaltete Mikro sowie je einen Knopf zur Aufforderung an den Redner, langsamer oder lauter zu sprechen (was nie funktionierte), und den zentralen Mikroschalter. Heute sind die Displays so kompliziert, dass ihre Bedienung ein hohes Maß an Konzentration erfordert, das dann für das Dolmetschen fehlt. Untersuchungen von Konferenztechnikanbietern haben gezeigt, dass einige Funktionen (z.B. die Wiederholtaste) redundant sind. Doch die Digitalisierung der Konferenztechnik wird vom Kunden gewünscht, ohne dass dies immer von Vorteil für das Dolmetschen wäre, wie die Einspielung von Musik bzw. Umgebungsgeräuschen in Rednerpausen belegt.

Die Nachteile von technisch hochgerüsteten Konferenzzentren zeigen sich weiterhin in Interferenzen, verursacht durch mobile Telefone, Blackberries, WLan etc. Technisch sind diese Probleme zu lösen, in der Praxis haben sie dennoch störende Auswirkungen.

Die Verfügbarkeit der verschiedensten elektronischen Tools in der Kabine hat dazu geführt, dass der gerade pausierende Dolmetscher mit einer Vielfalt anderer Tätigkeiten befasst ist – Dateneingaben auf dem Laptop, Abrufen oder Beantworten von Mails, Recherchen im Internet (und nicht immer für die gerade stattfindende Konferenz), Lesen oder Schreiben von SMS-Nachrichten etc. In seiner Erholungspause ist er also ständig beschäftigt, was dazu führt, dass er kaum die gerade laufende Präsentation verfolgt und dem Kollegen wenig oder gar nicht helfen kann (etwa durch Notieren von Zahlen, Namen, Aufschreiben eines Fachbegriffs). Letzteres ist aber eine der wichtigen Teamleistungen beim Simultandolmetschen. Die beschriebenen Beschäftigungen führen mitunter auch dazu, dass ein Dolmetscher, wenn er wieder an der Reihe ist und das Mikro übernimmt, nicht genau weiß, welche Argumente zuvor ausgetauscht wurden, und evtl. nicht erkennt, worauf sich ein Redner gerade bezieht. Damit werden wichtige Informationen verpasst, was wiederum die Kohärenz des Zieltextes gefährdet.

Doch die meisten Erschwernisse haben externe Ursachen. Immer häufiger werden unangekündigt Filme in Präsentationen eingespielt, ohne dass der Originalton in die Kabine übertragen wird; oft wird der Ton lediglich über die Saalmikrofone empfangen. Die Veranstalter erwarten natürlich dennoch, dass diese Filme, deren Skripte den Dolmetschern nicht vorliegen, gedolmetscht werden. Von den Problemen, die diese mit Einspielungen schlechter akustischer Qualität haben, machen sie sich keine Vorstellung.

4.2 Multimedia über alles

Seit vielen Jahren gehört das Einspielen von Videos zur Präsentationstechnik auf Konferenzen. Handelte es sich zunächst um Sequenzen, die mehr für das Auge als für das Ohr intendiert waren, so wurden solche Einspielungen bald als Multimedia-Bereicherung vieler Präsentationen weiterentwickelt, und je mehr Informationen die Audiospur enthielt, desto größer wurden die Probleme für die Dolmetscher.

Jede Audio-/Video-Einspielung ist laut Vertragsbedingungen den Dolmetschern vorab zugänglich zu machen, oder zumindest ist ein Skript davon zur Verfügung zu stellen. Videos von Produktionsabläufen (beliebt sind laut arbeitende Maschinen und/oder fetzige Musik) können nur gedolmetscht werden, wenn die Tonqualität des gesprochenen Textes ausreichend ist und dieser direkt in die Dolmetschkabinen eingespeist wird. Selbst dann ist eine qualitativ den üblichen Ansprüchen an Dolmetschleistungen genügende Verdolmetschung meist nicht möglich. Es ist schwierig, den Auftraggebern verständlich darzulegen, warum unter solchen Bedingungen die Qualität der Verdolmetschung leidet; Dolmetscher müssen daher Strategien entwickeln, wie sie ein Produkt abliefern, das dennoch für die Zuhörer in begrenztem Maße brauchbar ist (vgl. DG Interpretation, 2006).

Viele Veranstaltungen mit Simultanverdolmetschung sind heute als Show-Events aufgezogen, was bedeutet, dass häufig Lichtshows mit Musikeinspielungen produziert werden und die Musik den gesprochenen Ton überlagert, manchmal sogar ganz ausblendet. Animationen und Filme haben oft Musikunterlegungen, die in der Dolmetschkabine nicht ausgeblendet werden können. Event-Agenturen, die das Dolmetschen als nur einen Bestandteil des von ihnen gelieferten Pakets betrachten, setzen sich in der Regel kaum für die technischen Bedürfnisse der Dolmetscher ein, vor allem, wenn deren Erfüllung den Showcharakter des Events beeinträchtigen könnte. Dass Personenführungsanlagen (PFA), gar noch in Verbindung mit Flüster-dolmetschen, in keinem Fall als Ersatz für Kabinen missbraucht werden dürfen, bedarf keiner weiteren Erläuterung (vgl. Farwick 2009).

Auf Fachkonferenzen passiert es nicht selten, dass Filme und Grafiken als Links in PowerPoint-Dateien eingebaut werden, die Dateien hinter den Links aber nicht zu öffnen sind. Bei seinem Fachthema spricht der Redner dann weiter, ohne dass die Videosequenzen, Animationen, Abbildungen o.a. zu sehen wären. Für die Dolmet-scher ist dies besonders problematisch, da sie bei ihrer Vorbereitung zwar über die PowerPoint-Präsentation verfügen, nicht aber über die jeweiligen Links und so gerade die technischen Verfahren, die mit dem Link gezeigt werden sollten, nicht fachlich vorbereiten konnten.

Einspielungen aus dem Internet, z.B. live aus einer laufenden Veranstaltung, sind ebenfalls beliebt, sorgen aber beim Dolmetschen für Konfusion, wenn nicht zu erkennen ist, ob ein Kommentar aus der Internetquelle oder dem Konferenzraum am Ort stammt. Dass die Onlineverbindungen oft gestört sind oder abbrechen, ist dem Bemühen des Dolmetschers um Verständnis für die Sache ebenfalls abträglich. So wird trotz der technologischen Fortschritte bei der Tonübertragung das Dolmetschen nicht leichter, und in den Köpfen der Teilnehmer bleibt allzu leicht der Eindruck zurück, dass die Verdolmetschung eben schlecht gewesen sei.

4.3 Technologie und Konsekutivdolmetschen

Der Charakter von Sitzungen, die heutzutage konsekutiv gedolmetscht werden, ist ein ganz anderer als der von klassischen Konsekutivsitzungen früherer Zeiten. Waren es seinerzeit große politische Reden, formbetonte Ansprachen wie Tischreden etc., so wird heute bei formellen Anlässen dann konsekutiv gedolmetscht, wenn lediglich ein oder zwei kürzere Reden zu halten sind – mehr Zeit hierfür einzuplanen sind die Organisatoren von heutigen Events nicht bereit. Für solche formbetonten Reden ist die traditionelle Konsekutivtechnik nach wie vor sehr hilfreich, aber viele Kollegen trauen sich solche Einsätze nicht mehr zu. Notiert wird in den allermeisten Fällen noch nach alter Manier, mit Stenoblock und Bleistift oder Kugelschreiber.

Eine Technologie, die das Notieren fast gänzlich überflüssig macht, ist die sogenannte *SimulCons*-Software, mit deren Hilfe der Dolmetscher die zu dolmetschende Rede bzw. das Redesegment digital auf einer Art PDA speichert und für die Wiedergabe noch einmal abhört; er dolmetscht somit quasi simultan. Dies ist sicher der Traum all derjenigen, die keine Konsekutivtechnik mehr beherrschen, ist aber erst in wenigen Tests angewendet worden, und die Ergebnisse sind bisher nicht eindeutig (vgl. Ferrari 2001, Pöchhacker 2007). Für die Veranstalter bedeutet die Technik keine Zeitspar-nis, und für diejenigen, die noch immer mit Freude konsekutiv arbeiten, weil der Verstehensvorgang sich hierbei auf viel mehr Text und tiefere Verarbeitung stützen kann, ist die Vorstellung, sich auf eine quasi simultane Technik als Ersatz für ein funktionierendes Gedächtnis und Konsekutivtechnik zu verlassen, ein Alptraum.

5 Neue Übertragungstechniken

5.1 Videokonferenzschaltungen

Gedolmetschte Videokonferenzen (Zwei- oder Dreipunktsysteme) sind inzwischen Stand der Technik (vgl. Braun 2004). Bei Besprechungen, an denen wenige Personen beteiligt sind, kann die Videokonferenztechnik mit entsprechend geschulten Teilnehmern und Dolmetschern die Kommunikation erleichtern. Die Technik wird jedoch oft in Bedingungen eingesetzt, in denen das Dolmetschen nicht oder nur sehr eingeschränkt möglich ist. So wird eine Videoschaltung z.B. zwischen zwei Städten eingesetzt, um Reisekosten einzusparen. Manchmal gibt es an jedem der beiden Orte lediglich ein Mikrofon und nur eine feste Kameraeinstellung, nämlich die Totale auf den Konferenztisch, die alle am Tisch sitzenden Personen einfängt, so dass keine Gesichter zu erkennen sind. Die akustischen Bedingungen sind oft unzulänglich, Bildausfall ist an der Tagesordnung In solchen Settings können Dolmetscher nicht mehr für die Qualität ihrer Leistung garantieren. Außerdem neigen die Teilnehmer mehr zu separater Unterhaltung, wenn der Redner sie nicht sehen kann, was wiederum die Dolmetscher beim Hören behindert. Für Videokonferenzen, die als konsekutiv angesetzt sind, bei denen dann tatsächlich Flüsterdolmetschen praktiziert wird, verschärft sich diese Problematik noch.

Ebenfalls problematisch für die Tonqualität sind Zuschaltungen mit Skype-Technik (Internet-Telefonie). Hierbei kann ein Teilnehmer, der am persönlichen Erscheinen verhindert ist, sein Statement dennoch abgeben, was im einsprachigen Setting funktioniert, mit hinzukommender Verdolmetschung jedoch zum Problem wird. Wenn aus der Videokonferenz eine reine Telefonkonferenz wird, bei der das Audiosignal ohnehin von schlechter Qualität ist, kann eine verlässliche Dolmetschleistung nicht mehr erwartet werden.

Für größere Veranstaltung wird ebenfalls Videokonferenztechnik benutzt. Handelt es sich um einen zugeschalteten Redner, bleibt die Belastung der Dolmetscher in Grenzen, vor allem, wenn nur dieser (monologisch) spricht. Je mehr Personen aber die Leitung mitbenutzen, desto schlechter wird die Tonqualität, und die Sprache des übertragenen Redners kommt im Staccato-Rhythmus mit Aussetzern an, es kommt zu Rauschen und Frequenzschwankungen, und die Qualität der Dolmetschleistung leidet. Hier ist es wichtig, dass der beratende Dolmetscher im Vorfeld kompetent über alle technischen Eventualitäten und ihre Auswirkungen berät und die technischen Daten von geplanten Zuschaltungen (Bandbreite, Zahl der Leitungen) in Erfahrung bringt.

5.2 Ausgelagerte Dolmetscher: *Remote interpreting*

Mit ihren 23 Arbeitssprachen ist die EU eine Organisation, für die *remote interpreting* (Ferndolmetschen) eine sehr verlockende Alternative zur Präsenz aller Dolmetscher im Konferenzraum darstellt. Der Bedarf an Sitzungen mit vielen Kabinen steigt, und so wurden – als erste Schritte zum *remote interpreting* – bereits mehrere Großtagungen mit vielen Sprachen mit dieser Übertragungstechnik gedolmetscht. Das Europäische Parlament hat diverse Untersuchungen zur Belastung der Dolmetscher veranlasst, und gemeinsam mit Berufsverbänden wurden inzwischen erste Regeln und Beschränkungen für *remote interpreting* vereinbart.

5.3 Webstreaming

Wenn eine Sitzung, die über Intra- oder Internet für weitere, nicht anwesende Interessenten in Bild und Ton übertragen wird, gedolmetscht wird, so kann auch die Verdolmetschung ins Netz gestreamt werden. Die Internetzuhörer können das Geschehen in den gedolmetschten Sprachen verfolgen und auch aktiv partizipieren, d.h. in der Diskussion Fragen stellen. Die Dolmetscher müssen hiervon vorab unterrichtet sein, damit sie auch dann weiter dolmetschen, wenn im Saal selbst keiner mehr ihrer Kabine zuhört. Auch Hauptversammlungen und öffentliche Präsentationen oder Show-Events werden heute oft über das Internet übertragen und können dort auch später abgerufen werden. Webstream-Präsentationen können ohne größeren technischen Aufwand mitgeschnitten werden.

Ein technisches, sicherlich lösbares Problem bei vielen Konferenzen, die per Webstreaming ins Internet übertragen werden, ist die Geschwindigkeit der Kameras, wenn diese in der Mitte des Saales bzw. an den Saaldecken verankert sind. Sie bewegen sich zu langsam, um in der Diskussion bei schnellen Rednerwechseln sofort den jeweiligen Redner auf die Leinwand zu projizieren. Dem Internetzuhörer geht somit die Information über den Rednerwechsel verloren, er merkt lediglich, dass evtl. eine andere Dolmetscherstimme zu hören ist. Wenn hier die Verdolmetschung im *remote interpreting* erfolgt, führt dies zu Problemen. Redner beginnen mit ihren Ausführungen jeweils, bevor die Kamera sie im Fokus hat. Damit haben die Dolmetscher bei den ersten 10 – 20 Wörtern kein Bild. Wenn sich dies in kurzen Abständen bei fast jedem Redner wiederholt, führt es beim Dolmetschen zu erheblicher Verunsicherung.

Ein weiteres Phänomen hierbei ist, dass Redner zunehmend dazu neigen, Links in ihre PowerPoint-Präsentationen einzubauen, die sie an der jeweiligen Stelle ihrer Präsentation öffnen wollen, um ein Videoclip aus dem Internet zu streamen. Diese Links öffnen sich meist erst mit einiger Verzögerung, der Redner spricht aber weiter und kommentiert, als ob bereits etwas zu sehen sei. Für den Zuhörer des Originals ist dies noch nachvollziehbar, aber für die Dolmetscher steigt die Schwierigkeit an, da sie dem Redner ohnehin mit einem Zeitabstand folgen, und für die Zuhörer der Verdolmetschung wird die verbale Erklärung zum erst später eintreffenden visuellen Material vollends problematisch. Hier zeigt sich, dass ein „gefühlter" Missstand bei der Verdolmetschung in Wirklichkeit auf technische Mängel zurückzuführen ist.

Webstreaming wird auch von Medienunternehmen eingesetzt, wenn es um Live-Übertragungen aktueller Ereignisse geht, und auch hierbei wird gedolmetscht. Diese neue Kommunikationstechnologie ist äußerst attraktiv, und folglich ist auch das Dolmetschen im Rahmen ihrer Nutzung zukunftsträchtig. Hierfür müssen Regeln definiert werden, damit die Bedingungen, die in solchen Settings herrschen, die Qualität von Dolmetschleistungen nicht gefährden. Eine Zusammenarbeit von Berufsverbänden und Konferenzorganisatoren ist dringend geboten.

Bei der EU wird die Technik der Videokonferenzschaltung (*one-way*) mit der Kommunikation per *netmeeting* kombiniert, wenn z.B. ein Mitglied der Kommission sich im direkten Kontakt mit Bürgern der Mitgliedstaaten austauschen will. Schriftliche

Fragen werden online empfangen und mündlich vom Blatt in die Sprache des Adressaten übersetzt; die Antwort wiederum wird gedolmetscht oder ebenfalls per mündlicher Übersetzung online übertragen (vgl. DG Interpretation, 2006: 15). Es wird in verschiedenen Dolmetschmodi gearbeitet, und das Setting ist sehr interaktiv.

5.4 IT-Einsatz in anderen Dolmetscharten

Hier ist vor allem auf die ersten Bemühungen zu verweisen, Videokonferenztechnik oder *remote interpreting* für Dolmetschen bei Gericht und im medizinischen Beratungsgespräch einzusetzen (vgl. die einschlägigen Beiträge in diesem Band). In solchen Settings ist es vor allem wichtig, dass die Arbeitsbedingungen der Dolmetscher sich an denen orientieren, wie sie für das Konferenzdolmetschen gelten, d.h. Arbeitszeiten, Teamstärke, Vertrautheit mit der eingesetzten Technik und Einsatz von ausgebildeten Dolmetschern mit entsprechender Bezahlung. Ist all dies gegeben, kann die Technik hier möglicherweise zu einer Qualitätsverbesserung führen, da nämlich nicht die nächste verfügbare Person (Putzfrau oder Krankenpfleger) herangezogen wird, sondern der Spezialist, der jeweils kurzfristig zugeschaltet werden kann.

Eine Software, die von Gerichtsreportern in den USA für die Notation genutzt wird, ist *LiveNote* (www.livenote.com/manage.asp, 27.06.2009). Wenn die Transkripte auf Bildschirme übertragen werden, die von allen, auch den Gerichtsdolmetschern zu sehen sind, können die Dolmetscher sich an diesen Notizen orientieren, was eine große Erleichterung darstellt. Das Transkript wird vom Gerichtsreporter ständig korrigiert, so dass auch die Dolmetscher ihre Verdolmetschung ggf. korrigieren können.

Schlussfolgerung

Dolmetschen durch professionelle Dolmetscher ist wohl nicht in Gefahr, bald von technologischen Entwicklungen verdrängt zu werden, die in der Lage wären, qualifizierte Dolmetschleistungen zu ersetzen. Eine Gefahr bilden eher die mittelbaren Auswirkungen der technologischen Entwicklungen mit ihren Folgen für die Menschheit. Hierzu zählen mangelnde Voraussetzungen beim Nachwuchs an Dolmetschern, was sich bereits in den Nachwuchssorgen der EU-Dolmetschdienste und der fehlenden Bereitschaft zur Konsekutivleistung generell niederschlägt. Weltwissen, Belastungs- und Konzentrationsfähigkeit, Stressresistenz und Gedächtniskapazität, Gewissenhaftigkeit im Umgang mit Sprache und sprecherische/artikulatorische Differenzierungsfähigkeit haben bei der jungen Generation an Bedeutung verloren; an ihre Stelle sind technologische Fertigkeiten getreten. Den Chancen, die der technologische Wandel für einen durch die Globalisierung erst möglich gewordenen Berufsstand mit sich gebracht hat, stehen daher Risiken gegenüber, die dazu führen könnten, dass die hohe Qualität von Dolmetschleistungen in Zukunft kein erreichenswertes Ziel mehr darstellen wird. Dem hat der Berufsstand entgegenzuwirken, und dies ist eine Aufgabe des BDÜ. Die Konferenz „Übersetzen in die-Zukunft" dient diesem Ziel.

Bibliographie

Braun, S. (2004). Kommunikation unter widrigen Umständen? Fallstudien zu einsprachigen und gedolmetschten Videokonferenzen. Tübingen: Narr.

DG Interpretation (2006). Meetings' Manual – Guide for Interpreters and Heads of Interpretation Teams, Version 3.0 EN. (http://scic.ec.europa.eu/scicnet/upload/docs/application/pdf/manual_en_final_22_02_2007.pdf, 29.06.2009)

Farwick, J.S. (2009). „Mit der Kabine im Koffer. Dolmetschen mit Personenführungsanlagen", in: MDÜ 55(2009)1, S. 45-48.

Ferrari, M. (2001). „Consecutive simultaneous ? Consecutive, notes and digital tape or the foolproof consecutive: digital recording hardware as the ultimate back-up tool", in: SCICNEWS Newsletter N°26, November 2001. (http://158.169.50.67/scicnews/ 011121/news.05.htm, 25.11.01).

Kalina, S. (1998). Strategische Prozesse beim Dolmetschen. Theoretische Grundlagen, empirische Untersuchungen, didaktische Konsequenzen. Tübingen: Narr.

Pöchhacker, F. (2007). „'Going Simul?' Technology-assisted Consecutive Interpreting", in: Forum 5:2, S. 101-124.

WebInterpret – Simultan dolmetschen online

Dr. Annette Lang

SAS WebInterpret, Valbonne, Frankreich

Annette.l@webinterpret.com

Abstract

Der vorliegende Artikel beschäftigt sich mit den neuen beruflichen Horizonten, die DolmetscherInnen in einer Marktsituation im Wandel mit der WebInterpret-Plattform erschließen können. Nach einer praxisorientierten Analyse des Dolmetschermarktes in den ersten beiden Quartalen 2009 wird die Plattform für Simultandolmetschen Online vorgestellt, mit besonderer Berücksichtigung der Lösungsansätze, die die Plattform für die neuen Gegebenheiten des Marktes bietet. Auf eine kurze Typologie der häufigsten Interaktionsformen bei Online-Dolmetschereinsätzen folgt eine Diskussion der Anforderungen, die der neue Verdolmetschungsrahmen an DolmetscherInnen stellt. Der Artikel geht abschließend detailliert darauf ein, wie sich SprachmittlerInnen die WebInterpret-Plattform in ihrem beruflichen Alltag zu Nutze machen und so eine neue berufliche Haltung im Kundenkontakt entwickeln können.

1   Ein Sprachmittlermarkt im Wandel

Die zurückliegenden 20 Jahre zeichnen sich durch tiefgreifende Veränderungen des Sprachmittlermarktes aus. Neben technischen Neuerungen, die an anderer Stelle des Konferenzbandes ausführlich diskutiert werden (siehe Kalina, Sylvia: „Dolmetschen im Wandel – neue Technologien als Chance oder Risiko?"), der Banalisierung internationaler Kontakte und des Aufstiegs von „Globish" zu einer weit verbreiteten Mittlersprache trägt die aktuelle Wirtschaftskrise ihren Teil zum Wandel des Dolmetschermarktes bei. Im Folgenden werden die genannten Punkte im Einzelnen angesprochen.

1.1   Der Einfluss von Informations- und Kommunitationstechnologie

Noch vor einem halben Jahrhundert hätte man bei der bloßen Vorstellung, mit einer Maus auf eine Ikone zu klicken, zweifelnd die Stirn gerunzelt und keinen Sinn an diesem eigenartig anmutenden Zusammenwirken von Nagern und Heiligenbildern gefunden. Heute gehört genau dieser Vorgang täglich zu hundertfach wiederholten Routinen breiter Teile der Bevölkerung. Computer, Internet und E-Mail, Skype, VoIP Telefone und MP3-Dateien sind aus dem Alltag inzwischen kaum mehr wegzudenken.

Globales Informationsmanagement und Computertools sind stark in den beruflichen Alltag von ÜbersetzerInnen integriert, währen DolmetscherInnen IuK -Technologien vorwiegend zur Vorbereitung von Sprachmittlerauftritten, nicht aber bei deren Verwirklichung selbst, einsetzen.

Da es bei Dolmetschen um die mündliche Übertragung der Ausgangs- in die Zielsprache geht, können die folgenden Neuerungen eine wichtige Rolle im Dolmetscheralltag übernehmen:

- VoIP-Leitungen haben zu erheblichen Kostensenkungen bei internationalen Telefonaten geführt. Selbst bei transkontinentalen Gesprächen belaufen sich die Gebühren pro Minute lediglich auf Cent-Beträge.

- Dank der rasanten Geschwindigkeit von Internetverbindungen können Daten massiv und augenblicklich übertragen werden. Dies führt bei VoIP-Leitungen zu einwandfreier Klangqualität.

- Konferenzschaltungen sind verblüffend einfach anzulegen und fester Bestandteil von internationalen Arbeitsroutinen.

- In Industrieländern sind der Griff zum Telefon und die Benutzung von Computer und Internet alltägliche oder sogar instinktive Gesten in Berufs- und Privatleben. Menschen weltweit sind mit diesen Kommunikationsmedien so vertraut, dass sie diese nicht mehr aus ihrem Leben wegdenken können.

Aus technischer Sicht ist der Weg für neue Arbeitsmethoden im Dolmetscheralltag gelegt. Im zweiten Teil dieses Artikels wird erläutert, wie die WebInterpret-Plattform diese Gegebenheiten bei Online-Dolmetscherauftritten einsetzt.

1.2 Basta Globish!

Die „Weltsprache" Englisch hat in der Tat in vielen alltäglichen Situationen zur besseren Völkerverständigung auf privater Ebene und zur Kontaktaufnahme und Abwicklung gewisser Arbeitsvorgänge im Berufsalltag beigetragen. Über die Jahre hinweg hat sich so die Variante des „Globish", Kontraktion aus „Global" und „English", entwickelt, bei deren bloßen Erwähnung so manchen DolmetscherInnen die Haare zu Berge stehen. Ohne auf die soziolinguistischen Aspekte von Globish an dieser Stelle eingehen zu können, sind im Zusammenhang mit den Einsatzmöglichkeiten der WebInterpret-Plattform die folgenden Aspekte erwähnenswert:

- Durch die starke Vereinfachung sprachlicher Aspekte ist mit Globish eine getreue Übertragung von einer Sprache in die andere nicht möglich. Der Inhalt ist zwingend verfälscht, was zu massiven Kommunikationsproblemen führen kann.

- Sprachmittlung setzt hohe Interkulturkompetenzen voraus, die unter anderem die perfekte Beherrschung aller beteiligten Sprachen voraussetzt. Konversationen auf Globish beruhen oft auf der Illusionen, man verstünde einander auf einer gemeinsamen sprachlichen und "kulturfreien" Ebene. Dies kann zu fatalen Missverständnissen führen (siehe Giovannini, Arno: "Andere Länder, andere Sitten: Interkulturelle Kompetenz als strategischer Erfolgsfaktor").

Internationale Zusammenarbeit erfordert häufige und oft spontane Kontaktaufnahme, für die Globish aus den oben genannten Gründen nicht ausreicht, eine mehrsprachige Konferenz mit Dolmetscherkabinen aus Zeit- und Kostengründen jedoch nicht angelegt werden kann. Daraus resultiert ein Bedarf an professioneller Sprachmittlung, die ohne technischen Aufwand und lange Vorlaufzeit organisiert werden kann.

1.3 Der Dolmetschermarkt in Zeiten der Wirtschaftskrise 2009

Die ersten beiden Quartale des Jahres 2009 haben mit kaum verhohlener Eindringlichkeit gezeigt, dass es an der Zeit ist, neue Perspektiven für den Dolmetschermarkt zu öffnen. Viele Firmen sehen sich zu substantiellen Einsparungen gezwungen, denen in erster Reihe das Kommunikationsbudget, Geschäftsreisen und internationale Veranstaltungen zum Opfer fallen. Zahlreiche DolmetscherInnen hatten in den letzten Monaten mit Absagen von lang geplanten Einsätzen zu kämpfen und mussten zum Teil markante Umsatzeinbußen verzeichnen.

Andererseits bringt die neue Wirtschaftssituation neue Bedürfnisse an internationalen Verhandlungen mit sich, wie z.B.:

- Vertriebspläne im Ausland müssen an neue finanzielle Rahmenbedingungen angepasst werden. Um möglichst spontan auf das Konsumverhalten in einem gegebenen Land reagieren zu können, bestehen zahlreiche Firmen auf wöchentliche Absprachen mit ihren Vertriebsnetzen im Ausland.

- Internationale Unternehmen haben sich zu teils massiven Entlassungswellen entschlossen, die juristische und wirtschaftliche Absprachen zwischen den Mutterhäusern und jeweiligen Niederlassungen erfordern.

- Zahlreiche Firmen haben vermehrt versucht, Schwellenmärkte, wie z.B. China und Brasilien, zu erschließen, um die Umsatzeinbuße auf traditionellen Märkten ausgleichen zu können.

Es bietet sich daher für DolmetscherInnen an, eine neue berufliche Dynamik zu entwickeln. Diese Dynamik sollte es ihnen ermöglichen, eventuelle Umsatzeinbußen auszugleichen und andererseits auf den neuen Typ von Anfragen zu reagieren.

2   Die WebInterpret-Online-Plattform

Die WebInterpret-Plattform wurde von den Telekommunikationsingenieuren Patrick Smarzynski et Benjamin Cohen in enger Zusammenarbeit mit Konferenzdolmetschern entwickelt. Der Gründungsidee liegen dabei eigene Erfahrungen mit Berufskontakten auf internationaler Ebene zu Grunde. Patrick Smarzynski und Benjamin Cohen haben beide persönlich Erfahrung mit dem unbefriedigenden Ergebnis von Verhandlungen, die in der Drittsprache Englisch und ohne Interkulturkompetenzen geführt wurden, gesammelt. Der VoIP-Ingenieur Maciek Kaminski und Software-Entwickler Tomasz Nazar haben nach ihren Angaben die WebInterpret-Plattform entworfen und dank strenger Qualitätskontrollen mit MasterdolmetscherInnen ständig weiterentwickelt.

Die Online Plattform bietet Kunden die Möglichkcit, mehrsprachige Telefonkonferenzen mit bis zu 100 Teilnehmern und 10 Sprachen anzulegen, die wahlweise simultan oder konsekutiv von professionellen Sprachmittlern verdolmetscht werden. Im Folgenden werden die wichtigsten Eigenschaften der Plattform kurz erläutert.

2.1 Eine gekoppelte Technik: Telefon und Webportal

Die WebInterpret-Plattform verbindet optimale Benutzerfreundlichkeit für den Kunden mit optimalem Bedienungskomfort für den/die Dolmetscher(in). Im Standardfall von zwei Gesprächsteilnehmern mit jeweils einer Sprache sieht das wie folgt aus:

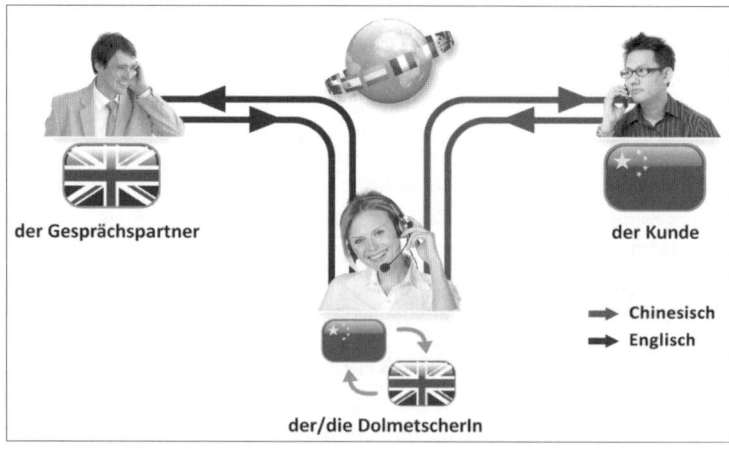

Abb. 1

- Der Kunde und sein Gesprächspartner benutzen herkömmliche Telefone, ein Kommunikationsmedium, mit dem sie vertraut sind und das sie täglich einsetzen. Beide sprechen und hören ihre eigene Sprache. Die Verdolmetschung erfolgt durch SprachmittlerInnen, die professionell für einen einwandfreien Konversationsfluss sorgen. Es ist keine besondere technische Ausrüstung für den Kunden erforderlich.

- Der/die DolmetscherIn arbeitet mit der Benutzeroberfläche des WebInterpret-Internetportals, das die wichtigsten Funktionen einer Dolmetscherkabine aufgreift. Über die Schaltfläche „Switch" kann die Richtung der Verdolmetschung geändert werden, z.B. von Englisch > Französisch oder Französisch > Englisch. Für eine optimale Klangqualität empfiehlt WebInterpret die Benutzung der Festnetznummer des Dolmetschers/der Dolmetscherin in Verbindung mit einem geeigneten Kopfhörer.

Abb. 2

2.2 Simultan oder konsekutiv

Auf besonderen Wunsch von DolmetscherInnen bietet die WebInterpret-Plattform wahlweise Simultan- oder Konsekutivdolmetschen an, was vor allem von Sprachmittlern asiatischer Sprachen erbeten wurde.

Bei simultaner Verdolmetschung hört der Sprecher den Dolmetscher, der seine Worte simultan in die Zielsprache überträgt, nicht. Auf Wunsch kann der Originalton ganz ausgeblendet oder auf 10% gesenkt werden, damit der Gesprächspartner die emotionale Verfassung des Sprechers an paraverbalen Parametern wie Intonation und Sprechgeschwindigkeit erkennen kann. Der/die Dolmetscher(in) wechselt, wie oben bereits erwähnt, die Richtung der Verdolmetschung über die „Switch"-Schaltfläche.

Bei konsekutiver Verdolmetschung erfolgt keine Schallisolierung, sodass sich alle Gesprächsteilnehmer ohne Unterbrechung hören.

2.3 Aktive und passive Teilnehmer

Die Plattform bietet beim Anlegen der Konferenz die Möglichkeit, so genannte „stumme" Teilnehmer anzulegen. Diese können zwar alle aktiven Gesprächspartner hören, jedoch nicht selbst das Wort ergreifen. Passive Teilnehmer können der Konfe-

renz auch über Raumton folgen, was sich bei einer großen Anzahl passiver Teilnehmer anbietet.

2.4 Arbeitsbedingungen

Die Online-Plattform wurde mit und für DolmetscherInnen entwickelt und achtet so
stets darauf, dass alle Richtlinien für die Arbeitsbedingungen von DolmetscherInnen
eingehalten werden. Die Plattform bietet selbstverständlich die Möglichkeit, im
Dolmetscherbinom zu arbeiten und sich alle 20 bis 30 Minuten abzulösen. Power-
Point-Präsentationen, Excel-Sheets, PDF-Dokumente und alle anderen computerunterstützten visuellen Elemente können allen beteiligten Teilnehmern über
Screensharing zugänglich gemacht werden, was dem/der Dolmetscher(in) den Einsatz
erheblich erleichtert.

Nach dieser kurzen Einführung in die Basisfunktionalitäten der WebInterpret-
Plattform wird im weiteren Verlauf des Artikels erläutert, wie DolmetscherInnen
dieses Sprachmittlertool in ihrem beruflichen Bereich gewinnbringend einsetzen
können.

3   WebInterpret zum Übersetzen in die Zukunft

Ohne in Einzelheiten auf die Selektionsmechanismen nach Charles Darwin eingehen
oder ihre Angemessenheit in jedem Kontext diskutieren zu wollen, kann 200 Jahre
nach Darwins Geburt mit Sicherheit gesagt werden, dass ein verändertes Umfeld eine
Anpassung seiner Bewohner mit sich bringen sollte. Dies gilt im weiteren Sinne auch
für die Weiterentwicklung, die eine Berufssparte durchlaufen kann, um sein Bestehen
in der Zukunft zu sichern. Weiterentwicklung besteht selbstverständlich keinesfalls
darin, auf bewährte Methoden gänzlich zu verzichten. Es geht vielmehr darum,
bewährtem Wissen neuen Ausdruck zu verleihen.

Wie zu Anfang dieses Artikels beschrieben bietet das 21. Jahrhundert Informations-
und Telekommunikationstechnologien an, die es DolmetscherInnen ermöglichen, auf
eine veränderte Wirtschaftssituation in angemessener Weise zu reagieren. Dies kann
am besten an Hand konkreter Beispiele erläutert werden.

3.1 Nutzungsbeispiele aus den letzten Monaten

Veranstaltungen vor Ort sind in vielen Kontexten die beste oder gar einzige Möglichkeit, einer mehrsprachigen Situation gerecht zu werden. So kann und will die WebInterpret-Plattform in keinem Fall medizinische Kongresse, Jahreshauptversammlungen
oder Wirtschaftsgipfel online verdolmetschen.

Die Erfahrung hat jedoch gezeigt, dass sich diese Lösung sowohl für die Vor- als auch
für die Nachbereitung anbietet. Einzelne Teilnehmer haben so die Möglichkeit, sich
vorab über bestimmte, eventuell vertrauliche Inhalte in begrenztem Teilnehmerrah-
men auszutauschen, wie die folgenden Beispiele aus den letzten Monaten zeigen:

- Ein brasilianischer Kinderarzt und eine französische Onkologin stellen ein
  gemeinsames Modell zur Behandlung von jungen Krebspatienten in Slum-
  Gebieten vor. Obwohl der eigentliche Vortrag in der Drittsprache Englisch

gehalten wird, ist es ihnen wichtig, im Vorfeld alle Punkte in der jeweiligen Muttersprache durchzugehen und genau zu besprechen.

- Ein internationales Unternehmen ist durch die wirtschaftliche Situation gezwungen, zahlreiche MitarbeiterInnen an einem französischen Standort der amerikanischen Firma zu entlassen. Die Rechtsberater beider Länder arbeiten in mehreren Online-Konferenzen den juristischen Rahmen der Entlassungswelle aus.

- Der deutsche Geschäftsführer bittet den Personaldienstleiter der chinesischen Niederlassung um die Übergabe vertraulicher Informationen vor Abhaltung der Jahreshauptversammlung, bei der wichtige Entscheidung im Bereich Personalpolitik vorgestellt werden.

In den beiden letzten Fällen haben die Online-Konferenzen dazu beigetragen, dass sich ein besonderes Vertrauensverhältnis zwischen DolmetscherInnen und Kunden entwickelt hat. Die jeweiligen Sprachmittler haben nach ihren Online-Konferenzen ebenfalls die Dolmetschereinsätze vor Ort ausgeführt.

Die beiden folgenden Nutzungsbeispiele zeigen auf, dass Online-Dolmetschen dann einspringen kann, wenn Einsätze vor Ort an ihre Grenzen gelangen:

- Im Gesundheitsbereich ist es durch die erhöhte internationale Mobilität häufig notwendig, Patienten aus dem Ausland zu behandeln. Drittsprachen wie Englisch oder die sprachlichen Kompetenzen der Beteiligten reichen bei medizinischen Sprechstunden oft nicht aus. Eine Schweizer Klinik fordert regelmäßig DolmetscherInnen für „Exotensprachen" wie Albanisch, Kurdisch und Tamil an, die bei Arbeitsunfähigkeits- oder Rentenversicherungsuntersuchungen über eine Freisprechanlage konsekutiv dolmetschen.

- Viele Firmen greifen auf Online-Schulungen zurück, die es ihnen erlauben, Personal im Ausland auf Distanz zu schulen. Dabei wird die WebInterpret-Plattform mit Screensharing-Programmen optimal gekoppelt.

- In drei Fällen ist eine Veranstaltung vor Ort durch eine Online-Konferenz ersetzt worden, da zahlreiche Teilnehmer die Reise wegen des Gesundheitsrisikos der H1A1-Grippe abgesagt hatten.

Anhand der oben genannten Beispiele ist es möglich, die von der Online-Plattform gebotenen Vorteile näher zu analysieren.

3.2 Benutzernahe und problemlose Handhabung

Über das Webportal können mehrsprachige Online-Konferenzen vom WebInterpret-Team, aber auch von Kunden und DolmetscherInnen selbst in wenigen Klicks angelegt werden. Auf diese Weise ist es möglich, binnen kurzer Zeit auf Situationen zu reagieren, die einen professionellen Dolmetschereinsatz erfordern.

3.3 Professionelle Sprachmittlerkompetenz

Die WebInterpret-Plattform kommt, unserer Erfahrung nach, unter anderem in Situationen zum Einsatz, für die Kunden zuvor selbst Lösungen in Drittsprachen wie das zuvor erwähnte „Globish" gesucht haben. Die perfekte Beherrschung der beteiligten Sprachen und echte Interkulturkompetenz sind dadurch jedoch nicht zu ersetzen. Gerade in der aktuell angespannten Wirtschaftssituation können durch die angeschnittenen Themen und das Ausmaß der zu treffenden Entscheidungen Stresssituationen entstehen, die professionelle Sprachmittlerkompetenz erfordern.

Die besonderen Eigenschaften von Online-Einsätzen stellen dabei Anforderungen an den/die DolmetscherInnen, die sich aus der besonderen Kommunikationssituation ableiten.

3.4 Charakteristiken von Online-Einsätzen

Ausgehend von den zuvor beschriebenen Beispielen, zeichnen sich Online-Einsätze durch die folgenden Eigenschaften aus:

- In den meisten Fällen umfasst das Kommunikationsschema eine begrenzte Anzahl von Teilnehmern, die aktiv am Gespräch beteiligt sind.

- Die Interaktionsstruktur ist grundlegend dialogisch: Die beteiligten Sprecher ergreifen abwechselnd das Wort.

- Die Inhalte der Konferenzen sind beruflicher Natur und betreffen häufig sensible Themen. Es werden vertrauliche Informationen ausgetauscht, Entscheidungen getroffen und Probleme gelöst.

- Die Gespräche erfolgen über das Telefon mit einem rein auditiven Informationsfluss ohne visuelle Elemente.

Online-Einsätze grenzen sich damit in vielerlei Hinsicht vom Konferenzdolmetschen ab. Die Verdolmetschung erfolgt simultan oder konsekutiv in anspruchsvollen Fachgebieten, aber der Redefluss ist bidirektional, da die verschiedenen Teilnehmer abwechselnd Sprecher und Hörer sind. Darüber hinaus liegt oft weniger Vorbereitungsmaterial für die DolmetscherInnen vor, da sich ein hoher Prozentsatz der Inhalte aus dem Gespräch selbst ergibt.

3.5 Anforderungsprofil an die Dolmetscher

Im Gegensatz zum Live- und zum Phone-Interpreting erfordern die Einsätze mit der WebInterpret-Plattform ausgeprägtes Fachwissen und solide Berufserfahrung als Dolmetscher.

Teilnehmer und DolmetscherInnen können einander nicht sehen. Allerdings sehen sich auch die Gesprächspartner gegenseitig nicht und tauschen alle Informationen, von Screensharing abgesehen, verbal oder paraverbal aus.

Der bidirektionale Redefluss erfordert, dass aktiv in beide Richtungen gedolmetscht wird und die DolmetscherInnen sehr spontan auf inhaltliche und emotionale Gegebenheiten reagiert.

Aus technischer Sicht ist WebInterpret äußerst bedienerfreundlich und auch mit wenigen technischen Vorkenntnissen problemlos zu benutzen. Dennoch ist eine offene und konstruktive Haltung gegenüber Informations- und Kommunikationstechnologien sicherlich hilfreich, um sich schnell in dieses neue Umfeld einarbeiten zu können. Sobald der/die Dolmetscher(in) gut mit der Plattform vertraut ist, ist die

Möglichkeit gegeben, diese neue Dolmetscherdienstleistung in die eigene Produktpalette einzugliedern und von sich aus Kunden anzubieten.

4   Ein neuer Platz für DolmetscherInnen

Wie zu Anfang dieses Artikels bereits erläutert, mussten viele DolmetscherInnen in den letzten Monat einen signifikanten Rückgang ihrer beruflichen Tätigkeit verzeichnen. Aus diesem Grunde soll an dieser Stelle die Überlegung angeregt werden, ob die Online Plattform DolmetscherInnen die Möglichkeit bietet, neue Horizonte zu erschließen.

Im normalen beruflichen Alltag erhalten Sprachmittler Anfragen für Dolmetschereinsätze, die sie je nach Verfügbarkeit, Fachgebiet und anderen Kriterien annehmen oder ablehnen können. Ihre Haltung auf dem Arbeitsbeschaffungsmarkt kann in dieser Hinsicht als „passiv" beschrieben werden. Internet und Websites wurden vor allem dazu eingesetzt, um berufliche Profile klar darzustellen und so von Kunden kontaktiert werden zu können. Es ist allerdings auch möglich, dass DolmetscherInnen ihren Aktionsradius in dieser Hinsicht aktiv erweitern.

4.1 Antwort auf Absagen

Die letzten Monate waren für zahlreiche DolmetscherInnen von Absagen zuvor geplanter Konferenzen durchzogen, die im Großen und Ganzen passiv entgegengenommen wurden. Mit der Online-Plattform haben DolmetscherInnen nun die Möglichkeit, solchen Absagen eine aktive Antwort entgegenzusetzen. So kann dem Kunden z.B. angeboten werden, an Stelle der abgesagten Veranstaltung vor Ort bestimmte Inhalte im Rahmen einer Online-Konferenz zu erbringen. Reise- und Hotelkosten entfallen, alle Teilnehmer können von einem Ort ihrer Wahl an einer Online-Konferenz teilnehmen. Dabei ist es wie zuvor erklärt möglich, aktive und passive Gesprächsteilnehmer und mehrere Sprachen zu verwalten.

Der/die Dolmetscher(in) kann also auf eine erhaltene Absage mit einem konkreten Vorschlag reagieren, der es ihm/ihr ermöglicht, sein/ihr Honorar ganz oder zum Teil beizubehalten.

4.2 Vor- und Nachbereitung von Aufträgen vor Ort

Die Online-Plattform bietet die Möglichkeit, Dolmetschereinsätze vor Ort vor- und nachzubereiten.

Erhält ein Sprachmittler eine Zusage für einen traditionellen Einsatz, kann er dem Kunden von sich aus eine Vor- oder Nachbereitung über eine Online-Konferenz vorschlagen.

Dem/der Dolmetscher(in) kann es auf diese Weise gelingen, regelmäßige Kunden für Online-Konferenzen zu gewinnen und sich eine neue Berufsnische aufzubauen.

Abschließend wird diese Arbeitsweise an einem konkreten Bespiel aus der WebInterpret-Dolmetschercommunity illustriert.

4.3 Fallbeispiel: Kaiko Miyazaki, Dolmetscherin zwischen japanisch und französisch

Kaiko ist seit zwanzig Jahren als Dolmetscherin etabliert und führt zahlreiche Einsätze bei traditionellen Aufträgen vor Ort aus.

Einer ihrer japanischen Stammkunden sah sich aus Budgetgründen gezwungen, Termine mit seinen französischen Partnern in Paris abzusagen und versuchte eine Zeit lang, Gespräche in Englisch abzuwickeln. Eine angespannte Wirtschaftslage, daraus resultierende Schwierigkeiten bei der Zusammenarbeit und ein sprachliches „Unwohlsein" in der Drittsprache führten dazu, dass beide Seiten ein Ende der Zusammenarbeit ins Auge fassten.

Als Kaikos Kunde sie um einen abschließenden Einsatz vor Ort bat, schlug Kaiko ihm eine Online-Konferenz vor, um bestimmte Fragen bereits im Vorfeld zu klären.

In den folgenden Wochen gelang es allen Beteiligten, einen konstruktiven Dialog herzustellen und Lösungsansätze für die gegebenen Probleme auszuarbeiten. In wöchentlichem Rhythmus finden ein- bis zweistündige Lagebesprechungen statt, die Kaiko konsekutiv verdolmetscht.

Zwischen Kaiko und dem Kunden hat sich ein starkes Vertrauensverhältnis entwickelt, und die Option der Online-Konferenz ist ein fester Bestandteil des japanisch-französischen Arbeitsalltags geworden.

5 Abschlussbemerkungen

Der vorliegende Artikel hatte das Ziel, die Möglichkeiten der WebInterpret-Online-Plattform als Ergänzung im Berufsleben von Dolmetschern aufzuzeigen.

Konferenzdolmetscher haben seit Jahrzenten zu einem reibungslosen und sinngebenden Ablauf internationaler Veranstaltungen beigetragen. Es wird gerade in den kommenden Jahren wichtig sein, dieses Wissen weiterzugeben und einer veränderten und sich verändernden Umwelt anzupassen. Die Online-Plattform versteht sich als Teil dieses Prozesses und beruht dabei auf der engen Zusammenarbeit mit DolmetscherInnen, ohne deren Beitrag selbstverständlich nichts möglich wäre.

Zu den Herausforderungen der kommenden Jahre gehören unter anderem die Einbettung der visuellen Komponente, die in manchen Situationen, die die Plattform bisher nicht abdeckt, nicht wegzudenken sind.

Darüber hinaus gilt unser Augenmerk der Funktionalität des Relaisdolmetschens für den Einsatz in europäischen Institutionen und den damit verbundenen 23 offiziellen Sprachen.

Bibliographie

Crystal, David, *English As A Global Language*, Cambridge: 1997.

Ende, Anne-Katrin, *Dolmetschen im Kommunikationsmarkt*, Berlin: 2006.

Garzone, Giulia und Maurizio Viezzi, *Interpreting in the 21st century: challenges and opportunities : selected papers from the 1st Forlì Conference on Interpreting Studies, 9-11 November 2000*, London: 2000.

Gschwend, Ragni Maria, *Der schiefe Turm von Babel: Geschichten vom Übersetzen, Dolmetschen und Verstehen*, Straelen: 2000.

Trompanaas, Fons und Charles Hampden-Turner, *Managing People Across Cultures*, Oxford: 2004.

Trompanaas, Fons und Charles Hampden-Turner, *Building the Waves of Culture*, London: 1998.

Wojtag, Gerd (Hg.), *Quo Vadis Translatologie?*, Berlin: 2007.

InterpretBank: Ein Tool zum Wissens- und Terminologiemanagement für Simultandolmetscher

Claudio Fantinuoli

Johannes Gutenberg-Universität Mainz, Germersheim

fantinuo@uni-mainz.de

1 Einleitung

1.1 Nutzergruppen und Aufgabenbereiche

Erfolgreiches Dolmetschen setzt qualifizierte Vorbereitung voraus. Dazu gehört auch die nutzeradäquate Gestaltung und kontinuierliche Pflege von Terminologiebeständen sowie die Möglichkeit, auf Informationen und Terminologie schnell und effizient zugreifen zu können. Als Fachgebietslaien müssen sich professionelle Dolmetscher auf einen bevorstehenden technischen Einsatz gezielt vorbereiten und sowohl fachliches als auch terminologisches Wissen aneignen. Da aufgrund der Fachlichkeit der Themen keine adäquaten Ressourcen zur Verfügung stehen, muss der Dolmetscher sie selbst erarbeiten.

Um diese Prozesse zu optimieren wird basierend auf den neuesten Erkenntnissen der Dolmetschwissenschaft und der Computerlinguistik der Versuch unternommen, eine speziell für die Dolmetscher konzipierte Anwendung Namens *InterpretBank* zu entwickeln und zu implementieren.

In diesem Artikel sollen die relevanten Grundlagen der Dolmetschwissenschaft und der Computerlinguistik sowie zwei der Module von *InterpretBank* vorgestellt werden.

1.2 Elektronische Datenverarbeitung

Während terminologische Daten und fachliche Informationen lange Zeit auf Papier verfasst und verbreitet wurden, bieten computerlinguistische Anwendungen und das Internet neue Möglichkeiten der Datenverarbeitung und -darstellung. Die Verfügbarkeit großer Mengen an frei zugänglichen Fachtexten im Internet (Kaligariff und Grafenstette 2003), die dynamische Datendarstellung und die unterschiedlichsten Möglichkeiten des Datenzugriffs mittels ausgereifter Suchverfahren sind nur einige der wichtigsten Vorzüge der elektronischen Datenverarbeitung.

Die starre und meist normative Struktur der gedruckten lexikographischen Werke, wie z.B. Wörterbücher und Lexika, oder die Inflexibilität der gedruckten Fachtexte, z.B. Fachzeitschriften oder -bücher, überlassen den dynamischen und linguistisch deskriptiven Ansätzen der computerunterstützten Wissens- und Terminologieverwaltung das Feld. Die Vernetzung von kontrollierten Datenbeständen (Glossare) mit automatisch gesammelten Fachtexten (Korpora), die automatische Extraktion von relevanten Fachbegriffen (Fantinuoli 2006), die Einbindung von Datensammlungen in speziell für die Bedürfnisse der Anwender programmierten Anwendungen, um z.B. aus den gewonnenen Datenmengen gezielt Informationen terminologischer und inhaltlicher Natur abrufen zu können, sowie die dynamische Erzeugung von Darstellungsformen (z.B. in der Form von semantischen Netzen oder Mind Maps), können die Möglichkeiten der *Knowledge Experience* – der Aneignung von Wissen und Terminologie – erweitern und ergänzen.

1.3 Computereinsatz bei Dolmetschern

In den letzten Jahren wurden zahlreiche Umfragen unter Konferenzdolmetschern zu deren Erfahrung mit Computern und Terminologietools durchgeführt. Die Arbeiten von Will (2000) und Valentini (2002) und die Umfrage vom Sprachen & Dolmetscher Institut München (2007) zeigen ein ernüchterndes Bild hinsichtlich der Verbreitung der für Dolmetscher entwickelten Tools. Die meisten Befragten benutzen heutzutage für die Terminologieverwaltung immer noch selbstproduzierte Lösungen, wie z.B. Word- oder Excel-Tabellen, nur selten aber Tools, die auch eine Simultanmodalität besitzen, so gut wie niemals computerlinguistische Anwendungen wie zum Beispiel Concordancer oder Terminologieextraktionswerkzeuge. Gleichzeitig aber zeichnet sich im Laufe der Jahre ein steig wachsendes Interesse an Computeranwendungen ab, die die Vorbereitung, Durchführung und Nachbearbeitung eins Dolmetscheinsatzes effizienter gestalten sollten. Nach dem gleichem Modell der Dolmetschwissenschaft, die zwischen *advance, last-minute* und *in-conference preparation* (Gile 1995) unterscheidet, muss eine dolmetschergerechte Anwendung die unterschiedlichen Phasen eines Dolmetscheinsatzes von der Vorbereitung bis zum Kabineneinsatz und zur Nachbearbeitung berücksichtigen und zum Tragen bringen.

1.4 Modelle und Methoden der Dolmetschwissenschaft

Die Dolmetschwissenschaft ist sich einig, dass

[...] before starting a conference, interpreters should acquire as much specific knowledge as possible (Gile 1995)

Die Vorbereitungsphase einer Fachkonferenz in einem dem Dolmetscher noch nicht bekannten Fachgebiet spielt eine entscheidende Rolle im Leben eines professionellen Dolmetschers. In dieser Phase muss sich der Dolmetscher eine Reihe von Informationen sprachlicher und inhaltlicher Natur aneignen, die notwendig sind um einen Dolmetscheinsatz erfolgreich durchzuführen.

Die terminologische und fachliche Vorbereitung wird von Kalina (1998) als Strategie beschrieben, die die kognitiven Prozesse auf die Zeit vor der Konferenz vorverlegt und somit den Dolmetscher während der Verdolmetschung entlastet. Die gewonnenen freien Kapazitäten bedeuten in der Regel ein besseres Output der Verdolmetschung. Darüber hinaus spielt die Anwendung einer nutzeradäquaten Terminologie in sehr fachlichen Konferenzen eine weitere wichtige Rolle: Einerseits schafft sie Vertrauen dem Dolmetscher gegenüber, andererseits vereinfacht sie die Fachkommunikation und erlaubt dem Dolmetscher präzisere und knappere Formulierungen. Und das verbessert wiederum die Qualität bzw. die Wahrnehmung der Qualität der Verdolmetschung.

Um sich in kürzester Zeit auf neue und komplexe Themen vorbereiten zu können, bedient sich der Dolmetscher unterschiedlicher Techniken. Im Wesentlichen beschränken sie sich aber auf die Bearbeitung der zur Verfügung gestellten Unterlagen und auf die Internetrecherchen. Diese Operationen werden vorwiegend sehr traditionell durchgeführt und zwar auf dem Medium Papier (Valentini 2002).

Nachdem die Dolmetschwissenschaft sich zuerst auf die reine Beschreibung des Verhältnisses zwischen Dolmetschern und Computern bzw. Vorbereitungsmustern beschränkt hat, erleben wir erst in den letzten Jahren, dass die Dolmetschwissenschaft einen Wandel vom rein deskriptiven zu einem eher konstruktiven Ansatz durchgemacht hat. Rütten (2007) zum Beispiel befasst sich auf eine detaillierte Art und Weise mit den strukturellen Prozessen der Organisation terminologischer Arbeit für Dolmetscher, während Will (2007) den Versuch unternimmt, Modelle und Methoden dafür zu entwickeln. Diese theoretischen dolmetschbezogenen Ansätze gekoppelt mit den Erkenntnissen der Korpuslinguistik im Bereich Spracherwerb und Übersetzungswissenschaft sowie der Computerlinguistik dienen als Grundlage für die Implementierung von *InterpretBank*.

2 InterpretBank – Die Struktur

InterpretBank ist ein neues, offenes und modulares Tool, welches den Dolmetscher im Bereich Wissens- und Terminologiemanagement vor, während und nach der Konferenz unterstützt. Die einzelnen Bauteile – die Module – sind unabhängige Anwendungen, die eine bestimmte Aufgabe erfüllen.

Unter anderem sind folgende Module vorgesehen:

- *ConferenceMode*: Modul zum Nachschlagen von Glossaren während des Simultaneinsatzes

- *TermMode*: Modul zur Erstellung und Pflege der Terminologiebestände

- *CorpusMode*: Modul zur automatischen Termextraktion und Informationssuche aus automatisch hergestellten Fachkorpora

- *DrillMode*: Modul zum aktiven und dolmetschspezifischen Lernen der Glossare

Alle Module sind mittels offener Formate miteinander und ggf. mit externen Anwendungen verbunden. Die im *TermMode* verwalteten terminologischen Einträge sind z.B. mit dem *Concordancer* des *CorpusMode* verbunden und ermöglichen somit das direkte Starten einer Kontextsuche aus einem bestimmten Glossar; aus dem *ConferenceMode* kann man neue Termini, die man während der Verdolmetschung zu den bestehenden Glossaren hinzufügen will, direkt eingeben, ohne die Konferenzmodalität verlassen zu müssen, usw. Um eine möglichst hohe Akzeptanz seitens der Dolmetscher zu erzielen, muss *InterpretBank* hohe Flexibilität und Leistungsfähigkeit mit einer einfachen, benutzerfreundlichen und selbsterklärenden Bedienungsoberfläche in Einklang bringen (Valentini 2002). Dieser kritische Balanceakt stellt für Design und Implementierung eine große Herausforderung dar.

Im Folgenden werden die wichtigsten Funktionalitäten zweier Module, *ConferenceMode* und *CorpusMode*, näher erläutert, die aus dolmetschwissenschaftlicher und computerlinguistischer Sicht innovativer sind.

2.1 ConferenceMode

ConferenceMode ermöglicht dem Konferenzdolmetscher den schnellen und bedarfsorientierten Zugriff auf bestehende mehrsprachige Terminologiedateien. Bedingt durch die Eigenschaften des Dolmetschprozesses – Zeitdruck, hohe Konzentration etc. – muss die Anwendung für den Einsatz in der Kabine vor allem Wert auf folgende Grundbeschaffenheiten legen (SDI 2007):

- schnelle und flexible Suchfunktion

- Übersichtlichkeit

- komfortable und schnelle Eingabe neuer Termini

- intuitive Bedienbarkeit

- Kompatibilität mit anderen Programmen

ConferenceMode verwendet als Datenbank eine einzige Txt-Datei, das so genannte *Aktive Glossar*. Diese Datei enthält alle Wortpaare, die im Vorfeld für einen Einsatz geladen wurden und bleibt unverändert, bis *ConferenceMode* für den nächsten Einsatz mit einem neuen Glossar geladen wird. Diese Lösung ermöglicht es dem Dolmetscher, das aktive Glossar zusammenzustellen, indem er ein oder mehrere Glossare aus *TermMode* oder aus anderen Programmen (MS Word, MS Excel, Multiterm, CSV-Dateien, etc.) nacheinander lädt. Dank dieser hohen Flexibilität kann der Dolmetscher am Einsatzort schnell und unproblematisch Glossare von Kunden oder Kollegen lesen und zum aktiven Glossar hinzufügen.

Auch die Eingabe von neuen Termini während des Einsatzes erfolgt schnell und komfortabel durch eine eigene Maske. Die neuen Termini werden direkt dem aktiven Glossar hinzugefügt, sodass diese gleich abrufbar sind. Damit diese Termini auch im eigenen Terminologieverwaltungstool eingetragen werden, werden sie in einer separaten Datei oder direkt in *TermMode* aufgenommen.

Um den Dolmetschprozess so wenig wie möglich zu beeinträchtigen und den Dolmetscher bei der Suche nach passenden Fachbegriffen auch während der Verdolmetschung zu unterstützen, ist es notwendig, dass einerseits das erforderliche Input so klein wie möglich ist und dass andererseits das Output so übersichtlich wie möglich gestaltet und auf das Minimum reduziert wird. Ziel ist es, dass der Dolmetscher mit wenig Aufwand möglichst wenige, aber gleichzeitig präzise Treffer angezeigt bekommt. Der gesuchte Begriff wird mittels Tastatur eingegeben, die Suche mit der Entertaste oder mit dem eigenen Suchalgorithmus (ohne Entertaste) begonnen. Dieser ermöglicht das Anzeigen der Treffer schon während der Eingabe. Sobald die eingestellte Anzahl von Treffern angezeigt wird, wird die Eingabemaske für die nächste Suche freigegeben. Dank dieser interaktiven Suchmethode wird der Dolmetscher bei der Suche erheblich entlastet. Die Reduzierung der angezeigten Treffer erfolgt u.a. durch den Einsatz von *Stopwords*. Wenn man zum Beispiel nach dem Wort „Dermatologie" sucht und die Buchstabenkette „d", „de" oder „der" eingibt, wird der Eintrag „Entzündung der Bauchspeicheldrüse" nicht angezeigt, weil der Artikel „der" auf der Stoppwortliste steht.

2.2 CorpusMode

CorpusMode unterstützt den Dolmetscher während der Vorbereitungsphase durch die Bereitstellung von fachlicher Terminologie und durch die Möglichkeit, in fachbezogenen Textsammlungen zu stöbern, um inhaltliche und terminologische Fragen zu vertiefen.

Das Grundprinzip von *CorpusMode* ist einfach: Aus wenigen Fachbegriffen – zum Beispiel aus Titeln oder Abstracts der Konferenzteilnehmer – wird automatisch nach der Methode von BootCaT (Baroni und Bernardini 2004) eine Sammlung von Fachtexten aus dem Internet heruntergeladen und als einfache Textdateien aufbereitet. Das erstellte Korpus dient dann zur automatischen Extraktion der Fachterminologie, die auf der Grundlage von statistischen und linguistischen Kriterien durchgeführt wird.

Ausgehend von den extrahierten Termkandidaten oder von den Fachtermini, die im Laufe der Einsatzvorbereitung getroffen werden, kann der Dolmetscher eine Suche im Fachkorpus starten. Die Ergebnisse dieser „browsing activity", (Bernardini, 2000 / Johns, 1988), die in Form einer Auflistung von sogenannten *Key Words In Context* (KWIK) angezeigt werden, können Informationen über Terminologie, Inhalt und Gebrauch von Begriffen in einem bestimmten Kontext verraten (Zanettin, 1998).

Sammlungen von Fachbegriffen, die das Ergebnis einer automatischen Termextraktion darstellen, können zum Beispiel als Basis für eine gezielte Vorbereitung verwendet werden:

The process of „knowledge acquisition/language learning" needed by interpreters in order to prepare themselves for a conference can be optimized by making it „terminology-driven", or „bottom-up": from the terminology to the conceptual structure of a particular domain. (Fantinuoli 2006)

Korpora können als Grundlage für einen nahezu unendlichen „serendipity process" (Johns 1988) dienen, da ein Wort oder ein Satz zum nächsten führen kann. Durch diesen Ansatz kann der Dolmetscher das Korpus – ausgehend von den Fachbegriffen – dynamisch erkunden und dabei Begriffe und deren Bedeutung lernen.

Für eine empirische Untersuchung der Qualität der automatisch erstellten Korpora und der extrahierten Terminologie im Bezug auf die Dolmetscherbedürfnisse wird hier auf die Arbeit von Fantinuoli (2006) verwiesen.

Nach dem Prinzip der Modularisierung verfügt *CorpusMode* über eine Rückkopplung zu den anderen Modulen. So ist es z.B. möglich, aus einem Eintrag in *TermMode*, dem Terminologie-Verwaltungsmodul von *InterpretBank*, direkt eine KWIK-Suche zu starten und eine Serie von Beispielen für das betroffene Wort zu erhalten. Das erspart einerseits viel Arbeit bei der Eingabe der Einträge, da Felder wie Definition oder Beispielsätze in den meisten Fällen nicht mehr nötig sind, andererseits erweitert es die Informationen, die mit einem Eintrag verbunden sind.

3. Ausblick

Während Computeranwendungen zum festen Bestandteil des Übersetzerberufs geworden und mittlerweile nicht mehr wegzudenken sind, bleibt das Dolmetschen von den neuesten Entwicklungen und Erkenntnissen im Bereich Translationswissenschaft und Computerlinguistik weiterhin unberührt. Da die möglichen Vorteile eines computergestützten Ansatzes auch für Dolmetscher auf der Hand liegen, will der Autor mit *InterpretBank* versuchen, eine erste Brücke zwischen diesen Disziplinen zu schlagen und praktizierenden oder angehenden Dolmetschern eine Lösung zu bieten, um die Qualität der eigenen Dienstleistung zu steigern und die kognitiven Kompetenzen zu fördern.

Bibliographie

Baroni, M. / Bernardini, S. (2004). BootCaT: Bootstrapping Corpora and Terms from the Web, in: *Proceedings of LREC*, Lisbon: ELDA, S. 1313-1316.

Bernardini, S. (2000). *Competence, capacity, corpora*. Bologna: CLUEB.

Gile, D. (1995). *Basic concepts and models for translator and interpreter training*. Amsterdam/Philadelphia: John Benjamins Publishing Company.

Kalina, S. (1998). Kognitive Verarbeitungsprozesse, in: Snell-Hornby, M. / Hönig, H. G. / Kußmaul, P. / Schmitt, P. A. (eds.) *Handbuch Translation*. Tübingen: Stauffenburg, S. 330-335.

Kilgarriff, A. / Grefenstette, G. (2003). Introduction to the web as corpus, in: *Computational Linguistics*, 29. S. 333-347.

Fantinuoli, C. (2006). Specialized Corpora from the Web for Simultaneous Interpreters, in: Baroni, M. / Bernardini, S. (eds.). *Wacky! Working papers on the Web as Corpus.* Bologna: GEDIT. S. 173-190.

Johns, T. (1988). Whence and whither classroom concordancing? In: Bongaerts et al. (eds.). *Computer applications in language learning.* Foris. S. 9–32.

Rütten, Anja (2007). *Informations- und Wissensmanagement im Konferenzdolmetschen.* Frankfurt: Lang.

Valentini, C. (2002). *Uso del Computer in Cabina di Interpretazione.* Tesi di Laurea, SSLiMIT, Bologna.

Will, M. (2000). Bemerkungen zum Computereinsatz beim Simultandolmetschen. In: Kalina, S. / Buhl, S. / Gerzymisch-Arbogast, H. (eds.). *Dolmetschen: Theorie-Praxis-Didaktik.* St. Ingbert: Röhrig. S. 125-135.

Will, M. (2007). Terminology Work for Simultaneous Interpreters in LSP Conferences: Model and Method. *MuTra 2007 – LSP Translation Scenarios: Conference Proceedings*

Sprachen & Dolmetscher Institut München (2007). Terminologietools für den Einsatz in der Simultankabine. In: *MDÜ* 3/2007. SS. 26 ff.

Übersetzungsprozesse und maschinengestütztes Übersetzen

Maschinelle Übersetzung bei Volkswagen

Jörg Porsiel

Dipl.-Übersetzer, Volkswagen AG, Fremdsprachenmanagement

extern.joerg.porsiel@volkswagen.de

1 Das Volkswagen Sprachenportal

Seit Sommer 2002 bietet das Intranet der Volkswagen AG das *Volkswagen Sprachenportal* an. Es bündelt zentral und für alle Konzernmitarbeiter zugänglich eine Vielzahl von Informationen zum Thema Sprache im Allgemeinen (u. a. bzgl. der neuen deutschen Rechtschreibung mit Links zu entsprechenden Websites) sowie Übersetzen und Dolmetschen im Besonderen. Darüber hinaus bietet es Zugriff auf eine umfangreiche mehrsprachige unternehmensspezifische Terminologiedatenbank mit über 16.000 Einträgen und auf maschinelle Übersetzung (nachfolgend als *„MT"* bezeichnet) in den Sprachen Deutsch, Englisch, Französisch, Russisch und Spanisch. Das Portal und seine Inhalte sind in diesen fünf Sprachen verfügbar.

1.1 Ausgangssituation und Rahmenbedingungen

Der Volkswagen Konzern, der weltweit rund 370.000 Mitarbeiter zählt, davon 174.000 in Deutschland, bietet seine Fahrzeuge in mehr als 150 Ländern an. An 61 Produktionsstandorten werden Fahrzeuge der Marken Volkswagen, Audi, Seat, Škoda, Bentley, Lamborghini, Bugatti, Volkswagen Nutzfahrzeuge und Scania gefertigt. 2008 wurden nahezu 6,26 Millionen Fahrzeuge ausgeliefert und der Umsatz auf 113,8 Milliarden Euro erhöht.

Das VW-interne *Fremdsprachenmanagement* in Wolfsburg wickelt jährlich ca. 30.000 Übersetzungsaufträge in bis zu 40 Sprachen sowie ca. 1.200 Dolmetschereinsätze ab.

Abb. 1: Das Volkswagen Sprachenportal in fünf Sprachen.

Ausschlaggebend für die Bereitstellung des Sprachenportals, der Terminologiedatenbank und der maschinellen Übersetzung waren mehrere Faktoren: Zum einen die wachsende Notwendigkeit im Zeitalter der Internationalisierung und Globalisierung, Texterstellungs- und Übersetzungsprozesse qualitativ zu optimieren und zu beschleunigen, indem u. a. das Bewusstsein für die (betriebswirtschaftliche) Bedeutung einer einheitlichen Unternehmenssprache geschärft sowie umfassendes Terminologiemanagement im Bereich der technischen Dokumentation weiter vorangetrieben wurde. Diese Ziele sollten durch die Bereitstellung einer möglichst unkomplizierten Anwendung zur Bewältigung des in den vergangenen Jahren extrem gestiegenen E-Mail-Aufkommens sowohl inner- als auch außerhalb des Konzerns erreicht werden. Darüber hinaus musste ebenfalls der starke Anstieg des Textvolumens der technischen Dokumentation aufgrund der Ausweitung der Fahrzeugmodellpalette sowie der Erschließung neuer Märkte bewältigt werden.

Weltweit werden täglich mehrere Milliarden E-Mails versandt (Spam-Mails nicht mitgerechnet). Im Durchschnitt erhält ein Mitarbeiter eines in den *Fortune 500* gelisteten Unternehmens, wozu auch Volkswagen gehört, pro Tag 80 E-Mails. Schätzungen zufolge können 70 % der Mitarbeiter eines Großunternehmens in Deutschland täglich 60 Minuten ihrer Arbeitszeit allein durch unverständliche E-Mails (dazu gehören auch fremdsprachige) verlieren. Zudem führt die steigende Zahl der Mails nicht zwangsläufig zu einer Verbesserung der Kommunikation bzw. des Informationsaustausches.

„Ineffizienter Informationsaustausch" durch *„unverständliche E-Mails"* kann auch darin bestehen, dass fremdsprachige E-Mails aufgrund unzureichender Sprachkenntnisse nicht bzw. missverstanden oder wegen der Wartezeit für eine notwendige Humanübersetzung (zu) spät beantwortet werden. Hier sorgt MT für erhebliche Prozessbeschleunigung: In Sekundenschnelle können Textmengen von einer Zeile bis hin zu mehreren Hundert Seiten übersetzt werden – wobei die Übersetzungsqualität zunächst von untergeordneter Bedeutung ist. Zeitgewinn ist das vorrangige Ziel beim Einsatz maschineller Übersetzung!

1.2 Ziele des Volkswagen Sprachenportals

Das Sprachenportal verfolgt mit seinem Angebot mehrere Ziele unterschiedlicher Tragweite. Neben der weiteren Verbesserung von Sprachqualität und Geschwindigkeit in der Kommunikation des Unternehmens sollen die im Portal verfügbaren Inhalte nachhaltig bewusstseinsbildend in Bezug auf das Thema *Sprache* im Allgemeinen und der Bedeutung einer einheitlichen und eindeutigen Unternehmenssprache im Besonderen wirken.

1.3 Betriebswirtschaftlicher Nutzen

Das Sprachenportal und dort vor allem MT wird von den Mitarbeitern gegenwärtig zur beschleunigten Abarbeitung täglicher Routineaufgaben, wie z. B. der Bearbeitung/Übersetzung von E-Mails, Sitzungsprotokollen oder Berichten eingesetzt. Dabei geht es um die Bereitstellung so genannter *gist* oder *indicative translations*, also von Rohübersetzungen. Obwohl die Qualität dieser Rohübersetzungen in Abhängigkeit von der Qualität der Ausgangstexte (GIGO-Prinzip, s. dazu unten *„Warum maschinelle Übersetzung ‚so schlecht' ist"*) zum Teil stark schwanken kann, reicht den Anwendern das Übersetzungsergebnis in der Regel aus, um innerhalb von Sekunden und in Verbindung mit dem eigenen Vor- und Fachwissen eine Entscheidung treffen zu können, wie weiter zu verfahren ist.

Aus der Konstellation von Informationsbedürfnis, -beschaffung und -verarbeitung – in Verbindung mit dem enormen Zeitgewinn durch MT – resultiert der primäre Nutzen für das Unternehmen. In Zeiten immer kürzer werdender Produktzyklen (*time-to-market*) und fortschreitender Globalisierung ist die beschleunigte Informationsbeschaffung, -aufbereitung und *„Veredelung"* zu Wissen von wesentlicher Bedeutung für die Sicherung von Wettbewerbsvorteilen. Insbesondere bei weltweit über alle Zeitzonen hinweg operierenden Unternehmen ist der Faktor *Zeit* entscheidend. Der Einsatz von MT bei Routineaufgaben, wie dem Lesen, Beantworten oder Weiterleiten von E-Mails o. Ä., führt zu einer bisher nicht gekannten Beschleunigung fremdsprachiger Kommunikations- und Entscheidungsfindungsprozesse, gleichzeitig verbunden mit einer erheblichen und nachhaltigen Senkung von Bearbeitungs- und Übersetzungskosten.

2 Maschinelle Übersetzung im Einsatz

Die im Sprachenportal eingesetzte maschinelle Übersetzung wurde nach umfangreichen Tests verschiedener Produkte ausgewählt. Ausdrücklich war (und ist) dabei *nicht* beabsichtigt, Humanübersetzer durch MT zu ersetzen oder MT in einem produktiven Umfeld zu nutzen, d. h. für die Übersetzung von Texten einzusetzen, die bisher von Humanübersetzern bearbeitet wurden. Vielmehr wird MT fast ausschließlich für die Übersetzung von Texten verwendet, die der Anwender bisher selbst, z. B. mit Hilfe eines handelsüblichen Wörterbuchs oder ähnlicher Hilfsmittel, und recht zeitaufwändig übersetzen musste.

Für alle angebotenen Sprachpaare wird ein so genanntes *regelbasiertes System* (rule-based machine translation [RBMT]) der Firma Lucy Software and Services GmbH eingesetzt. In den vergangenen Jahren verstärkt auf den Markt drängende statistische (statistical machine translation [SMT]) oder Hybridsysteme, also eine Mischung aus SMT und RBMT, waren Mitte 2002, dem Testzeitpunkt bei Volkswagen, in den Sprachen Deutsch, Englisch und Spanisch entweder noch nicht marktreif oder überhaupt nicht verfügbar, konnten folglich auch nicht geprüft werden.

2.1 Kennzahlen

Das Sprachenportal und damit die maschinelle Übersetzung sind konzern-, d.h. weltweit (auch auf Dienstreisen), erreichbar. Nach einer forcierten Erweiterung des Sprachenangebotes um Russisch (Februar 2008) und Französisch (Juli 2008) sowie der Integration von über 40.000 VW-spezifischen Begriffen (d. h. hauptsächlich aus Kfz-Technik und Maschinenbau) werden derzeit durchschnittlich 7.000 Übersetzungen pro Arbeitstag maschinell verarbeitet, wobei *eine Übersetzung* sowohl lediglich ein einziges Wort (s. dazu unten unter *„Warum maschinelle Übersetzung ,so schlecht' ist"*) als auch Texte mit Umfängen von mehr als 100 DIN-A4-Seiten umfassen kann. Insgesamt bedeutet dies umgerechnet ein Übersetzungsvolumen von ca. 1.500 Standardseiten pro Arbeitstag, wobei – das sei nochmals betont – die Qualität zunächst *keine* Rolle spielt. Hier geht es vorrangig und ausschließlich um Geschwindigkeit, also Zeitgewinn.

In den vergangenen zwei Jahren wurde das Sprachenportal inhaltlich stark erweitert, u. a. durch den Ausbau der dort zugänglichen Terminologiedatenbank, die nun in 20 Sprachen (mit ca. 15.000 deutschen Benennungen) zur Verfügung steht und ausschließlich konzerntypische Begriffe enthält. Darüber hinaus wurde die maschinelle Übersetzung um die Sprachen Französisch und Russisch ergänzt sowie die VW-Terminologie in den nunmehr fünf einsetzbaren Sprachen integriert, um die Übersetzungsergebnisse zu verbessern. Die Inhalte des Sprachenportals sind vollständig in den derzeit fünf Portalsprachen lokalisiert.

Abb. 2: Maschinelle Übersetzung im Sprachenportal.

2.2 Was maschinelle Übersetzung kann

Soll maschinelle Übersetzung sinnvoll eingesetzt werden, muss man sich vorher darüber im Klaren sein, wo deren Verwendung nützlich ist und was MT *nicht* zu leisten vermag und vor allem warum. Das bedeutet für den Portalbetreiber, in diesem Sinne bewusstseinsbildend tätig werden zu müssen.

Der Einsatz von MT *„lohnt"* unter folgenden Voraussetzungen: Es muss spezifische Unternehmensterminologie in möglichst großem Umfang und von möglichst guter Qualität sowohl in der jeweiligen Ausgangs- wie auch in der Zielsprache vorhanden sein. Jeder terminologische Begriff sollte eindeutig und darüber hinaus einem Sachgebiet zugeordnet sein. Idealerweise sollte es eine Schnittstelle zwischen Terminologiedatenbank und maschineller Übersetzung geben, oder es sollten doch wenigstens regelmäßige Updates neuer Terminologie durchgeführt werden, damit die Qualität der MT-Ergebnisse kontinuierlich und spürbar besser wird. Neben der erheblichen Zeitersparnis führt dies zu einer Steigerung der Akzeptanz seitens der Nutzer, die maschineller Übersetzung im Allgemeinen anfänglich eher skeptisch gegenüberstehen.

Den Anwendern wiederum muss das Vorhandensein einer standardisierten Unternehmensterminologie vermittelt werden, wobei der übergeordnete betriebswirtschaftliche, aber auch der persönliche Nutzen dazustellen sind. Des Weiteren müssen die Nutzer dazu angehalten werden, diese Terminologie auch tatsächlich für ihre tägliche Arbeit zu verwenden. In Bereichen wie der technischen Dokumentation wäre es darüber hinaus überaus hilfreich, maschinelle Lektoratssysteme einzusetzen, um die Effizienz zu erhöhen, (Übersetzungs-) Kosten zu senken und Sprachbewusstsein nachhaltig zu fördern.

Die Qualität der Übersetzungsergebnisse hängt bei MT – weitaus mehr noch als bei der Humanübersetzung – von der Qualität der Ausgangstexte ab. Hier schlägt das *garbage-in-garbage-out*-Prinzip (GIGO) voll durch.

2.3 Warum maschinelle Übersetzung „*so schlecht*" ist

Gelegentlich beschweren sich Anwender, dass die Ergebnisse der maschinellen Übersetzung „*so schlecht*" seien. Besonders zwei „Beweise" werden dafür angeführt: 1. Die Übersetzung einzelner Begriffe „*funktioniert nicht*". „*Ich habe ‚xy' eingegeben, aber keine Übersetzung erhalten.*" Variante: „*.... aber eine völlig falsche Übersetzung erhalten.*"; und 2. Einige Nutzer sind der Meinung, das ideale Messmittel für Übersetzungsqualität gefunden zu haben: nämlich die *Rückübersetzung*. Sie unterliegen aber hier mangels Sprachbewusstsein dem Trugschluss, Sprache sei in Aufbau und Funktionsweise mit Mathematik gleichzusetzen: Analog zur Gegenprobe in der Mathematik wird der gerade übersetzte Text rückübersetzt. Ist das Ergebnis nicht vollkommen oder wenigstens doch zu 90 % identisch mit dem Ursprungstext, handelt es sich nach Ansicht dieser Nutzer automatisch um eine „*schlechte Übersetzung*". Beide *Beweise* führen drastisch vor Augen, wo die Defizite auf Anwenderseite liegen bzw. wie viel Arbeit noch in Bezug auf das Verständnis von Sprache im Allgemeinen und (maschineller) Übersetzung im Besonderen weiterhin zu leisten ist.

Es ist festzustellen, dass eine der Hauptfehlerquellen bei der maschinellen Übersetzung (neben unzureichender Terminologie, Softwaremängeln, sonstigen technischen Problemen), der Anwender selbst ist. Einige Beispiele: Aufgrund fehlenden Sprachgefühls und meist nicht vorhandener Kenntnis dessen, was maschinelle Übersetzung leisten kann und was nicht, versuchen Nutzer häufig Einzelbegriffe (wie mit einem Wörterbuch oder einer Terminologiedatenbank) zu übersetzen. Das funktioniert manchmal, meistens aber nicht (richtig). Anwender geben häufig auch unvollständige Sätze ein, solche mit fehlender oder falscher Interpunktion (vor allem fehlendem Satzendezeichen), fehlerhafter, um nicht zu sagen beliebiger, Rechtschreibung oder mit unbekannten bzw. selbst erdachten und damit willkürlichen Abkürzungen. Sehr häufig kommen Texte vor, die größtenteils aus einem für einen Computer unverarbeitbarem Sprachenmischmasch aus Deutsch, Englisch, Denglisch o. Ä. bestehen – Textqualitäten also, bei denen selbst ein Humanübersetzer erhebliche Schwierigkeiten hätte, überhaupt zu verstehen, was gemeint sein *könnte*.

2.4 Was maschinelle Übersetzung *nicht* kann

Der Mehrheit der Anwender ist (zumindest anfänglich) nicht bewusst, was MT zu leisten vermag und was nicht – vor allem Letzteres erscheint schwer vermittelbar. So muss es Bestandteil der bewusstseinsbildenden Maßnahmen sein, den Anwendern zu verdeutlichen, was MT nicht kann, nämlich: *zwischen den Zeilen lesen*, ahnen, interpretieren, vermuten, assoziieren, Nichtübersetzbares paraphrasieren und vor allem fehlertolerant sein.

Beispiele

Fehlerhafter Ursprungstext:

habe u.g. HWMotor 4J0.367.832 hinsichtl. ENBaulage an drei Bsp. aktueller Neuprojekte gegengeprüft. demnach ist dieser HWMot. für uns zur Anfrage

Ergebnis:

> [u.g] has. [HWMotor 4J0.367.832] with regard to [ENBaulage] at three [Bsp]. current new projects' tested. accordingly this [HWMot] is. for us for the inquiry

Abb. 3: Übersetzungsergebnis bei fehlerhaftem Ausgangstext.

Einwandfreier Ursprungstext unter Verwendung von VW-Terminologie:

Der neue Passat CC steht unter anderem mit einem starken und agilen V6-Motor mit 220 kW (300 PS) zur Verfügung, der serienmäßig mit Doppelkupplungsgetriebe DSG und Allradantrieb 4MOTION ausgestattet ist (Kraftstoffverbrauch: 10,1 l/100 km; CO_2-Emission: 242 g/km). Im neuen Coupé kommt dazu ein innovatives System zum Einsatz: die Adaptive Fahrwerksregelung DCC.

Ergebnis:

> The new Passat [CC] is available among other things with a strong and agile V6 engine with 220 kilowatts (300 hp), [which | who] is equipped TO direct shift gearbox and to four-wheel drive 4MOTION in series with direct shift gearbox (Fuel consumption: 10,1 l/100 km; CO2-[emission | exhaust]: 242 g/km). In the new Coupé an innovative system is used for this purpose: the Adaptive Running Gear [Regulation | Arrangement] DCC.

Abb.4: Übersetzungsergebnis bei fehlerfreiem Ausgangstext.

2.5 Exkurs: Maschinelle Übersetzung im Internet

Im Gegensatz zum MT-Einsatz in einem Firewall-abgesicherten Unternehmensintranet birgt die Nutzung maschineller Übersetzungsangebote im World Wide Web Gefahren, die von der überwiegenden Mehrheit der Anwender bisher weitestgehend unterschätzt bzw. gar nicht wahrgenommen werden: nämlich die der Industriespionage. Mittlerweile existiert weltweit eine Vielzahl von Websites, die MT-Dienste unter Umständen „*von jeder Sprache in jede Sprache*" anbieten. Ein auf den ersten Blick verlockendes Angebot, da fast immer kostenlos zur Verfügung gestellt. Doch sollte man sich als potenzieller Nutzer vorher einige Fragen stellen: Wo steht der Server? Wer hat Zugriff auf ihn? Was geschieht mit meinen Daten? Wer ist der Anbieter? Warum bietet er diesen Dienst an? Welche Interessen verfolgt der Anbieter? Da diese Fragen vom Anwender kaum beantwortet werden können, sollte man sich die Nutzung solcher Angebote – vor allem wenn es um vertrauliche Textinhalte geht – sehr genau überlegen.

2.6 Nutzerreaktionen

Gegenwärtig verzeichnet das Volkswagen Sprachenportal durchschnittlich rund 1.200.000 Hits pro Monat mit stark steigender Tendenz. Obwohl es wie erwähnt gelegentlich Anwender gibt, die maschinelle Übersetzung an sich und die Übersetzungsergebnisse im Besonderen negativ beurteilen, ist die überwiegende Zahl der Rückmeldungen durchweg positiv. Die Mehrzahl positiver Rückmeldungen bringt sehr deutlich zum Ausdruck, welche große Unterstützung maschinelle Übersetzung für die tägliche Arbeit darstellt. Zahlreiche Nutzer bieten sogar ihre Mithilfe bei der Verbesserung der Übersetzungsergebnisse an, indem sie ihre fachbereichsspezifische Terminologie zur Verfügung stellen und sogar selbst in die Wörterbücher einpflegen wollen.

3   Ausblick – Was zu tun bleibt

Vorrangiges Ziel in Bezug auf den künftigen und vor allem erweiterten Einsatz maschineller Übersetzung ist der Ausbau des Angebotes und der Anwendungsbereiche. Dazu gehören neben der kontinuierlichen Erweiterung der unternehmensspezifischen Terminologie – auch aus nicht-Kfz-spezifischen Bereichen (wie z. B. BWL, Rechts- und Versicherungswesen) – die Einrichtung einer direkten Schnittstelle zwischen Terminologiedatenbank und MT und nicht zuletzt die Hinzufügung weiterer Sprachen wie etwa Chinesisch, Portugiesisch, Tschechisch oder Polnisch.

Was eine erweiterte Anwendung der maschinellen Übersetzung betrifft, so ist denkbar, MT in Bereichen sehr stark reglementierter bzw. standardisierter Texte wie Kurztexte von Diagnosegeräten o. Ä. einzusetzen. Absolute Grundvoraussetzung wäre in diesem Fall allerdings, dass die Quelltexte vorher mittels eines maschinellen Lektoratssystems erstellt wurden, da andernfalls der (Nach-) Bearbeitungsaufwand viel zu groß wäre, somit Kosten und Nutzen in keinem sinnvollen Verhältnis stünden.

Schließlich gilt es weiterhin, kontinuierlich und unternehmensweit das Bewusstsein für die (betriebswirtschaftliche) Bedeutung von *Sprache* in einem global agierenden Konzern zu schärfen und den Nutzen für den Einzelnen aber letztendlich auch für einen verbesserten (fremdsprachigen) Kommunikationsfluss und Informationsaustausch hervorzuheben. Ergebnisse derartiger Maßnahmen wären nicht nur eine spürbare Verbesserung der internen Kommunikation zwischen Mitarbeitern verschiedener, weltweit verteilter Standorte, sondern vor allem auch ein erheblicher Qualitätssprung bei der Kommunikation mit Lieferanten und Kunden.

Auswirkungen auf den Übersetzungsprozess durch die Einbindung maschineller Übersetzung in konventionelle Translation-Memory-Systeme

Hans Pich

Document Service Center GmbH

h.pich@dsc-translation.de

1 Maschinelle Übersetzung

Maschinelle Übersetzung (MÜ oder MT für engl. machine translation), auch automatische Übersetzung, bezeichnet die Übersetzung von Texten aus einer Ausgangssprache (in der MÜ als Quellsprache bezeichnet) in eine Zielsprache mit Hilfe eines Computerprogrammes. MÜ ist ein Teilbereich der künstlichen Intelligenz.[16]

Laut der deutschen Wikipedia ist die maschinelle Übersetzung ein Teilbereich der künstlichen Intelligenz. Das bedeutet zuerst einmal: Sie ist kein Teilbereich der Übersetzungswissenschaften und auch nicht der Sprachwissenschaften.

Diese Einordnung hat grundsätzliche Bedeutung für die Einbindung entsprechender Systeme in real existierende Übersetzungsworkflows. Es besteht ein deutliches Misstrauen in die Qualität der maschinell erstellten Übersetzungen. Dieses wird zudem noch durch praktische Erfahrungen mit den frei im Internet verfügbaren Systemen gestützt, deren Übersetzungsergebnisse mit konstanter Regelmäßigkeit Anlass zu Heiterkeit geben.

Auf der anderen Seite gibt es genügend Beispiele für einen funktionierenden Einsatz maschineller Übersetzungssysteme. Die in den aktuellen Versionen führender Translation-Memory-Systeme eingeführte praktisch nahtlose Integration interaktiver maschineller Übersetzungen in den bisherigen Übersetzungsprozess verändert die Bedeutung dieser Technologie für das Verhältnis zwischen Auftraggeber und Auftragnehmer jedoch grundlegend.

1.1 Einbindung maschineller Übersetzung in Translation-Memory-Systeme

Die Einbindung maschineller Übersetzungen in Übersetzungsprozesse unter Einsatz von Translation-Memory-Systemen ist eigentlich schon seit mehreren Jahren zumindest möglich und wurde auch genutzt. Generell kann man hier zwei Verfahren unterscheiden:

---

[16] http://de.wikipedia.org/wiki/Maschinelle_Uebersetzung

- Maschinelle Vorübersetzung der Texte und Einbindung der maschinellen Übersetzung in die Translation Memorys.
- Interaktive maschinelle Übersetzung während des normalen Übersetzungsprozesses für Segmente, die nicht im Translation Memory vorhanden sind.

Auch wenn die Qualität der maschinellen Übersetzungen nicht im Vordergrund steht, ist es doch wichtig, sich kurz zu vergegenwärtigen, welche Voraussetzungen für die Erreichung einer qualitativen Übersetzung erforderlich sind:

- Terminologie in einer für maschinelle Übersetzungssysteme geeigneten Aufbereitung
- Regeln bzw. Stilvorgaben

Je nach eingesetztem Übersetzungssystem wären dann auch noch ausreichend viele qualitativ hochwertige Referenzübersetzungen z.B. aus einem Translation Memory erforderlich.

Generell hat natürlich auch die Qualität der Quelltexte, genau wie bei einer *menschlichen* Übersetzung, eine große Bedeutung für das Ergebnis einer maschinellen Übersetzung.

1.2 Maschinelle Vorübersetzung vs. interaktive maschinelle Übersetzung

Bei der maschinellen Vorübersetzung wird der komplette Text oder der noch nicht in einem Translation Memory vorhandene Text in einer definierten Umgebung von einem maschinellen Übersetzungsprogramm übersetzt. Danach wird das Übersetzungsergebnis entweder direkt überarbeitet oder als abzugsbehaftete Menge von Übersetzungseinheiten in das Translation Memory integriert. Hierbei bestimmt nur der Kostenfaktor, wie viel Aufwand für die Umsetzung der Voraussetzungen für hohe Übersetzungsqualität betrieben wird. Auch wird normalerweise eine bewusste Entscheidung anhand nachprüfbarer Kriterien für ein konkretes Übersetzungsprogramm gefällt.

Im Gegenzug ist die interaktive maschinelle Übersetzung durch ihren dezentralen Ansatz viel schwieriger zu kontrollieren. Momentan entscheidet der Übersetzer (ggf. nach Anweisung), ob er sich während seiner Übersetzungen Vorschläge von einem maschinellen Übersetzungssystem machen lässt und wie er mit diesen dann verfährt. Eine echte Auswahl zwischen verschiedenen Übersetzungsprogrammen hat er nicht, da die Translation-Memory-Systeme in der Standardausführung noch keine Auswahl ermöglichen.

Üblicherweise geht man bei beiden Varianten davon aus, dass nach der maschinellen Übersetzung eine Überarbeitung durch den Übersetzer erfolgt, um letztendlich eine lieferfertige Übersetzung zu erhalten.

Die Integration der interaktiven maschinellen Übersetzung ist momentan zumeist so gelöst, dass der Übersetzer den vorgegebenen frei verfügbaren Übersetzungsserver in seiner Konfiguration aktiviert. Darauf schickt das Translation-Memory-System die

Segmente, für die es keine ausreichend guten Matches im Translation-Memory-System findet, an den Übersetzungsserver und erhält von dort eine maschinelle Übersetzung des Segments. Dieses Szenario ist zwar nicht für alle Sprachkombinationen verfügbar, die Anzahl der angebotenen Sprachkombinationen steigt jedoch stetig.

2 Problemfelder beim Einsatz der interaktiven maschinellen Übersetzung

Der Einsatz der interaktiven Übersetzung in diesem Szenario bietet eine Reihe unterschiedlicher Problembereiche.

Ein erster Bereich ist natürlich die Qualität. Aufgrund der freien Verfügbarkeit der Übersetzungsserver bestehen zumindest Zweifel an der Qualität. Schließlich heißt es im Volksmund nicht ganz zu Unrecht: Kost nix = Taugt nix. Auch wenn diese Redensart natürlich keine Basis für die Beurteilung der Qualität sein kann, bleiben zumindest Zweifel.

Aber selbst wenn man davon ausgeht, dass der Übersetzungsserver in der Lage ist (in Bezug auf die Erwartung an maschinelle Übersetzungen), hochwertige Übersetzungen zu liefern, bleibt die Frage nach der Terminologie und dem Stil. Bei den verfügbaren Lösungen werden momentan weder Terminologieinformationen noch Stilvorgaben an den Übersetzungsserver übertragen, so dass deren Einhaltung praktisch auszuschließen ist und lediglich Zufallstreffer möglich sind. In den modernen Translation-Memory-Systemen ist es zumindest möglich, bereits während der Übersetzung eine halbautomatische Terminologieprüfung durchzuführen, um ggf. vorhandene Terminologiefehler zu korrigieren.

Ein weiterer Problembereich ist die Sicherheit und Vertraulichkeit der zu übersetzenden Inhalte. Wenn wir annehmen, dass ein Übersetzer ein Dokument zur Übersetzung erhält, dass praktisch keine Matches zum Translation Memory hat, würde das Translation-Memory-System sukzessive die einzelnen Sätze nacheinander zum Übersetzungsserver schicken. Aus technischer Sicht ist es für den Betreiber des Übersetzungsservers leicht möglich, die übermittelten Inhalte wieder zu kompletten Dokumenten zusammenzusetzen. Da er in keinem Vertragsverhältnis zum Auftraggeber der Übersetzung steht, gibt es für ihn natürlich auch keine Vertraulichkeitsverpflichtungen. Es wäre also durchaus denkbar, dass vertrauliche Informationen in unbefugte Hände geraten können.

Auch der Faktor Mensch und die durchaus üblichen Gegebenheiten im Übersetzeralltag sind ein Problembereich. Viele Übersetzer stehen bei der Durchführung ihrer Aufträge unter einem nicht zu unterschätzenden Zeitdruck. Oft verbindet sich dies auch noch mit einer eher geringen Bezahlung. In diesem Kontext stellt sich die Frage, wie gründlich ein Übersetzer bei näher rückendem Abgabetermin die vom Übersetzungsserver gelieferten Übersetzungen überarbeitet. Wann beginnt er, auch die nicht so guten Übersetzungen *durchzuwinken*. Dieses Problem verschärft sich im Übrigen noch mit zunehmender sprachlicher Qualität der maschinellen Übersetzungsvorschläge. Wenn der Text in der Zielsprache korrekt aussieht, fällt es auch erfahrenen Übersetzern schwer, über einen längeren Zeitraum konzentriert nach Übersetzungsfehlern in Bezug zum Quelltext zu suchen.

Für den einzelnen Übersetzer und auch für Übersetzungsdienstleister ergibt sich zudem das Problem aus der Konkurrenzsituation zu Mitbewerbern. Es ist mit Sicherheit anzunehmen, dass es eine relevante Anzahl Anbieter gibt bzw. geben wird, die intensiv die Möglichkeiten der schnelleren *Erledigung* von Übersetzungsaufträgen nutzen werden und dies dementsprechend dann auch in ihre Angebotspreise einfließen lassen. Selbst wenn hier möglicherweise die Qualität auf der Strecke bleibt, werden diese Angebote doch im Markt präsent sein und auch in den Einkaufsabteilungen neben die Angebote von Übersetzern und Dienstleistern mit anderer Arbeitsweise gelegt werden. Es ist naheliegend, dass dies den Preisdruck im Markt noch weiter verschärfen wird.

3   Die Problematik aus Sicht der Auftraggeber

Für den Auftraggeber ist es beim Erhalt einer Übersetzung nicht auf den ersten Blick ersichtlich, ob der Übersetzer bei der Erstellung seiner Übersetzung auf maschinelle Übersetzungsvorschläge zurückgegriffen hat. Es war zwar auch früher schon möglich, dass ein Übersetzer die Dokumente maschinell vorübersetzt hat; die direkte Integration in ein Translation-Memory-System macht den Zugriff auf diese Art der Übersetzung allerdings so leicht verfügbar, dass mit einem ansteigenden Einsatz durch die Übersetzer zu rechnen ist.

Ein Auftraggeber, der hier ein Problem sieht, kann daher als erste Konsequenz einfach über eine vertragliche Vereinbarung den Einsatz von maschinellen Übersetzungssystemen ausschließen. Aber auch mit einer derartigen Vereinbarung werden viele Auftraggeber ihr schlechtes Gefühl nicht verlieren. Daher stellt sich die Frage, ob und wenn ja wie eine Überprüfung der gelieferten Übersetzungen erfolgen kann.

Wenn es nur um die Qualität der Übersetzung geht, kann hier ein auch allgemein sinnvolles Zweitkorrektorat (4-Augen-Prinzip) durchgeführt werden.

Zudem könnte man das Dokument noch einmal komplett durch den Übersetzungsserver übersetzen lassen und dann über einen Dokumentenvergleich der beiden Zieltexte überprüfen, wie hoch der Anteil des Textes ist, der unverändert von der maschinellen Übersetzung erstellt worden ist bzw. gleichlautend erstellt worden wäre.

Beide Verfahren bedeuten jedoch auf jeden Fall einen zusätzlichen Aufwand, der auch entsprechend mit kalkuliert werden muss. Gerade in Szenarien, wo das Zweitkorrektorat dem Kostenfaktor geopfert wurde, wird dieser zusätzliche Aufwand schwer durchzusetzen sein.

Auch für die Terminierung der Übersetzungen ist der entstehende Zusatzaufwand zu berücksichtigen. Im ungünstigen Fall kann dies dazu führen, dass der Übersetzer unter einen noch stärkeren Zeitdruck gerät und sich hierdurch die Problematik verschärft oder sogar erst konkret entsteht.

Wenn es allerdings um die Frage der Vertraulichkeit von Dokumenten geht, hilft dieser Ansatz leider überhaupt nicht weiter, denn spätestens wenn der Auftraggeber die maschinelle Übersetzung erzeugt, wird die eigentlich als vertraulich eingestufte Information doch an den Übersetzungsserver übermittelt.

Besser wäre es daher, wenn die Translation-Memory-Systeme integrierte Reports mit dieser Information erzeugen könnten, und die Information über die Verwendung

maschineller Übersetzungen über die komplette Prozesskette zuverlässig erhalten
bleiben würde.

Der Vergleich von Anbietern hinsichtlich der Art der Leistungserbringung und der zu
erwartenden Übersetzungsqualität wird für den durchschnittlichen Auftraggeber, der
selbst kein Experte für Übersetzungen ist, zunehmend schwerer. Praktisch alle
Anbieter führen in ihren Marketingaussagen die gleichen Argumente an und die
Komplexität der Übersetzungsprozesse und der möglichen Leistungen steigt stetig.
Selbst Übersetzungsdienstleister wissen manchmal nicht, ob ein Übersetzer eine
Übersetzung selbst macht oder sie noch unterbeauftragt. Auch der Verweis auf
qualitätsorientierte Standards z.B. im Rahmen einer Registrierung nach DIN EN
15038 bringt keine zusätzliche Entscheidungshilfe, denn die Registrierung bedeutet
lediglich die Überweisung einer geringen Gebühr und muss nicht mehr als ein Lip-
penbekenntnis sein. Allein die Vermutung, dass seine Übersetzungen evtl. nur *billige
Maschinenübersetzungen* sein könnten, wird das Vertrauen in seinen Übersetzer oder
Übersetzungsdienstleister empfindlich stören.

4 Fazit

Der Einsatz der interaktiven maschinellen Übersetzung führt zu relevanten Fragen im
Verhältnis zwischen Übersetzer und Auftraggeber. Es ist für beide Seiten wichtig, hier
zu verbindlichen und möglichst auch nachprüfbaren Vereinbarungen zu gelangen.

Darüber hinaus stellen sich auch weitergehende Anforderungen an die Hersteller der
Translation-Memory-Systeme. Für die Weiterentwicklung dieser neuen weiterführen-
den Funktionen sind auch Aspekte der Sicherheit und Verlässlichkeit sowie der
Qualitätssicherung in der gesamten Prozesskette zu berücksichtigen und entsprechend
in die Software zu integrieren. Die Hersteller haben hier auch so etwas wie Technik-
folgenabschätzung zu betreiben.

An die Betreiber der Übersetzungsserver, die oftmals auch direkt mit den Herstellern
der Translation-Memory-Systeme verbunden sind, stellt sich die Forderung zumindest
über eine Registrierung der Anwender und entsprechende Vertraulichkeitsvereinba-
rungen einen rechtlichen Rahmen für den Einsatz ihrer Dienste zu schaffen.

Insgesamt ist es nicht zu erwarten, dass die Einführung dieser neuen Funktionen
wieder rückgängig gemacht werden wird. Es ist daher die Aufgabe aller Beteiligten,
sich intensiv mit diesem Thema auseinanderzusetzen, um zu praxisnahen und verlässlichen Lösungen zu kommen. Gerade die Übersetzungsbranche lebt zu einem großen
Teil aus dem Vertrauen in die Übersetzer und ihre professionelle Leistungserbringung. Es ist von besonderer Bedeutung, dieses Vertrauen zu erhalten und nach Möglichkeit zu stärken.

Auf der anderen Seite ist es auch eine Anforderung an die Auftraggeber, sich intensi-
ver mit der Auswahl ihrer Übersetzungsdienstleister und der Art der Leistungserbringung ihrer Übersetzer zu beschäftigen. Das Annehmen oder Einfordern von
Dumpingangeboten hat direkte Auswirkungen auf die Qualität und die Art der
Leistungserbringung. Ein Mehr an Transparenz ermöglicht dem Auftraggeber, sich
genauer über die zu erwartende Leistung zu informieren und erhöht damit direkt auch
das Vertrauen in die Übersetzungen. Eine Zertifizierung des Übersetzers oder Über-

setzungsdienstleisters nach DIN EN 15038 ist zumindest ein Einstieg in eine neutrale Überprüfung. Für den qualifizierten Übersetzer eröffnen sich damit zudem bessere Möglichkeiten, sich im Markt mit seinem Angebot zu positionieren.

Der springende Punkt: Nichttextuale Elemente und ihre Behandlung in CAT-Systemen

Dino Azzano

Ludwig-Maximilians-Universität München / ITL AG

dino.azzano@gmail.com

1 Einführung

1.1 Überblick

In diesem Beitrag werden Elemente unter die Lupe genommen, die bei der Übersetzung eines Dokumentes entweder gleich bleiben oder nach bestimmten Regeln angepasst werden. Diese so genannten *nichttextualen Elemente*, für die mehrere Beispiele gegeben werden, stehen im Mittelpunkt einer vergleichenden Analyse unterschiedlicher CAT-Systeme.

Die Schwerpunkte der durchgeführten Tests liegen bei der Erkennung und Unterstützung der nichttextualen Elemente seitens der CAT-Systeme. Auf der Basis der Ergebnisse werden die Auswirkungen der nichttextualen Elemente auf Qualität und Kosten einer Übersetzung besprochen.

1.2 Definition

Bei nichttextualen Elementen handelt es sich um einen Arbeitsbegriff, der eingangs eine Definition benötigt. Nichttextuale Elemente sind Dokumenteinheiten, welche im Laufe der Übersetzung entweder gleich bleiben oder gemäß genauen Konventionen angepasst werden, sodass ihre Übersetzung voraussagbar ist. Diese Konventionen sind in erster Linie sprachspezifisch, können aber auch z.B. firmenspezifisch sein.

Folgende nichttextuale Elemente wurden identifiziert:

- Zahlen
- Datumsangaben
- URLs

- E-Mail-Adressen
- Interpunktionszeichen
- manche Eigennamen
- Grafiken in derselben Zeile wie der Text (Inline-Grafiken)
- Felder
- Tags

1.3 Bedeutung

Nichttextuale Elemente sind für die Übersetzung aus mehreren Gründen bedeutsam. Erstens sind sie in allen Texten häufig zu finden, obwohl Ausgangsformat und Textsorte ihre Verteilung beeinflussen: Technische Anleitungen verfasst mit FrameMaker® oder Produktbroschüren gestaltet mit InDesign® beinhalten in der Regel viele der oben genannten Elemente, z.B. im Gegensatz zu manchen reinen Textdateien.

Neben der Häufigkeit ihres Auftretens beruht die Wichtigkeit der nichttextualen Elemente jedoch noch auf weiteren Überlegungen. Zum Einen tragen sie wesentlich zur Textbedeutung bei (besonders bei Zahlen und Eigennamen). Zum anderen sind sie prozesstechnisch relevant: So können z.b. Änderungen bei den Tags die Konvertierung des Zieltexts in das Originalformat verhindern.

Diese Bedeutung wurde von den Herstellern von CAT-Systemen erkannt und deswegen bieten sie Funktionen an, um im Rahmen der Qualitätssicherung zumindest manche dieser Elemente überprüfen zu können, insbesondere Zahlen und Tags, aber auch Interpunktionszeichen.

2 Tests

2.1 Testrahmen

Im Rahmen einer vergleichenden Analyse wurden verschiedene CAT-Systeme im Hinblick auf ihren Umgang mit nichttextualen Elementen untersucht. Im Mittelpunkt standen drei Hauptfragestellungen:

- Wird das Element erkannt?
- Welche Auswirkungen auf den Ähnlichkeitswert haben Änderungen dieser Elemente?
- Inwieweit werden automatische Anpassungen vorgenommen?

Zu diesem Zweck wurden zahlreiche Beispiele aus einem deutschen Korpus extrahiert, ggf. angepasst und mit folgenden CAT-Systemen bearbeitet: Across (4.00), Déjà Vu (7.5), Heartsome (7.0), MemoQ (3.2), MultiTrans (4.3), SDL Trados (8.2), Transit (3.1) und Wordfast (5.53). Für die Tests wurden gelegentlich die Standardeinstellungen modifiziert, unter anderem in Hinsicht auf die verwendeten Abzüge. Eine Beschreibung dieser Anpassungen würde jedoch den Rahmen dieses Beitrags sprengen.

Zur eindeutigen Identifizierung mancher Sonderzeichen, die in den hier beschriebenen Tests vorkommen, wird ihr hexadezimaler Unicode-Codepoint in Klammern nachgestellt.

Da die durchgeführte Studie zum Redaktionsschluss noch nicht vollständig abgeschlossen war, beschränkt sich dieser Beitrag auf die bis dahin vorliegenden Erkenntnisse. Aus diesem Grund werden Inline-Grafiken, Felder und Tags nicht im Detail behandelt.

2.2 Erkennung nichttextualer Elemente

2.2.1 Zahlen

Zahlen sind nichttextuale Elemente, welche grundsätzlich von allen CAT-Systemen erkannt werden. Da sie wichtige Informationsträger sind, bieten mittlerweile alle CAT-Systeme entsprechende Qualitätssicherungsfunktionen, mit denen sie überprüft werden können. Die Tests haben jedoch Unzulänglichkeiten bei der Erkennung von Zahlen festgestellt.

Manche Zahlen werden nicht als Einheit erkannt, sondern als Abfolgen mehrerer Ziffern. Dies ist insbesondere der Fall, wenn unübliche Zeichen, beispielsweise der Apostroph (0027), als Tausendertrennzeichen oder Dezimaltrennzeichen verwendet werden. Diese ungenaue Erkennung kann zwei Auswirkungen haben: Einige CAT-Systeme bieten automatische Umwandlungen von Trennzeichen und legen dabei die erlaubten Trennzeichen fest; mit abweichenden Trennzeichen kann diese Funktion nicht greifen. Zweitens werden auch automatische Umrechnungen angeboten (z.B. Zentimeter in Zoll). In diesen Fällen ist eine unvollständige Erkennung der Zahl problematisch, da die Umrechnung ein falsches Ergebnis liefert.

Alphanumerische Sequenzen stellen ein grundsätzliches Problem dar. An dieser Stelle sind in den verschiedenen CAT-Systemen zwei Ansätze zu beobachten. Einige CAT-Systeme (wie Across und MemoQ) beschränken sich auf die Erkennung von Ziffern. Andere CAT-Systeme (wie SDL Trados und Wordfast) versuchen hingegen, kontextabhängig die Erkennung auf Buchstaben zu erweitern. Ein typischer Fall ist eine Zahl unmittelbar gefolgt von der Maßeinheit, z.B. „10KB". Manche Sequenzen sind jedoch problematisch, sodass auch die Ziffern nicht erkannt werden, beispielsweise „25ms", „J.41", „3x400V", „ISO9001-2000" und „RJ45". Wordfast kann alphanumerische Sequenzen vollständig erkennen, der Nachteil dabei sind Fehlinterpretationen des Kontexts, insbesondere wenn Bindestrichfügungen vorkommen, zum Beispiel „A4-Seiten".

Wenn Zahlen nicht erkannt werden können, wie dies häufig bei alphanumerischen Sequenzen der Fall ist, können sie auch nicht geprüft werden. Diese Unzulänglichkeit bei der Erkennung von Zahlen hat tief greifende Auswirkungen auf die Qualitätssicherung, die sich damit als lückenhaft erweisen kann.

2.2.2 Datumsangaben

Es gibt zwei Kategorien von Datumsangaben:

- rein numerisch: Tag, Monat und Jahr werden durch Ziffernfolgen ausgedrückt, z.B. 30.06.07, 21.1.2007, 12.2004.

- alphanumerisch: Der Monat (ggf. abgekürzt) wird ausgeschrieben, z.B. 1. Mai 2008, 1. Dez. 2006, 30. April.

Die ersteren weisen bestimmte Formate auf, welche bei Zahlen selten oder gar nicht zu finden sind, z.B. TT.MM.JJJJ oder TT/MM/JJJJ. Heartsome und MemoQ können diese Formate nicht erkennen und erkennen zwei getrennte Ziffernsequenzen, typischerweise TT.MM und JJJJ. Alle anderen getesteten CAT-Systeme erkennen übliche Datumsformate als eine Einheit, weshalb automatische Formatanpassungen (beispielsweise TT.MM.JJJJ > MM.TT.JJJJ) prinzipiell möglich sind.

Alphanumerische Datumsangaben werden nur von SDL Trados erkannt, obwohl abgekürzte Monatsnamen wiederum problematisch sind. Diese Einschränkungen sind dadurch erklärbar, dass solch eine Erkennung linguistisches Wissen voraussetzt, idealerweise für alle vom jeweiligen CAT-System unterstützten Sprachen.

2.2.3 E-Mail-Adressen und URLs

E-Mail-Adressen und URLs werden nicht erkannt, wenn sie als reiner Text in einem Dokument vorhanden sind. Die einzige Ausnahme stellt Wordfast dar, das URLs erkennen kann. Sind E-Mail-Adressen und URLs als Feldfunktionen vorhanden, dann werden sie wie Felder bearbeitet. Selbst in diesem Fall wird ihr Inhalt von einigen CAT-Systemen, z.B. Déjà Vu und Transit, als reiner Text angeboten.

Solche Elemente sollen bei Bedarf bearbeitbar sein. Oft sollen sie aber nur übernommen werden: Durch die Erkennung als platzierbares Element könnte dies effektiver erfolgen. Eine Erkennung könnte außerdem auch zu Qualitätssicherungszwecken verwendet werden: Man möchte z.B. prüfen, ob E-Mail-Adressen und URLs tatsächlich unverändert geblieben sind.

2.2.4 Interpunktionszeichen

Unter Interpunktionszeichen sind nicht nur Satzzeichen, sondern auch Anführungszeichen, horizontale Striche, Leerzeichen, Klammern und weitere Sonderzeichen wie Auslassungspunkte zu verstehen. In dieser Testreihe umfasste jeder Test ein Segmentpaar, dessen Segmente sich durch die Löschung, Ersetzung oder Hinzufügung eines Interpunktionszeichens voneinander unterschieden. Ziel dieser Testreihe war zunächst zu bewerten, ob und wie der Unterschied erkannt wurde.

Keins der getesteten CAT-Systeme zeigt Schwierigkeiten mit den üblichen Satzzeichen, andere Interpunktionszeichen stellen sich hingegen als problematisch heraus. Beispielsweise wird das geschützte Leerzeichen (00A0) von Leerzeichen (0020) nicht unterschieden. Die Auswirkung sind fehlerhafte 100%-Treffer. Diese Art von Fehlerkennungen ist gelegentlich bei Heartsome, MultiTrans und SDL Trados zu beobachten.

2.2.5 Eigennamen

Manche Eigennamen fallen in die Kategorie der nichttextualen Elemente, weil sie unverändert bleiben. Um ihre Erkennung seitens einiger CAT-Systeme zu beschreiben, sollen sie jedoch nicht semantisch betrachtet werden, sondern strukturell. Verschiedene Muster sind in dieser Hinsicht interessant:

- Komplette Großschreibung (Abkürzungen und Akronyme), z.B. DVB-T, IEEE, SDRAM.
- Gemischte Groß- und Kleinschreibung (mixed case), z.B. xDSL, MySQL, JavaScript.
- Alphanumerische Sequenzen, z.B. DDR2, A4.
- Vorkommen von Sonderzeichen, z.B. AAC+, #NICK#, %VERSION%.

Es handelt sich offenkundig um Verallgemeinerungen, welche Ausnahmen erlauben. Dabei werden nicht nur Eigennamen im engeren Sinne berücksichtigt, sondern auch Produktcodes, Variablennamen usw.

Zwei CAT-Systeme versuchen, diese Elemente zu erkennen. SDL Trados kann komplett groß geschriebene Wörter erkennen, wenn sie ausschließlich aus Buchstaben bestehen. Bei Wordfast ist die Erkennung mächtiger, weil sie auch alphanumerische Sequenzen, gemischte Groß- und Kleinschreibung sowie einige Sonderzeichen berücksichtigt. Außerdem kann der Benutzer die Liste der Sonderzeichen anpassen.

2.2.6 Übernahme

Alle CAT-Systeme erkennen Tags und zeigen sie gesondert an. Dabei sind insbesondere Tags berücksichtigt, welche innerhalb eines Segmentes vorkommen können (*interne Tags*), beispielsweise zur Kursivformatierung eines Ausdrucks (<i> und </i> in HTML). Mittels Tastaturkürzel können sie bequem in das Zielsegment übernommen werden.

Manche CAT-Systeme, wie SDL Trados und Wordfast, erkennen einige weitere nichttextuale Elemente als so genannte *platzierbare Elemente* (Placeables), d.h. sie werden ebenfalls als Einheiten behandelt, die in den Zieltext übernommen werden können.

2.3 Auswirkungen von Veränderungen auf den Ähnlichkeitswert

2.3.1 Abzüge bei nichttextualen Elementen

Änderungen, die nichttextuale Elemente betreffen, können spezifische Abzüge erhalten. Es ist im Allgemeinen sinnvoll, textuale Änderungen – bei gleich bleibender Anzahl geänderter Zeichen – mit höheren Abzügen zu versehen als nichttextuale Änderungen, weil textuale Änderungen in der Regel einen höheren Anpassungsaufwand nötig machen. Das ist bei fast allen CAT-Systemen standardmäßig der Fall.

Etliche CAT-Systeme bieten die Möglichkeit, die Abzüge für gewisse nichttextuale Systeme einzustellen, z.b. Across, SDL Trados und Wordfast. Benutzer können auch einstellen, dass gewisse Unterschiede gar keinen Abzug verursachen.

2.3.2 Anzeige des Unterschieds

Selbst bei korrekter Erkennung eines Unterschieds und Anwendung des entsprechenden Abzugs, wird der Unterschied nicht immer angezeigt. Während übliche Satzzeichen von diesem Problem nicht betroffen sind, ist die Anzeige bei Leerzeichen und horizontalen Strichen bei der Mehrzahl der untersuchten CAT-Systeme mangelhaft. Ein Beispiel liefert folgendes Segmentpaar, das sich durch das Leerzeichen zwischen 9 und € unterscheidet: ein geschütztes Leerzeichen (00A0) im ersten Segment, ein schmales Leerzeichen (2009) im zweiten.

1. Die Kosten für eine Installation betragen 289 €

2. Die Kosten für eine Installation betragen 289 €

Nur Heartsome und SDL Trados heben diesen Unterschied hervor. Andere CAT-Systeme wenden zwar einen Abzug an, markieren jedoch den Unterschied nicht. Das erschwert den Benutzern die Suche nach der Abweichung, wegen der nur ein Fuzzy-Treffer angeboten wird. Obwohl die Anzeige nur mit der Benutzerfreundlichkeit der CAT-Systeme zu tun hat, ist diese Erkenntnis in diesem Zusammenhang trotzdem interessant.

2.3.3 Ermittlung von Abzügen

Was die angewendeten Abzüge angeht, sind große Unterschiede zwischen den CAT-Systemen festzustellen. Across, Déjà Vu, MemoQ, MultiTrans wenden einen (ggf. benutzerdefinierten) Abzug unabhängig von der Segmentlänge an, während dieser Abzug bei den restlichen CAT-Systemen auch durch die Segmentlänge beeinflusst wird. Wenn das Segment besonders kurz ist, fällt der Abzug bei den CAT-Systemen, die längenabhängige Abzüge anwenden, besonders hoch aus. Aus diesem Grund führen feste Abzüge für dieselbe Art von Änderungen meistens zu angemesseneren Ähnlichkeitswerten. Folgende Beispiele verdeutlichen diese Erkenntnisse.

1. Nicht verstellen!

2   Nicht verstellen

Alle CAT-Systeme bieten hierfür Treffer oberhalb 90%, bis auf Transit, das nur einen 75%-Treffer anbietet. Das nächste Segmentpaar zeigt, wie die Segmentlänge den Abzug beim vorherigen Beispiel beeinflusst hat.

1. Die zulässigen Betriebsbedingungen gemäß Datenblatt (Spannung, Strom, Lufttemperatur) sind einzuhalten!

2. Die zulässigen Betriebsbedingungen gemäß Datenblatt (Spannung, Strom, Lufttemperatur) sind einzuhalten

Alle CAT-Systeme bieten wieder Treffer oberhalb 90%, wobei Transit einen 95%-Treffer errechnet, obwohl der Unterschied (und der Anpassungsaufwand für den Benutzer) gleich geblieben ist.

Neben der Segmentlänge spielt die Unterstützung von Sonderzeichen ebenfalls eine wichtige Rolle: Während für übliche Satzzeichen nachvollziehbare Ähnlichkeitswerte ermittelt werden, stellen sich andere Interpunktionszeichen als problematisch heraus, insbesondere Leerzeichen und horizontale Striche.

1. –Touchscreen-Farbbildschirm
2. Touchscreen-Farbbildschirm

Grundsätzlich bieten hier fast alle CAT-Systeme Treffer oberhalb 95%. Lediglich Wordfast schlägt für das zweite Segment keinen Treffer vor, obwohl die Mindestgrenze für Fuzzy-Treffer auf das Minimum gesetzt worden war. Weitere Tests lassen gelegentlich eine mangelhafte Unterstützung mancher weniger häufig auftretender Interpunktionszeichen vermuten, wobei dieses Problem ausschließlich diejenigen CAT-Systeme betrifft, welche keinen festen Abzug definieren.

2.3.4 Entwicklung des Abzugs

Die Entwicklung des Abzugs in Abhängigkeit von der Anzahl der Veränderungen ist ein wichtiger Punkt. Bei Across, Déjà Vu, MultiTrans und Transit ist zu beobachten, dass die Anzahl der Veränderungen für den Abzug irrelevant ist, soweit diese Veränderungen dieselben nichttextualen Elemente (horizontale Striche, Leerzeichen oder Anführungszeichen) betreffen. Für folgende Segmente wird z.B. immer derselbe Abzug angewendet.

1. Sind Sie mit Xyz zufrieden?
2. „Sind Sie mit Xyz zufrieden?"
3. „Sind Sie mit ‚Xyz' zufrieden?"

Diese Funktionsweise ist aus Übersetzersicht nicht optimal, weil sie den steigenden Anpassungsaufwand nicht berücksichtigt. Dabei wäre eine lineare Progression angemessener. Bei den restlichen CAT-Systemen sind Höhe des Abzugs und Anzahl der Unterschiede zwar gekoppelt, eine lineare Progression ist jedoch ebenfalls nicht zu beobachten.

2.3.5 Schlussfolgerungen

Zusammenfassend lassen sich bei der Ermittlung des Ähnlichkeitswertes Unzulänglichkeiten feststellen, welche hohe Abzüge auf Grund der Längenabhängigkeit oder der mangelhaften Unterstützung verursachen. Andererseits sind feste Abzüge teilweise ebenfalls nicht optimal, wenn sie die Anzahl der Änderungen nicht berücksichtigen und somit den Anpassungsaufwand außer Acht lassen.

2.4 Automatische Anpassungen

Automatische Anpassungen sind Veränderungen des Zieltextes, welche seitens der CAT-Systeme vorgenommen werden. Sie können in Form von Ersetzungen sowie Löschungen und Hinzufügungen vorkommen. Sie modifizieren den Fuzzy-Treffer, sodass keine oder weniger händische Anpassungen seitens der Benutzer notwendig sind, damit das Zielsegment dem neuen Ausgangstext entspricht. Im Idealfall kann durch diese Anpassungen aus einem Fuzzy-Treffer ein 100%-Treffer erzeugt werden.

Diese Modifizierungen setzen also einen Fuzzy-Treffer im Translation Memory voraus, brauchen aber kein linguistisches Wissen über Ausgangs- oder Zielsprache.

Insbesondere Interpunktionszeichen eignen sich prinzipiell für automatische Anpassungen, vorausgesetzt, dass ihre Position eindeutig ermittelbar ist. Dies ist typischerweise (jedoch nicht ausschließlich) am Anfang und am Ende eines Segments der Fall. Kommata mitten im Segment bleiben zum Beispiel ausgeschlossen.

Die meisten CAT-Systeme stellen solche automatischen Anpassungen überhaupt nicht zur Verfügung. Déjà Vu stellt eine Ausnahme dar: Dieses CAT-System kann in der Regel bei Interpunktionszeichen den Fuzzy-Treffer präzise anpassen. Neben Déjà Vu können manchmal MemoQ und vereinzelt MultiTrans und Wordfast automatische Anpassungen vornehmen. Die von diesen CAT-Systemen angebotene Hilfestellung ist aber im Vergleich zu Déjà Vu sehr eingeschränkt.

Für weitere Elemente, insbesondere für Felder und Tags, wird die Mächtigkeit der automatischen Anpassungen im weiteren Verlauf der Tests geprüft.

3 Schlussfolgerungen

Nichttextuale Elemente können auf verschiedenen Ebenen für die Übersetzungsarbeit relevant sein. Aus diesem Grund können eine korrekte und vollständige Erkennung, eine nachvollziehbare Ermittlung des Ähnlichkeitswertes sowie automatische Anpassungen zu Geschwindigkeit, Wirtschaftlichkeit und Qualität der Übersetzung beitragen. Diese drei Faktoren werden im Folgenden einzeln behandelt.

3.1 Zeitfaktor

Nichttextuale Elemente können die Geschwindigkeit der Übersetzung auf verschiedene Weisen beeinflussen.

In einem typischen Szenario, in dem kein Treffer aus dem Translation Memory kommt, müssen Benutzer die Übersetzung neu eintippen. Für Tags und platzierbare Elemente sind aber Tastaturkürzel vorhanden, welche die Übernahme in das Zielsegment gegenüber einem Copy&Paste-Verfahren wesentlich beschleunigen. Einige CAT-Systeme, z.B. Heartsome, bieten auch ein Tastaturkürzel an, welches die Übernahme aller in einem Ausgangssegment enthaltenen nichttextualen Elemente in das Zielsegment ermöglicht. Alternativ kann zwar auch das komplette Ausgangssegment in das Zielsegment kopiert werden, die Übersetzung muss aber durch Überschreiben angefertigt werden. Diese Arbeitsweise kann unter Umständen und je nach Benutzervorlieben weniger komfortabel sein.

Darüber hinaus nehmen automatische Anpassung (z.B. von Zahlen, Interpunktionszeichen und Tags) den Benutzern Kleinarbeit ab, die besonders fehleranfällig ist (Tippfehler, Flüchtigkeitsfehler). Damit wird nicht nur die Übersetzung beschleunigt, sondern es entsteht weniger Aufwand bei der Qualitätssicherungsschleife. Voraussetzung dafür sind korrekte und vollständige automatische Anpassungen.

3.2 Kostenfaktor

Die Anzahl an 100%-Treffern, Fuzzy-Treffern (unterteilt in verschiedene, ggf. benutzerdefinierte Ähnlichkeitswertintervalle) sowie Nichttreffern in einem Ausgangsdokument kann mittels einer Analyse ermittelt werden. Diese Analyse dient sowohl zur Einschätzung des Arbeitsaufwandes als auch als Basis für die Abrechnung. Wie im Abschnitt 2.3   Auswirkungen von Veränderungen auf den Ähnlichkeitswert beschrieben, hat die Unterstützung der nichttextualen Elemente Auswirkungen auf die Ermittlung des Ähnlichkeitswertes für Fuzzy-Treffer.

Der Abzug für gewisse nichttextuale Elemente kann zum Teil und bei gewissen CAT-Systemen vom Benutzer selbst definiert werden. Es liegt dann in seiner Verantwortung einen angemessenen Wert zu definieren; Abzüge können auch auf 0% heruntergesetzt werden, obwohl dies mehr als fraglich ist, weil der Anpassungsaufwand damit vollständig unberücksichtigt bleibt.

Beispiele aus den Tests zeigen, dass der Abzug bei Unterschieden, welche nichttextuale Elemente betreffen, manchmal wenig nachvollziehbar ist, siehe 2.3.3 Ermittlung von Abzügen und 2.3.4 Entwicklung des Abzugs. Dabei sind sowohl zu hohe als auch zu niedrige Werte möglich.

3.3 Qualitätsfaktor

Nichttextuale Elemente sind für die Qualität eines Textes maßgebend. Aus diesem Grund werden sie von den Qualitätssicherungsfunktionen der CAT-Systeme berücksichtigt.

Ohne Ausnahme bieten alle untersuchten CAT-Systeme eine Zahlenprüfung, auch wenn Zahlen während der Übersetzung nicht als platzierbare Elemente erkannt werden beziehungsweise nur im Nachhinein geprüft werden können. Was Zahlen angeht, schlagen sich die besprochenen Probleme mit der Erkennung (siehe 2.2.1 Zahlen) unmittelbar auf die Qualitätssicherung nieder. Die Zahlenprüfung ist lückenhaft und somit können Fehler auch nach der Prüfung bestehen bleiben. Diese Unzulänglichkeit ist für die Produkthaftung von Bedeutung, weil der Zieltext falsche Angaben liefert.

Tags als wichtige Bestandteile eines Dokuments können von den CAT-Systemen überprüft werden. Einige CAT-Systeme (z.B. Déjà Vu) bieten auch eine Überprüfung in Echtzeit, d.h. schon während der Übersetzung wird das Zielsegment markiert, wenn Tags aus dem Ausgangssegment fehlen oder in einer anderen Reihenfolge stehen (beides ist jedoch nicht notwendigerweise ein Fehler). Ansonsten kann diese Tag-Überprüfung im Anschluss an die Übersetzung durchgeführt werden.

Interpunktionszeichen können ebenfalls im Rahmen der Qualitätssicherung geprüft werden. Automatische Anpassungen für Interpunktionszeichen können zur Beschleunigung der anschließenden Qualitätssicherung beitragen, weil sie Flüchtigkeitsfehlern vorbeugen können.

Die Erkennung von Eigennamen/URLs/E-Mail-Adressen könnte zu Qualitätssicherungszwecken verwendet werden. Es wäre möglich, die Übereinstimmung von URLs und E-Mail-Adressen in Ausgangs- und Zielsegmenten zu prüfen, auch wenn sie im

Dokument als reiner Text vorhanden sind. Bisher ist diese Funktionalität noch in keinem CAT-System implementiert. Sinnvollerweise sollte diese Prüfung optional sein, weil diese nichttextualen Elemente unter Umständen lokalisiert werden müssen. Eine vollständige Erkennung von Eigennamen kann allerdings ohne linguistisches Wissen nicht realisiert werden. Trotzdem wäre eine teilweise Überprüfung nicht uninteressant, insbesondere für Texte, in denen viele solcher Elemente vorkommen.

Bibliographie

Friedl, J. E. F. (2006). Mastering Regular Expressions. Sebastopol: O'Reilly.

Goyvaerts, J. / Levithan, S. (2009). Regular Expressions Cookbook. Sebastopol: O'Reilly.

Korpela, J. K. (2006). Unicode Explained. Sebastopol: O'Reilly.

TM-Systeme: Fluch oder Segen?

Translation memories as technological productivity tools in the localization industry and their effects on translation

Érika Nogueira de Andrade Stupiello

PhD Student – Linguistic Studies Program, São Paulo State University, Brazil

erika@traducao-interpretacao.com.br

Introduction

Localization is an activity strongly connected to the new global economy and which has greatly expanded in the past twenty years. The Internet has not only shortened the distance between countries sharing the benefits of the electronic economy, but also integrated and promoted the active trade of products and services among them. The increase in trade has stimulated the demand for the simultaneous availability of information on a product in all languages of prospective target markets, especially since "the dissemination of information through globalized mass media or over the Web means that potential customers in different parts of the globe are aware of new models as soon as they come out" (Cronin, 2003:14-15).

The demand for translation is thus generated from the moment the information in the original language is made available and business accomplishments rely mostly on meeting this requirement at very limited turnarounds. According to Sprung (2000: 14), "the most effective way to make a product truly international is to make it look and feel like a native product in the target country - not merely to give it a facelift by translating the words of its documentation and user-interface". The stress seems to be on target-oriented translations, capable of being culturally adapted to intended markets, and not just mere duplicates of their original versions.

In this new scenario, the localization industry flourishes as it focuses on combining language and technology to bring onto the market products – ranging from web pages to various types of software program documentations – that would ideally be able to cross cultural and language barriers (ESSELINK, 2000). As the globalized market expands and becomes more mature, product life cycle, time-to-market, and the simultaneous shipment ("simship") of different language versions of a product at the time it is launched have turned into constantly pursued goals.

In order to achieve these objectives, the localization process has been undergoing many changes in the past years. One of them involves starting up translation projects while the product to be localized is still in its development cycle. Managing different languages in parallel with the development of a product requires standardization and control of the translation work, as well as the possibility of making changes and amendments during and after text production into different languages. This is one of the main applications for translation memory systems, which have been widely used in the localization industry for allowing terminology control and translation reuse in product updates or future releases.

The purpose of this paper is to analyze the effects of the use of translation memories in the translator's production with special focus on the localization industry. The proposed analysis is grounded on the work of translation scholars such as Cronin (2003), Pym (2004, 2006), and Bowker (2002, 2006) with a view on the discourse of localization (ESSELINK, 2000) and Folaron (2006). The aim is also to discuss the asymmetrical relations built between the discourse of the localization industry and the practice of translation that, in spite of being downplayed in the localization process, arguably plays a much larger role in the work in language and context recreation.

1 Work division in the localization industry and effects of translation memories in the concept of translation

In the process of localizing a product, large localization service providers often argue that translation constitutes just one of the stages a product has to go through in the much more complex and technological process of culture adaptation. For Folaron (2006:201), a Canadian localization professor and researcher, "conventional translation processes transferring linguistics and cultural content must accommodate technological transfer too, and the translation emerges as just one operational link in the chain of target end content production". According to this idea, in the workflow of a typical localization project, translation is supposed to be one of the least complex steps, since the most challenging aspects of the work would be prepared in advance during the terminology setup stage, when glossaries and multilingual equivalents are compiled.

This simplistic view of the translation work is responsible not only for the minor role assigned to the translator in the localization process, but also for the overestimation of the tools used, such as translation memories, to the disadvantage of the language skills and expertise of the professional. As Pym points out, the advent of localization, which itself carries out various forms of adaptation, could have effaced the age-old association between equivalence and translation, but, on the contrary, it has brought back a 1960s concept of translation, restricting the way the practice is conceived as "the replacing of natural-language strings" (2004: 57).

The achievement of multilingual equivalents would be one of the steps towards delivering translations tailored to their target markets in the shortest turnaround possible. Another would be the industry's demand on translators to standardize their production so as it may be stored and recycled in future projects. In order to meet such requirements and be able to fit in and compete in this largely growing translation market, translators are increasingly more adept at employing translation memories in their work for the localization industry. However, as Biau Gil and Pym (2006:10) indicate, "the possibility of reusing previous translations means that clients ask translators to work with translation memory systems and then reduce the translator's fees. The more exact and fuzzy matches there are (equal and similar segments already translated and included in the database), the less they pay".

Translation memory systems applications have been promoting irreversible changes in the practice of translation with direct impact in the way translation is conceived in the localization industry, mostly with regard to the question of ownership of the translation memory databases and the issue of payment for previously translated segments. As noted by Esselink (2000:364), in the localization industry, clients usually claim ownership over the translation memory database and, in general, pay 60% of the full word rate for fuzzy matches and only 30% for exact matches. Exact matches retrieved from the database are not remunerated, even if editing is required to adapt the match to its new context.

As we may infer, the same tools announced to be designed to aid translators and promote efficiency in their work are bringing back the image of translation as uncreative and inferior work of language manipulation and, as such, should be remunerated accordingly. Most purchasers of language services are unaware of the intellectual work involved in reconstructing meaning in other languages. As reported by Sprung (2000:12), translation has long had an image problem, and even "professional translation does not enjoy praise – it merely avoids criticism". This characterization seems to reverberate through the clear-cut distinction made between "localization" and "translation". The word "localization" has, from the very beginning, been associated with the concept of "locale", in a specific reference to produce work with the target market in view. Translation, on the other hand, has always been referred to as an incomplete work of language , in a very distinct way from the principle of localization in the discourse of this industry. According to Cronin (2003:62), this tendency is not wholly unintentional, and frequently leads to "negative and potentially damaging consequences" for the way translation is featured in the age of globalization. Translation is traditionally seen in its constant but frequently vain effort to approximate the target culture, an image that conflicts with the ideal concept of localization in its process to engage with the local markets, especially by disguising the "unpleasant imperial aftertaste left by agonistic conceptions of translation as conquest" (ROBINSON, 1997, apud CRONIN, 2003).

As a way to help control the possible undesirable effects translation may have on the expectations raised by localization, the practice of translation has forcibly been associated with the use translation memories and other computer-aid-translation (CAT) tools by the localization market, in an effort to normalize the work and ideally efface the translator's unwanted mediation. However, as Cronin aptly criticizes (2003:62) "the more successfully the 'process' itself can be automated, the more the translation problem can retreat to the margins of commercial attention".

Translation memory systems, designed to aid and partially automate the translator's work in localization projects, reflect the concept of translation, held by this industry of localization, as an activity of replacement of words, phrases and sentences preferably by those with equivalent meaning and number of characters in the target culture, in order to avoid supposedly unnecessary or costly changes or graphic layout resizing. The way source texts are presented for translation in the software interface are indicative of this narrow conception of the work with different languages. In the currently used systems, the translator is presented with a segmented source text to work on and, most of the time, is deprived of any contact with the full text design, which is suppressed in the user's interface. The layout of the system is a constant reminder that

> the translator's task is to change the words and nothing else. There is no clear view of what the text formatting looks like; there is no easy view of what the web site design looks like. Translators are not supposed to be interested in such things; they are certainly not supposed to know about the cultural values and effects involved. (PYM, 2004:163).

The way the source text is segmented and presented for translation in the interface of the system compels the translator to work exclusively with the segment at hand, disregarding the larger context it takes part. As past translation options are recovered from the database and showcased, they tend to induce the translator to reuse them to produce a translation that retakes past translations that may have been done by other translators and, as such, expressing less and less the individual choices and writing style of the translator. In addition, the absence of the full source text and the very design of the translation memory system do not encourage the translator to think beyond what is being presented or to research terminology even further.

The very conceptualization of the translation memory systems employed is based on controlling terminology use, while leaving out individual choices that might affect consistency and hinder future reuse of translated segments stored in the system databases. However, concentrated efforts on ensuring productivity gains by storing translated segments for reuse helps conceal the fact that translation memory database is firstly produced by humans and, as such, is just as unlikely to be error-free.

Moreover, since translation memories operate on the basis of string matching and texts are not stored as a whole in the database, when a match is presented to the translator as being an exact correspondence, no certainty is offered that the context is still the same, nor is it possible for the translator to know exactly the origin of the translation stored and thus guarantee its reusability. Thus, unsuitable terminological uses or constructions from previous translations may end up being continuously reproduced should the translation memory database not be constantly and thoroughly reviewed. Even in cases where translation memory databases are periodically reviewed and amended, there is still the possibility that the translator may be ill-informed about terminology changes and end up using translation options recovered from the database that may be deemed outdated over time.

Endorsing the possibility of producing translations for localization based on the recycling of previous translations arguably narrows the work involved in translation in the process of recreating meaning for a new target audience. According to Bowker,

> when it comes to producing a target text, translators must keep in mind that features of organization may be language and culture specific. For instance, language may have different strategies for achieving cohesion, and the overall level of cohesion that is desired may even differ between languages. As part of the

translation process, translators need to adjust the organizational features of the source text to create a target text that meets expectations of the way in which texts are organized in the target language. (BOWKER, 2006:176-177).

It is possible to argue that the way translation memory systems are currently being put to work, by retrieving past translations that may reoccur in texts so as to guarantee consistency, may cause the inverse effect, since they may be a distracting interference to text coherence. When facing only text strings and past translation options, it becomes difficult for the translator to build a network of conceptual and semantic relations in the text being translated.

The tendency to overlook the role of translation in the localization industry may, on the one hand, lead to more sophisticated technological tools to speed up language work while, on the other, separate translators even further from the sense of communicating something to someone. Esselink's (2000) vision of localization projects in the new millennium foreshadow the latter consequence. It may also be used to illustrate the point of how the enforced distinction between localization and translation is being employed to the detriment of the way translation is conceived and practiced in the contemporary world. As the author foresees, in order for the industry to gain competitiveness in the next years, "the number of steps between creation and translation will need to be reduced to a minimum" (2000:478). As Esselink explains, instead of working on source language texts with the help of a bilingual translation memory system maintained by the translator, the translation memory engine will soon be integrated with a multilingual database with both source and translated materials. The texts will then be first analyzed and automatically pre-translated and then sent out to translators, who would basically be in charge of dealing with fuzzy and no matches. In order for this system to be feasible, source texts would be prepared with the use of authoring or controlled source language (basically English) tools, so that language would be as consistent as possible. This systematization will allow the recombination and modification of textual elements in order to create new texts. As we may infer, this prospective localization strategy also aims to internationalize the work of translation and reduce workloads, for "all information is extracted from the database, processed by translation memory so only new text is translated" (ESSELINK, 2000: 479). Thus conceptualized, the translator's work would be restricted to rendering and editing new pieces of information, mostly because the database of a translation memory system made available for the translator will just allow the translator to have access to new segments of texts to be translated or edit fuzzy matches.

Seemingly far-fetched, Esselink's approach is restricted to how technology will be put in use to deal with linguistic contents of different languages and at no time does he refer to the complexity or challenges of the process of translating, which seems to remain in the periphery of the discussion in the field of localization.

As noted by Pym (2004:164), Esselink's vision of "some kind of brave new world, ruled by criteria of efficiency" may be closer than we are capable of conceiving. Changes in the practices of one of the largest translation consumption segments shall deepen the already existing asymmetries disguised in the work of localization, namely in the translation strategies employed to guarantee that large amounts of text materials are made available in various languages and in the shortest term possible.

2 Language asymmetries built through translation strategies for localization projects

The contemporary discourse that minimizes the work of translation in the localization industry, while attributing productivity gains and terminology consistency to the use of translation memory systems, foments the notion of a transparent exchange between languages. As Cronin (2003:62) highlights, "the post-Babelian condition is accepted but only on the condition that it can be engineered to produce a pre-Babelian illusion". The "pre-Babelian illusion" may be identified in the extensive localization projects for worldwide distribution of Microsoft products and applications. As reported by Cronin, language standardization policies put in practice by the company reflect the perception of the former Microsoft chairman Bill Gates, for whom localization is "just a linguistic process" and, by extension, echoes "the conception of translation process as secondary and capable of containment, de-dramatizing Babel through a vision of multilingualism as a minor hiccup in corporate planning" (2003:62).

Thus conceived, localization is planned and executed so as to guarantee high productivity. Overall costs are lower if the source product (usually software produced for the US market) is first prepared for later localization, with simplication of the source language mainly through the removal of specific local contents and separation of points that require translation or adaptation. Although at first sight these strategies may be carried out exclusively for operational purposes, in Pym's opinion, the practice of simplifying the source language specifically for localization enlarges the gap between those on the production side and those on the consumption end, generating

> a second technological divide, no longer between the haves and the have-nots of material machines, but between the active and passive users of language. In effect, the more condescending forms of localization would divide the world into text producers who will always be producers, text consumers who can only remain consumers, and the excluded, who remain unlocalized. (PYM, 2002:5)

The idea of neutralizing source culture particularities in a product in order to "acclimate" it to foreign target cultures constitutes a dissimulated strategy to ascertain the ownership of technology to the dominating culture in charge of producing and distributing technology. Following market interests, product documentation and distribution by those retaining the production power work in a way to keep users with the permanent status of receptors and consumers of the technological products thus produced. In order to illustrate my point, I take the localized versions of Microsoft Windows XP into Brazilian Portuguese. In general, the main commands, menus and dialogue boxes present their localized versions standardized by the company distributing the software and thus maintained when the system is updated. On the other hand, if we need to access more technical information on source codes or the technical language the program has been developed in, we need to resort to the source language English, since the knowledge of this language among technically-minded users seems to be taken for granted by the manufacturer of the program. Users of localized programs like this are conceived as "passive consumers" to whom limited access is granted to the language of technology.

The perspective through which translation is seen as mere language work to be automated and controlled, and as such restricted and characterized as just one of the stages in the much more complex work of localization, also works to conceal the adaptations, inclusions, exclusions and other changes through which a text inevitably goes through during translation. The fast pace imposed by the localization market for products like Microsoft Windows XP is apparent to have as many people in as many countries as possible using the same software, all the while disguising its intention of perpetuating the status of passive consumers of localized and ideally neutral products.

Final considerations

The requirement of adopting translation memory systems in the work for the localization industry is changing the very nature of the work of translation. In order to translate the overall text message, the translator often needs to work outside the artificial boundaries of sentences, so the sentence-by-sentence approach usually imposed by most translation memories seems to go against the need the translator has to refer to the context when reconstructing the meaning in a different language. Although much may be gained by translators using translation memories as productivity tools, particularly in the fast-paced localization industry, their employment does not make the translation process any less complex or the translator's task any simpler or less mediated in dealing with the inherent difference of languages and cultures.

Bibliography

BIAU GIL, José Ramón; PYM, Anthony. (2006). Technology and Translation (a pedagogical overview). In: PYM, A., A., PEREKRESTENKO, A., STARINK, B. *Translation Technology and its Teaching.* Tarragona, Spain. Available at: http://isg.urv.es/publicity/isg/publications/technology_2006/idex.htm. Consulted in June, 2007.

BOWKER, Lynne. (2002). *Computer-aided Translation: a Practical Introduction.* Ottawa, Canada: Ottawa University Press.

BOWKER, Lynne. (2006). "Translation memory and text". In: BOWKER, Lynne (Ed.). Lexicography, Terminology, and Translation: text-based studies in honour of Ingrid Meyer. Ottawa, Canada: Ottawa University Press, p. 175-187.

CRONIN, Michael. (2003). *Translation and Globalization.* London: Routledge.

ESSELINK, Bert. (2000). *A Practical Guide to Localization.* Amsterdam/Philadelphia: John Benjamins.

FOLARON, Debbie. (2006). A discipline coming of age in the digital age. In: DUNNE, K. J. (Ed.). *Perspectives on Localization.* American Translators Association Scholarly Monograph Series XIII. Amsterdam/Philadelphia: John Benjamins, p. 195-219.

PYM, Anthony. (2002) *Localization and the humanization of the technical discourse: Revising the suppositions.* 2002. Available at: www.tinet.org/~apym/online/translation/rimini.pdf. Consulted on: Aug. 10, 2008.

PYM, Anthony. (2004). *The Moving Text: Localization, Translation, and Distribution.* Benjamins Translation Library, v. 49, Amsterdam/Philadelphia: John Benjamins.

SPRUNG, Robert C. (2000). Introduction. In: Sprung, Robert C. (Ed.). *Translating into success: Cutting-edge strategies for going multilingual in a global age.* v. 6, ATA Scholarly Monograph Series, p. 9-22.

Durch den Einsatz eines Translation-Memory-Systems sowie einer Terminologiedatenbank umgehend von weniger Kosten, kürzerem Zeitaufwand und höherer Qualität profitieren? – Von wegen!

Anja Dohrn

B.A Mehrsprachige Kommunikation, M.A. Terminologie und Sprachtechnologie (BDÜ, DTT, tekom)

anja_dohrn@gmx.de

Selina Schmitz

Diplom-Übersetzerin (FH), M.A. Terminologie und Sprachtechnologie (BDÜ, DTT, tekom)

selina.schmitz@t-online.de

1   Am Anfang war das Wort...

...beziehungsweise der Satz, der nur einmal übersetzt werden sollte:

„Übersetzungen leicht gemacht", „Nie mehr redundant übersetzen", „Übersetzen ohne Grenzen", „Höhere Qualität, weniger Vorbereitung", „Weil Ihre Zeit wertvoll ist", „Profitieren Sie von schnellerem Umsatzwachstum, Kosteneinsparungen und geringerem Arbeitsaufwand"...

So oder so ähnlich lauten die Versprechen vieler Hersteller von Translation-Memory-Systemen. Bevor Sie jedoch einen Einblick in die wunschgemäße Erfüllung dieser Versprechen erlangen, folgt zunächst eine kurze Einführung in die unterschiedlichen

Komponenten und Funktionsweisen von Translation-Memory-Systemen, die auch gern TM-Systeme oder einfach TMS genannt werden. Unabhängig davon, ob es sich um das System eines großen, eines kleinen oder eines unabhängigen Herstellers handelt, die meisten TM-Systeme verfügen mittlerweile über folgende Hauptkomponenten:

- Einen Übersetzungsspeicher – das Translation-Memory (TM), in dem die ausgangssprachlichen Sätze zusammen mit ihren zielsprachlichen Entsprechungen gespeichert werden. Der Übersetzer kann dann während der Arbeit zu Referenzzwecken und auch zur Wiederverwendung auf den Inhalt des TMs zugreifen.

- Eine Terminologiekomponente, die für die Pflege, Verwaltung und Bereitstellung terminologischer Daten verwendet wird und je nach Hersteller zusätzliche für die Terminologiearbeit relevante Werkzeuge beinhaltet.

- Einen Editor, in dem die zu übersetzenden Texte unter Verwendung der zuvor genannten Komponenten bearbeitet werden.

- Eine Alignment-Komponente, mit der bereits außerhalb eines TM-Systems übersetztes Textmaterial für den Übersetzungsspeicher zur Wiederverwendung aufbereitet werden kann.

- Eine Projektmanagementkomponente, die dazu dient, komplexe Übersetzungsprojekte zu planen und zu verwalten.

Zu diesen Hauptkomponenten kommen immer mehr neue, unterschiedlichste Funktionen hinzu. Schließlich möchte sich jeder Hersteller von seinen Mitstreitern abgrenzen und möglichst innovative Lösungen anbieten. In diesem Zusammenhang versuchen die Hersteller oftmals auch die Wünsche und Anregungen ihrer Kunden mit in die Software-Entwicklung einzubinden. Diese Neuerungen werden dann, je nach Hersteller, dem Kunden in Form eines Updates, eines Upgrades, eines Patches oder einer neuen Vollversion angeboten. Zu den potenziellen Kunden der Tool-Hersteller zählen mittlerweile nicht mehr nur die Übersetzer bzw. Übersetzungsdienstleister. Auch technische Redakteure und „Direktkunden" (Unternehmen aus Industrie und Wirtschaft, die nicht zwingend in der Übersetzungsbranche tätig sein müssen), haben den Nutzen von TM-Systemen für sich erkannt. In Zeiten der Globalisierung spielt die internationale Präsenz eine immer wichtigere Rolle. Texte werden dem Markt in unterschiedlichen Formen und Formaten bereitgestellt. Ganz gleich, ob Sie bzw. Ihr Unternehmen nun international oder national präsent sind bzw. ist, die Verwendung einer einheitlichen, konsistenten Terminologie sollte für Sie bei der Erstellung Ihrer Texte höchste Priorität haben. Und hier kommen jetzt die TM-Systeme ins Spiel. Ein TM-System kann sehr hilfreich sein, wenn es darum geht, konsistentes Textmaterial zu produzieren. Sie können durchaus von geringeren Kosten, reduziertem Zeitaufwand und höherer Qualität profitieren, wenn Sie sich dazu entscheiden, ein TM-System in Ihren Texterstellungsprozess einzubinden. Allerdings gilt auch hier die Redensart „Ohne Fleiß kein Preis". Natürlich können Sie durch den Einsatz eines TM-Systems

- Produktionsfehler durch einheitliche Terminologie vermeiden,

- höhere Qualität durch konsistente Formulierungen und konsistenten Stil erzielen,

• sich durch die konsistente Verwendung Ihrer „Corporate Language" von anderen Anbietern abgrenzen.

Allerdings ist es wie bei anderen Software-Anwendungen auch: Das System ist nur so gut wie seine Anwender. Dieser Vortrag soll Ihnen Denkanstöße, Tipps und Ratschläge im Zusammenhang mit TM-Systemen liefern, damit Sie eine ungefähre Vorstellung davon bekommen, worauf Sie sich beim Kauf eines CAT-Tools dieser Art einlassen, und Sie nicht die Katze im Sack kaufen.

2 Die Entscheidung ist gefallen

2.1 Planung

Die Entscheidung ist gefallen. Sie haben sich für den Einsatz eines Translation-Memory-Systems, möglicherweise in Verbindung mit einer passenden Terminologieverwaltungslösung, entschieden, um so die Qualität Ihrer Übersetzungen zu steigern. Eine gute Entscheidung! Durch den richtigen Einsatz und die richtige Pflege werden Sie so mit Sicherheit Ihre Übersetzungsqualität verbessern und Ihre Übersetzungskosten senken. Natürlich müssen Sie hierfür aber auch ein bisschen was tun. Der alleinige Kauf und Einsatz eines TM-Systems ist leider nicht ausreichend. Vor dem Kauf eines TM-Systems der verschiedenen Hersteller steht die eigentliche Planung. Es wird eine Vielzahl von Tools angeboten, jedoch gibt es keines, das man als das Beste bezeichnen kann. Man muss entscheiden, welches Tool den persönlichen Anforderungen und Ansprüchen am besten entspricht.

Der erste Schritt ist, dass Sie sich überlegen, was genau Sie sich durch den Einsatz eines TM-Systems versprechen. Sind Sie momentan mit der Qualität Ihrer Texte unzufrieden? Fehlt Ihnen ein einheitlicher Stil? Kursieren in Ihrem Unternehmen viele unterschiedliche Benennungen für ein und dieselbe Sache? Fragen wie diese sollten Sie sich stellen und vielleicht auch eine Liste anfertigen, in der Sie Ihre aktuelle Situation der zukünftigen „Wunschsituation" gegenüberstellen. Dieser Schritt ist sehr wichtig. Bevor Sie wirklich loslegen, sollten Sie Ihre aktuelle Situation analysiert und Ihre Ziele klar definiert haben.

Nachdem Sie sich nun Gedanken über Ihre eigene Situation gemacht haben, sollten Sie sich ein paar Gedanken in Bezug auf Ihre Geschäftspartner machen. Mit welchen Tools arbeiten meine Kunden? Welche Dateiformate werden in meiner Branche eingesetzt? Welche Formate haben die ausgangssprachlichen Texte? Kann ich die Dateien problemlos mit meinen Geschäftspartner austauschen? In diesem Zusammenhang sollten Sie auch überlegen, wer schlussendlich mit dem Tool arbeiten wird. Wird allein der Übersetzer damit arbeiten? Werden zudem Projektmanager und Technische Redakteure das Tool einsetzen wollen?

Sie sehen, schon bevor Sie das eigentliche Tool kaufen, sollten Sie einige grundlegende Dinge klären. Es wird Sie nicht weiterbringen, wenn Sie ein Tool kaufen, mit dem Sie später nicht arbeiten können, da es Ihren Anforderungen nicht entspricht.

Haben Sie all diese Punkte geklärt und sind sich dessen bewusst, was Sie wollen, so können Sie nun unter all den Angeboten der verschiedenen Hersteller auf dem Markt das für Sie persönlich „beste" Tool auswählen. Auch wenn Sie sich bereits intensiv auf den unterschiedlichen Webseiten der Hersteller über deren Tools informiert haben, sollten Sie dennoch ein Beratungsgespräch mit einem Kundenbetreuer des jeweiligen Herstellers vereinbaren. Bestens vorbereitet sind Sie nach dieser Planung jedenfalls.

2.2 Einsatz

Auch wenn nun das Kapitel „Planung" abgeschlossen ist und sich dieses Kapitel mit dem tatsächlichen Einsatz des Tools beschäftigt, so sollte auch dieser Schritt gut durchdacht und geplant sein. Sie haben sich intensiv mit Ihrer Situation und Ihren Ansprüchen an das Tool auseinander gesetzt und sich für einen „Hersteller Ihres Vertrauens" entschieden. Dennoch sollten Sie sich einige weitere Fragen durch den Kopf gehen lassen: Wer wird die Software installieren? Wie viel Support bietet der Hersteller? Fallen zusätzliche Kosten für den Support an? Wer ist innerhalb Ihres Unternehmens für die Datenpflege verantwortlich? Wie sieht es mit Schulungen aus? Müssen nur Ihre „internen" Mitarbeiter geschult werden, oder sogar Ihre Kunden, „externe" Mitarbeiter oder andere Geschäftspartner? Wer trägt die Schulungskosten?

Sie sehen, auch beim Einsatz des TM-Systems bedarf es einiger Planung. Wichtig während der kompletten Einführung eines TM-Systems ist, dass Sie Verantwortliche bestimmen und auch an Krankheits- und Urlaubsvertretungen denken. Nicht nur, damit die entsprechenden Personen die Ihnen zugewiesenen Aufgaben erledigen, sondern auch, damit Sie für alle anderen einen Ansprechpartner für das Tool nennen können. So können Sie sicherstellen, dass sich jederzeit jemand findet, der sich mit dem Tool auskennt, bei eventuell auftretenden Problemen direkt reagieren kann und bei anfallenden Fragen „Rede und Antwort" steht.

2.3 Pflege

Auch wenn die Pflege des Tools bzw. der zugehörigen Datenbanken zeitlich gesehen auf die Planung und den Einsatz des TM-Systems folgt, so ist dieser Schritt nicht weniger wichtig. Denn auch bei der Pflege sollten einige wichtige Dinge beachtet und eingehalten werden. Zunächst ist festzulegen, wer für die Pflege der Tools verantwortlich sein wird. Bei Unternehmen empfiehlt es sich, dass maximal 2-3 Mitarbeiter für die Pflege eingesetzt werden. Zur Pflege eines TM-Systems zählen neben der Datenpflege, zu der wir später kommen, auch administrative Tätigkeiten. So sollten bestimmte Funktionen beispielsweise für freiberufliche Übersetzer oder andere externe Mitarbeiter gesperrt werden. Auf diese Weise stellen Sie sicher, dass die Übersetzer die von Ihnen vorgegebenen Einstellungen nicht ändern können.

Sie sollten für die Pflege Ihrer TM-Systeme feste Zeiten festlegen, ganz gleich, ob Sie als Übersetzungsdienstleister für Ihre Kunden oder als Freiberufler für sich selbst die Datenbanken erstellt haben. Projekte sollten erst dann, wenn sie als „final" angesehen werden können, in das TM-System gecleant werden. So können Sie sicherstellen, dass die Einträge im TM-System fehlerfrei und aktuell sind. Hierzu sollte in jedem Fall mit Attributen gearbeitet werden, damit diese zu einem späteren Zeitpunkt unter Einsatz der entsprechenden Filtereinstellungen die Suche bestimmter Einträge innerhalb des TMs und auch der Terminologiedatenbank erleichtern. Auf diese Weise kann sichergestellt werden, dass sich eventuell eingeschlichene Fehler beispielsweise über die Suche nach der Projektnummer oder des Projektnamens besser ermitteln lassen.

Wenn es um die eigentliche Datenpflege geht, also um die Pflege der Datenbankinhalte, ist es besonders wichtig, dass Duplikate aus den TM-Systemen entfernt werden. Dies gilt insbesondere für Einträge, die inkonsistent übersetzt wurden und somit mehr als eine zielsprachliche Entsprechung im TM gespeichert ist. Im TM sollte im besten Fall nur ein zielsprachiges Äquivalent enthalten sein, es sei denn, dass verschiedene Übersetzungen in verschiedenen Kontexten möglich sind. In diesem Fall sollte ebenfalls unbedingt mit Attributen gearbeitet werden, die Einträge also beispielsweise mit den Einsatzgebieten (Marketing, Technische Dokumentation etc.) attribuiert werden. Ansonsten sollte wirklich nur eine zielsprachliche Entsprechung im TM verbleiben, denn nur so kann sichergestellt werden, dass diese konsistent verwendet wird. Bei der Bereinigung der Inkonsistenzen sollte mit großer Sorgfalt vorgegangen werden, um bestmögliche Ergebnisse zu erzielen. Dies gilt natürlich auch für die Ausgangssprache. Schon bei der ausgangssprachlichen Texterstellung sollte auf eine konsistente Verwendung von Fachtermini und Formulierungen geachtet werden. Denn nur mit konsistenten ausgangssprachlichen Texten kann das TM-System die zuvor gespeicherten Übersetzungseinheiten wiedererkennen, dem Übersetzer die gespeicherte zielsprachliche Entsprechung anbieten und so dabei hilfreich sein, Ihre „Corporate Language" bestmöglich einzusetzen und den Wiedererkennungswert Ihrer Texte zu erhalten.

3   Das Beste zum Schluss

Der Einsatz eines TM-Systems ist mit jeder Menge Arbeit verbunden. Nun fragen Sie sich wahrscheinlich, ob die Anschaffung diese ganze Arbeit wert ist und ob Sie in der Lage sind, diese Aufgaben zu meistern. ABER NATÜRLICH! Lassen Sie sich nicht abschrecken! Vielmehr sollten Sie nun eine bessere Vorstellung von dem tatsächlichen Aufwand beim Einsatz eines Translation-Memory-Systems haben. Beim Verkaufsgespräch mit einem Vertreter des Tool-Herstellers können Sie jetzt vielleicht ein bisschen besser zwischen den Zeilen lesen und wissen, welche Fragen Sie stellen sollten. Da letztendlich jeder Fall ganz individuell ist, kann dieser Beitrag die persönliche Beratung durch einen unabhängigen Fachmann natürlich nicht ersetzen. Aber vielleicht hat er Ihnen ja insofern ein wenig geholfen, dass die Anschaffung Ihres CAT-Tools nicht für die Katz' war.

openTMS – Umstand oder Ausweg?

Thomas Wedde

Steuerungskreis openTMS / Steering Committee openTMS

thomas.wedde@openTMS.de

1 Einleitung

openTMS ist ein Open-Source-basiertes Translation-Memory-System. Handelt es sich dabei um ein weiteres Werkzeug, das der Übersetzer zusätzlich beherrschen muss? Oder bietet das Forum Open Language Tools (FOLT) mit openTMS einen Beitrag zur Industrialisierung, d.h. zur Vereinfachung, Vereinheitlichung und Automatisierung von Übersetzungsprozessen?

2 Grundlegendes Prinzip

Nachfolgend eine kurze Erläuterung der Funktionsweise von TMS – der versierte Anwender möchte bitte seine geneigte Aufmerksamkeit Punkt 3 zuwenden.

Translation-Memory-Systeme (TMS) speichern die Übersetzungen von in der Regel menschlichen Übersetzern und bieten dem Übersetzer bereits vorhandene Übersetzungen zur Wiederverwendung an. Hierbei können nicht nur identische, sondern auch ähnliche Ausgangstextsegmente erkannt werden. TMS dienen vor allem zur Sicherung der terminologischen, inhaltlichen, stilistischen und formalen Konsistenz von Übersetzungen. Ein weiterer Aspekt ist die Arbeitserleichterung und –beschleunigung und die damit verbundene Kostenreduzierung.

Besonders sinnvoll ist der Einsatz von TMS zur Übersetzung von Texten, in denen immer wiederkehrende identische oder ähnliche Formulierungen vorkommen, wie Bedienungsanleitungen, Rechenschaftsberichte, Bilanzen, Werbetexte und Kataloge. Grundsätzlich gilt: Je höher der Wiederholungsanteil im Textkörper ist, desto eher greift das Prinzip der TMS. Die Verwendung von Textbausteinen im redaktionellen Prozess bringt die Mächtigkeit von TMS besonders zur Geltung.

Diese Methodik ist um ein Vielfaches schneller als das herkömmliche Übersetzen. TMS reproduzieren zielsprachliche Inhalte und können, entsprechende Schnittstellen und Prozessdefinitionen vorausgesetzt, die redaktionelle Erstellung des ausgangssprachlichen Textes unterstützen. Diese Variante nennt sich Authoring Memory System (AMS).

3 Der Markt heute

TMS werden zur kommerziellen Verwendung seit über 20 Jahren entwickelt. Der Verbreitungsgrad ist hoch (> 70%). Der Markt wird von sehr wenigen kommerziellen Anbietern beherrscht. Seit der Übernahme von TRADOS durch SDL drängen eine Reihe neuer Hersteller in den Markt.

Die kommerziellen Translation-Memory-Systeme sind nicht oder nur sehr eingeschränkt kompatibel zueinander und ermöglichen keinen unproblematischen Datenaustausch. Dies hat insgesamt zu einem uneinheitlichen Zustand im Übersetzungsprozess mit TMS geführt. Übersetzer müssen sich entweder auf ein TMS spezialisieren oder eine Reihe unterschiedlicher Systeme beherrschen.

Da viele Auftraggeber nur eines der kommerziellen Systeme einsetzen bzw. eingesetzt wissen wollen, erfolgt die Auswahl von Fachübersetzern nach ihrer Qualifikation auf ein bestimmtes TMS. Die Übersetzer sind deshalb zunehmend gezwungen, ihre Kernkompetenzen mit zusätzlichen Aufgaben zu belasten. Programmhandhabung, Schulung und Release-Wechsel der kommerziellen Programme fordern immer höheren Zeitaufwand und Kosten, für die es keinen finanziellen Ausgleich gibt. Hinzu kommt, dass Anschaffungs- und Folgekosten für die gängigen kommerziellen Systeme unverhältnismäßig hoch sind. Der Wechsel von einem System zu einem anderen wird durch Inkompatibilität der Systeme erschwert. Der Aufwand für Konvertierungen bei einem Systemwechsel ist hoch.

4   Warum Open Source?

Ein Open-Source-Translation-Memory-System soll die Übersetzungsprozesse künftig vereinheitlichen und die bestehenden offenen Standards konsequent umsetzen.

Open Source heißt, die Software liegt neben der binären, vom Rechner ausführbaren Form zusätzlich immer in einer für den Menschen lesbaren und verständlichen Form vor: In der Regel handelt es sich bei dieser Form um die Quelltexte in einer höheren Programmiersprache. Diese Quelltexte werden frei zugänglich veröffentlicht.

Die Software darf beliebig kopiert, verbreitet und genutzt werden: Für Open-Source-Software gibt es bezüglich der Anzahl der Benutzer der Installationen keine Nutzungsbeschränkungen. Mit der Vervielfältigung und der Verbreitung von Open-Source-Software sind auch keine Zahlungsverpflichtungen an einen Lizenzgeber verbunden.

Die Software darf verändert und in der veränderten Form weitergegeben werden: Durch den offengelegten Quelltext ist Verändern theoretisch für jeden möglich. Open-Source-Software ist auf die aktive Beteiligung der Anwender an der Entwicklung geradezu angewiesen. So bietet sich Open-Source-Software zum Lernen, Mitmachen und Verbessern an. Ein Grund, warum die Hochschulen openTMS tatkräftig unterstützen.

Für Open-Source-Produkte gibt es unterschiedliche Lizenzen. openTMS unterliegt der Eclipse Public License (EPL), die neben der freien Verwendung ebenfalls die Integration veränderter Versionen in andere kommerzielle Produkte zulässt, beispielsweise im Rahmen einer Systemintegration mit Redaktionssystemen oder einer kundenspezifischen Anpassung. Letztlich erlaubt die EPL das zeitlich und räumlich nicht limitierte und nicht widerrufbare Nutzungsrecht und steht damit im krassen Gegensatz zu den üblichen Lizenzbedingungen kommerzieller Software-Hersteller.

5   FOLT und openTMS

openTMS ist das spannende Beispiel für die besondere Form der konsortialen Software-Entwicklung: Wettbewerber arbeiten mit einem bestimmten Ziel für eine unbestimmte Zeit zusammen. Im Forum Open Language Tools (FOLT) haben sich Sprachendienstleister, Redakteure, Übersetzer, Industrieunternehmen mit großen Übersetzungsvolumen, Hochschulen und die Bundesbehörden, vertreten durch das Bundessprachenamt, zusammengefunden, um an der Entwicklung von openTMS mitzuwirken. Sie alle bringen sich auf unterschiedliche Art und Weise ein: mit Wissen und Technologie, durch die Definition von Anwendungsfällen, mit Ideen für die Architektur und die Gestaltung der Oberfläche, mit wissenschaftlichen Abschlussarbeiten über das Datenbankmodell, durch intensives Testen und natürlich mit Entwicklungsarbeit und notwendigen Geldern.

FOLT ist 2005 als Arbeitskreis für den deutschsprachigen Raum gegründet worden und hat sich von Beginn an darauf konzentriert, die Diskussion über Standardisierung der Übersetzungsprozesse und Austauschformate zwischen den TMS, beispielsweise mittels XLIFF, anzuregen und weiterzubringen. Der Steuerungskreis von openTMS setzt sich aus den Teilnehmern von FOLT zusammen.

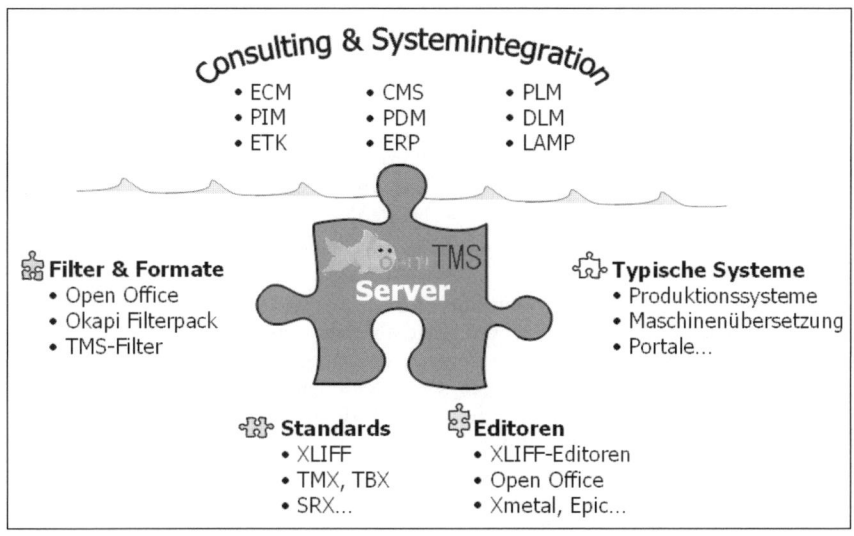

6 Übersetzungsdienstleister und openTMS

Der Einsatz von TMS bei vielen Sprachendienstleistern ist ein Abbild der Marktsituation. Ein großer Teil der Kunden erwartet den Einsatz von TRADOS, wenn überhaupt. Was das bedeutet? Viele Kunden machen keine echten Vorgaben, sondern wählen den bekanntesten TMS-Hersteller. Solange sie von den grundlegenden Prinzipien der TMS-Technologie profitieren, wie schnellerer Durchlauf, bessere Qualität und Einsparungen, scheint die tatsächlich eingesetzte Technologie nachrangig zu sein.

Sicherlich sind einige Kunden auf bestimmte Systeme festgelegt, wenn sie bei ihnen hausintern im Einsatz sind, zum Beispiel in einem eigenen Sprachendienst. Im Vergleich zu einer herkömmlichen Übersetzung, die extern geleistet wird, entstehen diesen Kunden Zusatzkosten für Lizenzen, Support, Pflege, Ausbildung, Vorhalten von zusätzlicher Hardware und Software. Dazu kommen die Kosten für zusätzliche Kenntnisse im hauseigenen HelpDesk, für die Pflege der Translation Memories, Datenauf- und Nachbereitung für den eigenen Sprachendienst oder externe Übersetzer. Selbst die Beschränkung auf nur ein TMS verursacht unnötige Zusatzkosten, sofern die Versionen der eingesetzten Werkzeuge bei den Beteiligten des Übersetzungsprozesses nicht einheitlich sind. Kann ein Hersteller selbst zwischen einzelnen Builds innerhalb einer Version seiner Software keine Kompatibilität gewährleisten, entstehen unüberschaubare Friktionen, die den gesamten Prozess stoppen können.

Ein freier, uneingeschränkter Austausch zwischen den proprietären TMS funktioniert noch weniger als der zwischen den Versionen einer Software. Dabei ist eine kalkulatorische Schwelle als kritisch anzusehen: Die zugehörigen Gemeinkosten werden nur in Ausnahmen vollständig erfasst, bleiben in verschiedenen Kostenstellen unterschiedlicher Abteilungen, sogar unterschiedlicher Geschäftsbereiche verborgen.

Setzt ein Kunde anstelle eigener Werkzeuge auf das breite Leistungsspektrum eines Sprachendienstleisters, verschieben sich die Kosten lediglich. Erwartet der Kunde den Einsatz bestimmter Werkzeuge, die er ebenfalls verwendet, steht der Dienstleister vor dem Dilemma, für viele Kunden unterschiedliche Werkzeuge vorzuhalten, diese zu pflegen und geeignete Prozesse - hier sind Transformationen gemeint - zu definieren. Diese Barriere ist wesentlich dafür verantwortlich, dass Übersetzer zunehmend nach dem eingesetzten TMS bzw. der richtigen Version, und nicht nach ihrem Fachgebiet, ihrer Qualifikation und Erfahrung ausgewählt werden.

Um dieses Phänomen einzuschränken, ist es aus Sicht eines Sprachendienstleisters notwendig, ständig zwischen den TMS und ihren Versionen hin- und her zu konvertieren. Diese Transformationskosten sind unnötig. Die Lösung liegt auf der Hand: Konsequente Einhaltung der Austauschformate seitens der Hersteller der TMS oder Vereinheitlichung der eigenen Übersetzungsprozesse durch ein Werkzeug, das in Gänze auf längst von internationalen Organisationen wie der ISO oder OASIS definierte Standards setzt und eine vollständig offene Architektur besitzt, um es in unterschiedliche Systeme und Prozesse zu integrieren. openTMS ist zur Zeit das einzige TMS-Projekt, das diesen Ansatz verfolgt.

Der Kern des Werkzeuges, die Translation Memory Engine, befindet sich seit April 2009 im Beta-Stadium und wird von einer Reihe von Unternehmen intensiv getestet. Der Source Code ist unter http://open-tms.sourceforge.net/ veröffentlicht. Die Version 1.0 ist zur tekom 2009 angekündigt.

7 openTMS und die Vision

Zurzeit setzen sich viele Experten unserer Branche mit großem Engagement dafür ein, mit Hilfe von openTMS den zuvor beschriebenen, überfälligen Ansatz zu verwirklichen: Der Kunde gibt, wenn überhaupt, lediglich das TMS vor, in dem er die Translation Memories lesen möchte. Der Sprachendienstleister zieht die Daten durch einen Transformationsfilter, hinter dem eine einheitliche Prozesskette mit einheitlichen Werkzeugen steht, die von allen Übersetzern verwendet werden.

Die Voraussetzungen dafür werden zurzeit entwickelt: openTMS umfasst einen XLIFF-Übersetzungseditor und ein einheitliches Datenbank-Modell mit einer leistungsstarken Translation Memory Engine, die in einer virtuellen Server-Umgebung betrieben werden kann. Online- wie Offline-Szenarien sind je nach Anforderung selbstverständlich. Der eigenständige Data Source Editor erlaubt eine optimale Aufbereitung von mono- und multilingualen Objekten aus unterschiedlichen Datenquellen für die eigentliche Übersetzung. Zurzeit entsteht ein plattformunabhängiger Webclient, der im Browser läuft.

Der naheliegende Schritt zu einem reinen Open-Source-basierten Übersetzer-arbeitsplatz ist klein...

Ein Teil der Definitionen von TMS und Open Source sind WIKIPEDIA entnommen. Weitere Informationen unter www.opentms.de bzw. den Source Code unter http://open-tms.sourceforge.net/.

Virtuelles Arbeiten – die praktischen und die sozialen Komponenten in der Zusammenarbeit

Ilona Wallberg

Siemens AG – IT Solutions and Services – Language Services
Generalsekretärin des Transforum

ilona.wallberg@siemens.com

1   Einleitung

"We are shaping the world faster than we can change ourselves, and we are applying to the present the habits of the past. " (Winston Churchill)

Als ich 1988 beim damaligen Nixdorf Sprachendienst anfing, legte mir mein Chef die zu bearbeitenden Texte auf den Schreibtisch, ich diktierte die Übersetzung, eine Gruppe von Phonotypistinnen schrieb sie, ich fügte Korrekturen ein und legte das Papier meinem Chef oder einem anderen Kollege zur Begutachtung vor, denn ich musste ja noch viel lernen, sowohl hinsichtlich des Übersetzens als auch hinsichtlich der fachlichen Inhalte. Die Sekretärinnen arbeiteten die Änderungen ein, ich machte die Endkontrolle und dann ging die Übersetzung, meistens sowohl in ausgedruckter Form als auch auf Floppydisk, zum Kunden zurück.

Bis auf den Kunden befanden sich alle Akteure in Sicht- und Rufweite, denn Heinz Nixdorf war ein Vorreiter in der Großraumbüro-Architektur.

Damals gab es also keine virtuelle Zusammenarbeit? Doch, aber natürlich in anderer Form als heute.

Denn der Kunde saß in einem anderen Stockwerk, einer anderen Stadt, einem anderen Land und konnte inhaltliche Fragen oder missverständliche Originaltexte nur per Telefon oder Fax klären. Aber auch damals war es für die Qualität der Lieferung wichtig, dass man ihn zur Klärung an die Strippe bekam, dass das Zeitmanagement, das damals natürlich auch noch nicht so hieß, im Büro klappte und dass das Miteinander der Kollegen vor Ort harmonisch funktionierte.

Heutzutage schickt der Kunde die Anfrage per E-Mail, eine Übersetzung in fünf Sprachen. Wenn man der Projektleiter oder direkte Auftragnehmer ist, spricht man mit (mindestens) fünf Kollegen, ob sie den Auftrag übernehmen können – stimmt die muttersprachliche und fachsprachliche Kompetenz, stehen die geforderten Tools zur Verfügung, passt der zeitliche Rahmen, reicht die Zeit auch noch für die geforderte 4-Augen-Prüfung. Man sammelt die qualitätsgesicherten Übersetzungen ein und schickt sie an den Kunden.

Gesehen hat man auch bei diesem heute üblichen Prozessablauf die direkt Beteiligten meistens nicht, miteinander telefoniert schon öfter.

In fast allen Stellenanzeigen, gleichgültig für welche Branche, wird „Teamfähigkeit" vorausgesetzt. Selbst wenn man jahrelang Mannschaftssport betrieben hat oder

Mitglied einer Band war, hat man das Motto der Musketiere wohl verinnerlicht, aber wie lässt es sich auf die Berufswelt übertragen und vor allem auf eine Berufswelt, in der der Kontakt häufig genug nur mit elektronischen Werkzeugen zu bewerkstelligen ist.

2 Definition und Zielsetzung

Virtuelle Teams

- sind Mitarbeiter an verschiedenen Standorten, Mitarbeiter verschiedener Gewerke und/oder Mitarbeiter verschiedener Projektabschnitte
- verstehen sich im Sinne einer gemeinsamen Identität und eines gemeinsamen Zieles
- müssen, um das gemeinsame Ziel zu erreichen, die verschiedenen Fähigkeiten und Kompetenzen der Mitglieder (aner)kennen und nutzen, damit die Aufgaben in kollektiver Verantwortung über die unterschiedlichsten Grenzen hinweg erfüllt werden können
- nutzen technische Hilfsmittel als Basis für die Zusammenarbeit
- arbeiten zeitlich begrenzt miteinander, sind geografisch verstreut und kommunizieren überwiegend telefonisch und elektronisch.

Damit unterscheiden sie sich zumindest durch die geografische Distanz und meistens auch zeitliche Begrenzung von Teams herkömmlicher Provenienz.

Machen wir uns doch zunächst einmal klar, was das Ziel des verteilten Arbeitens ist.

Es bietet Kunden und Mitarbeitern am Projekt die Möglichkeit, Wissen und Fähigkeiten des einzelnen Teammitglieds zu nutzen, auch über räumliche Grenzen hinweg, individuelle Leistungen zu bündeln und so eine qualitativ hochwertige Übersetzung zu erhalten.

Manchmal ist eine virtuelle Zusammenarbeit einfach notwendig, um einen Termin in den Griff zu kriegen, auch wenn dabei immer Qualitätsabstriche in Kauf genommen werden müssen, weil die Übersetzung zwar nur in eine Sprache erfolgt, aber die Textmenge so groß und der Zeitrahmen so eng ist, dass sie auf mehrere Kollegen aufgeteilt werden muss.

Durch die EN 15038 hat die Zahl der Kolleginnen und Kollegen, die ansonsten als Einzelkämpfer ein Zweierteam mit dem Kunden darstellen, sicherlich zugenommen. Das geforderte Vier-Augen-Prinzip vergrößert das Team sofort um 50%.

Manchmal ist es aber auch die Komplexität eines Auftrags, erhöhte Anforderung an DTP-Kenntnisse oder der plötzliche Wunsch des Kunden „Kennen Sie nicht einen Kollegen, der uns die Broschüre auch noch ins Französische übersetzen kann? Bitte organisieren Sie das doch, Sie würden uns sehr helfen", der die Zahl der Mitspieler in die Höhe schnellen lässt.

3 Erhöhte Anforderungen

Virtuelle Zusammenarbeit setzt bei allen Teammitgliedern Eigenverantwortung, Selbstorganisation und Eigeninitiative voraus.

Teamleiter müssen darüber hinaus eine direktere Führung mit unmittelbareren Handlungsanweisungen ausüben, als es beim Managen von natürlich gewachsenen Arbeitsgruppen notwendig ist. Deshalb müssen sie die Kompetenzen und Einstellungen der einzelnen Mitglieder sehr genau im aktuellen Anforderungskontext einordnen können.

Die Art der Kommunikation, der Umgang mit Konflikten und der Einsatz virtueller Kommunikationsmedien beeinflussen die Effektivität enorm.

4 Projektvorbereitung / Teamzusammenstellung

Wer sich ein eigenes Team zusammenstellen kann, muss natürlich in erster Linie auf die fachlichen Qualifikationen der Teammitglieder achten. Aber auch über die „sozialen Kompetenzen" des Teams sollte nachgedacht werden; soweit man das im Einzelfall beurteilen kann.

Einen guten Eindruck bietet sicherlich das erste Gespräch.

Folgende Fragen und Themen können Anhaltspunkte bieten:

- Akzeptieren mich alle als Teamleiter? Die Seniorität oder der Mangel daran kann ein entscheidender Aspekt für den Erfolg der Zusammenarbeit sein.

- Herrscht unter den möglichen Teammitgliedern ein Klima des Vertrauens oder gibt es aus der Vergangenheit noch offene Konflikte?

- Können alle mit Kritik umgehen (die immer sachbezogen geäußert werden sollte)?

- Können alle kurz und prägnant diskutieren und formulieren, damit Informationen umfassend ausgetauscht werden können, ohne dass ein zeitraubender Debattierclub entsteht?

- Nationalität und ethnische Abstammung haben einen direkten Einfluss auf das Kommunikations- und Diskussionsverhalten, auf zwischenmenschliche Beziehungen oder auch auf die individuelle Einstellung zur Zeit. Unsere Wertvorstellungen, Verhaltensweisen, Erwartungen und Einstellungen werden durch unsere Nationalität, unsere ethnische Abstammung und unsere Sozialisation bestimmt; aber auch unser Alter und unsere Stellung in einem Unternehmen oder einer Gruppe beeinflussen unsere kulturelle Identität.

Wenn man in einem Projekt ein bereits bestehendes Team leiten soll, erklärt sich vielleicht durch den einen oder anderen Aspekt, warum es bislang so gut läuft oder dauernd hakt. Bei Bedarf müssen die Probleme angesprochen werden (je nach Situation im Einzelgespräch oder in der Gruppe).

5 Vorbereitung der ersten (Telefon-) Konferenz

Das erste Zusammentreffen aller Teammitglieder findet idealerweise face-to-face statt; wenn das nicht möglich ist, müssen alle Unterlagen den Teilnehmern mindestens einen Tag vor der ersten Telefonkonferenz geschickt werden, damit sie sich vorbereiten können.

Der Teamleiter sollte eine Liste erstellen, in der folgende Daten enthalten sind:

- Namen der Teammitglieder und deren Funktionen im Team
- Telefonnummern
- E-Mail-Adressen
- Muttersprachen / Nationalitäten
- Zeiten der Erreichbarkeit, besonders bei unterschiedlichen Zeitzonen oder wenn Teammitglieder in Teilzeit arbeiten
- nach Möglichkeit Fotos, Hobbys, Persönliches (vorher beim Teammitglied erfragen und nicht im eigenen Schatzkästlein kramen)

Kleine Erinnerungskarten, auf denen die wichtigen Stichpunkte einzeln aufgeschrieben werden, erweisen sich häufig als hilfreich. Das sind zum Beispiel:

- Nachfragen: ob der besprochene Punkt von allen verstanden wurde; ein Nicken oder Kopfschütteln sieht keiner der Beteiligten.
- Zeit: eine angeregte Diskussion sollte nicht unterbrochen werden, aber der Teamleiters sollte die Aufmerksamkeit aber zurück zum Thema lenken, wenn sich die Argumente wiederholen; Folgebesprechungen sollten zeitlich klar durch eine Agenda strukturiert werden.
- Und natürlich die projektspezifischen Details.

6 Die erste Konferenz

In der ersten Konferenz sollten alle Teammitglieder ausreichend Zeit haben, sich einander vorzustellen.

Bei allen zeitlichen Einschränkungen sollte immer, auch bei den späteren Projektbesprechungen, Zeit für ein freundliches Wort, ein bisschen Smalltalk nach dem Wochenende sein, denn auch Emotionen bestimmen das reibungslose Zusammenspiel.

Bei der ersten Konferenz sollte das gemeinsame Ziel besprochen und geklärt werden, ob jeder seine eigene Rolle und die der anderen versteht und akzeptiert. Daraus ergeben sich Verantwortlichkeiten für einzelne Prozessabschnitte und Termine, die eindeutig vereinbart und dokumentiert werden sollten.

Insbesondere die Rolle des Teamleiters sollte klar definiert werden:

- einzige (!) Kontaktstelle zum Kunden
- Verteilung der Aufgaben

- Einberufung und Dokumentation der Besprechungen und Ergebnisse (kann delegiert werden, wenn die Gruppe so groß ist, dass der Teamleiter die Besprechungen moderieren muss (ab fünf Teilnehmer))
- Verabredungen einfordern

Bei der ersten Konferenz sollte auch die Häufigkeit und die Art und Weise der Folgebesprechungen und der sonstige Austausch von Informationen vereinbart werden.

Es sollte auch Verabredungen darüber geben, wie schnell auf Nachrichten geantwortet wird. Zeiten für die telefonische Erreichbarkeit sollten festgelegt werden, damit zu den anderen Zeiten die Konzentration auf das Projekt gelenkt werden kann.

Telefonkonferenzen mit mehr als fünf Teilnehmern sind sehr anstrengend, vor allem, wenn man die anderen nicht oder nicht sehr gut kennt. Es fällt dann noch schwerer, die Stimmen den Personen (ihren Rollen) zuzuordnen. Der Teamleiter muss auch hier die Moderatorenrolle übernehmen und die Kollegen mit Namen ansprechen und diejenigen, die sich nicht beteiligen zum Reden auffordern. Die Teammitglieder können zur Klarheit beitragen, indem sie ihren Redebeitrag einleiten „Hier ist Gundi, ich bin für die Überprüfung im Schwedischen zuständig, meine Meinung zu dem Thema ist…".

7 Die regelmäßigen Besprechungen

Je nach Dauer der Projektarbeit sollte mindestens einmal wöchentlich ein Gedankenaustausch stattfinden (jour fixe).

Der Termin und die Form sollte einvernehmlich und verbindlich festgelegt werden. Der Inhalt der Besprechung muss dokumentiert (Protokoll) und an alle Beteiligten zeitnah verteilt werden.

Manchmal kann ein Teammitglied überraschend nicht an einer Besprechung teilnehmen, am besten legt man vorher fest, wie eine solche Situation zu handhaben ist:

- bei kleineren Gruppen (bis vier Personen) sollte das absagende Teammitglied mit der Absage dem Teamleiter mindestens zwei neue Terminvorschläge machen
- bei größeren Gruppen (ab fünf Personen) sollte die Besprechung durchgeführt werden und ein Teammitglied bespricht die Ergebnisse mit der fehlenden Person
- Terminabstimmungen und sonstige Umfragen kann man übrigens hervorragend online mit www.doodle.ch realisieren.

Gemeinsam sollte ein Styleguide für Fragen und Antworten verabschiedet werden. Dieses Dokument bildet zusammen mit den Besprechungsprotokollen das Rückgrat des Projekts. Hier werden alle Fragen und Antworten eingetragen (z. B. „Abschnitt xyz ist sehr landesspezifisch, soll der überhaupt übersetzt werden?" oder „Für den Begriff abc finde ich in der Kundenterminologie keinen Eintrag, in der Fachliteratur werden 123 und 678 parallel verwendet; was will der Kunde?". Dieses wachsende Dokument kann z.B. eine EXCEL-Liste sein, die Spalten haben sollte für:

- Datum der Frage
- Kategorie (Terminologie, Verständnisfrage, technisches Problem)
- Name des Fragestellers
- Name des gewünschten Beantworters
- Frage
- Textstelle (Zitat oder genaue Seiten-/Abschnittsangabe)
- Datum der Antwort
- Name des Beantworters
- Antwort bzw. Weiterleitung an anderen Beantworter (dann sollte die Frage vielleicht in der nächsten Zeile wiederholt werden

Der Teamleiter vergibt farbige Markierungen (ist die Frage beantwortet worden, für welchen Personenkreis ist die Antwort wichtig etc.) und verteilt die Datei regelmäßig. Auch für die Aktualisierung sollten verbindliche Zeiten vereinbart werden, wenn der Zugriff nicht online möglich ist.

Es hat sich gezeigt, dass Fragen und Antworten für alle Beteiligten hilfreich sein können. Vielleicht ist man ja noch gar nicht zu der Textstelle vorgerückt oder man kennt eine Lösung aus einem früheren Projekt.

Dass man während einer Besprechung nicht Kaffee kocht oder E-Mails beantwortet – auch wenn es keine Zeugen per Webcam gibt – versteht sich von selbst. Die Konzentration aller ist bei virtuellen Teams in noch größerem Maße gefordert als bei Vor-Ort-Teams.

8 Stolpersteine

In jedem Projekt kann es zu Problemen kommen – die Technik versagt, jemand wird krank oder die Chemie im Team stimmt aus den unterschiedlichsten Gründen nicht.

Jedes Teammitglied sollte sich nicht nur für sein Teilprojekt, sondern auch für das große Ganze verantwortlich fühlen, deshalb muss ist es natürlich seine vorderste Aufgabe, absehbare Verzögerungen und eingetretene Problem umgehend an den Teamleiter zu melden, der, je nach Lage des Problems, evtl. auch mit dem Kunden und den anderen Teammitgliedern eine Lösung suchen muss.

Dem Teamleiter fällt auch bei der Beziehungspflege eine besondere Rolle zu. Er muss seine Sensoren dafür schärfen, Anzeichen für persönliche Konflikte frühzeitig zu erkennen.

Diese Konflikte sollten im Einzelgespräch geklärt werden, das von beiden Seiten sachlich geführt werden muss, auch wenn durch z. B. durch Termindruck die Nerven blank liegen.

Der Ton dieser Gespräche muss unbedingt von beiden Seiten sachlich gehalten werden und jeder sollte darauf achten, dass der andere sein Gesicht wahren kann.

Die Problemlösung sollte gemeinsam vereinbart, zeitlich festgelegt und dokumentiert werden.

Bei Verstoß gegen die Vereinbarung sollte der Teamleiter bei der nächsten Team-konferenz auf die Vereinbarung hinweisen und die Einhaltung sozusagen öffentlich einfordern.

Und jeder sollte sich immer wieder in Erinnerung rufen, dass entscheidende Elemente der Kommunikation bei virtuellen Teams fehlen.

Auch wenn die Webcam noch so gute Bilder liefert, bei 5 Teilnehmern hat man Wackelbilder in Briefmarkengröße. Die Chance, dass Mimik und Gestik richtig erkannt werden, setzt voraus, dass man sich gut kennt, aber selbst dann dürfte es schwierig sein.

Und das Gespräch im Pausenraum fehlt. Auch wenn ich spontan zu Telefonhörer greife, ich weiß nicht, ob mein Gegenüber gerade aufnahmefähig ist für Smalltalk oder auch das eine oder andere nicht so drängende Problem.

Das 1981 von Friedemann Schulz von Thun entwickelte Kommunikationsmodell verweist auf die vier Ebenen eines Gesprächs (Vier-Ohren-Gespräch).

• Sachebene (was wird durch gesprochene Worte ausgedrückt)

• Appellebene (wozu möchte man den Angesprochenen veranlassen)

• Beziehungsebene (wie steht man zu der am Gespräch beteiligten Personen)

• Selbstoffenbarungsebene (verborgene Werte wie Emotionen; Selbstdarstel-lung und unfreiwillige Selbstenthüllung inklusive)

Zu diesen vier (Sender-)Ebenen kommen aber bei jeder Kommunikation auch noch die Positionen des Empfängers. Versteht der Empfänger das Gemeinte oder eher das von ihm mit bestimmten Wörtern oder Aussagen Verbundene?

Und das alles per Telefon und mit (fast) Unbekannten? Es ist also doppelt schwierig. Aber es ist kein unüberwindbares Problem, man muss sich dessen nur bewusst sein und Strategien zum Gegensteuern entwickeln.

9 Das Projektende

Am Ende jedes Projekts sollte mit einem zeitlichen Abstand eine letzte gemeinsame Besprechung stehen.

Jeder der Beteiligten sollte Gelegenheit haben, sich zum Projektablauf zu äußern. Was hat gut geklappt, was sollte beim nächsten Mal geändert werden?

Der Teamleiter sollte das Feedback des Kunden an die Teammitglieder weitergeben.

Bei dieser Besprechung wird das Fundament für die zukünftige Zusammenarbeit in gleicher oder anderer Konstellation gelegt; deshalb kommt ihr eine ungeheure Bedeu-tung zu. Dessen sollten sich alle Teammitglieder bewusst sein.

10 Weiterbildung

Es gibt zahlreiche Weiterbildungsangebote. Hilfreich sind nach meiner Erfahrung Kurse zu folgenden Themen:

- Zeitmanagement
- Konfliktmanagement
- Moderatorenschulung
- Kommunikationstraining

Diese Kurse sind in der Regel steuerlich absetzbar. Übrigens auch für Arbeitgeber, die die Teilnahme als Incentive anbieten können oder anstelle einer Gehaltserhöhung, wenn sich dadurch die Steuerprogression negativ auswirken würde.

11 Telearbeit und Homeoffice

Die notwenige Technik ist da. Das Einsparpotenzial für die Arbeitgeber ist wissenschaftlich nachgewiesen. Der Motivationsschub bei den Mitarbeitern messbar.

Und dennoch eignet sich meines Erachtens nicht jeder für ein Einzelplatz-Dasein.

Freelancer und Telearbeiter müssen ein hohes Maß an Selbstmanagement und Eigenmotivation erbringen. Sie müssen sich selbst disziplinieren – nicht nur zur vereinbarten Zeit am Schreibtisch zu sitzen, sondern auch den Computer nach der vereinbarten Zeit auszuschalten und das Telefon außerhalb der Arbeitszeit auch mal klingeln zu lassen.

Die Kinderbetreuung oder Pflege von Angehörigen muss durch Dritte gewährleistet sein. Wenn die Arbeitszimmertür geschlossen ist, muss das auch den Kindern signalisieren, dass die Mama eigentlich nicht da ist und dass der Papa keine Zeit hat, das Fahrrad zu reparieren.

Nur so kann sichergestellt werden, dass jeder die Zeit bekommt, die ihm zusteht, die Familie und der Job.

12 Fazit

Wir tendieren dazu, Gewohnheiten aus einer Umgebung (Face-to-face-Teamarbeit) auf eine andere, neue Umgebung (virtuelle Teamarbeit) zu übertragen.

Virtuelle Zusammenarbeit ist viel schwieriger, weil man „zwischen den Zeilen lesen muss", man muss sowohl als Teamleiter als auch als Teammitglied vieles erahnen, was man in einem persönlichen Gespräch aus Mimik und Gestik interpretieren könnte. Man muss seine eigenen Emotionen in Worte kleiden können.

Es ist wichtig, die Unterschiede zu erkennen und sich entsprechend anzupassen.

Alle Mitglieder von virtuellen Teams sind gefordert, das Bewusstsein und die Akzeptanz für unterschiedliche kulturelle Identitäten zu entwickeln.

Vertrauensbildung ist hierbei der wichtigste Erfolgsfaktor.

Für alle Beteiligten ist es unerlässlich, kollaborative Technologien kennen (und lieben) zu lernen, die Teamarbeit trotz Distanz möglich machen.

TM-Systeme

Übersetzen in die Zukunft mit SDL Trados Studio 2009

Daniel Brockmann

Diplom-Übersetzer (BDÜ Landesverband Baden-Württemberg e.V.)
Senior Product Manager SDL TRADOS Technologies

dbrockmann@sdl.com

SDL Trados Studio 2009: Innovation Delivered

„Besser als Trados, besser als SDLX – plus Innovation" – so das Motto der neuen SDL Trados-Generation, die im Juni als SDL Trados Studio 2009 auf den Markt kam. Basierend auf dem über viele Jahre gesammelten Kundenfeedback – von Freiberufler-Innen über Sprachdienstleister bis hin zu Unternehmenskunden – wurde die SDL Trados-Übersetzungsumgebung in großen Teilen neu entwickelt mit der Zielsetzung, den veränderten Anforderungen der Anwender auf Dauer gerecht zu werden. Es handelt es sich hierbei also mit Sicherheit um den größten Versionssprung seit den ersten Trados- und SDLX-Versionen der 90er Jahre.

Auf der einen Seite wurden im Rahmen dieses ambitionierten Entwicklungsprojekt mehr als 100 Verbesserungswünsche der Kunden umgesetzt, z.B. die Abfrage mehrerer Translation Memories gleichzeitig und die Möglichkeit, Konkordanzsuchen in der Zielsprache durchzuführen. Auf der anderen Seite wartet SDL Trados Studio mit sehr innovativen, bisher nie dagewesenen Merkmalen auf. Auf diese soll in diesem Vortrag das Hauptaugenmerk liegen.

SDL Trados im neuen Gewand – integriert und vollständig anpassbar

Der augenfälligste Unterschied zu SDL Trados 2007 Suite: Anstelle von Einzel-anwendungen präsentiert sich SDL Trados Studio in einer neu gestalteten, integrierten Benutzeroberfläche, die Translation-Memory-, Editier- und Projektmanagement-Funktionen in sich vereint. Farben, mit denen beispielsweise die Unterschiede zwi-schen dem aktuellen und dem im TM gespeicherten Segment hervorgehoben werden, lassen sich benutzerspezifisch anpassen. Auch die Tastaturkürzel sind frei konfigu-rierbar.

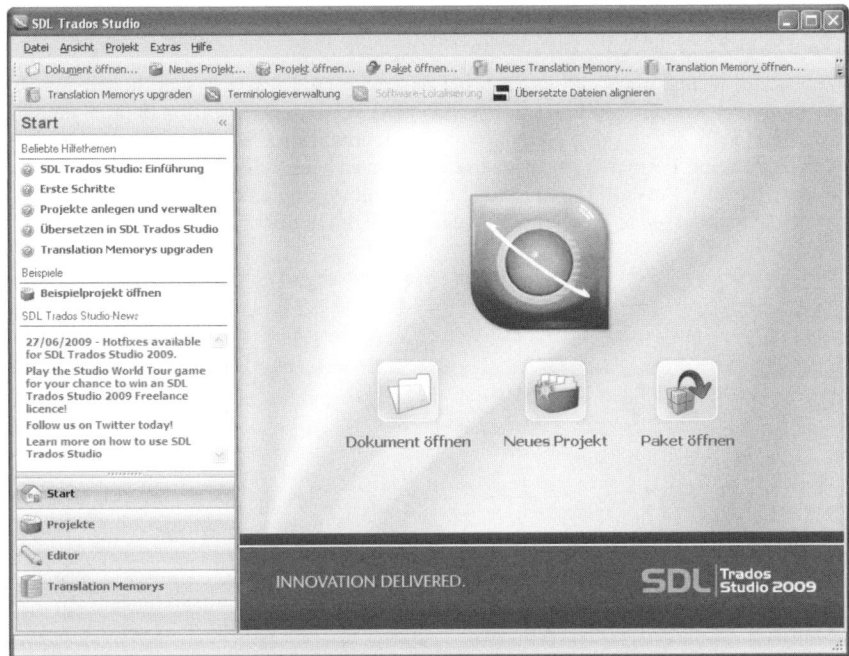

Abb. 1: Eine integrierte Oberfläche für Übersetzung, Review und Projektmanagement

Für Groß- und Kleinaufträge gerüstet

Über den Startbildschirm der Anwendung kann der Projektassistent aufgerufen werden. Dieser eignet sich für umfangreiche Projekte mit mehreren Dateien und/oder Zielsprachen. Mithilfe des Assistenten können Anwender Projekte Schritt für Schritt anlegen und die Ausgangsdateien automatisch konvertieren, analysieren und vorübersetzen. Alternativ kann aber auch nur das „Dokument öffnen"-Symbol verwendet werden. Dieses richtet sich an Benutzer, die unkompliziert Einzeldateien öffnen und übersetzen wollen - was im Freiberufleralltag nicht selten vorkommt.

Übersetzen in der neuen Editierumgebung

Die Übersetzung erfolgt in der neuen Editierumgebung von SDL Trados Studio. Im Gegensatz zu TagEditor setzt der neue Editor auf eine spaltenbasierte Darstellung. Die Übersetzungen werden direkt in die Zielspalte eingetragen. Anstelle externer Struktur-Tags zeigt der Editor eine gesonderte Spalte an, aus der hervorgeht, ob es sich beim aktuellen Segment um einen Tabelleninhalt, eine Überschrift usw. handelt. Der Editor wird außerdem durch eine weitere neue Komponente zur schnellen Navigation in komplexen Dokumenten ergänzt: Neben dem Editor lässt sich ein Document Explorer ein- und ausblenden, der das aktuelle Dokument als Baumstruktur darstellt. Ein Klick im Document Explorer bringt Sie direkt zum gewünschten Abschnitt, was Zeit raubendes Blättern im Text erspart.

Interessante Neuigkeiten gibt es auch bei den internen Tags, also den Steuerzeichen, die mitten im Segment auftauchen und meistens Formatierungsinformationen enthalten: Diese Tags werden nun (standardmäßig) überhaupt nicht mehr angezeigt, sofern es sich um reine Formatierungen wie fett, unterstrichen, Schriftart Tahoma 14 Punkt rot usw. handelt. Anstatt Tags in das Zielsegment zu kopieren, können Formatierungen per Mausklick oder Tastendruck in das Zielsegment übertragen werden.

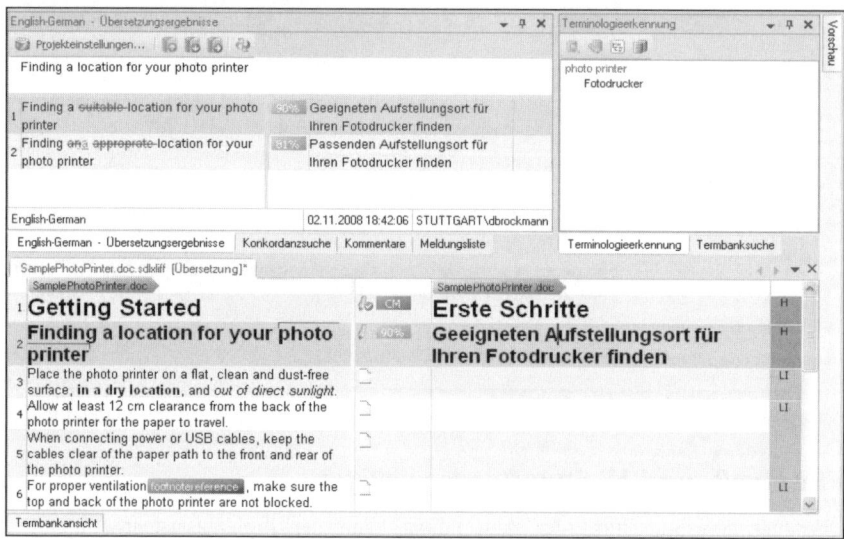

Abb. 2: Übersichtliche Darstellung von Quell- und Zieldokument mit deutlich weniger internen Tags

Lediglich Tags, die keine interne Formatierung speichern (z.B. Fußnotenreferenzen), werden nach wie vor angezeigt. Das Kopieren dieser Tags gestaltet sich allerdings deutlich einfacher als in TagEditor: So lässt sich beispielsweise per Tastaturkürzel eine Quicklist öffnen, aus der Sie das zu platzierende Tag dann auswählen.

Abfrage mehrerer Translation Memories gleichzeitig und Konkordanzsuche in der Zielsprache

Traditionell hat SDL Trados bisher die Segmentsuche in nur einem Translation Memory unterstützt. Diese Beschränkung wird in SDL Trados Studio vollständig aufgehoben. So lassen sich jetzt für ein Projekt bzw. Dokument pro Sprachrichtung beliebig viele Translation Memories auswählen. Dabei kann der Anwender festlegen, welche TMs nur abgefragt und welche aktualisiert werden sollen. So kann man beispielsweise definieren, dass ein TM zur Abfrage von Segmenten und für die

Konkordanzsuche verwendet werden soll, alle anderen TMs aber nur für die Konkordanzsuche. Diese lässt sich übrigens nun auch in der Zielsprache durchführen. Das ‚Umdrehen' von Translation Memories per Export/Import ist also nicht mehr notwendig (auch wenn es natürlich nach wie vor möglich ist).

Interaktive Qualitätssicherung und Rechtschreibprüfung

Die Rechtschreibkontrolle im Editor erfolgt jetzt in Echtzeit. Orthografische Fehler werden sofort bei der Eingabe erkannt und mit einer roten Unterringelung markiert. Ähnlich geht SDL Trados Studio vor, wenn das Zielsegment beispielsweise Zahlenfehler, Interpunktionsfehler usw. enthält. Der Editor weist beim Abschluss eines Segments unmittelbar auf solche Probleme hin und entfernt den Hinweis sofort wieder, wenn der Fehler behoben wurde.

Die Übersetzung Stück für Stück im fertigen Layout

Der Editor von SDL Trados Studio trennt auch weiterhin den zu übersetzenden Text vom Layout, wodurch sich der Anwender auf den Inhalt konzentrieren kann. Ähnlich wie in TagEditor ist es natürlich möglich, den Zieltext in einer Layout-Voranzeige zu sichten. Die Verbesserung in SDL Trados Studio: Die Voranzeige kann während der Übersetzung in Echtzeit aktualisiert werden, so dass Übersetzer Segment für Segment nachvollziehen können, wie der Zieltext im fertigen Layout aussieht. Ein Klick in die Microsoft Word-Ansicht bringt den Anwender zum entsprechenden Segment im Übersetzungseditor. Die Layout-Anzeige ist in SDL Trados Studio eingebettet, lässt sich aber an eine beliebige Stelle im Bildschirm oder auch auf einen zweiten Monitor ziehen.

In der aktuellen Version von SDL Trados Studio ist die Echtzeitvorschau übrigens für die Formate Microsoft Word, HTML und XML realisiert. Alle anderen Formate lassen sich weiterhin nativ in der jeweiligen Anwendung (z.B. Microsoft PowerPoint, Adobe FrameMaker bzw. InDesign) einsehen.

Wiederholungen schneller und konsistenter übersetzen mit AutoPropagate

Wiederholungen in einem Dokument können tückisch sein: Auf der einen Seite profitiert der Anwender davon, dass derselbe Satz dank TM nicht immer wieder neu übersetzt werden muss. Auf der anderen Seite ist es in einem umfangreichen Dokument nicht leicht, Wiederholungen einheitlich zu halten, z.B. wenn dem Übersetzer erst auf Seite 100 die optimale Formulierung für ein bereits vorher übersetztes Segment einfällt. In diesem Fall müssen per Suchen/Ersetzen alle davor übersetzten Vorkommen angeglichen werden.

Für diesen Fall bietet SDL Trados Studio jetzt die AutoPropagate-Funktion. Im oben genannten Beispiel würde SDL Trados Studio alle Vorkommen desselben Segments automatisch anpassen, sobald Ihnen im späteren Verlauf des Dokuments eine bessere Formulierung einfällt. AutoPropagate trägt aber auch dem Umstand Rechnung, dass derselbe Satz im Dokument eventuell anders übersetzt werden muss. Daher lässt sich diese Funktion auf Wunsch auch abschalten oder so einstellen, dass der Auto-Propagate-Vorgang manuell bestätigt bzw. unter bestimmten Bedingungen bestätigt werden muss.

Kontextabhängige TM-Matches

Bisher hat SDL Trados auf Segmentebene zwei Arten von Translation-Memory-Treffern gekannt: „Exact Matches" und „Fuzzy Matches". Bekanntermaßen bedürfen auch „Exact Matches" einer Überprüfung, weil ein in Kontext A übersetzter Satz in einem anderen Zusammenhang nicht zwangsläufig genauso übersetzt werden kann. Beispiel: Der Satz *„Please double-click it."* kann im Deutschen verschiedene Übersetzungen erfordern, je nachdem wie der vorausgehende Satz lautet, also ob sich das englische *„it"* auf ein weibliches, männliches oder sächliches Wort bezieht.

Dieses Problem löst SDL Trados Studio durch eine neue Match-Kategorie, dem „Context Match". Ein Context Match ist zuverlässiger als ein „Exact Match" (also ein 100%-Treffer), weil dieses nur dann vergeben wird, wenn das aktuelle und das vorausgehende Segment und dessen Übersetzung übereinstimmen.

Den Übersetzungsfortschritt im Blick

Einzelnen Segmenten lassen sich nun auch verschiedene Status zuordnen, z.B. bestätigt, akzeptiert, abgelehnt usw. SDL Trados Studio aktualisiert während der Übersetzung laufend eine Statusanzeige, anhand derer sich der Projektfortschritt auf einen Blick nachvollziehen lässt. Z.B. können Anwender jederzeit den prozentualen Anteil der bestätigten Segmente ablesen. Mithilfe eines Filters kann sich der Übersetzer beispielsweise nur alle unbestätigten Segmente anzeigen lassen, alle Segmente mit einem Kommentar oder alle Segmente, die ein bestimmtes Wort enthalten. Letzteres ist beispielsweise dann praktisch, wenn Sie schnell nachsehen wollen, ob das Wort „Dialogfeld" einheitlich übersetzt wurde, ohne Suchläufe durch das gesamte Dokument zu starten.

Komfortablere Termerkennung

SDL Trados Studio bietet natürlich weiterhin eine direkte Schnittstelle zu SDL MultiTerm, das seit Juni 2009 auch in einer runderneuerten Version, SDL MultiTerm 2009, vorliegt. So kann der Anwender weiterhin Funktionen wie Schnelleingabe von Benennungen aus dem Editor heraus und die aktive Termerkennung nutzen.

Die Anzeige im Termerkennungsfenster von SDL Trados Studio ist ebenfalls anpassbar. So kann der Übersetzer beispielsweise in der Termerkennung nicht nur die Ausgangs- und Zielbenennung anzeigen lassen, sondern auch ein Fachgebietsfeld auf Eintragsebene – und zwar in der bevorzugten Schriftgröße und -farbe.

Einfacher ist das Einfügen zielsprachlicher Benennungen in die Übersetzung geworden: Ab sofort reicht es, den Anfangsbuchstaben einer erkannten Benennung einzugeben. Wurde beispielsweise für *„distribution"* in MultiTerm *„Verteilung"* gefunden, muss der Übersetzer nur noch den Buchstaben „V" tippen und das System schlägt in einer Auswahlliste *„Verteilung"* und ggf. noch Synonyme vor, die durch Auswahl in der Liste einfach übernommen werden. Darüber hinaus kann der Anwender per Tastaturkürzel auch eine komplette Auswahlliste aller relevanten Termini öffnen.

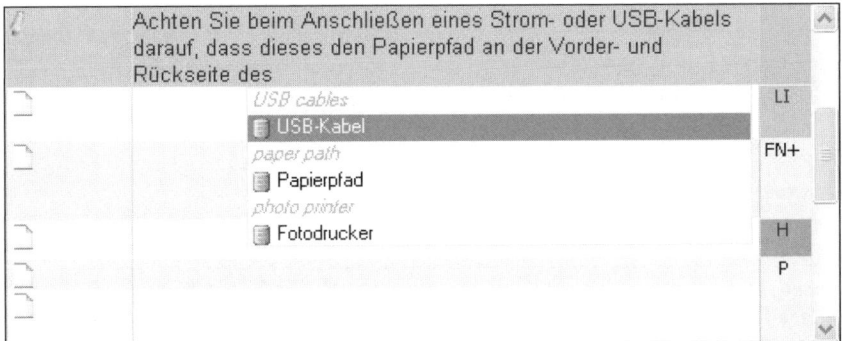

Abb. 3: Neue Quicklist zum schnelleren Einfügen relevanter Benennungen in den Zieltext

Produktivitätsschub durch intelligente Wiederverwendung von Satzfragmenten

Den wahrscheinlich stärksten Produktivitätsschub in SDL Trados Studio dürfte eine ganz besondere Innovation bieten: die zum Patent angemeldete *AutoSuggest*-Funktion. Bisher gab es in SDL Trados zwei Quellen von Übersetzungslösungen: Translation Memorys und Termbanken. SDL Trados Studio eröffnet quasi noch eine „dritte Dimension" der Übersetzung: eine neue Datenbank, die sich aus dem TM speist und die nicht mehr nur ganze Sätze, sondern auch relevante Satzfragmente vorschlägt. Auf diese Weise profitieren nun auch diejenigen Anwender von TM-Technologie, deren Texte auf Segmentebene kaum Wiederholungen aufweisen. Auch solche Texte enthalten nämlich fast immer wiederkehrende Formulierungen, z.B. *„Der Vorstand hat entschieden ...", „... Nachhaltigkeit gewährleisten ..."* usw.

SDL Trados Studio bietet einen intelligenten Mechanismus, der je nach Kontext der Ausgangssprache passende zielsprachliche Formulierungen vorschlägt und damit Tipparbeit und Zeit raubendes Nachschlagen erspart. Beispiel: Das Ausgangssegment enthält den Ausdruck *„... employee convention ..."*. Sobald der Anwender anfängt, die zielsprachliche Kombination, *„Mi..."* einzugeben, erkennt SDL Trados Studio, dass laut Ausgangssprache die Wörter *„Mitarbeiter", „Mitarbeiterversammlung"* usw. passen könnten und schlägt diese Wörter daher automatisch in einer Auswahlliste vor.

Dabei ist wichtig, die Anzahl der Vorschläge auf relevante Treffer zu begrenzen, da diese Funktion das TM als Datengrundlage nutzt. So würde im obigen Fall beispielsweise nicht *„Mittelstand"* vorgeschlagen, da der Ausgangssatz keine Entsprechung (also z.B. *„middle-sized businesses"*) hierfür enthält. Die AutoSuggest-Funktion in SDL Trados Studio bietet somit ein derzeit auf dem Markt neues und bislang nicht verfügbares Satzfragment-Matching. Neben deutlichen Geschwindigkeitsgewinnen durch Einsparung wiederkehrender Tipparbeit sorgt es natürlich auch für eine Konsistenzsteigerung, weil die Nutzer automatisch auch auf Ausdrücke aufmerksam gemacht werden, die nicht in einer Termbank erfasst sind, aber in der Vergangenheit auch auf TM-Ebene einheitlich übersetzt wurden.

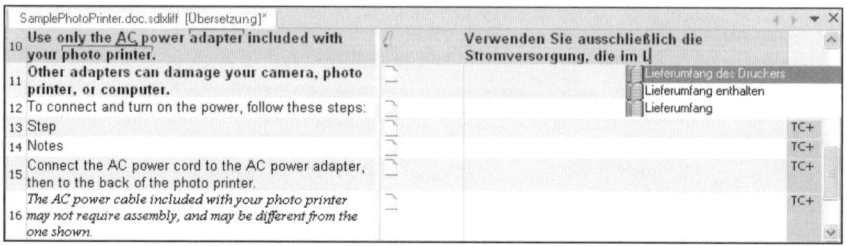

Abb. 4: Die AutoSuggest-Funktion in der Praxis: SDL Trados Studio erkennt interaktiv während der Eingabe, welches Satzfragment in den Zielsatz passen könnte – basierend auf dem aktuellen ausgangssprachlichen Segment.

Offene Standards ‚unter der Haube'

Einige technische Unterschiede ‚unter der Haube' von SDL Trados Studio: Das neue Produkt setzt voll auf offene Standards. So sind die herstellerspezifischen bilingualen Formate TTX (TradosTag) und ITD dem offenen und flexibleren XLIFF-Format gewichen. SDL Trados Studio unterstützt aus Kompatibilitätsgründen aber nach wie vor das TTX- und ITD-Format. Der Import und Export von Translation Memories basiert jetzt auf dem TM-Austauschformat TMX.

Fazit

Obwohl sich SDL Trados Studio sehr grundlegend vom altbewährten Translator's Workbench/TagEditor-Duo unterscheidet, sollte die Einarbeitung in die neue Version leicht fallen. Allein die übersichtlichere Darstellung der Dokumente mit sehr viel weniger Tags stellt eine von vielen Anwendern geforderte Erleichterung dar. Nicht mehr missen möchten Übersetzer vor allem Features wie die interaktive Rechtschreibprüfung und Qualitätskontrolle. Sehr spannend und interessant ist vor allem die intelligente AutoSuggest-Funktion: Hier wird erstmals das wahre Potenzial, das in Translation Memorys schlummert, nutzbar gemacht.

Mit diesem Funktionsumfang und den auf Kundenfeedback basierenden Innovationen hat die neue SDL Trados-Version das Potenzial, die Erstellung sowie das Lektorat von Übersetzungen auf eine neue, zukunftsfähige Grundlage zu stellen. ÜbersetzerInnen können nun benutzerfreundlicher, produktiver und fokussierter arbeiten.

Neue Formen der Zusammenarbeit von Industrie und Übersetzern – gewinnbringend für beide Seiten

Dr. Nicole Keller

Across Systems GmbH, Karlsbad

nkeller@across.net

Hans-Jürgen Strubel

Leiter Marketing Services, WAGO Kontakttechnik GmbH & Co. KG, Minden

hj.strubel@wago.com

Angesichts immer kürzerer Time-to-Market-Zeiten, zunehmend komplexer Produkt-beschreibungen und der wachsenden Zahl von Sprachen stehen Unternehmen und Übersetzer gleichermaßen vor derselben Herausforderung: Mehrsprachige Dokumentationen und Produktinformationen müssen zeitnah und effizient erstellt und verfügbar sein, um die geplante Produktauslieferung nicht zu verzögern. Und selbst kleine und mittlere Übersetzungsprojekte verursachen erhebliche Kosten und beinhalten ein hohes Potenzial zur Effizienzsteigerung. Es ist erforderlich, dass beide Welten – einerseits die der Kommunikationsverantwortlichen in Unternehmen und andererseits die der Übersetzer und Sprachdienstleister – eng verzahnt sind, auch um flexibel reagieren zu können.

Sogenannte Corporate-Translation-Management-Systeme, wie der Across Language Server, bieten hierbei gezielt Unterstützung. Mit dem Across Language Server lässt sich über Unternehmensgrenzen hinweg eine zentrale Plattform für alle Sprachressourcen und Übersetzungsprozesse realisieren. Die integrierte Lösung umfasst ein Translation Memory, ein Terminologiesystem und einen universellen Übersetzungs-editor. Auch leistungsfähige Werkzeuge für die Steuerung und Abwicklung von Übersetzungsprojekten und für die nahtlose Zusammenarbeit von Redakteuren, Übersetzern und Lektoren stehen als Standardfunktionen zur Verfügung. Die dem Übersetzungsprozess vor- und nachgelagerten Systeme können über offene Schnitt-stellen nahtlos angebunden werden.

1   Eine konsistente Begriffswelt schaffen

Wenn Unternehmen einen neuen ausländischen Markt erschließen wollen, müssen Marketing- und Vertriebsunterlagen, Broschüren, Angebote und Pflichtenhefte, Informations- und Konditionsblätter, Texte für Websites, Verträge, Korrespondenzen usw. in der jeweiligen Landessprache verfügbar sein. Unabhängig davon, ob Übersetzungen in-house oder durch externe Dienstleister stattfinden, gehen die Unternehmen vermehrt dazu über, ihr Translation Memory und ihre Terminologiedatenbank auf einem eigenen Systemen zentral vorzuhalten und so die Kontrolle über ihre wertvollen Sprachressourcen zu behalten. Durch optionale Schnittstellen zu Editoren sind Unternehmen zudem in der Lage, die Einträge des Translation Memory und des Terminologiesystems bereits bei der Erstellung des Ausgangstextes zu nutzen. Dieses sogenannte ‚übersetzungsgerechte Schreiben', die Optimierung des Quelltextes im Hinblick auf die spätere Übersetzung, sorgt für eine deutliche Effizienzsteigerung bei Lokalisierungsprojekten. Davon profitieren beide Seiten: Unternehmen, indem sie durch eine erhöhte Trefferquote bei dem Abgleich mit der Sprachdatenbank, dem Translation Memory, die Kosten für die Übersetzungen signifikant reduzieren können. Übersetzer insofern, als sie über konsistentes Ausgangsmaterial verfügen, so weniger Klärungsbedarf und damit auch Rückfragen entstehen. Entsprechend ist der Abstimmungs- und Finalisierungsprozess von Übersetzungen insgesamt mit weniger Aufwand verbunden. Eine weitere Möglichkeit, um die Konsistenz von Texten und Inhalten systemgestützt zu verbessern, besteht in der automatisierten Qualitätssicherung. Sie ist integraler Bestandteil der Across-Produktphilosophie. So verfügt der Language Server beispielsweise über leistungsfähige Funktionen zur Rechtschreibprüfung und Textlängenkontrolle sowie für die Gewährleistung konsistenter Formatierungen. Auch die automatisierte Prüfung der Vollständigkeit der Übersetzung und der Verwendung von Translation Memory und Terminologieeinträgen ist damit möglich.

2 Durchgehende Prozesse

Übersetzungsarbeit ist in vielen Fällen Teamarbeit. Es gibt eine Vielzahl von Akteuren, die mehr oder weniger intensiv mit übersetzungsrelevanten Themen beschäftigt sind oder zumindest auf die entsprechenden Ressourcen zugreifen müssen. Die komplexen Prozesse können aufgrund der Vielzahl der involvierten Personen und der sich teilweise überlagernden Arbeitsabläufe ohne entsprechende Systemunterstützung kaum effizient gestaltet werden. Integrierte Lösungen, wie der Across Language Server, der über Funktionen für das Projektmanagement und zur Workflow-Steuerung verfügt, unterstützen hier die nahtlose Abwicklung von Übersetzungsprojekten. Alle beteiligten Parteien können unmittelbar in die Prozesse eingebunden werden. Zudem können die vorab definierten Arbeitsabläufe automatisch angestoßen werden. Basis hierfür bilden die im System hinterlegten relevanten Übersetzungsdaten, beispielsweise die benötigten Zielsprachen oder das Abgabedatum des fertigen Textes.

3 Einfaches Daten-Handling

So vielfältig wie die beteiligten Akteure sind auch die Quellen, in denen die zu übersetzenden Inhalte im Unternehmen entstehen: Das Textverarbeitungsprogramm und das Katalogsystem liefern die Produktdaten, das Redaktionssystem die Technische Dokumentationen und das Content-Management-System die Web-Inhalte. Gleichzeitig kann der Übersetzer nicht Spezialist für MS Word, MS Excel, Adobe FrameMaker, XML/HTML, Softwareoberflächen etc. sein. Der Multi-Format-Editor des Across Language Server trägt dem Rechnung und abstrahiert sowohl vom Layout als auch vom Dokumentenformat. Gleichzeitig lässt er aber erkennen, wenn z. B. ein überlanger Text ein vorgegebenes Layout sprengen würde. Eine WYSIWYG-Vorschau in Across bietet dafür eine Layout-Kontrolle. Zusätzlich stehen absatzbezogene Kommentar-/Lesezeichen-Funktionen zur effizienten Kommunikation mit Lektoren zur Verfügung.

Mit Einsatz des Across Language Server ist jeder am Übersetzungsprozess Beteiligte in die sogenannte Linguistic Supply Chain eingebunden, die von der übersetzungsgerechten Quelltexterstellung bis zur detaillierten Termin- und Kostenkontrolle für alle Übersetzungen reicht. Entsprechend den unterschiedlichen Rollen und Anforderungen der beteiligten Akteure stehen unterschiedliche Zugangs- und Nutzungsvarianten für den Across Language Server zur Verfügung. Von der üblichen Client-Server-Installation über die Server-zu-Server-Verbindung zwischen Auftraggebern und Dienstleistern bis hin zu Web-Clients und webbasierten Sprachportalen reichen die Möglichkeiten. Für freiberufliche Übersetzer steht mit der Across Personal Edition ein Produkt zu Verfügung, das in einzigartiger Weise sowohl als voll umfängliches Einzelplatzsystem verwendet werden als auch sich als Client mit dem Language Server eines Auftraggebers verbinden kann.

4 Einblicke in die Praxis

Hans-Jürgen Strubel, Leiter Marketing Services bei WAGO Kontakttechnik GmbH & CO. KG berichtet:

Als international agierendes Unternehmen steht WAGO vor der Herausforderung, seine Informationen zu Produkten und Leistungen in 21 Sprachen lokalisieren zu müssen. Das Übersetzungsvolumen liegt bei circa 1,7 Millionen Wörtern extern und 0,3 Millionen Wörtern intern. Für die Außer-Haus-Übersetzungen arbeitet WAGO direkt mit über 40 Fachübersetzern zusammen, durchwegs mit Muttersprachlern mit Sitz im entsprechenden Land. Je Sprache gibt es mindestens einen Übersetzer. Für die Hauptsprachen wie Englisch, Französisch oder Spanisch wird die Last auf teilweise drei oder noch mehr Schultern verteilt.

Um die Übersetzungsprozesse zu optimieren und die Abläufe für alle Beteiligten zu verschlanken, führte WAGO bereits 2005 den Across Language Server ein. WAGO realisierte dadurch durchgängige Workflows, in die alle betreffenden Personen, sowohl Interne als auch Externe, eingebunden sind. Gleichzeitig arbeiten alle beteiligten Parteien auf Basis der gleichen, konsistenten Daten. Die Übersetzer greifen teils mit der Across Personal Edition direkt auf den Language Server bei WAGO zu, teils werden „Pakete geschnürt" die über einen FTP-Server oder per E-Mail ausgetauscht werden. Der Austausch von Dokumenten, Terminologie und Translation Memories erfolgt Client-/Server-basiert sofern die Voraussetzungen der Infrastruktur gegeben sind wie z.B. schnelle Datenverbindungen. Eine wichtige Voraussetzung für die Übersetzungsqualität und deren ständige Verbesserung ist die Trennung von Übersetzung und Lektorat. Letzteres wird ausschließlich von WAGO-Mitarbeitern in den Landesgesellschaften direkt in Across durchgeführt.

Mit dem Across Language Server erhält WAGO maximale Transparenz über Termine, Aufwände etc. und realisiert durchgängige Prozesse, auch über die Unternehmensgrenze hinweg. Der direkte Austausch von Terminologie und Translation-

Memory-Einträgen gewährleistet darüber hinaus konsistente Inhalte für alle Sprachvarianten, unabhängig vom Ausgabeformat.

Auf der anderen Seite verfügen die Übersetzer mit der Across Personal Edition über einen leistungsfähigen Multi-Format-Editor, der ihnen kostenfrei zur Verfügung gestellt wird und mit dem sie wahlweise standalone oder am Server ihrer Kunden arbeiten können.

Die Across Personal Edition können freiberufliche Übersetzer kostenlos nutzen. Es entstehen keine Lizenzkosten, weder im Einzelplatzbetrieb noch bei der Nutzung als Client an einem Language Server aufseiten des Übersetzers. Die Registrierung als freiberuflicher Übersetzer in der Übersetzerdatenbank des Across-Systems genügt, um eine kostenlose Lizenz zu erhalten. Auch Updates und Mail-Support werden für freiberufliche Übersetzer nicht berechnet.

Die Zahl der Across-Anwender auf Seiten der Industrie wächst stark. Übersetzer können deshalb durch den Einsatz von Across bestehende Kunden binden und neue Kunden gewinnen.

Die Rolle des Übersetzers oder Übersetzer quo vadis?

Christiane Gläser

STAR Deutschland GmbH, Böblingen

christiane.glaeser@star-group.net

Abstract

Der Vortrag beschäftigt sich mit der Rolle des Übersetzers im Wandel der Zeit und vor dem Hintergrund der Globalisierung sowie dem zunehmenden Einfluss von Software-Technik. Besonderes Augenmerk wird dabei auf die Anforderungen, Einflüsse und Herausforderungen gelegt, die das Berufsbild in den letzten drei Jahrzehnten mit sich gebracht hat, derzeit mit sich bringt und voraussichtlich zukünftig mit sich bringen wird.

Der diesbezügliche Schwerpunkt liegt auf den zunehmenden technischen Anforderungen und Tücken, die die Tätigkeit des Übersetzers zwangsläufig mit sich bringt, die aber nicht nur neue Herausforderungen sind, sondern auch Möglichkeiten und Chancen mit sich bringen.

Anforderungen an Übersetzungsmanager durch ansteigenden Technologieeinsatz

Hans Pich

Document Service Center GmbH

h.pich@dsc-translation.de

1 Technologische Entwicklungen im Übersetzungsworkflow

Die technologischen Entwicklungen des Übersetzungsworkflows werden durch eine Vielzahl unterschiedlicher Entwicklungen rund um die eigentliche Übersetzung mitbestimmt. Wesentlichen Einfluss haben hier vor allem die eingesetzten Technologien in den vorgelagerten Bereichen der Content-Erstellung.

Ein weiterer Bereich ist die Entwicklung von Technologien der direkten Übersetzungsunterstützung vom Translation-Memory-System über Terminologiedatenbanken bis hin zur automatischen bzw. maschinellen Übersetzung.

Als wenn dies nicht schon in sich komplex genug wäre, wird natürlich auch erwartet, dass Übersetzer die unterschiedlichsten Quellen im Internet für die Recherche nutzen können.

Für die Verwaltung der Übersetzungsaufträge wird selbstverständlich vorausgesetzt, dass Übersetzer geeignete Workflow- oder Verwaltungstools einsetzen, Informationen aus Portalen abrufen können bzw. diese dort wieder einstellen und die Buchhaltung stets passgenau zu den sich verändernden gesetzlichen Vorschriften gestaltet ist.

Insgesamt ein durchaus komplexes Umfeld, in dem die eigentliche Aufgabe der korrekten Umsetzung von textlichen Inhalten in eine andere Sprache manchmal kaum noch zu erkennen ist.

1.1 Von der Schreibmaschine zum Redaktionssystem

Vor noch nicht allzu langer Zeit war es für Übersetzer durchaus üblich, dass die zu übersetzenden Texte als Ausdruck zur Verfügung gestellt wurden und die Übersetzungen dann mittels einer Schreibmaschine oder gar handschriftlich angefertigt wurden. Lektoren verewigten ihre Korrekturen in Form von Korrekturfahnen auf dem Papier und spezialisierte Schriftsetzer kümmerten sich um das Layout bzw. das „Setzen" der Dokumente, bis sie dann von Druckern wieder auf Papier gebracht wurden.

Auch wenn dies immer noch das Bild ist, dass sich manche Zeitgenossen vom Alltag eines Übersetzers machen, hat sich schon vor geraumer Zeit die technologische Entwicklung in diese heile Welt eingeschlichen.

Bereits in den Achtzigern des letzten Jahrhunderts wurde die Erstellung der Dokumente über Text- und DTP-Systeme auf den Computer verlagert. Die Entwicklung dieser Programme hat oft dazu geführt, dass der spezialisierte Setzer aus dem Bearbeitungsworkflow herausgefallen ist. Die zu übersetzenden Texte waren im gleichen Maße zunehmend nur noch als Datei zum Übersetzer gelangt und wurden von diesem auch als Datei wieder an den Auftraggeber geliefert.

Die elektronische Verfügbarkeit der zu übersetzenden Inhalte hat zwangsläufig dazu geführt, dass auch Software zur Anfertigung von Übersetzungen entwickelt wurde. Aufgrund der Vielzahl unterschiedlicher Text- und DTP-Systeme war die Schnittstelle zwischen den Übersetzungstools eine der ersten technologischen Herausforderungen im modernen Übersetzungsworkflow.

Die folgenden Jahre wurden vor allem durch Weiterentwicklungen der jeweiligen Softwaretools hinsichtlich der Layout-Funktionalität, der Automatisierung von Dokumentationen und auch der Steigerung der Effizienz geprägt. Für den Übersetzer hatte dies vor allem zur Folge, dass er für erheblich größere Dokumentenvolumina mit deutlich geringeren Einnahmen rechnen musste. Es sollte jedoch nicht unerwähnt bleiben, dass er mit den Tools auch ein höheres Übersetzungsvolumen in vergleichbarer Zeit bewältigen konnte.

Der nächste größere Technologieschub war die Einführung strukturierter Dateiformate (z. B. SGML, XML, ...), die es möglich machen, die Inhalte deutlich stärker zu modularisieren und dabei gleichzeitig auch die Verwaltung dieser Module im Blick auf eine Wiederverwendung zu ermöglichen. Für den Übersetzer hat dies zur Folge, dass er nun wieder mit tendenziell sinkenden Übersetzungsvolumina rechnen kann. Technologisch bedeutet der Umstieg auf strukturierte Inhalte zum einen eine Vereinfachung der technologischen Komplexität. Auf der anderen Seite erhöhen sich aber die Anforderungen an die Bearbeitung der einzelnen Module hinsichtlich stilistischer und terminologischer Konsistenz deutlich. Die Antwort der Anbieter von Übersetzungstools sind hier z. B. immer umfangreichere Funktionen im Bereich der Qualitätssicherung. Das dies die Anforderungen an den Übersetzer deutlich erhöht, kann man z. B. daran ablesen, dass praktisch alle am Markt befindlichen Tools wie selbstverständlich vom Übersetzer erwarten, dass er komplexe Suchkriterien über die Definition regulärer Ausdrücke beschreiben kann.

1.2 Spezielle technologische Anforderungen

Auch wenn die Einführung neuer Technologien und insbesondere neuer Software die Bearbeitungsmöglichkeiten immer mehr erweitert hat, kann man feststellen, dass Software eigentlich immer unvollkommen ist und Probleme schafft, die man ohne die Software nicht hätte.

Ein typisches Beispiel hierfür sind die über viele Jahre bekannten Probleme im Bereich der Codierung von Zeichen. Da die Entwickler der marktführenden Software anscheinend vorwiegend dem englischsprachigen Spektrum zuzuordnen sind, wurden in ersten Versionen vorwiegend nur die für das Englische benötigten Zeichen verfügbar gemacht. Darauf aufbauend wurden dann auch Lösungen für zusätzliche Zeichen in den westeuropäischen Sprachen angehängt. Schon bei der Umsetzung weiterer Zeichen für osteuropäische Sprachen merkt man, dass hier die Umsetzung eher

Stückwerk war. Für den Übersetzer ergaben sich somit teilweise erhebliche Probleme, die nur mit viel Engagement, teilweise skurrilen Workarounds und auf jeden Fall fern jeder Übersetzungstätigkeit gelöst werden konnten.

Ein weiteres Beispiel für übersetzungsfremde technologische Anforderungen sind die Probleme, die sich aus der teilweise sehr mangelhaften Bearbeitbarkeit von trotzdem gerne verwendeten Dateiformaten ergeben. Das beste Beispiel hierfür dürfte immer noch der Versuch sein, PDF-Dateien übersetzen zu lassen.

Neben den Problemen des mangelhaften Zusammenspiels unterschiedlicher Programme gibt es aber auch noch ein weiteres Feld zusätzlicher Anforderungen. Moderne Text- und DTP-Programme bringen eine Fülle von Möglichkeiten der typografischen Gestaltung mit sich. Dies veranlasst viele Ersteller von Dokumenten, mal alles auszuprobieren, was das gerade verwendete Programm so her gibt. Vom Übersetzer wird nun ganz selbstverständlich erwartet, dass er die typografischen Anforderungen seiner Zielsprache genau kennt (auch wenn die Ersteller von Dokumenten das in der Quellsprache nicht ganz so genau nehmen). Darüber hinaus ist aber auch die reine Bedienung der entsprechenden Programme nicht immer so intuitiv, dass man sich hier „einfach mal dransetzen" kann.

1.3 Projektmanagement / Workflowtools

Eine aktuelle Entwicklung im Übersetzeralltag ist die zunehmende Entwicklung und Einführung von Tools zur Workflow-Unterstützung. Ursächlich hängt diese Übersetzung stark mit der Einführung von Redaktionssystemen zusammen, die im Gegensatz zu der früher üblichen Bearbeitung (weitgehend) kompletter Dokumente nun eine teilweise unübersichtlich große Anzahl vereinzelter Informationsmodule in den Übersetzungsworkflow gibt. Hierdurch entsteht ein deutlicher Bedarf an Tools um die Übersicht zu behalten. Eine weitere Motivation für die Einführung von Workflowtools ist der auch weiterhin vorhandene Kostendruck. Der inzwischen weitgehend etablierte Einsatz von spezialisierten Übersetzungstools lässt scheinbar kaum noch Raum für Einsparungspotenziale bei der reinen Übersetzung. So ist es konsequent, dass man die Einsparungspotenziale bei der Verwaltung der Übersetzungsaufträge energisch anzugehen versucht.

In dem von den Softwareherstellern angedachten Endausbau könnten Übersetzungsworkflows durch den Einsatz von Konnektoren, Portallösungen und automatisierten Workflowsystemen den menschlichen Faktor in der Übersetzung wieder soweit reduzieren, dass hier nur noch der Übersetzer wie am Fließband seine Arbeitslisten mit einer nicht endenden Kette einzelner Informationsmodule abarbeitet. Nur ein klein wenig weiter gedacht könnten dann vielleicht sogar automatische Übersetzungssysteme den Übersetzer auch noch von dieser Restarbeit befreien.

Auch neben der reinen Übersetzungstätigkeit stellen sich dem Übersetzer zusätzliche technologische Anforderungen für die Ausübung seiner Tätigkeit. Viele Unternehmen erwarten inzwischen, dass die Rechnungsstellung im Self-Service-Verfahren direkt über entsprechende Portale durch den Übersetzer selbst erfolgt. Und auch Vater Staat will hier nicht hinten anstehen und verlangt für die Abgabe von Steuererklärungen bzw. die Angabe von Sozialversicherungsmeldungen einen kontinuierlich steigenden Technologieeinsatz.

2 Aktuelle Anforderungen an ÜbersetzungsmanagerInnen

Wenn nun bisher ein durchaus in Teilen etwas düsteres Bild vom Arbeitsalltag der in der Übersetzung beschäftigten Menschen gezeichnet und vielleicht der Eindruck erweckt wurde, dieser Vortrag sei technologiefeindlich, soll jetzt doch noch einmal Bezug auf die konkrete Alltagssituation genommen werden.

Die in den letzten Jahren entwickelten Systeme haben trotz aller Kritik auch stets neue Möglichkeiten geschaffen und unbestreitbar die Effizienz im Übersetzungsbereich deutlich gesteigert. Die gestiegenen technologischen Anforderungen sind daher vor allem auch eine Konsequenz der zusätzlichen Möglichkeiten.

Eine direkte Folge der zusätzlichen Anforderungen ist die Einsetzung von spezialisierten Übersetzungsmanagern, die nicht zwangsläufig auch Übersetzer sein müssen. Ihr Aufgabenbereich ist es, den Übersetzern eine möglichst problemfreie Arbeitsumgebung zu schaffen, damit sich diese (wieder) auf ihre eigentliche Kernkompetenz konzentrieren können.

Zu diesen Aufgaben gehören daher folgende Teilbereiche:

- Analyse konkreter Auftragsanforderungen im Hinblick auf Technologieeinsatz

- Analyse inhaltlicher Anforderungen im Hinblick auf Terminologie, Stilistik und weiterführender Referenzen bzw. Bezüge auf externe Inhalte

- Optimieren der beigestellten Inhalte für den Einsatz der vorgesehenen Übersetzungstools inkl. der Rückführung geeigneter Formate an den Auftraggeber

- Gestalten effizienter Workflows

- Planung und Durchführung der konkreten Übersetzungsprojekte inkl. der entsprechenden Mitarbeiterauswahl, Terminplanung und -überwachung und Durchführung der entsprechenden Qualitätssicherung

- Beratung der Auftraggeber

Zu dieser bereits recht umfassenden Liste von Aufgaben gesellen sich oft noch die Bereiche Kalkulation und Vertrieb.

Aus der einleitenden Schilderung der technologischen Entwicklung und hieraus resultierender Anforderungen ist es offensichtlich, dass die Umsetzung dieser Anforderungen nur durch ein breites technologisches Wissen und Kenntnisse in Bezug auf aktuelle Softwaretools und Technologien ermöglicht werden kann. Darüber hinaus ist es jedoch von elementarer Bedeutung, dass sich der Übersetzungsmanager auch in die Arbeitsmethodik und -umgebung des Übersetzers hineinversetzen kann. Denn nur dann kann er Übersetzungsprojekte so gestalten, dass die Technologie den Menschen (in diesem Fall den Übersetzer) unterstützt und zudem die Workflows einen umsetzbaren Rahmen für die Durchführung der gewünschten Arbeiten bieten.

Diese Herangehensweise muss der Übersetzungsmanager auch seinen Auftraggebern vermitteln können und dabei einen Weg zwischen kurzfristigen Kosten- und Terminzielen und langfristigen Qualitätszielen aufzeigen.

3 Anforderungen an das Berufsbild

Für die Umsetzung dieser Anforderungen erscheint es zweckmäßig, das Berufsbild des Übersetzungsmanagers zu konkretisieren und entsprechende Ausbildungsmöglichkeiten zu schaffen.

Ansätze zu einer diesbezüglichen Ausbildung finden sich z. B. im Modellversuch MEUM (Modulentwicklung Übersetzungsmanagement) der Universität Hildesheim und der Fachhochschule Flensburg[17], im Localization Project Management Certification der California State University[18] und in Ansätzen auch im Rahmen der tekom-Zertifizierung für technische Redakteure[19].

Daneben wird die Ausbildung als Übersetzungsmanager auch weiterhin zu einem erheblichen Anteil als Weiterbildung z. B. für Übersetzer oder Redakteure erfolgen. Hierbei ist es für den einzelnen wichtig, sich durch die Kombination von Selbststudium und gezielter Weiterbildung einen möglichst umfassenden Einblick sowohl in die inhaltlichen und technologischen Grundlagen, das Handwerkszeug aus dem Bereich Projektmanagement und einen Überblick über die verfügbare Software zu verschaffen.

Diese Qualifikation ist auch die Basis für die Gestaltung funktionierender Übersetzungsworkflows aus den verfügbaren Ressourcen unter Berücksichtigung der konkreten Anforderungen.

4 Gestaltung von Übersetzungsworkflows

Ein Workflow ist, wie es der deutsche Name korrekt bezeichnet, ein Arbeitsablauf. Um hier funktionierende und aufeinander sinnvoll aufbauende Abläufe zu ermöglichen, ist es erforderlich, die einzelnen Arbeitsschritte mit den jeweiligen Voraussetzungen, Randbedingungen und dem zu erwartenden Arbeitsergebnis präzise zu definieren. Ein besonderes Augenmerk ist hierbei auf die Schnittstellen zwischen Auftraggeber und Auftragnehmer zu legen, da es hier auch zu einem Informations- und Wissensbruch kommen kann. Üblicherweise sind Auftraggeber nicht so detailliert über die Prozesse im Übersetzungsbereich informiert, dass Sie selbst die Auswirkungen bestimmter Anforderungen oder mangelnder Voraussetzungen umfassend beurteilen können.

Aus dem Katalog der sich so ergebenden Leistungsbausteine kann man dann den jeweils optimalen Workflow zusammen mit dem Auftraggeber gestalten. Eine umfassende Beschreibung ist auch die Voraussetzung für den Einsatz von funktionierender Workflow-Software.

---

[17] www.uni-hildesheim.de/~meum/aktuelles/archiv/pdfs/MEUM_final.pdf

[18] http://rce.csuchico.edu/localize/

[19] www.tekom.de/index_neu.jsp?url=/servlet/ControllerGUI?action=voll&id=1336

Modularisierte Workflows bieten neben der besseren Übersichtlichkeit auch die Option externe Leistungen reibungsärmer in den Workflow zu integrieren. Durch die präzise Beschreibung der jeweiligen Schnittstellen kann die Übergabe an externe Stellen, z.b. zur Durchführung von Incountry-Reviews wesentlich stressärmer organisiert werden. Selbstverständlich sollten auch für diese externen Arbeitsschritte konkrete Leistungsbeschreibungen erstellt werden.

Hilfreich für den Aufbau und die Beschreibung der Leistungsbausteine kann z. B. eine Zertifizierung nach DIN EN 15038 sein, da im Rahmen der Zertifizierung genau diese Verfahrensbeschreibungen und Arbeitsanweisungen zu erstellen sind.

Eine Zertifizierung ist unabhängig von der Größe des Übersetzungsdienstleisters möglich. Wie am Sonntag im Beitrag von Herrn Kurre dargelegt werden wird, besteht daher auch für freiberufliche Übersetzer die Möglichkeit der Zertifizierung.

Workshops und Podiumsdiskussionen

Basiswissen Internetpräsenz

Imen Mguedmini

Freiberufliche Übersetzerin, Lektorin und Lehrkraft für DaF

mguedmini@gmail.com

Workshop

Ziele

Ziel des Workshops ist es, Dolmetscher und Übersetzer mit dem notwendigen Hintergrundwissen zur Erstellung einer eigenen Präsenz im Internet auszustatten. Der Workshop-Teilnehmer soll in die Lage versetzt werden, einen sogenannten Hosting-Dienstleister auszuwählen, sich (rechtssicher) eine eigene Domain zu sichern und kostengünstig eine einfache Webseite mit Hilfe von geeigneter Software oder auf Basis eines Templates zu erstellen sowie diese auf dem Server zu installieren.

Inhalt des Workshops

- Was ist ein Hoster, welche Dienste kann/sollte mein Hoster bieten
- Was ist ein Nameserver, was ein Admin-C, worauf muss ich beim Registrieren einer Domain achten?
- Was ist HTML, was XHTML? Wie kann eine solche Datei bearbeitet werden (anhand eines Beispiels)?
- Was ist FTP/SFTP/SCP, und was bedeutet rwx?
- Impressumspflicht, rechtliche Vorgaben
- Wie kann ein Kunde mich über meine Homepage erreichen?

Ablauf

Jeder einzelne Punkt wird kurz erläutert, der Teilnehmer kann die Beispiele jeweils an seinem Rechner nachvollziehen. Um das Veröffentlichen der Webseite zu demonstrieren, legen wir im Vorfeld entsprechend viele Benutzeraccounts auf einem eigenen Server im Internet an. Die Teilnehmer können so eine erste einfache selbst erstellte Webseite direkt im Internet aufrufen.

Werkzeuge für die Softwarelokalisierung

Prof. Dr. Uta Seewald-Heeg

Hochschule Anhalt (FH), Köthen

uta.seewald-heeg@inf.hs-anhalt.de

Workshop

1 Einleitung

Wer Softwarelokalisierung als Dienstleistung in sein Portfolio aufnimmt, benötigt geeignete Werkzeuge, um die sehr verschiedenartigen Lokalisierungsaufgaben angemessen lösen zu können. Während Inhalte klassischer Web-Seiten auf der Basis von HTML in den meisten Fällen mit den gängigen Translation-Memory-Umgebungen sehr gut bearbeitet werden können, kann die Bearbeitung von Benutzungsoberflächen mit diesen Werkzeugen zum Teil nur eingeschränkt oder gar nicht erfolgen. Die Zahl der Dateiformate, in denen Dateien grafischer Benutzeroberflächen vorliegen können, ist sehr vielfältig, so dass eine umfassende Unterstützung in der Regel nur von spezialisierten Lokalisierungswerkzeugen geboten wird. Ferner sind besondere Routinen, die in der Vorbereitungsphase eines Lokalisierungsprojekts anfallen, wie beispielsweise das Schützen oder Verbergen einzelner Ressourcenelemente, die bei der Übersetzung nicht modifiziert werden dürfen, ebenso wie Funktionen zum Vergleich verschiedener Softwareversionen und bestimmter auf die Besonderheiten von Softwareoberflächen abgestimmter Prüfroutinen in der Regel nur in Softwarelokalisierungswerkzeugen in ausreichendem Umfang vorhanden.

2 Lokalisierungswerkzeuge

Für die sprachliche Anpassung der Bedienoberflächen von Softwareprodukten stehen spezielle Lokalisierungswerkzeuge zur Verfügung. Typischerweise kann mit diesen Werkzeugen der Umfang der zu übersetzenden Textsegmente ermittelt werden, mit Hilfe von Pseudoübersetzungsroutinen der Platzbedarf und die Darstellung zielsprachiger Schriftzeichen überprüft sowie Größenanpassungen für Schaltflächen vorgenommen werden (Abb. 1). Lokalisierungswerkzeuge verfügen in der Regel ferner über Vorschaumodi und Testfunktionen. Bei genauerer Betrachtung unterscheiden sich Softwarelokalisierungswerkzeuge aber in ihrer Handhabung und in ihrem Funktionsumfang zum Teil wesentlich voneinander. Schon beim Anlegen eines Lokalisierungsprojekts und dem damit verbundenen Import der zu lokalisierenden Dateien gibt es konzeptionelle Unterschiede zwischen den Werkzeugen. Aber auch hinsichtlich der unterstützten Dateiformate bzw. deren Dateiendungen bestehen wesentliche Unterschiede zwischen den Systemen.

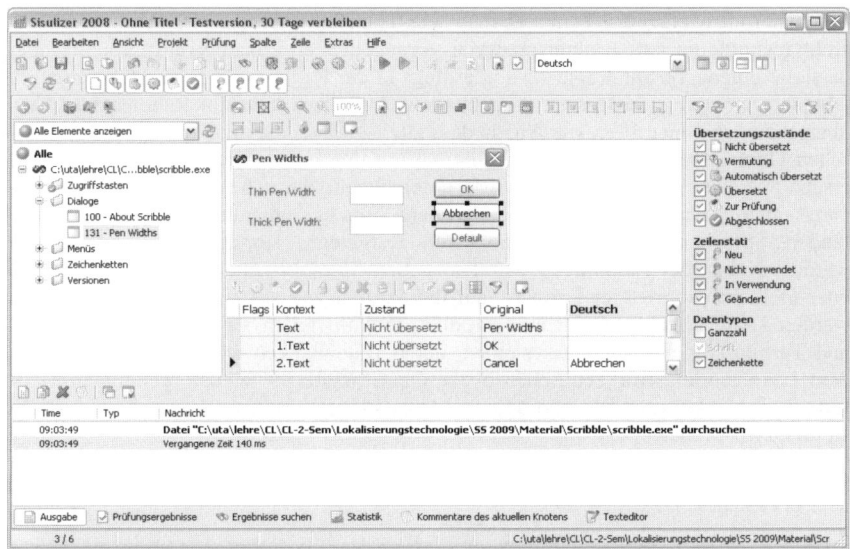

Abb. 1: Bearbeitungsoberfläche von Sisulizer mit grafischer Vorschau und der
Möglichkeit der Bearbeitung von Schaltflächen.

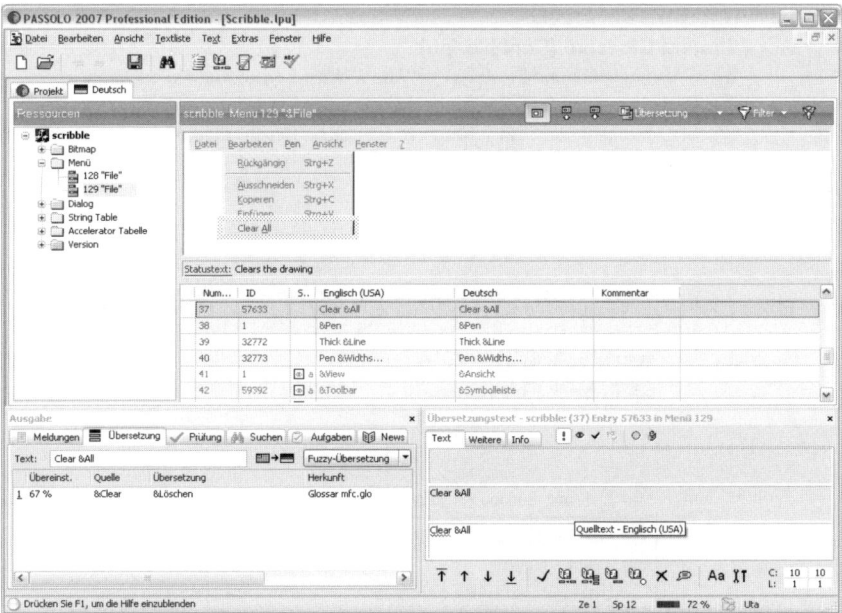

Abb. 2: Bearbeitungsoberfläche von Passolo mit grafischer Vorschau (oben) und
Vorschlag einer 67%igen Übereinstimmung aus dem Glossar (links unten).

Lokalisierungswerkzeuge bauen ebenso wie Translation-Memory-Systeme auf Satz-archivtechnologie auf. Referenzmaterial vorangehender Lokalisierungsprojekte oder herstellereigene Terminologie wird allerdings in der Regel in Form von Glossaren im tabulatorgetrennten Textformat eingebunden. Auf diese kann im Rahmen von Vor-übersetzungen zugegriffen werden, so dass alle Einträge, die mit Segmenten der grafi-schen Oberfläche übereinstimmen, automatisch durch ihr zielsprachiges Äquivalent ersetzt werden. Wo Systeme Glossare unterstützen, die neben der jeweiligen Aus-gangs- und Zielsprache beliebig viele weitere Sprachen enthalten, müssen die betref-fenden Sprachen durch systemspezifisch festgelegte Kopfzeilen gekennzeichnet werden. Neben der Einbindung von Translation-Memory-Dateien, als TMX-Dateien oder in Form proprietärer Formate, auf die ähnlich wie auf ein Glossar zugegriffen werden kann, bieten verschiedene Produkte Schnittstellen zu Translation-Memory-und Terminologieverwaltungssystemen, deren Datenbanken während der Arbeit mit dem Lokalisierungswerkzeug ebenso wie die Glossare im tabulatorgetrennten Text-format nach geeigneter Terminologie und Vorschlägen aus dem Satzarchiv durchsucht werden (vgl. Abb. 2).

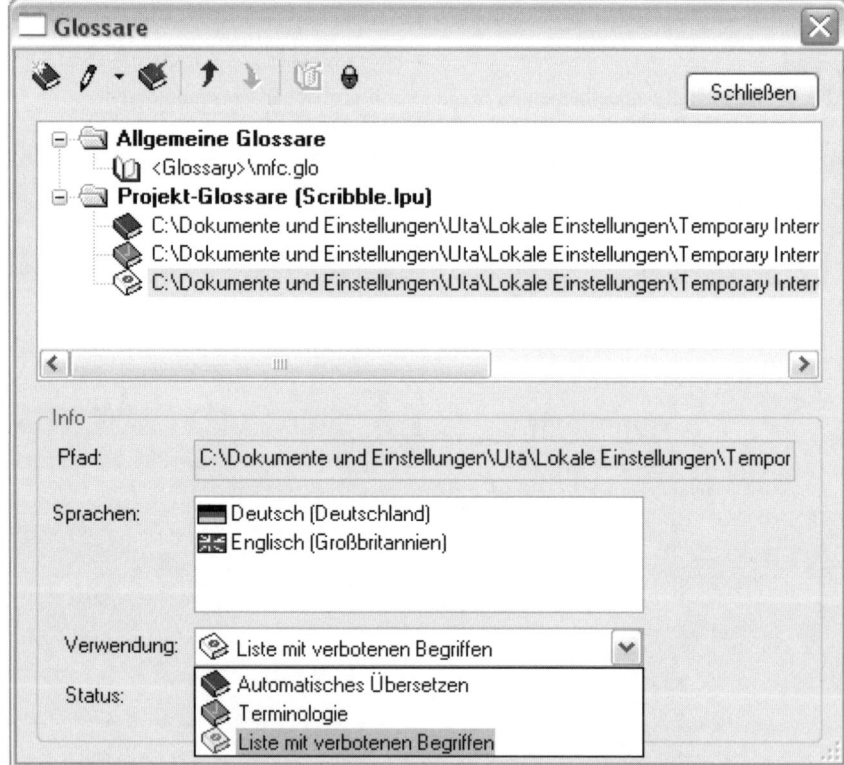

Abb. 3: Glossarverwaltung in Passolo mit einem Glossar, das zur Überprüfung nicht zugelassener Terminologie eingesetzt wird.

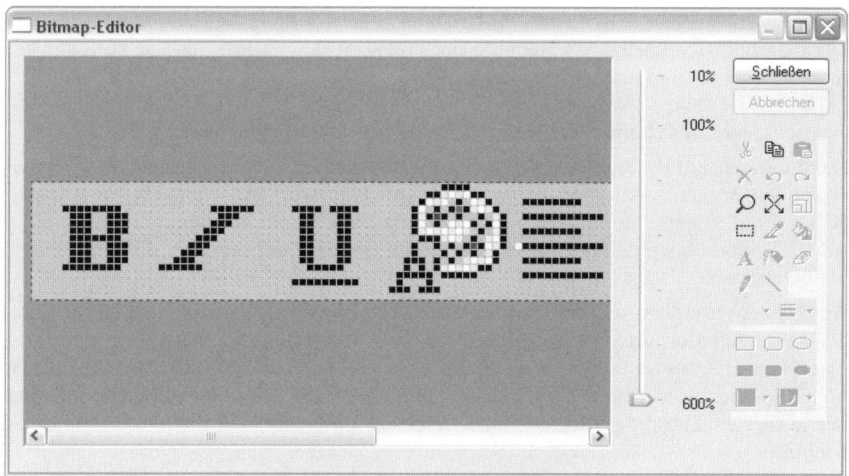

Abb. 4: Bitmap-Editor zur Bearbeitung von Grafikelementen in Passolo.

Terminologielisten können in einigen Systemen auch zur Terminologiekontrolle eingesetzt werden, um zu überprüfen, ob für einen Hersteller oder ein bestimmtes Produkt nichtzulässige Terminologie verwendet wurde (vgl. Abb. 3).

Mit einigen Systemen können zusätzlich zu den Standardroutinen in einem integrierten Grafikeditor auch Cursor und andere grafische Elemente der Benutzungsoberfläche angepasst werden (Abb. 4). Andere Werkzeuge sehen grundsätzlich den Export von Bildelementen in komfortable Grafikprogramme vor.

Die Stärken und Schwächen von Lokalisierungswerkzeugen wie Catalyst, Multilizer, Passolo, RC-WinTrans, Sisulizer oder Visual Localize lassen sich durch Evaluierungsanordnungen systematisch einander gegenüberstellen. Abhängig von den zu lokalisierenden Dateien eines Projekts stellen die Systeme immer aber auch Anforderungen an das informationstechnische Wissen der Nutzer.

3. Anforderungen an die Nutzer von Lokalisierungswerkzeugen

Um die Funktionen eines Lokalisierungswerkzeugs optimal ausnutzen zu können, bedarf es wie auch bei anderen Werkzeugtypen bei jedem einzelnen Werkzeug einer Einarbeitungszeit. Darüber hinaus ist aber zum Teil auch mehr oder weniger umfangreiches informationstechnisches Wissen notwendig. Das sei am Beispiel der Lokalisierung von XML-Dateien kurz erläutert: Während ein Word-Dokument von einem Übersetzer in vielen Fällen ohne das Wissen um die interne texttechnologische Repräsentation eines solchen Dokuments in einer Translation-Memory-Umgebung übersetzt werden kann, sind bei der Verarbeitung von XML-Dokumenten unbedingt

Kenntnisse über den Aufbau von XML-Dateien erforderlich. So muss der Nutzer des Lokalisierungswerkzeugs im Rahmen der Auswahl des Parsers für ein zu lokalisierendes XML-Dokument immer auch dokumentspezifische Parserregeln angeben (Abb. 5), die dem Lokalisierungsprogramm erlauben, aus dem Dokument nur jene Textsegmente zu extrahieren, die den zu lokalisierenden Text enthalten.

Dazu müssen in der Regel die Auszeichnungselemente (*Tags*) benannt oder in einem speziellen programminternen Editor gekennzeichnet werden (vgl. Abb. 6). Andernfalls gelingt es dem Nutzer entweder nicht, das Dokument einzulesen, oder aber auch solche Segmente werden bei der Bearbeitung angezeigt und geöffnet, die unverändert bleiben müssen.

Ähnliche Vertrautheit mit dem strukturellen Aufbau von Dokumenten ist häufig auch bei Textdateien erforderlich, bei denen jedes zu übersetzende Textsegment eindeutig einer Identifikationsnummer oder einem Symbol zugeordnet wird. Auch in diesen Fällen müssen vom Nutzer Regeln angelegt werden, die das Lokalisierungswerkzeug zur korrekten Extraktion der zu lokalisierenden Einheiten und nur dieser Einheiten benötigt.

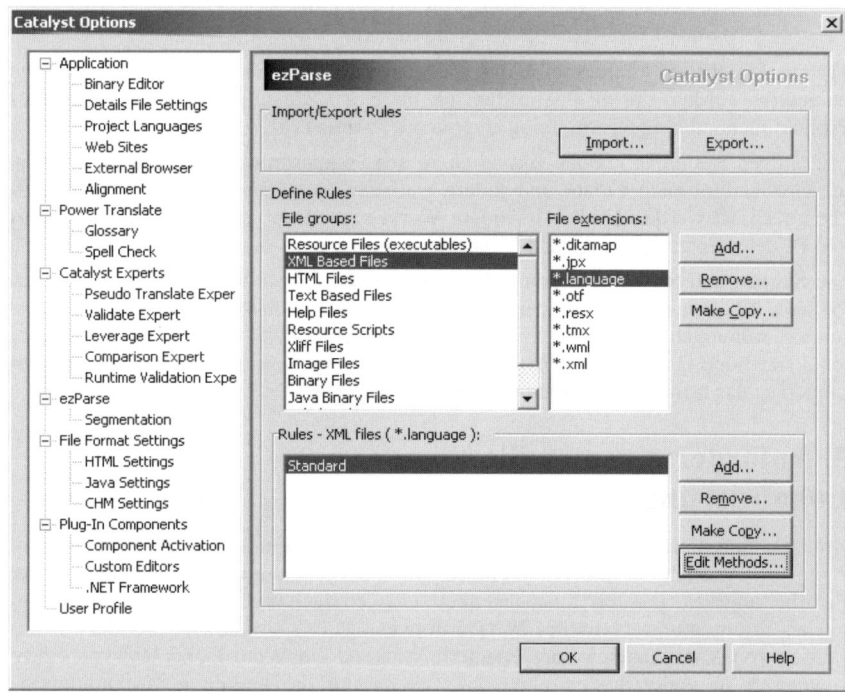

Abb. 5: Einstiegsdialog zur Einstellung von Parserregeln für ein XML-Dokument in Catalyst.

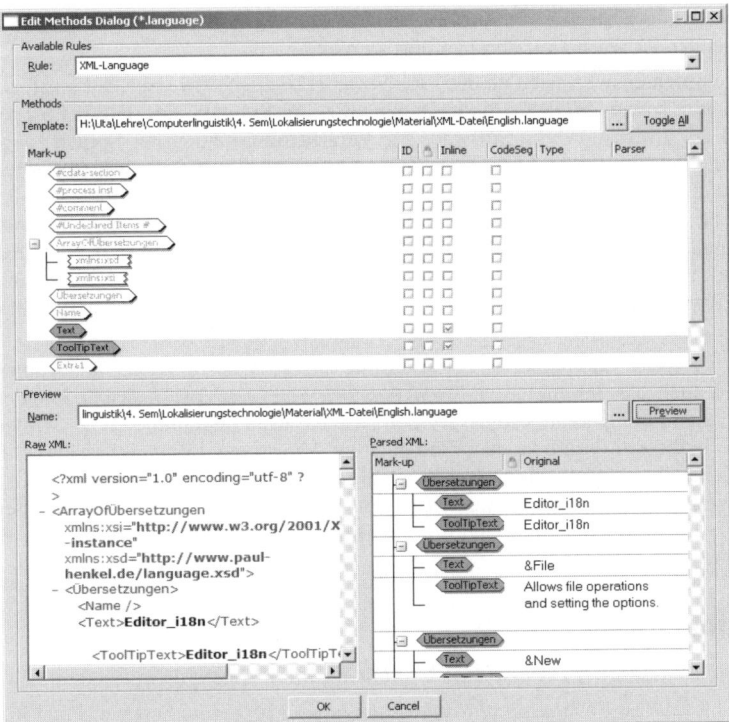

Abb. 6: Einstellung von Parserregeln für ein XML-Dokument in Catalyst.

In zahlreichen Fällen sind zudem umfassende Kenntnisse der Konventionen einzelner Betriebssysteme erforderlich, um ein Lokalisierungsprojekt erfolgreich zum Abschluss zu führen. Nur wenige Werkzeuge unterstützen neben Dateiformaten von Microsoft Windows auch Anwendungen anderer Betriebssysteme. Für Apple-Mac-OS-Anwendungen existieren ebenso wie für Linux-Anwendungen eigene Systeme. Bei der Lokalisierung von Software, für die die gängigen Lokalisierungswerkzeuge keine Parser bereithalten, muss der Lokalisierer entweder auf die Entwicklungsumgebung, in der die Anwendung programmiert wurde, oder auf die Arbeit in einem einfachen Texteditor zurückgreifen. In beiden Fällen stehen ihm in der Regel keine speziell an Lokalisierungsaufgaben orientierten Funktionen wie etwa der Zugriff auf Referenzmaterial oder Prüfroutinen zur Verfügung.

4. Methoden zur Evaluierung von Lokalisierungswerkzeugen

Um die Frage nach dem jeweils für individuelle Einsatzzwecke geeigneten Lokalisierungswerkzeug zu beantworten, müssen das Einsatzszenarium genau bestimmt und entsprechende Tests zur Überprüfung der Funktionalität sowie der Integration in den bestehenden Arbeitsablauf durchgeführt werden.

Es ist empfehlenswert, sich an der ISO-Norm 9126 zur Softwareproduktevaluation zu orientieren sowie an den Überlegungen, die im Rahmen des EAGLES-Projektes (1996) zur Evaluation von Software zur Verarbeitung natürlicher Sprache angestellt wurden. Danach müssen zunächst eine Bewertungsskala, eine Metrik sowie Evaluierungskriterien erarbeitet werden, anhand derer Funktionalität, Benutzertauglichkeit, Effizienz und Zuverlässigkeit, in größeren Unternehmen möglicherweise auch die Wartungsfreundlichkeit und Übertragbarkeit, der zur Auswahl stehenden Systeme ermittelt werden können. Bei den zur Überprüfung herangezogenen Kriterien hat sich in der Praxis die Orientierung an den Phasen typischer Softwarelokalisierungsprojekte bewährt, wie sie in Esselink (2000) oder Wahle (2000) skizziert werden.

Wurden Passolo oder Catalyst bereits in die engere Wahl gezogen, kann unter Umständen auch das Internetportal *Translatorstraining* von Jost Zetzsche bei der Entscheidungsfindung herangezogen werden (www.translatorstraining.com). Mittlerweile werden in diesem Portal, zu dem man über ein Abonnement Zugang erhält, neben den zahlreichen Translation-Memory-Umgebungen auch die beiden erwähnten Lokalisierungswerkzeuge jeweils in einem Kurzfilm dargestellt, der die Bedienung der Programme in zentralen Funktionen bei der Bearbeitung von EXE- und Dotnet-RESX-Dateien widergibt.

Bibliographie

Esselink, B. (2000). *A Pratical Guide to Localization.* Amsterdam: Benjamins.

EAGLES (1996): *Evaluation of Natural Language Processing Systems.* Final Report. EAGLES DOCUMENT EAG-EWG-PR.2. Version of October 1996. HTML-Version verfügbar unter: www.issco.unige.ch/projects/ewg96/ewg96.html.

ISO 9126: (1991). *International Standard ISO/IEC 9126. Information technology — Software product evaluation — Quality characteristics and guidelines for their use.* International Organization for Standardization, International Electrotechnical Commission, Geneva.

Hegner, M. (2003). *Methoden zur Evaluation von Software.* IZ-Arbeitsbericht Nr. 29, Mai 2003. Online im Internet: www.gesis.org/fileadmin/upload/forschung/publikationen/gesis_reihen/iz_arbeitsbe richte/ab_29.pdf.

Schmitz, K.-D. / Reineke, D. (eds.) (2005). *Einführung in die Softwarelokalisierung.* Tübingen: Stauffenburg Verlag.

Translatorstraining. Internetportal unter www.translatorstraining.com.

Wahle, K. (2000). Wie wird Software lokalisiert?. In: Schmitz, K.-D. /Wahle, K. (eds.). *Softwarelokalisierung.* Tübingen: Stauffenburg, S. 31-47.

Urheberrechte an Translation Memories

João Esteves-Ferreira

Tradulex; Moderator

Manuel Cebulla, LL.M.

Silvia Cerrella Bauer

Financial Operations Manager, Euroscript Switzerland AG

Podiumsdiskussion mit Impulsvortrag zur Einleitung der Diskussion

1 Einleitung

Die Globalisierung geht Hand in Hand mit einem zunehmenden Druck zu Beschleunigung der Übersetzungsprozesse und Senkung der Übersetzungskosten. Ein dazu immer häufiger eingesetztes Hilfsmittel sind Translation-Memory-Systeme (TMS). Sie gleichen in Sekundenschnelle neu zu übersetzende Texte mit gespeicherten Texten ab, zu denen bereits Übersetzungen vorliegen, ermitteln identische oder teilweise übereinstimmende Textpassagen und bieten sie dem Übersetzer an, damit er sie entweder unverändert übernehmen oder an den neuen Übersetzungsauftrag anpassen kann.

Für diesen Abgleich werden Ausgangstexte und die dazugehörigen Übersetzungen im TMS gespeichert. Somit dient eine Übersetzung nicht nur der Erfüllung des aktuellen Übersetzungsauftrages, sondern die Leistung des Übersetzers findet auch Eingang in spätere Übersetzungen oder dient zumindest als Material für spätere Abgleiche. Es kommt auch vor, dass Übersetzungsauftraggeber den Abgleich bereits selbst vornehmen und nur noch die Textabschnitte übersetzen lassen, für die es im TMS noch keine Übersetzung gibt.

Schon seitdem es das Übersetzen und Dolmetschen gibt, arbeitet jeder Sprachmittler mit einem Memory-System, nämlich seinem Gedächtnis. Seit langem nutzen Sprachmittler zudem selbst oder von anderen erstellte Fachglossare, Formulierungs- und Mustertextsammlungen. Das wesentlich Neue an den TMS sind ihre Leistungsfähigkeit, der Umfang der nutzbar zu machenden Texte und insbesondere auch die Tatsache, dass die Leistungen vieler Übersetzer in die TMS einfließen, und das in verstärktem Maße über nationale Grenzen hinweg.

Hier stellen sich eine Reihe von rechtlichen Fragen: Wem gehören die in das TMS eingehenden Leistungen? Darf ein Übersetzer die in ein TMS eingeflossene Übersetzung eines Anderen überhaupt nutzen? Ist es einem Übersetzungsbüro oder End-

kunden gestattet, Übersetzungen ohne Einwilligung des Übersetzers in TMS einzu-
speisen?

2 Vertragsrechtliche Grundlagen

Schaut man sich die vertraglichen Beziehungen zwischen Auftraggeber und Übersetzer an, ergibt sich zuerst einmal Folgendes: Der Übersetzungsauftrag ist ein
Werkvertrag zur Erstellung eines Zieltextes auf der Grundlage des Ausgangstextes
gemäß den im Übersetzungsauftrag spezifizierten Anforderungen. Ist vertraglich
nichts anderes vereinbart, dann darf der Auftraggeber die Übersetzung grundsätzlich
nach seinem Belieben und sooft er will nutzen, verändern oder weitergeben.

Diese Freiheit findet ihre Grenzen in anderen Gesetzen, zum Beispiel im Bundesdatenschutzgesetz oder im Strafgesetzbuch. Hier sei insbesondere an Geheimhaltungspflichten erinnert. Zum anderen ergeben sich Einschränkungen aus dem Vertragsrecht
selbst: Denn jeder Vertragspartner ist gesetzlich dazu verpflichtet, auf die Rechte,
Rechtsgüter und Interessen der anderen Vertragspartei Rücksicht zu nehmen.

Das können sowohl die Rechte, Rechtsgüter und Interessen des Autors des Ausgangstextes sein, als auch die des Übersetzers, der insbesondere ein Interesse an einer
angemessenen Vergütung für seine Leistung hat. Auf der anderen Seite hat der
Auftraggeber ein Interesse an einer möglichst uneingeschränkten Nutzung der Übersetzung. Diese Interessen gilt es, miteinander in Einklang zu bringen und im frei
aushandelbaren Werkvertrag einen gerechten Ausgleich zu finden. Damit dies möglich ist, müssen auch bestimmte Informationspflichten erfüllt werden, damit der
Übersetzer z.B. vorab weiß, welche Nutzung seiner Übersetzung beabsichtigt ist.

3 Das Urheberrecht des Übersetzers

Ein wichtiges Recht des Übersetzers, auf das Rücksicht zu nehmen ist, ist sein Urheberrecht. Vorausgesetzt, dass er ein solches Urheberrecht an seiner Übersetzung hat,
stehen ihm sowohl Urheberpersönlichkeitsrechte als auch Urheberverwertungsrechte
zu. Zu den Persönlichkeitsrechten zählen insbesondere das Namensnennungsrecht, der
Schutz vor Entstellung des Werkes und das Änderungsrecht.

Das Verwertungsrecht legt es in die Hand des Übersetzers, darüber zu bestimmen, wie
und wie häufig sein Werk genutzt wird. Will der Auftraggeber die Übersetzung also
nicht nur für seinen internen Gebrauch verwenden, so muss er sich für jede Art
von Nutzung ein entsprechendes Nutzungsrecht einräumen lassen, für das er den
Übersetzer auch vergüten muss. Entsprechend ist mit jedem Miturheber zu verfahren,
der an der Übersetzung mitgewirkt hat (Übersetzungsteam), und natürlich auch mit
dem Autor des Ausgangstextes.

3.1 Schutzfähige Übersetzungen

Damit dem Übersetzer im konkreten Fall solche Rechte zukommen, muss seine
Übersetzung die Voraussetzungen für den urheberrechtlichen Schutz erfüllen.

Das deutsche Urheberrecht setzt der Schutzfähigkeit von Werken bestimmte Grenzen: Es muss sich dabei um eine *persönliche geistige Schöpfung* handeln. Diese liegt nach der Rechtsprechung und dem urheberrechtlichen Schrifttum vor, wenn es das Werk eines Menschen ist, ein Immaterialgut, das einen Gedanken- oder Gefühlsinhalt überträgt und den Geist der Adressaten anregt. Unter einer *Schöpfung* wird etwas noch nicht Dagewesenes verstanden beziehungsweise etwas, das anders ist als das bisher Existierende. Zusätzlich wird von der Rechtsprechung und einem Teil des Schrifttums gefordert, dass das Werk schöpferische Eigentümlichkeit, Originalität oder Individualität besitzen müsse. Die untere Grenze, unter der die urheberrechtliche Schutzfähigkeit nicht erreicht wird, soll da liegen, wo es sich um eine *rein mechanische* und *schablonenmäßige* Leistung handelt, oder wo sie sich von der Masse des Alltäglichen und von lediglich *handwerklichen* oder *routinemäßigen* Leistungen nicht abhebt.

Die Eigenschaft der persönlichen geistigen Schöpfung wird Gebrauchstextübersetzungen zu Unrecht häufig abgesprochen. So heißt es oft, sie wären nur das genaue Abbild des Ausgangstextes, würden handwerksmäßig und wortwörtlich erstellt und erforderten keine stilistischen Fähigkeiten oder Einfühlungsvermögen des Übersetzers. Der Übersetzer habe gerade bei technischen Texten gar keinen sprachlichen Gestaltungsspielraum. Weiter wird häufig vorgetragen, dass von unterschiedlichen Übersetzern erstellte technische Übersetzungen im Ergebnis im Wesentlichen gleich lauten würden und daher nicht die Handschrift des Übersetzers zeigten.

Bei genauer Betrachtung der von den Urheberrechtskommentatoren und Teilen der Rechtsprechung gegebenen Beispiele für die Abgrenzung schutzfähiger von nicht schutzfähigen Übersetzungen stellt sich heraus, dass fast alle Übersetzungen urheberrechtlich schutzfähig sind. Schließlich liegt jeder Übersetzung eine komplexe kognitive und vor allem auch kreative Tätigkeit zugrunde, und fast jeder Text bietet hinreichenden Spielraum für persönliche übersetzerische Entscheidungen. Die Kreativität kann indes beim Einsatz von TMS eventuell eingeschränkt sein. Diese Einschränkung gilt aber jedenfalls nicht für die ins TMS einfließenden Erstübersetzungen.

3.2 Das europäische Urheberrecht

Das Europäische Urheberrecht stellt wesentlich niedrigere Anforderungen als das deutsche Urheberrecht an die sogenannte *Schöpfungshöhe* von schriftlichen Werken, während diese niedrigen Anforderungen auch in Deutschland bei anderen Werkarten anerkannt sind. Es ist damit zu rechnen, dass diese Ungleichbehandlung insbesondere durch den Einfluss des Europarechts in Zukunft schwinden wird, denn es macht auch auf Seiten deutscher Urheberrechtler ein Umdenken erforderlich. Das größte Problem bezüglich der Anerkennung der urheberrechtlichen Schutzfähigkeit von Gebrauchstextübersetzungen liegt indes darin, dass die wenigsten Juristen eine klare Vorstellung vom Übersetzen haben.

3.3 Textfragmente

Derzeit geht eine Entwicklung dahin, dass TMS auch Fragmente unter der Satzebene angeben. Das kann eine Auswirkung auf die urheberrechtliche Behandlung haben. Denn grundsätzlich spielt die Länge des Werks eine Rolle: Je kürzer das Werk, desto schwieriger ist es, dass es die für den Urheberrechtsschutz notwendige Eigenartigkeit aufweist. In diesem Zusammenhang ist jedoch zu beachten, dass nicht einzelne Fragmente in das TMS eingelesen werden, sondern ganze Übersetzungen. Dieses Einlesen ist urheberrechtlich als Form der Vervielfältigung eine gesondert zu vereinbarende und zu vergütende Nutzung. Ebenso ist die Einräumung des Rechts zu vergüten, die Übersetzung zum Abgleich zu verwenden. Grundlage dafür ist die Feststellung, dass der gesamte Text urheberrechtlich schutzfähig ist.

Werden einzelne Bausteine aus bestehenden Übersetzungen in eine neue Übersetzung eingefügt und für diese angepasst bzw. verändert, kann eine sogenannte *freie Benutzung* des Werkes vorliegen. Dann entsteht ein neues selbständiges Werk, das ohne Zustimmung des Urhebers des benutzten Werkes bzw. der benutzten Werke veröffentlicht und verwertet werden darf. Werden die Matches aber unverändert übernommen, muss bei jedem einzelnen Textbaustein geprüft werden, ob er für sich die urheberrechtliche Schutzfähigkeit erreicht.

4 Schluss

Bei der Podiumsdiskussion zum Urheberrecht an Translation Memory Systemen werden noch weitere Aspekte angesprochen werden, und wahrscheinlich werden nicht zu allen Fragen abschließende Antworten gegeben werden können. Die Podiumsdiskussion möge aber die Debatte in Wissenschaft und Lehre, im BDÜ und zwischen diesem und den Vereinigungen der Übersetzungsbüros und der Endkunden anregen und dazu beitragen, dass die am Übersetzungsprozess Beteiligten einen gerechten Ausgleich aller Interessen erzielen.

Manuel Cebulla, LL.M., m@cebulla-net.de

Bibliographie

Cebulla, M. (2007). *Das Urheberrecht der Übersetzer und Dolmetscher.* Berlin: Wissenschaftlicher Verlag Berlin. (Beziehbar über die BDÜ Service GmbH).

Who killed creativity? – Do we really need TM?

Hugh Keith

Moderator

hkeith@blueyonder.co.uk

Terence Oliver

Panel coordinator, freelance technical translator

olitrans@aol.com

Chris Durban, Ian Hinchliffe, Bill Maslen

Panel

Panel discussion

1   The background

To deny the blessings of technology would be absurd in an age like ours which benefits so much from the accuracy of laser surgery, the convenience of microwaved foods and the speed of broadband internet. But in all these cases we still need the skill of the surgeon to guide the laser scalpel, the experience of the cook to set the heat and timer on the oven, and the discernment of the individual to sift, sort and select the information presented.

Voice recognition software and computer-assisted translation tools can no doubt offer the same advantages of accuracy, convenience, speed and consistency. However, while it is irrefutable that translation memory (TM) software can improve terminological consistency and reduce confusion by standardising forms of expression, the downside is often a less fluent, a stilted, or even a syntactically flawed translation. For certain types of text this signals a significant deterioration in quality of the end result.

Translation buyers and translators themselves need to be aware that, in many instances, the quicker and less considered the initial translation, the more extensive and time-consuming the process of self-editing becomes. TM tools are merely a means to an end and not an end in themselves. As such, they do not necessarily lead to overall cost savings on the scale that is frequently anticipated.

Like many of the other technological aids that surround us today, TM tools relieve us of much of the burden of our work, but they can never relieve us of our professional responsibility for producing an end product that is in every way as fit for purpose as it is possible for it to be.

2   The debate

Why is it that some people, once they start using translation memory, stop creating translations that "sing"? Does the TM approach improve process quality at the expense of translation quality? Does the man-machine interface actually affect the thought processes of those using it? Is there anything we can do to prevent translation quality suffering? Are there certain kinds of texts that TM tools should not be used for on principle? Are people forgetting that TM tools are merely a means to an end, not an end in themselves? These and related questions will be discussed by a group of experienced translators who work in widely differing fields and who range from the highly sceptical to the convinced user of TM tools.

VI. Ausbildung heute

Spezialisierungen in der Lehre

Specialising in legal translation

Richard Delaney

City University, London

Conference@Delaneytranslations.com

1 Introduction

Legal translation is a curious field. On the one hand, as Šarčević pointed out, the need for competent legal translators is greater than ever in this age of globalisation (Šarčević/Legal Translation and Translation Theory*)*. On the other hand, there are very few courses that actually offer training focusing exclusively on legal translation. Among clients two approaches seem to be prevalent, neither of which is terribly helpful; there are those who feel that any translator will do, regardless of the field of specialization, and those who do not want to give any legal translation work to a translator unless that translator is also a qualified lawyer. While both approaches are somewhat problematic, the first approach is one that will be only too familiar to translators everywhere, who find potential clients basing their choice entirely on cost, not appreciating that specialist subject matter requires specialist translators. For that reason I shall focus on the latter approach. No translator would deny that a specialised translation requires a specialised translator. However, hardly anyone would expect a medical translator to be a qualified doctor, nor would one expect a literary translator to necessarily be an author in their own right. Why, therefore, should clients and employers expect legal translators to be qualified lawyers?

One explanation might be that the language of the law is seen as a separate language, 'legalese', containing plenty of terms and expressions that are not encountered in normal, everyday language, either because they are archaic (such as *mesne profits*, or *granting leave*), or because they have developed within the legal system (such as *Anton Pillar orders* or *Mareva injunctions*), while common terms that appear familiar are suddenly assigned different meanings (*consideration* referring to remuneration). As if this were not enough, legalese also seems to be riddled with Latin expressions (such as *locus standi, amicus curiae*, etc.). As a result, both lawyers commissioning translations and translation agencies looking for translators often take the view that only someone who is a lawyer himself can understand the text. This frequently leads to a situation where preference is given to lawyers who are not trained translators, as opposed to translators who are not trained lawyers.

2   Substance and style

Generally speaking, in legal translations substance will be more important than style, although some suggest that the ideal translation should read as though it had originally been drafted in that language (Pescatore / Das Konzipieren übersetzungsgerechter juristischer Dokumente 1999). While this is a noble aim, there are two difficulties with it. Firstly, the legal systems of the source language and target language frequently differ, as do the concepts in the respective legal systems, so that it is not always possible to find an exact equivalent, which may make it impossible to produce a translation that sounds as though it had been originally drafted in that language. Secondly, bearing in mind the fact that legal concepts may differ between source and target language, there is a danger in a translation that sounds as though it had been drafted in the target language; Beaupré gives the example of *Gulf Oil Can Ltd. V Canadien Pacifique Ltée* ([1979] C.S. 72), where the English text of an order referred to an *act of God*, while the French version made reference to *cas fortuit ou de force majeure*. The difficulty arose, because certain facts that qualify as *cas fortuit* under Quebec law, would not necessarily qualify as an *act of God* at common law. In that case, a truck had hit a locomotive- in interpreting the phrase *cas fortuit*, the court applied the civil law concept, which meant the accident was covered. In common law this would not have counted as an a*ct of God*. The court ruled according to the French version, explaining that if the common law concept had been meant, the translator ought to have translated the term literally as *acte de Dieu*, which would have alerted the court to the fact that it was the common law concept that was meant. However, since the civil law term *cas fortuit* had a defined meaning, the court ruled accordingly (Beaupré/ Interpreting Bilingual Legislation, 1986). This case is a prime illustration of what can happen if the legal concepts of the source and target language do not match exactly. Using *acte de Dieu* would not have been idiomatic, while *cas fortuit*, being the French term generally used, made the translation sound more as though it might have been originally drafted in French. Nevertheless, an unidiomatic translation would have been preferable, precisely because it would have been unidiomatic, thus alerting the reader to the likelihood that the concept referred to might differ from that of the target language. While this can cause problems in bilingual jurisdictions (such as Hong Kong or Canada), the difficulties are even more marked when translating between different legal systems. In other fields of specialised translation there tend to be common concepts (a broken leg is a broken leg, even though treatments might differ in different cultures), while legal concepts differ (the English concept of murder is not necessarily the same as Mord in German, nor does a Private Company limited by shares (Ltd.) have the same requirements as a German GmbH).

3   Challenges of legal translation

It can be seen, therefore, that a translator wishing to specialise in legal translation does not only have to be fully conversant in his language pair, he should also have a solid understanding of the legal systems and concepts of the jurisdictions of his source and target language (which means that different translations may be required when translating German texts from Austrian, Swiss or German sources, or when considering English texts from England, Scotland, Ireland, America, India, etc.). Ideally, it would appear, the legal translator should not only be a qualified lawyer, but be a qualified lawyer in both jurisdictions of the languages into which he translates. However, that in itself is not sufficient either, since a thorough understanding of the two systems and their terminology does not in itself make for a good translator.

Therefore, in addition to this knowledge, the translator will have to be aware of the nuances of language and have a theoretical framework within which to do the translation. However, as de Beaugrande put it (although admittedly in relation to poetic translation): *"it is inappropriate to expect that a theoretical model of translation should solve all the problems a translator encounters. Instead, it should formulate a set of strategies for approaching problems and for coordinating the different aspects entailed."* (de Beaugrande/ Factors in a Theory of Poetic Translating, 1978)

3.1 Linguistic and sociocultural problems

As mentioned above, different legal systems may have different concepts, and as if that were not enough, the law constantly changes and develops, creating not only new concepts, but also new terminology of which the translator needs to stay abreast (although frequently the translator will also have to be conversant with outdated terminology, since one may be called upon to translate texts originating before the latest changes). In addition to having different concepts and terminology, different legal systems frequently have very different styles as well. While the Lord Woolf reforms in England have started to introduce plain English and have tried to reduce the number of specifically legalese terms, such a concept is not (yet) known in Germany. This means that texts of a similar nature may be written in very different registers, and adapting them to the target culture may not always be appropriate.

Although there are often similar concepts in other languages, there is a question whether to translate these terms at all, or whether to leave them in the original, thus marking them as peculiarities, and providing an explanation, although some terms, such as 'common law', are well known as a concept, and often left untranslated, regardless of the fact that a translation would be possible.

Talking about leaving terms untranslated, the language of the law, at least when looking at English and German, frequently employs Latin terms. In view of the fact that this happens in both languages, and that the terms are borrowed from a third language, it is tempting to just transfer the Latin terms in the translation, thus leaving them untranslated. However, in many cases the Latin terms used in one language are not used in the other, and vice versa. Effectively, therefore, they will frequently need to be understood and translated in the same way as any other specialised technical term.

Of course it is important to bear in mind that any well-written text must be coherently ordered, and that to achieve this, the translator may need to make adjustments, to ensure that the target text is coherent in the target language. Contradiction and ambiguity should ideally be avoided, although particularly in the case of legal texts that is not always possible, or indeed desirable. While one should certainly not introduce any ambiguity, the translator should be very careful not to 'improve' the source text. Particularly in the case of a legal dispute, the decision of how to interpret any ambiguity ought to be decided by a judge, not the translator, so that it is important to retain any ambiguity that is in the source text, without adding or detracting from it.

4 How can one specialise in legal translation?

So far only very few qualifications are available in the field of legal translation. Admittedly, some general translation degrees and professional qualifications offer an option in legal translation, while other providers offer individual (CPD) courses specialising on one particular aspect of legal translation (e.g. contract law). These courses vary substantially, in content, length and recognition. While short courses are available that focus on legal terminology in a particular area of law, the difficulty with these is that they can only ever give a short overview, and are restricted to a particular area of law. However, the law is a wide field, and ideally one needs a comprehensive understanding of the whole of the law, in order to properly assess any individual aspect thereof.

Clearly experience is a vital component, and there are excellent legal translators who have never had the benefit of any formal legal training at all (just as there are excellent translators who have never had the benefit of any formal translation training). However, this is the exception, rather than the rule, and in any event will take years of practice until one is at a stage where one does not only manage to convince potential clients that one is qualified to do legal translations, but also feels confident to do so.

Since last year a specialised MA in Legal Translation is offered both in Hong Kong and at City University, London. It appears that the MA in Hong Kong focuses on the requirements of translators within that one legal system, since both Mandarin and English are official languages. As a result, although some knowledge of the English common law and of the law of mainland China will no doubt be helpful, essentially, as with any bilingual system, any translations are within the same jurisdiction, so that the reader will be familiar with the concepts expressed.

The MA at City, on the other hand, is aimed at translators who will translate between jurisdictions, so that the students are provided with information on both the legal systems with which they will have to deal.

4.1 Does a translator need to be a qualified lawyer?

As I have outlined above, it is my view that the legal translator certainly needs to have a comprehensive understanding of the legal systems of the languages with which he works. However, it is not necessary for the translator to have the same level of knowledge as a qualified lawyer, as the translator is not the one who needs to advise on the law. However, just as a qualified translator wishing to specialise on legal translation will need to ensure a solid grounding in law, so a qualified lawyer wishing to move into the area of translation will have to familiarise himself with the principles and practice of translation. The approach we have taken at City, is that we provide a comprehensive overview of the two legal systems our students need. While the course is quite clearly not a law course, there is a definite focus on law lectures, although for obvious reasons they do have a rather stronger focus on terminology and semantics that one would expect to find on a course aimed at aspiring lawyers.

Like other translation degrees, we do, of course, cover a certain amount of translation theory, and indeed parallel sessions focusing on translation theory are offered for those students who are qualified lawyers. However, apart from that, the focus is exclusively on legal translation, and students have lectures given by qualified lawyers in both their languages, as well as being taught in translation workshops by translators who specialise on legal translation. In this way, over the course of two years, we aim to provide our students with a solid foundation to enable them to understand the source text fully, and to translate it into appropriate language; using idiomatic language where appropriate, but also being aware of the dangers of using idiomatic language or similar concepts when they do not match completely.

One other point that is stressed is their role as translators (and this, perhaps, is more relevant to those of our students who are qualified lawyers). It is not the translator's role to correct or second-guess the source text. While a footnote might be included alerting the client to a potential error in the source text, even where the translator is absolutely sure that there is an error, he must not correct it (nor does he get paid for or is insured for providing legal advice).

It will of course help to know what the purpose of a translation is (Vermeer/ A Skopos Theory of Translation, 1996), and in legal translation I find that texts can roughly be divided into "originals in the source language", and "originals in the target language". An "original in the source language" is a text which is already in use, which may already be the subject of litigation, and which is translated for information purposes. Regardless of who the client is, there is clearly no leeway in translating this. Any error must be retained, any ambiguity translated with similar ambiguity, and any logical flaws recreated in the translation. If an entire dispute hinges on the fact of whether a certain term ought to be interpreted in one way or the other, then the translator cannot short-circuit that process by choosing a translation which allows only one interpretation.

Originals in the target language, on the other hand, allow for a little more flexibility. What I mean when I refer to "originals in the target language", is the translation of texts that are intended to become binding in the target language version in the future. A prime example would be templates of contracts, or indeed any contract, which is drafted in one language, but which is to be signed in another language. Once the translated version is signed, that then becomes the original document, while the source language text has no further relevance. In this case it will be possible for the translator to clarify certain matters with the client (depending on the client, of course), and to ensure that the meaning that was intended by the client is translated accurately. In a way, the translator here also takes on the role of a proof-reader, and in this case it is possible, and may even be desirable, to disambiguate and to remove errors.

This division between originals in the source language and originals in the target language is one of the aspects that gives legal translation its special position. While a translator would normally adapt a translation to its target audience and culture, a legal translation can only really do so, if it is intended to be an original in the target language. Even then, this might be problematic, as can be seen from the Gulf Oil case cited above. The challenge is that a translator must *"understand not only what the words mean and what a sentence means, but also what legal effect it is supposed to have, and how to achieve that legal effect in the other language"* (Shroth/ Legal

Translation, 1986). This means that the translator has to be sufficiently familiar with the legal concepts of both jurisdictions, to realise where the most idiomatic translation might give a misleading impression, and where it may be most appropriate to chose a different translation, one that sounds odd to the reader of the target language text, thus alerting him to the fact that the concept referred to may differ to that with which he is familiar in his jurisdiction.

While this also applies in the case of the translation of originals in the source language, it is here that the legal translator is most seriously fettered. Although Alcaraz & Hughes suggest that *"it seems good practice to avoid reproducing unwanted ambiguity wherever possible"*, this can lead to serious misunderstandings. Their example is: *"Harrelson contends now that the admission of this testimony was irreversible error because it had been hypnotically induced"*- Does the 'it' refer to the testimony or the admission? (Alcaraz & Hughes/ Legal Translation Explained 2002) The question arises whether it would be permissible for the translator to remove that ambiguity by taking a decision on the probable meaning of the sentence.

5   How to train legal translators

As can be seen, legal translation presents a variety of challenges. The MA at City University aims to provide its students with the tools to master these challenges, by providing them with an overview of the relevant legal systems, increasing their awareness of the specific potential difficulties in translations, and discussing to what extent the various translation theories are applicable to legal translation. In view of the different backgrounds of our students, the design of the course also poses certain difficulties. Although all students have to write the same assignments, those with a legal background will obviously have different requirements from those with a translation background. In both cases it will be necessary for the students to do a certain amount of unlearning. The lawyer needs to realise that he cannot give legal advice, while the translator will need to become accustomed to a far more restrictive type of translation than he may be used to. Parts of the course are effectively run in parallel, with the lawyers receiving more translation input, while the translators learn about the law. That said, in the joint sessions all the students benefit, since having such a varied group means that questions are asked that might not even have occurred to a more homogenous group, while the students also have the opportunity of benefiting from each other's experience.

6.   Conclusion

In view of the challenges posed by legal translation, is it necessary to be a trained lawyer in order to translate legal texts successfully? It is certainly necessary to have an understanding of the law, and the concepts raised therein. That said, it is even more important for the translator to know how to go about finding the most appropriate translation, that the translator is aware of the difficulties arising, and that one has the confidence to depart from the idiomatic where necessary. A legal translation need not be elegant, but it is absolutely crucial that it is accurate. Overinterpretation, or unwarranted improvement of a text (which is wonderfully expressed by the German term

"Verschlimmbesserung") is as dangerous as an incomplete understanding of the source text. Just because a text was written by a lawyer does not mean that it will be free from error, and translating a source text in a way that makes sense, but does not accurately reflect the source text can have significant consequences. Of course taking an MA alone is not going to turn a student into a perfect legal translator, only years of practice will achieve that. Nevertheless, it will provide the student with the tools to work towards this.

Bibliography

Alcaraz, Enrique; Hughes, Brian: *Legal Translation explained.* Manchester UK: St Jerome Publishing, 2002

de Beaugrande, R. (1978): *Factors in a Theory of Poetic Translating,* van Gorcum, Assen

Beaupré, Michael (1986)*: Interpreting Bilingual Legislation*, Toronto, Carswell

Pescatore, Pierre (1999): "Das Konzipieren übersetzungsgerechter juristischer Dokumente", G. R. de Groot and R. Schulze (ed.) *Recht und Übersetzen*, Nomos, Baden-Baden

Šarčević, Susan (2000), "Legal Translation and Translation Theory: A Receiver-oriented Approach", in Gémar, J.-Cl. (ed.) *La traduction juridique, Histoire, théorie(s) et pratique,* Université de Genève

Shroth, Peter (1986) Legal Translation *"American Journal of Comparative Law"*

Vermeer, Hans (1996): *A Skopos Theory of Translation*, Heidelberg, TEXTconTEXT

International Terminology Summer School: Eine arbeitsbegleitende Fachausbildung im Terminologiebereich ist möglich

Blanca Nájera

TermNet – Internationales Terminologienetz

termnet@termnet.org

1 Terminologie als Wirtschaftsfaktor auf dem Übersetzungsmarkt heute

Terminologie ist einer der Hauptschwerpunkte auf dem aktuellen Übersetzungsmarkt. Das Bewusstsein von Übersetzungsdienstleistern für Terminologiemanagement ist geweckt und hat im vergangenen Jahrzehnt an Bedeutung gewonnen. Wer an wichtige Kunden herankommen möchte, wer mehr Profit aus Daueraufträgen gewinnen möchte, wer einen Mehrwert für seine Kunden anbieten möchte, der weiß, dass Investitionen in Terminologieausbildung für Mitarbeiter, Übersetzer und Projektmanager innerhalb des Betriebes wichtig sind. Eine richtige Terminologieverwaltung innerhalb der Arbeitsprozesse hat eine neue Relevanz auf dem Übersetzungsmarkt gewonnen. Welche Optionen bietet der Markt und warum ist die International Terminology Summer School (kurz TSS) so erfolgreich? Der folgende Beitrag will diesen Fragen genauer nachgehen und ein Erfolgsmodell für eine berufsbegleitende Ausbildung näher vorstellen.

2 TSS und das Ausbildungsangebot

Der Ausbildungsmarkt im Bereich Terminologie bietet bereits verschiedene Möglichkeiten zur Aus- und Fortbildung. Die meisten davon sind in diversen Studiengängen der Universitäten oder Fachhochschulen verankert und benötigen von den Teilnehmern daher viel Zeit und vor allem Präsenz. Sie sind somit eher für Studenten, vor allem der Übersetzungswissenschaften, geeignet als für Berufstätige. Daneben gibt es die verschiedensten Seminare und Workshops, die von Herstellern von CAT-Tools mit und über ihre jeweils eigenen Produkte angeboten werden. Diese sind allerdings naturgemäß toolabhängig und relativ produktspezifisch gehalten. In den meisten Fällen ist bereits ein Hintergrundwissen über die Arbeit mit der entsprechenden Software erforderlich.

Das Konzept der International Terminology Summer School basiert auf dem Vermitteln von Grundlagen, Prinzipien und Methoden der Terminologie und des Terminologiemanagements. Dabei wird nicht speziell differenziert, in welchem Arbeits- oder Tätigkeitsbereich (Übersetzer, Projektmanager oder Terminologen) diese zum Einsatz kommt. Weiterhin ist der Kurs unabhängig davon, mit welcher Software gearbeitet wird. Die International Terminology Summer School ist ein fünftägiges Kompaktseminar, das jedem Teilnehmer mit verschiedensten Berufshintergründen die Möglichkeit bietet, sich fortbilden zu können.

2.1 TSS: Grundlagen für die Terminologiearbeit

Bereits vor über 25 Jahren begann das Internationale Informationszentrum für Terminologie (Infoterm), mit Hauptsitz in Wien, Kurse für Terminologen auszurichten und zu organisieren. Diese Kurse fanden zumeist in Wien, aber auch an anderen Orten statt. Die Zielgruppe damals unterschied sich noch stark von der heutigen. An erster Stelle nahmen Mitarbeiter öffentlicher Institutionen teil, die Terminologieplanung betrieben. Aber auch damals war schon ein stark internationaler Charakter erkennbar. Teilnehmer aus China, Malaysia, Südamerika und Afrika ließen sich von Infoterm zu Grundlagen der Terminologiearbeit ausbilden.

Über die Jahre erlebte der Kurs wechselhafte Zeiten. Sowohl inhaltlich als auch gemessen an Teilnehmerzahlen. Begonnen hatte alles als Grundlagenkurs. Später gab es einige Versuche, spezielle Gruppen mit den *Summer Schools* oder *Summer Academies* anzusprechen. So wurden zum Beispiel Ausbilderseminare für Terminologie und Lokalisierung entwickelt und durchgeführt. Solche Überlegungen, der Ausbildung verschiedene andere und spezialisiertere Ausrichtungen zu geben, führten nicht immer zu Erfolg und so versickerte das Interesse langsam.

Seit dem Jahr 2005 erlebt das Seminar jedoch wieder verstärkten Zulauf. Gründe dafür sind nicht zuletzt das „neue" Konzept und Management. Da sich immer wieder der große Bedarf an Grundlagenvermittlung und Austausch zeigte, wurde in jenem Jahr begonnen, sich auf diesen Bereich rückzubesinnen, um diesen Bedarf zu decken.

Behandelt werden unter anderem folgende Themen:

- Terminology theory: models, objects, concepts, terms
- Introduction to terminology work
- Applied principles of terminology work
- Retrieving and validating relevant online information for terminology work
- Data categories and modelling principles for terminology management
- Terminology management systems
- Creating a database for terminology work
- From terminologies to ontologies
- Project management workshop
- Terminology and technical documentation
- Economic issues of terminology management
- Terminology and software localization
- Copyright issues for terminology management

Sowohl inhaltlich als auch didaktisch entwickelt sich die International Terminology Summer School stetig weiter, um sich dem gegenwärtigen Stand der Technik und der Wissenschaft, sowie den Bedürfnissen der Teilnehmer anzupassen. Neue Anwendungsbereiche, wie Lokalisierung oder semantische Interoperabilität, sind zu den „traditionellen" Themen, wie Normung und Übersetzen, hinzugekommen.

Die verschiedenen Lerneinheiten werden von einigen der renommiertesten Experten im Bereich Terminologie abgehalten, darunter Prof. Dr. Klaus-Dirk Schmitz, Prof. Dr. Gerhard Budin, Prof. Dr. Sue Ellen Wright, Dr. Heribert Picht, Prof. Dr. Frieda Steurs und Dr. Gabriele Sauberer[20]. Alle Trainer sind international aktiv tätig in verschiedenen Netzwerken, Projekten und Initiativen im Bereich Terminologie. Dadurch bereichern sie die TSS jedes Jahr mit neuen Einflüssen. Diese weitgehende Vernetzung sorgt nicht nur für Aktualität. Sie bewirkt außerdem eine breite und interdisziplinäre Ausrichtung. Die Bedeutung von Kooperation und Vernetzung ist auch eines der grundlegenden Ziele, die den Teilnehmern des Kurses vermittelt werden sollen. Gleichzeitig bietet der Kurs die Möglichkeit, solche Netzwerke zu gestalten oder bestehenden beizutreten.

2.2 Teilnehmerspektrum

Was die TSS zu etwas Besonderem macht, ist nicht nur ihre Kompaktheit, das Programm oder ihre Experten, sondern die Teilnehmer selbst: Übersetzer, Wissenschaftler, Praktiker, studentischer Nachwuchs, Inhaber von Übersetzungsbüros und Universitätslehrer aus aller Welt.

Das wachsende Interesse lässt sich anhand der Teilnehmerzahlen belegen:

Während es 2006 noch 50 Teilnehmer waren, stieg die Zahl im Jahr darauf bereits auf 60 und 2008 sogar auf 77. Im Jahr 2009, dem Jahr der weltweiten Wirtschaftskrise, sank die Teilnehmerzahl ebenfalls nicht wesentlich und blieb mit etwa 60 Teilnehmern nahezu konstant. Wenige Änderungen gab es hinsichtlich der Herkunftsländer der Teilnehmer. Die Mehrzahl stammt aus europäischen Ländern, doch sind beinahe alle anderen Kontinente unterschiedlich stark vertreten. Die Zusammensetzung schwankt dabei von Jahr zu Jahr. Die nachfolgende Abbildung spiegelt die Internationalität sehr gut wieder.

Hinsichtlich des professionellen Hintergrundes gab es während der letzten 5 Jahre eine balancierende Entwicklung. Im Jahr 2005 noch bestand der überwiegende Teil aus Studenten und Akademikern, daneben war vor allem der Übersetzungsmarkt vertreten, sowohl mit freien als auch firmeninternen Mitarbeitern. Über die Jahre hinweg hat sich der Anteil an Studenten verringert, während sich gleichzeitig der Anteil an Terminologen und anderer Sprachdienstleister aus Wirtschaft, Freiberuflichkeit und öffentlichen Institutionen erhöht hat. Heute hat sich das Verhältnis der Teilnehmer weitgehend eingependelt. Sie gehören im Großen und Ganzen 3 verschiedenen Sektoren an: Universitäten, Vertreter regionaler, nationaler und internationaler Organisationen, und kommerziellen Firmen. Letztere sind sowohl direkt dem Sprachdienstleistungsmarkt zuzuordnen als auch großen, global agierenden Privatfirmen mit Übersetzungsabteilungen.

---

[20] Information über die TSS Ausbilder: www.termnet.org/english/events/tss_2009/instructors.php

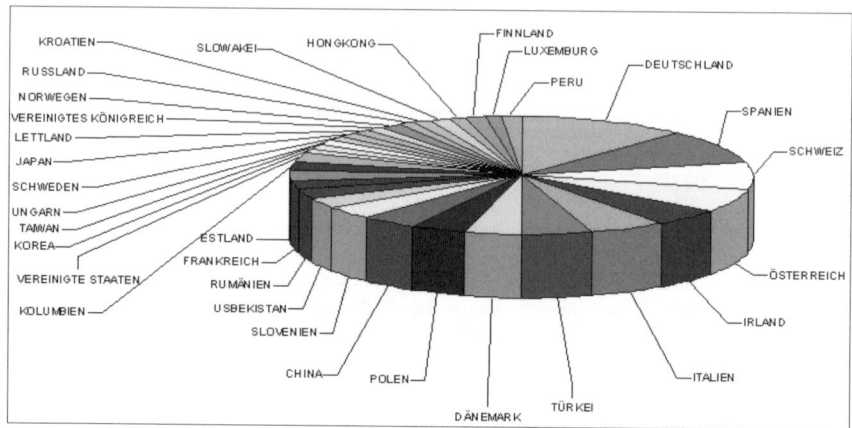

Abb. 1: Herkunftsländer der International Terminology Summer School 2008 Teilnehmer

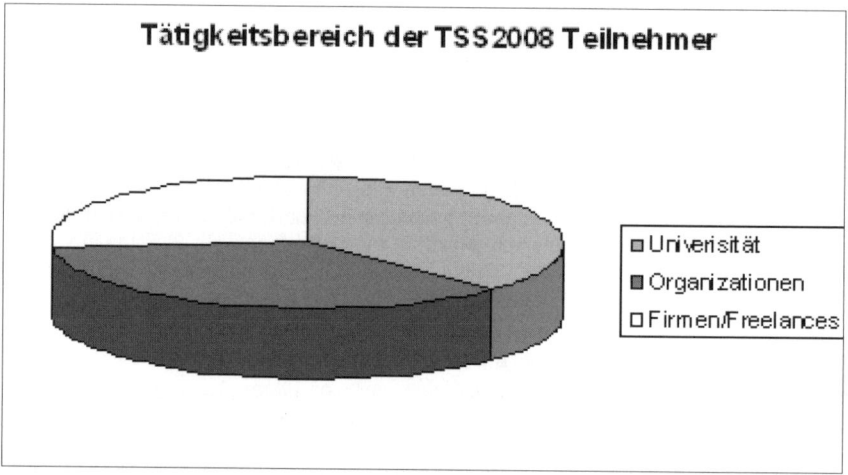

Abb. 2: Tätigkeitsbereich der TSS2008-Teilnehmer

Das Problem der Heterogenität der Gruppe besteht seit Anbeginn und nach wie vor, hat sich aber insofern gemäßigt, als dass die Teilnehmer zwar über unterschiedliches, aber dennoch vergleichbares Praxiswissen verfügen. Homogene Gruppen sind beinahe unmöglich, vor allem im internationalen Sektor. Vielfach wird eine gewisse Heterogenität auch von den Teilnehmern als Bereicherung empfunden, solange man sie bei der Gestaltung des Kurses berücksichtigt und in das didaktische Konzept integriert.

Die Ausbildung von Übersetzern und Terminologen ist sowohl inhaltlich als auch formell im weltweiten Vergleich unterschiedlich. Terminologiemanagement ist, auch dank der Bemühungen des BDÜ in dieser Hinsicht, an deutschsprachigen Universitäten heute Bestandteil fast jeder Übersetzerausbildung. Die Situation in anderen Teilen der Welt ist dagegen oft vollkommen anders. Nicht überall gibt es separate Übersetzerausbildungen, von Terminologie ganz zu schweigen. Weiterhin hat nicht jeder, der als Terminologe in einer Organisation beschäftigt ist, einen Übersetzerhintergrund.

Aus dieser Situation ergab sich eine Lücke an Qualifizierungsmöglichkeiten, die von der TSS erfolgreich gefüllt wird.

Anhand der Teilnehmerbefragung von 2008 lässt sich feststellen, dass nur 18% zuvor schon einmal an einem Kurs oder Seminar dieser Art teilgenommen haben.

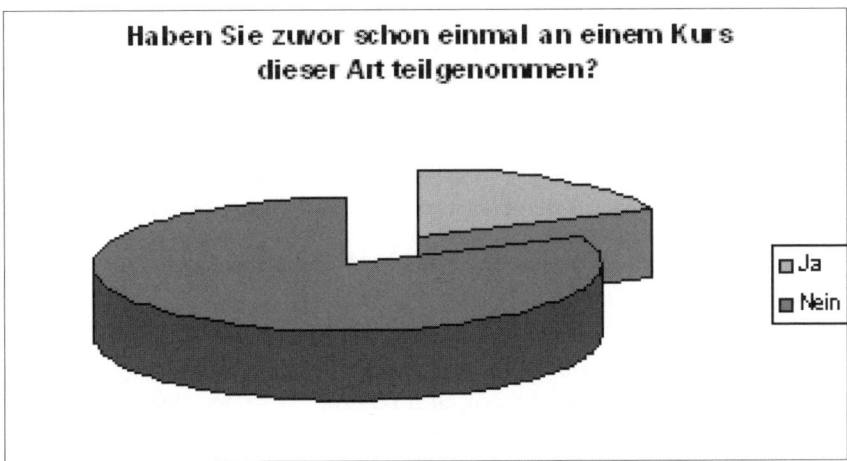

Abb. 3: Teilnahme an Kursen/Seminaren dieser Art

Dies ist besonders relevant, um zu erkennen, welche Bedürfnisse auf dem Markt herrschen und was für eine besondere Rolle die TSS mit ihrem Angebot spielt.

Ebenso wurde die Frage nach der Motivation für die Teilnahme an der TSS 2008 gestellt. Die am häufigsten genannten Gründe sind: a) Grundkenntnisse über Terminologie zu verbessern, b) den Wissensstand zu aktualisieren, c) mehr über die Tendenzen auf dem Markt zu erfahren und Kontakte zu Berufskollegen zu knüpfen.

2.3 Was die TSS darüber hinaus noch bietet?

Das Programm der TSS entspricht nicht nur einer klassischen Ausbildung in Terminologie, sondern bietet auch die Gelegenheit für die Teilnehmer, sich auszutauschen über ihre Erfahrungen mit Terminologie in Debatten und Diskussionen, in denen man einzelne Schwerpunkte vertiefen und konkreten Fragen nachgehen kann. Der Kontakt mit anderen Kollegen ermöglicht, dass das Selbstbewusstsein von Übersetzern und Terminologen gestärkt wird. Noch viel zu wenige Übersetzer und Terminologen haben gelernt, bei ihrer Arbeit „über den Tellerrand zu blicken". Die Erkenntnis, dass ihre Kollegen ähnliche oder sogar gleiche Probleme bei ihrer täglichen Arbeit haben, kommt für viele Teilnehmer überraschend und wird als inspirierend und motivierend empfunden. Durch diese Erfahrung des Austausches lassen sich schneller und leichter gemeinsame Lösungen finden, Tipps und Tricks werden weitergegeben.

Interaktion, Kommunikation, Zusammenarbeit und Kooperation spielen eine besonders große Rolle innerhalb der TSS und werden bewusst gefördert.

Für Studenten ist eine Teilnahme auch wegen der Möglichkeit, ECTS[21] für ihr Studium zu sammeln und sich damit die Teilnahme anrechnen zu lassen, besonders attraktiv. Dies wird durch die Kooperation mit europäischen Universitäten mit renommierten Übersetzer- und Terminologiecurricula erreicht.

2.4 Was bringt die Zukunft der TSS?

Wie oben bereits erwähnt entwickelt sich die TSS jedes Jahr gemeinsam mit ihren Teilnehmern weiter. Sie ist kein starres System und ist bemüht um eine Balance zwischen bewährten Methoden und Neuerungen. Es scheint jetzt an der Zeit zu sein, TSS einen weiteren Schritt nach vorne gehen zu lassen.

TermNet, das Internationale Terminologienetz – Mitorganisator der TSS, entwickelt derzeit im Rahmen des Projekts EUCERT[22] Schlüsselqualifikation und Querschnittskompetenzen für das Berufsprofil von Terminologiemanagern[23]. Gleichzeitig entsteht derzeit an der Fachhochschule Köln im Rahmen eines Pilotprojekts ein E-Learning-Kurs zum Terminologiemanagement, ELCAT[24] *Innovatives E-Learning: Contentaufbereitung von Terminologie-Lernmodulen für die Automobilindustrie* (Juli 2008 bis Dezember 2010; ein Projekt der Fachhochschule Köln, Leiter des Projekts ist Prof. Dr. Klaus-Dirk Schmitz), bei dem auch TermNet als Partner mitarbeitet.

Bei diesem Projekt entsteht eine E-Learning-Plattform unter Anwendung digitaler, auf Internettechnologie basierender Medien. Sie soll „Nichtspezialisten", wie Ingenieuren, Marketingexperten oder Juristen eine Einführung in die Prinzipien und Methoden der Terminologielehre und Terminologiearbeit geben, um Arbeitsprozesse effizienter und besser nach terminologischen Prinzipien auszurichten.

Durch diese enge Kooperation aus Universitäten und Organisationen wird sich auch das Konzept der International Terminology Summer School weiter entwickeln, hin zu einem noch größeren Mehrwert für die Teilnehmer, die sich in Zukunft neben der regulären Teilnahme auch im Rahmen eines Zertifizierungsprogrammes zum EU-weit anerkannten Terminologiemanager qualifizieren können.

---

[21] Information über die European Credits (ECTS) bei Teilnahme an der TSS:
www.termnet.org/english/events/tss_2009/students.php

[22] Informationen zu EUCERT: www.eu-certificates.org/

[23] Certified Terminology Manager Beschreibung: www.iscn.com/projects/eu_cert/index.php?id=52

[24] Näheres über ELCAT unter: www.f03.fh-koeln.de/fakultaet/iim/forschungsprojekte/aktuelle/

3   Über TermNet und die International Terminology Summer School

TermNet, das Internationale Terminologienetz, ist ein internationales Kooperationsforum für Firmen, Universitäten, Institutionen und Verbände, die sich für die Weiterentwicklung des weltweiten Terminologiemarktes einsetzen. Die Produkte und Dienstleistungen dieses Marktes betrachtet und bewirbt TermNet als integrale, qualitätssichernde Bestandteile jedes Produkts und jeder Dienstleistung in den Bereichen a) Information & Kommunikation, b) Klassifikation & Kategorisierung, sowie c) Übersetzen & Lokalisieren.

Die International Terminology Summer School wird von TermNet in Zusammenarbeit mit verschiedenen europäischen Universitäten seit dem Jahr 2005 erfolgreich durchgeführt.

TSS ist ein generalistischer Grundlagenkurs zum Terminologiemanagement, der als solcher Vor- und Nachteile besitzt, welche in diesem Beitrag erläutert wurden. Doch bestehen auch Bedürfnisse für lokal und thematisch stärker spezialisierte Terminologieausbildung. Für und gemeinsam mit diesen Zielgruppen konzipiert TermNet maßgeschneiderte Ausbildungen vom In-House-Seminar bis zum multimodalen Aufbaukurs.

Weitere Informationen können sie dieser Website entnehmen:

www.termnet.org/english/events/tss_2009

www.termnet.org/

VII. Neue Anforderungen an die Berufsverbände

Europäische Fragen

CIUTI und EMT – Qualitätssiegel für die Ü/D-Ausbildung

Prof. Dr. Peter A. Schmitt

Universität Leipzig, BDÜ-Bundesreferent Übersetzungswissenschaft, CIUTI-Vizepräsident, Mitglied der EMT-Expertengruppe

pas@paschmitt.eu

1 Einkommen, Ansehen, Kompetenz, Qualität der Ausbildung – alles hängt mit allem zusammen

Das Ansehen und Einkommen eines Berufsstandes korreliert bekanntlich auch mit der Kompetenz seiner Akteure und der von ihnen gelieferten Produkt- und Dienstleistungsqualität. Eine zentrale Rolle spielt dabei die Qualität der Ausbildung. Diese wiederum wird von zahlreichen Faktoren beeinflusst, wozu neben den Studieninhalten unter anderem auch die materielle und personelle Infrastruktur gehören. Letztere hängt auch von der Verfügbarkeit kompetenter Lehrer ab. Die Ü/D-Ausbildungsstätten haben daher sowohl die Aufgabe, berufsqualifizierte Absolventen hervorzubringen, als auch für geeigneten Ausbildernachwuchs zu sorgen. Kontrovers diskutierte Aspekte sind dabei das von Absolventen und Ausbildern zu erwartende Kompetenzspektrum angesichts eines sehr heterogenen Marktes, die Rolle der Übersetzungstheorie bzw. Translatologie in diesem Kontext, aber auch der Einfluss der Europäischen Hochschulreform („Bologna-Prozess") mit den daraus resultierenden neuen Bachelor- und Masterstudiengängen. Es gibt unterschiedliche Ansätze, wie auf internationaler Ebene (unter Berücksichtigung heterogener nationaler Rahmenbedingungen) eine hohe Ausbildungsqualität stimuliert werden kann; die drei wichtigsten (aus eurozentrischer Perspektive) und aktuellsten sind die Europäische Hochschulreform, das EMT-Netzwerk der Generaldirektion Übersetzen der Europäischen Kommission und die CIUTI.

2 Die Europäische Hochschulreform

Die Europäische Hochschulreform, besser bekannt unter dem Schlagwort „Bologna-Prozess", steht nicht im Titel und Zentrum dieses Beitrags, denn darüber ist schon viel geschrieben wurden – vor allem in letzter Zeit, weil die Reform ja bestimmungsgemäß bis zum Jahr 2010 umgesetzt werden musste und man daher inzwischen erste

Erfahrungen mit dem neuen Bachelor- und Mastersystem gesammelt hat. Diese Erfahrungen sind offenbar überwiegend negativ, wenn man den Tenor dessen nimmt, was man in den Medien liest und hört. Aber auch an den Hochschulen selbst hört man von Lehrenden und Studierenden oft nur vernichtende Kommentare: Das zentrale Schlag- und Schimpfwort ist „Verschulung"; geklagt wird auch über zu hohen Leistungsdruck, zu hohen Prüfungsaufwand, starre Module, unflexible Studienabläufe, mangelnde Möglichkeit, im Ausland zu studieren, letztlich geringere Mobilität, und die fehlende Garantie auf einen Studienplatz im Masterstudium.

Vor dem Hintergrund dieser aktuellen und oft ebenso heftig wie unsachlich geäußerten Kritik ist es angebracht, kurz die Ziele der Hochschulreform in Erinnerung zu rufen, die von den Europäischen Bildungsministern in ihrer gemeinsamen Erklärung am 19. Juni 1999 in Bologna formuliert wurden. Ein zentraler Punkt ist die Mobilität; zwei der Ziele nennen konkret die Qualitätssteigerung der Ausbildung bzw. der Hochschulabsolventen (www.bmbf.de/pub/bologna_deu.pdf; meine Hervorhebung)[25]:

* Einführung eines Systems leicht verständlicher und vergleichbarer Abschlüsse, auch durch die Einführung des Diplomzusatzes (Diploma Supplement) mit dem Ziel, die arbeitsmarktrelevanten Qualifikationen der europäischen Bürger ebenso wie die internationale Wettbewerbsfähigkeit des europäischen Hochschulsystems zu fördern.

* Einführung eines Systems, das sich im Wesentlichen auf zwei Hauptzyklen stützt: einen Zyklus bis zum ersten Abschluss (undergraduate) und einen Zyklus nach dem ersten Abschluss (graduate). Regelvoraussetzung für die Zulassung zum zweiten Zyklus ist der erfolgreiche Abschluss des ersten Studienzyklus, der mindestens drei Jahre dauert. Der nach dem ersten Zyklus erworbene Abschluss attestiert eine für den europäischen Arbeitsmarkt relevante Qualifikationsebene. Der zweite Zyklus sollte, wie in vielen europäischen Ländern, mit dem Master und/oder der Promotion abschließen.

* Einführung eines Leistungspunktesystems – ähnlich dem ECTS – als geeignetes Mittel der Förderung größtmöglicher Mobilität der Studierenden. Punkte sollten auch außerhalb der Hochschulen, beispielsweise durch lebenslanges Lernen, erworben werden können, vorausgesetzt, sie werden durch die jeweiligen aufnehmenden Hochschulen anerkannt.

* Förderung der Mobilität durch Überwindung der Hindernisse, die der Freizügigkeit in der Praxis im Wege stehen, insbesondere – für Studierende: Zugang zu Studien- und Ausbildungsangeboten und zu entsprechenden Dienstleistungen – für Lehrer, Wissenschaftler und Verwaltungspersonal: Anerkennung und Anrechnung von Auslandsaufenthalten zu Forschungs-, Lehr- oder Ausbildungszwecken, unbeschadet der gesetzlichen Rechte dieser Personengruppen.

* Förderung der europäischen Zusammenarbeit bei der Qualitätssicherung im Hinblick auf die Erarbeitung vergleichbarer Kriterien und Methoden.

---

[25] Siehe auch http://ec.europa.eu/education/policies/educ/bologna/bologna.pdf und die Kommentare im Abschnitt „The Bologna Declaration: an explanation".

• Förderung der erforderlichen europäischen Dimensionen im Hochschulbe-
reich, insbesondere in Bezug auf Curriculum-Entwicklung, Zusammenarbeit
zwischen Hochschulen, Mobilitätsprojekte und integrierte Studien-, Ausbil-
dungs- und Forschungsprogramme.

Wenn es heute Bachelor- und Masterstudiengänge gibt, die diese Ziele nicht oder
schlechter erfüllen als die vorhergehenden Studiengänge, dann liegt das (sofern die
Infra- oder Personalstruktur nicht verschlechtert wurde, was allerdings leider oft der
Fall ist) nicht an „Bologna", sondern am Studiengangdesign. In den sechs Jahren
meiner zwei Amtszeiten als Studiendekan an der Universität Leipzig (in diese Zeit fiel
die Planung und Einführung der neuen Studiengänge) sowie als Gutachter in Akkredi-
tierungsverfahren zeigte sich immer wieder, dass Institute die Ziele der Reform
torpedieren, indem sie in den neuen Studiengängen, vor allem, ein mobilitätsschädli-
ches „Modul"-Konzept verwenden.

Der Grundgedanke der Modularität ist der Bausteincharakter der Module, also ihre
Austauschbarkeit. Was primär nichts mit Beliebigkeit der Inhalte oder deren Reihenfolge zu tun hat, sondern schlicht damit, dass es möglich sein soll, gewisse zusammenhängende Teile des Lehrangebots „en bloc" auszuwählen oder durch andere
(passende) Blöcke (Bausteine, Module) zu ersetzen. Zum Beispiel durch passende
Lehrangebote in einem anderen Studiengang, an einem anderen Institut, an einer
anderen Fakultät, oder gar an einer anderen Hochschule in einem anderen Land.
Wenn man freilich „Module" implementiert, die sich über mehr als ein Semester
erstrecken (es gibt Fälle, wo viersemestrige „Module" eingerichtet wurden, oder
„Module", die mit Unterbrechungen in diversen Semestern stattfinden sollten), dann
funktioniert die Austauschbarkeit nicht – und man muss sich über mangelnde Mobilität nicht wundern.

Es war auch nicht Sinn der Sache, bestehende Studiengänge und ihre alte Struktur
einfach umzuetikettieren. Manche Institute konnten in der Tat nicht „der Versuchung
[…] widerstehen", ihre alten Studiengänge „lediglich durch geschickte Umbenennung
Bologna-fähig zu machen" (Forstner 2007: 124). Die Hochschulreform war, im
Gegenteil, eine vielleicht für lange Zeit einmalige Chance, bestehende Studiengänge
gründlich, d.h. wirklich von Grund auf, zu entrümpeln, zu renovieren (vgl. Schmitt
2007). Und, quasi *en passant*, in den Studiengängen ein Qualitätssicherungssystem
einzuführen, das diesen Namen verdient. Wenn man heute gefordert ist, für jedes
Modul und die darin gebündelten Lehrveranstaltungen Lernziele zu formulieren,
wenn man nun spezifizieren muss, mit welchen Lehrinhalten man gedenkt, diese Ziele
zu erreichen und wie man das Erreichen der Lernziele am Ende des Moduls prüft,
dann bedeutet das für manche Lehrende an den Hochschulen ein Umdenken, und für
Viele mehr Vorbereitungs- und Prüfungsaufwand. Ein klares und auch für die Studierenden transparentes didaktisches Konzept zu haben[26] ist aber nicht die Apokalypse
der akademischen Lehrfreiheit.

Richtig verstanden und richtig umgesetzt liefert die Europäische Hochschulreform
den Anlass und die Grundlage dafür, endlich alle Forderungen an die Ausbildung von

---

[26] Dieses Konzept sollte den Studierenden jederzeit zugänglich sein, z.B. auf der Website des Instituts; das ist
übrigens eines der vielen Prüfkriterien für das EMT-Netzwerk.

Übersetzern und Dolmetschern zu erfüllen, die schon anno 1986 im BDÜ-*Memorandum* genannt wurden. Das Memorandum wurde bekanntlich vom „Koordinierungsausschuss Praxis und Lehre" verfasst, einem vom BDÜ initiierten Vorläufer des heutigen Transforum (siehe dazu www.transforum.de), und an diesem Memorandum waren daher Vertreter aller deutschen Ü/D-Institute und Repräsentanten der Ü/D-Praxis beteiligt.

Hans J. Vermeer beispielsweise hat in den KA-Sitzungen schon damals immer wieder betont, dass eine translatorische Ausbildung keine „Sprachausbildung" ist und gefordert, dass eine hohe Kompetenz in den gewählten Arbeitssprachen bereits bei Studienbeginn gegeben sein müsse: Ü/D-Institute sind keine „Sprachschulen". Diese Forderung galt damals als utopisch und wurde als unrealistisch abgetan. Fast überall konnte man bis vor kurzem noch die „Nichtschulsprachen" an den Ü/D-Instituten ohne Vorkenntnisse erwerben; aber Sprachkurse auf dem Niveau von „me Tarzan, you Jane" haben ebenso wenig mit Universität zu tun wie die Schreibmaschinenkurse der 50er bis 70er Jahre im letzten Jahrhundert. Dieses „Sprachschul"-Image haftet manchen Instituten bis heute an und ist auch dem Berufsbild der Dolmetscher und Übersetzer nicht förderlich.

Im Zuge der Hochschulreform, vielleicht sogar ausgelöst durch den Bologna-Prozess, wurde vielerorts Schluss damit gemacht: Am IALT in Leipzig beispielsweise ist seit Inkrafttreten der Bachelor- und Masterstudiengänge als Zugangsvoraussetzung ein Sprachkompetenzniveau[27] von B1 nachzuweisen (für Englisch sogar B2). Zusätzlich gibt es eine obligatorische Eignungsfeststellungsprüfung (in deren Deutschteil fallen erfahrungsgemäß 60 % der Bewerber mit Muttersprache Deutsch durch)[28]. Der Wegfall elementarer Sprachkurse schafft den nötigen Freiraum für zeitgemäßere Lehrinhalte und die Vermittlung aktuell nötiger Kompetenzen.

Zu Zeiten des Memorandums waren die Wörter *Translation* und *Translationswissenschaft* sogar im akademischen Umfeld noch ziemlich extravagant und gingen nur wenigen Wissenschaftlern locker über die Lippen[29]. Die europäische Hochschulreform und die damit einhergehende Pflicht zur Akkreditierung der neuen Studiengänge hat auch in dieser Hinsicht einen Stimulus geliefert. Inzwischen führen die meisten Ü/D-Institute im deutschsprachigen Raum ein „T" wie „Translation" „im Schilde"; seit Juli 2009 heißt auch der Fachbereich 06 in Germersheim „Translations-, Sprach- und Kulturwissenschaft" (FTSK)[30]. Auch dies setzt ein Zeichen – für das wachsende Selbstbewusstsein unserer Disziplin.

---

[27] Nach dem Europäischen Referenzrahmen; eine Übersicht der Kompetenzstufen s. z.B. http://de.wikipedia.org/wiki/Gemeinsamer_Europäischer_Referenzrahmen

[28] Und dies, obwohl es in der Regel genügt, im Test nur 55 % der maximal erreichbaren Punkte zu erzielen. Siehe dazu auch Schmitt 2009.

[29] Im gleichen Rahmen wurde von Justa Holz-Mänttäri das etwas sperrige *Botschaftsträgerverbund* (statt *Text*) propagiert – das hat sich seither jedoch nicht durchgesetzt.

[30] Die Entwicklung der Disziplin zeigt sich in Namen: Zunächst „Auslands- und Dolmetscherinstitut" (ADI), dann „Fachbereich angewandte Sprachwissenschaft" (FAS), danach „Fachbereich angewandte Sprach- und Kulturwissenschaft" (FASK).

3 Das EMT-Netzwerk

Ein weiterer Ansatz, auf europäischer Ebene eine hohe Qualifikation von Übersetzern zu fördern, ist das EMT-Projekt der Generaldirektion Übersetzen (DGT) der Europäischen Kommission in Brüssel. Ausführliche Informationen hierzu liefert die Website der DGT[31]; hier nur einige zentrale Punkte.

„EMT" steht für „European Master in Translation". Das Projekt betrifft also Übersetzer, nicht Dolmetscher (dafür gibt es seit 1997 ein anders konzipiertes Projekt der Generaldirektion Dolmetschen, den European Master in Conference Interpreting, EMCI, auf den ich hier nicht eingehe)[32]. Beim EMT handelt es sich auch nicht, wie gelegentlich angenommen wird, um einen eigenen Masterstudiengang oder Masterabschluss der EU (die EU-Kommission hat nicht das Recht, akademische Grade zu vergeben). „EMT" ist ein Gütesiegel, repräsentiert durch ein geschütztes Logo, mit dem Studiengänge ausgezeichnet werden können, die bestimmte Qualitätskriterien erfüllen. Hochschulen mit einem Masterstudiengang mit EMT-Gütesiegel bilden das sogenannte EMT-Netzwerk. Dessen Ziel ist es nicht, sich „elitär" gegen andere Studiengänge abzuschotten. Im Gegenteil, das EMT-Netzwerk ist ein offenes System; dessen Mitglieder sollen als exemplarische Modellfälle für „best practice" im Bereich der Übersetzerausbildung auf Masterniveau dienen. Im Idealfall sollten also letztlich sämtliche Master-Übersetzerstudiengänge in Europa dieses Qualitätsniveau erreichen.

Nicht trivial war (und ist) die Frage, wie man die Qualität eines Studiengangs beurteilt, auch wenn solche Beurteilungen für sogenannte Hochschulrankings[33] seit Jahrzehnten international gang und gäbe sind. Hochschulen, die in Rankings gut platziert sind, haben natürlich keinen Anlass, die Aussagekraft solcher Qualitätsurteile öffentlich in Frage zu stellen. Gleichwohl mehren sich Stimmen, die die Methodik der Datenerhebung und die Validität der Bewertungen kritisieren, und laut einem Bericht in der *Welt Online*[34] ist auch die Elite-Universität Harvard nicht mehr bereit, Daten für diese Rankings zur Verfügung zu stellen. Ein binäres Qualitätsbeurteilungssystem, das nur eine JA/NEIN-Entscheidung (über die Zulassung zum EMT-Netzwerk) zulässt, ist also inhärent etwas heikel.

Außerdem sind, selbst bei Eingrenzung auf die Europäische Union, und sogar nach Abschluss der Europäischen Hochschulreform, die jeweils nationalen Verhältnisse so verschieden, dass es unmöglich ist, einen einheitlichen Studiengang vorzuschreiben, der für sich in Anspruch nehmen könnte, die gewünschte Ausbildungsqualität an jedem Ort in Europa sicherzustellen. Selbst der Begriff „Masterstudiengang", um nur ein Beispiel zu nennen, ist unscharf, denn in Europa gibt es unterschiedliche Kombinationen von Bachelor- und Masterstudiengängen, und die Masterstudiengänge können sich über ein bis zwei Jahre erstrecken.

---

[31] http://ec.europa.eu/dgs/translation/external_relations/universities/emt_network_join_de.htm

[32] Näheres dazu auf www.emcinterpreting.org

[33] In Deutschland am bekanntesten ist das CHE-Ranking, das von der Bertelsmann-Stiftung initiiert wurde und von der deutschen Hochschulrektorenkonferenz (HRK) unterstützt wird; Näheres siehe www.che-ranking.de

[34] Vom 5. Juli 2009; siehe http://www.welt.de/wams_print/article4060480/Uni-Kiel-steigt-aus-dem-Hochschulranking-aus.html

Vor diesem heterogenen Hintergrund beauftragte die DGT eine *ad personam* benannte achtköpfige „Expertengruppe"[35] damit, geeignete Qualitätskriterien auszuarbeiten. Das Ergebnis ist ein Katalog von Kompetenzen, über die die Absolventen eines solchen Masterstudiengangs verfügen sollen. Auf welchem Weg durch den Studiengang sie diese Kompetenzen erworben haben, ist unerheblich. Das deckt gegebenenfalls die Option ab, diesen Masterstudiengang an einen translatorischen Bachelorstudiengang (am selben oder einem anderen Institut) anzuschließen, oder (sofern die betreffende Studienordnung das zulässt) auf einen andersartigen (nichttranslatorischen, nichtphilologischen) Bachelorstudiengang aufzusetzen (z.B. auf einen Bachelor of Science in Mechanical Engineering[36]).

Gerade letzterer Fall macht deutlich, dass dies einige konzeptionelle Überlegungen aufwirft, wenn man sicherstellen will, dass am Ende sowohl die translatologisch-theoretischen als auch die translatorisch-praktischen Kompetenzen erworben wurden. Mit einem starren Studiengangdesign ist dies kaum realisierbar; umgekehrt macht ein von diversen Wahlmöglichkeiten geprägtes Studiengangkonzept wie zum Beispiel das am IALT eine Quantifizierung und „Messung" von Studieninhalten schwieriger – es kommt eben darauf an, welche Optionen im Einzelfall gewählt werden und mit welchen Vorkenntnissen jemand in diesen Studiengang eintritt.

Unstrittig ist, dass es ausgeschlossen ist, jemanden in einem einjährigen Masterstudiengang ohne vorheriges translatologisches Fundament zu einem Fachübersetzer zu machen, der über die heute verlangten Kompetenzen verfügt. Sofern man nicht „geradlinig" zunächst einen translatorischen Bachelorstudiengang absolviert und danach am selben Institut einen translatorischen Master aufsetzt (z.B. zum Konferenzdolmetschen oder Fachübersetzen), wird man nicht umhin können, vor Eintritt in den Masterstudiengang eine Eignungsfeststellungsprüfung zu absolvieren.

Das EMT-Kompetenzraster[37] umfasst 48 Kompetenzen, gruppiert in die Kategorien „Dienstleistungskompetenz", „Sprachenkompetenz", „interkulturelle Kompetenz", „Recherchekompetenz", „Fachkompetenz" und „Kompetenz im Umgang mit technischen Hilfsmitteln". Im Einzelnen wird beispielsweise Folgendes erwartet:

- Imstande sein, sich den Markterfordernissen und den Beschäftigungsprofilen anzupassen (die Nachfrageentwicklung zu verfolgen)

- Kontakte zu seinen Kunden bzw. potenziellen Auftraggebern knüpfen und pflegen können (Marketing)

---

[35] Die Mitglieder der Expertengruppe kommen aus verschiedenen EU-Staaten und haben, aufgrund diverser Funktionen, einen guten Überblick sowohl über die Ausbildungssituation als auch über den Arbeitsmarkt für Übersetzer. Näheres dazu unter: http://ec.europa.eu/dgs/translation/external_relations/universities/emt_dgt_emt_expert_group_de.htm

[36] Dass diese in der Reform ausdrücklich vorgesehene Option oft ignoriert wird, erkennt man auch daran, dass oft von „BA/MA" gesprochen und geschrieben wird, wenn eigentlich Bachelor/Master gemeint sein sollte, man aber nur den Bachelor bzw. Master of Arts (B.A. bzw. M.A.) und nicht auch den B.Sc. bzw. M.Sc. im Blick hat.

[37] Herunterladbar unter: http://ec.europa.eu/dgs/translation/external_relations/universities/emt_network_join_de.htm

- Mit Auftraggebern verhandeln können (um Termine, Honorare/Fakturierung, Arbeitsbedingungen, Zugang zu Informationen, Vertragsbedingungen, Rechte und Pflichten, Anforderungen an die Übersetzung, Aufgaben usw. festzulegen)

- Seine Zeit, seine Kräfte, seine Arbeit, seine finanziellen Möglichkeiten einteilen und seine Weiterbildung (um die verschiedenen Kompetenzen aufzufrischen) organisieren können

- Sein Leistungsangebot und seine Vorzüge benennen und beziffern können

- In der Lage sein, Anweisungen, Termine, Verpflichtungen, Umgangsformen, Teamzwänge einzuhalten bzw. zu wahren

- Die Normen und Standards für die Erbringung von Übersetzungsdienstleistungen kennen

- Imstande sein, unter Zeitdruck und auch in einem mehrsprachigen Umfeld mit anderen Fachleuten oder einem Projektleiter zusammenzuarbeiten (Kontaktfähigkeit, Fähigkeit zur Zusammen- und zur Mitarbeit)

- In der Lage sein, eine Übersetzung anzufertigen und anzubieten, die dem Bedarf des Kunden, d. h. dem Zweck (Skopos) und dem Kontext der Übersetzung gerecht wird

- Die einschlägige Metasprache beherrschen (um seine Arbeit, seine Vorgehensweise, seine Entscheidungen zu beschreiben)

- Eine Übersetzung gegenlesen und überprüfen (revidieren) können (Verfahren und Strategien des Gegenlesens und Revidierens beherrschen)

- In der Lage sein, (in den A- und B-Sprachen) schnell und gut zu redigieren, umzuformulieren, umzustrukturieren, zu verdichten und nachzubearbeiten

- In der Lage sein, mehrere Korrektur-, Übersetzungs-, Terminografie-, DTP- und Dokumentensuchprogramme effizient, schnell und parallel zu nutzen (zum Beispiel Textverarbeitung, Rechtschreib- und Grammatikprüfung, Internet, Übersetzungsspeicher, Terminologiedatenbank, Spracherkennung)

- Imstande sein, sich an neue Werkzeuge anzupassen und sich mit ihnen vertraut zu machen, insbesondere im Bereich der Übersetzung im audiovisuellen und Multimediabereich

- Eine Übersetzung in verschiedenen Formaten und auf verschiedenen Datenträgern anfertigen können

- Die Möglichkeiten und Grenzen der maschinellen Übersetzung kennen

Auch wenn das nur eine kleine Auswahl ist[38]: Man sieht, heutzutage wird von einem Übersetzer allerhand erwartet. Und die Botschaft dieser Kompetenzenliste richtet sich auch an die Auftraggeber und Bedarfsträger von Übersetzungen: Seht her, das kann man von einem gut ausgebildeten Übersetzer erwarten (und der ist nicht zum Dumpingpreis zu haben).

---

[38] Es ist auch für „gestandene Übersetzer" durchaus interessant, die ganze Liste zu lesen.

Das antragstellende Institut muss angeben, ob es diese Kompetenzen vermittelt und die Lehrveranstaltungen konkret benennen, in denen diese Vermittlung erfolgt (hier können natürlich manche Veranstaltungen mehrfach auftauchen; in Seminaren zum technischen Übersetzen beispielsweise können sehr komplexe „Bündel" von Kompetenzen vermittelt werden). Auch wenn es sich nach Ansicht der Expertengruppe um Minimalforderungen(!) handelt, so ist es doch schwierig, all dies unter den jeweils gegebenen Rahmenbedingungen zu realisieren.

Zum Antrag gehört daher auch der Nachweis, dass das antragstellende Institut über die nötige personelle und materielle Infrastruktur verfügt. Also z.b. eine ausreichende Anzahl aktueller Computerarbeitsplätze mit einschlägiger translationsrelevanter Software, eine Bibliothek mit einem angemessenen Angebot translationswissenschaftlicher Bände und Zeitschriften (wie etwa *Fachsprache, Lebende Sprachen, MDÜ*, *meta, target*), Räume mit den nötigen didaktisch-technischen Einrichtungen, genügend und entsprechend qualifiziertes Lehrpersonal. Es muss auch dokumentiert werden, welcher Prozentsatz des Lehrangebots durch Lehrende mit translatorischer Berufserfahrung erfolgt.

Last but not least muss der betreffende Studiengang ein staatlich anerkannter Studiengang sein, der bereits Absolventen hervorgebracht hat, und es muss dokumentiert werden (z.B. durch Alumni-Befragungen), welcher Prozentsatz der Absolventen erfolgreich berufstätig ist[39]. Die Dokumentation eines EMT-Antrags erfordert daher einen relativ hohen Aufwand für alle Beteiligten (der durchaus abschreckend sein könnte), und die Mitgliedschaft im EMT-Netzwerk ist befristet (denn erfahrungsgemäß verändern sich Studiengänge, oft steht und fällt die Qualität mit bestimmten Personen) – in bestimmten Intervallen muss eine Fortführung der Mitgliedschaft beantragt werden. Trotz der hohen Hürden haben zum Start des Programms Anfang 2009 über 90 Institute aus der EU diesen Antrag gestellt. Hierzu wurden pro Institut kartonweise Unterlagen eingereicht, die von der Expertengruppe mit Unterstützung durch DGT-Mitarbeiter im Juni 2009 geprüft wurden[40]. Die Ergebnisse werden im Herbst durch die DGT bekanntgegeben.

4   Die CIUTI

Das im Wesentlichen gleiche Ziel verfolgt die CIUTI. Diese Organisation geht auf eine Initiative der Universitäten Genf, Heidelberg, Mainz/Germersheim und Paris-Sorbonne zurück und wurde 1960 in Genf zusammen mit den weiteren Partnern Universität des Saarlandes und Universität Triest gegründet unter der Bezeichnung

---

[39] Auf die vielen Detailprobleme kann hier nicht eingegangen werden; hier nur der Hinweis, dass es angesichts der vielfältigen Arbeitsmöglichkeiten für Absolventen translatorischer Studiengänge oft schwierig ist zu sagen, ob eine bestimmte Erwerbstätigkeit in ursächlichem Zusammenhang mit dem Studium zu sehen ist: Der Übergang zwischen den Tätigkeiten Übersetzer zu, beispielsweise, Terminologe, Technischer Redakteur, Softwareentwickler, Schulungsleiter, Reisebüroleiter, Reiseführer, Animateur, Table Dancer ist fließend und nur in den Extremfällen einfach entscheidbar.

[40] Am wenigsten Mühe machten die Anträge von Studiengängen, die nach den „Bologna"-Richtlinien konzipiert, akkreditiert und dokumentiert waren. Hier gab es klare und formal weitgehend einheitliche Beschreibungen der Qualifikationsziele des Studiengangs insgesamt sowie der Module, ihrer Inhalte, Ziele und Prüfungsmodalitäten. Die anderen Fälle zeigten ebenso deutlich das bildungspolitische Spektrum (oder: Durcheinander), das in Europa vorher herrschte.

Conférence Internationale Permanente de Directeurs d'Instituts Universitaires pour la formation de Traducteurs et d'Interprètes, kurz: CIUTI[41]. Es handelt sich um einen Verein nach belgischem Recht, mit folgenden in den Statuten, Artikel 3, festgelegten Zielen (s. www.CIUTI.org):

- d'harmoniser les programmes de cours et les examens en vue de faciliter la mobilité des étudiants entre les instituts membres et de permettre ainsi l'exploitation totale des ressources offertes du point de vue de la formation;

- de promouvoir et de développer les échanges d'étudiants et de professeurs;

- d'assurer la collaboration de ses membres dans le domaine de la recherche, dans le développement de nouvelles méthodes d'enseignement et d'instituer une assistance réciproque dans l'élaboration de documentation;

- d'instituer et de poursuivre une action concertée parmi ses membres pour ce qui concerne leurs relations avec les organisations internationales et leurs services linguistiques, les autres institutions à caractère international portant intérêt à la formation d'interprètes et de traducteurs, ainsi que les associations internationales d'interprètes et de traducteurs.

Man sieht, dass die CIUTI zentrale Ziele der Europäischen Hochschulreform – vor allem die Förderung der Mobilität von Studierenden und Lehrenden – bereits vor 50 Jahren antizipiert und formuliert hat und auch das Ziel des EMT-Netzwerks schon lange verfolgt, nämlich eine translatorische Ausbildung auf dem neuesten Stand der Wissenschaft, Didaktik und Praxis.

Es gibt freilich auch elementare Unterschiede.

Die CIUTI ist, wie schon das „I" im Namenskürzel – im Gegensatz zum „E" in EMT – signalisiert, nicht auf Europa beschränkt, sondern sie operiert auf internationaler Ebene weltweit. Zu den CIUTI-Mitgliedern gehören daher auch Institute in Beirut, Minsk, Monterey (Kalifornien), Montréal, Peking, Sankt Petersburg, Schanghai, Seoul und, um noch ein weiteres Nicht-EU-Mitglied zu nennen, Genf.

Auch die Tatsache, dass die CIUTI nach nunmehr 50 Jahren „erst" 39 Mitglieder hat, während das EMT-Netzwerk trotz der regionalen Beschränkung voraussichtlich schon *ab ovo* mehr als 50 Mitglieder haben wird, weist auf einen weiteren Unterschied hin: Das Aufnahmeverfahren in die CIUTI ist noch selektiver und strenger als beim EMT-Netzwerk.

Eine Einschränkung ergab sich ursprünglich durch das „U" in CIUTI: Nichtuniversitäre Hochschulinstitute waren zunächst nicht im Blickfeld; inzwischen können jedoch auch Fachhochschulen Mitglied werden. Des Weiteren können sich nach den bislang geltenden Statuten nur solche Hochschulinstitute um eine Mitgliedschaft bewerben, die sowohl Konferenzdolmetscher als auch Übersetzer ausbilden, ungeachtet einer vielleicht hervorragenden Qualität in nur einem der beiden Bereiche. Mit diesem – innerhalb der CIUTI mit jeweils guten Gründen kontrovers diskutierten – Junktim sind bisher sehr viele Institute (wie z.B. an der FH Flensburg) von vornherein ausgeschlossen.

---

[41] Näheres dazu unter www.CIUTI.org

Ein wichtiger Unterschied besteht darin, dass das EMT-Gütesiegel nur für einen konkreten Masterstudiengang beantragt werden kann – nicht für das Institut als Ganzes. Bei der CIUTI hingegen wird ein Institut als Einheit Mitglied, d.h., die CIUTI-Mitgliedschaft bürgt dafür, dass das ganze Institut mit seinem u.u. breitgefächerten Studienangebot (man denke z.b. an so große Institute wie in Germersheim oder Seoul) hohen Qualitätsansprüchen in Forschung und Lehre genügt. Hierzu gehören – ganz im Gegensatz zum EMT-Netzwerk – auch der Nachweis von Forschungsleistungen im Bereich der Übersetzungs- und/oder Dolmetschwissenschaft (z.b. durch Publikationen, Durchführung von Konferenzen), eine mindestens nationale, aber idealerweise internationale Reputation als erstklassige Adresse für Forschung und Lehre, und der Nachweis der Förderung des wissenschaftlichen Nachwuchses (z.b. durch die Anzahl und Qualität von Promotionen, Doktorandenprogramme etc.)[42]. Entsprechend höher ist der Dokumentations- und Prüfungsaufwand im CIUTI-Aufnahmeverfahren.

Das CIUTI-Aufnahmeverfahren dauert ab Eingang des Aufnahmeantrags im Generalsekretariat rund ein Jahr. Zusätzlich zur Prüfung der Dokumentation (ähnlich wie bei EMT) wird das antragstellende Institut auf dessen Kosten von zwei neutralen[43] Hochschullehrern besucht. Diese besichtigen die Einrichtungen und didaktisch-technischen Anlagen (z.B. Dolmetschtrainingsanlagen, Sprachlabore, Computerarbeitsplätze, Hörsäle und Seminarräume mit Beamern etc.), prüfen die Ausstattung und Zugänglichkeit der Bibliothek, sprechen mit Lehrenden und Studierenden, hospitieren im Unterricht, nehmen an Dolmetschprüfungen teil, nehmen Einsicht in Prüfungsklausuren, Diplom-, Bachelor- und Masterarbeiten. Die Ergebnisse der Auswertung von Dokumentation und Besuchen vor Ort werden von einer Aufnahmekommission zu einer Empfehlung über Aufnahme oder Nichtaufnahme zusammengefasst und auf der jährlichen CIUTI-Generalversammlung den Mitgliedern zur Entscheidung vorgelegt.

Im Lichte dieses Anspruchs und Aufwandes ist es durchaus verständlich, dass der CIUTI-Mitgliederkreis sich nur langsam weitet und dass der CIUTI ein gewisses elitäres Image anhaftet, welches von manchen Mitgliedern durchaus kultiviert wird.

5 Der BDÜ

Der gemeinsame Nenner zwischen dem bisher Dargelegten und dem BDÜ ist der Begriff „Qualität". Ein Berufsverband wie der BDÜ vertritt die Interessen einer bestimmten Berufsgruppe, und dies gelingt umso besser, je kompetenter die Akteure dieser Berufsgruppe und dieses Verbandes sind. Insofern ist alles, was der Qualität der Ausbildung dient, alles, was die Kompetenzen der Absolventen verbessert – ob Bologna, EMT oder CIUTI, im Interesse aller qualitätsorientierten Beteiligten auf dem Translationsmarkt – seien es wir selbst als Übersetzer, Dolmetscher oder deren

---

[42] Irgendwoher müssen ja die Lehrer kommen, die dann ihrerseits die künftigen Übersetzer- und Dolmetschergenerationen ausbilden sollen.

[43] Das heißt, die Besucher sollen so unparteiisch wie möglich sein, kommen daher in der Regel aus einem anderen Land und nicht aus einem Institut, das mit dem antragstellenden Institut in irgendeiner Konkurrenzsituation stehen könnte.

Ausbilder, seien es die Institute, die ihre Daseinsberechtigung und Budgets ständig neu rechtfertigen müssen, seien es die Übersetzungsagenturen in ihrem Spannungsfeld zwischen Kundenerwartungen, Wettbewerb und Freiberuflern, seien es die Auftraggeber und Kunden von Übersetzungen und Dolmetschleistungen, oder letztlich diejenigen, die unsere Übersetzungen lesen oder hören.

Bibliographie

Forstner, M. (2007): Paralipomena zur Diskussion über die Qualität von Translationsstudiengängen unter dem Bologna-Regime, in: Schmitt, P.A. / Jüngst, H. (eds.), *Translationsqualität*. Leipziger Studien zur angewandten Linguistik und Translatologie. Frankfurt am Main u.a.: Peter Lang, 124-157.

Schmitt, P. A. (2007): Der Bologna-Prozess als Chance zur Qualitätssteigerung der neuen Bachelor- und Master-Studiengänge, in: Schmitt, P.A. / Jüngst, H. (eds.), *Translationsqualität*. Leipziger Studien zur angewandten Linguistik und Translatologie. Frankfurt am Main u.a.: Peter Lang, 520-536.

Schmitt, P. A. (2009): Bemerkungen zur Translatologie-Modulprüfung im Bachelor-Studiengang Translation am IALT, in: Wotjak, G. / Ivanova, V. / Tabares, E. (eds.). *Translatione via facienda. Festschrift für Christiane Nord zum 65. Geburtstag.* Frankfurt am Main u.a.: Peter Lang. (in Druck)

FIT Europe: Aims and activities

Reiner Heard

Chairman, FIT Europe Steering Committee

chair@fit-europe.org

1 Introduction

Nowadays a trend towards fragmentation is discernible, with more and more specialised associations for translators and interpreters emerging. Yet strength surely lies in unity, or at least in cooperation. FIT Europe can be regarded as a form of institutionalised cooperation at European level.

But what exactly is FIT Europe? What are its goals, the projects it handles, the challenges faced, and the prospects for the future?

2 History / structure

The International Federation of Translators / Fédération Internationale des Traducteurs (FIT), founded in Paris in 1953, brings together over 100 associations of translators, interpreters and terminologists in more than 60 countries, thus representing some 80,000 professionals. This global organisation, which has French and English as its working languages and whose website can be found at www.fit-ift.org, maintains formal consultative relations with UNESCO.

FIT has several regional centres. One of them is FIT Europe, which was established in 1994 and in turn unites 43 of those associations. It has a lean structure, setting up working groups ad hoc and being run by a steering committee. The present steering committee, elected for the 2008-2011 term, consists of members coming from Belgium (Patricia Alarcon), Finland (Liisa Laakso-Tammisto), Germany (Reiner Heard), Norway (Kevin Quirk), Romania (Cristiana Coblis), Spain (Javier Sancho Duran) and the UK (Eyvor Fogarty). Thus all four corners of Europe – north, south, east, west – and the centre are represented!

FIT Europe holds general meetings once per annum. This year's took place here in Berlin yesterday morning.

3 Mission / aims

The general mission of FIT Europe, as stated in its mission statement, is to further the interests of professionally active translators[44] in Europe. This breaks down into the following goals:

- coordinate the work done by European member associations,
- serve as a clearing house for collecting and disseminating information regarding European members,
- provide collective representation for European members,
- take initiatives on specific issues and publish recommendations,
- foster translators' awareness that they belong to a specific profession,
- achieve convergence in the standards and practices applied by translators in European countries,
- promote the image of translators in Europe.

4 Projects / activities

Over the years FIT Europe has carried out various projects. Here I shall confine myself to the main projects and other activities that are currently being pursued or are at the planning stage. They largely continue or build on the achievements of past steering committees (chaired by João Esteves-Ferreira, Anne Verbeke and Jeannette

---

[44] The term "translator" as used by FIT generally covers translators, interpreters, terminologists and other language professionals.

Ørsted) and of ad hoc working groups. Further details on most of these activities can be found on the FIT Europe website at www.fit-europe.org.

4.1 Survey on translators' working conditions and rates

Given the increasing Europeanisation or even globalisation of the translation market, it was decided to carry out a pan-European survey on the types of rates, qualifications and working conditions of translators belonging to FIT Europe associations. A working group was set up for this purpose, and the online survey was conducted in May 2009, leading to replies from respondents in many FIT Europe member countries. A report on the results of the survey will be made available on the FIT Europe website.

4.2 Bad payers

Although most companies and individuals that ask for translation services are reliable enough, there is still a small percentage of them who do not observe the agreed payment terms and conditions. FIT Europe has collected the information that member associations have on methods for claiming a debt nationally (standard letters demanding payment, small claims court procedures etc.). This enables that information to be shared with other members so that they, too, become aware of the resources available in Europe to claim a debt in a different country.

4.3 Admission criteria

Increasing numbers of translators working for clients outside their own country are seeking membership of more than one professional association – both in their country of residence and in the markets where they do business. Yet the admission criteria of national associations vary considerably. A considerable amount of information has been collected and is to be examined with a view to simplifying/harmonising admission requirements. This will speed up and reduce the cost of admission procedures.

4.4 Code of professional practice

On the basis of the codes of conduct or codes of ethics of national associations, a draft European Code of Professional Practice has been prepared. It lays down the basic rights and obligations of translators and interpreters as a non-exhaustive guide for its member associations. Its five sections deal with general conduct (confidentiality etc.), qualifications, relations with fellow translators/interpreters, disputes and performance of work. It is hoped that the working document will be adopted after making the changes agreed at the last General Meeting in Paris last year.

4.5 Standards (especially EN 15038)

FIT Europe was involved from the outset in the drafting of the European standard EN 15038 „Translation Services – Service requirements". It provides a framework that can be used to improve quality control in the translation process and therefore offers great potential for enhancing the service provided and raising the status of the translation profession as a whole. A working group was set up and issued recommendations on criteria for assessing compliance with the requirements of the standard and for carrying out certification (i.e. confirmation of compliance as a result of a third-party audit). The aim now is to collect information on types of certification in individual countries and also to provide practical guidance for freelancers on preparing their business for certification.

4.6 Dissemination of information

Another task of FIT Europe is to spread information on new developments, such as the envisaged establishment in November 2009 of EULITA, the European Legal Interpreters and Translators Association (www.eulita.eu). It aims to represent the interests of its members vis-à-vis national, European and international organisations and institutions. Its membership will comprise professional associations of legal interpreters and translators in EU countries, general associations that include such interpreters and translators among their membership, and individual legal interpreters and translators from EU countries where such associations have not yet been set up.

4.7 Cultivation of contacts

It goes without saying that it is imperative for FIT Europe to cultivate contacts with other European bodies, such as the European Union, the Council of Europe, the European Union of Associations of Translation Companies (EUATC) and the European Council of Literary Translators' Associations (CEATL). In addition, it has been involved in a consultative capacity in the European Master's in Translation (EMT) project, which serves to ensure high-quality training of translators, especially for the purposes of EU institutions and other employers.

4.8 Support for conferences

FIT Europe assists in the planning and/or organisation of seminars and conferences. One such example is the technical seminar on copyright, intellectual property and translation tools held in Barcelona in 2007, the results of which are available on the FIT Europe website. It has also granted its auspices to the forthcoming IALB/ASTTI conference in Geneva entitled „The World in Crisis – And the Language Industry?".

4.9 Planned activities

Various other activities are envisaged, including the following:

- exchange of information on continuing professional development,
- conduct of a pan-European survey on interpreting,
- establishment of contact with newly formed associations, especially in eastern Europe,
- examination of the consequences of the EU Services Directive,
- development of a professional translator's profile.

5   Challenges

These diverse activities show that FIT Europe is seeking to respond to the requirements of the 21st century. However, in doing so it faces various challenges, both internally and externally.

5.1 Resources

Like many voluntary organisations, FIT Europe has to cope with certain constraints: a shortage of time, funds and human resources (there are no permanent staff). It must therefore seek to act efficiently and not become overstretched through involvement in too many projects. Yet it has to be able to react quickly and effectively to members' needs and to new developments. After all, our profession is changing in many respects: in terms of structures (e.g. more and more international service providers), technologies (translation memories, for example, have almost become the norm) and the legal framework (e.g. the EU Services Directive).

5.2 Communication / information

Needless to say, effective communication and the swift exchange of information are vital. Obviously, modern technology (e-mail, telephone conferences, electronic discussion groups) has facilitated communication between members and reduced the need for costly and time-consuming travel. The general meetings are usually held on the fringes of conferences that many delegates are attending anyway.

In order to avoid duplication of work it is essential to liaise with FIT bodies, not least with other FIT regional centres and with the committees that operate globally and have been set up on a wide spectrum of subjects including legal translation & court interpreting, community-based interpreting, literary translation, translation & cultural adaptation, translation technology, the media, terminology, copyright, human rights, standards and training.

Externally, the information has to reach its target through various channels, such as the internet platform, contacts and liaison with the appropriate bodies and participation in the relevant conferences.

5.3 Representation

There are still some national associations that are not members of FIT Europe (and indeed many translators do not belong to any association at all). It is therefore essential to ensure wider representation. Greater size makes for greater clout and credibility, especially when engaging in lobbying or otherwise seeking to assert one's legitimate interests. This will also enhance FIT Europe's capacity for playing a proactive role and seizing the initiative on specific issues.

5.4 New developments

As already indicated, various developments – reflected in the themes of this conference – are occurring:

- in the marketplace: changing customer requirements, stiffer international competition, etc.,

- technologically: for instance, increasing use of translation memories and other tools, possibly even machine translation,

- in work methods: for example, virtual teamwork and project management and thus the need for new job profiles,

- etc.

FIT Europe and the national associations have to play their part in enabling their members to respond appropriately, not least through networking and continuing professional development.

6 Outlook

If FIT Europe manages to meet the challenges just described (which is indeed no mean feat!), it can surely fulfil its purpose of serving as a forum for exchanging information, experience and best practice, finding solutions to shared problems and arriving at measures to heighten public awareness of this profession.

It can do so best as part of a global organisation that allows adequate scope for the pursuit of regional interests and then combines the strength and resources of its regional centres to form a powerful whole.

Yet ultimately the success of FIT Europe depends to a large extent on the input and involvement of the member associations themselves. A strong sense of commitment on the part of all participants is indispensable. But, as the benefits of collaboration are surely self-evident, it makes sense for the members to join forces for the common cause: promoting the interests of translators, interpreters, terminologists and other language professionals throughout Europe.

Europäische Dienstleistungsrichtlinie – Chancen und Risiken für Sprachmittler

Dörte Stielow

Bundesgeschäftsführerin des Bundesverbandes
der Dolmetscher und Übersetzer e.V. (BDÜ)

stielow@bdue.de

Abstract

Die EU-Dienstleistungsrichtlinie (Richtlinie 2006/123/EG) soll bürokratische Hindernisse abbauen, den grenzüberschreitenden Handel mit Dienstleistungen fördern und damit zur Verwirklichung des einheitlichen Binnenmarktes beitragen. Sie ist ein Reformvorhaben im Rahmen der Umsetzung der sogenannten „Lissabon-Strategie", die die EU bis 2010 zum wettbewerbsfähigsten und dynamischsten wissensgestützten Wirtschaftsraum der Welt machen will.

Da die Dienstleistungsrichtlinie insbesondere das Ziel verfolgt, den freien Verkehr von Dienstleistungen – also auch Übersetzungs- und Dolmetschleistungen – zwischen den EU-Mitgliedsländern zu fördern, ergeben sich hieraus erweiterte Möglichkeiten für die Niederlassung deutscher Übersetzungsdienstleister im europäischen Ausland; gleichzeitig zeichnet sich eine weitere Verschärfung des Wettbewerbs auf dem deutschen Markt durch erleichterte Niederlassung ausländischer Übersetzungsdienstleister ab.

Die Umsetzung der Vorgaben der Dienstleistungsrichtlinie in nationales Recht soll bis Ende Dezember 2009 abgeschlossen sein, sie umfasst folgende Bereiche:

1. Einheitlicher Ansprechpartner
2. Normenprüfung
3. IT-Umsetzung
4. Qualitätssicherung

Zu 1. „Einheitliche Ansprechpartner"

sollen künftig ermöglichen, dass jeder Dienstleistungserbringer über eine Kontaktstelle bzw. -person verfügt, über die alle Verfahren und Formalitäten, die zur Aufnahme seiner Tätigkeit notwendig sind, abgewickelt werden können. Diese sogenannten „One-Stop-Shops" müssen gemäß Dienstleistungsrichtlinie keine physischen sein, alles kann „elektronisch aus der Ferne" abgewickelt werden.

In Deutschland sind die Bundesländer für die Einrichtung und Ausgestaltung der Einheitlichen Ansprechpartner zuständig.

Der BDÜ hat im Rahmen von Arbeitsgruppen und -kreisen des Bundesverbandes der Freien Berufe (BFB) an den Diskussionen zur „Verortung" der Einheitlichen Ansprechpartner teilgenommen.

Zu 2. Normenprüfung

Die Mitgliedsstaaten sind verpflichtet, ihren gesamten dienstleistungsbezogenen Rechtsbestand auf seine Vereinbarkeit mit der Dienstleistungsrichtlinie zu überprüfen (Bund prüft Bundesrecht, Land prüft Landesrecht, Kammern und Kommunen das von ihnen gesetzte Satzungsrecht). Das BMWi hat ein Prüfraster erarbeitet, es wird zahlreiche Anpassungen des deutschen Rechts geben.

Zu 3. IT-Umsetzung

Die mit der IT-Umsetzung (insbesondere den elektronischen Verwaltungsverfahren) verbundenen Fragen werden im Rahmen eines so genannten „prioritären Deutschland-Online-Projekts" (www.deutschland-online.de) unter Federführung der Bundesländer Schleswig-Holstein und Baden-Württemberg aufbereitet.

Zu 4. Qualitätssicherung

Berufsorganisationen sind aufgefordert, sich für gemeinsame Verhaltenskodizes auf europäischer Ebene einsetzen. „Diese würden dazu beitragen, den freien Verkehr von Dienstleistungserbringern zu vereinfachen, da sie sich auf detaillierte, im Voraus bekannte Verhaltensregeln stützen könnten, und die Wahlfreiheit des Verbrauchers zu stärken." (aus: Pressemitteilung der Kommission vom 04.06.2007)

Das Arbeitsdokument der Kommission „Qualität der Dienstleistungen - die Rolle von europäischen Verhaltenskodizes", das unter dem Link:

http://ec.europa.eu/internal_market/services/services-dir/conduct_de.htm

auf Deutsch, Englisch und Französisch abrufbar ist, beinhaltet Informationen darüber, wie ein europäischer Kodex erarbeitet werden kann bzw. was er beinhalten soll und was nicht. Es wurde von der Generaldirektion Binnenmarkt und Dienstleistungen erarbeitet.

Ein von der FIT-Europe erarbeiteter „Code of Professional Practice" liegt in Entwurfsform vor.

Der Vortrag gibt einen Überblick über die oben genannten vier Aspekte der Umsetzung der Dienstleistungsrichtlinie und ihre Auswirkungen auf Sprachmittler und beleuchtet diesbezügliche Aufgaben der Berufsverbände der Dolmetscher und Übersetzer in Europa.

Weitere Informationen: www.dienstleistungsrichtlinie.de.

Neue Aufgaben der Berufsverbände

Übersetzen zwischen Gewerbe und Nachschöpfung. Versuch der gewerberechtlichen Reglementierung des Übersetzerberufs in Österreich

Mag. Florika Griessner

Österreichischer Dolmetscher- und Übersetzerverband
UNIVERSITAS (Universität Graz) / ITAT Graz

florika.griessner@uni-graz.at

1 Die Rahmenbedingungen

Einleitend ein Zitat: „... so scheint uns doch zwischen der historischen Rolle der Translation im Informationszeitalter und ihren aktuellen Aufgaben in den multikulturellen Gesellschaften auf der einen, dem Stellenwert der Translation im akademischen Diskurs und schließlich dem Image, das die Translatoren in den meisten europäischen Gesellschaften genießen, auf der anderen Seite eine unübersehbare Diskrepanz zu herrschen." (Prunc, 1997) Die in dem Artikel dargestellten Interessens- und Machtkonstellationen, die zur Perpetuierung dieses Zustandes beitragen, die Produktions- und Rezeptionsbedingungen in der jeweils vorherrschenden Translationskultur sind hilfreiche Analysemodelle, entheben jedoch die TranslatorInnen nicht ihrer Verantwortung, als selbstverantwortliche HandlungspartnerInnen ihren Stellenwert zu reflektieren und gegebenenfalls zu verändern. Und diese Reflexion anhand eines österreichspezifischen Einzelaspekts ist Inhalt des vorliegenden Artikels, da der Stellenwert der TranslatorInnen nun nicht nur ein abstraktes Konstrukt darstellt, das von der Translationswissenschaft beleuchtet, analysiert und kritisiert wird, sondern an konkreten gesellschaftlichen und wirtschaftspolitischen Gegebenheiten festzumachen ist. Wie sehen diese nun in Österreich aus? Betrachten wir zunächst die wirtschaftspolitische und sozialversicherungsrechtliche Einbettung des Berufs.

1.1 Selbstverwaltungskörperschaften und Sozialversicherungspflicht

Traditionell gibt es in Österreich zum einen Kammerorganisationen für die Freien Berufe (z.B. Ärztekammer, Anwaltskammer, etc.) und zum anderen die Wirtschaftskammer, die die Gewerbeberufe vertritt. Bei den Gewerbeberufen wiederum unterscheidet die Österreichische Gewerbeordnung reglementierte Gewerbe, nämlich solche, die einen Befähigungsnachweis erfordern, von freien Gewerben, für deren Anmeldung kein Befähigungsnachweis zu erbringen ist.

Ein wichtiger Aspekt der Kammerordnung besteht gerade darin, dass diese eng mit dem Sozialversicherungssystem verknüpft ist. Gewerblich Selbstständige werden „ ... mit dem Erwerb der Berufsbefugnis automatisch Kammermitglieder und [sind] somit nach GSVG versichert." (Yoshiba-Karlhuber, 2006: 138). Mit Kammermitgliedschaft ist hier die Zugehörigkeit zur Kammer der gewerblichen Wirtschaft gemeint. Auch die Kammern der Freien Berufe sehen für ihre Mitglieder eine Sozialversicherungspflicht vor, die z.t. von den Kammern selbst organisiert wird, wie z.b. die Krankenversicherung für ÄrztInnen oder über andere Sozialversicherungsträger erfolgt. Alle Kammerorganisationen verpflichten ihre Mitglieder zu irgendeiner Art der Selbstbzw. Pflichtversicherung, entweder nach dem Allgemeinen Sozialversicherungsgesetz (ASVG), dem Gewerblichen Sozialversicherungsgesetz (GSVG) oder dem Freiberuflichen Sozialversicherungsgesetz (FSVG). Soweit eine Kurzdarstellung der traditionellen beruflichen Selbstverwaltungskörperschaften und deren Verknüpfung mit dem Sozialversicherungssystem in Österreich.

Nun hat der wirtschaftliche Wandel in den letzten dreißig Jahren des 20. Jahrhunderts zur Entstehung völlig neuer Berufe geführt und viele ehemals als Angestellte tätige Personen in eine erzwungene Selbstständigkeit gedrängt. So waren viele nicht durch die Gewerbeordnung erfasste oder als FreiberuflerInnen in Kammern organisierte Berufsgruppen entstanden, die als selbstständig Erwerbstätige ihren Lebensunterhalt verdienten und nicht in das auf der Kammerordnung aufgebaute Sozialversicherungssystem integriert waren. Für diese „neuen freiberuflichen Selbständigen" galt der Automatismus Kammerorganisation = Pflichtversicherung also nicht. Es stellte sich daher die Frage, wie diese Berufe im wirtschaftlichen und sozialversicherungsrechtlichen Gefüge zu verankern seien.

Zum Teil sind die „neuen Berufe" wie z. B. die EDV-Berater, Meinungsforscher und Wirtschaftsberater – trotz ihrer Freiberuflichkeit – Mitglieder der Wirtschaftskammer (vgl. Yoshiba-Karlhuber, 2006), zum Teil haben sie sich in Form eines Beirats und von „Listen der zur selbstständigen Ausübung des Berufs befugten Personen" eigene Selbstverwaltungskörper geschaffen, wie z.B. die Psychotherapeuten (vgl. Kierein et.al. 1991).

Auch die Sozialversicherungsfrage wurde sehr individuell gelöst. Bis 1998 haben die Angehörigen dieser Berufsgruppen sich individuell selbst versichert oder sie standen zusätzlich zu ihrer freiberuflichen Tätigkeit in einem versicherungspflichtigen Dienstverhältnis. „Erst durch die Einführung der Sozialversicherungspflicht im Jahre 1998 hat der Staat den ersten Schritt gesetzt, die selbständig Erwerbstätigen außerhalb der Gewerbeordnung in das Gefüge der sozialen Sicherheit zu integrieren." (Yoshiba-Karlhuber, 2006: 2)

Wie haben ÜbersetzerInnen und DolmetscherInnen auf diese Situation reagiert? Der Beruf der ÜbersetzerInnen und DolmetscherInnen ist zwar kein neuer Beruf, allerdings haben die internationalen wirtschaftlichen und politischen Verflechtungen und der gestiegene Bedarf an Übersetzungen den Beruf in Wirtschaft und Gesellschaft „sichtbarer" gemacht. In den 80er Jahren des letzten Jahrhunderts haben die im

Österreichischen Übersetzer- und Dolmetscherverband Universitas organisierten ÜbersetzerInnen und DolmetscherInnen die Schaffung einer eigenen Kammer betrieben. Dieses Vorhaben scheiterte allerdings mangels politischer Unterstützung.

Viele ÜbersetzerInnen und DolmetscherInnen haben sich 1998 dafür entschieden, den neu entstandenen Arbeitsmarktstatus der Neuen Selbstständigkeit zu wählen und als „Neue Selbstständige" ihren Beruf auszuüben, da damit eine sozialen Absicherung bei der Gewerblichen Sozialversicherung verbunden ist.

2 Übersetzen und Dolmetschen in der österreichischen Gewerbeordnung

Innerhalb der österreichischen Gewerbeordnung fällt das gewerblich betriebene Übersetzen und Dolmetschen in die Kategorie der freien Gewerbe. Das sind nach der gesetzlichen Definition in § 5 Abs. 2 GewO 1994 Tätigkeiten, die nicht als reglementierte Gewerbe (vgl. § 94 GewO 1994) ausdrücklich angeführt sind. Zur Ausübung eines freien Gewerbes ist kein Befähigungsnachweis zu erbringen. Die Tätigkeiten, für die diese Bestimmungen gelten, werden vom Österreichischen Bundesministerium für Wirtschaft und Arbeit auf der Grundlage der Gewerbeordnung (GewO 1994) in einer „Liste der freien Unternehmenstätigkeiten" angeführt (www.bmwa.gv.at/ BMWA/default.htm).

Nun verstärken sich in letzter Zeit die Bemühungen, v.a. seitens der Wirtschaftskammer Wien und Niederösterreich, freiberuflich als „Neue Selbstständige" tätige ÜbersetzerInnen davon zu überzeugen, dass sie einen Gewerbeschein – wie man so schön sagt – zu lösen haben. Zu diesem Thema gab es einige Gespräche und eine Podiumsdiskussion zwischen Vertretern der Wirtschaftskammer und Vertretern des Österreichischen Übersetzer- und Dolmetscherverbandes UNIVERSITAS (s. Universitas Mitteilungsblatt 2007, 5). Das Hauptargument der Wirtschaftskammervertreter lautet, die „literarischen Übersetzer" seien explizit von der Gewerbeordnung ausgenommen und daher fielen – in einer Art Umkehrschluss – alle nicht streng genommen als literarisch zu wertenden Übersetzungstätigkeiten (Zitat: „Übersetzen von Bedienungsanleitungen") automatisch unter die Gewerbeordnung, womit auch eine (Pflicht-) Mitgliedschaft bei der Österreichischen Wirtschaftskammer verbunden ist. Verständlich ist, dass sich die Wirtschaftskammer einen Zuwachs an Mitgliedern wünscht. Geworben wird natürlich auch mit dem breiten Serviceangebot, das für nur 58,– EUR an jährlichem Mitgliedsbeitrag bereitsteht.

Es ist anzunehmen, dass es nicht die 58,– EUR Mitgliedsbeitrag sind, die überzeugte FreiberuflerInnen davon abhalten, einen Gewerbeschein zu lösen. Es geht, wie Dagmar Jenner in ihrem Beitrag im Mitteilungsblatt ausführt, zum einen Teil um eine Glaubensfrage (Universitas Mitteilungsblatt 2007: 5), die sich an der Tatsache entzündet, dass das so genannte Übersetzergewerbe als „freies Gewerbe" definiert ist und somit keinerlei Befähigungsnachweis zu dessen Ausübung erforderlich ist, was gleichzeitig auch bedeutet, dass die Anmeldung eines Gewerbes mit keinerlei Qualitäts- oder Berufsschutz verbunden ist.

Tatsächlich handelt es sich nicht nur um eine Glaubensfrage, sondern um eine äußerst unklare Situation mit einer ganzen Reihe von Diskrepanzen, deren erste bereits in der Liste der freien Unternehmenstätigkeiten selbst zu finden ist.

2.1 Die Diskrepanz zwischen der Auflistung der „freien Gewerbe" und der beruflichen Realität im Tätigkeitsfeld Translation

Grundsätzlich lassen sich im Hinblick auf die Berufspraxis 4 Gruppen unterscheiden, persönlich und eigenverantwortlich tätige ÜbersetzerInnen (die keine Vermittlungstätigkeit ausüben), persönlich und eigenverantwortlich tätige DolmetscherInnen (die keine Vermittlungstätigkeit ausüben, in den meisten Fällen aber auch als ÜbersetzerInnen arbeiten), Übersetzungs- und Dolmetschbüros, deren InhaberInnen selbst den Beruf ausüben und auch Aufträge an Kollegen/Kolleginnen vermitteln sowie Übersetzungs- und Dolmetschbüros, die sich ausschließlich der Vermittlung widmen und deren InhaberInnen selbst nicht übersetzen oder dolmetschen.

Nun finden sich in der vom Bundesministerium für Wirtschaft und Arbeit veröffentlichten „Liste der freien Unternehmenstätigkeiten" zum einen „Dolmetsche", dann „Übersetzungsbüros" und eine Zeile weiter „Übersetzungsbüros und Dolmetsche" mit dem Zusatz („ausgenommen literarische Übersetzer).

Die o.a. Auflistung erscheint also nicht nur inkonsistent, sondern auch praxisfern. So fehlt die Gruppe der persönlich und eigenverantwortlich tätigen ÜbersetzerInnen (die keine Vermittlungstätigkeit ausüben) völlig, während die „Dolmetsche" [sic] sich einer zweimaligen Anführung erfreuen.

Gleichzeitig kann damit das Argument der Wirtschaftskammervertreter entkräftet werden, dass DolmetscherInnen ohnehin von der Gewerbeordnung ausgenommen seien. Da die DolmetscherInnen laut einer im Jahr 2003 durchgeführten Umfrage „großteils auch als Übersetzer tätig [sind]" (Yoshiba-Karlhuber, 2006: 10) ist eine strikte Unterscheidung zwischen ÜbersetzerInnen und DolmetscherInnen gewerberechtlich nicht sinnvoll.

2.2 Die Diskrepanz zwischen dem österreichischen Einkommenssteuergesetz und der Gewerbeordnung

Das österreichische Einkommensteuergesetz 1988, BGBl. Nr. 400/1988, zuletzt geändert durch BGBl. I Nr. 7/2002, nennt in § 22 Einkommen aus selbstständiger Arbeit ausdrücklich sowohl Übersetzer als auch Dolmetscher, nicht hingegen Übersetzungsbüros, wie durch den nachstehenden Auszug belegt wird.

§ 22 Selbständige Arbeit (§ 2 Abs. 3 Z 2)

§ 22. Einkünfte aus selbständiger Arbeit sind:
1. Einkünfte aus freiberuflicher Tätigkeit. Zu diesen Einkünften gehören nur
a) Einkünfte aus einer wissenschaftlichen, künstlerischen, schriftstellerischen, unterrichtenden oder erzieherischen Tätigkeit.
b) Einkünfte aus der Berufstätigkeit der staatlich befugten und beeideten Ziviltechniker oder aus einer unmittelbar ähnlichen Tätigkeit sowie aus der

Berufstätigkeit der
- *Ärzte, Tierärzte und Dentisten,*
- *Rechtsanwälte, Patentanwälte, Notare und Wirtschaftstreuhänder,*
- *Unternehmensberater, Versicherungsmathematiker, Schiedsrichter im Schiedsgerichtsverfahren,*
- *Bildberichterstatter und Journalisten,*
- *Dolmetscher und Übersetzer*

Vermutlich handelt es sich hierbei um eine der häufigen Inkonsistenzen der Gesetzgebung, oder um ein Versäumnis des Gesetzgebers im Hinblick auf die Harmonisierung der verschiedenen Sektoralbestimmungen. Die Tatsache, dass diese Inkongruenz bisher nicht „entdeckt" und behoben wurde, kann jedoch zumindest als Hinweis dafür gewertet werden, dass es der allgemein gesellschaftlichen Auffassung der Tätigkeit des Übersetzens entspricht, diese den freien Berufen zuzuordnen. Noch mehr Gewicht in diesem Zusammenhang ist wohl dem Faktum beizumessen, dass auch FinanzjuristInnen, SteuerberaterInnen, FinanzbeamtInnen die Nennung der Übersetzungstätigkeit unter den „freiberuflichen Tätigkeiten" offensichtlich nicht als störend empfinden. Dies führt uns zu einer weiteren Diskrepanz.

2.3 Die Diskrepanz zwischen den beruflichen Anforderungen und der Zuordnung zu einem „freien Gewerbe" ohne Befähigungsnachweis

Die Lektüre der o.a. 27-seitigen Auflistung der freien Unternehmenstätigkeiten des Bundesministeriums für Wirtschaft und Arbeit ergibt, dass sich dort, außer dem Gewerbe der EDV-Dienstleister und des Buchverlags, unter den mehreren 100 „freien Gewerben" keine im Hinblick auf das Qualifikationsprofil mit der Translation vergleichbaren Tätigkeiten finden lassen. Zudem enthält die Liste nicht einen einzigen Beruf, der über eine eigene wissenschaftliche Disziplin verfügt und für den es in Österreich eine universitäre Ausbildung gibt. Zur Veranschaulichung mag dienen, dass dort neben einer ganzen Reihe von Vermietungs- und Vermittlungsunternehmen Tätigkeiten aufgelistet werden, wie Abdecker, Babysitter, Call-Center, Dachpappenherstellung (jeweils die ersten Einträge unter den ersten vier Buchstaben des Alphabets).

Auf die Anfrage des Österreichischen Übersetzer- und Dolmetscherverbandes UNIVERSITAS vom 18. August 2006 an das österreichische Bundesministerium für Wirtschaft und Arbeit, welche Gründe es für die Einstufung der Übersetzertätigkeit zu den „nicht reglementierten Gewerben" gebe, wurde folgendermaßen geantwortet: „Die Einstufung des Berufes als freies Gewerbe ist eine gewerbepolitische Entscheidung des Gesetzgebers. Der Bedarf nach einer Reglementierung wird insbesondere dann gegeben sein, wenn diese zur Sicherung eines entsprechenden Leistungsniveaus und zum Schutz potenzieller Auftraggeber vor unqualifizierten Dienstleistern erforderlich scheint. Im Fall der Dolmetsche und Übersetzungsbüros sieht das Bundesministerium für Wirtschaft und Arbeit die genannten Schutzinteressen als nicht gefährdet an, sodass derzeit an die Einführung eines Befähigungsnachweises nicht gedacht ist." (Brief vom 28.08.2006 des Bundesministers Mag. Dr. iur. Christian Forstner an die UNIVERSITAS.)

Inwieweit die „Sicherung eines entsprechenden Leistungsniveaus" und der „Schutz potenzieller Auftraggeber vor unqualifizierten Dienstleistern" auf dem österreichischen Markt dadurch gefährdet sind, dass es keines Kompetenznachweises bedarf, um ein Übersetzungsbüro zu eröffnen, wäre ein interessanter Gegenstand einer eigenen Untersuchung. Allein die Tatsache, dass es unqualifizierten Dienstleistern ermöglicht wird, Übersetzungsleistungen einzukaufen und wieder zu verkaufen, legt die Vermutung nahe, dass dabei in vielen Fällen berufsethische Überlegungen und Qualitätserfordernisse in den Hintergrund gedrängt werden – oder gar nicht bekannt sind – und es in erster Linie um die Profitspanne zwischen Ein- und Verkauf geht.

2.4 Die Diskrepanz zwischen der historisch gewachsenen Begrifflichkeiten der Freiberuflichkeit und der Gewerbetätigkeiten

Abgesehen von der historischen Begrifflichkeit der „artes liberalis", mit der ihnen eigenen Freiheit vom Zunftzwang und ihrer Ausbildung an den Universitäten, findet sich ein Hinweis auf die „freien Berufe" in der österreichischen Rechtsordnung lediglich im § 2 Abs. 3 Z 2 EStG (vgl. Karlhuber-Yoshiba, 2006).

Da sie in Österreich nicht fündig wird, zitiert Yoshiba-Karlhuber folgende Entscheidung des EuGH: „Die … Freien Berufe sind Tätigkeiten, die ausgesprochen intellektuellen Charakter haben, eine hohe Qualifikation verlangen und gewöhnlich einer genauen und strengen berufsständischen Regelung unterliegen. Bei der Ausübung einer solchen Tätigkeit hat das persönliche Element besondere Bedeutung, und diese Ausübung setzt auf jeden Fall eine große Selbständigkeit bei der Vornahme der beruflichen Handlungen voraus." (EuGH, C-267/99, vom 11.10.01) und führt weiter aus: „Diese Ausführungen decken sich weitgehend mit der Begriffsbestimmung des deutschen Bundesverbandes der Freien Berufe (BFB)" (Yoshiba-Karlhuber, 2006: 6).

In ihrem Selbstverständnis zählen sich viele ÜbersetzerInnen und DolmetscherInnen in Österreich zu den „freien Berufen". Sie sind allerdings nicht in einer Kammer organisiert, wie andere freie Berufe, sondern ausschließlich in freiwilligen Berufsverbänden. Es sind dies der als Absolventenverband des Dolmetschinstituts der Universität Wien entstandene Österreichische Übersetzer- und Dolmetscherverband UNIVERSITAS Austria, der Österreichische Verband der Gerichtsdolmetscher und die Übersetzergemeinschaft als Organisation der literarischen ÜbersetzerInnen.

2.5 Die Diskrepanz zwischen der Situation der „freiberuflich tätigen ÜbersetzerInnen und DolmetscherInnen" in Österreich und jener im Nachbarstaat Deutschland

Vergleichen wir die österreichische Situation mit der unserer BerufskollegInnen in Deutschland, stellen wir fest, dass das Bundesministerium für Wirtschaft unter den gewerblichen Tätigkeiten nur den „Übersetzungsbüro-Inhaber, der selbst nicht über Kenntnisse der Sprachen verfügt, in die oder aus denen innerhalb des Geschäftsbetriebs (durch Angestellte) übersetzt wird" nennt, während „Übersetzer", also solche, die selbst über die Kenntnis der Sprachen verfügen und selbstständig Aufträge ausführen, unter den so genannten „freien Kulturberufen" (www.bmwi.de) aufscheinen – neben Autoren, Journalisten, Pädagogen, Yogalehrern etc.

Weiters führt das bundesdeutsche Wirtschaftministerium aus: „Das wichtigste Kennzeichen für einen Freiberufler ist die enge Verknüpfung zwischen persönlicher Ausbildung und beruflicher Selbständigkeit." "Die Freien Berufe haben im allgemeinen auf der Grundlage besonderer beruflicher Qualifikation oder schöpferischer Begabung die persönliche, eigenverantwortliche, und fachlich unabhängige Erbringung von Dienstleistungen höherer Art im Interesse der Auftraggeber und der Allgemeinheit zum Inhalt." (§1 (2) PartGG).

Zusammenfassend ergeben sich daraus für unser Nachbarland folgende Unterscheidungsmerkmale zwischen der gewerblich ausgeübten Tätigkeit im Bereich des Übersetzens und der freiberuflichen Übersetzertätigkeit, die im Schlussteil noch einmal besprochen werden.

Übersetzen als gewerbliche Tätigkeit	Übersetzen als freier Beruf
Übersetzungsbüro-Inhaber; verfügt nicht über Kenntnisse der Sprachen, in die oder aus denen übersetzt wird;	persönliche und eigenverantwortliche Erbringung von Übersetzungsleistungen; spezifische berufliche Qualifikation

Es ist also offensichtlich in der BRD sehr wohl möglich, anhand weniger, nachvollziehbarer Kriterien eine Trennung zwischen Übersetzen und Dolmetschen als freiem Beruf und als gewerbliche Tätigkeit vorzunehmen.

3 Wo liegen nun wirklich die Unterschiede?

Wie oben erwähnt, wird von der Österreichischen Wirtschaftskammer unter Hinweis auf die Liste der freien Unternehmenstätigkeiten die Auffassung vertreten, die Unterscheidung zwischen gewerblicher und freiberuflicher Tätigkeit könne anhand der übersetzten Textsorten erfolgen. So sei die Übersetzung von Literatur, Werbetexten u.Ä. als freiberufliche, weil eigenschöpferische Tätigkeit einzuordnen, während das Übersetzen von „technischen und wirtschaftlichen Texten" als gewerbliche Tätigkeit gelten soll, da dies keine „kreative" Leistung sei.

Das Kriterium der Textsortenspezifik als Unterscheidungsmerkmal zwischen gewerblicher und freiberuflicher Tätigkeit ist in der Praxis allerdings nicht anwendbar. Viele ÜbersetzerInnen sind in ihrem Berufsalltag mit einer großen Bandbreite von Textsorten und Aufträgen konfrontiert und übersetzen sowohl technische und wirtschaftliche als auch literarische und essayistische Texte (vgl. Kurz/Moisl, 1997).

Die mit der Literarizität der Texte eng verknüpfte und immer wieder als Kriterium angeführte Urheberrechtsfrage ist für viele Textsorten nach wie vor ungelöst, wie Alfred Noll in seinem 1994 erschienenen Handbuch zum Übersetzungsrecht und Übersetzer-Urheberrecht ausführt. Für einen urheberrechtlichen Schutz ist grundsätzlich der „Werkcharakter" eines Textes ausschlaggebend. Ist dieses Kriterium erfüllt, sind ÜbersetzerInnen Inhaber eines Urheberrechtsschutzes an dem von ihnen erstellten „Werk". (vgl. Noll, 1994).

Grundsätzlich gilt, dass laut Urheberrecht Bearbeitungen (und sohin auch die Übersetzung) auf jeden Fall dann Werkcharakter haben, wenn auch der Ausgangstext urheberrechtlichen Schutz genießt. (vgl. § 5 Abs. 1 UrhG, zitiert nach Noll 1994: 46). Die Frage des Werkcharakters ist aber nicht eindeutig zu klären. Daher lautet eine Schlussfolgerung Nolls: „Dabei ist in jedem einzelnen Fall anhand des vorliegenden Textes – und nicht etwa nach statistischen Grundsätzen – zu prüfen, ob ein Sprachwerk eine eigentümliche geistige Schöpfung ist." (Noll, 1994: 42). Raschauer führt dazu in einem für den Österreichischen Übersetzer- und Dolmetscherverband erstellten Rechtsgutachten Folgendes aus: „Entsprechend der bisherigen Lehre und Praxis darf der Begriff der eigenschöpferischen Tätigkeit nicht allzu eng ausgelegt werden. Daher sind auch die Tätigkeiten der Schauspieler und Dirigenten davon erfasst. [...] sofern nachgestaltende schöpferische Fähigkeiten erforderlich sind. [...] Nichts anderes gilt aber auch für sprachmittlerische Leistungen." (Raschauer, 1997: 8).

Eine Überprüfung des Werkcharakters anhand jedes einzelnen Textes ist wohl kaum durchführbar. Auch eine statistische Gewichtung der bearbeiteten Textsorten lässt sich jeweils erst a posteriori ermitteln und kann somit keine Entscheidungsgrundlage für die Frage „Gewerbeschein ja oder nein" darstellen.

Da als Unterscheidungskriterium zwischen „freiberuflicher" und gewerblicher Übersetzungstätigkeit jenes der Textsorten aus den o.a. Gründen nicht anwendbar ist, bliebe noch das in der Bundesrepublik Deutschland angewandte Kriterium der Sprachkenntnis. Für gewerblich tätige Übersetzer nennt das Bundesministerium für Wirtschaft u. a. als Charakteristikum: „verfügt nicht über Kenntnisse der Sprachen, in die oder aus denen übersetzt wird" (s.o.). Diese Bestimmung meint wohl, dass die Sprachkompetenz für das Anbieten von Übersetzungsdienstleistungen nicht unbedingt erforderlich ist.

Tatsächlich sind ca. 90% der gewerblich tätigen ÜbersetzerInnen in Österreich einschlägig ausgebildet und übersetzen einen großen Teil der Texte selbst. (vgl. Kurz/Moisl, 1997). Für eine gewerbliche Tätigkeit haben sich einige entweder aus sozialversicherungstechnischen Gründen entschieden oder weil sie doch auch einen gewissen Anteil an Übersetzungen gegen Entgelt weitervermitteln.

Auf Grund der Unschärfe der o.a. Unterscheidungskriterien und der Vielgestaltigkeit der beruflichen Positionierung und des Tätigkeitsprofils im Translationsbereich bleibt wohl als einzig praktikables Kriterium jenes der „Vermittlung von Übersetzungsleistungen mit Kostenaufschlag". Sobald also Übersetzungsleistungen nicht persönlich und eigenverantwortlich erbracht, sondern an andere ÜbersetzerInnen vergeben und mit Kostenaufschlag weiterverkauft werden, läge somit eine gewerbescheinpflichtige Tätigkeit vor.

3.1 Vermittlung als springender Punkt

Das Kriterium der Vermittlung, d.h. die Fragestellung „Wird das Einkommen aus der Übersetzungstätigkeit ausschließlich aus Eigenleistung oder auch aus Fremdleistungen erzielt?" ist ein einfach zu befolgendes und leicht zu überprüfendes Kriterium und würde zum einen Klarheit in die unbefriedigende Situation in Österreich bringen, zum anderen aber auch dem Selbstverständnis einer Gruppe von ÜbersetzerInnen und DolmetscherInnen entsprechen, die sich den akademischen freien Berufen zugehörig fühlen.

Fazit: Wenn wir davon ausgehen, dass eine Grenzziehung zwischen „freiberuflicher" und „gewerblicher" Tätigkeit im Wesentlichen über das Kriterium der Vermittlungstätigkeit möglich ist, dürfte die „Liste der freien Unternehmenstätigkeiten" nur den Eintrag „Übersetzungsbüros" und gegebenenfalls „Dolmetschbüros" enthalten.

Bibliographie

Kierein, M./Pritz, A./Sonnek, G. (1991) *Psychologengesetz, Psychotherapiegesetz – Kurzkommentar*, Orac-Verlag: Wien

Kurz, I./Moisl, A. (eds.) (1997) *Berufsbilder für Übersetzer und Dolmetscher. Perspektiven nach dem Studium*. WUV: Wien

Jenner, D. (2007) *Podiumsdiskussion – FreiberuflerInnen und/versus UnternehmerInnen*, in: Universitas Mitteilungsblatt 2/2007, Österreichischer Übersetzer- und Dolmetscherverband UNIVERSITAS: Wien

Noll, A. J., (1994) *Handbuch zum Übersetzungsrecht und Übersetzer- Urheberrecht*, Verlag Österreich Edition juristische Literatur: Wien

Prunc, E. (1997) *Translationskultur (Versuch einer konstruktiven Kritik des translatorischen Handelns)*, in: Tct 11, S 99 – 127,

Raschauer, B. (1997) *Rechtsgutachten zur Anwendbarkeit der GewO auf Sprachmittler (Dolmetscher und Übersetzer)*, Österreichischer Übersetzer- und Dolmetscherverband UNIVERSITAS: Wien

Yoshiba-Karlhuber, M. (2006) *Interessenvertretung und Soziale Sicherheit für Angehörige Freier Berufe als Neue Selbständige*, Dissertation Rechtswissenschaftliche Fakultät der Universität Wien: Wien

ATA at 50: Challenges and opportunities

Dr. Nicholas Hartmann

American Translators Association

nh@nhartmann.com

The American Translators Association (ATA) will hold its 50th annual conference October 28-31, 2009. This milestone represents a useful opportunity to summarize what the Association has achieved, and present some ideas about its future.

The first 50 years

ATA was established in 1959 in New York City, a circumstance commemorated by the site selected for this year's conference. The Association's founders were a small group of professional translators, many of them operators of what were then known as translation bureaus, and all of them located in the eastern United States. Their purpose was to exchange information, provide mutual benefit, and promote their nascent profession.

ATA has grown and changed in many ways since that first core of professionals came together, perhaps most strikingly in its internal governance. In its infancy, the Association was personally managed and administered by its members on a strictly volunteer basis. As membership grew, those volunteers gave way first to a single paid administrator and a few part-time assistants still located in the vicinity of New York City, and then to an office near Washington, D.C., staffed by full-time employees. Our present executive director is a professional in his own right, certified by the American Society of Association Executives, who supervises almost a dozen staffers responsible for information technology, Certification, chapter and division relations, member benefits, conference and seminar planning, and the Association's publications. ATA's office is located in Alexandria, Virginia, which is home to thousands of other U.S. associations and offers easy access to decision-makers at the highest levels of government.

This evolution in governance has been accompanied, and largely driven, by a steady increase in size. ATA's membership recently exceeded the 10,000 mark, and may reach 11,000 by the end of this calendar year. With this increase in size has come a commensurate growth in scope and reach. The Association now has members in all 50 states of the U.S. and in almost 90 other countries, and ATA's professional breadth and coverage is now equally wide: Certification exams are offered in almost 30 language combinations, there is now much greater emphasis on meeting the needs of interpreters as well as translators, conference presentations address hundreds of different subject specialties, and programs and services have been developed to meet the needs of independent contractors, in-house translators and interpreters, translation company owners and project managers, academics, and students.

Despite all these changes, ATA's purpose remains the same: to serve its members and promote their interests, and give them value for the dues money they pay each year. Some of the pivotal areas in which the Association works to achieve this are communication, the Certification program, and effective governance. It is also in these areas that ATA may face its greatest challenges and opportunities.

The next 50 years

The translator

Like all translators and interpreters, ATA's members will face many challenges both in the near future and over the next 50 years. The two most fundamental of these are "globalization" – the rapid elimination of physical distance as a governing factor in human relationships around the world – and recent explosive growth in information-processing power and communication capabilities. These two developments, and the complex ways in which they interact with and reinforce one another, are creating a new world in which people can interact more easily and more rapidly than ever before.

This revolution in global communication represents a double-edged sword as far as translators are concerned. We all benefit from these developments in many ways: clients are easier to acquire and contact and cultivate, and translations can be delivered with the touch of a button. With the advent of e-mail and now of networking sites, contact among professional colleagues has become even more immediate and extensive, with mutual advantages that are just beginning to be understood. Last but not least, the volume of reference information now available through Internet search engines is quickly making the translator's physical library obsolete.

But progress in this area, as everywhere, also creates difficulties that must be overcome. The ability to communicate so much more quickly, and to be accessible almost everywhere, creates a corresponding expectation of instant response, constant availability, and sometimes unreasonable turnaround. A subtler but perhaps greater risk is that of sheer information overload: we can now find out so much, so quickly, from so many sources, about everything, that information itself may become devalued.

The organization

Even beyond the significant issues of globalization and electronic communication that each individual practitioner must deal with, every voluntary association faces challenges of a different nature and magnitude. One important challenge is that of maintaining relevance, in other words, staying useful to its members. This requires constant self-examination, and an attitude of exploration and flexibility. New programs and services must always be under development so that the members' attention can be retained in today's increasingly distracting information-rich society. A sharp eye must always be kept on the money, especially during economic downturns such as the present one, and ways must always be found to work as efficiently as possible. None of this can be achieved without the right people, and perhaps the greatest organizational challenge is therefore to identify, cultivate, motivate, and retain the volunteers who make all good associations function, and to coordinate their efforts with those of an expert and permanent professional staff.

Another issue that ATA, in particular, must consider over the longer term – and it is a very good problem to have – is membership growth. Having broken the 10,000 barrier only two years ago, the Association already has twice as many members as it did only 15 years ago, and while constant efforts are made to change and adapt, some procedures and structures will always lag behind. By one estimate dating back to 2006, there are approximately 30,000 "professional" translators and interpreters in the United States. If ATA convinced all of them to join, our membership would be three times what it was in 2008. This possibility raises two questions: How would the Association need to change in order to provide that many people with the same level of service and benefit presently enjoyed by only 11,000 members? And would an ATA of that size really be desirable? Arriving at plausible answers to these questions, and taking concrete action on that basis, is essential.

ATA and the future

The author of this paper begins a two-year term as ATA President in October, 2009, on the occasion of the Association's 50th-anniversary Conference. Two years is not much time to accomplish anything, especially when translation customers and real life must also be accommodated; but there are three broad areas in which one can hope to make at least some impact. Those areas are governance and especially the role of specialty groups within the Association, the Certification program, and communication.

Governance

Significant progress has already been made in optimizing the Association's governing documents (policies, procedures, and especially Bylaws), mostly in order to ensure that the documents represent useful tools rather than procedural dead weight. This process will continue, with greater emphasis on regular and transparent reviews and updates as an integral part of ATA's governance.

A second aspect requiring close attention is the relationship between volunteers and the professional staff. The Headquarters staff already include specialists in Certification, education and professional development, publications, member services, and information technology Every one of those functions was once handled by a volunteer, until it became obvious that the job had become too complex and important to be entrusted to an overworked amateur; in every case, adding the professional has not only relieved the load on volunteers, but also improved the service provided to members. This process of transition to professional staff will continue; in a few months, for example, a person responsible for public relations, marketing, and other external communications will join the staff. Increasing professionalization of member services and programs also changes the nature of the work done by volunteers: committee chairs, working group members, Directors, and Officers can increasingly devote their time and energy to thinking and strategizing and creating policy, supported by professionals whose job is to implement those ideas.

The other side of this coin is, of course, the volunteers themselves. Headquarters staffers can be hired, but volunteers must... volunteer. It is literally essential to ensure that as ATA continues to grow and adapt, it remains an association that its members care about enough to work on its behalf. The Association's ingrained culture of collegiality and service helps to keep the pool of future leaders topped up, but specific actions are also being taken in this direction, including a shift in the role of the Nominating Committee toward long-term leadership development and cultivation.

Divisions

ATA's first Division was created in 1978, and there are now more than two dozen such interest groups. Their broadest purpose is to provide an individual and more intimate "home," within what is becoming a rather large Association, for translators and interpreters who work in a particular language pair or subject specialty. The Divisions constitute a source of strength for ATA, attracting members with specific interests and contributing specialized expertise especially in the context of the annual Conference. There has, however, always been the potential for separatism, a risk that Divisions may lose sight of their status as subgroups **within** the larger Association that supports and funds them. A delicate balance must be maintained, in which financial and procedural discretion is distinguished from autonomy, and collegiality and support are not allowed to degenerate into arbitrary central control. This is another area in which success is critical: an ATA that, with regard to its Divisions, is not quite federal but less than imperial, will be strong and diverse and beneficial to all its member. Action is already underway, in the form of Bylaws revisions to redefine the financial situation, but a great deal is left to be done.

Certification

The Certification program, initiated in 1973, is one of ATA's crown jewels, a credential of increasing prestige with a constant demand for examination sittings. The program gives translators an opportunity to acquire an objective qualification that demonstrates competence in a particular language pair (from or into English). Applicants must meet educational and other requirements before taking the test, and those who are successful can add the designation "CT" (Certified Translator) after their name. A lot has been accomplished in the last few years: a tremendous effort to develop a keyboard-based test adaptable to every language combination is about to come to fruition, and the number of such combinations is constantly being expanded. Originated and, for many years, administered entirely by volunteers, the program is now run by a hybrid group of dedicated volunteers and headquarters staff members. An important area consideration here is whether, and if so how, to professionalize this particular program even further, once again in the interest of better service to candidates.

A major issue with regard to Certification for the next few years will be external validation. The Certification program was devised exclusively within ATA and has been developed and expanded largely on an in-house basis. That is likely to change in the near future. Extensive research over almost half a decade has indicated that while the program in general, and the examination in particular, do meet many of the criteria applied by experts in testing and evaluation, certain steps still need to be taken.

Fortunately those steps are relatively simple and can be taken fairly quickly. One option would then be to submit the program for external review and eventual accreditation by a standards organization. Another route that could be taken would be simply to establish the program on a firm footing in accordance with accepted practices, and begin to promote its value more assertively than has been done in the past.

This drive toward validation has already produced some very useful side-effects, mostly with regard to better understanding of the program among those who work with it every day. The benefits of a robust and well-founded program are becoming apparent, and as this initiative progresses it is likely to further enhance communication and commitment. If the option of true external validation is selected, and if the laborious (and expensive) process of seeking accreditation culminates in actual approval by a standards organization, there will be even further benefits: greater prestige internationally for the credential; a leadership role for ATA among translators' associations, since it would be the first such association to gain this type of accreditation; and the possibility of international reciprocity with other organizations in terms of credentials, creating greater mobility for professional translators and interpreters.

A final decision on the particular approach to validation has yet to be made, but a definite commitment exists to proceeding along whichever route is felt to be the most effective one with the greatest benefit.

Communication

Translators and interpreters are in the communication business, so the way in which ATA itself communicates is of course a concern. Particular attention will be devoted to refining and optimizing communication both internally (within the Association and among its members) and externally (between ATA and the outside world).

Internal communication

This category embraces all the educational and other information distributed by the Association to its members, much of which in fact consists of communication among members themselves. ATA's internal communication media include its award-winning monthly magazine (The ATA Chronicle), along with weekly and monthly e-mail bulletins. The Association also provides online connectivity via networking systems such as LinkedIn and Twitter, and supports individual e-mail lists for each of the twenty-odd language- and subject-specific Divisions, through which members can communicate with one another. The annual Conference is ATA's principal educational offering and the high point of each year. Attendance now routinely exceeds 1,500, and over 2,000 are expected for the upcoming 50th-anniversary event in New York City. Each Conference represents an extraordinary opportunity for information exchange among members, with other professionals, and between ATA leaders and the membership. In addition ATA holds professional development seminars throughout the rest of the year on a variety of topics, often coordinated with a particular location (energy and petroleum development in Houston, Texas; entertainment in Los Angeles, etc.) All of these opportunities to acquire and exchange information will continue to be supported and enhanced.

External communication

The purpose of ATA's highly successful public-relations effort is to create greater awareness and positive opinions of the Association, the translating and interpreting professions, and the language industry in general. The present strategy is based not on advertising but on unpaid media exposure, supported by a corps of virtuoso volunteers who put in long hours to achieve these goals. A consistent message has been established and refined, and the circle of expert spokespersons is being expanded. A headquarters staff person responsible solely for external communication should come on board early in 2010. A number of other programs are also devoted to external communication: a school outreach project has rewarded and publicized efforts by individual translators to talk about what they do to young people, and an analogous client outreach program is just being finalized, based on a standardized presentation that members can use when speaking to local chambers of commerce or other groups of potential customers. This is felt to be an extremely useful member benefit especially in today's difficult economic circumstances. Lastly, the searchable online services database represents another valuable tool for individual members, providing external communication to potential customers in a context, and on a scale, that would not otherwise be feasible.

All of these efforts are directed toward creating value and benefit for translators and interpreters. Ideally, the results will be cumulative and mutually reinforcing: translators and interpreters who avail themselves of the many educational opportunities offered by ATA become better translators. The Certification program gives each of them a way to demonstrate his or her expertise, and thereby to enhance his or her professional status. The interest groups within the Association foster specialized capabilities that in turn let each practitioner concentrate in a particular subject area in which he or she excels. Lastly, a properly targeted program of public relations, marketing, and other external communication tells the outside world, including translators' customers, about all the specialized, certified, quality-conscious members of ATA, establishing translation and interpreting as a specialized business service that is worth paying for, rather than a commodity to be procured solely on the basis of price.

Summary

Each of these major aspects of the Association's future – governance with particular attention to interest groups, Certification, and communication – deserves individual attention in the immediate future and for years to come. Even greater benefit to the Association and its members, and to translators and interpreters everywhere, will come if they can be addressed synergistically rather than in isolation. For example, the manner in which ATA governs itself will influence how effectively its volunteer leaders and professional staff can function in all of the other areas. A balance between individuality and unity with regard to Divisions will encourage more members, from a greater diversity of backgrounds, to contribute their time and expertise as volunteers. A validated Certification program can be presented to the world very differently, creating new opportunities for marketing the Association as a whole. These and many other interrelated possibilities and correlations are the real challenge for the next 50 years and beyond, requiring constant effort and attention, assiduous training of leaders, an awareness of how external developments affect the profession and the Association, and most of all, an understanding that the purpose of ATA is to give value to its members.

BDÜ 2.0 – oder: Berufsverbände reloaded

Wolfram Baur

Vizepräsident des Bundesverbandes der Dolmetscher und Übersetzer e.V. (BDÜ); Freier Übersetzer

baur@bdue.de

Dr. oec. Stanisław Gierłicki

Bundesreferent IT des Bundesverbandes der Dolmetscher und Übersetzer e.V. (BDÜ); Konferenzdolmetscher

gierlicki@bdue.de

Das Internet und die Entwicklung des „Web 2.0"

Auch wenn der Prozess der Globalisierung schon vor den Anfängen des Internets begann, ermöglichte doch erst das Internet das heutige Ausmaß der Globalisierung und hat den Prozess der weiteren Globalisierung enorm beschleunigt.

Die Anfänge des Internets reichen zurück bis Ende der 60er Jahre. Neben E-Mail hat insbesondere das World Wide Web (WWW), das 1989 von Tim Berners-Lee am CERN entwickelt und ab Mitte der 90er Jahre durch grafikfähige Web-Browser einer breiten Öffentlichkeit zugänglich wurde, als Teil des Internets eine enorme praktische Bedeutung für unseren Berufsstand gewonnen.

War die Nutzung des Internets noch in den 90er Jahren eher auf technikbegeisterte Kolleginnen und Kollegen beschränkt, so ist für Übersetzer (u.a. E-Mail, Recherche-möglichkeiten im WWW) und Dolmetscher (universelle Erreichbarkeit, Recherche-möglichkeiten, Einsatz webbasierter Technologien wie Dolmetschen bei Video-konferenzen) eine professionelle Berufsausübung ohne Internet heute undenkbar geworden.

Internet und World Wide Web unterlagen und unterliegen jedoch auch selbst einer ständigen Weiterentwicklung. Wurden in der Anfangsphase Inhalte vorwiegend zentral von sogenannten „Content Providern" bereitgestellt, so haben sich Wahrneh-mung und Nutzung des Internets vor allem seit Ende der 90er Jahre gewandelt:

Erstellung von Inhalten durch die Nutzer selbst, Wiki-Projekte, Foren und soziale Netzwerke sind zu wesentlichen Merkmalen des heutigen WWW geworden, Web-Browser haben sich inzwischen sprichwörtlich zur „eierlegenden Wollmilchsau" gewandelt und der Web-Benutzer wandelt sich mehr und mehr vom Konsumenten von Inhalten zum Akteur:

> *„Die Benutzer erstellen, bearbeiten und verteilen Inhalte in quantitativ und qualitativ entscheidendem Maße selbst, unterstützt von interaktiven Anwendungen. Die Inhalte werden nicht mehr nur zentralisiert von großen Medienunternehmen erstellt und über das Internet verbreitet, sondern auch von einer Vielzahl von Nutzern, die sich mit Hilfe sozialer Software zusätzlich untereinander vernetzen.*[45]

Diese Entwicklung wird gemeinhin als „Web 2.0" bezeichnet, wobei es für den Zweck dieses Vortrags müßig ist, darüber zu streiten ob es jemals ein „Web 1.0" gab, oder ob das, was wir heute sehen, bereits das ursprüngliche Netzverständnis war, wie Tim Berners-Lee selbst vertritt. Tatsache ist: Ausmaß der Nutzung, technische Möglichkeiten und Nutzungsgewohnheiten haben sich drastisch geändert, die überwiegende Mehrheit der Teilnehmer dieser Konferenz dürfte sich heute mehr Stunden pro Tag mit dem World Wide Web als mit Printmedien, Fernsehen und klassischen Telekommunikationsmitteln beschäftigen, und die Erstellung von Inhalten durch die Nutzer selbst, Wiki-Projekte, Foren und soziale Netzwerke wurden zu wesentlichen Merkmalen des World Wide Web, wie wir es heute kennen.

Ein kurzer Blick zurück: die „BDÜ-Mailbox"

Bereits in den 90er Jahren hatte der BDÜ versucht, mit einem Mailbox-System, genannt „BDÜ-Mailbox", diese Entwicklung auch für die Verbandsarbeit nutzbar zu machen. Da jedoch die damals genutzte Mailbox-Technik Mängel insbesondere hinsichtlich der Benutzerfreundlichkeit aufwies (viele potenzielle Nutzer scheiterten damals schon allein an der Installation der hierfür erforderlichen besonderen Software) und die Nutzergewohnheiten noch stark auf das „Konsumieren" fertiger Inhalte ausgerichtet waren, blieb die Nutzung dieses damals zukunftsweisenden Systems auf eine kleine Zahl von Funktionsträgern und Aktiven im Verband beschränkt.

Berufsverbände durch universelle Vernetzung im World Wide Web obsolet?

Seit Ende der 90er Jahre wurde immer wieder die Ansicht vertreten, angesichts der neu entstandenen Vielzahl von Möglichkeiten zur Vernetzung und Diskussion über das World Wide Web seien Berufsverbände „obsolet" geworden. Im Internet entstand nach und nach eine fast unüberschaubare Vielfalt an Mailinglisten und „Communities", wie z.B. www.proZ.com und zahlreiche Gruppen bei Yahoo-Groups. Daneben sehen wir in jüngster Zeit auch ein zunehmendes Aufkommen sogenannter „Marktplätze" für Übersetzungsdienstleistungen, die mit einigen wenigen Ausnahmen wohl eher kritisch zu betrachten sind: Das bei manchen dieser Plattformen angewendete

---

[45]http://de.wikipedia.org/wiki/Web_2.0

„Reverse Auctioning"-Verfahren für die Auftragsvergabe ignoriert sämtliche Qualifi-kations- und Qualitätsaspekte und erhebt den (niedrigsten) Preis einer Übersetzung zum einzigen Vergabekriterium; bei anderen Plattformen, die auf Provisionsbasis für die Vermittlung von Aufträgen funktionieren, wird offenbar versucht, die leidige „Umtüter"-Praxis ins Internetzeitalter hinüberzuretten.

Die Ansicht, durch das Aufkommen virtueller Marktplätze, Communities und sozialer Netzwerke würden Berufsverbände überflüssig, verkennt zwei grundlegende Aspekte:

- Ein Berufsverband ist von Natur aus mehr als ein „Netzwerk" zum Erfah-rungs- und Wissensaustausch oder eine „Werbegemeinschaft" bzw. ein Vehi-kel zur Akquise – auch wenn die Aspekte des Netzwerkens und der praktischen Hilfe beim Markteintritt aufgrund des unmittelbaren praktischen Nutzens im subjektiven Empfinden der Mitglieder unter den Beweggründen für eine Mitgliedschaft häufig im Vordergrund stehen. Satzungszweck von Berufsverbänden ist regelmäßig gerade auch eine effiziente Interessenvertre-tung der Gesamtheit ihrer Mitglieder und des Berufsstandes – und dazu bedarf es eben mehr als „Stammtischdiskussionen", wobei es egal ist, ob es sich da-bei um Diskussionen an realen Stammtischen oder in Communities in der „virtuellen Welt" handelt.

- In öffentlich zugänglichen Foren, die meist für jedermann zugänglich sind, der sich selbst für die Berufsausübung als Dolmetscher oder Übersetzer qualifi-ziert hält, teilen qualifizierte Sprachmittler ihr während der Ausbildung ange-eignetes Wissen und ihren hart erarbeiteten Erfahrungsschatz stets auch mit unzureichend qualifizierten Möchtegern-Sprachmittlern, die ihnen dann am Markt unter Verwendung des in den Foren oberflächlich aufgeschnappten Fachwissens als Konkurrenten begegnen und damit am Markt ihre Qualifika-tionsdefizite maskieren. Um Missverständnissen vorzubeugen: Wir wollen hier keiner „Closed Shop"-Politik das Wort reden, aber: Berufsschutz fängt auch „im Kleinen" an, bei der Frage nach der Qualifikation derer, mit denen wir unser Wissen teilen. Nicht umsonst legt der BDÜ – wie auch die übrigen Berufsverbände in Deutschland – viel Wert auf die Weiterentwicklung und Einhaltung seiner Aufnahmebedingungen.

Als Antwort auf die oben beschriebenen Entwicklungen hat der BDÜ mit dem Start seiner Mitgliederplattform „MeinBDÜ" im Jahr 2007 Elemente des „Web 2.0" zur Organisierung eines Meinungs-, Wissens- und Erfahrungsaustauschs unter den Verbandsmitgliedern – ausnahmslos qualifizierten Sprachmittlern – in seine Ver-bandsarbeit eingeführt. Innerhalb kurzer Zeit hat sich MeinBDÜ zu einem der größten und lebendigsten Foren in der Sprachmittlerbranche in Deutschland entwickelt. Daneben wurde – gleichfalls in 2007 – der öffentliche Web-Auftritt des BDÜ unter www.bdue.de neu gestaltet und die interne „Integrierte Mitgliederdatenbank" syste-matisch zu einem elektronischen Verbandsverwaltungssystem weiterentwickelt. Diese Bemühungen wurden im Jahr 2008 anlässlich des Weltkongresses der Fédération Internationale des Traducteurs (FIT) in Shanghai durch Verleihung des FIT-Preises für den besten Web-Auftritt anerkannt. Der vorliegende Beitrag gibt einen kurzen Überblick über den derzeitigen Stand der Verbandsarbeit in Sachen Web-Nutzung und Überlegungen zur weiteren Entwicklung.

MeinBDÜ

Innerhalb weniger Wochen konzipiert und eingerichtet, wurde MeinBDÜ unter der URL www.mein.bdue.de am 01.04.2007 nach einer ca. fünfmonatigen Erprobungs- und Ausbauphase für alle Mitglieder freigeschaltet.

Wesentliche Elemente von MeinBDÜ sind: Diskussionsforen (grob unterteilt in allgemeine Foren, fach- und sprachgruppenbezogene Foren, Foren von Verbandsgremien und -arbeitsgruppen), Modul zur Übermittlung persönlicher Nachrichten zwischen Mitgliedern, Wissensdatenbank (in der zahlreiche berufs- und verbandsbezogene Dokumente, Gutachten usw. bereitgestellt und durch eine Suchfunktion erschlossen werden), persönliche Profile der Nutzer (wahlweise auch mit Foto und Angaben zum persönlichen Werdegang/fachlichen Hintergrund), persönlicher Kalender (einschließlich Anzeige anstehender Seminare und Veranstaltungen des Verbandes), Möglichkeit zur Bearbeitung bestimmter Mitgliederdaten durch das Mitglied selbst und, für Funktionsträger, Zugang zu den jeweils zugeordneten Funktionen des Verbandsverwaltungssystems.

Für die Einrichtung von MeinBDÜ wurde bewusst eine weit verbreitete Open-Source Community Software verwendet (phpBB), zum einen, um den erforderlichen Programmieraufwand zu minimieren und zum anderen, um den Benutzern auf Grundlage ihrer Erfahrung aus anderen Foren den Einstieg so leicht wie möglich zu machen.

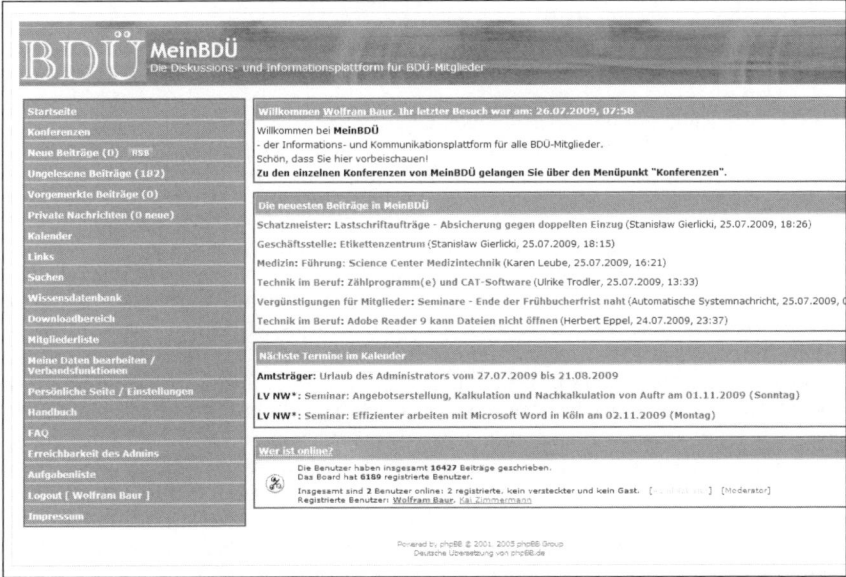

Abb. 1: Startseite von MeinBDÜ, links das Hauptmenü, das die einzelnen Module erschließt.

Fachkonferenzen

	Thema	Fäden	Beiträge	Neuester Beitrag
	Dolmetschen/Übersetzen allgemein Die Konferenz für alle Themen des Dolmetschens/Übersetzens, für die es in den Fachkonferenzen keine spezielle Konferenz gibt **Moderator** Fachkonferenzmoderatoren	103	533	Vorschlag für die BDÜ-Hymne 24.07.2009, 14:20 Tamara Dieterle ➜◻
	Chinesisch Konferenz für Chinesisch **Moderator** Fachkonferenzmoderatoren	33	225	Chinesische Lyrik in elf deuts... 04.07.2009, 13:18 Anja Kirsch ➜◻
	Deutsch Eine Konferenz für alle Fragen, die sich auf Deutsch beziehen **Moderator** Fachkonferenzmoderatoren	11	48	Saarland: Deutschlehrer für c... 01.07.2009, 14:29 Thorsten Vogt ➜◻
	Englisch Konferenz für Englisch **Moderator** Fachkonferenzmoderatoren	214	947	Zusatzqualifikation TEFL/TESOL 24.07.2009, 16:19 Ulrike Trodler ➜◻
	Französisch Konferenz für Französisch **Moderator** Fachkonferenzmoderatoren	76	302	Abkürzung "EPS APTE"... 21.07.2009, 14:43 Helgard Drechsel ➜◻
	Japanisch Konferenz für Dolmetscher und Übersetzer der japanischen Sprache **Moderator** Fachkonferenzmoderatoren	2	15	Wer macht denn hier Japanisch? 18.04.2009, 22:29 Yukari Wollboldt-Komazaki ➜◻
	Spanisch Konferenz für Spanisch **Moderator** Fachkonferenzmoderatoren	82	335	Juzgado del 3er turno 23.07.2009, 15:23 Antje Eckart ➜◻
	Sprachen Konferenz für alle Sprachen, für die es keine speziellen Konferenzen gib **Moderator** Fachkonferenzmoderatoren	66	198	Russische Schrift mit Betonung... 15.07.2009, 10:49 Berit Haritonow ➜◻
	Computerunterstütztes Übersetzen (CAT) Hier können alle Fragen aus dem Bereich des computergestützten Übersetzens diskutiert werden **Moderator** Fachkonferenzmoderatoren	121	591	Trados: Clean-up erfolgreich, ... 06.07.2009, 21:26 Birthe El Yaaqoubi ➜◻
	§-Dolmetscher und -Übersetzer Hier tauschen sich beeidigte/vereidigte/öffentliche bestellte/ermächtigte (usw. usf.) Dolmetscher und Übesetzer zu allen Themen und Fragen der Beeidigung/Bestellung/Ermächtigung und der Tätigkeit als §-D/Ü aus **Moderator** Fachkonferenzmoderatoren	144	828	EU entwirft Rahmenbeschluss f... 23.07.2009, 11:29 Leon Adoni ➜◻

Abb. 2: Ausschnitt aus der Übersicht von Fachkonferenzen in MeinBDÜ, die Zahlen in den mittleren Spalten geben die Anzahl der Diskussionsfäden bzw. geschriebenen Beiträge an, rechts ist der jeweils neueste Beitrag genannt.

Die nachfolgenden Diagramme illustrieren die quantitative Entwicklung der Nutzung von MeinBDÜ. Bei der Einführung von MeinBDÜ hat sich einmal mehr gezeigt, dass für eine lebendige Auseinandersetzung in einem solchen Forum eine „kritische Masse" an (tatsächlichen) Nutzern erforderlich ist. Mussten in den ersten Monaten zahlreiche Beiträge von einigen wenige Initiatoren von MeinBDÜ selbst verfasst werden, um die Diskussion in Gang zu bringen und zu „pflegen", so wurde im Fall von MeinBDÜ eine kritische Masse bei ca. 1.000 Nutzern pro Monat erreicht, ab der eine sich selbst tragende, dynamische Auseinandersetzung unter den Mitgliedern in Gang kam. Auch aus diesem Grund begannen wir zunächst mit wenigen Fachforen, um die anfangs relativ geringe Zahl von Beiträgen und Nutzern nicht unnötig auf zu viele Fachforen zu zersplittern, bevor die Anzahl von Foren in MeinBDÜ im Einklang mit dem Wachstum der Benutzerzahl nach und nach auf inzwischen 107 erhöht wurde. Derzeit liegt die Zahl der regelmäßigen MeinBDÜ-Nutzer bei 20 – 25% der BDÜ-Mitglieder. Sicher, Größe ist bei Berufsverbänden nicht alles was zählt, aber unter den Dolmetscher- und Übersetzerverbänden in Deutschland dürfte der BDÜ mit seinen inzwischen über 6.000 Mitgliedern der einzige Verband sein, der seinen

Mitgliedern einen Mehrwert in Form eines solchen Mitgliederforums, das tatsächlich von den Beiträgen der Nutzer selbst lebt, bieten kann.

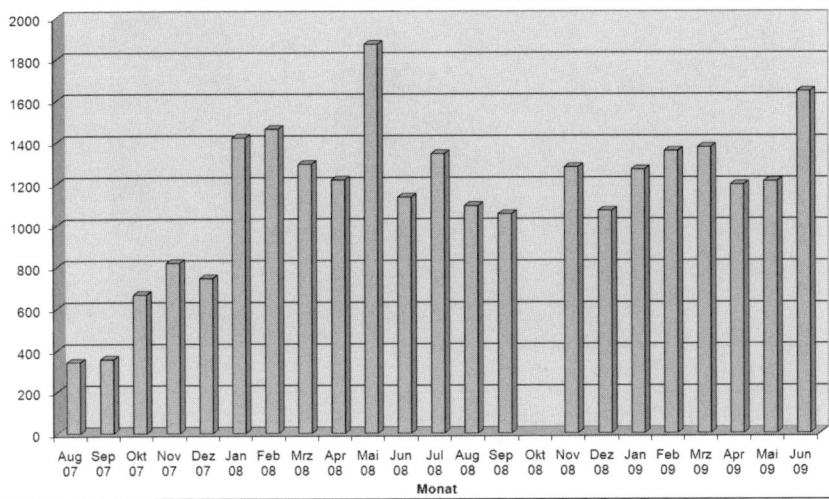

Abb. 3: Anzahl der Mitglieder, die MeinBDÜ pro Monat genutzt haben

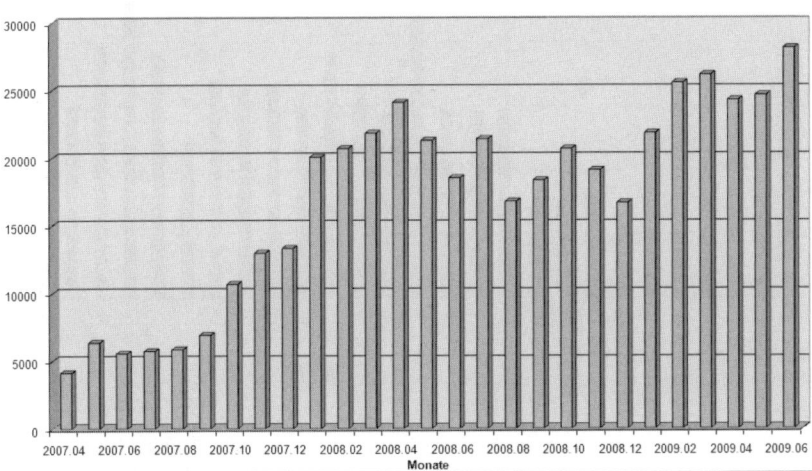

Abb. 4: Anzahl der Seitenaufrufe auf www.mein.bdue.de

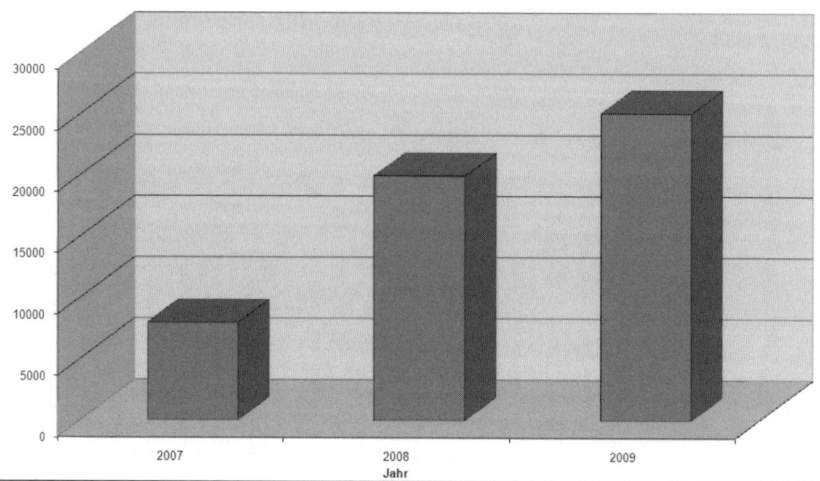

Abb. 5: MeinBDÜ-Besucher (durchschnittliche monatliche Seitenaufrufe pro Jahr)

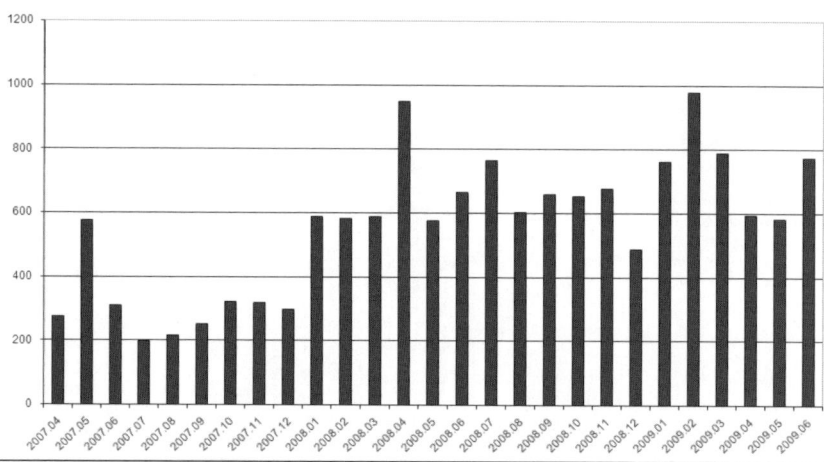

Abb. 6: Anzahl der Beiträge in MeinBDÜ seit April 2007

Stil der Auseinandersetzung in MeinBDÜ und Umgang der Nutzer untereinander heben sich wohltuend von dem in vielen öffentlichen Foren und Mailinglisten gepflegten Stil ab: Unter den inzwischen verfassten mehr als 16.000 Beiträgen ist es (auch ohne Eingriffe von Seiten der Administratoren) schwer, die ansonsten in Foren verbreitete besserwisserische Schulmeisterei zu finden, und die Beiträge sind von einem hohen Maß an Sachkunde, Sachlichkeit, kollegialem Teilen von Wissen und gegenseitiger Hilfsbereitschaft geprägt.

Die Bedeutung von MeinBDÜ für die Entwicklung der Verbandsarbeit besteht, kurz gesagt, vor allem in sechs Punkten:

- Der in MeinBDÜ stattfindende ständige Austausch von Wissen, Erfahrungen und Meinungen zwischen den Mitgliedern trägt der Tatsache Rechnung, dass unser Beruf komplexer, vielseitiger und „schneller" geworden ist. Die Fülle der hier behandelten Fragen könnte beim besten Willen nicht auf monatlichen Treffen oder von einer kleinen Gruppe Verbandsfunktionäre behandelt werden, sondern erfordert neben dem aktiven Engagement möglichst vieler Mitglieder auch die „kollektive Intelligenz" des Verbandes.

- Die Verfolgung der Auseinandersetzung in MeinBDÜ ist für die Verbandsleitung unschätzbar wertvoll, denn sie gibt Aufschluss darüber, bei welchen Themen den Mitgliedern „der Schuh drückt", wo also der Verband in seiner Interessenvertretung besonders gefordert ist.

- MeinBDÜ fördert die Entwicklung der Kommunikationskultur im Verband. Eine aktuellere Information der Mitglieder „von oben nach unten" wird ergänzt durch unmittelbares Feedback „von unten nach oben".

- MeinBDÜ fördert die „Aktivierung" einer größeren Zahl von Verbandsmitglieder zur aktiven Mitwirkung am Verbandsleben/an der Verbandsarbeit, als dies durch „physische Präsenzveranstaltungen" zu erreichen wäre.

- MeinBDÜ fördert den kollegialen Umgang der Mitglieder untereinander, fördert die Vernetzung und professionelle Zusammenarbeit zwischen den Mitgliedern.

- MeinBDÜ beschleunigt die Meinungsbildung und Entscheidungsfindung in dezentral aufgestellten Verbandsgremien und Arbeitsgruppen, da der Meinungsaustausch auch zwischen physischen Sitzungen geführt werden kann, und Verlauf und Ergebnisse der Entscheidungsfindungsprozesse automatisch in den einzelnen Diskussionsfäden bzw. Abstimmungsmodulen dokumentiert sind.

Der öffentliche Web-Auftritt des BDÜ

Zeitgleich mit der Einführung von MeinBDÜ wurde im April 2007 auch der öffentliche Web-Auftritt des BDÜ unter www.bdue.de neu gestaltet. Handelte es sich zuvor – abgesehen von der Online-Suche nach Dolmetschern und Übersetzern und dem Online-Shop für Publikationen der BDÜ-Service GmbH – um eine „statische Präsentationsseite", wurden nun über die Präsentation des Verbandes und des Berufsstandes hinaus auch aktuelle Nachrichten, eine Übersicht bevorstehender Seminare mit Online-Buchungsmöglichkeit für alle Seminare des Verbands sowie Umfragen (wie die jährliche Honorarumfrage des BDÜ) aufgenommen. Dabei geht die Steigerung der Zugriffszahlen auf die Website von 5.248.169 im Jahr 2006 auf 7.205.342 im Jahr 2008 und die Steigerung der Zugriffszahlen auf die Online-Suche auf 470.318 im Jahr 2008 (und schon 300.533 bisher im Jahr 2009) insbesondere auf die Verzahnung der verstärkten Interaktivität der Website mit einer systematischeren Presse- und Öffentlichkeitsarbeit zurück (z.B. Pressemitteilungen zu Weihnachtsgrußaktion, Online-

Suche nach Dolmetschern und Übersetzern, „Exotenliste" und Honorarumfrage). Mit der inzwischen vollzogenen Einrichtung „sprechender" Subdomains (www.mein. bdue.de, www.mdue.bdue.de, www.service.bdue.de) werden weitere Ansatzpunkte für eine enge Verzahnung zwischen konventioneller Presse/Öffentlichkeitsarbeit und Web-Auftritt geschaffen.

Anlässlich der Konferenz „Übersetzen in die Zukunft" wurde auch erstmals für ein Projekt des Verbandes eine eigene Website eingerichtet, auf der einige (für uns) neue interaktive Elemente ausprobiert wurden, so die „Favoritenwahl" aus den zur Konferenz eingereichten Vortragsvorschlägen (die wichtige Hinweise zur Gestaltung des Konferenzprogramms ergab), die Verbindung von Rundmails an die Teilnehmer mit eindeutig zuordenbaren Links, über die z.b. die Wahl des Abendprogramms oder die Anmeldung zu Workshops automatisiert datenbankmäßig erfasst werden konnten.

Für die Zukunft ist an die verstärkte Nutzung weiterer zeitgemäßer Content-Elemente wie z.b. Podcasts (beispielsweise von dieser Konferenz) oder auch „Live Chats" mit Verbandsvertretern gedacht.

Effizientes Verbandsverwaltungssystem

Bei Übernahme der Verantwortung für den IT-Bereich konnten sich die Autoren dieses Beitrags auf die von ihren Vorgängern entwickelte „Integrierte Mitgliederdatenbank" stützen, die bereits zahlreiche Funktionen für ein effizientes Verbandsmanagement beinhaltete.

Das heutige hohe Serviceniveau der Mitgliedsverbände des BDÜ für ihre über 6.000 Mitglieder ist bei beschränkten personellen Ressourcen überhaupt nur möglich durch eine effiziente webbasierte Nutzung der Datenbanktechnik, die den Routineverwaltungsaufwand weitestgehend minimiert und damit ehrenamtliche und bezahlte Arbeitskraft für die Beratung von Mitgliedern, aber auch für die Öffentlichkeitsarbeit zur Imagebildung für unseren Berufsstand und für Interessenvertretung z.B. durch Lobbyarbeit freisetzt.

Das Verbandsverwaltungssystem gibt den Mitgliedern die Möglichkeit, alle nicht qualifikationsbezogenen Daten (wie angebotene Sprachrichtungen, Auftragsannahme ja/nein, Kontaktdaten) selbst zu bearbeiten. Neben der damit bewirkten Entlastung der Geschäftsstellen bleiben die Mitglieder damit in gewisser Weise auch Herr über ihre eigenen Daten.

Mittels eines Systems der Zugriffssteuerung auf die einzelnen Funktionen und auf Teilmengen von Daten kann die administrative Arbeit in Bundesverband und Mitgliedsverbänden unter Erfüllung von Datenschutzerfordernissen effizient auf viele (meist ehrenamtliche) Schultern verteilt und die Führung separater Listen für einzelne Funktionen (z.B. bezüglich Berechnung und Einzug von Mitgliedsbeiträgen) reduziert werden. Dabei ist der Aufwand zur Administration und laufenden Pflege der Systemfunktionen auf ein Minimum beschränkt, wodurch sich der Systemadministrator auf die systematische Weiterentwicklung des Systems und die Einrichtung neuer Funktionen konzentrieren kann.

Die Bereitstellung einer einheitlichen Verbandsverwaltungsplattform wirkt bei richtiger Ausrichtung auch festigend auf den Zusammenhalt zwischen den Mitgliedsverbänden des BDÜ, der ja mit derzeit 13 Mitgliedsverbänden föderal organisiert ist. Damit die Stärken der föderalen Organisation voll zum Tragen kommen können, müssen die Besonderheiten und besonderen Anliegen der einzelnen Verbände berücksichtigt werden. Trotz einer zentralen, einheitlichen technischen Plattform, die von allen Verbänden genutzt werden kann, müssen die einzelnen Verbände weiterhin „Eigentümer" ihrer Daten bleiben und jederzeit die uneingeschränkte Verfügungsgewalt über diese behalten.

Nutzung der neuen Aspekte der Web-Technologie – nicht nur eine Frage der technischen Kompetenz

Natürlich sind zur Nutzung der oben beschriebenen Aspekte des „Web 2.0" technische Kenntnisse und Fertigkeiten erforderlich – all das programmiert sich schließlich (noch) nicht von alleine. Als ebenso wichtig erwiesen sich in den vergangenen Jahren aber auch „weiche Faktoren", wie

- Abschied zu nehmen von Vorstellungen, die Verbandsleitung könnte oder müsste jede Diskussion im Verband irgendwie „steuern". Administrative Eingriffe in Diskussionen sind auf ein Minimum zu beschränken, z.B. wenn Auseinandersetzungen in persönliche Angriffe abgleiten (bei inzwischen über 16.000 Beiträgen in MeinBDÜ war ein solches Eingreifen bisher nur in 3 Fällen erforderlich).

- Keine Angst vor vielleicht unliebsamen Meinungen zu haben, die im Forum geäußert werden – es ist besser, solche Meinungen kommen beizeiten zum Vorschein und können diskutiert werden, als wenn es irgendwann „knallt";

- Sich die Mühe zu machen, auch bei auf der Hauptseite falschen Meinungen oder ungerechtfertigten Kritiken spätestens beim zweiten Nachdenken „das kleine Körnchen Wahrheit" zu suchen, aufzugreifen und für die weitere Entwicklung der Verbandsarbeit zu nutzen;

- Das geflügelte Wort „Make a system idiot-proof and they will invent a better idiot" als Naturgesetz zu akzeptieren und geduldig an einer ständigen Verbesserung arbeiten, statt in Frustration zu verfallen, wenn einmal etwas nicht im ersten Anlauf so klappt, wie von den Erfindern vorgesehen;

- Vorhaben nach einer ersten grundsätzlichen Klärung nach und nach umzusetzen, nicht auf den „einen großen Befreiungsschlag" durch ein allumfassendes Konzept zu warten.

Mit der immer umfassenderen Einführung webbasierter Technologien und erweiterter Datenbanknutzung erhält auch der Schutz persönlicher und personenbezogener Daten eine immer größere Bedeutung. Der BDÜ e.V. hat sich deshalb kürzlich einem freiwilligen Datenschutzaudit unterzogen, das uns grundsätzlich einen verantwortungsbewussten Umgang mit den Daten der Mitglieder bestätigt hat und Hinweise auf weitere Verbesserungsmöglichkeiten gab. In den nächsten Monaten werden Bundesvorstand und die Vorstände der Mitgliedsverbände darüber beraten, welche konkreten Maßnahmen angezeigt sind, um die Datensicherheit noch weiter zu erhöhen.

Ausblick

Im Verlauf der letzten Jahre hat der BDÜ in Sachen Nutzung der Web-Technologie mit einigem Erfolg drei Elemente geschaffen:

- Öffentlicher Web-Auftritt mit einigen zeitgemäßen, interaktiven Elementen,

- Community-Plattform für die Mitglieder zum Austausch von Wissen, Erfahrungen und Meinungen, und

- Einrichtung eines recht umfassenden, effizienten Verbandsverwaltungssystems.

Diese Elemente werden in den nächsten Jahren zu stabilisieren und weiterzuentwickeln sein.

Darüber hinaus denken wir seit einiger Zeit über ein weiteres, neues Element der Web-Nutzung durch den Verband nach, nämlich die Bereitstellung eines Systems, mit dem jedes Verbandsmitglied selbst sein eigenes professionelles Netzwerk organisieren kann – über das es also direkt seine berufliche Zusammenarbeit mit Kollegen realisieren und seinen Kunden einen Mehrwert bieten kann. Hierbei müsste es sich um ein einfaches, intuitiv zu nutzendes System handeln, das ohne großes technisches Verständnis oder „Erlernen" besonderer Software, wie z.B. FTP-Software, bedient werden kann.

Ein solches System müsste aus unserer Sicht zunächst unter anderem die folgenden Funktionen/Tools umfassen:

- Einrichtung persönlicher Verzeichnisse im Web, in Verbindung mit einer Rechteverwaltung für Schreib- und/oder Lesezugriff durch Dritte (freie Mitarbeiter im Netzwerk, Kunden) auf bestimmte Verzeichnisse und Dateien,

- System zur Übermittlung sehr großer Dateien,

- Dateiarchiv – z.B. Bereitstellung auftragsbezogener Terminologielisten und Glossare, TMs,

- Fortschrittsverfolgung für laufende Aufträge,

- Öffentlich zugänglicher „Verfügbarkeitskalender", z.B. zur Einbindung in die eigene Website.

Wie in der Vergangenheit bereits erfolgreich praktiziert, wäre auch ein solches System nach anfänglicher Klärung grundlegender Aspekte wie Struktur, Datensicherheit, Gewährleistung usw. schrittweise zu entwickeln und nach und nach gemäß den Nutzeranforderungen und den mit vertretbarem technischem Aufwand realisierbaren Möglichkeiten auszubauen.

Fazit

Die neuen technischen Möglichkeiten und veränderten Nutzergewohnheiten, die allgemein mit dem Schlagwort „Web 2.0" beschrieben werden, können und müssen für eine innovative, demokratischere und effizientere Verbandsarbeit genutzt werden. Sie erschließen Möglichkeiten, den Mitgliedern einen nach heutigen Maßstäben erforderlichen Mehrwert ihrer Verbandsmitgliedschaft zu bieten. Bereits heute hat die

Aufnahme einzelner Elementen des sogenannten „Web 2.0" in die Verbandsarbeit das Verbandsleben des BDÜ belebt und für mehr Dynamik in der Entwicklung des Verbands gesorgt. Dabei spielen sowohl technische Fähigkeiten als auch soziale Kompetenzen der Verbandsleitung eine Rolle.

Bibliographie

Berners-Lee, Tim und Fischetti, Mark (2000). *Weaving the Web: The Past, Present and Ultimate Destiny of the World Wide Web by its Inventor.* New York: Harper-Collins Publishers Inc.

Anhang

Call for papers (de)

**Bundesverband der Dolmetscher und Übersetzer e.V. (BDÜ),
Berlin, den 15.07.2008**

Der größte europäische Berufsverband für Dolmetscher und Übersetzer, BDÜ, veranstaltet im September 2009 eine dreitägige internationale Konferenz mit dem Titel „Übersetzen in die Zukunft – Herausforderungen der Globalisierung für Dolmetscher und Übersetzer". Vorträge, Workshops, eine Fachmesse und eine Stellenbörse sollen Industriekunden, Behörden, Hochschullehrer, Anbieter von Softwarewerkzeugen, Studierende und professionelle Sprachmittler einander näherbringen.

Sind Übersetzer und Dolmetscher für die Herausforderungen der Globalisierung gewappnet? Immer kürzere Termine zur Übersetzung mehrsprachiger Dokumentationen, Kostendruck, Zusammenarbeit in virtuellen Teams, Beherrschung einer Vielzahl technischer Werkzeuge, Dolmetschen bei Videokonferenzen – dies sind nur einige der neuen Anforderungen an den Berufsstand.

Der BDÜ veranstaltet vom 11.–13. September 2009 eine **internationale Konferenz** im Henry-Ford-Bau der Freien Universität Berlin, um über den Wandel der Berufe und die sich daraus ergebenden Herausforderungen für Sprachmittler zu diskutieren. Die **Vorträge** werden simultan in mehrere Sprachen gedolmetscht, **Workshops** laden zur aktiven Mitarbeit ein.

Auf der begleitenden **Fachmesse** können sich die Besucher über die neuesten Nachschlagewerke, Werkzeuge zum Informationsmanagement, Translation-Mcmory-Systeme, Dienstleistungsangebote für Übersetzer und Dolmetscher und vieles mehr informieren. Darüber hinaus bietet die Konferenz Sprachmittlern auch die Möglichkeit, direkten Kontakt zu potenziellen Arbeit- und Auftraggebern aufzunehmen: Im Rahmen einer Stellenbörse können sich Interessierte namhaften Unternehmen und Institutionen vorstellen.

Experten aus den Bereichen Übersetzen und Dolmetschen sind eingeladen, bis 6. Januar 2009 Vorschläge für Vorträge oder Workshops zu folgenden Themenfeldern einzureichen:

Auswirkungen der Globalisierung auf den Übersetzungs- und Dolmetschmarkt
Steigende Übersetzungsvolumina, Einkauf von Leistungen weltweit, kürzere Lieferfristen, Rolle international operierender Übersetzungsunternehmen und „Multilanguage Vendors", veränderter Bedarf an Sprachen, Erosion von Honoraren, Existenzgründung in einem globalisierten Markt, neue unternehmerische Herausforderungen usw.

Neue Berufsprofile, neue Perspektiven
Technische Redaktion, Überprüfer, Softwarelokalisierung, Untertitelung usw.

Neue Herausforderungen beim Übersetzen
Effizientes Projektmanagement, Qualitätssicherung, Arbeit in virtuellen Teams, Übersetzen von Textbausteinen ohne Kontext, Fachjargon und fachliche Spezialisierung, Wissensmanagement, nationale und internationale Qualitätsnormen usw.

Neue Herausforderungen beim Dolmetschen
Veränderte Arbeitsbedingungen beim Konferenzdolmetschen, Englisch als Lingua franca?, Videodolmetschen, Community Interpreting usw.

Neue Technologien
Maschinelle Übersetzung, rechnergestütztes Übersetzen, Translation-Memory-Systeme, Terminologieverwaltung, Sprachtechnologien, Urheberrechte an Translation Memories usw.

Ausbildung heute
Neue BA/MA-Studiengänge, Mobilität der Studierenden usw.

Neue Anforderungen an die Berufsverbände
Lobbyarbeit unter veränderten politischen Rahmenbedingungen, Weiterbildung, Networking usw.

Interessenten werden gebeten, bis zum 6. Januar 2009 ein Abstract von bis zu 2.000 Zeichen für einen Vortrag zu einem der genannten Themenkreise einzureichen. Bei Workshops sind die Ziele sowie Inhalte in Stichworten, der Ablauf und die benötigten Medien zu beschreiben. Verwenden Sie hierzu bitte das Formular im Menüpunkt „Abstract einreichen" auf der Konferenz-Website. Die Vorträge haben eine Dauer von maximal 30 Minuten; an die einzelnen Vortragsblöcke schließt sich eine Diskussion an. Für Workshops ist eine Dauer von 90 Minuten vorgesehen. Vortragssprachen sind Deutsch, Englisch und Französisch. Eine Übertragung aus anderen Vortragssprachen wird bei Bedarf geprüft. Alle angenommenen Vorträge werden in einem Tagungsband veröffentlicht, der zum Termin der Konferenz erhältlich ist.

Wir benachrichtigen Sie bis zum 30. Januar 2009, ob Ihr Vorschlag angenommen wurde. Am 1. März 2009 wird das detaillierte Programm der Konferenz bekannt gegeben. Zur Aufnahme in den Tagungsband müssen die ausgearbeiteten Vorträge bis 1. Juli 2009 eingereicht werden.

Weitere Informationen finden Sie im Internet unter: www.uebersetzen-in-die-zukunft.de oder senden Sie uns eine E-Mail an: konferenz2009@bdue.de.

Call for papers (en)

**Bundesverband der Dolmetscher und Übersetzer e.V. (BDÜ),
Berlin, July 15, 2008**

In September 2009, Europe's largest professional association for interpreters and translators, BDÜ, is hosting a three-day international conference entitled "Interpreting the Future — Challenges for Interpreters and Translators Arising from Globalisation". A programme of events en- compassing presentations, workshops, a trade exhibition and job exchange will bring together corporate clients, public authorities, university teachers, software tool providers, students and translation practitioners.

Are translators and interpreters ready for the challenges of globalisation? The emerging demands on the profession include ever-shorter deadlines for translating documents into several languages, cost pressures, working in virtual teams, a command of numerous technical tools, and video- conference interpreting, to mention just a few. From September 11—13, 2009, the BDÜ is hosting an **international conference** in the Henry Ford Building of Freie Universität Berlin, to discuss the transformation that is taking place within the professions and the associated challenges facing translation practitioners. The **presentations** are to be simultaneously interpreted into several languages, and participants will be encouraged to play an active part in the **workshops**.

The accompanying **trade exhibition** will give those attending the conference an opportunity to learn about the latest reference works, information management tools, translation memory systems, service offerings for translators and interpreters, among other things. The event will also enable translation practitioners to establish direct contact with prospective employers and customers. The forum provided by the **job exchange** will allow candidates to present themselves to leading companies and institutions.

Experts in the fields of translation and interpreting are invited to submit proposals for presentations or workshops on the following subjects by January 06, 2009:

Effects of globalisation on the translation and interpreting markets
Rising translation volumes, global procurement of services, shorter deadlines, role of international translation companies and multi-language vendors, demand for different languages, fee erosion, setting up business in a global market, new business challenges etc.

New job profiles, new perspectives
Technical editing, revising, software localisation, subtitling etc.

Emerging practical challenges for translators
Efficient project management, quality assurance, working in virtual teams, translating template wording without any context, jargon and subject speciali-

sation, knowledge management, national and international quality standards etc.

Emerging practical challenges for interpreters
Changing working conditions for conference interpreters, English as a lingua franca?, video-interpreting, community interpreting etc.

New technologies
Machine translation, computer-aided translation, translation memory systems, terminology management, language technologies, copyright in translation memories etc.

Education today
New BA/MA courses, student mobility etc.

New demands on professional associations
Lobbying in a changing political framework, continuing professional development, networking etc.

Interested persons are invited to submit an abstract of the proposed presentations on one of the forenamed subjects, containing no more than 2,000 characters, by January 06, 2009. An abstract for a workshop must indicate the goals and subject matter in abbreviated form, the structure and the required media. To send an abstract, please use the form provided under the "Submit abstract" button on the conference website. Presentations are not to exceed 30 minutes; each presentation session will be wrapped up by a discussion. Workshops are expected to last 90 minutes. Presentations can be delivered in German, English or French. Translation from other languages may be offered if necessary. All accepted presentations will appear in the conference proceedings, which will be available at the time of the conference.

We will let you know whether your proposal has been accepted by January 30, 2009. The detailed conference programme will be announced on March 1, 2009. For inclusion in the conference proceedings, manuscripts must be submitted by July 1, 2009.

Further information is available on the internet at: www.interpreting-the-future.com. You can also email us at: conference2009@bdue.de.

Appel à contribution

**Bundesverband der Dolmetscher und Übersetzer e.V. (BDÜ),
Berlin, 15/07/2008**

Le BDÜ, la plus grande organisation professionnelle européenne d'interprètes et de traducteurs organise une conférence internationale en septembre 2009 qui durera trois jours intitulée « La traduction projetée dans l'avenir – Les défis de la mondialisation pour les interprètes et les traducteurs ». Conférences, ateliers ainsi qu'un salon professionnel et une bourse de l'emploi se proposent de rapprocher les clients du secteur industriel, les administrations, les professeurs d'université, les fournisseurs de logiciels, les étudiants ainsi que les professionnels de la traduction et de l'interprétariat.

Les traducteurs et les interprètes sont-ils armés pour répondre aux défis de la mondialisation ? Des délais de plus en plus courts pour traduire des documentations en plusieurs langues, la pression exercée sur les coûts, la collaboration en équipes virtuelles, la maîtrise d'un grand nombre d'outils techniques, l'interprétariat lors de vidéoconférences sont autant d'exigences nouvelles qui sont posées à la profession. Le BDÜ organise du 11 au 13 septembre 2009 **une conférence internationale** dans les locaux annexes Henry Ford de l'Université Libre de Berlin où il sera question de l'évolution des métiers et des défis qui en découlent pour les professionnels de la traduction et de l'interprétariat. Une traduction simultanée des **interventions** en plusieurs langues est assurée, les **ateliers proposés sont axés sur une participation active des visiteurs.**

Au **salon professionnel** qui a lieu parallèlement, les visiteurs peuvent se renseigner sur les derniers ouvrages de référence parus, les outils de gestion de l'information les plus récents, les derniers logiciels de traduction assistée par ordinateur sortis, les offres de prestations actuelles pour traducteurs et interprètes et bien d'autres choses encore. Cette rencontre internationale est l'occasion pour les professionnels de la traduction et de l'interprétariat d'entrer directement en contact avec des employeurs et donneurs d'ordre potentiels. Les personnes intéressées ont la possibilité de se présenter à des entreprises et institutions de renom par le biais de la **bourse de l'emploi.**

Les spécialistes travaillant dans le domaine de la traduction et de l'interprétariat sont invités à soumettre leurs propositions pour les conférences et ateliers d'ici le 06 janvier 2009 qui devront porter sur les thèmes suivants:

Effets de la mondialisation sur le marché de la traduction et de l'interprétariat

> Volumes de traduction croissants, achats de prestations à une échelle mondiale, délais de livraisons plus courts, rôle des sociétés de traduction opérant à l'international et des « multilanguage vendors », évolution des besoins en langue, importante diminution des honoraires, création de sa propre entreprise sur un marché mondialisé, défis nouveaux posés aux entreprises etc.

Profils professionnels nouveaux, perspectives nouvelles
Rédaction technique, réviseurs, localisation de logiciel, sous- titrage etc.

Défis nouveaux posés aux traducteurs
Gestion de projet efficace, assurance qualité, travail en équipes virtuelles, traduction de blocs de texte sans contexte, jargon des spécialistes, spécialisation
professionnelle, gestion des con- naissances, normes de qualité nationales et
internationales etc.

Défis nouveaux posés aux interprètes
Evolution des conditions de travail dans le domaine de l'interprétariat de conférence ; l'anglais, une nouvelle lingua franca ? ; interprétariat lors de vidéoconférences, médiation linguistique, etc.

Technologies nouvelles
Traduction automatique, traduction assistée par ordinateur, systèmes d'aide à
la traduction, gestion de la terminologie, technologies linguistiques, droits
d'auteur en rapport avec les systèmes d'aide à la traduction etc.

Formation aujourd'hui
Nouvelles filières Licence, Master, Doctorat (LMD), mobilité des étudiants
etc.

Exigences nouvelles posées aux organisations professionnelles
Le lobbying dans un contexte où les conditions politiques générales se sont
transformées ; formation continue, travail en réseau etc.

**Il est demandé aux personnes intéressées de nous faire parvenir d'ici le 06
janvier 2009 un résumé d'intervention ne dépassant pas les 2.000 caractères
concernant l'un des thèmes précités.** S'agissant des ateliers, indiquer objectifs et
contenu sous forme de mots-clés en précisant le déroulement et les médias nécessaires. Pour ce faire, veuillez utiliser S.V.P. le formulaire à votre disposition à la
rubrique « Soumission de résumé » sur le présent site web. La durée des interventions
est de 30 minutes au maximum et chaque volet d'interventions est suivie d'une
discussion. Quant aux ateliers, une durée de 90 minutes est prévue. Les langues
d'intervention sont l'allemand, l'anglais et le français. En cas de besoin, toute demande de traduction d'une intervention dans une autre langue que les trois langues
mentionnées ci-avant sera examinée. Toutes les interventions acceptées seront
publiées dans un recueil de publications qui sera disponible sur les lieux de la conférence.

**Nous vous ferons savoir d'ici le 30 janvier 2009 si votre proposition a été retenue.
Le programme détaillé de la conférence sera publié le 1er mars 2009. Le délai de
sou- mission du texte des interventions pour qu'il puisse figurer dans le recueil
des publications de la conférence est le 1er juillet 2009.**

**Si vous souhaitez de plus amples renseignements, consultez S.V.P. notre site web
en tapant : www.uebersetzen-in-die-zukunft.de** ou envoyez-nous un e-mail à
l'adresse suivante : konferenz2009@bdue.de.

Verzeichnis der Redner, Referenten, Moderatoren und Podiumsteilnehmer

Mitglieder der Programmkommission

Wolfram Baur, Essen

*Vizepräsident des Bundesverbandes der Dolmetscher und
Übersetzer e.V. (BDÜ); Freier Übersetzer*

baur@bdue.de

Prof. Dr. phil. Sylvia Kalina, Köln

*Institut für Translation und Mehrsprachige Kommunikation (ITMK)
an der Fachhochschule Köln; Diplom-Dolmetscherin*

Sylvia.Kalina@fh-koeln.de

Prof. Dr. phil. Felix Mayer, München

*Präsident der Hochschule für Angewandte Sprachen des SDI,
Direktor des SDI München; Diplom-Übersetzer*

mayer@sdi-muenchen.de

Dipl.-Übers. Jutta Witzel, Nürtingen

*Chefredakteurin des MDÜ – Fachzeitschrift für Dolmetscher und Übersetzer;
Fachjournalistin und Sprachtrainerin*

witzel@bdue.de

11.–13. SEPTEMBER 2009
FREIE UNIVERSITÄT BERLIN • HENRY-FORD-BAU

BDÜ

Herausforderungen der Globalisierung für Dolmetscher und Übersetzer

ÜBERSETZEN IN
DIE ZUKUNFT

Internationale Fachkonferenz • Fachmesse • Stellenbörse
des Bundesverbands der Dolmetscher und Übersetzer e.V. (BDÜ)

www.uebersetzen-in-die-zukunft.de

Unter der Schirmherrschaft von:

Bundesministerium
für Wirtschaft
und Technologie

Unterstützt von:

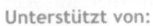

Acolada
Content Language
Data Management

LICS®
Language Industry Certification System

across
www.across.net

MGDenzer
Unabhängiger Versicherungsmakler

TermNet
International Network for Terminology

BOSS
ASSEKURANZ

STAR

Langenscheidt
Fachverlag

In der Schriftenreihe des BDÜ sind bisher folgende Bücher erschienen:

31   Gerichts- und Behördenterminologie – von Prof.   **€ 17,00**
Ulrich Daum, Umfang: 180 Seiten, ISBN 9783938430231, Erscheinungsjahr: 2009

Gerichts- und Behördenterminologie von Ulrich Daum ist eine Handreichung zur Sprache von Gericht und Verwaltung und ein Vademecum angehender Gerichtsdolmetscher. Kandidaten der Staatsprüfung für Übersetzer und Bewerber um Beeidigung als Dolmetscher finden hier die wichtigsten einschlägigen Informationen und sprachlichen Besonderheiten.

30   Deutsche Landeskunde – von Prof. Ulrich Daum, Umfang: 169   **€ 16,00**
Seiten, ISBN: 9783938430224, Erscheinungsjahr: 2009

Ob für Dolmetscher und Übersetzer in der Ausbildung, für im Beruf stehende Sprachmittler im deutschsprachigen Raum oder für Einbürgerungswillige: Die „Deutsche Landeskunde" von Ulrich Daum bietet ein Grundwissen über die Realien in Deutschland, das für diese Zielgruppen unabdingbar ist. Das Buch eignet sich als Lehrwerk im Unterricht wie auch zum Eigenstudium und dient als Handreichung für Prüfungen im Sprachmittlerbereich. Schließlich kann es auch zur Vorbereitung für die Tests für Einbürgerungswillige verwendet werden.

29   Honorarspiegel für Übersetzungs- und Dolmetschleistungen,   **€ 15,00**
Umfang: 83 Seiten, Erscheinungsjahr: 2008

Anders als für Leistungen in anderen freien Berufen – z.B. Leistungen von Rechtsanwälten, Architekten oder Ingenieuren – gibt es in Deutschland für die Leistungen von Übersetzern und Dolmetschern keine Gebühren- oder Honorarordnungen. Um dennoch in einem preislich für Auftraggeber und Auftragnehmer gleichermaßen weitgehend unübersichtlichen Markt für ein gewisses Maß an Transparenz zu sorgen, führt der BDÜ ab dem Jahr 2008 jährliche Umfragen über die im Vorjahr in Deutschland erzielten Honorare für Dolmetsch- und Übersetzungsleistungen durch.

28   Erb- und Immobilienrecht: Wörterbuch Deutsch–Spanisch/   **€ 35,00**
Spanisch–Deutsch – von Katrin Berty; Juan Fernández-Nespral; Norbert Lösing, Anna-Karola Rosse, Erscheinungsjahr: 2009

Das Wörterbuch deckt pro Sprachrichtung etwa 350 Termini ab. Von üblichen zweisprachigen (Fach-) Wörterbüchern unterscheidet es sich durch seine Konzeption als terminologisches Nachschlagewerk: Definitionen, Kontextbeispiele sowie sprach- und kulturspezifische Informationen stellen eine fundierte Entscheidungsgrundlage für die

Wahl des treffenden Terminus dar. Diese Kombination von Sprach-
und Sachinformationen macht das Wörterbuch zum Erb- und Immobilienrecht zu einem Fachwörterbuch im besten Sinne, das seinen
Nutzern einen entscheidenden Mehrwert bietet.

27   Der Zivilprozess: Eine Einführung für Gerichtsdolmetscher und -   € 14,00
übersetzer – von Helia Daubach; Claus Sprick, Umfang: 155
Seiten, ISBN: 9783938430033, Erscheinungsjahr: 2007

Verfasst von Richterin am Landgericht Dr. Helia-Verena Daubach
und Richter am Bundesgerichtshof Claus Sprick gibt dieser Band
Dolmetschern und Übersetzern, die für die Gerichte tätig sind oder
werden möchten, eine zusammenhängende Einführung in den Zivilprozess. Neben der Vermittlung eines grundlegenden Verständnisses
des Zivilprozesses und der in diesem Zusammenhang wesentlichen
juristischen Begriffe zeichnen sich die beiden in diesem Band zusammengefassten Beiträge („Der Zivilprozess erster Instanz" und
„Das Verfahren in den Rechtsmittelinstanzen") insbesondere dadurch
aus, dass hier zwei Richter, also „Abnehmer" der Leistungen von
Sprachmittlern, Hinweise darauf geben, worauf es ihnen besonders
ankommt. Fragen wie z.B. „Wie frei oder wortgetreu soll ich dolmetschen?" werden hier im Verfahrenszusammenhang erörtert und ganz
praktisch beantwortet.

26   Dolmetschen im medizinischen Bereich – Diplomarbeit von Marja   € 18,00
Barkowski, Umfang: 190 Seiten, ISBN: 9783938430194, Erschei-
nungsjahr: 2007

Gehört Krankenhausdolmetschen zum so genannten Community
Interpreting? Welche Kompetenzen muss ein professioneller Krankenhausdolmetscher aufweisen? Welche Rolle spielt medizinisches
und institutionelles Hintergrundwissen für einen Krankenhausdolmetscher? Dieses Buch zeigt spezifische Kompetenzen und Anforderungen an professionelle Krankenhausdolmetscher auf. Weiterhin werden
der aktuelle Forschungsstand des Krankenhausdolmetschens, die Art
der Einsatzmöglichkeiten und die derzeitige Arbeitsmarktsituation
beleuchtet.

25   Sprachdidaktik und Computer: MT-Dictionaries: Ein Beitrag zur   € 13,00
Usability-Forschung – von Martina Schwanke, Umfang: 144
Seiten, ISBN: 9783938430156, Erscheinungsjahr: 2007

In dieser Studie werden die Instruktionen zum Aufbau und zur
Erweiterung der Lexika in maschinellen Übersetzungssystemen
untersucht. Der Schwerpunkt der Analysen liegt auf der Flexion der
deutschen Substantive.

24   **Übersetzen und Globalisierung: Globalisierung und ihre Auswir-**   € 13,00
          kungen auf die Übersetzungs- und Lokalisierungsindustrie" –
          Diplomarbeit von Florian Willer, Umfang: 143 Seiten, ISBN:
          9783938430187, Erscheinungsjahr: 2007

Welche Vorteile entstehen mit der fortschreitenden Technisierung und
Vernetzung in der Übersetzungs- und Lokalisierungsindustrie für den
freiberuflichen Übersetzer? Wie reagieren die Auftraggeber und
welchen Nutzen sehen sie in dieser Entwicklung? Eine empirische
Studie über globale Entwicklungen und Veränderungen in der Übersetzerbranche als Folge der unaufhaltsamen Technisierung bei der
Abwicklung von Übersetzungs- und Lokalisierungsprojekten.

23   **Dieser Titel ist nicht mehr erhältlich.**

22   **Glossar der Gefängnissprache: Materialien für Gerichtsdolmet-**   € 10,00
          scher – von Anja Pachel, Umfang: 110 Seiten, ISBN:
          9783938430040, Erscheinungsjahr: 2006

Was tun, wenn ein Strafgefangener bei einem Gerichtstermin plötzlich
davon redet, dass er sich „blankmachen" musste, um sich einer „84-2"
zu unterziehen, dass der „Pop Shop" viel zu früh ist und er nun nach
seiner Erfahrung im „Kahn" sicher weiß, dass er nie wieder etwas
„eintüten" wird. Was ist der Unterschied zwischen einem Be- und
einem Angeschuldigten oder zwischen Außenbeschäftigung, Ausführung, Freigang und Ausgang? Dieses Nachschlagewerk soll Dolmetschern helfen, sich auf einen Einsatz vor Gericht vorzubereiten.

21   **Die Bedeutung von Fachwissen für das Simultandolmetschen:**   € 12,00
          Eine empirische Untersuchung – Diplomarbeit von Silke Fritz,
          Umfang: 132 Seiten, ISBN: 9783938430149, Erscheinungsjahr:
          2006

Dolmetscher finden in dieser Diplomarbeit eine Analyse der wichtigsten Bausteine für eine gute Arbeitsleistung. Dieses Buch zeigt auf,
inwieweit Vorwissen wesentlich für das Verstehen eines Textes ist
und wie wichtig es für Dolmetscher ist, sich hierfür nicht nur Fachvokabular, sondern auch Fachwissen anzueignen. Weiterhin wird
beleuchtet, wie Verstehensdefizite durch geschickte Dolmetsch-
strategien ausgeglichen werden können.

**20   Wörterbuch zur Unternehmensfinanzierung: Deutsch–Spanisch /   € 43,00
Spanisch–Deutsch" – von Juan Fernández-Nespral; Julia Fritz;
Anke Lutz; Sylvia Thebes, Umfang: 437 Seiten, ISBN:
9783938430118, Erscheinungsjahr: 2006**

Das „Wörterbuch zur Unternehmensfinanzierung: Deutsch–Spanisch/
Spanisch–Deutsch" durchleuchtet pro Sprachrichtung etwa 650
Termini. Durch seine Konzeption unterscheidet sich das vorliegende
Wörterbuch von üblichen (Groß-)Wörterbüchern, die zwar eine
Vielzahl von Termini beleuchten, meist aber keine Sachinformation
zur Verfügung stellen. Definitionen, Kontextbeispiele sowie sprach-
und kulturspezifische Informationen bieten dem Nutzer dieses
Wörterbuchs eine fundierte Entscheidungsgrundlage für die Wahl des
treffenden Terminus. Gerade das Zusammenspiel von Sprach- und
Sachinformationen macht das Wörterbuch zur Unternehmensfinanzierung zu einem Fachwörterbuch im besten Sinne, das seinen Nutzern
einen entscheidenden Mehrwert bietet.

**19   Wer übersetzt was – Ausgabe 2006/2007: Ein Kompendium mit   € 26,00
Angaben über Ausbildung, Werdegang und Berufspraxis von
über 900 BDÜ-Mitgliedern, Umfang: 246 Seiten, ISBN:
9783938430019, Erscheinungsjahr: 2006**

Dieses Verzeichnis enthält ausführliche Angaben über Dolmetscher
und Übersetzer. Erstmals werden hier in Buchform auch Bildungswe-
ge, Erfahrungen und Kenntnisse von Mitgliedern veröffentlicht. Auch
wenn es zwei Dutzend Datenbanken gibt, aus denen die eine oder
andere Information gewonnen werden kann, geht doch nichts über ein
Buch, das direkt griffbereit hinter dem Schreibtisch steht. Das Verzeichnis richtet sich an Behörden, Hochschulen, Wissenschaftsinstitu-
te, Verlage, Gerichte, Verbände, Bibliotheken, Sprachendienste,
Großunternehmen sowie Dolmetscher und Übersetzer selbst.

**18   Strafbefehle und Anklagen, Materialien für Dolmetscher – von   € 13,00
Norbert Zänker (Hrsg.), Umfang: 146 Seiten, ISBN:
9783938430026, Erscheinungsjahr: 2006**

Was schreibt ein Staatsanwalt denn wirklich, wenn er einem Angeklagten Betrug, Diebstahl oder Körperverletzung vorwirft? Hier
finden Sie Materialien für Gerichtsdolmetscher, d.h. zur Vorbereitung
von Einsätzen dienende konkrete Texte des Strafverfahrens. Strafbefehle und Anklagen sind die bei weitem häufigste, im Gericht vom
Blatt übersetzte bzw. gedolmetschte Textsorte.

17   Dieser Titel ist nicht mehr erhältlich.

16 Aufsätze und Beiträge: Theoretische Einsichten und praktische   € 22,00
Ausblicke – von Prof. Dr. Albrecht Neubert, Umfang: 223 Seiten,
ISBN: 9783938430088, Erscheinungsjahr: 2006

In seinen Artikeln und Aufsätzen aus den Jahren 2003 bis 2005 widmet sich der langjährige Direktor des Leipziger Dolmetscherinstituts dem Zusammenhang zwischen Theorie und Praxis. Dies ist eine weitere vom BDÜ aufgelegte Zusammenstellung (auch) theoretischer Überlegungen und Ansätze.

15 Theoria cum Praxi: Theoretische Einsichten und praktische   € 29,00
Ausblicke – von Prof. Dr. Albrecht Neubert, Umfang: 287 Seiten,
ISBN: 9783938430071, Erscheinungsjahr: 2006

In seinen Artikeln und Aufsätzen aus den Jahren 1986 und 2002 widmet sich der langjährige Direktor des Leipziger Dolmetscherinstituts dem Zusammenhang zwischen Theorie und Praxis. Viele der hier vorgelegten, früher bereits einzeln erschienenen Beiträge sind in englischer Sprache.

14 Deutsche Urteile in Strafsachen, Materialien für Dolmetscher –   € 20,00
von Norbert Zänker (Hrsg.), Umfang: 206 Seiten, ISBN:
9783938430064, Erscheinungsjahr: 2006

Dieser Band enthält authentische, aber anonymisierte Urteile der bundesdeutschen Strafgerichtsbarkeit. Vom Diebstahl über die Körperverletzung bis zum Raub und Mord sind hier Urteile abgedruckt, die angehenden Gerichtsdolmetschern die Einarbeitung in ihr neues Tätigkeitsfeld erleichtern sollen.

13 Terminologie und Lexikographie, Reprint 3 (2005), Umfang: 172   € 20,00
Seiten, ISBN: 9783980824293, Erscheinungsjahr: 1974

Beizeiten hat sich der BDÜ mit übersetzungsrelevanten Themen der Terminologie befasst. Der hier als Nachdruck vorgelegte Tagungsband des BDÜ-Fachseminars „Terminologie und Lexikographie, Frankfurt am Main, 23.–25.10.1974", galt als „Quelle der Weisheit" für den Übersetzer draußen im Lande. Er war lange Zeit vergriffen, weswegen er – ob seiner grundlegenden Bedeutung – in neuer Aufmachung noch einmal vorgelegt wird. Schaut man sich an, wer vor gut dreißig Jahren die Sprachendienste der Industrie und der Behörden vertrat, kommt man leider nicht umhin festzustellen, dass viele dieser Abteilungen nicht mehr existieren. Die Themen und Probleme sind jedoch ähnliche geblieben, nur werden sie heute mehr an Hochschulen und bei den Übersetzern und anderen Sprachdienstleistern selbst bearbeitet. Sicher, die Entwicklung, zumal in der rechnergestützten Terminologiearbeit, ist weit vorangeschritten. Ein

Blick zurück hilft aber zu sehen, wo wir herkommen. Dieses Buch behandelt:

- Die Ausbildung in Terminologie und terminologischer Lexikographie
- Die vier Dimensionen der Terminologiearbeit
- Die internationale terminologische Grundsatzarbeit
- Infoterm – Das Internationale Informationszentrum für Terminologie
- Gemeinsprachen, Fachsprachen und Übersetzen
- Terminologie und Übersetzen
- Die Terminologiearbeit in der Übersetzungsabteilung der Firma E. Merck, Chemisch-Pharmazeutische Fabrik, Darmstadt
- Die Terminologiearbeit der Sprachendienste der Europäischen Gemeinschaften
- Terminologiearbeit in einem Fachwörterbuchverlag
- Die Dezimalklassifikation und ihre Bedeutung für die Arbeit des Übersetzers

12 **Dolmetscher und Übersetzer im Landesrecht: Das Recht der Dolmetscher und Übersetzer in den Ländern der Bundesrepublik Deutschland – von Norbert Zänker (Hrsg.), Umfang: 346 Seiten, ISBN: 9783938430002, Erscheinungsjahr: 2005** € 35,00

Prüfung, Beeidigung, Ermächtigung bzw. Bestellung von Dolmetschern und Übersetzern sind – wie auch zum Teil die Ausbildung für diese Berufe – in Deutschland landesrechtlich geregelt. Der BDÜ legt hier eine erste Übersicht über die Vielfalt an Gesetzen und Verordnungen der Bundesländer vor.

11 **Dieser Titel ist nicht mehr erhältlich.**

10 **Übersetzen und Dolmetschen im 20. Jahrhundert: Schwerpunkt deutscher Sprachraum – von Prof. Dr. Wolfram Wilss, Nachdruck (2005), Umfang: 300 Seiten, ISBN: 9783980824286, Erscheinungsjahr: 1999** € 15,00

„Übersetzen und Dolmetschen im 20. Jahrhundert" von Prof. Dr. Wolfram Wilss ist innerhalb weniger Jahre zum Standardwerk geworden. Angehenden Dolmetschern und Übersetzern, Berufspraktikern und Philologen wird es zur Lektüre empfohlen.

9 **4. Deutscher Gerichtsdolmetschertag: 28./29.**   € 12,00
Oktober 2004, München, Umfang: 115 Seiten, ISBN: 9783980824279, Erscheinungsjahr: 2004

Im Jahr der Einführung des Justizvergütungs- und -entschädigungsgesetzes (JVEG) und den damit verbundenen Einkommenseinbußen für öffentlich bestellte und beeidigte Übersetzer und Dolmetscher erscheint es eine dringende Notwendigkeit, die Bedeutung dieses Berufsfeldes herauszustellen. Durch die Vorträge gewähren wir einen Einblick in das weite Einsatzgebiet von beeidigten Dolmetschern und Übersetzern bei Justiz, Staatsanwaltschaft und Polizei, verbunden mit den dadurch gestellten hohen Anforderungen an Wissen, Kommunikationsfähigkeit und Vermittlungsgeschick, nicht nur hinsichtlich der Sprachen, sondern auch in Bezug auf die unterschiedlichen Rechtssysteme. Die Vorträge behandeln wichtige Aspekte dieses Berufs und eignen sich hervorragend sowohl für Berufsanfänger, weil sie zahlreiche Fragen aus der täglichen Praxis beleuchten, als auch für erfahrene Kollegen, die sich über den neuesten Stand der Dinge informieren möchten.

8 **Das berufliche Umfeld des Dolmetschers und Übersetzers: Aus**   € 18,00
der Praxis für die Praxis, Reprint 1 (2004), Umfang: 350 Seiten, ISBN: 9783980824262, Erscheinungsjahr: 1993

In der Reihe REPRINT, Nachdrucke wichtiger Veröffentlichungen, legt der BDÜ hier den Tagungsband des Kongresses „Das berufliche Umfeld des Dolmetschers und Übersetzers: Aus der Praxis für die Praxis", Bonn 1993, vor. Bei diesem größten BDÜ-Kongress wurden alle wichtigen beruflichen Themen der Dolmetscher und Übersetzer von sachkundigen Referenten behandelt. Viele der Beiträge sind noch immer wegweisend und verdienen, gelesen zu werden. Einige sind historisch interessant und zeigen, wie weit wir über die Jahre gekommen sind. Oder auch nicht.

7 **2. Deutscher Gerichtsdolmetschertag. Berlin, 1997, Reprint 2**   € 14,00
(2004), Umfang: 130 Seiten, ISBN: 9783980824255, Erscheinungsjahr: 1997

Zivilverfahren, Strafverteidigung, Daktyloskopie, Psychiatrische Gutachten, BTM-Untersuchungen, Asylrecht und Alkoholgutachten sind nur einige Themen, die bei diesem Kongress behandelt wurden. Keine andere Zusammenstellung dieser Art geht so auf die Bedürfnisse der Gerichtsdolmetscher ein und vermittelt ihnen Grundlagenwissen, welches sie im Kriminalgericht, aber auch bei Verkehrszivilsachen, Betreuungsfällen oder polizeilichen Ermittlungen nutzen können.

6   Codice Penale: Das italienische Strafgesetzbuch, Umfang: 245   € 25,00
Seiten, ISBN: 9783980824231, Erscheinungsjahr: 2004

Auch Gerichtsdolmetscher für Italienisch schlagen gern einmal in der
Quelle der Erkenntnis – hier im italienischen Strafgesetzbuch – nach,
wenn sie Anklagen, Strafbefehle, Urteile und ähnliche Texte zu
übersetzen haben. Diesen unkommentierten Originaltext stellt man
sich am besten griffbereit in Augenhöhe ins Regal.

5   Justizvergütungs- und -entschädigungsgesetz (JVEG): Materia-   € 6,00
lien für Dolmetscher – von Norbert Zänker (Hrsg.), 2. Auflage,
Umfang: 60 Seiten, ISBN: 9783980824248, Erscheinungsjahr:
2005

Ab 1.Juli 2004 führt das mit seiner Begründung abgedruckte Justiz-
vergütungs- und -entschädigungsgesetz (JVEG) für Dolmetscher und
Übersetzer bei Gericht erstmals das Vergütungsprinzip ein. Gesetzes-
text und Begründung sind für beeidigte Dolmetscher bzw. ermächtigte
Übersetzer unentbehrlich und gehören auf den Schreibtisch jedes
freiberuflichen Sprachmittlers.

4   Dolmetscher und Übersetzer in deutschen Gesetzen: Auszüge aus   € 14,00
deutschen Gesetzen, die sich auf Dolmetscher und Übersetzer
beziehen – von Norbert Zänker (Hrsg.), 2. Auflage, Umfang: 145
Seiten, ISBN: 9783980824224, Erscheinungsjahr: 2005

Wer darf die Richtigkeit und Vollständigkeit von Übersetzungen
bescheinigen? Wo ist die Geheimhaltung geregelt? Was verdient ein
Gerichtsdolmetscher? Wann kann ein Dolmetscher vor Gericht
abgelehnt werden? Wie lang ist die Zeile einer Übersetzung? All' das
und mehr steht im Gesetz. Der 4. Band der Schriftenreihe des BDÜ
beinhaltet Auszüge aus deutschen Gesetzen, die sich auf Dolmetschen
und Übersetzen beziehen.

3   Gerichtsdolmetscher in Berlin, 2006: Für die Berliner Gerichte   € 40,00
und Notare allgemein beeidigte Dolmetscher (und Übersetzer),
Umfang: 180 Seiten, ISBN: 9783938430101, Erscheinungsjahr:
2006

Dies ist eine Liste von in Berlin allgemein beeidigten Dolmetschern
(und Übersetzern). Die Eintragungen sind nach Sprachen geordnet,
innerhalb der Sprachen nach Namen und Vornamen. Für die Richtigkeit und Vollständigkeit dieser öffentlichen Daten wird keinerlei
Gewähr übernommen. Dies ist kein Mitgliederverzeichnis.

2   **Das Praktikum im Dolmetschen und Übersetzen: Ein Leitfaden**   € 10,00
        für Schüler, Studenten, Freiberufler sowie Firmen, 2. überarbei-
        tete Auflage, Umfang: 73 Seiten, ISBN: 9783980824217, Erschei-
        nungsjahr: 2003

Dieser Band der BDÜ-Schriftenreihe gibt Studenten des Dolmet-
schens, Übersetzens und verwandter Disziplinen einen umfassenden
Einblick in Sinn und Nutzen eines Praktikums. Der umfangreiche
Adressteil erleichtert es dem Berufsnachwuchs, ein für ihn sinnvolles
Praktikum erfolgreich zu gestalten.

1   **Erfolgreich selbstständig als Dolmetscher und Übersetzer: Ein**   € 20,00
        Leitfaden für Existenzgründer, 3. überarbeitete Auflage, Umfang:
        140 Seiten, ISBN: 9783980824200, Erscheinungsjahr: 2005

Inhaltlich deckt das Werk sämtliche Bereiche ab, mit denen ein
unternehmerisch denkender Freiberufler zu Beginn und im Laufe
seiner beruflichen Tätigkeit konfrontiert wird. Angefangen bei der
Frage nach der persönlichen Eignung über praktische Überlegungen
zu Betriebsausstattung, Arbeitsmitteln, Auftragsabwicklung, Qualitätssicherung, Versicherungs-, Steuer- und Haftungsfragen bis hin zu
Erwägungen, in welcher Form und mit welcher Spezialisierung sich
der Beruf ausüben lässt. Der Anhang enthält neben aussagekräftigen
Musterformularen auch nützliche Adressen und eine umfassende
Bibliographie.

Alle Preise sind Bruttopreise und verstehen sich zzgl. Porto und Verpackung (€ 4,00). Bestellungen erbitten wir über:
www.publikationen.bdue.de.